Unicode
Demystified

Unicode Demystified

A Practical Programmer's Guide to the Encoding Standard

RICHARD GILLAM

✦✦Addison-Wesley

Boston • San Francisco • New York • Toronto • Montreal
London • Munich • Paris • Madrid
Capetown • Sydney • Tokyo • Singapore • Mexico City

The publisher offers discounts on this book when ordered in quantity for special sales. For more information, please contact:

U.S. Corporate and Government Sales
(800) 382-3419
corpsales@pearsontechgroup.com

For sales outside of the U.S., please contact:

International Sales
(317) 581-3793
international@pearsontechgroup.com

Visit Addison-Wesley on the Web: www.aw.professional.com

Library of Congress Cataloging-in-Publication Data

Gillam, Richard.
    Unicode demystified : a practical programmer's guide to the encoding standard /
  Richard Gillam.
      p.   cm.
  Includes bibliographical references and index.
  ISBN 0-201-70052-2
  1. Computer programming.   2. Unicode (Computer character set)—Standards.   I. Title.

  QA76.6 .G5535 2002
  005.7'2—dc21

2002018544

Pearson Education, Inc.
Rights and Contracts Department
75 Arlington Street, Suite 300
Boston, MA 02116
Fax: (617) 848-7047

ISBN 0-201-70052-2
Text printed on recycled paper
1 2 3 4 5 6 7 8 9 10—MA—0605040302
First printing, September 2002

To Mark, Kathleen, Laura, Helena,
Doug, John F, John R, Markus, Bertrand, Alan,
Eric, and the rest of the old JTCSV Unicode crew,
without whom this book would
not have been possible

and

To Ted and Joyce Gillam,
without whom the author would
not have been possible

Contents

Foreword

Unicode began with a simple goal: to unify the many hundreds of separate character encodings into a single, universal standard. These character encodings were incomplete and inconsistent: Two encodings would use the same number for two *different* characters, or use different numbers for the *same* character. Any given computer (especially servers) needed to support many different encodings, yet whenever data was passed between different encodings or platforms, that data always ran the risk of corruption.

Unicode was designed to fix that situation: to provide a *unique* number for every character, no matter what the platform, no matter what the program, no matter what the language.

Unfortunately, Unicode has not remained quite as simple as we originally planned. Most of the complications derive from three unavoidable sources. First, written languages are complex: They have evolved in strange and curious ways over the centuries. Many oddities end up being reflected in the way characters are used to represent those languages, or reflected in the way strings of characters function in a broader context. Second, Unicode did not develop in a vacuum: We had to add a number of features—and a great many characters— for compatibility with legacy character encoding standards. Third, we needed to adapt Unicode to different OS environments: allowing the use of 8-, 16-, or 32-bit units to represent characters, and either big- or little-endian integers. Of course, in addition to these three factors, there are in hindsight parts of the design that could have been simpler (true of any project of such magnitude).

Luckily you, a typical programmer, are shielded from most of these complexities. Just to put two strings in alphabetic order according to the conventions of any given language or country, for example, involves a lot of heavy lifting. Sometimes accents are important, sometimes not; sometimes two characters compare as one, sometimes one character compares as two, sometimes characters even swap. The software has to twist and hop between multiple code paths to make the simple cases absolutely as fast as possible, while still making every comparison absolutely accurate. All these gyrations are done by "the man behind the curtain"—you just call up a library routine in Windows, Java, ICU, or some other library, magic happens, and you get the right result.

You are not shielded from all of the complexities, however. There are still pitfalls. An English-speaking programmer might assume, for example, that given the three characters X, Y, and Z, that if X sorts before Y, then XZ sorts before YZ. This works for English, but fails for many languages. These are the things that a library can't do for you; you need to understand enough of the differences between the way characters behave in various environments so you can avoid stumbling into the traps.

So how do you learn more? The Unicode Standard and associated Technical Reports are available, but they often start at too high a level, or are aimed at a different audience—programmers implementing the standard, rather than programmers using pre-built implementations. The FAQs on the Unicode site (http://www.unicode.org) should help a good deal, but they jump from topic to topic, and don't provide a smooth exposition of the issues involved.

That brings us to this book and its author. For many years, Rich was part of the ICU team, which supplies one of the premier Unicode-enablement libraries. During that time, Rich was the "man behind the curtain" for parts of ICU, including pieces that were incorporated into the standard Java versions. He did some very interesting work there, and became intimately familiar with data structures and mechanisms used to support implementations of Unicode. Because ICU offers the same functionality across Java and cross-platform C/C++, he also has a solid grasp of the issues involved in those environments. That led him to becoming a columnist for *C++ Report*.

The ICU team got an inside look at Rich's work as successive drafts of his columns would float across our internal net for feedback. We still use his

"Anatomy of the Assignment Operator" column as a basis for asking questions of interviewees—it is remarkable just how tricky some of the nuts and bolts issues are in C++!

Rich left the ICU team a couple of years ago (after all, when Texas beckons, who can refuse her), but has continued to develop as a writer. He has a clear, colloquial style that allows him to make even complex matters understandable.

This book covers many of the important issues involved in dealing with Unicode: the basic character architecture, combining characters, encoding forms, normalization, searching, and sorting. It provides a solid foundation for understanding the structure and usage of Unicode, and the implications for most programmers. I'm glad that Rich has poured so much of his time and energy into this effort over the past few years, and hope you find the book as useful as I think you will.

Dr. Mark Davis,
President, The Unicode Consortium
(Chief Globalization Architect, IBM)
http://www.macchiato.com

Preface

As the economies of the world continue to become more connected together, and as the American computer market becomes more saturated, computer-related businesses are increasingly looking to markets outside the United States to grow their businesses. At the same time, companies in other industries are not only beginning to do the same thing (or, in fact, have been doing so for a long time), but are also turning to computer technology, especially the Internet, to grow their businesses and streamline their operations.

The convergence of these two trends means that it's no longer just an English-only market for computer software. To an ever greater extent, computer software is being used not just by people outside the United States or by people whose first language isn't English, but by people who don't speak English at all. As a result, interest in software internationalization is growing in the software development community.

Many things are involved in software internationalization: displaying text in the user's native language (and in different languages depending on the user), accepting input in the user's native language, altering window layouts to accommodate expansion or contraction of text or differences in writing direction, displaying numeric values according to local customs, indicating events in time according to the local calendar system, and so on.

This book isn't about any of these things. It's about something more basic, which underlies most of the issues listed above: representing written language in a computer. There are many different ways to do this; in fact, several approaches exist for just about every language that's been represented in computers. And that's the problem, too. Designing software that's flexible enough to handle data in multiple languages (or at least multiple languages that use different writing systems) has traditionally meant not just keeping track of the text, but also keeping track of which encoding scheme is being used to represent it. If you want to mix text in multiple writing systems, this bookkeeping becomes even more cumbersome.

The Unicode standard was designed specifically to solve this problem. It aims to be the *universal* character encoding standard, providing unique, unambiguous representations for every character in virtually every writing system and language in the world. The most recent version of Unicode provides representations for more than 90,000 characters.

Unicode has been around for 12 years now and is in its third major revision, with support for more languages being added with each revision. It has gained widespread support in the software community and in a wide variety of operating systems, programming languages, and application programs. Each of the semiannual International Unicode Conferences is better attended than the previous one, and the number of presenters and sessions at the conferences grows correspondingly.

Representing text isn't as straightforward as it appears at first glance; it's not merely as simple as picking out a bunch of characters and assigning numbers to them. First, you have to decide what a "character" is, which isn't as obvious in many writing systems as it is in English. In addition, you have to contend with issues such as how to represent characters with diacritical marks applied to them, how to represent clusters of marks that represent syllables, when differently shaped marks on the page are considered different "characters" and when they're considered just different ways of writing the same "character," and in what order to store the characters when they don't proceed in a straightforward manner from one side of the page to the other (for example, some characters stack on top of each other or appear in two parallel lines, or the reading order of the text on the page may zigzag around the line because of differences in natural reading direction).

The decisions you make on each of these issues for every character affect how various processes, such as comparing strings or analyzing a string for word boundaries, are performed, making them more complicated. Also, the sheer number of different characters that can be represented using the Unicode standard complicates many processes on text.

For all of these reasons, the Unicode standard is a large, complex affair. Unicode 3.0, the last version published as a book, is 1,072 pages long. Even at this length, many of the explanations are fairly concise and assume the reader already has some degree of familiarity with the problems to be solved. It can be kind of intimidating.

This book aims to provide an easier entrée into the world of Unicode. It arranges things in a more pedagogical manner, takes more time to explain the various issues and how they're solved, fills in pieces of background information, and adds information on implementation and existing Unicode support. It is this author's hope that this book will be a worthy companion to the standard itself, and will provide the average programmer and the internationalization specialist alike with all the information they need to effectively handle Unicode in their software.

▪ ABOUT THIS BOOK

There are a few things you should keep in mind as you go through this book:

- This book assumes that the reader either is a professional computer programmer or is familiar with most computer-programming concepts and terms. Most general computer science jargon isn't defined or explained here.
- It's helpful, but not essential, if the reader has some understanding of the basic concepts of software internationalization. Many of those concepts are explained here, but if they're not central to one of the book's topics, they're not given a lot of time.
- This book covers a lot of ground, and it isn't intended as a comprehensive and definitive reference for every single topic it discusses. In particular, it does not repeat the entire text of the Unicode standard; the idea is

to complement the standard, not replace it. In many cases, this book summarizes a topic or attempts to explain it at a high level, leaving it to other documents (typically the Unicode standard or one of its technical reports) to fill in all the details.

- The Unicode standard changes rapidly. New versions come out yearly, and small changes, new technical reports, and other things happen even more quickly. In Unicode's history, terminology has changed many times, and this will probably continue to happen occasionally. In addition, many other technologies use or depend on Unicode, and they are also constantly changing. I'm certainly not an expert on every single topic I discuss here. (In my darker moments, I'm not sure I'm an expert on any of them!) I have made every effort to ensure that this book is complete, accurate, and up-to-date, but I can't guarantee I've succeeded in every detail. In fact, I can almost guarantee that some information given here is either outdated or just plain wrong. Nevertheless, I have made every effort to minimize this problem, and I pledge to continue, with each future version, to try to bring it closer to being fully accurate.

- At the time of this writing (January 2002), the newest version of Unicode, Unicode 3.2, was in beta and thus still in flux. The Unicode 3.2 specification is scheduled to be finalized in March 2002, well before this book actually hits the streets. With a few exceptions, I don't expect major changes between now and March, but they're always possible. As a consequence, the Unicode 3.2 information in this book may wind up wrong in some details. I've tried to flag all of the Unicode 3.2-specific information, and I've tried to indicate the areas that I think are still in the greatest amount of flux.

- Sample code in this book is almost always in Java. This choice was made partially because Java is the language I use in my regular job, and thus the programming language I think in these days. I also chose Java because of its increasing importance and popularity in the programming world in general and because Java code tends to be somewhat easier to understand than, say, C (or at least no more difficult). Because of Java's syntactic similarity to C and C++, I also hope the examples will be reasonably accessible to C and C++ programmers who don't also program in Java.

- The sample code is provided for illustrative purposes only. I've gone to the trouble, at least with the examples that can stand alone, to ensure that the examples compile, and I've tested them to verify that I didn't make any obvious stupid mistakes, but they haven't been tested comprehensively. They were also written with more of an eye toward explaining a concept than being directly usable in any particular context. Incorporate them into your code at your own risk!

- I've tried to define jargon the first time I use it or to indicate a full explanation is coming later. There's also an enormous glossary at the end of this book to which you can refer if you come across an unfamiliar term that isn't defined.

- Numeric constants—especially numbers representing characters—are generally shown in hexadecimal notation. Hexadecimal numbers in the text are always written using the 0x notation familiar to C and Java programmers.

- Unicode code point values are shown using the standard Unicode notation, U+1234, where "1234" is a hexadecimal number containing four to six digits. In many cases, a character is referred to by both its Unicode code point value and its Unicode name: for example, "U+0041 LATIN CAPITAL LETTER A." Code unit values in one of the Unicode transformation formats are shown using the 0x notation.

THE AUTHOR'S JOURNEY

Like many people in the field, I fell into software internationalization by happenstance. I've always been interested in language—written language in particular—and (of course) in computers. But my job had never really dealt with this issue directly.

In the spring of 1995, that situation changed when I went to work for Taligent. Taligent, you may remember, was the ill-fated joint venture between Apple Computer and IBM (later joined by Hewlett-Packard) that was originally formed to create a new operating system for personal computers using state-of-the-art object-oriented technology. The fruit of our labors, CommonPoint, turned out to be too little too late, but it spawned many technologies that found their places in other products.

For a while, Taligent enjoyed a cachet in the industry as the place where Apple and IBM sent many of their best and brightest. If you managed to get a job at Taligent, you had "made it."

I almost didn't make it. I had wanted to work at Taligent for some time and eventually got the chance, but turned in a rather unimpressive interview performance (coworkers kidded me about that for years afterward) and wasn't offered the job. About that same time, a friend of mine *did* get a job there, and after the person who got the job for which I interviewed originally turned it down for family reasons, my friend put in a good word for me and I got a second chance. I probably would have taken almost any job there, but the specific opening was in the text and internationalization group. Thus began my association with Unicode.

One thing almost everyone who ever worked at Taligent will agree on is that working there was a wonderful learning experience—an opportunity, as it were, to "sit at the feet of the masters." The Taligent experience made me the programmer I am today. My C++ and OOD skills improved dramatically, I became proficient in Java, and I went from knowing virtually nothing about written language and software internationalization to . . . well, I'll let you be the judge.

My team was eventually absorbed into IBM, and I enjoyed a little more than two years as an IBMer before deciding to move on in early 2000. During my time at Taligent/IBM, I worked on four sets of Unicode-related text handling routines: the text-editing frameworks in CommonPoint, various text-storage and internationalization frameworks in IBM's Open Class Library, various internationalization facilities in Sun Microsystems' Java Class Library (which IBM wrote under contract to Sun), and the libraries that eventually came to be known as the International Components for Unicode (ICU).

ICU began life as an IBM developer-tools package based on the Java internationalization libraries. It has since morphed into an open-source project and taken on a life of its own. ICU is gaining ever more popularity and showing up in an increasing number of operating systems and software packages, and it's acquiring a reputation as a great demonstration of how to implement the various features of the Unicode standard. I had the twin privileges of contributing frameworks to Java and ICU and of working alongside those who developed the other frameworks and learning from them. I got to watch the Unicode standard develop, work with some of the people who were developing it, occasionally rub shoulders with the others, and occasionally contribute a tidbit or two to the effort myself. It was a fantastic experience, and I hope that at least some of their expertise rubbed off on me.

■ ACKNOWLEDGMENTS

It's been said that it takes a village to raise a child. I don't really know about that, but it *definitely* takes a village to write a book like this one. The person whose name is on the cover gets to take the credit, but an army of people actually contribute to the content.

Acknowledgments sections have a bad tendency to sound like acceptance speeches at the Oscars, as the authors go on forever thanking everyone in sight. This set of acknowledgments will be no different. If you're bored or annoyed by that sort of thing, I recommend that you skip to the next section now. You have been warned.

First and foremost, I'm indebted to the various wonderful and brilliant people I worked with on the internationalization teams at Taligent and IBM: Mark Davis, Kathleen Wilson, Laura Werner, Doug Felt, Helena Shih, John Fitzpatrick, Alan Liu, John Raley, Markus Scherer, Eric Mader, Bertrand Damiba, Stephen Booth, Steven Loomis, Vladimir Weinstein, Judy Lin, Thomas Scott, John Jenkins, Deborah Goldsmith, Clayton Lewis, Chen-Lieh Huang, and Norbert Schatz. Whatever I know about either Unicode or software internationalization, I learned from these people. I'd also like to thank the crew at Sun with whom we worked: Brian Beck, Norbert Lindenberg, Stuart Gill, and John O'Conner.

I'd also like to thank my management and coworkers at Trilogy, particularly Robin Williamson, Chris Hyams, Doug Spencer, Marc Surplus, Dave Griffith, John DeRegnaucourt, Bryon Jacob, and Zach Roadhouse, for their understanding and support as I worked on this book. I especially appreciate their letting me continue to participate in various Unicode-related activities, especially the conferences, on company time and with company money.

Numerous people have helped me directly in my efforts to put this book together, by reviewing parts of it and offering advice and corrections, by answering questions and giving advice, by helping me put together examples or letting me use examples they'd already put together, or simply by offering an encouraging word or two. I'm tremendously indebted to all who helped out in these ways: Jim Agenbroad, Matitiahu Allouche, Christian Cooke, John Cowan, Simon Cozens, Mark Davis, Roy Daya, Andy Deitsch, James Do, Martin Dürst, Tom Emerson, Franklin Friedmann, David Gallardo, Pat Glenski, Tim Greenwood, Jarkko Hietaniemi, Martin Hosken, Richard Ishida, John Jenkins, Charlie Jolly, Kent Karlsson, Koji Kodama, Mike Ksar, Alain LaBonté, Mike Lambert, Ken Lunde, Rick McGowan, John O'Conner, Dan Poirier, Chris Pratley, John Raley, Jonathan Rosenne, Yair Sarig, Dave Thomas, Jonathan Walden, and Garret Wilson.

I'd also like to acknowledge all the people at Addison-Wesley who've had a hand in putting this thing together: Ross Venables, my current editor; Julie DiNicola, my former editor; Tyrrell Albaugh, the production manager; Jill Hobbs, who copyedited the manuscript and ruthlessly zapped extraneous words from my prose; Kim Arney Mulcahy, who had the unenviable task of designing and typesetting the manuscript and cleaning up all my diagrams and examples; Tom Dinse, who put together the index; Karin Hansen, who designed the cover; and Mike Hendrickson, who oversaw the whole thing. I greatly appreciate their professionalism and their patience in dealing with this first-time author.

Last but not least, I'd like to thank the family members and friends who've had to sit and listen to me talk about this project for the last couple years: my parents Ted and Joyce Gillam; Leigh Anne and Ken Boynton, Ken Cancelosi, Kelly Bowers, Bruce Rittenhouse, and many of the people listed earlier.

I couldn't have finished the book without all these people. If this book is good, they deserve the lion's share of the credit. If it isn't, I deserve the blame and owe them my apologies.

■ A PERSONAL APPEAL

For a year and a half, I wrote a column on Java for *C++ Report* magazine. For much of that time, I wondered if anyone was actually reading the thing and what they thought of it. I would occasionally get an e-mail from a reader commenting on something I'd written, and I was always grateful, whether the feedback was good or bad, because it meant that someone was reading my work and took it seriously enough to let me know what he or she thought.

I'm hoping there will be more than one edition of this book, and I really want it to be as good as possible. If you read it and find it less than helpful, I hope you won't just throw it on a shelf somewhere and grumble about the money you wasted on it. If this book fails to adequately answer your questions about Unicode, or if it wastes too much time answering questions you don't care about, I want to know. The more specific you can be about just what isn't doing it for you, the better. Please write me at `rtgillam@concentric.net` with your comments and criticisms.

Of course, if you *like* what you see here, I wouldn't mind hearing from you either. God knows, I can use the encouragement.

R. T. G.
Austin, Texas
January 2002

1

Unicode in Essence

An Architectural Overview of the Unicode Standard

Language, Computers, and Unicode

1

Words are amazing, marvelous things. They have the power both to build up and to tear down great civilizations. Words make us who we are. Indeed, many have observed that our use of language is what separates humans from the rest of the animal kingdom. Humans have the capacity for symbolic thought, the ability to think about and discuss things we cannot immediately see or touch. Language is our chief symbolic system for doing this. Consider even a fairly simple concept such as "There is water over the next hill." Without language, this idea would be an extraordinarily difficult thing to convey.

There's been a lot of talk in recent years about "information." We face an "information explosion" and live in an "information age." Maybe so, but when it comes right down to it, we are creatures of information. Language is simply one of our main ways of sharing information with one another and, often, of processing information.

We often hear that we are in the midst of an "information revolution," surrounded by new forms of "information technology," a phrase that didn't even exist a generation or two ago. These days, the term "information technology" is generally used to refer to technology that helps us perform one or more of three basic processes: the storage and retrieval of information, the extraction of higher levels of meaning from a collection of information, and the transmission of information over large distances. The telegraph, and later the telephone, represented a quantum leap in the last of these three processes, and the digital computer in the first two, and these two technologies form the cornerstone of the modern "information age."

By far, the most important advance in information technology occurred many thousands of years ago and can't be credited to one particular inventor. That advance (like so many technological revolutions, really a series of smaller advances) was written language. Think about it: Before written language, storing and retrieving information over a long period of time relied mostly on human memory, or on precursors of writing, such as making notches in sticks. Human memory is unreliable, and storage and retrieval (or storage over a time longer than a single person's lifetime) involved direct oral contact between people. Notches in sticks and the like avoid this problem, but don't allow for much nuance or depth in the information being stored. Likewise, transmission of information over a long distance also required memorization or relied on technology such as drums or smoke signals that also had limited range and bandwidth.

Writing made both of these processes vastly more powerful and reliable. It enabled storage of information in dramatically greater concentrations and over dramatically longer time spans than was ever thought possible. It also made possible transmission of information over much greater distances, with greater nuance and fidelity, than had ever been imagined.

In fact, most of today's data processing and telecommunications technologies have written language as their basis. Much of what we do with computers today is use them to store, retrieve, transmit, produce, analyze, and print written language.

Information technology didn't begin with the computer, and it didn't begin with the telephone or telegraph. It began with written language.

This is a book about how computers are used to store, retrieve, transmit, manipulate, and analyze written language.

▪ ▪ ▪

Language makes us who we are. The words we choose speak volumes about who we are and about how we see the world and the people around us. They tell others who "our people" are: where we're from, which social class we belong to, and possibly even to whom we're related.

The world is made up of hundreds of ethnic groups, who constantly do business with, create alliances with, commingle with, and go to war with each other. The whole concept of an "ethnic group" is actually rooted in language. Who "your people" are is reflected not only in which language *you* speak, but in which language or languages *your ancestors* spoke. As a group's subgroups become separated, the languages the subgroups speak will begin to diverge, eventually giving rise to multiple languages that share a common heritage (for example, classical Latin diverged into modern Spanish and French). As different groups come into contact with one another, their respective languages will change as a result of the other's influence (for example, much of modern English vocabulary was borrowed from French). Much of a group's history is encoded in its language.

We live in a world of languages. Today, some 6,000 to 7,000 different languages are spoken in the world, each with countless dialects and regional variations.[1] Humans may be united by *language*, but we're divided by our *languages*.

Yet the world of computing is strangely homogeneous. For decades now, the language of computing has been English—specifically, American English. Thankfully, this situation is changing. Information technology is increasingly making possible contact between people in different parts of the world. In particular, it is facilitating the conduct of business in different parts of the world. As information technology invades more and more of the world, people are becoming increasingly unwilling to speak the language of information technology—they want information technology to speak *their* language.

This is a book about how all, or at least most, written languages—not just English or Western European languages—can be used with information technology.

■   ■   ▩

Language makes us who we are. Almost every human activity has its own language, a specialized version of a normal human language adapted to the de-

---

1. SIL International's Ethnologue Web site (www.ethnologue.com) lists 6,800 "main" languages and 41,000 variants and dialects.

mands of discussing a particular activity. As a consequence, the language you speak also says much about what you do.

Every profession has its jargon, which is used both to provide a more precise method of discussing the various aspects of the profession and to help tell "insiders" from "outsiders." The information technology industry has always had a reputation as one of the most jargon-laden professional groups around. This reputation probably isn't warranted, but it looks that way because of the way computers have come to permeate our lives: Now that noncomputer people have to deal with computers, they have to deal with the language that computer people use.

It's interesting to watch as the language of information technology starts to infect the vernacular: "I don't have the bandwidth to deal with that right now." "Joe, can you spare some cycles to talk to me?" My personal favorite came from a TV commercial from a few years back: "No shampoo helps download dandruff better."

Each subspecialty within information technology also has its own jargon that isn't shared by computer people outside that subspecialty. In the same way that a bit of culture clash is occurring as the language of computers enters the language of everyday life, so a bit of culture clash is occurring as the language of software internationalization enters the language of general computing.

This trend is a good development, because it shows the increasing interest of the computing community in developing computers, software, and other products that can deal with people in their native languages. We're slowly moving from (with apologies to Henry Ford) "your native language, as long as it's English" to "your native language." The challenge of writing one piece of software that can deal with users in multiple human languages involves many different problems that need to be solved, and each of those problems has its own terminology.

This is a book about some of that terminology.

■   ■   ■

One of the biggest problems to be dealt with in software internationalization is that the ways human language has been traditionally represented inside computers don't often lend themselves to many human languages, and they lend themselves especially badly to multiple human languages in the same document.

Over time, systems have been developed for representing quite a few different written languages in computers, but each scheme is generally designed for only a single language, or at best a small collection of related languages. These systems are often mutually incompatible. Interpreting a series of bits encoded with one standard using the rules of another yields gibberish, so software that handles multiple languages has traditionally had to do a lot of extra bookkeeping to keep track of the various different systems used to encode the characters of those languages. This juggling act is difficult to do well, and few pieces of software attempt it, leading to a Balkanization of computer software and the data it manipulates.

Unicode solves this problem by providing a *unified* representation for the characters in the various written languages. By providing a unique bit pattern for every single character, you eliminate the problem of having to keep track of which of many different characters this specific instance of a particular bit pattern is supposed to represent.

Of course, each language has its own peculiarities and presents its own challenges for computerized representation. Dealing with Unicode doesn't necessarily mean dealing with all the peculiarities of the various languages, but it can—it depends on how many languages you want to support in your software as well as how much you can rely on other software (such as the operating system) to perform that work for you.

In addition, because of the sheer number of characters it encodes, dealing with Unicode-encoded text in software presents challenges that go beyond those of dealing with the various languages Unicode allows you to represent. The aim of this book is to help the average programmer find his or her way through the jargon and understand how to work with Unicode.

This is a book about Unicode.

▪ WHAT UNICODE IS

Unicode is a standard method for representing written language in computers. So why do we need it? After all, probably dozens, if not hundreds, of ways of handling this issue already exist. That's exactly the point. Unicode isn't just another entry in the endless parade of text-encoding standards; it's an attempt to do away with all the others, or at least simplify their use, by creating a *universal* text encoding standard.

Let's back up for a second. The best-known and most widely used character encoding standard is the American Standard Code for Information Interchange (ASCII). The first version of ASCII was published in 1964 as a standard way of representing textual data in computer memory and sending it over communication links between computers. ASCII is based on a 7-bit byte. Each byte represents a character, and characters are represented by assigning them to individual bit patterns (or, if you prefer, individual numbers). A 7-bit byte can have 128 different bit patterns. Because 33 of these patterns were set aside for use as control signals of various types (start- and end-of-transmission codes, block and record separators, and so on), 95 were left free for representing characters.

Perhaps the main deficiency in ASCII comes from the *A* in its name: American. ASCII is an American standard, and it was designed for the storage and transmission of English text. Although 95 characters are (barely) sufficient for representing English text, that's it. On early teletype machines, ASCII could also be used to represent the accented letters found in many European languages, but this capability disappeared during the transition from teletypes to CRT terminals.

As computer use became more widespread in various parts of the world, alternative methods of representing characters in computers arose for representing other languages. This proliferation led to the situation we have today, where generally three or four different encoding schemes are available for every language and writing system in use today.

Unicode is the latest of several attempts to solve this Tower of Babel problem by creating a universal character encoding. Its primary approach to this issue is to increase the size of the possible encoding space by increasing the number of bits used to encode each character. Most other character encodings are based on an 8-bit byte, which provides enough space to encode a maximum of 256 characters (in practice, most encodings reserve some of these values for control signals and encode fewer than 256 characters). For languages that have more than 256 characters, such as Japanese, most encodings are still based on the 8-bit byte, but use sequences of several bytes to represent most of the characters, with relatively complicated schemes being employed to manage the variable numbers of bytes used to encode the characters.

Unicode uses a 16-bit word to encode characters, allowing up to 65,536 characters to be encoded without resorting to more complicated schemes involving multiple machine words per character. This set of 65,536 characters, with careful management, is enough to allow encoding of the vast majority of characters in the vast majority of written languages in use today. The current version of Unicode, version 3.2, actually encodes 95,156 different characters— it represents the less common characters by using two 16-bit units. Of course, with 50,212 characters actually encoded using only a single unit, you rarely encounter the two-unit characters. In fact, these 50,212 characters include all of the characters representable with virtually all of the other character encoding methods that are in reasonably widespread use.

This approach provides two main benefits. First, a system that wants to allow textual data (either user data or items such as messages and labels that may need to be localized for different user communities) to be in any language would, without Unicode, have to keep track of not just the text itself, but also of the character encoding method being used. In fact, mixtures of languages might require mixtures of character encodings. This extra bookkeeping means you couldn't look directly at the text and know, for example, that the value 65 was a capital letter A. Depending on the encoding scheme used for that particular piece of text, the value might represent some other character or even be simply part of a character (that is, it might have to be considered along with an adjacent byte so as to be interpreted as a character). This system might also mean you would need different logic to perform certain processes on text depending on which encoding scheme that happened to be used, or you might be required to convert pieces of text between different encodings.

Unicode does away with this chaos. It allows all of the same languages and characters to be represented using only one encoding scheme. Every character has its own unique, unambiguous value. The value 65, for example, *always* represents the capital letter A. You don't need to rely on extra information about the text to interpret it, you don't need different algorithms to perform certain processes on the text depending on the encoding or language, and you don't (with some relatively rare exceptions) need to consider context to correctly interpret any given 16-bit unit of text.

Second, Unicode gives you a pivot point for converting between other character encoding schemes. Because it's a superset of all of the other common character encoding systems, you can convert between any other two encodings by converting from one of them to Unicode, and then from Unicode to the other encoding. Thus, if you have to provide a system that can convert text between any arbitrary pair of encodings, the number of converters you have to provide can be dramatically smaller. If you support n different encoding schemes, you only need $2n$ converters, not n^2 converters. Also, when you need a system that can interact with the outside world using several different non-Unicode character representations, the system can do its internal processing in Unicode and convert at the boundaries, rather than potentially having to have alternative code to do the same things for text in the different outside encodings.

■ What Unicode Isn't

It's also important to keep in mind what Unicode isn't. First, Unicode is a standard scheme for representing *plain text* in computers and data communication. It is not a scheme for representing *rich text* (sometimes called "fancy text" or "styled text"). This distinction is important. Plain text is the words, sentences, numbers, and so forth themselves. Rich text is plain text plus information about the text, especially information on the text's visual presentation (for example, the fact that a given word is in italics), the structure of a document (for example, the fact that a piece of text is a section header or footnote), or the language (for example, the fact that a particular sentence is in Spanish). Rich text may also include nontext items that travel with the text, such as pictures.

It can be difficult to draw a line between what qualifies as plain text, and therefore should be encoded in Unicode, and what is really rich text. In fact, debates on this very subject flare up from time to time in the various Unicode discussion forums. The basic rule is that plain text contains all of the information necessary to carry the semantic meaning of the text—the letters, spaces, digits, punctuation, and so forth. If removing it would make the text unintelligible, then it's plain text.

This is still a slippery definition. On the one hand, italics and boldface carry semantic information, and discarding them may lose some of the meaning of a sentence that uses them. On the other hand, it's perfectly possible to write intelligible, grammatical English without using italics and boldface, but it would be impossible, or at least extremely difficult, to write intelligible, grammatical English without the letter m, or the comma, or the digit 3. Some of the distinction may also come down to user expectations—you can write intelligible English with only capital letters, but it's generally not considered grammatical or acceptable.

There's also a certain amount of document structure you need to be able to convey in plain text, even though document structure is generally considered the province of rich text. The classic example is the paragraph separator. You can't really get by without a way to represent a paragraph break in plain text without compromising legibility, even though it's technically something that indicates document structure. Many higher-level protocols that deal with document structure, however, have their own ways of marking the beginnings and endings of paragraphs. For this reason, the paragraph separator, is one of a number of characters in Unicode that are explicitly disallowed (or ignored) in rich-text representations that are based on Unicode. HTML, for example, allows paragraph marks, but they're not recognized by HTML parsers as paragraph marks. Instead, HTML uses the <P> and </P> tags to mark paragraph boundaries.

When it comes down to it, the distinction between plain text and rich text is a judgment call. It's kind of like Potter Stewart's famous remark on obscenity—"I may not be able to give you a definition, but I know it when I see it." Still, the principle is that Unicode encodes only plain text. Unicode may be used as the basis of a scheme for representing rich text, but it isn't intended to provide a complete solution to this problem on its own.

Rich text is an example of a "higher-level protocol," a phrase you'll run across a number of times in the Unicode standard. A higher-level protocol is anything that starts with the Unicode standard as its basis and then adds additional rules or processes to it. XML, for example, is a higher-level protocol that uses Unicode as its base and adds rules that define how plain Unicode text can be used to represent structured information through the use of various kinds of markup tags. To Unicode, the markup tags are just Unicode text like everything else; to XML, though, they delineate the structure of the document. You can, in fact, have multiple layers of protocols: XHTML is a higher-level protocol for representing rich text that uses XML as its base.

Markup languages such as HTML and XML offer one example of how a higher-level protocol may be used to represent rich text. The other main class of higher-level protocols involves the use of multiple data structures, one or more of which contain plain Unicode text, and which are supplemented by other data structures that contain the information on the document's structure, the text's visual presentation, and any other nontext items that are included with the text. Most word processing programs use such schemes.

Unicode also isn't a complete solution for software internationalization. Software internationalization is a set of design practices that lead to software that can be adapted for various international markets ("localized") without having to modify the executable code. The Unicode standard in all of its details includes a lot of stuff, but it doesn't include everything necessary to produce internationalized software. In fact, it's perfectly possible to write internationalized software without using Unicode at all; conversely, it's perfectly possible to write completely non-internationalized software that uses Unicode.

Unicode is a solution to one particular problem in writing internationalized software: representing text in different languages without getting tripped up in dealing with the multiplicity of encoding standards. This issue is an important one, but it's not the only problem that needs to be solved when developing internationalized software. An internationalized piece of software might also have to worry about the following:

- Presenting a different user interface to the user depending on what language he or she speaks. This may involve not only translating any text in the user interface into the user's language, but also altering screen layouts to accommodate the size or writing direction of the translated text, changing icons and other pictorial elements to be meaningful (or not offensive) to the target audience, changing color schemes for the same reasons, and so forth.

- Altering the ways in which binary values such as numbers, dates, and times are presented to the user, or the ways in which the user enters these values into the system. This involves not only relatively small things, such as changing the character that's used for a decimal point (it's a comma, not a period, in most of Europe) or the order of the various pieces of a date (day-month-year is common in Europe), but possibly larger-scale changes (Chinese uses a completely different system for writing numbers, for example, and Israel uses a completely different calendar system).

- Altering various aspects of your program's behavior. For example, sorting a list into alphabetical order may produce different orders for the same list depending on language because "alphabetical order" is a language-specific concept. Accounting software might need to work differently in different places because of differences in accounting rules.

To those programmers who are experienced in software internationalization, this is all obvious, of course, but those who are less experienced often seem to use the words "Unicode" and "internationalization" interchangeably. If you're in this camp, be careful: If you're writing in C++, storing all of your character strings as arrays of `wchar_t` doesn't make your software internationalized. Likewise, if you're writing in Java, the fact that it's in Java and the Java `String` class uses Unicode doesn't automatically make your software internationalized. If you're unclear on the internationalization issues you might run into that Unicode *doesn't* solve, you can find an excellent introduction to the subject at `http://www.xerox-emea.com/globaldesign/paper/paper1.htm`, along with a wealth of other useful papers and other goodies.

Finally, Unicode isn't a glyph registry. We'll get into the Unicode character–glyph model in Chapter 3, but it's worth the effort to provide a quick synopsis here. Unicode draws a strong, important distinction between a **character**, which is an abstract linguistic concept such as "the Latin letter A" or "the Chinese character for 'sun,'" and a **glyph**, which is a concrete visual presentation of a character, such as A or ⊟. There isn't a one-to-one correspondence between these two concepts. A single glyph may represent more than one character (such a glyph is often called a **ligature**), such as the fi ligature, a single mark that represents the letters f and i together. Also, a single character might be represented by two or more glyphs: The vowel sound *au* in the Tamil language (ெளா) is represented by two marks, one that goes to the left of a consonant character, and another on the right; nevertheless, it's still thought of as a single character. In addition, a character may be represented using different glyphs in different contexts: The Arabic letter heh has one shape when it stands alone (ه) and another when it occurs in the middle of a word (ﻬ).

You'll also see what we might consider typeface distinctions between different languages using the same writing system. For instance, both Arabic and Urdu use the Arabic alphabet, but Urdu is generally written in the more ornate Nastaliq style, while Arabic frequently isn't. Japanese and Chinese are both written using Chinese characters, but some characters have a different shape in Chinese (for example, 骨 in Japanese is 骨 in Chinese).

Unicode, as a rule, doesn't care about any of these distinctions. It encodes underlying semantic concepts, not visual presentations (characters, not glyphs) and relies on intelligent rendering software (or the user's choice of fonts) to draw the correct glyphs in the correct places. Unicode does sometimes encode glyphic distinctions, but only when necessary to preserve interoperability with some preexisting standard or to preserve legibility (i.e., if smart rendering software can't pick the right glyph for a particular character in a particular spot without clues in the encoded text itself). Despite these exceptions, Unicode by design does not attempt to catalogue every possible variant shape for a particular character. It encodes the character and leaves the shape to higher-level protocols.

■ THE CHALLENGE OF REPRESENTING TEXT IN COMPUTERS

The main body of the Unicode standard is 1,040 pages long, counting indexes and appendices, and there's even more supplemental information—addenda, data tables, related substandards, implementation notes, and so on—on the Unicode Consortium's Web site. That's an awful lot of verbiage. And now this book offers another 800 pages on the subject. Why? After all, Unicode's just a character encoding. Sure, it includes a lot of characters, but how hard can it be?

Let's look at this issue for a few minutes. The basic principle is simple: If you want to be able to represent textual information in a computer, you make a list of all the characters you want to represent and assign a number to each one.[2] Now you can represent a sequence of characters with a sequence of numbers. Consider the simple number code we all learned as kids, where A is 1, B is 2, C is 3, and so on. Using this scheme, the word

food

would be represented as 6-15-15-4.

---

2. Actually, you assign a bit pattern to each one, but numbers are useful surrogates for bit patterns, because there's a generally agreed-upon mapping from numbers to bit patterns. In fact, some character encoding standards, including Unicode, offer several alternative ways to represent each character in bits, all based on the same numbers, so the numbers you assign to them become useful as an intermediate stage between characters and bits. We'll look at this point more closely in Chapters 2 and 6.

Piece of cake. This also works well in Japanese,

日本語

although you need a lot more numbers (which introduces its own set of problems, as we'll see in a minute).

In real life, you may choose the numbers fairly judiciously, to facilitate things like sorting (it's useful, for example, to make the numeric order of the character codes follow the alphabetical order of the letters) or character-type tests (it makes sense, for example, to put all the digits in one contiguous group of codes and the letters in another, or even to position them in the encoding space such that you can check whether a character is a letter or digit with simple bit-masking). But the basic principle is still the same: Just assign each character a number.

It gets more difficult, or at least less clear-cut, as you move to other languages. Consider this phrase:

à bientôt

What do you do with the accented letters? You have two basic choices: You can either just assign a different number to each accented version of a give letter, or you can treat the accent marks as independent characters and give them their own numbers.

If you take the first approach, a process examining the text (comparing two strings, perhaps) can lose sight of the fact that a and à are the same letter, possibly causing it to do the wrong thing, without code that knows from extra information that à is just an accented version of a. If you take the second approach, the letter a keeps its identity, but you then have to decide where the code for the accent goes in the sequence relative to the code for the letter a, and what tells a system that the accent belongs on top of the a and not some other letter.

For European languages, the first approach (just assigning a new number to the accented version of a letter) is generally considered to be simpler. But consider another situation:

הֹדוּ לַיהוָה כִּי-טוֹב: כִּי לְעוֹלָם חַסְדּוֹ

In this Hebrew example, that approach breaks down. Here, most of the letters have marks on them, and the same marks can appear on any letter. Assigning a unique code to every letter–mark combination quickly becomes unwieldy, and you have to give the marks their own codes.

In fact, Unicode prefers the give-the-marks-their-own-codes approach, but in many cases it also provides unique codes for the more common letter–mark combinations. Thus many combinations of characters can be represented more than one way. The à and ô in "à bientôt," for example, can be represented either with single character codes, or with pairs of character codes, but you want "à bientôt" to be treated the same no matter which set of codes is used to represent it. This requires a whole bunch of equivalence rules.

The whole idea that you number the characters in a line as they appear from left to right doesn't just break down when you add accent marks and the like into the picture. Sometimes, it's not even straightforward when you're only dealing with letters. The sentence

Avram said מזל טוב and smiled.

is in English with some Hebrew words embedded. It presents an ordering quandary: The Hebrew letters don't run from left to right, but from right to left. That is, the first letter in the Hebrew phrase, מ, is the one farthest to the right. This poses a problem for representation order. You can't really store the characters in the order in which they appear on the line (in effect, storing either the English or the Hebrew "backward"), because it messes up the determination of which characters go on which line when you break text across lines. If you store the characters in the order they're read or typed, you need to specify just how they are to be arranged when the text is displayed or printed.

The ordering thing can go to even wilder extremes. Consider this Hindi example:

$$पूर्ति$$

The letters in Hindi knot together into clusters representing syllables. The syllables run from left to right across the page like English text does, but the arrangement of the marks within a syllable can be complicated and doesn't necessarily follow the order in which the sounds they correspond to are actually spoken (or the characters themselves are typed). There are six characters in this word, arranged like this:

Many writing systems have this kind of complicated ordering or shaping behavior, and each presents unique challenges in determining how to represent the characters as a linear sequence of bits.

You also run into interesting decisions as to just what you mean by "the same character" or "different characters." For example, in the Greek word

$$Χριστος$$

the letter σ and the letter ς are really both lowercase versions of letter sigma (Σ)—it's written one way when it occurs at the end of a word and a different way when it occurs at the beginning or in the middle. Two distinct shapes representing the same letter. Do they get one character code or two? This issue comes up over and over again, as many writing systems have letters that change shape depending on context. In our Hindi example, the hook in the upper-right corner normally looks like this:

$$र$$

It can take some very different forms (including the hook) depending on the characters surrounding it.

You also have the reverse problem of the same shape meaning different things. Chinese characters often have more than one meaning or pronunciation.

Does each different meaning get its own character code? The letter Å can either be a letter in some Scandinavian languages or the symbol for the angstrom unit. Do these two uses get different codes, or is it the same character in both places? What about this character:

3

Is this the number 3 or the Russian letter z? Do these share the same character code just because they happen to look a lot like each other?

For all of these reasons and many more, Unicode is more than just a collection of marks on paper with numbers assigned to them. Every character has a story, and for every character or group of characters, someone had to sit down and decide whether it was the same as or different from the other characters in Unicode, whether several related marks were assigned a single number or several, just what a series of numbers in computer memory would look like when you draw them on the screen, just how a series of marks on a page would translate into a series of numbers in computer memory when neither mapping was straightforward, how a computer performing various types of processes on a series of Unicode character codes would do its job, and so on.

For every character code in the Unicode standard, there are rules about what it means, how it should look in various situations, how it is arranged on a line of text with other characters, what other characters are similar but different, how various text-processing operations should treat it, and so on. Multiply all these decisions by 95,156 unique character codes, and you begin to see why the standard is so big and to realize just how much labor, how much energy, and how much heartache, on the part of so many people, went into this thing. Unicode is the largest, most comprehensive, and most carefully designed standard of its type, and the toil of hundreds of people made it that way.

■ WHAT THIS BOOK DOES

The definitive source on Unicode is, not surprisingly, the Unicode standard itself. The main body of the standard is available in book form as *The Unicode Standard, Version 3.0,* published by Addison-Wesley and available wherever you bought this book. *The Unicode Standard, Version 3.0,* is supplemented by

various tables of character properties covering the exact semantic details of
each individual character, and by various technical reports that clarify, supplement, or extend the standard in various ways. A snapshot of this supplemental
material is on the CD that accompanies *The Unicode Standard, Version 3.0.* The
most current version of this supplemental material, and the definitive source for
the most up-to-date material on the Unicode standard, is the Unicode Web site,
located at `http://www.unicode.org`.

For a long time, the Unicode standard was not only the definitive source on
Unicode, but also the *only* source. The problem with this is that the Unicode standard is just that: a standard. Standards documents are written by and for people
who will implement the standard. They assume extensive domain knowledge and
are designed to define as precisely as possible every aspect of the thing being
standardized. This approach makes sense: The whole purpose of a standard is to
ensure that a diverse group of corporations and institutions all do some particular
thing in the same way so that things produced by these different organizations can
work together properly. If the definition of the standard has holes, or passages that
are open to interpretation, you could wind up with implementations that conform
to the standard, but still don't work together properly.

Because of this requirement, and because they're generally written by committees whose members have different and often conflicting agendas, standards
tend by their very nature to be dry, turgid, legalistic, and highly technical documents. They also tend to be organized in a way that presupposes considerable
domain knowledge—if you're coming to the topic with no prior experience,
you'll often find that to understand any particular chapter of a standard, you'll
have read every other chapter first.

The Unicode standard is better written than most, but it's still good bed-
time reading—at least if you don't mind having nightmares about canonical reordering or the bi-di algorithm. That's where this book comes in. It's intended
to act as a companion to the Unicode standard and supplement it by doing the
following:

- Providing a more approachable, and more pedagogically organized, introduction to the salient features of the Unicode standard
- Capturing in book form changes and additions to the standard since it
  was last published in book form, and additions and adjuncts to the standard that haven't been published in book form

- Filling in background information about the various features of the standard that are beyond the scope of the standard itself
- Providing an introduction to each of the various writing systems Unicode represents and the encoding and implementation challenges presented by each
- Providing useful information on implementing various aspects of the standard, or using existing implementations

My hope is to provide a good enough introduction to "the big picture" and the main components of the technology that you can easily make sense of the more detailed descriptions in the standard itself—or know you don't have to.

This book is for you if you're a programmer using any technology that depends on the Unicode standard. It will give you a good introduction to the main concepts of Unicode, helping you to understand what's relevant to your situation and what things to look for in the libraries or APIs on which you depend.

This book is also for you if you're doing programming work that actually involves implementing part of the Unicode standard and you're relatively new to either Unicode itself or software internationalization in general. It will give you most of what you need and enough of a foundation to be able to find complete and definitive answers in the Unicode standard and its technical reports.

■ HOW THIS BOOK IS ORGANIZED

This book is organized into three parts. Part I, Unicode in Essence, provides an architectural overview of the Unicode standard, explaining the most important concepts in the standard and the motivations behind them. Part II, Unicode in Depth, goes deeper, taking a close look at each of the writing systems representable using Unicode and the unique encoding and implementation problems they pose. Part III, Unicode in Action, takes an in-depth look at what goes into implementing various aspects of the standard, writing code that manipulates Unicode text, and understanding how Unicode interacts with other standards and technologies.

Part I: Unicode in Essence

Part I provides an introduction to the main structure and most important concepts of the standard—the things you need to know to deal properly with Unicode whatever you're doing with it.

Chapter 1 is the book's introduction. It gives a very high-level account of the problem Unicode is trying to solve, the goals and nongoals behind the standard, and the complexity of the problem. It also sets forth the goals and organization of this book.

Chapter 2 puts Unicode into historical context and relates it to other character encoding standards. It discusses ISO 10646, Unicode's sister standard, and its relationship to the Unicode standard.

Chapter 3 provides a more complete architectural overview. It outlines the structure of the standard, Unicode's guiding design principles, and the definition of what it means to conform to the Unicode standard.

Often, it takes two or more Unicode character codes to get a particular effect, and some effects can be achieved with two or more different sequences of codes. Chapter 4 considers this concept, the combining character sequence, and the extra rules that specify how to deal with combining character sequences that are equivalent.

Every character in Unicode has a large set of properties that define its semantics and how it should be treated by various processes. These properties are all set forth in the Unicode Character Database. Chapter 5 introduces this database and all of the various character properties it defines.

The Unicode standard actually consists of two layers: a layer that defines a transformation between written text and a series of abstract numeric codes, and a layer that defines a transformation between those abstract numeric codes and patterns of bits in memory or in persistent storage. The lower layer, from abstract numbers to bits, comprises several different mappings, each optimized for different situations. Chapter 6 introduces and discusses these mappings.

Part II: Unicode in Depth

Unicode doesn't specifically deal in languages; instead, it deals in **scripts**, or writing systems. A script is a collection of characters used to represent a group of related languages. Generally, no language uses all the characters in a script. For example, English is written using the Latin alphabet. Unicode encodes 819 Latin letters, but English only uses 52 (26 uppercase and lowercase letters). Part II goes through the standard script by script, looking at the features of each script, the languages that are written with it, and the way in which it's represented in Unicode. It groups scripts into families according to their common characteristics.

For example, in Chapter 7 we discuss the scripts used to write various European languages. These scripts generally don't pose any interesting ordering or shaping problems, but are the only scripts that have special uppercase and lowercase forms. They're all descended from (or otherwise related to) the ancient Greek alphabet. This group includes the Latin, Greek, Cyrillic, Armenian, and Georgian alphabets, as well as various collections of diacritical marks and the International Phonetic Alphabet.

Chapter 8 looks at the scripts of the Middle East. The major feature shared by these scripts is that they're written from right to left rather than left to right. They also tend to use letters only for consonant sounds, using separate marks around the basic letters to represent the vowels. Two scripts in this group are cursively connected, even in printed text, which poses interesting representational problems. These scripts are all descended from the ancient Aramaic alphabet. This group includes the Hebrew, Arabic, Syriac, and Thaana alphabets.

Chapter 9 examines the scripts of India and Southeast Asia. The letters in these scripts knot together into clusters that represent whole syllables. The scripts in this group all descend from the ancient Brahmi script. This group includes the Devanagari script used to write Hindi and Sanskrit, plus 18 other scripts, including Thai and Tibetan.

In Chapter 10, we look at the scripts of East Asia. The interesting things here are that these scripts comprise tens of thousands of unique, often complicated characters (the exact number is impossible to determine, and new characters are created all the time). These characters are generally all the same size, don't combine with one another, and can be written either from left to right or vertically. This group includes the Chinese characters and various other writing systems that either are used with Chinese characters or arose under their influence.

While most languages of the world are written using a writing system that falls into one of the above groups, not all of them do. Chapter 11 discusses the other scripts, including Mongolian, Ethiopic, Cherokee, and the Unified Canadian Aboriginal Syllabics, a set of characters used for writing a variety of Native American languages. In addition to the modern scripts, Unicode encodes a growing number of scripts that are *not* used now but are of scholarly interest. The current version of Unicode includes four of these scripts, which are also discussed in Chapter 11.

Of course, you can't write only with the characters that represent the sounds or words of spoken language. You also need things like punctuation marks, numbers, symbols, and various other nonletter characters. These characters are covered in Chapter 12, along with various special formatting and document-structure characters.

Part III: Unicode in Action

Part III examines various techniques that can be used in code to implement or make use of the Unicode standard.

Chapter 13 provides an introduction to the subject, discussing a group of generic data structures and techniques that are useful for various types of processes that operate on Unicode text.

Chapter 14 explains in detail how to perform various types of transformations and conversions on Unicode text. These operations include converting between the various Unicode serialization formats, performing Unicode compression and decompression, performing Unicode normalization, converting between Unicode and other encoding standards, and performing case mapping and case folding.

Chapter 15 zeros in on two of the most complex text-analysis processes: searching and sorting. It talks about both language-sensitive and language-insensitive string comparisons and how searching and sorting algorithms build on language-sensitive string comparison.

Chapter 16 discusses the most important operations performed on text: drawing it on the screen (or other output devices) and accepting it as input, otherwise known as rendering and editing. It considers dividing text up into lines, arranging characters on a line, figuring out what shape to use for a particular character or sequence of characters, and various special considerations one must deal with when writing text-editing software.

Finally, in Chapter 17 we look at how Unicode intersects with other computer technologies. This chapter discusses Unicode and the Internet, Unicode and various programming languages, and Unicode and various operating systems.

2

A Brief History of Character Encoding

*T*o understand Unicode fully, it's helpful to have a good sense of where we came from and what the whole business of character encoding involves. Unicode didn't just spring fully grown from the forehead of Zeus; it's the latest step in a history that actually predates the digital computer, having its roots in telecommunications. Unicode is not the first attempt to solve the problem it addresses, and Unicode is also in its third major revision. To understand the design decisions that led to Unicode 3.0, it's useful to understand what worked and what didn't work in Unicode's many predecessors.

This chapter is entirely background material. If you want to jump right in and start looking at the features and design of Unicode itself, feel free to skip it.

▪ PREHISTORY

Unlike with written language itself, the history of electronic (or electrical) representations of written language doesn't go back very far. Of course, that's largely because the history of the *devices* using these representations doesn't go back very far.

The modern age of information technology does, however, start earlier than one might think at first—a good century or so before the advent of the modern

25

digital computer. We can date the beginning of modern information technology from Samuel Morse's invention of the telegraph in 1837.[1]

The telegraph is more than just an interesting historical curiosity. Telegraphic communication has never really disappeared, although it's morphed into different forms. Long after the invention and popularization of the telephone, the successors to the telegraph continued to be used to send written communication over a wire. Telegraphic communication was used to send large volumes of text, especially when it needed ultimately to be put into written form (news stories, for example), or when human contact wasn't especially important and saving money on bandwidth was very important (especially for routine business communications such as orders and invoices). Today, e-mail and EDI are more or less the logical descendants of the telegraph.

The Telegraph and Morse Code

So our story starts with the telegraph. Morse's original telegraph actually worked on numeric codes, not the alphanumeric code with which we're familiar today. The idea was that the operators on either end of the line would have a dictionary that assigned a unique number to each *word,* not each letter, in English (or a useful subset). The sender would look up each word in the dictionary and send the number corresponding to that word; the receiver would do the opposite. (The idea was probably to automate this process in some way, perhaps with some kind of mechanical device that would point to each word in a list or something.)

This approach had died out before Morse's famous "WHAT HATH GOD WROUGHT" demonstration in 1844. By this time, the device was being used to send the early version of what we now know as "Morse code," which was probably actually devised by Morse's assistant Alfred Vail.

Morse code was in no way digital in the sense we think of the term—you can't easily turn it into a stream of 1 and 0 bits the way you can with many of the succeeding codes. But it was "digital" in the sense that it was based on a

---

1. My main source for this section is Tom Jennings, "Annotated History of Character Codes," found at `http://www.wps.com/texts/codes`.

circuit that had only two states, on and off. This step is Morse's big innovation; telegraph systems had existed prior to Morse, but they were based on sending varying voltages down the line and deflecting a needle on a gauge of some kind.[2] The beauty of Morse's scheme is a higher level of error tolerance—it's a lot easier to tell "on" from "off" than it is to tell "half on" from "three-fifths on." This, of course, is also why modern computers are based on binary numbers.

Morse code is based not on a succession of "ons" and "offs," however, but on a succession of "ons" of different lengths, with some amount of "off" state separating them. It uses two types of signal: a long "on" state, usually represented with a dash and pronounced "dah," and a short "on" state, usually represented by a dot and pronounced "dit." Individual letters were represented with varying-length sequences of dots and dashes.

The lengths of the codes were designed to correspond roughly to the relative frequencies of the characters in a transmitted message. Letters were represented with anywhere from one to four dots and dashes. The two one-signal letters were the two most frequent letters in English: E was represented with a single dot and T with a single dash. The four two-signal letters were I (. .), A (. –), N (– .), and M (– –). The least common letters were represented with the longest codes: Z (– – . .), Y (– . – –), J (. – – –), and Q (– – . –). Digits were represented with sequences of five signals, and punctuation, which was used sparingly, was represented with sequences of six signals. The dots and dashes were separated by just enough space to keep everything from running together, individual characters by longer spaces, and words by even longer spaces.

As an interesting sidelight, the telegraph was designed as a recording instrument—the signal operated a solenoid that caused a stylus to dig shallow grooves in a moving strip of paper. (The interpretation of Morse code by listening to beeping, as we've all seen in World War II movies, came later, with radio, although experienced telegraph operators could interpret the signal by listening to the clicking of the stylus.) This system was a historical antecedent to the punched-tape systems used in teletype machines and early computers.

---

2. This tidbit comes from Steven J. Searle, "A Brief History of Character Codes," found at http://www.tronweb.super-nova.co.jp/characcodehist.html.

The Teletypewriter and Baudot Code

Of course, what you *really* want isn't grooves on paper, but actual writing on paper. One problem with Morse's telegraph was that the varying lengths of the signals didn't lend themselves well to driving a mechanical device that could put actual letters on paper. The first big step in this direction was Emile Baudot's "printing telegraph," invented in 1874.

Baudot's system didn't use a typewriter keyboard, but rather a pianolike keyboard with five keys, each of which controlled a separate electrical connection. The operator operated two keys with the left hand and three with the right and sent each character by pressing down some combination of these five keys simultaneously. (The "chording keyboards" that are somewhat in vogue today as a way of combating RSI aren't a new idea—they go all the way back to 1874.)

Thus the code for each character is some combination of the five keys, so you can think of it as a 5-bit code. Of course, this system gives you only 32 combinations to play with, a meager allotment for encoding characters. You can't even get all the letters and digits in 32 codes.

The solution devised for this problem persisted for many years: You have two separate sets of characters assigned to the various key combinations, and you steal two key combinations to switch between them. As a result, you end up with a LTRS bank, consisting of 28 letters (the 26 you'd expect, plus 2 French letters), and a FIGS bank, also consisting of 28 characters (the 10 digits and various punctuation marks and symbols). The three left-hand-only combinations have the same function in both banks: Two of them switch back and forth between LTRS and FIGS, and one (both left-hand keys together) means "ignore the last character" (this eventually evolved into the ASCII DEL character). The thirty-second combination, no keys at all, didn't mean anything—"no keys at all" separated one character code from the next. (The FIGS and LTRS signals doubled as spaces.)

The operator would go along in LTRS mode, sending letters. When a number or punctuation mark was reached, the Baudot operator would send FIGS, send the number or punctuation, send LTRS, and return to sending words again. For example, "I have 23 children." would be sent as follows:

I HAVE **[FIGS]** 23 **[LTRS]** CHILDREN **[FIGS]**.

It would have been possible to get the same effect by just adding a sixth key, of course, but this was considered too complicated mechanically.

Even though Baudot's code (actually invented by Johann Gauss and Wilhelm Weber) can be thought of as a series of 5-bit numbers, it isn't laid out as you might arrange a similar thing today: If you lay out the code charts according to the binary-number order, it looks jumbled. As with Morse code, characters were assigned to key combinations in such a way as to minimize fatigue, both to the operator and to the machinery. More-frequent characters, for example, used fewer fingers than did less-frequent characters.

Other Teletype and Telegraphy Codes

The logical next step from Baudot's apparatus would be a system that used a normal typewriterlike keyboard instead of the pianolike keyboard employed by Baudot. Such a device was invented by Donald Murray sometime between 1899 and 1901. Murray kept the 5-bit, two-state system Baudot had used, but rearranged the characters. As there was no longer a direct correlation between the operator's hand movements and the bits being sent over the wire, there was no need to worry about arranging the code to minimize operator fatigue; instead, Murray designed his code entirely to minimize wear and tear on the machinery.

Some interesting developments occur first in the Murray code. First, it debuts what later became known as "format effectors" or "control characters"— the CR and LF codes, which return the typewriter carriage to the beginning of the line and advance the platen by one line, respectively.[3] Second, a few codes from Baudot moved to the positions where they have stayed ever since (at least until the introduction of Unicode, by which time the positions no longer mattered): the NULL or BLANK all-bits-off code and the DEL all-bits-on code. All bits off, fairly logically, meant that the receiving machine shouldn't do anything; it was essentially used as an idle code for when no messages were being sent. On real equipment, you also often had to pad codes that took a long time to execute with NULLs. If you issued a CR, for example, it would take a while

---

3. I'm taking my cue from Jennings here: These code positions were apparently marked "COL" and "LINE PAGE" originally; Jennings extrapolates back from later codes that had CR and LF in the same positions and assumes that "COL" and "LINE PAGE" were alternate names for the same functions.

for the carriage to return to the home position, and any "real" characters sent during this time would be lost; for this reason, you would send extra NULLs after the CR. This tactic would put enough space after the CR so that the real characters wouldn't go down the line until the receiving machine could print them, and it would not have any effect (other than maybe to waste time) if the carriage got there while they were still being sent.

The DEL character would also be ignored by the receiving equipment. The idea here was that if paper tape was being used as an intermediate storage medium (as we still see today, it became common practice to compose a message while off line, store it on paper tape, and then log on and send the message from the paper tape rather than "live" from the keyboard) and you made a mistake, the only way to blank out the mistake was to punch out all the holes in the line with the mistake. So a row with all the holes punched out (or a character with all the bits set, as we think of it today) was treated as a null character.

Murray's code formed the basis of most of the various telegraphy codes of the next 50 years or so. Western Union picked it up and used it (with a few changes) as its encoding method until the 1950s. The CCITT (Consultative Committee for International Telephone and Telegraph, a European standards body) picked up the Western Union code and, with a few changes, blessed it as an international standard, International Telegraphy Alphabet #2 (ITA2). The ITA2 code is often referred to today as "Baudot code," although it's significantly different from Baudot's code. It does, however, retain many of the most important features of Baudot's code.

Among the interesting differences between Murray's code and ITA2 were the addition of more "control codes". An explicit space character was introduced, rather than using the all-bits-off signal, or the LTRS and FIGS signals, as spaces. A new BEL signal rang a bell or produced some other audible signal on the receiving end. Also, for the first time a code existed explicitly to control the communications process itself—the WRU, or "Who are you?" code, which would cause the receiving machine to send some identifying stream of characters back to the sending machine (which enabled the sender to make sure that he or she was connected to the right receiver before sending sensitive information down the wire, for example).

At this point, inertia set in throughout the industry. By the time ITA2 and its national variants came into use in the 1930s, a significant number of teletype machines had been deployed and the weight of an international standard had been placed behind one encoding method. ITA2 would be the code used by teletype machines into the 1960s. When computers started communicating with the outside world in real time using some kind of terminal, the terminal would be a teletype machine, and the computer would communicate with it using the teletype codes of the day. (The other main way computers dealt with alphanumeric data was through the use of punched cards, which had their own encoding schemes.)

FIELDATA and ASCII

The teletype codes were all 5-bit codes with two separate banks of characters, which meant that they all included the concept of "state." That is, the interpretation of a particular code depended on the last bank-change signal (some operations also included an implicit bank change—a carriage return, for example, often switched the system back to LTRS mode). This system makes sense if you're dealing with a completely serial medium where you don't have random access into the middle of a character stream and as long as you're working with a mechanical system (LTRS and FIGS would just shift the print head or the platen to a different position). In computer memory, where you might want random access to a character and prefer to avoid having to scan backward an arbitrary distance for a LTRS or FIGS character to find out what you're looking at, it generally makes more sense to use an extra bit to store the LTRS or FIGS state. This approach produces a 6-bit code. Indeed, for a long time, characters were thought of as 6-bit units. (Punched-card codes of the day were also six bits in length, so you've got that, too.) This is one reason why many computers of the time had word lengths that were multiples of 6. As late as 1978, for example, Kernighan and Ritchie mention that the `int` and `short` data types in C were 36 bits wide on the Honeywell 6000, implying that it had a 36-bit word length.[4]

By the late 1950s, the computer and telecommunications industries were both starting to chafe under the limitations of the 6-bit teletype and punched-card codes of the day, and a new standards effort was begun that eventually

---

4. See Brian W. Kernighan and Dennis M. Ritchie, *The C Programming Language* (Prentice-Hall, 1978), p. 34.

led to the ASCII code. An important predecessor of ASCII was the FIELD-ATA code used in various pieces of communications equipment designed and used by the U.S. Army starting in 1957. (It bled out into civilian life as well; UNIVAC computers of that era were based on a modified version of the FIELDATA code.)

FIELDATA was a 7-bit code, but was divided into layers in such a way that you could think of it as a 4-bit code with either two or three control bits appended, similar to punched-card codes. It's useful[5] to think of it has having a 5-bit core similar to the ITA2 model with two control bits. The most significant, or "tag," bit is used similarly to the LTRS/FIGS bit discussed earlier; it switches the other six bits between the "alphabetic" and "supervisory" banks. The next-most-significant bit shifted the five core bits between two sub-banks: The alphabetic bank was shifted between uppercase and lowercase sub-banks, and the supervisory bank was shifted between a supervisory and a numeric/symbols sub-bank.

In essence, the extra bit made it possible to include both uppercase and lowercase letters for the first time, and it also allowed the inclusion of a wide range of control, or supervisory, codes. The latter codes were used for tasks such as controlling the communication protocol (there were various handshake and termination codes) and separating various units of variable-length structured data. Also, within each 5-bit bank of characters, we finally see the influence of computer technology: The characters are ordered in binary-number order.

FIELDATA had a profound influence on ASCII, which was being designed at the same time. Committee X3.4 of the American Standards Association (now the American National Standards Institute, or ANSI) had been convened in the late 1950s, about the time FIELDATA was deployed, and consisted of representatives from AT&T, IBM (which, ironically, didn't actually use ASCII until the IBM PC came out in 1981), and various other companies from the computer and telecommunications industries.

The first result of this committee's efforts was what we now know as ANSI X3.4-1963, the first version of the American Standard Code for Information Interchange, our old friend ASCII. ASCII-1963 kept the overall structure of

---

5. Or at least *I* think it's useful, looking at the code charts—my sources don't describe things this way.

FIELDATA and regularized some things. For example, this pure 7-bit code is laid out in such a way as to make it possible to reasonably sort a list into alphabetical order by comparing the numeric character codes directly. ASCII-1963 didn't officially include the lowercase letters, although it had a big undefined space where they would later go, and it featured some weird placements, such as a few control codes in the printing-character range. These problems were fixed in ASCII-1967, which is more or less the ASCII we all know and love today. It standardized the meanings of some of the control codes that were left open in ASCII-1963, moved all of the control codes (except for DEL) into the control-code area, and added the lowercase letters and some special programming-language symbols. It also discarded certain programming-language symbols from ASCII-1963 in a bow to international usage: The upward-pointing arrow used for exponentiation turned into the caret (which did double duty as the circumflex accent), and the left-pointing arrow (used sometimes to represent assignment) turned into the underscore character.

Hollerith and EBCDIC

As we see, ASCII has its roots in telegraphy codes that date back to the nineteenth century and, in fact, was designed in part as telegraphy code itself. The other important category of character codes encompasses the punched-card codes. For many years, punched cards were the main way computers dealt with alphanumeric data. In fact, the use of the punched card for data processing predates the modern computer, although not by as long as the telegraph.

Punched cards date back at least to 1810, when Joseph-Marie Jacquard used them to control automatic weaving machines. Charles Babbage proposed adapting Jacquard's punched cards for use in his "analytical engine." Punched cards weren't actually used for data processing until the 1880s, when Herman Hollerith, a U.S. Census Bureau employee, devised a method of using punched cards to collate and tabulate census data. His punched cards were first used on a national scale in the 1890 census, dramatically speeding the tabulation process. The 1880 census figures, calculated entirely by hand, had taken seven years to tabulate. The 1890 census figures took six weeks. Flush with the success of the 1890 census, Hollerith formed the Tabulating Machine Company in 1896 to market his punched cards and the machines used to punch, sort, and count them. This company eventually merged with two others, diversified into actual computers, and grew into what we now know as the world's largest computer company, International Business Machines.[6]

The modern IBM rectangular-hole punched card was first introduced in 1928 and has since become recognized as the standard punched-card format. It had 80 columns, each representing a single character (it's no coincidence that most text-based CRT terminals had 80-column displays). Each column had 12 punch positions. This format would seem to indicate that Hollerith code, the means of mapping from punch positions to characters, was a 12-bit code, which would give you 4,096 possible combinations.

This assumption is wrong, however. You didn't actually want to use all of the possible combinations of punch positions—doing so would put too many holes in the card and weaken its structural integrity (not a small consideration when these things are flying through the sorting machine at a rate of a few dozen per second). The system worked as follows: You had 10 main rows of punch holes, numbered 0 through 9, and two "zone" rows, 11 and 12 (row 0 also did double duty as a zone row). The digits were represented by single punches in rows 0 through 9, and the space was represented with no punches at all.

The letters were represented with two punches: a punch in row 11, 12, or 0 plus a punch in one of the rows from 1 to 9. This system divided the alphabet into three nine-letter "zones." A few special characters were represented with the extra one-punch combinations and the remaining two-punch combination. The others were represented with three-punch combinations: Row 8 would be pressed into service as an extra zone row and the characters would be repre-sented with a combination of a punch in row 8; a punch in row 11, 12, or 0; and a punch in one of the rows from 1 to 7 (row 9 wasn't used). This system sup-ported three banks of seven symbols each (four banks if you included a bank that used row 8 as a zone row without an additional punch in row 11, 12, or 0). The grand total was 67 unique punch combinations. Early punched-card sys-

---

6. Much of the information in the preceding paragraph is drawn from the Searle article; the source for the rest of this section is Douglas W. Jones, "Punched Cards: An Illustrated Technical History" and "Doug Jones' Punched Card Codes," both found at http://www.cs.uiowa.edu/~jones/cards.

tems didn't use all of these combinations, but later systems filled in until all of the possible combinations were being used.

In memory, the computers used a 6-bit encoding system tied to the punch patterns. The four least-significant bits would specify the main punch row (meaning 10 of the possible 16 combinations would be used), and the two most-significant bits would identify which zone row was punched. (Actual systems weren't always quite so straightforward, but this was the basic idea.) This approach was sufficient to reproduce all of the one- and two-punch combinations in a straightforward manner and was known as the Binary Coded Decimal Information Code (BCDIC, or just BCD for short).

IBM added two more bits to BCD to form the *Extended* Binary Coded Decimal Information Code (EBCDIC), which first appeared with the introduction of the System/360 in 1964. It was backward compatible with the BCD system used in the punched cards, but added the lowercase letters and several control codes borrowed from ASCII-1963 (you didn't really need control codes in a punched-card system, because the positions of the columns on the cards, or the division of information between cards, gave you the structure of the data, and you didn't need codes for controlling the communication session). This code was designed both to allow a simple mapping from character codes to punch positions on a punched card and, like ASCII, to produce a reasonable sorting order when the numeric codes were used to sort character data. (Note that you don't get the *same* order with EBCDIC as with ASCII—digits sort after letters instead of before them, and lowercase sorts before uppercase instead of the reverse.)

One consequence of EBCDIC's lineage is that the three groups of nine letters in the alphabet used in the punched-card codes are numerically separated from each other in the EBCDIC encoding. For example, I is represented by 0xC9 and J by 0xD1, leaving an eight-space gap in the numerical sequence. The original version of EBCDIC encoded only 50 characters in an 8-bit encoding space, leaving large numbers of gaping holes with no assigned characters. Later versions of EBCDIC filled in these holes in various ways, but retained the backward compatibility with the old punched-card system. Although ASCII is finally taking over in IBM's product line, EBCDIC survives in the current models of IBM's System/390, even though punched cards are long obsolete. Backward compatibility is a powerful force.

■ SINGLE-BYTE ENCODING SYSTEMS

ANSI X3.4-1967 (ASCII-1967) went on to be adopted as an international standard, first by the European Computer Manufacturers' Association as ECMA-6 (which actually came out in 1965, two years before the updated version of ANSI X3.4), and then by the International Organization for Standardization (ISO) as ISO 646 in 1972. (ISO serves as an umbrella organization for most national standards bodies and generally creates international standards by taking various national standards, modifying them to be more palatable to an international audience, and republishing them as international standards.)

A few interesting things happened to ASCII on its way to turning into ISO 646. First, it formalized a system for applying the various accents and other diacritical marks used in European languages to the letters. It did this not by introducing accented variants of all the letters—there was no room for that—but by pressing several punctuation marks into service as diacritical marks. The apostrophe did double duty as the acute accent, the opening quote mark as the grave accent, the double quotation mark as the diaeresis (or umlaut), the caret as the circumflex accent, the swung dash as the tilde, and the comma as the cedilla. To produce an accented letter, you'd follow the letter in the code sequence with a backspace code and then the appropriate "accent mark." On a teletype machine, the letter would be overstruck with the punctuation mark, producing an ugly but serviceable version of the accented letter.

ISO 646 also left the definitions of 12 characters open—the so-called national-use code positions (in ASCII, these 12 characters are #, $, @, [, \,], ^, `, {, |, }, and ~). An International Reference Version of ISO 646 gives the American meanings to the corresponding code points, but other national bodies were allowed to assign other characters to these 12 code values. (Some national bodies did put accented letters in these slots.) The various national variants have generally given way to more-modern standards such as ISO 8859 (described later), but vestiges of the old system remain. For example, many Japanese systems treat the code for \ as the code for ¥.[7]

---

7. The preceding information comes partially from the Jennings paper, and partially from Roman Czyborra, "Good Old ASCII," found at `http://www.czyborra.com/charsets/iso646.html`.

Eight-Bit Encoding Schemes and the ISO 2022 Model

ASCII gave us the 8-bit byte. All earlier encoding systems (except for FIELD-ATA, which can be considered an embryonic version of ASCII) used a 6-bit byte. ASCII extended that to 7, and most communication protocols tacked on an eighth bit as a parity-check bit. As the parity bit became less necessary (especially in computer memory) and 7-bit ASCII codes were stored in 8-bit computer bytes, it was only natural that the 128 bit combinations not defined by ASCII (the ones with the high-order bit set) would be pressed into service to represent more characters.

This need was anticipated as early as 1971, when the ECMA-35 standard was first published.[8] This standard later became ISO 2022. ISO 2022 sets forth a method of organizing the code space for various character encoding methods. An ISO 2022-compliant character encoding can have up to two sets of control characters, designated C0 and C1, and up to four sets of printing ("graphic") characters, designated G0, G1, G2, and G3.

The encoding space can either be seven or eight bits wide. In a 7-bit encoding, the byte values from 0x00 to 0x1F are reserved for the C0 controls, and the byte values from 0x20 to 0xFF are used for the G0, G1, G2, and G3 sets. The range defaults to the G0 set, and escape sequences can be used to switch it to one of the other sets.

In an 8-bit encoding, the range of values from 0x00 to 0x1F (the "CL area") constitutes the C0 controls, and the range from 0x80 to 0x9F (the "CR area") constitutes the C1 controls. The range from 0x20 to 0x7F (the "GL area") always represents the G0 characters, and the range from 0xA0 to 0xFF (the "GR area") can be switched between the G1, G2, and G3 characters.

Control functions (signals to the receiving process, as opposed to printing characters) can be represented either as single control characters or as sequences of characters usually beginning with a control character (usually that control character is ESC and the multicharacter control function is an "escape sequence"). ISO 2022 uses escape sequences to represent C1 controls in the 7-bit systems, and to switch the GR and GL areas between the various sets of

---

8. The information in this section is taken from Peter K. Edberg, "Survey of Character Encodings," *Proceedings of the 13th International Unicode Conference,* session TA4, September 9, 1998, and from a quick glance at the ECMA-35 standard itself.

printing characters in both the 7- and 8-bit versions. It also specifies a method of using escape sequences to associate the various areas of the encoding space (C0, C1, G0, G1, G2, and G3) with actual sets of characters.

ISO 2022 doesn't actually apply semantics to most of the code positions–the major exceptions are ESC, DEL, and the space, which are given the positions they have in ASCII. Other character semantics are taken from other standards, and escape sequences can be used to switch an area's interpretation from one standard to another (a registry specifies the auxiliary standards and the escape sequences used to switch between them).

An ISO 2022-based standard can impose whatever semantics it wants on the various encoding areas and can choose whether to use the escape sequences for switching things. As a practical matter, most ISO 2022-derived standards put the ISO 646 IRV (i.e., U.S. ASCII) printing characters in the G0 area and include the C0 control functions from ISO 6429 (which defines a whole mess of control functions, along with standardized C0 and C1 sets—the C0 set is the same as the ASCII control characters) into the C0 area.

ISO 8859

By far, the most important of the ISO 2022-derived encoding schemes is the ISO 8859 family.[9] The ISO 8859 standard comprises 14 separate ISO 2022-compliant encoding standards, each covering a different set of characters for a different set of languages. Each counts as a separate standard. ISO 8859-1, for example, is the near-ubiquitous Latin-1 character set you see on the Web.

Work on the ISO 8859 family began in 1982 as a joint project of ANSI and ECMA. The first part was originally published in 1985 as ECMA-94. It was adopted as ISO 8859-1, and a later edition of ECMA-94 became the first four parts of ISO 8859. The other parts of ISO 8859 likewise originated in various ECMA standards.

---

9. Much of the information in this section is drawn from Roman Czyborra, "ISO 8859 Alphabet Soup," found at `http://www.czyborra.com/charsets/iso8859.html`, supplemented with information from the ISO Web site, the ECMA-94 standard, and the Edberg article.

The ISO 8859 series is oriented, as one might expect, toward European languages and European usage, as well as certain languages around the periphery of Europe that are used frequently there. It aimed to do three things:

1. Do away with the use of backspace sequences as a way to represent accented characters (the backspace strategy works on a teletype, but doesn't work at all on a CRT terminal without some pretty fancy rendering hardware)
2. Do away with the varying meanings of the "national use" characters from ISO 646, replacing them with a set of code values that would have the same meaning everywhere and still include everyone's characters.
3. Unify other national and vendor standards that were attempting to do the same thing.

All of the parts of ISO 8859 are based on the ISO 2022 structure, and all have a lot in common. Each part assigns the ISO 646 printing characters to the G0 range, and the ISO 6429 C0 and C1 control characters to the C0 and C1 ranges. Thus each standard, whatever else it includes, includes the basic Latin alphabet and is downward compatible with ASCII. (That is, pure 7-bit ASCII text, when represented with 8-bit bytes, conforms to any of the 8859 standards.) Where the standards differ is in their treatment of the G1 range. None defines anything in the G2 or G3 areas or uses escape sequences to switch interpretations of any of the code points, although you can use the registered ISO 2022 escape sequences to assign the G1 repertoire from any of these standards to the various GR ranges in a generalized ISO 2022 implementation.

The 14 parts of ISO 8859 are as follows:

ISO 8859-1	Latin-1	Western European languages (French, German, Spanish, Italian, the Scandinavian languages, and so on)
ISO 8859-2	Latin-2	Eastern European languages (Czech, Hungarian, Polish, Romanian, and so on)
ISO 8859-3	Latin-3	Southern European languages (Maltese and Turkish, plus Esperanto)
ISO 8859-4	Latin-4	Northern European languages (Latvian, Lithuanian, Estonian, Greenlandic, and Sami)

ISO 8859-5	Cyrillic	Russian, Bulgarian, Ukrainian, Belarusian, Serbian, and Macedonian
ISO 8859-6	Arabic	Arabic
ISO 8859-7	Greek	Greek
ISO 8859-8	Hebrew	Hebrew
ISO 8859-9	Latin-5	Turkish (replaces Latin-3)
ISO 8859-10	Latin-6	Northern European languages (unifies Latin-1 and Latin-4)
ISO 8859-11	Thai	Thai
ISO 8859-13	Latin-7	Baltic languages (replaces Latin-4; supplements Latin-6)
ISO 8859-14	Latin-8	Celtic languages
ISO 8859-15	Latin-9	Western European languages (replaces Latin-1; adds the euro symbol and some forgotten French and Finnish letters)
ISO 8859-16	Latin-10	Eastern European languages (replaces Latin-2; adds the euro symbol and a few missing Romanian letters)

The ISO 8859 family of standards reveals how constraining an 8-bit encoding space can be. You have many different versions of the Latin alphabet with considerable overlap, each optimizing for a slightly different collection of alphabets. Likewise, the standards for the non-Latin alphabets tend to make do with fairly constrained collections of characters from their writing systems. Even so, they're a lot better, and a lot more standard, than the mishmash that came before.

Other 8-Bit Encoding Schemes

Many other 8-bit encoding standards exist. They include a wide variety of vendor-developed encodings (many vendors, including IBM and Microsoft, call these "code pages") that cover the same set of languages as the 8859 series, but generally predate it and put things in a different order. Some code pages add other nonletter characters, such as the old DOS box-drawing characters. These encodings include the old Macintosh and DOS code pages that predate ISO 8859, as well as some code pages that follow and extend ISO 8859. While most of these are downward compatible with ASCII, they're not always compliant with ISO 2022. Windows code page 1252, the Western European encoding for Windows, for example, is a superset of ISO 8859-1. It includes all of the Latin-1 characters, but then fills the C1 space with additional printing characters. (Sometimes you even see this happen to the C0 space: The old standard IBM PC code page not only had box-drawing and other characters in the C1/G1 range, but also put printing characters in the C0 range where they could be confused with control characters.) IBM also created numerous EBCDIC-derived code pages devoted to the languages covered by the ISO 8859 family.

Other 8-bit encoding standards focus on languages outside the ISO 8859 family. They include the TIS 620 standard for Thai, an ISO 2022-derived standard that puts the Thai letters in the G1 range, and the ISCII (Indian Script Code for Information Interchange) standard, which places any of several sets of characters for writing Indian languages in the G1 area. (The various Indian writing systems are all so closely related that the meanings of the code points are common across all of them—you can often transliterate from one Indian writing system to another simply by changing fonts.) The VISCII (Vietnamese Standard Code for Information Interchange, an Internet RFC) and TCVN 5712 (a Vietnamese national standard) standards are used for writing Vietnamese and are ASCII-derived, but invade both the C0 and C1 areas with Vietnamese letters (it's a big set). One version of TCVN 5712 complies with ISO 2022, but it relies on combinations of codes to represent the letters.

The Japanese JIS X 0201 (JIS-Roman) standard is also an ISO 2022-derived 8-bit standard. It places the Japanese Katakana syllabary in the G1 area. Here, though, the G0 area isn't exactly the same as American ASCII. A few of the "national use" code positions from ISO 646 have Japanese-specific meanings. For example, the code position normally occupied by the backslash (\) is instead occupied by the yen sign (¥), so DOS path names on Japanese computers come out with yen signs between their components.

▪ CHARACTER ENCODING TERMINOLOGY

Before we move on to talk about more character encoding standards, we need to take a break and define some terms. This effort will make the discussion in the next section easier and help crystallize some of the fuzzy terminology in the sections we just finished.

It's useful to think of the mapping of a sequence of written characters to a sequence of bits in a computer memory or storage device or in a communication link as taking places in a series of stages, or *levels,* rather than all at once. The Internet Architecture Board (IAB) proposed a three-level encoding model. The Unicode standard, in Unicode Technical Report (UTR) #17, proposes a five-level model, explicitly discussing one level that was merely implied in the IAB model, and interposing an extra level between two of the IAB levels. This discussion borrows the terms from UTR #17, as it was designed specifically to make it easier to talk about Unicode.

The first level is the **abstract character repertoire,** a collection of characters to be encoded. It can usually be expressed simply in words: Such phrases as "the Latin alphabet" or "the union of the English, Spanish, French, German, Italian, Swedish, Danish, and Norwegian alphabets" define repertoires. For most Western languages, this kind of thing is pretty straightforward and usually takes the form "The blah-blah alphabet, plus this set of special characters and digits." For East Asian languages, matters are more complicated.

One of the other things you must think about when defining a character repertoire is just what constitutes a "character." Here, "character" can simply mean "a semantic unit that has its own identity when encoded." An encoding standard can decide, for example, whether accented letters are first-class characters that get their own identity when encoded, or whether the accents themselves are first-class characters that get their own identity and combine with unaccented letters to form the accented letters. Another example would be whether the different shapes a character can assume in different contexts are each treated as a separate "character" or whether the underlying and unchanging semantic unit these shapes represent is treated as a "character."

Unicode defines a "character" as an independent abstract semantic unit, explicitly eschewing glyph variants and presentation forms. It explicitly encodes accents and other combining marks as first-class characters. Other encoding standards made different decisions. Throughout the rest of the book, we'll use "character" the way Unicode does, distinguishing it from "glyph," rather than simply to mean "something deemed worthy of encoding."

The second level is the **coded character set,** a mapping between the characters in an abstract repertoire and some collection of coordinates. Most coded character sets map the characters to *x* and *y* positions in a table, although these coordinates can always be mapped to a set of single numbers.

Allied with the concept of a coded character set is the idea of an **encoding space,** basically the dimensions of the table containing all the characters. It can be expressed as a pair of numbers ("a 16 × 16 encoding space") or as a single number ("a 256-character encoding space"). Often (but not always) the encoding space is constrained by the size of the storage unit used to represent a character, which is used as a shorthand way of describing the encoding space ("an 8-bit encoding space"). Sometimes the encoding space is broken down into subsets. Depending on the subset and the standard, these subsets go by various names (e.g., "row," "plane," "column").

A position in the encoding space is called a **code point.** The position occupied by a particular character is called a **code point value.** A coded character set is a mapping of characters to code point values.

The third level of the encoding model is the **character encoding form,** also called a "storage format." It maps the abstract code point values to sequences of integers of a specific size, called **code units.** For a fixed-size encoding, this is usually a null mapping, but it doesn't have to be. For variable-length encodings, the mapping is more complicated, as some code points will map to single code units and some code points will map to sequences of code units.

The fourth level of the encoding model is the **character encoding scheme,** also referred to as the "serialization format." This mapping goes from code unit values to actual sequences of bits. Two things happen here. First, code units that are more than a byte long are converted to sequences of bytes, meaning that which byte goes first when the encoded text is sent over a communications link or written to a storage medium becomes important. Second, a character encoding scheme may tie together two or more character encoding forms, defining extra bytes that get written into the serialized data stream to switch between them, or some additional transformation that happens to the code units from one of the encoding forms to make their numeric ranges disjoint. The "charset" parameter that shows up in a variety of Internet standards (see Chapter 17) specifically refers to a character encoding scheme.

A character encoding standard usually defines a stack of all four of these transformations: from characters to code points, from code points to code units, and from code units to bytes, although some of the transformations might be implicit. Sometimes, different layers in the model are defined separately. This often happens with East Asian encodings, for example.

The fifth level, the **transfer encoding syntax,** is more or less orthogonal to the other four levels, and is usually defined separately from (and independent of) the others. This additional transformation might be applied ex post facto to the bytes produced by a character encoding scheme. Transfer encoding syntaxes are typically used for one of two things: They either map a set of values into a more-constrained set of values to meet the limitations of some environment (think Base64 or quoted-printable, both of which are discussed in Chapter 17), or they're compression formats, mapping sequences of bytes into shorter sequences of bytes (think LZW or run-length encoding).

Let's go back and apply these terms to the encoding standards we've mentioned so far. The telegraph codes, such as ITA2, divided their repertoires into two coded character sets, FIGS and LTRS, each of which mapped half the repertoire into a 5-bit encoding space, usually expressed as a table of two rows of 16 cells each. The character encoding forms were straightforward transformations, mapping the coordinates into 5-bit binary numbers in a straightforward manner. The character encoding schemes mapped the 5-bit code units into bytes in an equally straightforward manner, and added the concept of using the FIGS and LTRS codes for switching back and forth between the two coded character sets. (If you consider the character encoding scheme to comprise the transformation to physical media, this scheme is also where it was decided whether the most significant bit in the byte was the leftmost hole or the rightmost hole on the paper tape.)

ASCII is actually simpler, mapping its repertoire of characters into a 7-bit, 128-character encoding space, usually expressed as an 8×16 table. It comprised a character encoding form that mapped the table positions into integer code units in an obvious manner, and an encoding scheme that mapped these code units to bytes in an equally obvious manner (with an 8-bit byte, the character encoding scheme can be said to comprise the padding of the value out to eight bits).

ISO 2022 doesn't actually define any coded character sets, but simply specifies the layout of the 256-character encoding space. It does specify a character encoding scheme for switching back and forth between, say, the G1 and G2 sets, and for associating actual coded character sets (for example, Latin-1 and Latin-2) with the G1 and G2 sets.

■ MULTIPLE-BYTE ENCODING SYSTEMS

These distinctions between layers become more interesting when you start talking about East Asian languages such as Chinese, Japanese, and Korean. These languages all make use of the Chinese characters. No one is really sure how many Chinese characters exist, although the total probably exceeds 100,000. Most Chinese speakers have a working written vocabulary of some 5,000 characters or so. Japanese and Korean speakers, who depend more on auxiliary writing systems to augment the Chinese characters, have a somewhat smaller vocabulary.

East Asian Coded Character Sets

With that many characters, you must start by officially defining particular sets of Chinese characters in which you're interested. The Japanese government, for example, publishes the Gakushu Kanji, a list of 1,006 Chinese characters (the Japanese call them *kanji*) everyone learns in elementary school; the Joyo Kanji, a list of another 1,945 characters used in government documents and newspapers (and, presumably, learned in secondary school); and the Jinmei-yo Kanji, a list of 285 characters officially sanctioned for use in personal names.[10] (Think of these lists as analogous to the vocabulary lists that school boards and other educational institutions in the United States put together to standardize which words a child should know at which grade level.) The other countries that use the Chinese characters publish similar lists. These lists are examples of character set standards that just standardize an abstract character repertoire—there's no attempt (so far) to assign numbers to them.

---

10. My sources for this section are parts of Ken Lunde, *CJKV Information Processing* (O'Reilly, 1999), as well as the Edberg paper, op. cit.

The Japanese Industrial Standards Commission (JISC, Japan's counterpart to ANSI) led the way in devising coded character set standards for representing the Chinese characters in computers (earlier Japanese telegraph codes existed, but we don't consider them here). The first, JIS X 0201, was published in 1976. It doesn't actually encode the Chinese characters; rather, this ISO 2022-derived encoding places a Japanese variant of ISO 646 in the G0 area and the Japanese Katakana syllabary in the G1 area. It's a fixed-length, eight-bit encoding, and it becomes important later.

The first Japanese standard to actually encode the kanji characters was JIS C 6226, first published in 1978 and later renamed JIS X 0208 (the work on this standard actually goes back to 1969). JIS X 0208 uses a much larger encoding space than we've looked at so far: a 94 × 94 table. The choice of 94 as the number of rows and columns isn't coincidental: It's the number of assignable code points in the G0 area according to ISO 2022. This arrangement produces an ISO 2022-compliant 7-bit encoding scheme. Each character is represented with a pair of 7-bit code units (in effect, you have a single 14-bit code point expressed as a coordinate in a 94 × 94 space being mapped into two 7-bit code units).

JIS X 0208's repertoire includes not only 6,355 kanji, divided into two "levels" by frequency and importance, but also the Latin, Greek, and Cyrillic alphabets, the Japanese Hiragana and Katakana syllabaries, and a wide variety of symbols and punctuation marks.

JIS X 0208 was supplemented in 1990 by JIS X 0212, which adds another 5,801 kanji, as well as more symbols and some supplementary characters in the Latin and Greek alphabets. The later standard is based on the same 94 × 94 encoding space used in JIS X 0208. JIS X 0213, published in 2000, adds in another 5,000 kanji and follows the same structure as the other two standards.

The other countries that use the Chinese characters followed the JIS model when designing their own national character set standards. These include the People's Republic of China's GB 2312, first published in 1981; Taiwan's CNS 11643, published in 1992; and South Korea's KS X 1001 (also known as KS C 5601), first published in 1987. All of these standards make use of a 94 × 94 encoding space, laid out in roughly similar ways (although the actual allocation of individual characters, especially the Chinese characters and the native-language characters in each standard, varies quite a bit).

CNS 11643, the most ambitious of all of these efforts, encodes a whopping 48,027 characters across 16 "planes" (only seven of which are currently used). The "planes" correspond roughly to the different parts of the ISO 8859 standard; they're more or less independent standards that put different characters in the same encoding space. In CNS 11643, characters at corresponding positions in each plane are variants of each other. In theory, you could take a text consisting of characters from all the planes, encode it using only plane 1, and it would still be legible.

All of these standards define coded character sets. If you take the row and column numbers of the code points and shift them up into ISO 2022's G0 space (by adding 32), you have a simple ISO 2022-derived encoding form. You can then have two encoding schemes based on this system—one that encodes the row number before the column number, and another that encodes the column number before the row number. Piece of cake.

Character Encoding Schemes for East Asian Coded Character Sets

Here's where things start to get interesting. Rather than just treat the East Asian standards as two-byte encodings along the lines above, various packing schemes have been developed, either to save space or to combine characters from two or more of the coded character set standards described earlier. Four major categories of these character encoding schemes exist.

The most familiar scheme, **Shift-JIS**, combines the JIS X 0201 and JIS X 0208 coded character sets. The JIS X 0201 code point values are represented as-is as single-byte values. The byte values not used by 201 (the C1 range and the top two rows of the G1 range: 0x80–0x9F and 0xE0–0xEF) are used as leading byte values for two-byte sequences representing the characters from 208. (The second byte would be in the range 0x40–0x7E or 0x80–0xFC.) The transformation from row and column numbers in JIS X 0208 to a two-byte Shift-JIS sequence isn't straightforward, but it's enough to cover all the characters. In fact, Shift-JIS also adds a space for user-defined characters; these are represented with two-byte sequences, the leading byte of which runs from 0xF0 to 0xFC.

One interesting consequence of Shift-JIS (and the other encodings we'll examine) is that it includes both JIS X 0201 and JIS X 0208, even though all the characters in 201 are also included in 208. The two have come to have different meanings: The codes from 201 (the single-byte sequences) are often thought of as "half-width" (taking up half the horizontal space of a typical kanji character), whereas the codes from 208 (the two-byte sequences) are thought of as "full-width" (taking up the full horizontal space of a kanji character).

The next most familiar encoding scheme is **Extended UNIX Code (EUC),** which, as the name suggests, was originally developed for use with UNIX systems and was standardized in 1991 by a group of UNIX vendors. It includes variable-length sequences ranging from one to four bytes and is based on the ISO 2022 structure. EUC defines four separate code sets. Code set 0 is always ASCII (or some other national variant of ISO 646) and is represented as-is in the C0 and G0 spaces. Code sets 1, 2, and 3 are represented using the values in the G1 space. Characters in code set 1 are represented unadorned. Characters in code set 2 are preceded with a C1 control character, the SS2 character, 0x8E. Characters in code set 3 are preceded with a different C1 control character, 0x8F, called SS3. Characters in code set 0 are always represented with one-byte sequences; characters in code sets 2 and 3 are always sequences of at least two bytes (and can be as many as four bytes, because of the SS2 or SS3 byte appended to the front). Characters in code set 1 may be sequences of from one to three bytes.

The assignment of specific characters to the three EUC code sets is locale-specific, so variants of EUC for each locale exist:

EUC-JP (Japan):

Code set 0:	JIS Roman (the Japanese variant of ISO 646) [one byte]
Code set 1:	JIS X 0208, with the row and column numbers shifted up into the G1 range [two bytes]
Code set 2:	Katakana from JIS X 0201 [SS2 plus one byte]
Code set 3:	JIS X 0212, with the row and column numbers shifted up into the G1 range [SS3 plus two bytes]

EUC-CN (China):

Code set 0:	Chinese ISO 646 [one byte]
Code set 1:	GB 2312, with the row and column numbers shifted up to the G1 range [two bytes]
Code sets 2 and 3:	Not used

EUC-TW (Taiwan):

Code set 0:	Taiwanese ISO 646 [one byte]
Code set 1:	CNS 11643, plane 1, with the row and column numbers shifted into the G1 range [two bytes]
Code set 2:	All of CNS 11643, the row and column numbers as above, preceded by the plane number, also shifted into the G1 range [SS2 plus three bytes]
Code set 3:	Not used

EUC-KR (Korea):

Code set 0:	Korean ISO 646 [one byte]
Code set 1:	KS X 1001, with the row and column numbers shifted up into the G1 range [two bytes]
Code sets 2 and 3:	Not used

Then there's the family of 7-bit **ISO 2022** encodings. Here you use the standard ISO 2022 machinery and the normal framework of 7-bit ISO 2022 code points to represent the characters. Again, depending on locale, you get different default behavior. The system is modal, so you can use the ASCII SI and SO (shift in and shift out, 0x0F and 0x0E) to switch back and forth between single-byte mode and double-byte mode. You can also use the SS2 and SS3 codes from ISO 2022 (here in their escape-sequence incarnations, as we're staying within seven bits) to quote characters from alternative two-byte character sets. The national variants of ISO 2022 then make use of escape sequences (often running to four bytes) to switch the two-byte mode from one coded character set to another. The various versions give you access to the following character sets:

ISO-2022-JP	JIS-Roman and JIS X 0208
ISO-2022-JP-1	
and ISO-2022-JP-2	ISO-2022-JP plus JIS X 0212
ISO-2022-CN	ASCII, GB 2312, CNS 11643 planes 1 and 2
ISO-2022-CN-EXT	ISO-2022-CN plus the rest of CNS 11643
ISO-2022-KR	ASCII and KS X 1001

The actual specifications differ widely from one variant to the next, and they don't all strictly follow the ISO 2022 standard (despite the name). See Ken Lunde's *CJKV Information Processing* for all the gory details.

Finally, there's **HZ,** another 7-bit encoding. It uses sequences of printing characters to shift back and forth between single-byte mode (ASCII) and double-byte mode (GB 2312). The sequence ~{ would switch into double-byte mode, and the sequence ~} would switch back.

Other East Asian Encoding Systems

Two more important encoding standards don't fit neatly into the coded-character-set/character-encoding-scheme division we've been considering.

The Taiwanese **Big5** standard (so named because it was backed by five large computer manufacturers) predates CNS 11643, the "official" Taiwanese standard, which was introduced in 1984. (CNS 11643 is downward compatible with Big5, and can be thought of as an extended and improved version of it.) Big5 uses a 94×157 encoding space, providing room for 14,758 characters. This variable-length encoding is compatible with the ISO 2022 layout: The Taiwanese version of ISO 646 is represented as-is in the C0 and G0 spaces with single-byte sequences. The Chinese characters (and all the usual other stuff) are represented with two-byte sequences: The first byte is in the G1 range; the second byte can be in either the G1 or the G0 range (although not all G0 values are used as trailing bytes).

CCCII (Chinese Character Code for Information Interchange) is another Taiwanese industry standard that predates Big5 (it was published in 1980) and also influenced CNS 11643. In this fixed-length encoding, each code point maps to *three* 7-bit code units. It has a $94 \times 94 \times 94$ encoding space: sixteen *layers,* each consisting of six 94×94 planes. The first byte of the code point is the layer and plane numbers, the second the row number, and the third the column number.

Johab is an alternative encoding scheme described in the KS X 1001 standard. KS X 1001 normally encodes only the 2,350 Hangul syllables (see Chapter 10 for more on Hangul) actually used in modern Korean, but it proposes an alternative method that permits encoding of all 11,172 possible modern Hangul syllables. (The Korean Hangul script is an alphabetic system, but the letters are commonly grouped into syllabic blocks, which are encoded as units in most Korean systems in a manner analogous to that used for the Chinese characters.) Johab takes advantage of the alphabetic nature of Hangul. Instead of just giving each syllable an arbitrary number, the syllable is broken down into its component letters, or *jamo* (as many as three in a syllable), each of which can be encoded in five bits. The resulting 15-bit character code can be encoded in a two-byte sequence. The G0 space in the leading byte is taken up with the Korean version of ISO 646, as always, but the leading byte of a two-byte sequence invades the C1 range and the second byte can be from the G0, C1, or G1 range. Thus, the Johab encoding doesn't fit the ISO 2022 structure.

■ ISO 10646 AND UNICODE

It should be fairly clear by now that we have a real mess on our hands. Literally hundreds of different encoding standards exist, many of which are redundant, encoding the same characters but encoding them differently. Even the ISO 8859 family includes 10 different encodings of the Latin alphabet, each containing a slightly different set of letters.

As a consequence, you have to be very explicit about which encoding scheme you're using, lest the computer interpret your text as characters other than the ones you intend, garbling it in the process (log onto a Japanese Web site with an American computer, for example, and it's likely you'll see garbage rather than Japanese). About the only thing that's safely interchangeable across a wide variety of systems is 7-bit ASCII, and even then you're not safe—you might run into a system using one of the national variants of ISO 646, mangling the "national use" characters from ASCII, or your text might pass through an EBCDIC-based system and get completely messed up.

You also can't easily mix characters from different languages (other than English and something else) without having auxiliary data structures to keep track of the encodings used for the different pieces of the text. Your other choice is to use a code switching scheme such as the one specified in ISO 2022, which is cumbersome both for the user and for the processing software.

Thus you have a bunch of problems it would be really nice to fix:

- A wide variety of mutually incompatible methods of encoding the various languages exist, but there is no foolproof way to tell from the data itself which encoding standard is being followed.
- A limited encoding space leads to an even wider variety of conflicting encoding standards, none of which is terribly complete.
- Variable-length encoding schemes don't use numerically disjoint code unit values for the different pieces of a multibyte character, making it difficult to count characters or locate character boundaries, and rendering the data highly susceptible to corruption. (A missing byte can trigger the wrong interpretation of every byte that follows it.)
- Stateful in-band code-switching schemes such as ISO 2022 are complicated, make encoded text in memory more difficult to process, and require arbitrary-length look-back to understand how to interpret a given byte on random access.

Clearly, what is needed is a universal character encoding system, one that will solve these problems and assign a unique code point value to every character in common use. A group formed in 1984 under the auspices of the International Organization for Standardization and the International Electrotechnical Commission to create such a thing. This group goes by the rather unwieldy name of ISO/IEC JTC1/SC2/WG2 (ISO/IEC Joint Technical Committee #1 [Information Technology], Subcommittee #2 [Coded Character Sets], Working Group #2 [Multioctet codes]), or just "WG2" for short. Its members began working on what became known as ISO 10646 (the connection between 10646 and 646 is not accidental: the number signifies that 10646 is an extension of 646).[11]

In 1988, a similar effort got under way independently of WG2. It was sparked by a paper written by Joe Becker of Xerox, which set forth the prob-

---

11. This section draws on Mike Ksar, "Unicode and ISO 10646: Continual Convergence," *Proceedings of the 20th International Unicode Conference,* session C2, and the Edberg paper, op. cit. The information on the early history of ISO 10646 comes from contributions by Mark Davis and Ken Whistler to online discussions by the IETF's Internationalized Domain Names task force, and were forwarded to me by Mark Davis. I also consulted Mike Ksar, "Untying Tongues–ISO/IEC 10646 Breaks Down Barriers in Processing Worldwide Languages," *ISO Bulletin*, June 1993.

lems listed above and proposed a list of desirable characteristics for a universal character encoding standard. The Becker paper was the first to use the name "Unicode," which has stuck. An informal group of internationalization experts from Xerox, Apple, and a few other companies got together to begin work on the Unicode standard (beginning from Xerox's earlier XCCS encoding standard). This group grew into the Unicode Consortium of today.

Although they had similar goals, the two groups went about achieving them in very different ways. The original version of ISO 10646 was based on 32-bit abstract code point values, arranged into a $256 \times 256 \times 256 \times 256$ encoding space. Not all code point values were actually possible: Byte values from 0x00 to 0x1F and from 0x80 to 0x9F, corresponding to the C0 and C1 areas in ISO 2022, were illegal in any position in the four-byte code point values, effectively yielding a $192 \times 192 \times 192 \times 192$ encoding space. This was referred to as 192 "groups" of 192 "planes" of 192 "rows" of 192 "cells."

Recognizing that a scheme with four-byte character codes, involving a quadrupling of the space required for a given piece of text, probably wouldn't go over well, the early versions of ISO 10646 had a whopping five encoding forms. These forms were based on code units ranging from one to four bytes in size, plus a variable-length scheme, which allowed single code points to be represented with sequences of one-byte code units of varying lengths. There were also encoding schemes for the shorter encoding forms that used ISO 2022-style escape sequences to switch the meanings of the code units from one part of the encoding space to another.

The division into "planes" was intended to facilitate the use of shorter encoding forms. That is, if all your characters came from the same plane, you could omit the plane and group numbers from the code unit and just have it consist of the row and cell numbers. A "basic multilingual plane" (BMP) contained the characters from most of the modern writing systems, with the major exception of the Han characters. The Han characters were organized into several planes of their own: for Traditional Chinese, Simplified Chinese, Japanese, and Korean. There were also provisions for special-purpose and private-use planes.

The original version of ISO 10646, with these features, failed to win approval on its first ballot attempt. The prohibition of C0 and C1 byte values not only restricted the available space too much (especially in the basic multilingual plane), but it also caused problems for C implementations because zero-extended ASCII values weren't legal 10646 code points, making it difficult or impossible to use wchar_t to store 10646 code points and still maintain backward compatibility. No one liked the multitude of different encoding forms and the escape sequences used with them. Also, the Asian countries didn't like having their writing systems relegated to their own planes.[12]

Meanwhile, the Unicode Consortium started with a 16-bit code point length, equivalent to a single plane of the ISO 10646 encoding space, and declared no byte values off limits. There were no separate encoding forms or schemes, and no ambiguous interpretations of variable lengths—just Unicode. (Encoding forms such as UTF-8 were a later development.)

A major difference between Unicode and ISO 10646 was the treatment of the Chinese characters. Even though there are certainly significant differences in the *use* of the Chinese characters in China, Japan, Korea, Vietnam, and Taiwan, they're still essentially the same characters. Great overlap exists between the five sets of Chinese characters, and it doesn't make sense to encode the same character once for each language any more than it makes sense to encode the letter A once each for English, Spanish, French, Italian, and German.

Work had already been going on at Xerox and Apple to devise a unified set of Chinese characters, following on the heels of ongoing work in China (CCCII, for example, attempted to unify the various national versions of the Chinese characters, and another effort was under way in China). The Apple/Xerox effort went into early drafts of Unicode and was proposed to ISO as a possible addition to ISO 10646. The Apple/Xerox efforts eventually merged with the various Chinese efforts to form the CJK Joint Research Group, which produced the first version of the unified Chinese character set in ISO 10646 in 1993. This group, now called the Ideographic Rapporteur Group (IRG), is still responsible for this section of ISO 10646 and Unicode and is now a formal subcommittee of WG2.

In addition to unifying the set of Chinese characters, the original idea was to further conserve encoding space by building up Korean syllables, rarer Chi-

---

12. One of Ken Whistler's messages on this issue actually quotes the Chinese national body's objections. The Chinese not only didn't like having their codes in a separate plane, but didn't like the idea that a single Han character could have one of several code point values depending on the language of the text. This group advocated a unified Han area located in the BMP. This seems to put the lie rather effectively to the allegations you hear every so often that Han unification was forced on the Asians by the Americans. For more on Han unification, see Chapter 10.

nese characters, rarer accented-letter combinations, and other items out of pieces: You'd take more than one code point to represent them, but each code point value would have a defined meaning independent of the others. Unicode also had a Private Use Area, which could be used for characters with more specialized applications (writing systems no longer in common use, for example). A higher-level protocol outside of Unicode would be used to specify the meaning of private-use code points.

After the initial ISO 10646 ballot failed, talks began between the two groups to merge their technologies. 10646 retained its 32-bit-ness and its organization into groups, planes, rows, and cells, but it removed the prohibition against C0 and C1 byte values, opening up the entire 32-bit space for encoding. (Actually, it turned into a 31-bit space, because code point values with the sign bit turned on were prohibited. This change made it possible to store an ISO 10646 code point in either a signed or an unsigned data type without worrying about mangling the contents.) The multitude of encoding forms and schemes was simplified. For example, the ISO 2022-style escape sequences were eliminated, as were the one-byte, three-byte and variable-byte encodings. That change left just UCS-4, a straightforward representation of the code point values in bytes, and UCS-2, which allowed the BMP to be represented with two-byte code unit values.

Both ISO 10646 and Unicode wound up adding and moving characters around. Unicode was forced to give up the idea of exclusively building up Korean syllables and rare Chinese characters out of pieces; ISO 10646 moved to a unified Chinese-character repertoire and located it in the BMP. From this point in 1991 on forward, Unicode and ISO 10646 have had their character repertoires and the code points those characters are assigned to synchronized. Unicode 1.1, minus the unified Chinese repertoire, was the first standard published after the merger. The unified Chinese repertoire was finished in 1993, at which point the first version of 10646 was published as ISO/IEC 10646-1:1993. The standards have remained synchronized ever since.

Neither standard went away in the merger. Indeed Unicode and ISO 10646 still exist as separate, distinct standards. Nevertheless, great effort is being expended to ensure that the two standards remain in sync with each other. There's a lot of overlapping membership on the two governing committees, and both sides care a lot about staying in step. From the time of the merger until now, the character repertoires of the two standards have effectively remained identical.

ISO 10646's organization into planes eventually had to be adopted into Unicode to accommodate the rapidly growing character repertoire. Unicode 2.0 added the "surrogate mechanism" (now known as UTF-16) to permit representation of characters outside the BMP in a 16-bit framework (a range of code point values was set aside to be used in pairs to represent characters outside the BMP). This mechanism permitted access to the first 17 planes of ISO 10646. WG2 agreed to declare the planes above plane 16 off limits, and the encoding spaces were also synchronized.

Starting in Unicode 2.0, then, Unicode's encoding space has expanded from a single 256×256 plane, corresponding to 10646's BMP, to seventeen 256×256 planes, corresponding to planes 0 to 16 in ISO 10646. Thus a Unicode code point value is now a 21-bit value. Unicode and ISO 10646 both now define a set of three character encoding forms—UTF-32, UTF-16, and UTF-8—which map the 21-bit code points into single 32-bit code units, variable-length sequences of one or two 16-bit code units, and variable-length sequences of from one to four 8-bit code units, respectively. They also define seven encoding schemes (UTF-8 and three flavors each of UTF-16 and UTF-32, arranged for machine architectures with different byte ordering).

Although both define the same coded character set and character encoding forms and schemes, Unicode and ISO 10646 differ in content and in how updates are issued. Among the important differences are the following:

- ISO 10646 defines a formalized method of declaring which characters are supported by an implementation; Unicode leaves this declaration to ad hoc methods.
- Unicode defines a host of semantic information about each of the characters and provides a wealth of implementation guidelines and rules; ISO 10646 basically just lists the characters and their code point assignments.
- The Unicode standard can be picked up in any bookstore (or accessed for free on the Web); ISO 10646 has to be ordered from an ISO member organization.
- The ISO 10646 standard is divided into two parts: ISO 10646-1, which defines the basic architecture and standardizes the code assignments in the BMP, and ISO 10646-2, which standardizes the code assignments in the other 16 planes. Unicode is published as a single unified standard.

The other important difference is the way the standards are updated. Unicode employs a version-numbering scheme; minor updates (where the number to the right of the decimal point increases) are published as technical reports, whereas major updates result in the publication of a new edition of the book. New editions of ISO 10646 are published far less often, but amendments and corrigenda are issued more frequently.

As a consequence, one standard can occasionally get ahead of the other. Usually 10646 runs a little ahead as amendments get adopted—every so often, a bunch of amendments are gathered together to make a new Unicode version. Still, there's always a direct mapping from a particular version of one standard to a particular version of the other. For the versions that have been published to date, that mapping is as follows:

Unicode 1.0   (*pre-merger*)

Unicode 1.1   ISO 10646-1:1993

Unicode 2.0   ISO 10646-1:1993, plus amendments 1 through 7

Unicode 2.1   ISO 10646-1:1993, plus amendments 1 through 7 and 18

Unicode 3.0   ISO 10646-1:2000 (which was formed from ISO 10646-1:1993 and amendments 1 through 31)

Unicode 3.1   ISO 10646-1:2000 and ISO 10646-2:2001

Unicode 3.2   ISO 10646-1:2000 and amendment 1, plus ISO 10646-2:2001

▪ HOW THE UNICODE STANDARD IS MAINTAINED

Before we look at the nuts and bolts of Unicode itself, it's worth taking a few minutes to look at how the Unicode Consortium actually works and the process by which changes are made to the standard.[13]

The Unicode Consortium is a nonprofit corporation located in Silicon Valley. It's a membership organization—members pay dues to belong and have a

---

13. The information in this section is drawn from Rick McGowan, "About Unicode Consortium Procedures, Policies, Stability, and Public Access," published as an IETF Internet-Draft, http://search.ietf.org/internet-drafts/draft-rmcgowan-unicode-procs-01.txt.

say in the development of the standard. Membership is relatively expensive, so full voting members are generally corporations, research and educational institutions, and national governments. (There are also various levels of nonvoting membership, many of which include individuals.)

The Unicode Consortium exists to maintain and promote the Unicode standard. The actual work of maintaining this standard falls to the Unicode Technical Committee (UTC). Each member organization can appoint one principal and one or two alternate representatives to the UTC. Nonvoting members can also send people to the UTC who can participate in discussion but not vote. Other people are sometimes permitted to observe but not participate.

The UTC meets four or five times each year to discuss changes and additions to the standard, make recommendations to other standard-setting bodies, issue resolutions, and occasionally issue new standards. A change to the standard requires a majority vote of the UTC, and a precedent-setting change requires a two-thirds vote.

The UTC doesn't take its job lightly; only the most trivial of actions goes through the whole process in a single committee meeting. Often proposals are sent back to their submitters for clarification or referred to various outside organizations for comment. Because many other standards are based on the Unicode standard, the organizations responsible for these dependent standards have a prominent place at the table whenever architectural changes that might affect them are discussed. Additions of new writing systems (or significant changes to old ones) require input from the affected user communities. For certain areas, either the UTC or WG2 (or both) maintains standing subcommittees. For example, the IRG is a WG2 subcommittee charged with maintaining the unified Chinese-character repertoire.

A lot of work also goes into keeping Unicode aligned with ISO 10646. Because the Unicode Consortium is an industry body, it has no vote with ISO, but it works closely with the U.S. national body, Technical Committee L2 of the National Committee on Information Technology Standards (NCITS), an ANSI organization. L2 *does* have a vote with ISO; its meetings are held jointly with the UTC meetings, and most UTC members are also L2 members.

ISO 10646 is maintained by ISO JTC1/SC2/WG2, which is made up of representatives from various national bodies, including L2. Many WG2 members are also UTC members. On issues that affect both Unicode and 10646, such as the addition of new characters, both the UTC and WG2 have to agree—effectively, each organization has a veto over the other's actions. Only after both the UTC and WG2 agree on something does it go through the formal ISO voting process. A typical proposal takes two years to wend its way through the whole process, from submission to WG2 or the UTC to being adopted as an international standard (or amendment) by an international ballot.

The Unicode Consortium maintains two Internet mailing lists: the "unicore" list, which is limited to Unicode Consortium members, and the "unicode" list, which is open to anyone (go to the Unicode Web site for information on how to join). Many proposals start as informal discussions on one of these two lists and turn into formal proposals only after being thoroughly hashed out in one of these informal discussions. In fact, it's generally recommended that an idea be floated on the mailing lists before being submitted formally—this procedure cuts down on the back-and-forth after the proposal has been sent to the UTC.

Anyone—not just UTC or Unicode Consortium members—can submit a proposal for a change or addition to the Unicode standard. You can find submission forms and instructions on the Unicode Web site. Don't make submissions lightly, however. To be taken seriously, you should understand Unicode well enough first to make sure the submission makes sense within the architecture and under the constraints that apply to Unicode, and you'll need to be prepared to back up the proposal with evidence of why it's the right thing to do and who needs it. You also need patience. It takes a long time for a proposal to be adopted, and shepherding a proposal through the process can be time-consuming.

More background than you really wanted, huh? Well, it'll be helpful to be armed with this information as we march ahead to explore the Unicode standard in depth. Onward!

3

Architecture: Not Just a Pile of Code Charts

*I*f you're used to working with ASCII or other similar encodings designed for European languages, you'll find Unicode noticeably different from those other standards. You'll also find that when you're dealing with Unicode text, various assumptions you may have made in the past about how you deal with text don't hold. If you've worked with encodings for other languages, at least some characteristics of Unicode will be familiar to you, but even then, some pieces of Unicode will be unfamiliar.

Unicode is more than just a big pile of code charts. To be sure, it *includes* a big pile of code charts, but Unicode goes much further. It doesn't just take a bunch of character forms and assign numbers to them; it adds a wealth of information on what those characters mean and how they are used.

Unlike virtually all other character encoding standards, Unicode isn't designed for the encoding of a single language or a family of closely related languages. Rather, Unicode is designed for the encoding of *all* written languages. The current version doesn't give you a way to encode *all* written languages (and in fact, this concept is such a slippery thing to define that it probably never will), but it does provide a way to encode an extremely wide variety of languages. The languages vary tremendously in how they are written, so Unicode must be flexible enough to accommodate all of them. This fact necessitates rules on how Unicode is to be used with each language. Also, because the same encoding standard can be used for so many different languages, there's a higher likelihood that they will be mixed in the same document, requiring rules on how text in the different languages should interact. The sheer number of characters requires special attention, as does the fact that Unicode often provides multiple ways of representing the same thing.

The idea behind all the rules is simple: to ensure that a particular sequence of code points will get drawn and interpreted the same way (or in semantically equivalent ways) by all systems that handle Unicode text. In other words, it's not so important that there should be only one way to encode "à bientôt," but rather a particular sequence of code points that represents "à bientôt" on one system will also represent it on any other system that purports to understand the code points used. Not every system has to handle that sequence of code points *in exactly the same way,* but merely must interpret it as meaning the same thing. In English, for example, you can follow tons of different typographical conventions when you draw the word "carburetor," but someone who reads English would still interpret all of them as the word "carburetor." Any Unicode-based system has wide latitude in how it deals with a sequence of code points representing the word "carburetor," as long as it still treats it as the word "carburetor."

As a result of these requirements, a lot more goes into supporting Unicode text than supplying a font with the appropriate character forms for all the characters. The purpose of this book is to explain all these other things you have to be aware of (or at least *might* have to be aware of). This chapter will highlight the things that are special about Unicode and attempt to tie them together into a coherent architecture.

▪ THE UNICODE CHARACTER–GLYPH MODEL

The first and most important thing to understand about Unicode is what is known as the *character–glyph model*. Until the introduction of the Macintosh in 1984, text was usually displayed on computer screens in a fairly simple fashion. The screen would be divided up into a number of equally sized *display cells*. The most common video mode on the old IBM PCs, for example, had 25 rows of 80 display cells each. A video buffer in memory consisted of 2,000 bytes, one for each display cell. The video hardware contained a **character generator chip** that contained a bitmap for each possible byte value, and this chip was used to map from the character codes in memory to a particular set of lit pixels on the screen.

Handling text was simple. There were 2,000 possible locations on the screen, and 256 possible characters to put in them. All the characters were the same size, and were laid out regularly from left to right across the screen. There was a one-to-one correspondence between character codes stored in memory and visible characters on the screen, and there was a one-to-one correspondence between keystrokes and characters.

We don't live in that world anymore. One reason is the rise of the WYSI-WYG ("what you see is what you get") text editor, where you can see on the screen exactly what you want to see on paper. With such a system, video displays have to be able to handle proportionally spaced fonts, the mixing of different typefaces, sizes, and styles, and the mixing of text with pictures and other pieces of data. The other reason is that the old world of simple video display terminals can't handle many languages, which are more complicated to write than the Latin alphabet is.

As a consequence, there's been a shift away from translating character codes to pixels in hardware and toward doing it in software. And the software for doing this has become considerably more sophisticated.

On modern computer systems (Unicode or no), there is no longer always a nice, simple, one-to-one relationship between character codes stored in your computer's memory and actual shapes drawn on your computer's screen. This point is important to understand because Unicode *requires* this flexibility—a Unicode-compatible system cannot be designed to assume a one-to-one correspondence between code points in the backing store and marks on the screen (or on paper), or between code points in the backing store and keystrokes in the input.[1]

Let's start by defining two concepts: character and glyph. A character is an atomic unit of text with some semantic identity; a glyph is a visual representation of that character.

---

1. Technically, if you restrict the repertoire of characters your system supports enough, you actually *can* make this assumption. At that point, though, you're likely back to being a fairly simplistic English-only system, in which case why bother with Unicode in the first place?

Consider the following examples:

13   thirteen 1.3×10^1

dreizehn

$0C   κγ   十三

١٢

treize   卌卌 ||| ӨӨ

These forms are 11 different visual representations of the number 13. The underlying semantic is the same in every case: the concept "thirteen." These examples are just different ways of depicting the concept of "thirteen."

Now consider the following:

g g *g* **g**

Each of these examples is a different presentation of the Latin lowercase letter g. To go back to our terms, these are all the same *character* (the lowercase letter g), but four different *glyphs*.

Of course, these four glyphs were produced by taking the small g out of four different typefaces. That's because there's generally only one glyph per character in a Latin typeface. In other writing systems, however, that isn't true. The Arabic alphabet, for example, joins cursively even when printed. This isn't an optional feature, as it is with the Latin alphabet; it's the way the Arabic alphabet is *always* written.

ه ه ه ه

These are four different forms of the Arabic letter heh. The first shows how the letter looks in isolation. The second depicts how it looks when it joins only to a letter on its right (usually at the end of a word). The third is how it looks when it joins to letters on both sides in the middle of a word. The last form illustrates how the letter looks when it joins to a letter on its left (usually at the beginning of a word).

Unicode provides only one character code for this letter,[2] and it's up to the code that draws it on the screen (the **text rendering process**) to select the appropriate glyph depending on context. The process of selecting from among a set of glyphs for a character depending on the surrounding characters is called **contextual shaping**, and it's required to draw many writing systems correctly.

There's also not always a one-to-one mapping between character and glyph. Consider the following example:

$$\text{fi}$$

This, of course, is the letter f followed by the letter i, but it's a single glyph. In many typefaces, if you put a lowercase f next to a lowercase i, the top of the f tends to run into the dot on the i, so the typeface often includes a special glyph called a ligature that represents this particular pair of letters. The dot on the i is incorporated into the overhanging arch of the f, and the crossbar of the f connects to the serif on the top of the base of the i. Some desktop-publishing software and some high-end fonts will automatically substitute this ligature for the plain f and i.

In fact, some typefaces include additional ligatures. Other forms involving the lowercase f are common, for example. You'll often see ligatures for a–e and o–e pairs (useful for looking erudite when using words like "archæology" or "œnophile"), although software rarely forms these automatically (æ and œ are actually separate letters in some languages, rather than combinations of letters), and some fonts include other ligatures for decorative use.

Again, though, ligature formation isn't just a gimmick. Consider the Arabic letter lam (ل) and the Arabic letter alef (ا). When they occur next to each other, you'd expect them to appear like this if they followed normal shaping rules:

$$\text{لا}$$

---

2. Technically, this isn't true—Unicode actually provides separate codes for each glyph in Arabic, although they're included only for backward compatibility. These "presentation forms" are encoded in a separate numeric range to emphasize this point. Implementations generally aren't supposed to use them. Almost all other writing systems that have contextual shaping don't have separate presentation forms in Unicode.

Actually, they don't. Instead of forming a U shape, the vertical strokes of the lam and the alef actually cross, forming a loop at the bottom:

لا

Unlike the f and i in English, these two letters *always* combine this way when they occur together. It's not optional. The form that looks like a U is just plain wrong. So ligature formation is a required behavior for writing many languages.

A single character may also split into more than one glyph. This happens in some Indian languages, such as Tamil. It's very roughly analogous to the use of the silent e in English. The e at the end of "bite," for example, doesn't have a sound of its own; it merely changes the way the i is pronounced. Since the i and the e are being used together to represent a single vowel sound, you could think of them as two halves of a *single* vowel character. Something similar happens in languages like Tamil. Here's an example of a Tamil split vowel:

கொ

This looks like three letters, but it's really only two. The middle glyph is a consonant, the letter ப. The vowel கொ is shown with a mark on either side of the ப. This kind of thing is required for the display of a number of languages.

As we see, there's not always a simple, straightforward, one-to-one mapping between characters and glyphs. Unicode assumes the presence of a character rendering process capable of handling the sometimes complex mapping from characters to glyphs. It doesn't provide separate character codes for different glyphs that represent the same character, or for ligatures representing multiple characters.

Exactly how this process works varies from writing system to writing system (and, to a lesser degree, from language to language within a writing system). For the details on just how Unicode deals with the peculiar characteristics of each writing system it encodes, see Part II (Chapters 7 to 12).

■ CHARACTER POSITIONING

Another faulty assumption is the idea that characters are laid out in a neat linear progression running in lines from left to right. In many languages, this isn't true.

Many languages also employ diacritical marks that are used in combination with other characters to indicate pronunciation. Exactly where the marks are drawn can depend on what they're being attached to. For example, look at these two letters:

ä Ä

Each of these examples is the letter a with an umlaut placed on top of it. The umlaut needs to be positioned higher when attached to the capital A than when attached to the small a.

This positioning can be even more complicated when multiple marks are attached to the same character. In Thai, for example, a consonant with a tone mark might look like this:

If the consonant also has a vowel mark attached to it, the tone mark has to move out of the way. It actually moves up and becomes smaller when there's a vowel mark:

Mark positioning can get quite complicated. In Arabic, a whole host of dots and marks can appear along with the actual letters. Some dots are used to differentiate the consonants from one another when they're written cursively, some diacritical marks modify the pronunciation of the consonants, vowel marks may be present (Arabic generally doesn't use letters for vowels—they're either left out or shown as marks attached to consonants), and reading or chanting marks may be attached to the letters. In fact, some Arabic calligraphy includes marks that are purely decorative. There's a hierarchy of how these various marks are placed relative to the letters that can get quite complicated when all the various marks are actually being used.

Unicode expects that a text rendering process will know how to position marks appropriately. It generally doesn't encode mark position at all—it adopts a single convention that marks follow in memory the characters they attach to, but that's it.[3]

Diacritical marks are not the only characters that may have complicated positioning; sometimes the letters themselves do. For example, many Middle Eastern languages are written from right to left rather than from left to right (in Unicode, the languages that use the Arabic, Hebrew, Syriac, and Thaana alphabets are written from right to left). Unicode stores these characters in the order they'd be spoken or typed by a native speaker of one of the relevant languages, known as **logical order**.

Logical order means that the "first" character in character storage is the character that a native user of that character would consider "first." For a left-to-right writing system, the "first" character is drawn farthest to the left. (For example, the first character in this paragraph is the letter L, which is the character farthest to the left on the first line.) For a right-to-left writing system, the "first" character would be drawn farthest to the right. For a vertically oriented writing system, such as that used to write Chinese, the "first" character is drawn closest to the top of the page.

Logical order contrasts with **visual order**, which assumes that all characters are drawn progressing in the same direction (usually left to right). When text is stored in visual order, text that runs counter to the direction assumed (usually the right-to-left text) is stored in memory in the reverse of the order in which it was typed.

Unicode doesn't assume any bias in layout direction. The characters in a Hebrew document are stored in the order they are typed, and Unicode expects that the text rendering process will know that because they're Hebrew letters, the first one in memory should be positioned the farthest to the right, with the succeeding characters progressing leftward from there.

---

3. The one exception to this rule has to do with multiple marks attached to a single character. In the absence of language-specific rules governing how multiple marks attach to the same character, Unicode adopts a convention that marks that would otherwise collide radiate outward from the character to which they're attached in the order they appear in storage. This is covered in depth in Chapter 4.

This process gets really interesting when left-to-right text and right-to-left text are mixed in the same document. Suppose you have an English sentence with a Hebrew phrase embedded into the middle of it:

Avram said מזל טוב and smiled.

Even though the dominant writing direction of the text is from left to right, the first letter in the Hebrew phrase (מ) still goes to the right of the other Hebrew letters—the Hebrew phrase still reads from right to left. The same thing can happen even when you're not mixing languages: In Arabic and Hebrew, for example, even though the dominant writing direction is from right to left, numbers are still written from left to right.

This issue can be even more fun when you throw in punctuation. Letters have inherent directionality; punctuation doesn't. Instead, punctuation marks take on the directionality of the surrounding text. In fact, some punctuation marks (such as the parentheses) actually *change shape* based on the directionality of the surrounding text (called **mirroring**, because the two shapes are usually mirror images of each other). Mirroring is another example of how Unicode encodes meaning rather than appearance—the code point encodes the meaning ("starting parenthesis") rather than the shape (either "(" or ")" depending on the surrounding text).

Dealing with mixed-directionality text can become quite complicated, not to mention ambiguous, so Unicode includes a set of rules that govern just how text of mixed directionality is to be arranged on a line. The rules are rather involved, but are required for Unicode implementations that claim to support Hebrew or Arabic.[4]

The writing systems for the various languages used on the Indian subcontinent and in Southeast Asia have even more complicated positioning requirements. For example, the Devanagari alphabet used to write Hindi and Sanskrit treats vowels as marks that are attached to consonants (which are treated as "letters"). A vowel may attach not just to the top or bottom of the consonant, but

---

4. This set of rules, the Unicode Bidirectional Text Layout Algorithm, is explained in more detail later in this book. Chapter 8 provides a high-level overview, and Chapter 16 looks at implementation strategies.

also to the left or right side. Text generally runs left to right, but when a vowel attaches to the left-hand side of its consonant, you get the effect of a character appearing "before" (i.e., to the left of) the character it logically comes "after."

$$\text{क} \ + \ \text{ि} \ = \ \text{कि}$$

In some alphabets, a vowel can actually attach to the left-hand side of a group of consonants, meaning this "reordering" may actually involve more than just two characters switching places. Also, in some alphabets, such as the Tamil example we looked at earlier, a vowel might actually appear on *both* the left- and right-hand sides of the consonant to which it attaches (called a "split vowel").

Again, Unicode stores the characters in the order they're spoken or typed; it expects the display engine to do this reordering. For more on the complexities of dealing with the Indian scripts and their cousins, see Chapter 9.

Chinese, Japanese, and Korean can be written either horizontally or vertically. Again, Unicode stores them in logical order, and the character codes encode the semantics. Many of the punctuation marks used with Chinese characters have a different appearance when used with horizontal text than when used with vertical text (some are positioned differently, some are rotated 90 degrees). Horizontal scripts are sometimes rotated 90 degrees when mixed into vertical text and sometimes not, but this distinction is made by the rendering process and not by Unicode.

Japanese and Chinese text may also include annotations (called "ruby" or "furigana" in Japanese) that appear between the lines of normal text. Unicode includes ways of marking text as ruby and leaves it up to the rendering process to determine how to draw it. For more on vertical text and ruby, see Chapter 10.

■ THE PRINCIPLE OF UNIFICATION

The bottom-line philosophy you should draw from the discussions on the character–glyph model and on character positioning is that *Unicode encodes semantics, not appearances*. In fact, the Unicode standard specifically states that the pictures of the characters in the code charts are for illustrative purposes only—

the pictures of the characters are intended to help clarify the meaning of the character code, not to specify the appearance of the character having that code.

The philosophy that Unicode encodes semantics and not appearances also undergirds the principle that Unicode is a plain-text encoding, which we discussed in Chapter 1. The fact that an Arabic letter looks different depending on the letters around it doesn't change what letter it is, and thus it doesn't justify having different codes for the different shapes. The fact that the letters lam and alef combine into a single mark when written doesn't change the fact that a word contains the letters lam and alef in succession. The fact that text from some language might be combined on the same line with text from another language whose writing system runs in the opposite direction doesn't justify storing either language's text in some order other than the order in which the characters are typed or spoken. In all of these cases, Unicode encodes the underlying meaning and leaves it up to the process that draws it to be smart enough to do so properly.

The philosophy of encoding semantics rather than appearance also leads to another important Unicode principle: the principle of **unification**.

Unlike most character encoding schemes, Unicode aims to be comprehensive. It aims to provide codes for all the characters in all the world's written languages. It also aims to be a superset of all other character encoding schemes (or at least the vast majority). By being a superset, Unicode can be an acceptable substitute for any of those other encodings (technical limitations aside, anyway), and it can serve as a pivot point for processes converting text between any of the other encodings.

Other character encoding standards are Unicode's chief source of characters. The designers of Unicode sought to include all the characters from every computer character encoding standard in reasonably widespread use at the time Unicode was designed. They have continued to incorporate characters from other standards as it has evolved, either as important new standards emerged, or as the scope of Unicode widened to include new languages. The designers of Unicode drew characters from every international and national standard they could get their hands on, as well as code pages from the major computer and software manufacturers, telegraphy codes, various other corporate standards, and even popular fonts, in addition to noncomputer sources. As an example of their thoroughness, Unicode includes code-point values for the glyphs that the old IBM PC code pages would show for certain ASCII control characters. As another example, Unicode assigns values to the glyphs from the popular Zapf Dingbats typeface.

This wealth of sources led to an amazingly extensive repertoire of characters, but also produced redundancy. If every character code from every source encoding retained its identity in Unicode (say, Unicode kept the original code values and just padded them to the same length and prefixed them with some identifier for the source encoding), they would never fit in a 16-bit code space. You would also wind up with numerous alternative representations for things that anyone with a little common sense would consider to be the same thing.

For starters, almost every language has several encoding standards. For example, there might be one national standard for each country where the language is spoken, plus one or more corporate standards devised by computer manufacturers selling into that market. Think about ASCII and EBCDIC in American English, for example. The capital letter A encoded by ASCII (as 0x41) is the same capital letter A that is encoded by EBCDIC (as 0xC1), so it makes little sense to have these two source values map to different codes in Unicode. In that case, Unicode would have two different values for the letter A. Instead, Unicode *unifies* these two character codes and says that both sources map to the same Unicode value. Thus, the letter A is encoded only once in Unicode (as U+0041), not twice.

In addition to the existence of multiple encoding standards for most languages, most languages share their writing system with at least one other language. The German alphabet is different from the English alphabet—it adds ß and some other letters, for example—but both are really just variations on the Latin alphabet. We need to make sure that the letter ß is encoded, but we don't need to create a different letter k for German—the same letter k we use in English will do just fine.

A truly vast number of languages use the Latin alphabet. Most omit some letters from what English speakers know as the alphabet, and most add some special letters of their own. Just the same, there's considerable overlap between their alphabets. The characters that overlap between languages are encoded only once in Unicode, not once for every language that uses them. For example, both Danish and Norwegian add the letter ø to the Latin alphabet, but the letter ø is encoded only once in Unicode.

Generally, characters are not unified across writing system boundaries. For instance, the Latin letter B, the Cyrillic letter B, and the Greek letter B are not unified, even though they look the same and have the same historical origins. This is partly because their lowercase forms are all different (b, б, and β, respectively), but mostly because the designers of Unicode didn't want to unify across writing-system boundaries.[5] It made more sense to keep each writing system distinct.

The basic principle is that, wherever possible, Unicode unifies character codes from its various source encodings, whenever they can be demonstrated beyond reasonable doubt to refer to the same character. One big exception exists: respect for existing practice. It was important to Unicode's designers (and probably a big factor in Unicode's success) for Unicode to be interoperable with the various encoding systems that came before it. In particular, for a subset of "legacy" encodings, Unicode is specifically designed to *preserve round-trip compatibility.* That is, if you convert from one of the legacy encodings to Unicode and then back to the legacy encoding, you should get the same thing you started with. Many characters that would have been unified in Unicode actually aren't because of the need to preserve round-trip compatibility with a legacy encoding (or sometimes simply to conform to standard practice).

For example, the Greek lowercase letter sigma has two forms: σ is used in the middle of words, and ς is used at the end of words. As with the letters of the Arabic alphabet, this example involves two different glyphs for the same letter. Unicode would normally just have a single code point for the lowercase sigma, but because all standard encodings for Greek give different character codes to the two versions of the lowercase sigma, Unicode has to do so as well. The same thing happens in Hebrew, where the word-ending forms of several letters have their own code point values in Unicode.

If a letter does double duty as a symbol, this generally isn't sufficient grounds for different character codes either. The Greek letter pi (π), for example, is still the Greek letter pi even when it's being used as the symbol of the

---

5. There are a few exceptions to this base rule: One that comes up often is Kurdish, which when written with the Cyrillic alphabet also uses the letters Q and W from the Latin alphabet. Because the characters are a direct borrowing from the Latin alphabet, they weren't given counterparts in Unicode's version of the Cyrillic alphabet, a decision that still arouses debate.

ratio between a circle's diameter and its circumference, so it's still represented
with the same character code. Some exceptions exist, however: The Hebrew
letter aleph (א) is used in mathematics to represent the transfinite numbers, and
this use is given a separate character code. The rationale here is that aleph-as-a-
mathematical-symbol is a left-to-right character like all the other numerals and
mathematical symbols, whereas aleph-as-a-letter is a right-to-left character.
The letter Å is used in physics as the symbol of the angstrom unit. Å-as-the-
angstrom is given its own character code because some of the variable-length
Japanese encodings did.

The business of deciding which characters can be unified can be complicated. Looking different is definitely not sufficient grounds by itself. For instance, the Arabic and Urdu alphabets have a very different look, but the Urdu
alphabet is really just a particular calligraphic or typographical variation of the
Arabic alphabet. The same set of character codes in Unicode, therefore, is used
to represent both Arabic and Urdu. The same thing happens with Greek and
Coptic,[6] modern and old Cyrillic (the original Cyrillic alphabet had different
letter shapes and some letters that have since disappeared), and Russian and
Serbian Cyrillic (in italicized fonts, some letters have a different shape in Serbian from their Russian shape to avoid confusion with italicized Latin letters).

By far the biggest, most complicated, and most controversial instance of
character unification in Unicode involves the Han ideographs. The characters
originally developed to write the various Chinese languages, often called "Han
characters" after the Han Dynasty, were also adopted by various other peoples
in East Asia to write their languages. Indeed, the Han characters are still used
(in combination with other characters) to write Japanese (who call them *kanji*)
and Korean (who call them *hanja*).

Over the centuries, many of the Han characters have developed different
forms in the different places where they're used. Even within the same written
language—Chinese—different forms exist: In the early 1960s, the Mao regime
in the People's Republic of China standardized or simplified versions of many
of the more complicated characters, but the traditional forms are still used in
Taiwan and Hong Kong.

---

6. The unification of Greek and Coptic has always been controversial, because they're generally
considered to be different alphabets, rather than just different typographical versions of the same
alphabet. It's quite possible that Greek and Coptic will be disunified in a future Unicode version.

Thus the same ideograph can have four different forms: one each for Traditional Chinese, Simplified Chinese, Japanese, and Korean (and when Vietnamese is written with Chinese characters, you might have a fifth form). Worse yet, it's very often not clear what really counts as the "same ideograph" between these languages. Considerable linguistic research went into coming up with a unified set of ideographs for Unicode that can be used for both forms of written Chinese, Japanese, Korean, and Vietnamese.[7] In fact, without this effort, it would have been impossible to fit Unicode into a 16-bit code space.

In all of these situations where multiple glyphs are given the same character code, it either means the difference in glyph is simply the artistic choice of a type designer (for example, whether the dollar sign has one vertical stroke or two), or it's language dependent and a user is expected to use an appropriate font for his or her language (or a mechanism outside Unicode's scope, such as automatic language detection or some kind of tagging scheme, would be used to determine the language and select an appropriate font).

The opposite situation—different character codes being represented by the same glyph—can also happen. One notable example is the apostrophe ('). There is one character code for this glyph when it's used as a punctuation mark and another when it's used as a letter (it's used in some languages to represent a glottal stop, such as in "Hawai'i").

Alternate-Glyph Selection

One interesting blurring of the line that can happen from time to time is the situation where a character with multiple glyphs needs to be drawn with a particular glyph in a certain situation, the glyph to use can't be algorithmically derived, and the particular choice of glyph needs to be preserved even in plain text. Unicode has taken different approaches to solving this problem in different situations. Much of the time, the alternate glyphs are simply given different

---

7. One popular misconception about Unicode is that Simplified and Traditional Chinese are unified. This isn't true; in fact, it's impossible, because the same Simplified Chinese character might be used as a stand-in for several different Traditional Chinese characters. Most of the time, Simplified and Traditional Chinese characters have different code point values in Unicode. Only small differences that could be reliably categorized as font-design differences, analogous to the difference between Arabic and Urdu, were unified. For more on Han unification, see Chapter 10.

code points. For example, five Hebrew letters have different shapes when they appear at the end of a word from the shapes they normally have. In foreign words, these letters keep their normal shapes even when they appear at the end of a word. Unicode gives different code point values to the regular and "final" versions of the letters. Examples like this can be found throughout Unicode.

Two special characters, U+200C ZERO WIDTH NON-JOINER (ZWNJ for short) and U+200D ZERO WIDTH JOINER (ZWJ for short), can be used as hints of which glyph shape is preferred in a particular situation. ZWNJ prevents formation of a cursive connection or ligature in situations where one would normally happen, and ZWJ produces a ligature or cursive connection where one would otherwise not occur. These two characters can be used to override the default choice of glyphs.

The Unicode Mongolian block takes yet another approach. Many characters in the Mongolian block have or cause special shaping behavior to happen, but sometimes the proper shape for a particular letter in a particular word can't be determined algorithmically (except with an especially sophisticated algorithm that recognizes certain words). The Mongolian block includes three "variation selectors," characters that have no appearance of their own, but change the shape of the character that precedes them in some well-defined way.

Beginning in Unicode 3.2, the variation-selector approach has been extended to all of Unicode. Unicode 3.2 introduces 16 general-purpose variation selectors, which work the same way as the Mongolian variation selectors: They have no visual presentation of their own, but act as "hints" to the rendering process that the preceding character should be drawn with a particular glyph shape. The list of allowable combinations of regular characters and variation selectors is given in a file called StandardizedVariants.html in the Unicode Character Database.

For more information on the joiner, non-joiner, and variation selectors, see Chapter 12.

▪ MULTIPLE REPRESENTATIONS

Having discussed the importance of the principle of unification, we must also consider the opposite property—the fact that Unicode provides alternate representations for many characters. As we saw earlier, Unicode's designers placed a high premium on respect for existing practice and interoperability with existing character encoding standards. In many cases, they sacrificed some measure of architectural purity in pursuit of the greater good (i.e., people actually using Unicode). As a result, Unicode includes code point assignments for a lot of characters that were included solely or primarily to allow for round-trip compatibility with some legacy standard, a broad category of characters known more or less informally as **compatibility characters**. Exactly which characters are compatibility characters is somewhat a matter of opinion, and there isn't necessarily anything special about the compatibility characters that flags them as such. An important subset of compatibility characters *are* called out as special because they have alternate, preferred representations in Unicode. Because the preferred representations usually consist of more than one Unicode code point, these characters are said to **decompose** into multiple code points.

There are two broad categories of decomposing characters: those with **canonical decompositions** (these characters are often referred to as "precomposed characters" or "canonical composites") and those with **compatibility decompositions** (the term "compatibility characters" is frequently used to refer specifically to these characters; a more specific term, "compatibility composite," is better). A canonical composite can be replaced with its canonical decomposition with no loss of data: the two representations are strictly equivalent, and the canonical decomposition is the character's preferred representation.[8]

Most canonical composites are combinations of a "base character" and one or more diacritical marks. For example, we talked about the character positioning rules and how the rendering engine needs to be smart enough so that when it sees, for example, an a followed by an umlaut, it draws the umlaut on top of the a: ä. Much of the time, normal users of these characters don't see them as the combination of a base letter and an accent mark. A German speaker sees ä

---

8. I have to qualify the word "preferred" here slightly. For characters whose decompositions consist of a single other character ("singleton decompositions"), this is true. For multiple-character decompositions, there's nothing that necessarily makes them "better" than the precomposed forms, and you can generally use either representation. Decomposed representations are somewhat easier to deal with in code, though, and many processes on Unicode text are based on mapping characters to their canonical decompositions, so they're "preferred" in that sense. We'll untangle this terminology in Chapter 4.

simply as "the letter ä" and not as "the letter a with an umlaut on top." A vast number of letter–mark combinations are consequently encoded using single character codes in the various source encodings, and these are very often more convenient to work with than the combinations of characters would be. The various European character encoding standards follow this pattern—for example, assigning character codes to letter–accent combinations such as é, ä, å, û, and so on—and Unicode follows suit.

Because a canonical composite can be mapped to its canonical decomposition without losing data, the original character and its decomposition are freely interchangeable. The Unicode standard enshrines this principle in law: On systems that support both the canonical composites and the combining characters that are included in their decompositions, the two different representations of the same character (composed and decomposed) are required to be treated as identical. That is, there is no difference between ä when represented by two code points and ä when represented with a single code point. In both cases, it's still the letter ä.

Most Unicode implementations must be smart enough to treat the two representations as equivalent. One way to do this is by **normalizing** a body of text to always prefer one of the representations. The Unicode standard actually provides four different normalized forms for Unicode text.

All of the canonical decompositions involve one or more **combining marks**, a special class of Unicode code points representing marks that combine graphically in some way with the character that precedes them. If a Unicode-compatible system sees the letter a followed by a combining umlaut, it draws the umlaut on top of the a. This approach can be a little more inconvenient than just using a single code point to represent the a-umlaut combination, but it does give you an easy way to represent a letter with *more than one* mark attached to it, such as you find in Vietnamese or some other languages: Just follow the base character with multiple combining marks.

Of course, this strategy means you can get into trouble with equivalence testing even without having composite characters. There are plenty of cases where the same character can be represented multiple ways by putting the various combining marks in different orders. Sometimes, the difference in ordering can be significant (if two combining marks attach to the base character in the same place, the one that comes first in the backing store is drawn closest to the character and the others are moved out of the way). In many other cases, the ordering isn't significant—you get the same visual result whatever order the combining marks come in. The different forms are then all legal and required—once again—to be treated as identical. The Unicode standard provides for a **canonical ordering** of combining marks to aid in testing such sequences for equivalence.

The other class of decomposing characters is **compatibility composites**, characters with compatibility decompositions.[9] A character can't be mapped to its compatibility decomposition without losing data. For example, sometimes alternate glyphs for the same character are given their own character codes. In these cases, a preferred Unicode code point value will represent the character, independent of glyph, and other code point values will represent the different glyphs. The latter are called **presentation forms**. The presentation forms have mappings back to the regular character they represent, but they're not simply interchangeable; the presentation forms refer to specific glyphs, while the preferred character maps to whatever glyph is appropriate for the context. In this way, the presentation forms carry more information than the canonical forms. The most notable set of presentation forms are the Arabic presentation forms, where each standard glyph for each Arabic letter, plus a wide selection of ligatures, has its own Unicode character code. Although rendering engines often use presentation forms as an implementation detail, normal users of Unicode are discouraged from using them and are urged to use the nondecomposing characters instead. The same goes for the smaller set of presentation forms for other languages.

Another interesting class of compatibility composites represent stylistic variants of particular characters. They are similar to presentation forms, but instead of representing particular glyphs that are contextually selected, they represent particular glyphs that are normally specified through the use of additional styling information (remember, Unicode represents only plain text, not styled text). Examples include superscripted or subscripted numerals, or letters with special styles applied to them. For example, the Planck constant is

---

9. There are a few characters in Unicode whose canonical decompositions include characters with compatibility decompositions. The Unicode standard considers these characters to be *both* canonical composites *and* compatibility composites.

represented using an italicized letter *h*. Unicode includes a compatibility character code for the symbol for the Planck constant, but you could also just use a regular h in conjunction with some non-Unicode method of specifying that it's italicized. Characters with adornments such as surrounding circles fall into this category, as do the abbreviations sometimes used in Japanese typesetting that consist of several characters arranged in a square.

For compatibility composites, the Unicode standard not only specifies the characters to which they decompose, but also information intended to explain what nontext information is needed to express exactly the same thing.

Canonical and compatibility decompositions, combining characters, normalized forms, canonical accent ordering, and related topics are all dealt with in excruciating detail in Chapter 4.

▪ FLAVORS OF UNICODE

Let's take a minute to go back over the character-encoding terms from Chapter 2:

- An **abstract character repertoire** is a collection of characters.
- A **coded character set** maps the characters in an abstract character repertoire to abstract numeric values or positions in a table. These abstract numeric values are called *code points*. (For a while, the Unicode 2.0 standard referred to code points as "Unicode scalar values.")
- A **character encoding form** maps code points to series of fixed-length bit patterns known as *code units*. (For a while, the Unicode 2.0 standard referred to code units as "code points.")
- A **character encoding scheme,** also called a *serialization format*, maps code units to bytes in a sequential order. (This may involve specifying a serialization order for code units that are more than one byte long, specifying a method of mapping code units from more than one encoding form into bytes, or both.)
- A **transfer encoding syntax** is an additional transformation that may be performed on a serialized sequence of bytes to optimize it for some situation (transforming a sequence of 8-bit byte values for transmission through a system that handles only 7-bit values, for example).

For most Western encoding standards, the transforms in the middle (i.e., from code points to code units and from code units to bytes) are so straightforward that they're never thought of as distinct steps. The standards in the ISO 8859 family, for example, define coded character sets. Because the code point values are a byte long already, the character encoding forms and character encoding schemes used with these coded character sets are basically null transforms: You use the normal binary representation of the code point values as code units, and you don't have to do anything to convert the code units to bytes. (ISO 2022 does define a character encoding scheme that lets you mix characters from different coded character sets in a single serialized data stream.)

The East Asian character standards make these transforms more explicit. JIS X 0208 and JIS X 0212 define coded character sets only; they just map each character to row and column numbers in a table. You then have a choice of character encoding schemes for converting the row and column numbers into serialized bytes: Shift-JIS, EUC-JP, and ISO 2022-JP are all examples of character encoding schemes used with the JIS coded character sets.

The Unicode standard makes each layer in this hierarchy explicit. It comprises the following:

1. An abstract character repertoire that includes characters for an extremely wide variety of writing systems.

2. A single coded character set that maps each character in the abstract repertoire to a 21-bit value. (The 21-bit value can also be thought of as a coordinate in a three-dimensional space: a 5-bit plane number, an 8-bit row number, and an 8-bit cell number.)

3. Three character encoding forms known as Unicode Transformation Formats (UTF):

   - UTF-32, which represents each 21-bit code point value as a single 32-bit code unit. UTF-32 is optimized for systems where 32-bit values are easier or faster to process and space isn't at a premium.

   - UTF-16, which represents each 21-bit code point value as a sequence of one or two 16-bit code units. The vast majority of characters are represented with single 16-bit code units, making it a good general-use compromise between UTF-32 and UTF-8. UTF-16, the oldest Unicode encoding form, is the form specified by the Java and

JavaScript programming languages and the XML Document Object Model APIs.

- UTF-8, which represents each 21-bit code point value as a sequence of one to four 8-bit code units. The ASCII characters have exactly the same representation in UTF-8 as they do in ASCII, and UTF-8 is optimized for byte-oriented systems or systems where backward compatibility with ASCII is important. For European languages, UTF-8 is also more compact than UTF-16; for Asian languages, UTF-16 is more compact than UTF-8. UTF-8 is the default encoding form for a wide variety of Internet standards.

4. Seven character encoding schemes. UTF-8 is a character encoding scheme unto itself because it uses 8-bit code units. UTF-16 and UTF-32 each have three associated encoding schemes:

- A "big-endian" version that serializes each code unit most-significant-byte first.
- A "little-endian" version that serializes each code unit least-significant-byte first.
- A self-describing version that uses an extra sentinel value at the beginning of the stream, called the "byte order mark," to specify whether the code units are in big-endian or little-endian order.

In addition, some allied specifications aren't officially part of the Unicode standard:

- UTF-EBCDIC is a version of UTF-8 designed for use on EBCDIC-based systems that maps Unicode code points to series of from one to five 8-bit code units.
- CESU-8 is a modified version of UTF-8 designed for backward compatibility with some older Unicode implementations.
- UTF-7 is a mostly obsolete character encoding scheme for use with 7-bit Internet standards that maps UTF-16 code units to sequences of 7-bit values.

- Standard Compression Scheme for Unicode (SCSU) is a character encoding scheme that maps a sequence of UTF-16 code units to a compressed sequence of bytes, providing a serialized Unicode representation that is generally as compact for a given language as that language's legacy encoding standards and that optimizes Unicode text for further compression with byte-oriented compression schemes such as LZW.
- Byte-Order Preserving Compression for Unicode (BOCU) is another compression format for Unicode.

We'll delve into the details of these encoding forms and schemes in Chapter 6.

■ CHARACTER SEMANTICS

Because Unicode aims to encode semantics rather than appearances, simple code charts aren't sufficient. After all, they merely show pictures of characters in a grid that maps them to numeric values. The pictures of the characters can certainly help illustrate the semantics of the characters, but they can't tell the whole story. The Unicode standard goes well beyond just pictures of the characters, providing a wealth of information on every character.

Every code chart in the standard is followed by a list of the characters in the code chart. For each character, an entry gives the following information:

- Its Unicode code point value.
- A representative glyph. For characters that combine with other characters, such as accent marks, the representative glyph includes a dotted circle that shows where the main character would go—making it possible to distinguish COMBINING DOT ABOVE from COMBINING DOT BELOW, for example. For characters that have no visual appearance, such as spaces and control and formatting codes, the representative glyph is a dotted square with some sort of abbreviation of the character name inside.
- The character's name. The name, and not the representative glyph, is the normative property (the parts of the standard that are declared to be

"normative" are the parts you have to follow exactly to conform to the standard; parts declared "informative" are there to supplement or clarify the normative parts and don't have to be followed exactly to conform). This reflects the philosophy that Unicode encodes semantics, although sometimes the actual meaning of the character has drifted since the earliest drafts of the standard and no longer matches the name. Such cases are very rare, however.

In addition to the code point value, name, and representative glyph, an entry may include the following:

- Alternate names for the character
- Cross-references to similar characters elsewhere in the standard (which helps to distinguish them from each other)
- The character's canonical or compatibility decomposition (if it's a composite character)
- Additional notes on its usage or meaning (for example, the entries for many letters include the languages that use them)

The Unicode standard also includes chapters on each major group of characters in the standard, with information that's common to all of the characters in the group (such as encoding philosophy or information on special processing challenges) and additional narrative explaining the meaning and usage of any characters in the group that have special properties or behavior that needs to be called out.

The Unicode standard actually consists of more than just *The Unicode Standard Version 3.0*. That is, there's more to the Unicode standard than just the book. The standard includes a comprehensive database of all the characters, a copy of which is included on the CD that's included with the book. Because the character database changes more frequently than the rest of the standard, it's usually a good idea to get the most recent version of the database from the Unicode Consortium's Web site at `http://www.unicode.org`.

Every character in Unicode is associated with a list of properties that define how the character is to be treated by various processes. The Unicode

Character Database comprises a group of text files that give the properties for each character in Unicode. Among the properties that each character has are the following:

- The character's code point value and name.
- The character's general category. All of the characters in Unicode are grouped into 30 categories. The category tells you things like whether the character is a letter, numeral, symbol, whitespace character, control code, and so forth.
- The character's decomposition, along with whether it's a canonical or compatibility decomposition, and for compatibility composites, a tag that attempts to indicate what data are lost when you convert to the decomposed form.
- The character's case mapping. If the character is a cased letter, the database includes the mapping from the character to its counterpart in the opposite case.
- For characters that are considered numerals, the character's numeric value (that is, the numeric value the character represents, not the character's code point value).
- The character's directionality (e.g., whether it is left-to-right, is right-to-left, or takes on the directionality of the surrounding text). The Unicode Bidirectional Layout Algorithm uses this property to determine how to arrange characters of different directionalities on a single line of text.
- The character's mirroring property. It says whether the character takes on a mirror-image glyph shape when surrounded by right-to-left text.
- The character's combining class. It is used to derive the canonical representation of a character with more than one combining mark attached to it (it's used to derive the canonical ordering of combining characters that don't interact with each other).
- The character's line-break properties. This information is used by text rendering processes to help figure out where line divisions should go.

For an in-depth look at the various files in the Unicode Character Database, see Chapter 5.

■ UNICODE VERSIONS AND UNICODE TECHNICAL REPORTS

The Unicode standard includes a group of supplementary documents known as Unicode Technical Reports. A snapshot of these is also included on the CD that comes with the book *The Unicode Standard, Version 3.0,* but the CD accompanying the Unicode 3.0 standard is now so out of date as to be nearly useless. You can always find the most up-to-date slate of technical reports on the Unicode Web site (`http://www.unicode.org`).

There are three kinds of technical reports:

- **Unicode Standard Annexes (UAX)** are actual addenda and amendments to the Unicode standard.
- **Unicode Technical Standards (UTS)** are adjunct standards related to Unicode. They're not normative parts of the standard itself, but carry their own conformance criteria.
- **Unicode Technical Reports (UTR)** include various types of adjunct information, such as text clarifying or expanding on parts of the standard, implementation guidelines, and descriptions of procedures for doing things with Unicode text that don't rise to the level of official Unicode Technical Standards.

Other types of reports exist as well:

- **Draft Unicode Technical Reports (DUTR).** Technical reports are often published while they're still in draft form. DUTR status indicates that an agreement has been reached in principle to adopt the proposal, but details must still be worked out. Draft technical reports don't have any normative force until the Unicode Technical Committee votes to remove "Draft" from their name, but they're published early to solicit comments and give implementers a head start.
- **Proposed Draft Unicode Technical Reports (PDUTR).** These technical reports are published before an agreement in principle has been reached to adopt them.

The status of the technical reports is constantly changing. Here's a summary of the slate of technical reports as of this writing (January 2002).

Unicode Standard Annexes

All of the following Unicode Standard Annexes are officially part of the Unicode 3.2 standard:

- **UAX #9: The Unicode Bidirectional Algorithm.** This report specifies the algorithm for laying out lines of text that mix left-to-right characters with right-to-left characters. It supersedes the description of the bidirectional layout algorithm in the Unicode 3.0 book. For an overview of the bidirectional layout algorithm, see Chapter 8. For implementation details, see Chapter 16.
- **UAX #11: East Asian Width.** It specifies a set of character properties that determine how many display cells a character takes up when used in the context of East Asian typography. For more information, see Chapter 10.
- **UAX #13: Unicode Newline Guidelines.** There are some interesting issues regarding how you represent the end of a line or paragraph in Unicode text, and this document clarifies them. This information is covered in Chapter 12.
- **UAX #14: Line Breaking Properties.** This document specifies how a word-wrapping routine should treat the various Unicode characters. Word-wrapping is covered in Chapter 16.
- **UAX #15: Unicode Normalization Forms.** Because Unicode has multiple ways of representing a lot of characters, it's often helpful to convert Unicode text to some kind of normalized form that prefers one representation for any given character over all the others. There are four Unicode Normalization Forms, described in this document. The Unicode Normalization Forms are covered in Chapter 4.
- **UAX #19: UTF-32.** It specifies the UTF-32 encoding form. UTF-32 is covered in Chapter 6.
- **UAX #27: Unicode 3.1.** This official definition includes the changes and additions to Unicode 3.0 that form Unicode 3.1. This document officially incorporates the other Unicode Standard Annexes into the standard and gives them a version number. It also includes code charts and character lists for all new characters added to the standard in Unicode 3.1.

Unicode Technical Standards

- **UTS #6: A Standard Compression Scheme for Unicode.** It defines SCSU, a character encoding scheme for Unicode that results in serialized Unicode text of comparable size to the same text in legacy encodings. For more information, see Chapter 6.
- **UTS #10: The Unicode Collation Algorithm.** It specifies a method of comparing character strings in Unicode in a language-sensitive manner and a default ordering of all characters to be used in the absence of a language-specific ordering. For more information, see Chapter 15.

Unicode Technical Reports

- **UTR #16: UTF-EBCDIC.** It specifies a special 8-bit transformation of Unicode for use on EBCDIC-based systems. This topic is covered in Chapter 6.
- **UTR #17: Character Encoding Model.** It defines a set of useful terms for discussing the various aspects of character encodings. This material was covered in Chapter 2 and reiterated in this chapter.
- **UTR #18: Regular Expression Guidelines.** It provides some guidelines for how a regular-expression facility should behave when operating on Unicode text. This material is covered in Chapter 15.
- **UTR #20: Unicode in XML and Other Markup Languages.** It specifies some guidelines for how Unicode should be used in the context of a markup language such as HTML or XML. This topic is covered in Chapter 17.
- **UTR #21: Case Mappings.** It gives more detail than the standard itself on the process of mapping uppercase to lowercase, and vice versa. Case mapping is covered in Chapter 14.
- **UTR #22: Character Mapping Tables.** It specifies an XML-based file format for describing a mapping between Unicode and some other encoding standard. Mapping between Unicode and other encodings is covered in Chapter 14.
- **UTR #24: Script Names.** It defines an informative character property: the script name, which identifies the writing system (or "script") to which each character belongs. The script name property is discussed in Chapter 5.

Draft and Proposed Draft Technical Reports

- **PDUTR #25: Unicode Support for Mathematics.** It gives a detailed account of the various considerations involved in using Unicode to represent mathematical expressions, including issues such as spacing and layout, font design, and interpretation of Unicode characters in the context of mathematical expressions. This technical report also includes a heuristic for detecting mathematical expressions in plain Unicode text, and proposes a scheme for representing structured mathematical expressions in plain text. We'll look at math symbols in Chapter 12.

- **DUTR #26: Compatibility Encoding Scheme for UTF-16: 8-bit (CESU-8).** It documents a UTF-8-like Unicode encoding scheme that's being used in some existing systems. We'll look at CESU-8 in Chapter 6.

- **PDUTR #28: Unicode 3.2.** Together with UAX #27, this official definition gives all the changes and additions to Unicode 3.0 that define Unicode 3.2, including revised and updated code charts with the new Unicode 3.2 characters. Unicode 3.2 is scheduled to be released in March 2002, so this technical report will likely be UAX #28 by the time you read these words.

Superseded Technical Reports

The following technical reports have been superseded by (or absorbed into) more recent versions of the standard:

- **UTR #1: Myanmar, Khmer, and Ethiopic.** Absorbed into Unicode 3.0.

- **UTR #2: Sinhala, Mongolian, and Tibetan.** Tibetan was in Unicode 2.0; Sinhala and Mongolian were added in Unicode 3.0.

- **UTR #3: Various Less-Common Scripts.** This document includes exploratory proposals for historical or rare writing systems. It has been superseded by more recent proposals. Some of the scripts in this proposal have been incorporated into more recent versions of Unicode: Cherokee (Unicode 3.0), Old Italic (Etruscan; Unicode 3.1), Thaana

(Maldivian; 3.0), Ogham (3.0), Runic (3.0), Syriac (3.0), Tagalog (3.2), Buhid (3.2), and Tagbanwa (3.2). Most of the others are in various stages of discussion, with another batch scheduled for inclusion in Unicode 4.0. This document is mostly interesting as a list of writing systems that will probably be in future versions of Unicode. For more information on this subject, check out `http://www.unicode.org/ unicode/alloc/Pipeline.html`.

- **UTR #4: Unicode 1.1.** Superseded by later versions.
- **UTR #5: Handling Non-spacing Marks.** Incorporated into Unicode 2.0.
- **UTR #7: Plane 14 Characters for Language Tags.** Incorporated into Unicode 3.1.
- **UTR #8: Unicode 2.1.** Superseded by later versions.

The missing numbers belong to technical reports that have been withdrawn by their proposers, have been turned down by the Unicode Technical Committee, or haven't been published yet.

Unicode Versions

Many of the technical reports either define certain versions of Unicode or are superseded by certain versions of Unicode. Each version of Unicode comprises a particular set of characters, a particular version of the character-property files, and a certain set of rules for dealing with them. All of these things change over time (although certain things are guaranteed to remain the same—see "Unicode Stability Policies" later in this chapter).

This point brings us to the question of Unicode version numbers. A Unicode version number consists of three parts—for example, "Unicode 2.1.8." The first number is the **major version number**. It gets bumped every time a new edition of the book is released. That happens when the accumulation of technical reports becomes too unwieldy or when a great many significant changes (such as lots of new characters) are incorporated into the standard at once. A new major version of Unicode appears every several years.

The **minor version number** gets bumped whenever new characters are added to the standard or other significant changes are made. New minor versions of Unicode don't get published as books, but do get published as Unicode

Standard Annexes. There has been one minor version of Unicode between each pair of major versions (i.e., there was a Unicode 1.1 [published as UTR #4], a Unicode 2.1 [UTR #8], and a Unicode 3.1 [UAX #27]), but this pattern was broken with the release of Unicode 3.2 (PDUTR #28 at the time of this writing, but most likely UAX #28 by the time you read this).

The **update version number** gets bumped when changes are made to the Unicode Character Database. Updates are published as new versions of the database; there is no corresponding technical report.

The current version of Unicode at the time of this writing (January 2002) is Unicode 3.1.1. Unicode 3.2, which includes a whole slate of new characters, is currently in beta and will likely be the current version by the time this book is published.

One has to be a bit careful when referring to a particular version of the Unicode standard from another document, particularly another standard. Unicode changes constantly, so it's seldom a good idea to nail yourself to one specific version. It's generally best either to specify only a major version number (or, in some cases, just major and minor version numbers) or to specify an open-ended range of versions (e.g., "Unicode 2.1 or later"). Generally, this approach is okay, as future versions of Unicode will only add characters—because you're never required to support a particular character, you can pin yourself to an open-ended range of Unicode versions and not sweat the new characters. Sometimes, however, changes are made to a character's properties in the Unicode Character Database that could alter program behavior. Usually, this is a good thing—changes are made to the database when the database is deemed to have been *wrong* before—but your software may need to deal with this modification in some way.

Unicode Stability Policies

Unicode will, of course, continue to evolve. Nevertheless, you can count on some things to remain stable:

- Characters that are in the current standard will never be removed from future standards. They may, in unusual circumstances, be deprecated (i.e., their use might be discouraged), but they'll never be eliminated and their code point values will never be reused to refer to different characters.

- Characters will never be reassigned from one code point to another. If a character has ambiguous semantics, a new character may be introduced with more specific semantics, but the old one will never be taken away and will continue to have ambiguous semantics.
- Character names will never change. Occasionally a character with ambiguous semantics will get out of sync with its name as its semantics evolve, but this is very rare.
- Text in one of the Unicode Normalized Forms will always be in that normalized form. That is, the definition of the Unicode Normalized Forms will not change between versions of the standard in ways that would cause text that is normalized according to one version of the standard not to be normalized in later versions of the standard.
- A character's combining class and canonical and compatibility decompositions will never change, as that would break the normalization guarantee.
- A character's properties may change, but not in a way that would alter the character's fundamental identity. In other words, the representative glyph for "A" won't change to "B", and the category for "A" won't change to "lowercase letter." You'll see property changes only to correct clear mistakes in previous versions.
- Various structural aspects of the Unicode character properties will remain the same, as implementations depend on some of these things. For example, the standard won't add any new general categories or any new bi-di categories, it will keep characters' combining classes in the range from 0 to 255, noncombining characters will always have a combining class of 0, and so on.

You can generally count on characters' other normative properties not changing, although the Unicode Consortium certainly reserves the right to fix mistakes in these properties.

The Unicode Consortium can change a character's informative properties more or less at will, without changing version numbers, because you don't have to follow them anyway. Again, this type of change shouldn't happen much, except when consortium members need to correct a mistake of some kind.

These stability guarantees are borne out of bitter experience. Characters *did* get removed and reassigned and characters' names *did* change in Unicode 1.1 as a result of the merger with ISO 10646, and it caused serious grief. This problem won't happen again.

▪ ARRANGEMENT OF THE ENCODING SPACE

Unicode's designers tried to assign the characters to numeric values in an orderly manner that would make it easy to tell something about a character just from its code point value. As the encoding space has filled up, this has become more difficult to do, but the logic still comes through reasonably well.

Unicode was originally designed for a 16-bit encoding space, consisting of 256 *rows* of 256 characters each. ISO 10646 was designed for a 32-bit encoding space, consisting of 128 *groups* of 256 *planes* containing 256 rows of 256 characters. Thus the original Unicode encoding space had room for 65,536 characters, and ISO 10646 had room for an unbelievable 2,147,483,648 characters. The ISO encoding space is clearly overkill (experts estimate that perhaps 1 million or so characters are eligible for encoding), but it was clear by the time Unicode 2.0 came out that the 16-bit Unicode encoding space was too small.

The solution was the **surrogate mechanism**, a scheme whereby special escape sequences known as **surrogate pairs** could be used to represent characters outside the original encoding space. It extended the number of characters that could be encoded to 1,114,112, leaving ample space for the foreseeable future (only 95,156 characters are actually encoded in Unicode 3.2, and Unicode has been in development for 12 years). The surrogate mechanism was introduced in Unicode 2.0 and has since become known as UTF-16. It effectively encodes the first 17 planes of the ISO 10646 encoding space. The Unicode Consortium and WG2 have agreed never to populate the planes above plane 16, so for all intents and purposes, Unicode and ISO 10646 now share a 21-bit encoding space consisting of 17 planes of 256 rows of 256 characters. Valid Unicode code point values run from U+0000 to U+10FFFF.

Organization of the Planes

Figure 3.1 shows the Unicode encoding space.

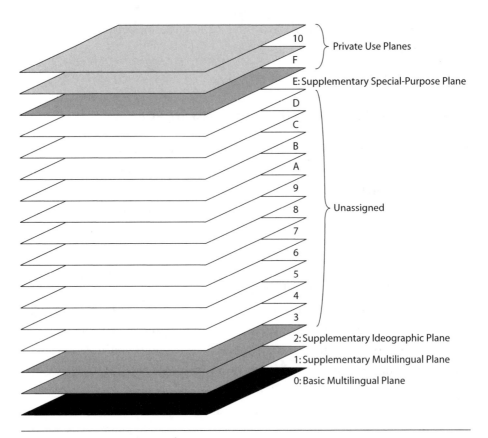

Figure 3.1   The Unicode Encoding Space

Plane 0 is the **Basic Multilingual Plane (BMP)**. It contains the majority of the encoded characters, including all of the most common ones. In fact, prior to Unicode 3.1, no characters were encoded in any of the other planes. The characters in the BMP can be represented in UTF-16 with a single 16-bit code unit.

Plane 1 is the **Supplementary Multilingual Plane (SMP)**. It is intended to contain characters from archaic or obsolete writing systems. Why encode them at all? They are here mostly for the use of the scholarly community in papers where they write about these characters. Various specialized collections of symbols will also go into this plane.

Plane 2 is the **Supplementary Ideographic Plane (SIP)**. This extension of the CJK Ideographs Area from the BMP contains rare and unusual Chinese characters.

Plane 14 (E) is the **Supplementary Special-Purpose Plane (SSP)**. It's reserved for special-purpose characters—generally code points that don't encode characters as such but are instead used by higher-level protocols or as signals to processes operating on Unicode text.

Planes 15 and 16 (F and 10) are the **Private Use Planes**, an extension of the Private Use Area in the BMP. The other planes are currently unassigned, and will probably remain that way until Planes 1, 2, and 14 start to fill up.

The Basic Multilingual Plane

The heart and soul of Unicode is plane 0, the BMP. It contains the vast majority of characters in common use today, and those that aren't yet encoded will go here as well. Figure 3.2 shows the allocation of space in the BMP.

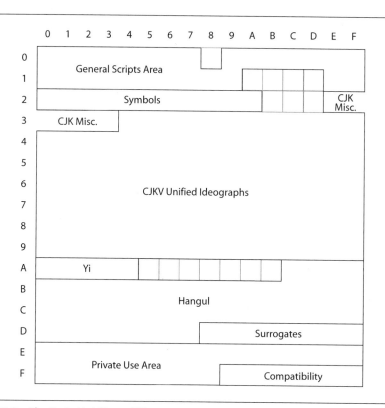

Figure 3.2   The Basic Multilingual Plane

The characters whose code point values begin with 0 and 1 form the **General Scripts Area**. This area contains the characters from all of the alphabetic writing systems, including the Latin, Greek, Cyrillic, Hebrew, Arabic, Devanagari (Hindi), and Thai alphabets, among many others. It also contains a collection of combining marks that are often used in conjunction with the letters in this area. Figure 3.3 shows how the General Scripts Area is allocated.

There are a few important things to note about the General Scripts Area. First, the first 128 characters (those from U+0000 to U+007F) are exactly the same as the ASCII characters with the same code point values. Thus you can convert from ASCII to Unicode simply by zero-padding the characters out to 16 bits (in fact, in UTF-8, the 8-bit version of Unicode, the ASCII characters have exactly the same representation as they do in ASCII).

	00	20	40	60	80	A0	C0	E0	00	20	40	60	80	A0	C0	E0
00/01	ASCII				Latin-1				Lat. Ext. A				Lat. Ext. B			
02/03	Lat. Ext. B		IPA		Mod. Ltrs.				Comb. Diac.				Greek			
04/05	Cyrillic										Armenian			Hebrew		
06/07	Arabic								Syriac				Thaana			
08/09									Devanagari				Bengali			
0A/0B	Gurmukhi				Gujarati				Oriya				Tamil			
0C/0D	Telugu				Kannada				Malayalam				Sinhala			
0E/0F	Thai				Lao				Tibetan							
10/11	Myanmar						Georgian		Hangul Jamo							
12/13	Ethiopic												Cherokee			
14/15	Canadian Aboriginal Syllablics															
16/17			Ogham	Runic		Phillipine Scripts				Khmer				
18/19	Mongolian															
1A/1B																
1C/1D																
1E/1F	Latin Extended Additional								Greek Extended							

Figure 3.3 The General Scripts Area

Second, the first 256 characters (those from U+0000 to U+00FF) are exactly the same as the characters with the same code point values from the ISO 8859-1 (ISO Latin-1) standard. (Latin-1 is a superset of ASCII; its lower 128 characters are identical to ASCII.) You can convert Latin-1 to Unicode by zero-padding out to 16 bits. (Note, however, that the non-ASCII Latin-1 characters have two-byte representations in UTF-8.)

For those writing systems that have only one dominant existing encoding, such as most of the Indian and Southeast Asian ones, Unicode keeps the same relative arrangement of the characters as their original encoding had. Conversion back and forth can be accomplished by adding or subtracting a constant.

We'll be taking an in-depth look at all of these scripts in Part II. The Latin, Greek, Cyrillic, Armenian, and Georgian blocks, as well as the Combining Diacritical Marks, IPA Extensions, and Spacing Modifier Letters blocks, are covered in Chapter 7. The Hebrew, Arabic, Syriac, and Thaana blocks are covered in Chapter 8. The Devanagari, Bengali, Gurmukhi, Gujarati, Oriya, Tamil, Telugu, Kannada, Malayalam, Sinhala, Thai, Lao, Tibetan, Myanmar, Khmer, and Philippine blocks are covered in Chapter 9. The Hangul Jamo block is covered in Chapter 10. The Ethiopic, Cherokee, Canadian Aboriginal Syllables, Ogham, Runic, and Mongolian blocks are covered in Chapter 11.

The characters whose code point values begin with 2 (with a few recent exceptions) form the **Symbols Area.** This area includes all kinds of stuff, such as a collection of punctuation that can be used with many different languages (this block actually supplements the punctuation marks in the ASCII and Latin-1 blocks), collections of math, currency, technical, and miscellaneous symbols, arrows, box-drawing characters, and so forth. Figure 3.4 shows the Symbols area, and Chapter 12 covers the various blocks.

The characters whose code point values begin with 3 (with Unicode 3.0, this group has now slopped over to include some code point values beginning with 2) form the **CJK Miscellaneous Area.** It includes all of the characters used in the East Asian writing systems, except for the three very large areas immediately following. For example, it includes punctuation used in East Asian writing, the phonetic systems used for Japanese and Chinese, various symbols and abbreviations used in Japanese technical material, and a collection of "radicals," component parts of Han ideographic characters. These blocks are covered in Chapter 10 and shown in Figure 3.4.

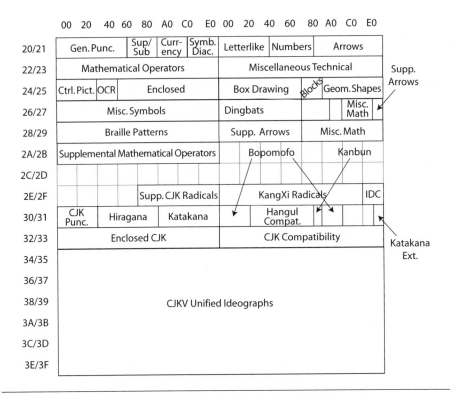

Figure 3.4   The Symbols and CJK Miscellaneous Areas

The characters whose code point values begin with 4, 5, 6, 7, 8, and 9 (in Unicode 3.0, this area has slopped over to include most of the characters whose code point values begin with 3) constitute the **CJKV Unified Ideographs Area**. This is where the Han ideographs used in Chinese, Japanese, Korean, and (much less frequently) Vietnamese are located.

The characters whose code point values range from U+A000 to U+A4CF form the **Yi Area**. It contains the characters used for writing Yi, a minority Chinese language.

The characters whose code point values range from U+AC00 to U+D7FF form the **Hangul Syllables Area**. Hangul is the alphabetic writing system used (sometimes in conjunction with Han ideographs) to write Korean. Hangul can be represented using the individual letters, or jamo, which are encoded in the General Scripts Area. The jamo are usually arranged into ideograph-like blocks representing whole syllables, and most Koreans look at whole syllables as single characters. This area encodes all possible modern Hangul syllables using a single code point for each syllable.

We look at the CJKV Unified Ideographs, Yi, and Hangul Syllables Areas in Chapter 10.

The code point values from U+D800 to U+DFFF constitute the **Surrogates Area**. This range of code point values is reserved and will never be used to encode characters. Instead, values from this range are used in pairs as code-unit values by the UTF-16 encoding to represent characters from planes 1 through 16.

The code point values from U+E000 to U+F8FF form the **Private Use Area (PUA)**. This area is reserved for the private use of applications and systems that use Unicode, which may assign any meaning they wish to the code point values in this range. Private-use characters should be used only within closed systems that can apply a consistent meaning to these code points; text that is supposed to be exchanged between systems is prohibited from using these code point values (unless the sending and receiving parties have a private agreement stating otherwise), as there's no guarantee that a receiving process would know what meaning to apply to them.

The remaining characters with code point values beginning with F form the **Compatibility Area**. This catch-all area contains characters that are included in Unicode simply to maintain backward compatibility with the source encodings. It includes various ideographs that would be unified with ideographs in the CJK Unicode Ideographs except that the source encodings draw a distinction, presentation forms for various writing systems, especially Arabic, and half-width and full-width variants of various Latin and Japanese characters, among other things. This section isn't the only area of the encoding space containing compatibility characters; the Symbols Area includes many blocks of compatibility characters, and some others are scattered throughout the rest of the encoding space. This area also contains a number of special-purpose characters and noncharacter code points. Figure 3.5 shows the Compatibility Area.

The Supplementary Planes

Planes 1 through 16 are collectively known as the Supplementary Planes. They include rarer or more specialized characters.

Figure 3.6 depicts plane 1. The area marked "Letters" includes a number of obsolete writing systems and will expand to include more. The area marked

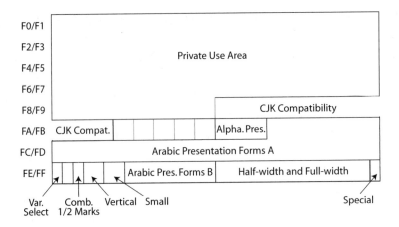

Figure 3.5   The Compatibility Area

"Music" includes a large collection of musical symbols, and the area marked "Math" includes a special set of alphanumeric characters intended to be used as symbols in mathematical formulas.

Figure 3.7 depicts plane 2. It's given over entirely to Chinese ideographic characters, acting as an extension of the CJKV Unified Ideographs Area in the BMP.

Figure 3.8 shows plane 14. It currently contains only a small collection of "tag" characters intended to be used for things like language tagging.

Although few unassigned code point values are left in the BMP, there are thousands and thousands in the other planes. Except for the Private Use Areas, Unicode implementations are not permitted to use the unassigned code point values for anything. All of them are reserved for future expansion, and they may be assigned to characters in future versions of Unicode. Conforming Unicode implementations can't use these values for any purpose or emit text purporting to be Unicode that uses them. This restriction also applies to the planes above plane 16, even though they may never be used to encode characters. It's also illegal to use the unused bits in a UTF-32 code unit to store other data.

Noncharacter Code Point Values

The code point values U+FFFE and U+FFFF, plus the corresponding code point values from all the other planes, are also illegal. They're not to be used in Unicode text at all. U+FFFE can be used in conjunction with the Unicode byte-

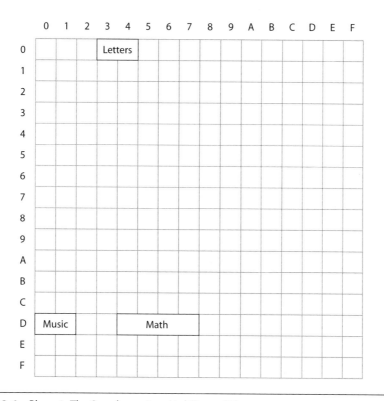

Figure 3.6 Plane 1: The Supplementary Multilingual Plane

order mark (U+FEFF) to detect byte-ordering problems (for example, if a Unicode text file produced on a Wintel PC starts with the byte-order mark, a Macintosh program reading it will read the byte-order mark as the illegal value U+FFFE and know that it has to byte-swap the file to read it properly).

U+FFFF is illegal for two main reasons. First, it provided a non-Unicode value that can be used as a sentinel value by Unicode-conformant processes. For example, the `getc()` function in C has to have a return type of `int` even though it generally returns only character values, which fit into a `char`. Because all `char` values are legal character codes, no values that are available to serve as the end-of-file signal. The `int` value -1 is the end-of-file signal—you can't use the `char` value -1 as end-of-file because it's the same as `0xFF`, which is a legal character. The Unicode version of `getc()`, on the other hand, could return unsigned short (or `wchar_t` on many systems) and still have a noncharacter value of that type—U+FFFF—available to use as the end-of-file signal.

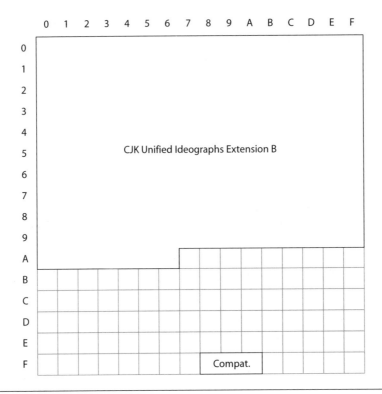

Figure 3.7   Plane 2: The Supplementary Ideographic Plane

Second, U+FFFF isn't a legal Unicode code point value for the reason given in the following example: Say you want to iterate over all of the Unicode code point values. You write the following (in C):

```
unsigned short c;
for (c = 0; c <= 0xFFFF; ++c) {
    // etc...
```

The loop will never terminate, because the next value after 0xFFFF is 0. Designating U+FFFF as a non-Unicode value enables you to write loops that iterate over the entire Unicode range in a straightforward manner without having to resort to a larger type (and a lot of casting) for the loop variable or other funny business to make sure the loop terminates.

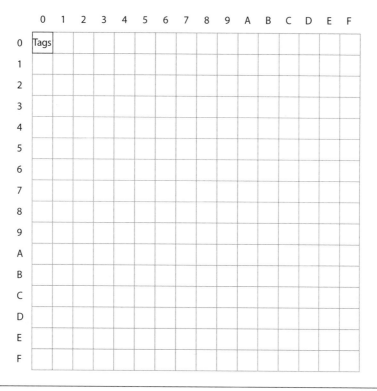

Figure 3.8   Plane 14: The Supplementary Special-Purpose Plane

The corresponding code points in the other planes were reserved for the same reasons, although this is mostly a historical curiosity now. In the original design of ISO 10646, each plane was expected to function as a more or less independent encoding space. If you dealt with characters from only one plane, you might have had to represent them with 16-bit units (effectively chopping off the plane and group numbers) and encountered the same problem as described above.

Unicode 3.1 sets aside 32 additional code point values, U+FDD0 to U+FDEF, as noncharacter code points. This change makes these values available to implementations for their internal use as markers or sentinel values without the implementations having to worry about their being assigned to characters in the future. These values are *not* private-use code points and therefore aren't supposed to be used to represent characters. Like the other noncharacter code points, they're never legal in serialized Unicode text.

■ CONFORMING TO THE STANDARD

What does it mean to say that you conform to the Unicode standard? The answer to this question varies depending on what your product does. The answer tends to be both more and less than what most people think.

First, conforming to the Unicode standard does *not* mean that you have to be able to properly support every single character that the Unicode standard defines. The Unicode standard simply requires that you declare which characters you do support. For the characters you claim to support, *then* you have to follow all the rules in the standard. In other words, if you declare your program to be Unicode conformant (and you're doing that if you use the word "Unicode" anywhere in your advertising or documentation) and say "Superduperword supports Arabic," then you must support Arabic the way the Unicode standard says you should. In particular, you've got to be able to automatically select the right glyphs for the various Arabic letters depending on their context, and you've got to support the Unicode bidirectional text layout algorithm. If you don't do these things, then as far as the Unicode standard is concerned, you don't support Arabic.

Following are the rules for conforming to the Unicode standard. They differ somewhat from the rules as set forth in Chapter 3 of the actual Unicode standard, but they produce the same end result. There are certain algorithms that you have to follow (or mimic) in certain cases to be conformant. I haven't included those here, but will go over them in future chapters. There are also some terms used here that haven't been defined yet; all will be defined in future chapters.

General

For most processes, it's not enough to say you support Unicode. By itself, this statement doesn't mean very much. You'll also need to say:

- **Which version of Unicode you're supporting.** Generally, this declaration is just a shorthand way of saying which characters you support. In cases where the Unicode versions differ in the semantics they give to characters, or in their algorithms to do different things, you're specifying which versions of those things you're using as well. Typically, if you support a given Unicode version, you also support all previous versions.[10]

Informative character semantics can and do change from version to version. You're not required to conform to the informative parts of the standard, but saying which version you support is also a way of saying which set of informative properties you're using.

It's legal and, in fact, often a good idea to say something like "Unicode 2.1.8 and later" when specifying which version of Unicode you use. This is particularly true when you're writing a standard that uses Unicode as one of its base standards. New versions of the standard (or conforming implementations) can then support new characters without going out of compliance. It's rarely necessary to specify which version of Unicode you're using all the way out to the last version number; rather, you can just indicate the major revision number ("This product supports Unicode 2.x").

- **Which transformation formats you support.** This information is relevant only if you exchange Unicode text with the outside world (including writing it to disk or sending it over a network connection). If you do, you must specify which of the various character encoding schemes defined by Unicode (the Unicode Transformation Formats) you support. If you support several, you need to specify your default (i.e., which formats you can read without being told by the user or some other outside source what format the incoming file is in). The Unicode Transformation Formats are discussed in Chapter 6.

- **Which normalization forms you support or expect.** Again, this point is important if you're exchanging Unicode text with the outside world. It can be thought of as a shorthand way of specifying which characters you support, but is specifically oriented toward telling people what characters can be in an incoming file. The normalization forms are discussed in Chapter 4.

---

10. Technically, this is guaranteed only as far back as Unicode 2.0— some radical changes, including removal and movement of characters, occurred between some of the earlier versions as Unicode and ISO 10646 were brought into sync with each other.

- **Which characters you support.** The Unicode standard doesn't require you to support any particular set of characters, so you need to say which sets of characters you know how to handle properly (of course, if you're relying on an external library, such as the operating system, for part or all of your Unicode support, you support whatever characters it supports). The ISO 10646 standard has formal ways of specifying which characters you support; Unicode doesn't. Instead, Unicode asks that you state these characters, but allows you to specify them any way you want, and you can specify any characters that you want.

  Part of the reason that Unicode doesn't provide a formal way of specifying which characters you support is that this statement often varies depending on what you're doing with the characters. Which characters you can display, for example, is often governed by the fonts installed on the system you're running on. You might also be able to sort lists properly only for a subset of languages you can display. Some of this information you can specify in advance, but you may be limited by the capabilities of the system you're actually running on.

Producing Text as Output

If your process produces Unicode text as output, either by writing it to a file or by sending it over some type of communication link, there are certain things you can't do. (Note that this constraint refers to *machine-readable* output; displaying Unicode text on the screen or printing it on a printer follow different rules, as outlined later in this chapter.)

- Your output can't contain any code point values that are unassigned in the version of Unicode you're supporting.
- Your output can't contain U+FFFE, U+FFFF, or any of the other noncharacter code point values.
- Your output *is* allowed to include code point values in the Private Use Area, but this technique is strongly discouraged. As anyone can attach any meaning desired to the private-use code points, you can't guarantee that someone reading the file will interpret the private-use characters in the same way you do (or interpret them at all). You can, of course, exchange things any way you want within the universe you control, but that

doesn't count as exchanging with "the outside world." You can get around this restriction if you expect the receiving party to uphold some kind of private agreement, but then you're technically not supporting Unicode anymore; you're supporting a higher-level protocol that uses Unicode as its basis.

- You can't produce a sequence of bytes that's illegal for whatever Unicode transformation format you're using. Among other things, this constraint means you have to obey the shortest-sequence rule. If you're putting out UTF-8, for example, you can't use a three-byte sequence when the character can be represented with a two-byte sequence, and you can't represent characters outside the BMP using two three-byte sequences representing surrogates.

Interpreting Text from the Outside World

If your program reads Unicode text files or accepts Unicode over a communications link (from an arbitrary source, of course—you can have private agreements with a known source), you're subject to the following restrictions:

- If the input contains unassigned or illegal code point values, you must treat them as errors. Exactly what this statement means may vary from application to application, but it is intended to prevent security holes that could conceivably result from letting an application interpret illegal byte sequences.
- If the input contains malformed byte sequences according to the transformation format it's supposed to be in, you must treat that problem as an error.
- If the input contains code point values from the Private Use Area, you can interpret them however you want, but are encouraged to ignore them or treat them as errors. See the caveats above.
- You must interpret every code point value you purport to understand according to the semantics that the Unicode standard gives to those values.
- You can handle the code point values you don't claim to support in any way that's convenient for you, unless you're passing them through to another process (see the following page).

Passing Text Through

If your process accepts text from the outside world and then passes it back out to the outside world (for example, you perform some kind of process on an existing disk file), you can't mess it up. Thus, with certain exceptions, your process can't have any side effects on the text—it must do to the text only what you say it's going to do. In particular:

- If the input contains characters that you don't recognize, you can't drop them or modify them in the output. You *are* allowed to drop illegal characters from the output.
- You *are* allowed to change a sequence of code points to a canonically equivalent sequence, but you're *not* allowed to change a sequence to a compatibility-equivalent sequence. This will generally occur as part of producing normalized text from potentially unnormalized text. Be aware, however, that you can't claim to produce normalized text unless the process normalizing the text can do so properly on any piece of Unicode text, regardless of which characters you support for other purposes.[11] (In other words, you can't claim to produce text in Normalized Form D if you only know how to decompose the precomposed Latin letters.)
- You *are* allowed to translate the text to a different Unicode transformation format, or a different byte ordering, as long as you do it correctly.
- You *are* allowed to convert U+FEFF ZERO WIDTH NO-BREAK SPACE to U+2060 WORD JOINER, as long as it doesn't appear at the beginning of a file.

Drawing Text on the Screen or Other Output Devices

You're not required to be able to display every Unicode character, but for those you purport to display, you've got to do so correctly.

---

11. This caveat guarantees you produce normalized text according to whatever version of Unicode you support. If someone passes text that includes characters from *later* Unicode versions, you may still not normalize them properly. That is okay, as long as you're clear about what version of Unicode you support.

- You can do more or less whatever you want with any characters encountered that you don't support (including illegal and unassigned code point values). The most common approach is to display some type of "unknown character" glyph. In particular, you're allowed to draw the "unknown character" glyph even for characters that don't have a visual representation, and you're allowed to treat combining characters as noncombining characters. It's better, of course, if you don't do these things. Even if you don't handle certain characters, if you know enough to know which ones not to display (such as formatting codes) or can display a "missing" glyph that gives the user some idea of what kind of character it is, that's a better option.

- If you claim to support the non-spacing marks, they must combine with the characters that precede them. In fact, multiple combining marks should combine according to the accent-stacking rules in the Unicode standard (or in a more appropriate language-specific way). Generally, this consideration is governed by the font being used—application software usually can't influence this ability much.

- If you claim to support the characters in the Hebrew, Arabic, Syriac, or Thaana blocks, you have to support the Unicode bidirectional text layout algorithm.

- If you claim to support the characters in the Arabic block, you have to perform contextual glyph selection correctly.

- If you claim to support the conjoining Hangul jamo, you have to support the conjoining jamo behavior, as set forth in the standard.

- If you claim to support any of the Indic blocks, you have to do whatever glyph reordering, contextual glyph selection, and accent stacking is necessary to properly display that script. Note that the phrase "properly display" gives you some latitude—anything that is legible and correctly conveys the writer's meaning to the reader is good enough. Different fonts, for example, may include different sets of ligatures or contextual forms.

- If you support the Mongolian script, you have to draw the characters vertically.

- When word-wrapping lines, you have to follow the mandated semantics of the characters with normative line-breaking properties.

- You're not allowed to assign semantics to any combination of a regular character and a variation selector that isn't listed in the Standardized-Variants.html file. If the combination isn't officially standardized, the variation selector has no effect. You can't define ad hoc glyph variations with the variation selectors. (You can, of course, create your own "variation selectors" in the Private Use Area.)

Comparing Character Strings

When you compare two Unicode character strings for equality, strings that are canonically equivalent should compare as equal. Thus you're not supposed to do a straight bitwise comparison without normalizing the two strings first. You can sometimes get around this problem by declaring that you expect all text coming in from outside to already be normalized or by not supporting the nonspacing marks.

Summary

In a nutshell, conforming to the Unicode standard boils down to three rules:

- If you receive text from the outside world and pass it back to the outside world, don't mess it up, even if it contains characters you don't understand.
- To claim to support a particular character, you have to follow all the rules in the Unicode standard that are relevant to that character and to what you're doing with it.
- If you produce output that purports to be Unicode text, another Unicode-conformant process should be able to interpret it properly.

4

Combining Character Sequences and Unicode Normalization

One feature of Unicode we've talked a lot about is combining characters. Indeed, this ability is one of the features that gives Unicode its power. At the same time, it may be the single greatest contributor to Unicode's complexity. In this chapter, we'll take an in-depth look at combining characters and all of the issues that arise because of them.

Consider the following collection of characters:

á	à	ä	â
é	è	ë	ê
í	ì	ï	î
ó	ò	ö	ô
ú	ù	ü	û

These characters are the Latin vowels with various diacritical marks added to them. Most of these letters occur fairly often in various European languages. The group includes 20 letters, but what's interesting to note is that all of the letters in each row have something in common and all of the letters in each column have something in common. Each row consists of characters sharing the same basic letter, and each column consists of characters sharing the same diacritical mark. We can take advantage of this commonality to cut down on the number of characters in the encoding. We already have codes for the basic letters:

a e i o u

All we really need to do is add codes for the diacritical marks:

′   `   ¨   ^

If we use these marks in combination with the regular letters, we can produce all 20 of the characters in our original chart, and we've had to allocate only four additional character codes. Using this system, you'd represent the letter ö using the code for the letter o and the code for the umlaut together.

The ASCII character encoding was originally designed to work that way. On a teletype machine, the backspace control code would cause the carriage of the teletype to back up one space, causing the next character to be printed over the top of the preceding character. The carriage return code originally returned the teletype carriage to the beginning of the line without advancing the platen, allowing you to overtype a whole line. A number of ASCII characters were designed to be used in conjunction with the backspace and carriage return. For example, the underscore character with which we're all familiar today in computers ("_") was originally intended to be used with the backspace and carriage return characters to underline words. In the same way, you could get ô by sending the letter o, followed by a backspace, followed by the caret or circumflex character "^". ASCII provided characters for the circumflex (^), tilde (~), and grave accent (`). The apostrophe/single-quote character did double duty (or maybe that's triple duty) as the acute accent, the double-quote character did double duty as the diaeresis or umlaut (the terms "diaeresis" and "umlaut" are more or less interchangeable—they refer to the same mark used for two different things), and the comma did double duty as the cedilla.

Unfortunately, this way of representing accented characters disappeared with the advent of the CRT terminal. Early CRTs weren't sophisticated enough to show two characters in the same display cell. Thus, if they encountered two characters separated by a backspace, the second character would just replace the first one on the screen. As a result, the diacritical marks in ASCII lost their meaning as diacritical marks and just turned into symbols, and the backspace fell into disuse (it was still the code transmitted when you hit the backspace key, but you no longer saw it used inside stored or transmitted text to glue characters together).

For CRT display, it became necessary to have a separate character code for each combination of letter and diacritical mark. This situation still prevails in most character encodings in use today, at least for European languages.

There are a few problems with this approach. One issue is that it can be limiting. If you have an unusual combination of base letter and accent that's not encoded, you're out of luck. Every combination of letter and mark requires the allocation of another code. In any given European language, the number of letter–mark combinations is relatively small, but the number of them for *all* languages that use the Latin alphabet is quite large—witness the large number of different "Latin alphabet" encodings in the ISO 8859 standard, for example.

Furthermore, for some other languages, base letters and diacritical marks can legitimately occur in almost any arbitrary combination. Almost any Hebrew letter, for example, can occur with almost any Hebrew vowel point. It can get worse: You can have combinations that include multiple marks applied to the same base letter. In Thai, for example, you can have arbitrary combinations of a consonant (the base letter), a vowel mark, and a tone mark.

Unicode dispenses with the idea that a single code point always maps to a single "display cell" on the screen. A single code point might map to a single "display cell," or perhaps multiple code points will, as in the cases we examined earlier.

Unicode includes a class of characters known as "combining marks" or "non-spacing marks." (The term "non-spacing mark" also comes from teletype machines—some European teletype machines were designed so that the carriage wouldn't advance to the next position when they received an accent mark, allowing the operator to send an accented letter without using a backspace. This practice goes back to the use of "dead keys" on European typewriters for the same purpose.) A non-spacing mark doesn't display as a self-contained unit; instead, it combines typographically with another character. A sequence of code points consisting of a regular character and one or more non-spacing marks is called a **combining character sequence**.

■ How Unicode Non-spacing Marks Work

Three rules govern the behavior of Unicode non-spacing marks:

1. **A non-spacing mark always combines with the character that precedes it.** If the backing store contains the character codes

   ```
   U+006F LATIN SMALL LETTER O
   U+0302 COMBINING DIAERESIS
   U+006F LATIN SMALL LETTER O
   ```

   they represent the sequence

   öo

   and not the sequence

   oö

   In other words, the diaeresis attaches to the o that precedes it.
   Unicode's designers could have gone either way with this decision. It really doesn't make much difference whether the mark attaches to the character before it or the one after it. Having the mark attach to the character after it is consistent with keyboards that use "dead key" combinations for entering accented letters, but having the mark attach to the character before it makes certain types of text analysis easier and is a little easier to understand when multiple combining marks are attached to the same character.

2. **To show a non-spacing mark appearing by itself, apply it to a space.** Unicode provides spacing versions of some non-spacing marks, generally for backward compatibility with some legacy encoding. Nevertheless, you can get any non-spacing mark to appear alone by preceding it with a space. In other words, U+0020 SPACE followed by U+0308 COMBINING DIAERESIS gives you a spacing (i.e., non-combining) diaeresis.

3. **When multiple non-spacing marks that interact typographically with the base character in the same way are applied to the same character, the marks occurring closest to the base character in the backing store also occur closest to it typographically, unless a different language-specific behavior is more appropriate.** This issue is a little complicated. Unicode allows you to apply arbitrarily many combining marks to a character. If they attach to different parts of the character (say, the top and the bottom), their ordering in the backing store isn't important. In other words, the sequence

```
U+006F LATIN SMALL LETTER O
U+0302 COMBINING CIRCUMFLEX ACCENT
U+0323 COMBINING DOT BELOW
```

and the sequence

```
U+006F LATIN SMALL LETTER O
U+0323 COMBINING DOT BELOW
U+0302 COMBINING CIRCUMFLEX ACCENT
```

are equivalent. Both look like this:

If the two marks attach to the *same* part of the character (say, they both attach to the top), then the order *is* important. In this case, the marks radiate outward from the character in the order in which they appear in the backing store. In other words, the sequence

```
U+0075 LATIN SMALL LETTER U
U+0308 COMBINING DIAERESIS
U+0304 COMBINING MACRON
```

looks like this:

ǖ

However, the sequence

```
U+0075 LATIN SMALL LETTER U
U+0304 COMBINING MACRON
U+0308 COMBINING DIAERESIS
```

looks like this:

ǖ

Note that the marks never collide typographically! Proper display of a Unicode combining character sequence includes positioning all of the marks so that they don't crash into one another.

This default behavior isn't necessarily required. In particular, some cases involve language-specific behavior that differs from the default behavior—usually with multiple marks appearing side by side instead of stacked. For example, in Vietnamese, when a vowel has both a circumflex and an acute or grave accent on it, instead of stacking,

ấ

the accent marks appear next to each other, like this:

ấ

In Greek, when a vowel has both an accent and a diaeresis mark on it, the accent is drawn between the dots of the diaeresis:

ΰ

If a vowel has a breathing mark and an accent on it, they appear side by side:

ὕ

Unicode doesn't explicitly specify this kind of behavior (although you can usually tell you're supposed to do it from looking at the representative glyph pictures in the Unicode standard), partially because accent placement on the same letters can vary depending on the language being displayed. If you're designing a font for a particular language, you need to know what the characters should look like for that language.

Dealing Properly with Combining Character Sequences

Systems handling Unicode text need to be careful when dealing with combining character sequences. Generally speaking, they should be thought of as single characters that happen to be stored using multiple code points, just as supplementary plane characters are represented using two code units in UTF-16 (the "surrogate pair"). That is, they should travel as units.

For example, deleting a base character without deleting the non-spacing marks that follow it will cause those marks to attach themselves to the character that precedes the one that was deleted. Inserting characters into the middle of a combining character sequence can have similarly weird consequences. Nothing in Unicode or in most string-handling libraries prevents you from doing this kind of thing, just as you aren't prevented from breaking up surrogate pairs; code that manipulates Unicode strings has to be careful to respect combining-character-sequence boundaries.

Unicode also doesn't say anything about what happens when a string or file begins with a non-spacing mark, or when a non-spacing mark follows a paragraph boundary or some kind of control character. These situations shouldn't arise if combining character sequences are treated as units, but again nothing prevents them. A good text-display engine might display the non-spacing marks as though they were attached to a space, but this outcome isn't required or guaranteed.

This point means, for example, that if you're editing a document and have the insertion point to the right of an accented character, and that character is represented in memory with a combining character sequence, hitting the left arrow should *not* simply back up one code unit in the backing store. That would let the user insert a character between the base letter and the accent or delete the base letter without also deleting the accent.

Similarly, search routines have to be careful when dealing with this issue. Searching for "resume" shouldn't find "résumé" just because the é is represented with a combining character sequence that starts with a normal e. You have to be careful to make sure that search hits land on combining-character-sequence boundaries.

Other than the sheer number of characters you have to deal with, combining character sequences may be the single biggest challenge to implementing truly Unicode-friendly text processing code. Even before the introduction of surrogate pairs in Unicode 2.0, Unicode was still effectively a variable-length encoding because of combining character sequences.

The trick is, again, to disabuse yourself of the idea that a one-to-one correspondence exists between "characters" as the user is used to thinking of them and code points (or code units) in the backing store. Unicode uses the term "character" to mean more or less "the entity that's represented by a single Unicode code point," but this concept doesn't always match the user's definition of "character." For instance, a French speaker doesn't see é as two characters stacked on top of each other; he or she sees it as a single character.

A lot of writing about Unicode uses the term "grapheme" to mean "character as the user understands it." Sometimes this term is somewhat ambiguous— is an Indic syllable cluster (see Chapter 9) a single "grapheme" or multiple "graphemes"? Even so, it's important for Unicode-friendly applications to deal with text in their user interfaces as a series of graphemes and not as a series of Unicode code points (or, worse, a series of UTF-16 or UTF-8 code units). Unicode 3.2 introduces a new concept, the "grapheme cluster," which can be used to help applications do the right thing. We look at grapheme clusters later in this chapter.

■ CANONICAL DECOMPOSITIONS

Combining character sequences are great for cutting down on encoding space and allowing for representation of combinations of marks you never thought of, but they have some big disadvantages. They take up more space, and they're more difficult to process, requiring more sophisticated display technology, among other things.

For these reasons, Unicode also contains a large number of "precomposed characters," code point values representing the combination of a base character and one or more non-spacing marks. Many character encoding standards, including the Latin-1 encoding used in most of Europe, use precomposed characters instead of combining character sequences. Users of these encodings know that they need only a single code point to represent characters such as é and ä, and implementations based on these encodings can adhere to the simple one-to-one relationship between code points and glyphs. Going to Unicode represents a significant step in either complexity or encoding size.

With Latin-1, there's the additional consideration that this encoding forms the basis of Unicode's representation of the Latin alphabet. You can convert between Latin-1 and Unicode simply by zero-padding to 16 bits or truncating to 8 bits. This conversion wouldn't be possible if Unicode didn't have precomposed characters.

In Unicode, all precomposed characters are compatibility characters. In other words, everything you can represent using precomposed characters, you must also be able to represent without them. Thus, every precomposed character in Unicode has an equivalent combining character sequence. This correspondence is known as its canonical decomposition, and a character with a canonical decomposition is known as a **canonical composite**.

For instance, consider the letter é. It can be represented using a single code point:

```
U+00E9 LATIN SMALL LETTER E WITH ACUTE
```

This representation is, technically speaking, only there for compatibility. It *decomposes* into the letter é's *canonical* representation:

```
U+0065 LATIN SMALL LETTER E
U+0301 COMBINING ACUTE ACCENT
```

Thus Unicode permits two legal representations for the same character. One is the canonical representation, but the other is also perfectly valid (and, in practice, much more likely to be used). And here's the big gotcha: *The two representations are absolutely equivalent.* In other words, a conforming Unicode implementation that supports all three code point values under discussion here should display the same thing on the screen for both representations (although few implementations actually do right now) and, more importantly, *is supposed to compare the two different sequences as equal.*

There's an important reason for this requirement. The average user doesn't have any direct control over how what he or she types is stored in memory; that's the province of the programmers who wrote the software being used. Suppose I'm writing a document using WhizBangWord, and WhizBangWord stores a combining character sequence in the document when I type the letter é. I decide to quote something a friend wrote to me in an e-mail; that e-mail program (SuperDuperMail) stores a canonical composite when you type the letter é. I paste in some text from my friend's e-mail that includes the word "résumé." Now I do a search for the word "résumé" in my document. WhizBangWord doesn't find "résumé" in the document even though my friend clearly used it in the section I pasted.

The problem, of course, is that WhizBangWord is searching for "résumé" using only the representation it produces. Because SuperDuperMail uses an alternative representation, WhizBangWord doesn't recognize it. Meanwhile, I—the naive user who doesn't know or care anything about how my writing is represented inside the computer—simply think my word processor is broken. The Unicode standard is trying to prevent exactly this behavior. We'll talk more about this issue in Chapter 15, but the basic rule states that code that compares strings has to be smart enough to account for the different possible representations of the same thing in Unicode.

By definition, every canonical composite character in Unicode has a canonical decomposition. The decomposition may be more than two code points long, if, for example, the original character has more than one accent mark. The Unicode Character Database saves space by giving a one- or two-code-point decomposition for every canonical composite. If a character's decomposition is more than two code points long, the first character in its decomposition will be another canonical composite. Implementations following this approach have to repeatedly look up decompositions until they arrive at a sequence consisting exclusively of noncomposite characters.

■ CANONICAL ACCENT ORDERING

Combining characters let you attach an arbitrary number of combining marks to a base character, leading to arbitrarily long combining character sequences.

As many languages permit a single base character to have at least two diacritical marks attached to it, these combinations do occur in practice. In some cases, even precomposed characters may include multiple diacriticals.

One of the crazy things about having precomposed characters *and* combining character sequences is that *both* can be used together to represent the same character. Consider the letter o with a circumflex on top and a dot beneath, which occurs in Vietnamese. This letter has *five* possible representations in Unicode:

```
U+006F LATIN SMALL LETTER O
U+0302 COMBINING CIRCUMFLEX ACCENT
U+0323 COMBINING DOT BELOW

U+006E LATIN SMALL LETTER O
U+0323 COMBINING DOT BELOW
U+0302 COMBINING CIRCUMFLEX ACCENT

U+00F4 LATIN SMALL LETTER O WITH CIRCUMFLEX
U+0323 COMBINING DOT BELOW

U+1ECD LATIN SMALL LETTER O WITH DOT BELOW
U+0302 COMBINING CIRCUMFLEX ACCENT

U+1ED9 LATIN SMALL LETTER O WITH CIRCUMFLEX AND DOT BELOW
```

All five of these representations are equivalent. All produce the following display:

You should get this glyph for any of these five internal representations. If you compare any two of these sequences, they should be regarded as equal.

Generally, you deal with the problem of comparing alternative representations of the same thing by converting all of them to their canonical representations and then comparing the canonical representations. This effort normally involves taking any composite characters and decomposing them, but the preceding example shows that this task isn't always that simple.

As it turns out, the canonical decomposition of U+1ED9 LATIN SMALL LETTER O WITH CIRCUMFLEX AND DOT BELOW is the second representation in the example: U+006F U+0323 U+0302—the letter o, followed by the underdot, followed by the circumflex.

How do we map the other alternative representations to this one? Well, there's another step we must go through in addition to decomposing any canonical composites. Every Unicode character has a property called its **combining class**, which is a number between 0 and 255. All noncombining characters have a combining class of 0. Some combining characters also have a combining class of 0, but most combining characters have some other number for their combining class.

The combining class specifies how the combining character interacts with its base character. For example, all non-spacing marks that appear above their base character but don't attach to it have a combining class of 230. All marks that attach to the bottom of their base character have a combining class of 202.

To get the canonical representation for some character, you first decompose the first character in the sequence. Next, you take all combining marks that follow it (which may include additional marks that followed the character you decomposed) and sort them in numerical order by their combining classes. In our example, the underdot has a combining class of 220 and the circumflex has a combining class of 230, so the underdot goes first. (Note that this ordering is arbitrary—there's no special reason *why* the underdot has to go first; it's just that *something* has to go first and the committee decided to have the combining classes go from bottom to top.)

Now remember the part about picking up combining characters that weren't in the original decomposition. If you start with o-circumflex followed by the combining underdot (U+00F4 U+0323), you'd begin by decomposing o-circumflex, giving U+006F U+0302 U+0323. You'd then have to notice that the sequence also includes the underdot (U+0323), even though it actually follows the character you decomposed (U+006F U+0302), and *then* sort them into the correct order. The basic rule is that a combining character sequence goes from one character with a combining class of 0 to the next character with a combining class of 0.[1]

Characters that have the *same* combining class aren't reordered relative to one another when deriving the canonical version of a combining character sequence, because characters with the same combining class interact typographically. As a result of this interaction, their relative order is important: The one that occurs first in the backing store gets drawn closest to the base character.

◼ DOUBLE DIACRITICS

One other interesting oddity is that some combining characters in Unicode attach to *two* characters. There's a tilde, for example, that is meant to be drawn over a pair of letters, like so:

$$\widetilde{aa}$$

These special characters, which are used in Tagalog and in the International Phonetic Alphabet, are treated as normal non-spacing marks. That is, they are stored after the first of the two characters they appear over and are just drawn so that they hang over whatever comes next.

For compatibility with some legacy encodings, the standard also includes pairs of combining characters that when drawn next to each other (i.e., when applied to succeeding characters) produce the same effect. You generally shouldn't use them.

---

1. This rule actually applies to comparing characters. Text-rendering engines must consider longer sequences from time to time, because there are combining characters with a combining class of 0. Many of these, such as Indic vowel signs, are treated as noncombining characters; a few, such as U+20DD COMBINING ENCLOSING CIRCLE, interact typographically with all other combining marks. The circle must maintain its position in the backing store relative to the other marks so that the rendering engine knows which marks to draw inside the circle and which to draw outside it.

◼ COMPATIBILITY DECOMPOSITIONS

Canonical composites are just one kind of compatibility character; in fact, they're only one kind of composite character. Unicode is also rife with compatibility composites, which account for 3,165 assigned code point values in Unicode 3.1. All of these characters have assigned code point values in some encoding standard in reasonably widespread use. They are characters from those standards that wouldn't have made it into Unicode on their own merits, but were given their own code point values in Unicode to allow text to be converted from the source encodings to Unicode and back again without losing any of the original information (this ability is usually referred to as "round-trip compatibility").

A few important differences separate canonical and compatibility decompositions:

- Compatibility decompositions may lose information. Many compatibility composites decompose to some other Unicode character plus some formatting information. The decomposition will revert to the canonical characters; because Unicode doesn't encode formatting information, the additional formatting is lost. (Theoretically, a styled-text system using Unicode as its character encoding could preserve the formatting information, but this is beyond the scope of Unicode.)
- Canonical composites can always be decomposed into pairs of characters, with a full decomposition being achieved by repeatedly splitting characters into pairs of characters until no more splitting is possible. The same isn't necessarily true with compatibility composites—the intermediate forms necessary to make this possible aren't all encoded as they are with canonical decompositions.

The compatibility decompositions are classified into the following categories:

1. **Superscripts and subscripts.** The encoding block from U+2070 to U+209F contains superscripted and subscripted versions of the Western digits and various math symbols. Others are scattered in the Latin-1 block and other places. The preferred representation of these digits/symbols is

the normal character codes with additional out-of-band formatting information indicating the subscripting or superscripting.

2. **Font variants.** The Letterlike Symbols block from U+2100 to U+214F includes symbols that are essentially letters with some kind of graphic variation. Many are just letters in some particular kind of font. They are marked as compatibility composites. The preferred representation is the regular letter plus out-of-band information indicating the font.[2]

3. **Circled characters.** Unicode includes many characters with circles around them. Some are encoded in the Enclosed Alphanumerics block from U+2460 to U+24FF, and others are encoded in the Enclosed CJK Letters and Months block from U+3200 to U+327F. The preferred representation is the normal representation plus out-of-band information indicating that the character is circled. (You could also represent many of them using U+20DD COMBINING ENCLOSING CIRCLE, but the official decompositions don't include this character.)

4. **Half-width and full-width.** The legacy East Asian standards include "full-width" variants of the ASCII characters. They normally map to fixed-width glyphs that are sized to fit in the display cells occupied by CJK ideographs, allowing them to be mixed better with ideographs in text that is laid out vertically. Various Japanese and Korean characters are also sized to fill up half a display cell, allowing them to be laid out in pairs in vertical text. These characters live in the Half-width and Full-width Forms block from U+FF00 to U+FFEF. Again, the preferred representation is the normal representation for the characters with out-of-band information indicating how they are to be laid out.

5. **Square forms.** The legacy Japanese standards include a large number of abbreviations—some in Japanese characters, others in Latin letters—specially laid out so as to fit in a single display cell. (Many consist of

---

2. With many of the letterlike symbols, going to an alternative representation featuring a regular Unicode letter with styling information attached may *still* lose data, even though you get the same appearance. This is because the Unicode general category changes: The character goes from being a symbol to being a letter. Many times there won't be a practical difference, but it could cause operations such as search functions to work differently—searching for the word "I" in a mathematical paper, for example, might find the italicized *i* used to represent imaginary numbers.

three or four Katakana characters arranged in a little square—hence the name.) These characters are found in the CJK Compatibility block from U+3300 to U+33FF. Again, the preferred representation is the normal characters with additional out-of-band information indicating how they are to be laid out.

6. **Vertical forms.** The CJK Compatibility Forms block from U+FE30 to U+FE4F contains a number of Japanese punctuation marks and symbols rotated 90 degrees for use in vertically laid-out text. The preferred representations for these symbols are the same as for horizontally laid-out text. The rendering engine should be smart enough to pick the appropriate glyph based on the directionality of the text.

7. **Small forms.** The Small Form Variants block from U+FE50 to U+FE6F includes a number of ASCII punctuation marks. Taken from the Taiwanese national standard, they are intended to be drawn in a full CJK display cell, but using a much-smaller-than-normal glyph. As with most other compatibility composites, these characters should be represented using the normal character codes and out-of-band information indicating the desired layout.

8. **Initial, medial, final, and isolated forms.** The Arabic alphabet is always written cursively, with most letters in a word joining to their neighbors and changing shape slightly depending on how they join. In Arabic printing, each letter is generally considered to have four visual forms: initial, medial, final, and isolated, depending on how the letter joins to its neighbors. Unicode encodes just the letters, leaving it up to the rendering engine to select the appropriate glyph for each letter. It also includes the Arabic Presentation Forms B block (U+FE70 to U+FEFE), which has a separate code point value for each glyph, for backward compatibility with systems whose rendering engines don't do this automatic glyph selection. The preferred representations of these characters are, of course, the glyph-independent versions.

9. **Non-breaking characters.** A few characters, such as U+00A0 NON-BREAKING SPACE and U+2011 NON-BREAKING HYPHEN, have non-breaking semantics. That is, paragraph-layout engines are not supposed to put these characters either immediately before or after a line boundary. These characters are considered compatibility composites,

with the preferred representation being the normal version of the character plus out-of-band information preventing the line breaks. (Any character can be given non-breaking semantics by surrounding it with U+2060 WORD JOINER on either side, but these characters' decompositions don't include this character.)

10. **Fractions.** Unicode includes a number of fractions encoded as single code points. The preferred representation of these fractions uses normal digits and U+2044 FRACTION SLASH.

11. **Miscellaneous.** Most of the remaining compatibility composites are, like the fractions, multiple characters encoded using a single code point. Some, such as the characters in Arabic Presentation Forms A, are ligatures, or special glyphs representing the combination of two or more characters. Others, such as the Roman numerals in the Number Forms block or the parenthesized numbers in the Enclosed Alphanumerics block, are just multiple characters laid out normally. In both cases, the preferred representations use multiple characters. (In the case of the ligatures, the rendering engine is supposed to be smart enough to form the ligature automatically when it sees the appropriate pair of characters.)

A handful of characters are *both* canonical composites *and* compatibility composites (that is, they have both canonical and compatibility decompositions, and they're different). This situation can arise when a character has a canonical decomposition that includes a compatibility composite. The character's canonical decomposition would leave this character intact, whereas the character's compatibility decomposition would start with the canonical decomposition and then find the compatibility decomposition of the composite character within it.

▪ SINGLETON DECOMPOSITIONS

A small number of compatibility characters have one-character canonical decompositions, often referred to as "singleton decompositions." These characters count as canonical composites, but are fundamentally different from the precomposed characters—the other canonical composites—because they don't actually represent the composition of anything. They're more akin to the compatibility composites, but they have canonical decompositions because replacing one of these characters with its decomposition doesn't lose any data. You see this kind of thing when a character, for historical reasons, is assigned two code point values in Unicode, usually because this duplication had happened in some source standard and Unicode's designers wanted to maintain round-trip compatibility.

By giving one of the two code points a singleton canonical decomposition to the other one, the Unicode standard effectively discourages its use by preventing it from appearing in normalized Unicode text (we'll get to normalization in a minute). Generally speaking, unless you're specifically trying to maintain round-trip compatibility with some other standard, you should avoid characters with singleton decompositions.

For example, the CJK Compatibility Ideographs block includes about two hundred Chinese characters that are also encoded in the CJK Unified Ideographs area. The duplicates in the compatibility area are, for all intents and purposes, identical to their counterparts in the main CJK area. Unicode provides this second set of code point assignments for these characters because some source standard included duplicate encodings for these characters. The majority come from the Korean KS C 5601 standard, which gave a separate code point assignment to each alternate pronunciation of the character. Unicode rejects this approach to encoding these characters, as they don't differ in appearance or semantics, but retains the duplicate encodings for round-trip compatibility with KS C 5601. All of the CJK compatibility characters have singleton decompositions to their counterparts in the main CJK Ideographs area, indicating that they really shouldn't be used in Unicode text unless such interoperability is really important.

■ HANGUL

Hangul is the name of the Korean writing system. Some linguists consider it the most perfect writing system in common use. Invented in the fifteenth century by King Sejong, it's basically an alphabetic system, but the letters, called *jamo,* are arranged into blocks representing whole syllables, probably because of the influence of the Chinese characters. Hangul syllables look somewhat like Chinese characters and are laid out on the page in a similar fashion (in fact, Korean writing often uses Chinese characters in addition to Hangul syllables).

Hangul jamo are classified into three categories, reflecting the structure of Korean pronunciation: *choseong,* which are initial consonants; *jungseong,* which are vowels; and *jongseong,* which are trailing consonants. A Korean syllable consists of a sequence of choseong, followed by a sequence of jungseong, optionally followed by a sequence of jongseong, all arranged to fit into a single square display cell.

Unicode provides two alternative methods of encoding Hangul. It includes a complete collection of precomposed Hangul syllable blocks, encoded in the range from U+AC00 to U+D7FF, as well as codes for the individual jamo in the range from U+1100 to U+11FF. A modern Korean syllable can be represented either with a single code point representing the whole syllable, or with a sequence of code points for the individual jamo.

The jamo code points have conjoining semantics—they're intended to be used together to represent whole syllables (another set of jamo, encoded from U+3130 to U+318F, stands alone, but these characters are considered compatibility composites). The precomposed syllables are considered to be canonical composites—they all have canonical decompositions into conjoining jamo.

The opposite isn't true, however—it's possible to produce sequences of conjoining jamo that can't be represented using the precomposed syllables. Many are mere nonsense, or sequences intended to give special effects (invisible filler characters can be used to represent isolated jamo or syllable blocks with missing jamo). However, some archaic Korean syllables can be represented only using the conjoining jamo. For this reason, as well as to provide consistency with the rest of Unicode, the conjoining jamo are the canonical representation of Korean Hangul, even though the precomposed syllables are more commonly used.

A sequence of conjoining Hangul jamo is a combining character sequence, but it differs from other Unicode combining character sequences in that it doesn't consist of a noncombining character followed by one or more combining characters. Instead, all of the jamo sometimes function as combining characters and sometimes as noncombining characters. Basically, all of the jamo are noncombining characters except when they appear together.

When they appear together, the Unicode standard gives an algorithm for locating syllable breaks. The algorithm is quite simple: Leading consonants are followed by vowels, which are followed by trailing consonants. The appearance of a character out of that sequence marks the beginning of a new syllable. Because every syllable is supposed to have an initial consonant and a vowel, Unicode provides invisible filler characters to allow the representation to be more regular.

The canonical decomposition of a precomposed syllable always consists of a single leading consonant, a single vowel, and, optionally, a single trailing consonant. This structure is possible even for syllables like *krang,* because all of the compound consonants and all of the diphthongs in Korean are encoded as single code points. The precomposed syllables and conjoining jamo are encoded in such a way as to allow for algorithmic conversion between the two representations. Extra work may still have to be done for some archaic Hangul syllables or nonstandard decomposed representations, such as representing the *kr* in *krang* using the separate *k* and *r* jamo. (The handling of nonstandard representations of modern syllables is neither specified nor required by the standard, although very early versions had this ability—it's an additional language-specific thing an application can handle if it wishes.)

Finally, there's a side effect of the decomposition of precomposed Hangul syllables into conjoining jamo. If you *mix* precomposed syllables and conjoining jamo in the same passage of text, they can combine with *each other.* To see why, consider this character:

뢴

It can be represented as

U+B8B4 HANGUL SYLLABLE ROEN

or

U+1105 HANGUL CHOSEONG RIEUL
U+116C HANGUL JUNGSEONG OE
U+11AB HANGUL JONGSEONG NIEUN

Likewise, the character

로|

can be represented as

U+B878 HANGUL SYLLABLE ROE

or

U+1105 HANGUL CHOSEONG RIEUL
U+116C HANGUL JUNGSEONG OE

Notice that the second sequence is a subset of the first. So if you have the sequence

U+B878 HANGUL SYLLABLE ROE
U+11AB HANGUL JONGSEONG NIEUN

and you decompose U+B878 into conjoining jamo

U+1105 HANGUL CHOSEONG RIEUL
U+116C HANGUL JUNGSEONG OE
U+11AB HANGUL JONGSEONG NIEUN

then you get the sequence we started with: the decomposed version of 뢴. This means that the sequence

U+B878 HANGUL SYLLABLE ROE
U+11AB HANGUL JONGSEONG NIEUN

has to be another alternate representation for 뢴. So precomposed Hangul syllables have to combine with conjoining jamo.

For more information on Hangul, see Chapter 10.

■ UNICODE NORMALIZATION FORMS

Of course, an encoding that provides so many alternative ways of representing characters can give rise to text that is much more difficult than necessary to process. In particular, comparing strings for equality is a big challenge when significantly different sequences of bits are supposed to be treated as equal. One way to deal with this problem is to require that text be *normalized,* or represented in a uniform manner, or to normalize text at some well-defined point so as to simplify operations such as comparing for equality.

Of course, by defining something as the "canonical representation" of a particular idea, you essentially nominate it as the form to which you normalize. In this way, Unicode 1.x and 2.x could be thought to have either one or two normalized forms:

- **Normalized Form D** is the traditional normalized form of Unicode, where all canonical composites (including Hangul syllables) are represented using their canonical decompositions.
- **Normalized Form KD** also eliminates the compatibility composites (the K stands for "kompatibility"), representing everything using both compatibility and canonical decompositions. Form KD is not recommended for general use (e.g., for transmitting things around on the Internet) because it potentially loses data.

Using the decomposed forms of everything, of course, makes everything bigger, which is a common objection in areas where the cost of every additional code point is significant, such as when transmitting data over the Internet, or for people familiar with using character encodings that have only precomposed characters. As a consequence, there was a strong call for a version of Unicode that favors the composed forms of everything over the decomposed forms. Two additional normalized forms were added to Unicode 3.0 in response to this need:

- **Normalized Form C** favors the canonical composite forms of the characters in Unicode. Of course, this approach is more complicated than decomposition because some things can *only* be represented using combining character sequences; there is no composite form that can be used as an alternative. For this reason, you obtain Normalized Form C by first converting to Normalized Form D and then composing everything it's possible to compose.

Another additional complication with using composed characters comes if more canonical composites are added to the standard in the future. Text that is in Normalized Form C with version 3.0 of Unicode might not be in Normalized Form C under a future Unicode version with more canonical composites if the definition of Normalized Form C amounted to "compose everything you can." To keep the definition of Normalized Form C consistent, the allowable canonical composites are fixed for all time to be just the ones in Unicode 3.0.[3] One ironic side effect is that a hypothetical Unicode 4.0 canonical composite would be represented by its *decomposed* form in Normalized Form C.

The Internet is an excellent example of an environment where Unicode normalization comes in handy. XML is a Unicode-based standard and, without requiring text to be normalized, matching up XML tags would be very difficult if XML followed the Unicode equivalence rules. The World Wide Web Consortium (W3C) deals with this complication by declaring a rule known as Uniform Early Normalization, which requires that all processes that produce text in the Internet environment produce it in Normalized Form C. Processes that consume or pass text through (which are generally expected to be way more common) can assume that the text they receive is already in normalized form and don't have to take this step themselves. Thus they can depend on character sequences always being represented with the same sequences of code points, making it possible to compare two strings for equality by doing a simple binary comparison based on the code points.

- **Normalized Form KC** is the counterpart of Normalized Form KD, taking compatibility decompositions into account as well. It's a little silly to favor the compatibility composites over the regular characters (would you want to convert two capital I's in a row into U+2161 ROMAN

---

3. Actually, this set isn't even all the precomposed characters in Unicode 3.0. A fair number of Unicode 3.0 characters with canonical decompositions are excluded from Normalized Form C because the decomposed alternatives were actually considered preferable. We talk about this issue more in Chapter 5.

NUMERAL TWO everywhere you encountered them, for example?), and Normalized Form KC doesn't do that. Rather, it does the opposite. To obtain Normalized Form KC, you first convert to Normalized Form KD (compatibility-decompose everything), then substitute precomposed characters (canonical compositions) where possible.

We'll take an in-depth look at implementation strategies for the various pieces of Unicode normalization—canonical decomposition, compatibility decomposition, canonical composition, and canonical reordering—in Chapter 14.

■ GRAPHEME CLUSTERS

Unicode 3.2 introduces a new concept called the "grapheme cluster." Actually, the concept isn't all that new; Unicode 3.2 merely formalizes a concept that was already out there, nailing down a more specific definition and some related character properties and giving it a new name.

A **grapheme cluster** is a sequence of one or more Unicode code points that should be treated as a single unit by various processes:

- Text-editing software should generally allow placement of the cursor only at grapheme cluster boundaries. Clicking the mouse on a piece of text should place the insertion point at the nearest grapheme cluster boundary, and the arrow keys should move forward and back one grapheme cluster at a time.
- Text-rendering software should never put a line break in the middle of a grapheme cluster. (Because the individual characters in a grapheme cluster generally interact typographically in ways that make it difficult to separate out the pieces, you generally couldn't put a line break in the middle of a grapheme cluster without deforming it visually in some way.)
- Sort orders for different languages generally give a relative ordering for grapheme clusters, not necessarily individual characters. For instance, in Spanish, the sequence ch is treated as a separate letter that sorts between c and d. Therefore, in Spanish, ch would generally be considered a grapheme cluster.

- Search algorithms should count a matching sequence in the text being searched as a hit only if it begins and ends on a grapheme cluster boundary.

Exactly what constitutes a grapheme cluster may vary from language to language. Unicode 3.2 simply attempts to set down a default definition of grapheme cluster that can then be tailored as necessary for specific languages.

The term "grapheme cluster" is new in Unicode 3.2;[4] in earlier versions of Unicode, the same concept was generally called a "grapheme," although other phrases such as "logical character" and "user character" were also thrown around. The problem with "grapheme" is that it has a specific meaning in linguistics, and the Unicode definition didn't agree completely with the common linguistic definition. A **grapheme** is essentially the smallest meaning-bearing unit of a writing system, as understood by the average user of that writing system.

This definition is necessarily subjective and language-specific: Is ö a single grapheme or two? An English speaker would probably say two: an o and an umlaut. A Swede would probably say one: ö is a separate letter of the Swedish alphabet. A German speaker could go either way. Also, a clump of letters that you might want a text editor to treat as a single unit, such as a Hindi syllable cluster, might still be recognized by an average Hindi speaker as several letters—a cluster of graphemes.

Thus exactly what constitutes a grapheme cluster may vary from language to language, from user to user, or even from process to process. Unicode sets forth a default definition of a grapheme cluster that should prevail in the absence of a more application-specific definition. A default grapheme cluster is one of the following things:

- A base character followed by zero or more combining marks (i.e., a normal combining character sequence).
- A Hangul syllable, whether represented using a precomposed-syllable code point, a series of conjoining-jamo code points, or a combination of the two.

---

4. This term may change before you read this book, although that's somewhat doubtful. There is widespread revulsion to this name in the Unicode community; no one really likes it (a fairly common complaint is that it sounds like some kind of breakfast cereal—"Have you tried new Grapheme Clusters? Now with more fiber!"), but no one has yet come up with anything better.

- An "orthographic syllable" in one of the Indic scripts. Such a sequence consists of a single consonant or an independent vowel, or a series of consonants joined together with *virama* marks, optionally followed by a dependent vowel sign. (For more information, see Chapter 9.)
- The CRLF sequence (i.e., U+000D U+000A, the ASCII carriage-return-line-feed combination).
- A user-defined grapheme cluster, which uses U+034F COMBINING GRAPHEME JOINER to "glue" together what would otherwise be separate grapheme clusters.

Generally speaking, grapheme cluster boundaries don't affect the way text is drawn, but there are a few situations where it does:

- An enclosing mark surrounds all the characters that precede it, up to the nearest preceding grapheme cluster boundary. U+034F COMBINING GRAPHEME JOINER can thus be used to get an enclosing mark to enclose more than one character:

```
U+0031 DIGIT ONE
U+0032 DIGIT TWO
U+20DD COMBINING ENCLOSING CIRCLE
```

is drawn like this:

1②

The 1 and the 2 are separate grapheme clusters, so the circle surrounds only the 2. If you put a grapheme joiner between them,

```
U+0031 DIGIT ONE
U+034F COMBINING GRAPHEME JOINER
U+0032 DIGIT TWO
U+20DD COMBINING ENCLOSING CIRCLE
```

you get this:

⑫

The grapheme joiner eliminates the grapheme cluster boundary between the 1 and the 2, binding them together as a single grapheme cluster. The circle then surrounds both numbers.

- A non-spacing mark applies to all characters up to the nearest preceding grapheme cluster boundary, provided they're not a conventional combining character sequence (if they are, the non-spacing mark is just part of that combining character sequence). This rule mainly states that non-spacing marks following Hangul syllables apply to the whole syllable, regardless of how it's represented.

The second definition is rather nebulous: What should you get with the following, for example?

```
U+0061 LATIN SMALL LETTER A
U+034F COMBINING GRAPHEME JOINER
U+0065 LATIN SMALL LETTER E
U+0303 COMBINING TILDE
```

The answer seems to be that the tilde goes over the e; the grapheme joiner would have no effect in this case. But it's equally reasonable to assume that the tilde would be centered between the a and the e, or even stretched to extend over both the a and the e. This approach would be a way to get more double diacritics without having to encode them separately. Neither seems to be the intent of Unicode, however. Indeed, there's been talk of achieving this effect by taking advantage of the enclosing-mark behavior. You'd introduce a new INVISIBLE ENCLOSING MARK character and apply the non-spacing mark to *that:* In the same way that a non-spacing mark after an enclosing mark would go outside the enclosing mark (and effectively be applied to it), the invisible enclosing mark would cause any non-spacing marks that follow it to be applied to the entire sequence of characters it "encloses." This rule isn't in Unicode 3.2, but it might appear in a future version of Unicode.

The Unicode 3.2 version of the Unicode Character Database specifies three new character properties to aid in the determination of grapheme cluster boundaries. First, a grapheme cluster consists of a Grapheme_Base character followed by zero or more Grapheme_Extend characters, optionally followed by a Grapheme_Link character, another Grapheme_Base character, and zero or more Grapheme_Extend characters, and so on. Second, on top of this basic definition, you have to layer some extra rules to get Hangul syllables and the CRLF sequence to be treated as grapheme clusters. Third, Join_Control characters are defined as transparent to the algorithm: They neither cause nor prevent grapheme cluster boundaries.

At the time of this writing (January 2002), the exact semantics and behavior of grapheme clusters haven't been completely nailed down. This discussion may well deviate from how it is ultimately settled in the final version of Unicode 3.2.

Character Properties and the Unicode Character Database

One of the things that makes Unicode unique is that it goes well beyond just assigning characters to numbers. The Unicode standard also provides a wealth of information on how the characters are to be used, both together and individually. It comprises not just the information in the Unicode book, but also the Unicode Character Database, a collection of files included on the CD that comes with the book.

The Unicode Character Database is the most active part of the standard, actually changing more frequently than the book does. In fact, changes to the database happen more often than Unicode Technical Reports are issued. If there are significant changes to the standard, such as new characters added, then a technical report will be issued or a new book will be put out. Error fixes and clarifications, however, can be made to the database without changes to any other documents. Changes to the database do cause Unicode's update version number (the third number) to be bumped. As of this writing (January 2002), the current Unicode version is 3.1.1, with version 3.2 in beta.

The Unicode Character Database may fairly be considered the heart of the standard. Implementations of many processes that operate on Unicode text are based on tables of data that are generated from the database. This chapter will take an in-depth look at the database and at the various properties that each Unicode character has.

■ WHERE TO GET THE UNICODE CHARACTER DATABASE

As the Unicode Character Database is updated relatively frequently, it's a good idea not to rely too heavily on the version on the CD that comes with the Unicode standard. In fact, it's almost obsolete right now, as the structure of the data files was changed when Unicode 3.1 came out. It'll be mostly right, but may differ in some particulars from the most current version, and it'll be organized differently.

You can always find the most current version on the Unicode Web and FTP sites. The URL of the Unicode Data page, which includes links to all the files, is

```
http://www.unicode.org/unicode/onlinedat/online.html
```

The current version of the Unicode Character Database is always at

```
http://www.unicode.org/Public/UNIDATA/
```

The parent directory also includes a number of other useful folders of data. Among these are the following:

- `http://www.unicode.org/Public/MAPPINGS/` contains files that map characters between Unicode and other encoding standards. The most interesting part of this section is the VENDORS folder, which contains mappings between Unicode and various vendor-defined encoding schemes. The other sections are useful as well, but haven't been updated in a long time.
- `http://www.unicode.org/Public/PROGRAMS/` contains sample code to do various interesting things. It includes demonstration code in C for converting between the Unicode encoding forms, a demonstration program for converting from SHIFT-JIS to Unicode, a sample implementation (in Java) of the Standard Compression Scheme for Unicode, and some other stuff.
- `http://www.unicode.org/Public/TEXT/` contains some old Unicode Technical Reports and some other stuff of mainly historical interest.
- `http://www.unicode.org/Public/BETA/` contains early versions of data files proposed for future versions of the Unicode Character Database.

In addition to these folders, other folders with version numbers in their names contain old updates to the Unicode Character Database. These are mainly of historical interest, but are also useful for figuring out what changed from version to version. For instance, if you have code based on an old version of Unicode, you can compare the files for that version to the ones for the current version to figure out how you need to change your own data tables to make them consistent with the current version of Unicode.

▪ THE **UNIDATA** DIRECTORY

The UNIDATA folder on the Unicode FTP/Web site (`http://www.unicode.org/Public/UNIDATA/`) is the official repository of the Unicode Character Database. Here's a quick rundown of what's in this directory:

- **ArabicShaping.txt** groups Arabic and Syriac letters into categories depending on how they connect to their neighbors. The data in this file can be used to put together a minimally correct implementation of Arabic and Syriac character shaping.
- **BidiMirroring.txt** is useful for implementing a rudimentary version of mirroring. For the characters whose glyphs in right-to-left text are supposed to be the mirror image of their glyphs in left-to-right text (the characters with the "mirrored" property), this file identifies those that have another character in Unicode that has the correct glyph in left-to-right text (or a similar glyph). You can implement mirroring for many (but not all) Unicode characters by simply mapping them to other characters that have the right glyph.
- **Blocks.txt** breaks the Unicode encoding space down into named blocks (e.g., "C0 Controls and Basic Latin" or "Miscellaneous Symbols") and specifies which block each Unicode character is in.
- **CaseFolding.txt** can be used to implement case-insensitive string comparison. It maps every Unicode code point to a case-insensitive representation—a code point or sequence of code points that represent the same character with case distinctions taken out (this file was basically derived by converting each character to uppercase and then converting the result to lowercase).

- **CompositionExclusions.txt** lists characters with canonical decomposi-tions that should not appear in normalized Unicode text.
- **EastAsianWidth.txt** assigns every character to a category that describes how it should be treated in East Asian typography. It is the data file for UAX #11.
- **Index.txt** is a soft copy of the character names index from the Unicode standard book. It gives you a way to quickly look up a character's code point value if you know its name.
- **Jamo.txt** assigns each of the conjoining Hangul jamo characters a "short name," which is used to derive names for the precomposed Hangul syllables.
- **LineBreak.txt** assigns every Unicode character to a category that deter-mines how it should be treated by a process that breaks text up into lines (i.e., a line-breaking process uses the character categories defined in this file to determine where to put the line breaks). It is the data file for UAX #14.
- **NamesList.txt** is the source file used to produce the code charts and character lists in the Unicode standard. **NamesList.html** explains its structure and use.
- **NormalizationTest.txt** is a test file that can be used to determine whether an implementation of Unicode normalization conforms to the standard. It includes unnormalized test strings along with what they should turn into when converted to each of the Unicode normalized forms.
- **PropertyAliases.txt,** which is new in Unicode 3.2, gives abbreviated and long names for all the Unicode character properties. These names can be used in regular-expression languages and other search facilities to identify groups of characters with a given property.
- **PropertyValueAliases.txt** is also new in Unicode 3.2. For each property listed in PropertyAliases.txt that isn't a numeric or Boolean property, it gives abbreviated and long names for all the possible values of that prop-erty. These names are intended to be used with the names in Property-Aliases.txt to provide shorthand ways of referring to sets of characters with common properties for regular-expression engines and similar facilities.
- **PropList.txt** is one of the two main files defining character properties. It acts as a supplement to the UnicodeData.txt file. **PropList.html** explains what's in it.

- **ReadMe.txt** gives the version number for the files in the directory and points to other files that explain its contents.
- **Scripts.txt** groups the Unicode characters by "script"—that is, by the writing system they are used in.
- **SpecialCasing.txt** gives complex case mappings for various Unicode characters. It lists all the characters that have a non-straightforward case mapping.
- **StandardizedVariants.html,** which is new in Unicode 3.2, indicates which combinations of regular character and variation selector are legal and which glyphs they represent.
- **UnicodeCharacterDatabase.html** gives an overview of all the files in the Unicode Character Database and provides references to the sections of the Unicode standard that deal with each of them.
- **UnicodeData.txt** is the original, and still primary, data file in the Unicode Character Database, defining most of the most important character properties for each character. **UnicodeData.html** explains the contents of UnicodeData.txt.
- **Unihan.txt** is a huge data file containing a wealth of information about the various Han (Chinese) characters.

In addition to the files listed above, you'll find many files with the word "Derived" in their names. Each of these files contains information that can be derived from information in one or more of the files listed above (most often, UnicodeData.txt). Generally, each file isolates a single character property from UnicodeData.txt and lists the characters in groups according to the value they have for that property. This arrangement can make it easier to figure out which characters are in certain groups and makes some of the Unicode data easier to work with. The derived-data files include the following:

- **DerivedAge.txt** is new in Unicode 3.2. It gives, for each character in Unicode, the version of Unicode in which it was introduced.
- **DerivedBidiClass.txt** groups the Unicode characters according to their directionality (i.e., how they're treated by the Unicode bidirectional layout algorithm). The normative versions of these properties are in UnicodeData.txt.

- **DerivedBinaryProperties.txt** lists groups of characters that have a value of "yes" for various properties that have yes/no values. Right now, this file lists only the characters that have the "mirrored" property, the one binary property given in UnicodeData.txt. PropList.txt gives more binary properties, but is already formatted the same way as this file.
- **DerivedCombiningClass.txt** groups characters according to their combining class, which is officially specified in UnicodeData.txt.
- **DerivedCoreProperties.txt** lists characters belonging to various general groups (e.g., letters, numbers, identifier-starting characters, identifier-body characters, and so on). The information in this file is derived from information in UnicodeData.txt and PropList.txt.
- **DerivedDecompositionType.txt** groups characters with decompositions according to the kind of decomposition they have (canonical versus compatibility). For the compatibility composite characters, it further breaks them down according to the type of their compatibility decomposition (that is, what information it loses). This information is derived from UnicodeData.txt.
- **DerivedJoiningGroup.txt** and **DerivedJoiningType.txt** both present information in the ArabicShaping.txt file organized in a different way. DerivedJoiningGroup.txt groups Arabic and Syriac letters according to their basic shapes, and DerivedJoiningType.txt groups them according to the way they join to their neighbors.
- **DerivedLineBreak.txt** presents the same information as LineBreak.txt, but organizes it differently. Instead of listing the characters in code point order and giving each one's line-break category, it lists the categories and then lists the characters in each category.
- **DerivedNormalizationProperties.txt** gives groups of characters that can be used to optimize implementations of Unicode normalization.
- **DerivedNumericType.txt** and **DerivedNumericValues.txt** group various characters that represent numeric values. DerivedNumericType.txt organizes them based on whether they are decimal digits or something else, and DerivedNumericValues.txt groups them by the numeric values they represent. Both are derived from UnicodeData.txt.
- **DerivedProperties.html** is an overview document explaining the contents of the other derived-data files.

You'll often see the filenames of the files in the UNIDATA directory with version numbers appended (there are also version numbers in the comments in the files). These version numbers are keyed to a particular version of Unicode: UnicodeData-3.1.1.txt, for example, would be the version of UnicodeData.txt that goes with version 3.1.1 of the Unicode standard. You can't always rely on this number, however, as not every file changes with every new version of Unicode (there is no UnicodeData-3.1.1.txt, for example—the Unicode 3.1.1 data changes were in other files). You'll also sometimes see one-digit version numbers on some of the files—originally some of the files, especially those that are keyed to Unicode Technical Reports, used a different numbering scheme. The numbering changed for each data file as its corresponding Technical Report was adopted into the standard (i.e., turned into a Unicode Standard Annex).

In the next sections, we'll take a closer look at the most important files in the Unicode Character Database and the properties they define.

■ UNICODEDATA.TXT

The "nerve center" of the Unicode Standard is the UnicodeData.txt file, which contains most of the Unicode Character Database. As the database has grown, and as supplementary information has been added to the database, various pieces of it have been split out into separate files. Nevertheless, the most important parts of the standard continue to reside in UnicodeData.txt.

The designers of Unicode wanted the database to be as simple and universal as possible, so it's maintained as a simple ASCII text file (we'll gloss over the irony of having the Unicode Character Database stored in an ASCII text file). For ease of parsing, this file is a simple semicolon-delimited text file. Each record in the database (i.e., the information pertaining to each character) is separated from the next by a newline (ASCII LF, hex 0x0B), and each field in a record (i.e., each property of a single character) is separated from the next by a semicolon.

It's not beautiful, and it's not cutting-edge, but it has the major advantage of being a format that is readable and parsable by just about anything. Today, of course, the Unicode Consortium could have also used XML, and this switch is discussed from time to time. However, compatibility with existing software that reads this file and easy differentiation between versions are compelling reasons to keep it in the current format. Besides, it's almost trivially easy to write a program to convert between this format and an XML-based format.

Here are a few sample records from the database:

```
0028;LEFT PARENTHESIS;Ps;0;ON;;;;;Y;OPENING PARENTHESIS;;;;
0033;DIGIT THREE;Nd;0;EN;;3;3;3;N;;;;;
0041;LATIN CAPITAL LETTER A;Lu;0;L;;;;;N;;;;0061;
022C;LATIN CAPITAL LETTER O WITH TILDE AND MACRON;Lu;0;L;
    00D5 0304;;;;N;;;;022D;
0301;COMBINING ACUTE ACCENT;Mn;230;NSM;;;;;N;NON-SPACING ACUTE;
    Oxia;;;
2167;ROMAN NUMERAL EIGHT;Nl;0;L;<compat> 0056 0049 0049 0049;;;
    8;N;;;;2177;
```

A fair amount of the information is immediately accessible (or at least gets that way with practice), but it's easy to get lost in the semicolons. Figure 5.1 shows the record for the letter A with the fields labeled.

Figure 5.1 tells us that the Unicode code point value U+0041 has the name LATIN CAPITAL LETTER A. It has a general category of "uppercase letter" (abbreviated "Lu"); it's not a combining mark (its combining class is 0); it's a left-to-right character (abbreviated "L"); it's not a composite character (no decomposition); it's not a numeral or digit (the three digit-value fields are all empty); it doesn't mirror (abbreviated "N"); its name in Unicode 1.0 was the same as its current name (empty field); it maps to itself when being converted to uppercase or titlecase (empty fields); and it maps to U+0061 (LATIN SMALL LETTER A) when being converted to lowercase.

In order from left to right, the properties are defined in UnicodeData.txt:

- The character's code point value (technically, not a property, but rather the value to which we're assigning properties), expressed as a four- to six-digit hexadecimal numeral.
- The character's name.
- The character's general category. It tells you whether the character is a letter, a digit, a combining mark, and so on.

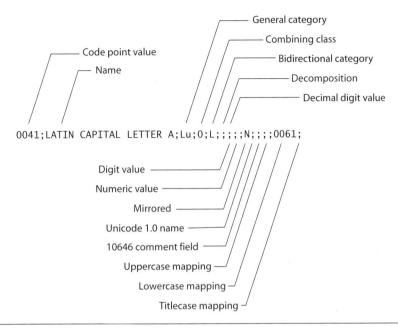

Figure 5.1   The UnicodeData.txt entry for the letter A

- The character's combining class. This value is used to order combining marks when converting Unicode text to one of the Unicode normalized forms.

- Bidirectional category. This value specifies the character's directionality and is used by the bidirectional text layout algorithm.

- Decomposition. For composite characters, it gives the characters in the decomposition a tag indicating the decomposition type.

- Decimal digit value. If the character can be used as a decimal digit, it is the numeric value the character represents.

- Digit value. If the character can be used as a digit (decimal or not), it is the numeric value the character represents.

- Numeric value. If the character can be used alone as a numeral, it is the numeric value the character represents.

- Mirrored. It says whether the character adopts a mirror-image glyph when surrounded by right-to-left text.

- Unicode 1.0 name. If the character existed in Unicode 1.0 and had a different name, this value is its old name.

- 10646 comment field. If the character has a comment attached to it in the ISO 10646 standard, it's given here.
- Uppercase mapping. If the character maps to a different character when converted to uppercase, that character is given here.
- Lowercase mapping. If the character maps to a different character when converted to lowercase, that character is given here.
- Titlecase mapping. If the character maps to a different character when converted to titlecase, that character is given here.

If we go back to the sample database records on page 146, we can now interpret them a little more clearly:

- U+0028's current name is LEFT PARENTHESIS, but it used to be STARTING PARENTHESIS. It's a member of the "starting punctuation" ("Ps") category, has a combining class of 0, does mirror ("Y"), and has neutral ("ON") directionality.
- U+0033 DIGIT THREE is a decimal digit ("Nd"), has weak left-to-right directionality ("EN"), doesn't mirror ("N"), and has a numeric value of 3.
- U+0041 LATIN CAPITAL LETTER A is an uppercase letter ("Lu"), has strong left-to-right directionality ("L"), and maps to U+0061 LATIN SMALL LETTER A when converted to lowercase.
- U+022C LATIN CAPITAL LETTER O WITH TILDE AND MACRON is an uppercase letter with strong left-to-right directionality, maps to U+022D when converted to lowercase, and has a canonical decomposition to U+00D0 U+0304.
- U+0301 COMBINING ACUTE ACCENT is a non-spacing mark ("Mn") with a combining class of 230 (which means it appears above the base character), it's transparent to the bi-di algorithm ("NSM"), and is the same as the Greek *oxia* according to ISO 10646.
- U+2167 ROMAN NUMERAL EIGHT is a letter number ("Nl") with a numeric value of 8. It maps to a Roman numeral made out of lowercase letters (U+2177) when mapped to lowercase, and it has a compatibility decomposition to "VIII" (U+0056 U+0049 U+0049 U+0049).

We'll take a closer look at each of these properties and how they're specified later in this chapter.

▪ PROPLIST.TXT

The UnicodeData.txt file is supplemented with a variety of other files that supply information about Unicode characters. Many of these properties (e.g., East Asian width, Jamo short name, and so on) have their own files, but others are given in PropList.txt. In particular, PropList.txt lists "binary" properties—categories a character either is or isn't in. (For example, it's either a digit or it isn't.)

PropList.txt has the same format used for most of the other files. Each line represents either a single character (in which case it starts with that character's code point value) or a range of characters (in which case it starts with the starting and ending code point values in the range, separated with ".."). A semicolon and the property's value follow. Usually the line ends with a comment that gives the character's name for readability. (Comments are set off with pound signs.)

For example, here are the first two entries in PropList.txt:

```
0009..000D    ; White_space # Cc    [5] <control>..<control>
0020          ; White_space # Zs        SPACE
```

The first line assigns the property "White_space" to the code point values from U+0009 to U+000D. The comment indicates the code points in this range have the "Cc" general category (we'll explain that terminology later in this chapter), the range includes five characters, and the characters at the beginning and end of the range are control characters.

The second line assigns the property "White_space" to the code point value U+0020. The comment indicates that U+0020's name is SPACE and that it belongs to the "Zs" category.

Files with this format are ordered either by code point value (e.g., Line-Break.txt) or by category value. PropList.txt is sorted by category.

Here's a rundown of the properties defined in PropList.txt:

- **White_space.** Characters that are considered "white space." They include spaces and line and paragraph separators, along with control characters that had these functions in older standards.
- **Bidi_Control.** Invisible formatting codes that affect the behavior of the bidirectional layout algorithm.
- **Join_Control.** Invisible formatting codes that affect the glyph selection process (by causing characters to join together or split apart).

- **Dash.** Dashes and hyphens.
- **Hyphen.** Hyphens and characters that behave like hyphens.
- **Quotation_Mark.** Quotation marks.
- **Terminal_Punctuation.** Punctuation marks that occur at the end of a sentence or clause.
- **Other_Math.** Characters that can be used as mathematical operators but weren't placed in the "Mathematical symbol" ("Sm") general category.
- **Hex_Digit.** Characters that are used as digits in hexadecimal numerals.
- **ASCII_Hex_Digit.** ASCII characters in the Hex_Digit category.
- **Other_Alphabetic.** Alphabetic characters that weren't assigned to one of the "letter" general categories.
- **Ideographic.** The Han characters and radicals. All of the characters with the Radical and Unified_Ideograph properties also have this property.
- **Diacritic.** Diacritical marks.
- **Extender.** Characters that elongate, either graphically or phonetically, the letters that precede them.
- **Other_Lowercase.** Characters that weren't assigned to the "lowercase letter" ("Ll") general category that are still considered lowercase.
- **Other_Uppercase.** Characters that weren't assigned to the "uppercase letter" ("Lu") general category that are still considered uppercase.
- **Noncharacter_Code_Point.** Code point values that are specifically called out by the standard as not representing characters and not being legal in Unicode text.

The Unicode 3.2 version of PropList.txt adds a number of new character properties. The final list of properties may change, as may the characters assigned to them. As of the beta version of Unicode 3.2, however, they included the following:

- **Other_Grapheme_Extend.** Characters with the Grapheme_Extend property that don't automatically get this property by virtue of belonging to some class. Grapheme extenders are characters that always occur in the same grapheme cluster as the character that precedes them.
- **Grapheme_Link.** Characters that cause both the preceding and following characters to be considered part of the same grapheme cluster.

- **IDS_Binary_Operator.** Ideographic description characters that take two operands. This property is included to aid code that interprets ideographic description sequences. See Chapter 10 for more on ideographic description sequences.
- **IDS_Trinary_Operator.** Ideographic description characters that take three operands. This property is included to aid code that interprets ideographic description sequences. See Chapter 10 for more on ideographic description sequences.
- **Radical.** Characters that are parts of Han characters. This property also exists mostly to aid in interpreting ideographic description sequences.
- **Unified_Ideograph.** Full-blown Han characters.
- **Other_Default_Ignorable_Code_Point.** Invisible formatting characters and other special characters that should be ignored by processes that don't know specifically how to handle them (instead of, say, trying to draw them). This category also includes a range of unassigned code points that are being set aside now to represent only characters that should also be ignored by processes that don't recognize them.
- **Deprecated.** Characters whose use is strongly discouraged. Because of Unicode's stability policies, this property is as close as you can get to simply removing a character from the standard.
- **Soft_Dotted.** Characters whose glyphs include a dot on top that disappears when a top-joining diacritical mark is applied. These characters are all variants of the Latin lowercase i and j.
- **Logical_Order_Exception.** Characters that break Unicode's normal rule about representing things in logical order. This category currently consists of the Thai and Lao left-joining vowel marks, which, unlike all other Indic vowel marks, precede the consonants they modify instead of following them. For more on this, see the Thai and Lao sections of Chapter 9.

GENERAL CHARACTER PROPERTIES

Each character has a set of properties that serve to identify the character. These include the name, Unicode 1.0 name, Jamo short name, ISO 10646 comment, block, and script.

Standard Character Names

First among these properties, of course, is the character's name, which is given both in the book and in the UnicodeData.txt file. The name is always in English, and the only legal characters for the name are the 26 Latin capital letters, the 10 Western digits, and the hyphen. The name is important, as it's the primary guide to just what character is meant by the code point. The names generally follow some conventions:

- For those characters that belong to a particular script (writing system), the script name is included in the character name.
- Combining marks usually have "COMBINING" in their names. Within certain scripts, combining marks' names may contain the word "MARK" instead. Vowel signs have the phrase "VOWEL SIGN" in their names.
- Letters have names containing the word "LETTER." Syllables have names that usually include either the word "LETTER" or the word "SYLLABLE." Ideographs have names that contain the word "IDEO-GRAPH."
- Uppercase letters have the word "CAPITAL" in their names. Lowercase letters have the word "SMALL" in their names.
- Digits have the word "DIGIT" in their names.

Unicode 2.0 was the first version of Unicode that was unified with the ISO 10646 Universal Character Set standard. As part of the unification process, many characters received new names. For instance, U+0028 LEFT PAREN-THESIS was called OPENING PARENTHESIS in Unicode 1.0. Sometimes the new names are more European-sounding than the old ones. For example, U+002E PERIOD became U+002E FULL STOP. For those characters that changed names in Unicode 2.0, their original names are shown in the "Unicode 1.0 name" field in UnicodeData.txt. If this field is blank, the character either didn't exist in Unicode 1.0 or it had the same name then that it does now.

The renaming that happened as part of the unification with ISO 10646 was a very unusual occurrence. The names are now carved in stone. No character's name will ever be changed in future versions of the standard. Although a character's semantics may occasionally drift out of sync with its name, such an event is very rare.

Algorithmically Derived Names

You'll notice some entries in UnicodeData.txt that look like the following:

```
4E00;<CJK Ideograph, First>;Lo;0;L;;;;;N;;;;;
9FA5;<CJK Ideograph, Last>;Lo;0;L;;;;;N;;;;;
```

The "name" is enclosed in angle brackets. These entries always occur in pairs. The first entry in the pair has a "name" that ends in "First," and the second entry has a "name" ending in "Last." These pairs of entries mark the beginning and end of ranges of characters that have exactly the same properties. Rather than have nearly identical entries for every code point from U+4E00 to U+9FA5, for example, the database abbreviates the range by using a pair of entries such as these. The properties shown for these entries apply to every character in the range. The lone exception is the name property, which is algorithmically generated according to rules in the Unicode standard.

Ten elided ranges of characters are given in the Unicode 3.1.1 database:

- The CJK Unified Ideographs Area, running from U+4E00 to U+9FA5.
- The CJK Unified Ideographs Extension A area, running from U+3400 to U+4DB5.
- The Hangul Syllables area, running from U+AC00 to U+D7A3.
- The high-surrogate values for non–private-use characters (i.e., planes 1 through 14), which run from U+D800 to U+DB7F.
- The high-surrogate values for private-use characters (i.e., planes 15 and 16), which run from U+DB80 to U+DBFF.
- The low-surrogate values, which run from U+DC00 to U+DFFF.
- The Private Use Area, running from U+E000 to U+F8FF.
- The CJK Unified Ideographs Extension B area, running from U+20000 to U+2A6D6.
- The Plane 15 Private Use Area, running from U+F0000 to U+FFFFD.
- The Plane 16 Private Use Area, running from U+100000 to U+10FFFD.

The code points in some of the elided ranges don't have character names (or any other properties, really—their code point values are simply assigned to a special category). The private-use characters just have a "private use" property. The surrogate code units aren't really characters at all, but the code point values corresponding to them are placed in one of a few special "surrogate" categories for the benefit of UTF-16-based applications that want to treat surrogate pairs as combining character sequences.

The other elided ranges have algorithmically derived character names. For the three CJK Unified Ideographs ranges, the algorithm for deriving the name of an individual character is simple: "CJK UNIFIED IDEOGRAPH–," plus the code point value in hex. For example, the name of U+7E53 is "CJK UNIFIED IDEOGRAPH–7E53."

The characters in the final elided range, the Hangul syllables, use a more complicated algorithm for deriving their names. It takes advantage of another property of Unicode characters, the "Jamo short name," which is given in the Jamo.txt file.

Most characters' Jamo short names are blank because they're not Hangul jamo (the alphabetic units that combine together to make Hangul syllables). The characters in the Hangul Jamo block, however, do use this property. For them, this property specifies an abbreviated name for that character.

You can obtain the name of a Hangul syllable by decomposing it into jamo and then concatenating the short names together. For example, consider the character U+B8B4 (뢴). This character decomposes into three characters, as follows:

```
U+1105 HANGUL CHOSEONG RIEUL (ㄹ)
U+116C HANGUL JUNGSEONG OE (ㅚ)
U+11AB HANGUL JONGSEONG NIEUN (ㄴ)
```

U+1105 has the short name R, U+116C has the short name OE, and U+11AB has the short name N. You concatenate these short names together and add "HANGUL SYLLABLE" to get the name of the syllable, so the name of the character U+B8B4 (뢴) is HANGUL SYLLABLE ROEN.

Control-Character Names

The code points corresponding to the C0 and C1 ranges from ISO 2022 (U+0000 to U+001F and U+0080 to U+009F) also get special treatment. They appear in a special "control character" category and aren't given names (the UnicodeData.txt file gives "<control>" as their names). Officially, Unicode doesn't assign semantics to these code points, but preserves them for backward compatibility with the various ISO 2022-compatible standards.

Unofficially, these code points usually retain the semantics described in ISO 6429, just as most one-byte character encodings do. This practice is reflected in their Unicode 1.0 names, which follow that convention. Over time, various pieces of the Unicode standard have begun officially assigning specific semantics to these code points—the Unicode line-breaking algorithm treats U+000D and U+000A as carriage return and line feed characters, for example, and the Unicode bidirectional layout algorithm treats U+0009 as the tab character. Despite their lack of official names and their assignment to the special "control character" category, these characters have, over time, picked up other properties that show their true meanings.

ISO 10646 Comments

In a few cases, comments are attached to a character in the ISO 10646 code charts. These comments typically give alternate names for the character, similar to the informative notes in the character listings in the Unicode standard. For example, U+1095 LATIN SMALL LETTER HV has an ISO 10646 comment of "hwair," the common name for this letter. These comments from ISO 10646 are preserved in the "ISO 10646 comment" field in UnicodeData.txt.

Block and Script

The 21-bit Unicode encoding space is divided into "blocks," or ranges of code point values with similar characteristics. For example, the range of code point values from U+0000 to U+007F is the C0 Controls and Basic Latin block, U+0400 to U+04FF is the Cyrillic block, U+20A0 to U+20CF is the Currency Symbols block, and so on. The official names and boundaries of all the blocks in the Unicode standard appear in the Blocks.txt file.

In the past, implementations have attempted to identify the more important characteristic—the writing system to which a character belongs—by finding out what block it's in. This practice is dangerous, because sometimes not everything in a block matches the name of the block. There are currency symbols outside the Currency Symbols block, for example. The Basic Latin block doesn't include just Latin letters, but some other characters (e.g., digits, punctuation marks) as well. The Arabic Presentation Forms A block contains two characters (the ornate parentheses) that are "real" characters and not just presentation forms.

What people are usually seeking when they ask which block a character is in is the writing system, or "script," to which the character belongs. For example, is this code point a Latin letter, a Greek letter, a Chinese ideograph, a Hangul syllable, or what? This information is given in the Scripts.txt file, which assigns every character to a script. Instead of treating the entire Basic Latin (i.e., ASCII) block as belonging to the Latin script, for example, only the letters A through Z and a through z are assigned to the Latin script.

Only letters and diacritical marks are assigned to scripts. The combining and enclosing marks are given a special "script" property, "INHERITED," that indicates that these code points take on the script of the characters to which they're attached.

Scripts.txt doesn't include every character in Unicode. Symbols, punctuation marks, and digits that are used with more than one writing system aren't assigned to a script. In effect, their "script" property is blank.

■ GENERAL CATEGORY

After the code point value and the name, the next most important property that a Unicode character has is its general category. Seven primary categories exist: letter, number, punctuation, symbol, mark, separator, and miscellaneous. Each is subdivided into additional categories.

Letters

The Unicode standard uses the term "letter" rather loosely in assigning things to this general category. Whatever counts as the basic unit of meaning in a particular writing system, whether it represents a phoneme, a syllable, or a whole word or idea, is assigned to the "letter" category. The major exception to this rule comprises marks that combine typographically with other characters, which are categorized as "marks" instead of "letters." They include not only diacritical marks and tone marks, but also vowel signs in those consonantal writing systems where the vowels are written as marks applied to the consonants.

Some writing systems, such as the Latin, Greek, and Cyrillic alphabets, also have the concept of "case." That is, two series of letterforms are used together, with one series, the "uppercase," used for the first letter of a sentence or a proper name, or for emphasis, and the other series, the "lowercase," used for most other letters.

Uppercase Letter (Lu) In cased writing systems, the uppercase letters are placed in this category.

Lowercase Letter (Ll) In cased writing systems, the lowercase letters are placed in this category.

Titlecase Letter (Lt) Titlecase is reserved for a few special characters in Unicode. These characters are basically examples of compatibility characters—characters that were included for round-trip compatibility with some other standard. Every titlecase letter is actually a glyph representing two letters, the first of which is uppercase and the second of which is lowercase. For example, the Serbian letter nje (Њ) can be thought of as a ligature of the Cyrillic letter n (Н) and the Cyrillic soft sign (Ь). When Serbian is written using the Latin alphabet (as is done in Croatian, which is almost the same language), this letter is written using the letters nj. Existing Serbian and Croatian standards were designed to provide a one-to-one mapping between every Cyrillic character used in Serbian and the corresponding Latin character used in Croatian. This approach required using a single character code to represent the nj digraph in Croatian, and Unicode carries that character forward. Capital Nje in Cyrillic (Њ) thus can convert to either NJ or Nj in Latin depending on the context. The fully uppercase form, NJ, is U+01CA LATIN CAPITAL LETTER NJ, and the combined upper-lower form, U+01CB LATIN CAPITAL LETTER N WITH SMALL LETTER J, is considered a "titlecase" letter. Three Serbian characters have a titlecase Latin form: Љ (lje, which converts to lj), Њ (nje, which converts to nj), and Џ (dzhe, which converts to dž). These characters were the only three titlecase letters in Unicode 2.x.

Unicode 3.0 added several Greek letters to this category. Some early Greek texts represented certain diphthongs by writing a small letter iota underneath the other vowel rather than after it. For example, you'd see "ai" written as ᾳ. If you just capitalized the alpha ("Ai"), you'd get the titlecase version: ᾼ. In the fully uppercase version ("AI"), the small iota becomes a regular iota again: AI. These characters are all in the Extended Greek section of the standard and are used only in writing ancient Greek texts. In modern Greek, these diphthongs are written using a regular iota; for example, "ai" is written as αι.

Modifier Letter (Lm) Just as some things you might conceptually think of as "letters" (vowel signs in various languages) are classified as "marks" in Unicode, the opposite also occurs. The modifier letters are independent forms that don't combine typographically with the characters around them, which is why Unicode doesn't classify them as "marks" (Unicode marks, by definition, combine typographically with their neighbors). Instead of carrying their own sounds, the modifier letters generally modify the sounds of their neighbors. In other words, conceptually they're diacritical marks. Because they occur in the middle of words, most text-analysis processes treat them as letters, so they're classified as letters.

The Unicode modifier letters are generally either International Phonetic Alphabet characters or characters that are used to transliterate certain "real" letters in non-Latin writing systems that don't seem to correspond to a regular Latin letter. For example, U+02BC MODIFIER LETTER APOSTROPHE is typically used to represent the glottal stop, the sound made by (or, more accurately, the *absence* of sound represented by) the Arabic letter alef, so the Arabic letter is often transliterated as this character. Likewise, U+02B2 MODIFIER LETTER SMALL J is used to represent palatalization, and thus is sometimes used in transliteration as the counterpart of the Cyrillic soft sign.

Other Letter (Lo) This catch-all category includes everything that's conceptually a "letter," but that doesn't fit into one of the other "letter" categories. Letters from uncased alphabets such as Arabic and Hebrew fall into this category, as do syllables from syllabic writing systems like Kana and Hangul and the Han ideographs.

Marks

Like letters, marks are part of words and carry linguistic information. Unlike letters, marks combine typographically with other characters. For example, U+0308 COMBINING DIAERESIS may look like ¨ when shown alone, but is usually drawn on top of the letter that precedes it. That is, U+0061 LATIN SMALL LETTER A followed by U+0308 COMBINING DIAERESIS isn't drawn as "a¨", but rather as "ä". All of the Unicode combining marks do this kind of thing.

Non-spacing Mark (Mn)   Most of the Unicode combining marks fall into this category. Non-spacing marks don't take up any horizontal space along a line of text—they combine completely with the character that precedes them and fit entirely into that character's space. The various diacritical marks used in European languages, such as the acute and grave accents, the circumflex, the diaeresis, and the cedilla, fall into this category.

Combining Spacing Mark (Mc)   Spacing combining marks interact typographically with their neighbors, but still take up horizontal space along a line of text. All of these characters are vowel signs or other diacritical marks in the various Indian and Southeast Asian writing systems. For example, U+093F DEVANAGARI VOWEL SIGN I (ि) is a spacing combining mark. Thus U+0915 DEVANAGARI LETTER KA followed by U+093F DEVANAGARI VOWEL SIGN I is drawn as कि—the vowel sign attaches to the left-hand side of the consonant.

Not all spacing combining marks reorder, however: U+0940 DEVANAGARI VOWEL SIGN II (ी) is also a combining spacing mark. When it follows U+0915 DEVANAGARI LETTER KA, you get की—the vowel attaches to the right-hand side of the consonant, but the two combine typographically.

Enclosing Mark (Me)   Enclosing marks completely surround the characters they modify. For example, U+20DD COMBINING ENCLOSING CIRCLE is drawn as a ring around the character that precedes it. These ten characters are generally used to create symbols.

Numbers

The Unicode characters that represent numeric quantities are given the "number" property (technically, it should be called the "numeral" property, but that's life). The characters in these categories have additional properties that govern their interpretation as numerals. This category is subdivided as follows.

Decimal-Digit Number (Nd) The characters in this category can be used as decimal digits. This category includes not only the digits with which we're all familiar ("0123456789"), but similar sets of digits used with other writing systems, such as the Thai digits ("๐ ๑ ๒ ๓ ๔ ๕ ๖ ๗ ๘ ๙").

Letter Number (Nl) The characters in this category can be either letters or numerals. Many are compatibility composites whose decompositions consist of letters. The Roman numerals and the Hangzhou numerals are the only characters in this category.

Other Number (No) All of the characters that belong in the "number" category, but not in one of the other subcategories, fall into this one. This category includes various numeric presentation forms, such as superscripts, subscripts, and circled numbers; various fractions; and numerals used in various numeration systems other than the Arabic positional notation used in the West.

Punctuation

This category attempts to make sense of the various punctuation characters in Unicode. It breaks down as follows.

Opening Punctuation (Ps) For punctuation marks, such as parentheses and brackets, that occur in opening-closing pairs, the "opening" characters in these pairs are assigned to this category.

Closing Punctuation (Pe) For punctuation marks, such as parentheses and brackets, that occur in opening-closing pairs, the "closing" characters in these pairs are assigned to this category.

Initial-Quote Punctuation (Pi) Quotation marks occur in opening-closing pairs, just like parentheses do. The problem is that which is which depends on the language. For example, both French and Russian use quotation marks that look like this: «», but they use them differently.

> «In French, a quotation is set off like this.»
> »But in Russian, a quotation is set off like this.«

This category is equivalent to either Ps or Pe, depending on the language.

Final-Quote Punctuation (Pf) The counterpart to the Pi category, Pf is also used with quotation marks whose usage varies depending on language. It's equivalent to either Ps or Pe depending on language. It's always the opposite of Pi.

Dash Punctuation (Pd) This category is self-explanatory. It includes all hyphens and dashes.

Connector Punctuation (Pc) Characters in this category, such as the middle dot and the underscore, get treated as part of the word in which they appear. That is, they "connect" series of letters together into single words: This_is_all_one_word. An important example is U+30FB KATAKANA MIDDLE DOT, which is used like a hyphen in Japanese.

Other Punctuation (Po) Punctuation marks that don't fit into any of the other subcategories, including obvious things like the period, comma, and question mark, fall into this category.

Symbols

This group of categories contains various symbols.

Currency Symbol (Sc)   Self-explanatory.

Mathematical Symbol (Sm)   Mathematical operators.

Modifier Symbol (Sk)   This category contains two main types of characters: the "spacing" versions of the combining marks and a few other symbols whose purpose is to modify the meaning of the preceding character in some way. Unlike modifier letters, modifier symbols don't necessarily modify the meanings of letters, and they don't necessarily get counted as parts of words.

Other Symbol (So)   This category contains all symbols that didn't fit into one of the other categories.

Separators

These characters mark the boundaries between units of text.

Space Separator (Zs)   This category includes all of the space characters (yes, there's more than one space character).

Paragraph Separator (Zp)   There is exactly one character in this category: the Unicode paragraph separator (U+2029). As its name suggests, it marks the boundary between paragraphs.

Line Separator (Zl)   There's also only one character in this category: the Unicode line separator (U+2028). As its name suggests, it forces a line break without ending a paragraph.

Even though the ASCII carriage-return and line-feed characters are often used as line and paragraph separators, they're not placed in either of these categories. Likewise, the ASCII tab character isn't considered a Unicode space character, even though it probably should be. They're all put in the "Cc" category.

Miscellaneous

A number of special character categories don't really fit in with the others.

Control Characters (Cc)   The codes corresponding to the C0 and C1 control characters from the ISO 2022 standard appear in this category. The Unicode standard doesn't officially assign any semantics to these characters (which include the ASCII control characters), but most systems that use Unicode text treat these characters the same way as they treat their counterparts in the source standards. For example, most processes treat the ASCII line-feed character as a line or paragraph separator.

The original idea was to leave the definitions of these code points open, as ISO 2022 does. Over time, however, various Unicode processes and algorithms have attached semantics to these code points, effectively nailing the ISO 6429 semantics to many of them.

Formatting Characters (Cf)   Unicode includes some "control" characters of its own: characters with no visual representation of their own that are used to control how the characters around them are drawn or handled by various processes. These characters are assigned to this category.

Surrogates (Cs)   The code points in the UTF-16 surrogate range belong to this category. Technically, the code points in the surrogate range are treated as unassigned and reserved, but Unicode implementations based on UTF-16 often treat them as characters, handling surrogate pairs the same way as combining character sequences are handled.

Private-Use Characters (Co)   The code points in the private-use ranges are assigned to this category.

Unassigned Code Points (Cn)   All unassigned and noncharacter code points, other than those in the surrogate range, are given this category. These code points aren't listed in the Unicode Character Database—their omission gives them this category—but are listed explicitly in DerivedGeneralCategory.txt.

▪ OTHER CATEGORIES

Over time, it's become necessary to draw finer distinctions between characters than the general categories let you do. It's also been noticed that some overlap exists between the general categories. Another set of categories, defined mostly in PropList.txt, has been created to capture these distinctions.

- **Whitespace.** Many processes that operate on text treat various characters as "whitespace," important only insofar as it separates groups of other characters from one another. In Unicode, "whitespace" can be thought of mainly as consisting of the characters in the Z (separator) categories. This is one case in which the ISO control characters have real meaning—most processes want the code points corresponding to the old ASCII and ISO 8859 whitespace characters (TAB, CR, LF, FF, and NEL) treated as whitespace as well. This property encompasses all of these characters.
- **Bi-di control** and **join control.** These categories isolate a few of the characters in the format control (Cf) category that control the behavior on certain specific text processes (in this case, the bi-di algorithm and the glyph selection process).
- **Dash** and **hyphen.** These categories not only break down the dash punctuation (Pd) category into dashes and hyphens, but also encompass a few characters from the connector punctuation (Pc) category that are used as hyphens (specifically, the Katakana middle dot).
- **Quotation marks** brings together all the characters from the Ps, Pe, Pi, Pf, and Po categories that represent quotation marks.
- **Terminal punctuation** isolates those characters in the other punctuation (Po) category that represent sentence- or clause-ending punctuation.
- **Math** brings together the characters that represent mathematical symbols. They include not only those characters assigned to the math symbol (Sm) category, but also characters from the other categories that have uses beyond math symbols. The non-Sm characters with the Math property are assigned to the "Other_Math" property in PropList.txt.
- **Hex digit** and **ASCII hex digit** single out the characters that can be used as digits in hexadecimal numerals.
- **Alphabetic** singles out alphabetic and syllabic characters. It encompasses everything in the "letter" (L) categories other than the characters with the "ideographic" property, plus all the combining marks and vowel signs used with them. PropList.txt lists all the characters with the "alpha-

betic" property that aren't in one of the L categories and assigns them to the "Other_Alphabetic" category.

- **Ideographic** isolates those characters in the "other letter" (Lo) category that represent whole words or ideas (basically, the Chinese characters).

- **Diacritic** brings together those characters from the modifier letter (Lm), modifier symbol (Sk), non-spacing mark (Mn), and combining spacing mark (Mc) categories that are used as diacritical marks.

- **Extender** isolates those characters from the modifier letter (Lm) category, plus one character—the middle dot—from the other punctuation (Po) category, that elongate, either phonetically or graphically, the letter that precedes them.

- **Uppercase** and **lowercase** bring together all the uppercase and lowercase letters. PropList.txt supplements the characters assigned to these general categories (Lu and Ll) with characters from other categories whose forms are the forms of uppercase or lowercase letters (it assigns these extra characters to the "Other_Uppercase" and "Other_Lowercase" categories).

- **Noncharacter code points** isolates the code point values from the "unassigned" (Cn) category that are illegal code point values in Unicode text (as opposed to merely not having a character assigned to them yet).

Once again, Unicode 3.2 adds a few new properties to the mix. At the time Unicode 3.2 entered beta, they included the following:

- **Default-ignorable code points** are code points or characters that should be ignored by processes that don't know about them. For example, the default behavior of a rendering process, when confronted with a code point it doesn't recognize, is to draw some kind of "missing" glyph. If the character has this property, it should instead draw nothing. This category consists of characters in the "formatting character" (Cf) or "control character" (Cc) general categories, plus a bunch of characters called out specifically in PropList.txt as "Other_Default_Ignorable_Code_Point." This is one of the few properties that is actually given to *unassigned* code points; it allows current implementations to "do the right thing" even with future default-ignorable characters that may be added to the standard.

- **Soft-dotted** calls out characters whose glyphs include a dot that disappears when certain diacritical marks are applied. They include the lowercase Latin letters i and j. If you apply an acute accent to the letter i, for example, the dot disappears: í. This property exists to make case-mapping algorithms easier.
- **Logical-order exceptions** are the few characters that break Unicode's logical-order rule. They include the left-joining Thai and Lao vowel marks, which precede in memory the consonants to which they attach, rather than following them, as every other Indic vowel mark does. This property exists to make life easier for the Unicode Collation Algorithm, some rendering algorithms, and possibly other processes that care about backing-store order. For more on Thai and Lao, see Chapter 9.
- **Deprecated** characters are characters that Unicode's designers would remove from the standard if they could. They're retained for backward compatibility, but their use and interpretation are strongly discouraged.
- **Radical, CJK_Unified_Ideograph, IDS_Binary_Operator,** and **IDS_Trinary_Operator** are used to help interpret ideographic description sequences. See Chapter 10 for more information on ideographic description sequences.

The DerivedCoreProperties.txt file explicitly lists the characters in the Math, Alphabetic, Uppercase, and Lowercase categories, along with the characters that are legal in various positions in a programmatic identifier according to the Unicode identifier guidelines (see Chapter 17).

■ PROPERTIES OF LETTERS

In the preceding sections, we looked at a bunch of letter-related properties. First, there were the various subdivisions of the "letter" category (Lu, Ll, Lt, Lm, and Lo). Then there were the Alphabetic and Ideographic categories. Finally, there's the case, defined by the Lu, Ll, and Lt general categories and by the separate Uppercase and Lowercase categories.

For cased letters (i.e., characters in the Lu, Ll, and Lt categories), Unicode provides additional information about how the characters in the different cases relate to each other. In particular, it provides information on how to map a character to its counterpart in the opposite case (or in titlecase) as well as a set of mappings that allow you to normalize away case differences when comparing strings.

Each character has uppercase, lowercase, and titlecase mappings in Unicode-Data.txt. If the character should be replaced with another character when converted to uppercase, lowercase, or titlecase, the code point value for the character that should replace it appears in the appropriate place in UnicodeData.txt.

For example, the entry for U+0061 LATIN SMALL LETTER A (a) gives U+0041 (A) as its uppercase and titlecase mappings. (The titlecase mapping is the same as the uppercase mappings for all but a handful of characters.) The entry for U+0393 GREEK CAPITAL LETTER GAMMA (Γ) gives U+03B3 (γ) as its lowercase mapping.

Converting a string to uppercase or lowercase is simple—just replace every character in the string with is uppercase or lowercase mapping (if it has one). Converting to titlecase is almost as simple—replace the first letter of every word with its titlecase mapping and the rest with their lowercase mappings.

SpecialCasing.txt

The case mappings aren't always as simple as they appear at first glance. The mappings in the UnicodeData.txt file are always single-character mappings. Sometimes a character expands into two characters when its case is changed. Sometimes a mapping is conditional—that is, it differs depending on the context or language.

These special mappings are relegated to their own file—SpecialCasing.txt. Like UnicodeData.txt, SpecialCasing.txt is structured as a series of one-line entries for the characters, each consisting of a semicolon-delimited series of fields. The first field is the code point value for which the mappings are being specified. The next three fields are the lowercase, titlecase, and uppercase mappings for the characters, each of which is a space-delimited series of code point values. An optional fifth field contains a comma-delimited series of tags indicating the context in which that particular set of mappings happens. As always, the line may end with a comment, which is set off from the actual data with a pound sign (#).

Here's an example entry:

```
00DF; 00DF; 0053 0073; 0053 0053; # LATIN SMALL LETTER SHARP S
```

This entry applies to the German ess-zed character (ß), which generally functions like a double s (in classical German spelling, the ss form was used after short vowels and the ß form after long vowels, although the ss form is gradually being used for both, while the ß form is gradually falling into disuse). First, we have the character itself, U+00DF. Next, we have its lowercase mapping. Since it's already a lowercase letter, its lowercase mapping is also 00DF. The titlecase mapping (which should never occur in practice, because ß never occurs at the beginning of a word) is Ss, U+0053 U+0073. The uppercase mapping is SS, U+0053 U+0053.

Several tags are used for context-sensitive mappings:[1]

- `Final_Sigma` is used for the Greek letter sigma and indicates that the mapping is effective when it is the last letter in the word but not the *only* letter in the word.
- `More_Above` indicates that the mapping is effective only when the character has one or more top-joining combining marks after it.
- `After_Soft_Dotted` indicates that the mapping is effective only when the character follows a Soft_Dotted character (basically, an i or j).
- `Before_Dot` indicates that the mapping is effective only when the character precedes U+0307 COMBINING DOT ABOVE.

In addition, the condition list may include one or more two-letter abbreviations for languages (the abbreviations come from the ISO 639 standard), which state that a particular mapping happens only if the text is in that language.

The last three conditions are used in Lithuanian-specific case mappings. In Lithuanian, the letter i keeps its dot when an accent is applied to it, an effect that can be achieved by adding U+0307 COMBINING DOT ABOVE. These

---

1. These tags appear in the Unicode 3.2 version of SpecialCasing.txt, which simplifies the approach used in the Unicode 3.1 version (but produces the same effect). It's possible that these tags will change before Unicode 3.2 becomes final.

conditions are used to control when this extra character should be added and removed.

Here's a classic example of the use of the special conditions:

```
03A3; 03C2; 03A3; 03A3; Final_Sigma; # GREEK CAPITAL LETTER SIGMA
# 03A3; 03C3; 03A3; 03A3; # GREEK CAPITAL LETTER SIGMA
```

These two entries are for the Greek capital letter sigma (Σ, U+03A3). This letter has two lowercase forms: one (ς, U+03C2) that appears only at the ends of words, and another (σ, U+03C3) that appears at the beginning or in the middle of a word. The FINAL_SIGMA at the end of the first entry indicates that this mapping applies only at the end of a word (and when the letter isn't the only letter in the word). The second entry, which maps to the initial/medial form of the lowercase sigma, is commented out (begins with a #) because this mapping is in the UnicodeData.txt file.

Here's the other classic example:

```
0049; 0131; 0049; 0049; tr Not_Before_Dot; # LATIN CAPITAL LETTER I
0069; 0069; 0130; 0130; tr; # LATIN SMALL LETTER I
# 0131; 0131; 0049; 0049; tr; # LATIN SMALL LETTER DOTLESS I
# 0130; 0069; 0130; 0130; tr; # LATIN CAPITAL LETTER I WITH DOT ABOVE
```

The "tr" in the conditions column tells us that these entries are language-specific mappings for Turkish. The Turkish alphabet includes an extra letter (ı, U+0131) that looks like a lowercase i with the dot missing. This letter's uppercase counterpart is what we'd normally think of as the capital I: U+0049. The regular lowercase i (U+0069) keeps the dot when converted to uppercase so that you can tell the two letters apart (İ, U+0130). Again, the last two mappings in the example are commented out because they're covered in UnicodeData.txt.

CaseFolding.txt

CaseFolding.txt is used for case-insensitive string comparisons. It prescribes a language-independent mapping for each character that erases case distinctions. Generally, it maps each character to its lowercase equivalent, but also includes some extra mappings that map some lowercase letters to variant forms (for example, ß maps to ss). Generally, the mappings were derived by converting everything to uppercase by using the mappings in the UnicodeData.txt and SpecialCasing.txt files and then converting back to lowercase by using just the UnicodeData.txt file. Each entry consists of the original code point value, a code (C, F, S, or I) indicating the type of mapping, and the mapping (one or more code point values). The code tells you whether the mapping causes the text to get bigger (F) or not (C). In cases where the standard mapping causes the text to expand, a second mapping that doesn't change the text length is provided (and tagged with S). (The Turkish I mappings are called out with an I tag, because they can cause funny things to happen.)

For more information on case mapping, see Chapter 14. For more information on string comparisons, including case folding, see Chapter 15.

■ **PROPERTIES OF DIGITS, NUMERALS, AND MATHEMATICAL SYMBOLS**

We looked at several number-related properties earlier in this chapter: First, we examined the various numeric general categories (Nd, Nl, and No). We also considered the hex-digit properties and the Math property.

For characters in the N categories (characters that are used to represent numeric values), three additional properties indicate the numeric values they represent. These properties are given in the UnicodeData.txt file.

Characters that can be used as decimal digits (generally, the characters in the Nd category, although some No characters as well) have a **decimal-digit value** property indicating the value that the character has when used as a decimal digit. It is shown in the UnicodeData file as an ASCII decimal digit. For example, the Western digit "2", the Arabic digit "٢", and the Thai digit "๒" all represent the value 2 in numeration systems that use Arabic positional notation, and thus all have the decimal-digit value property of 2. All characters with a decimal-digit value property are identified as "decimal" in the DerivedNumericProperties.txt file.

Characters that can be used as digits in any numeration system, including decimal, have a **digit value** property indicating their numeric value when used as digits. It is shown in the UnicodeData file as a decimal numeral using ASCII digits. The decimal-digit characters all have a digit value that's the same as their decimal-digit value. The only characters that have a digit value but not a decimal-digit value are certain presentation forms of the decimal digits (circled, parenthesized, followed by a period, and so on). These characters represent whole numerals, not just digits, but are technically still decimal digits. The DerivedNumericProperties.txt file identifies these characters as "digit."

Finally, all other characters representing numeric values have a **numeric value** property that gives the numeric values they represent. It is given in the UnicodeData.txt file as a decimal numeral using ASCII digits. These characters also show up in DerivedNumericProperties.txt as "numeric." Characters in this category include digits from numeration systems that don't use Arabic positional notation, such as the Ethiopic 10 symbol (፲) and the Tamil 100 symbol (௱); presentation forms of numbers 10 and above (such as the circled 13); Roman numerals; and fractions. If the numeric value is a fraction, it's shown as a fraction in the UnicodeData file, using the ASCII slash as the fraction bar. For example, the character ½ has a numeric value of "1/2", as shown in the Unicode-Data file. The DerivedNumericValues.txt file lists all characters with the numeric property according to their numeric values.

Sometimes, characters in the "letter" categories are used as digits or numerals. For instance, the Latin letters are often used as digits in numerals with radices above 10 (such as the letters A through F being used to represent digit values from 11 to 15 in hexadecimal notation). The Latin letters are also used in Roman numerals. Ancient Greek and Hebrew texts used the letters in their respective alphabets to form numerals. Various Han ideographs are also used to represent numeric values (and sometimes even used as decimal digits). All of these applications are considered specialized uses by Unicode, and the Unicode standard gives none of these characters numeric properties.

We'll look more closely at the various number characters in Unicode in Chapter 12.

■ LAYOUT-RELATED PROPERTIES

The Unicode characters are associated with several properties that specify how various processes related to text rendering (i.e., drawing text on the screen or on paper) should handle them.

Bidirectional Layout

The Unicode standard includes a very detailed specification of how characters from right-to-left and left-to-right writing systems are to be arranged when intermixed in a single line of text. Central to this specification are the characters' bi-di categories, which are given in the UnicodeData.txt file using these codes:

L	Strong left-to-right characters.
R or AL	Strong right-to-left characters.
EN and AN	Digits, which have weak left-to-right directionality.
ES, ET, and CS	Punctuation marks used with numbers. Treated like digits when they occur as part of a number and like punctuation the rest of the time.
WS and ON	Neutrals. Whitespace and punctuation, which take on the directionality of the surrounding text.
NSM	Non-spacing marks, which take on the directionality of the characters to which they attach.
B and S	Block and segment separators, which break text into units that are formatted independently of each other by the bi-di algorithm.
BN	Invisible formatting characters that are invisible to the bi-di algorithm.
LRE, RLE, LRO, RLO, and PDF	Special formatting characters that override the default behavior of the bi-di algorithm for the characters they delimit.

The bi-di category is officially specified in the UnicodeData.txt file. It is also listed in the DerivedBidiClass.txt file, which groups characters according to their bi-di category.

The characters in the LRE, RLE, LRO, RLO, and PDF categories—the invisible control characters that affect the bi-di algorithm's treatment of other characters—have the "Bidi_Control" property in PropList.txt.

For a conceptual overview of the bi-di algorithm, see Chapter 8. For in-depth information on implementing the bi-di algorithm, including more detailed treatment of these categories, see Chapter 16.

Mirroring

Another important property related to the bi-di algorithm is the "mirrored" property. It is also specified in the UnicodeData.txt file as a "Y" or "N" in the "mirrored" column. (The DerivedBinaryProperties.txt file lists all characters with the "mirrored" property.) A "Y" means that the character has the "mirrored" property. Characters with the "mirrored" property have a different glyph shape when they appear in right-to-left text than when they appear in left-to-right text. Usually the two glyphs are mirror images of each other, which is where the word "mirrored" comes from.

Consider the parentheses. The same code, U+0028, is used to represent the mark at the beginning of a parenthetical expression (the character is called "LEFT PARENTHESIS" rather than "STARTING PARENTHESIS," its old name—an unfortunate side effect of the ISO 10646 merger) regardless of the direction of the surrounding text. The concave side always faces the parenthetical text (the text that comes after it). In left-to-right text that means it looks like this: (. In right-to-left text, it has to turn around, so it looks like this:).

Not all of the characters that mirror come in pairs. For those that do, the BidiMirroring.txt file gives the code point value of the character with the mirror-image glyph (for U+0028 LEFT PARENTHESIS, it would, of course, be U+0029 RIGHT PARENTHESIS, and vice versa). Some of the mappings in BidiMirroring.txt are tagged as "[BEST FIT]," meaning the match is only approximate. The file also lists all the characters with the "mirrored" property that can't be mirrored simply by mapping them to another character.

Arabic Contextual Shaping

The letters of the Arabic and Syriac alphabets join together cursively, even in printed text. For this reason, they adopt a different shape depending on the surrounding characters. The ArabicShaping.txt file provides information that can be used to implement a simple glyph-selection algorithm for Arabic and Syriac.

Each line gives information for one character and consists of four fields separated with semicolons:

- The code point value.
- An abbreviated version of the character's name.

- A code indicating the character's joining category. R means the character can connect to the character on its right, D means the character can connect to characters on both sides, and U means the character doesn't connect to characters on either side. L could conceivably be used for characters that connect only to their neighbors on the left, but this category currently contains no characters. C is also used for characters that cause surrounding characters to join to them but don't change shape themselves. (There's also a T category for characters that are transparent to the shaping algorithm, but they're not listed in this file.)
- The name of the character's joining group. Many Arabic letters share the same basic shape and are differentiated from one another by adding dots in various places. This column identifies the character's basic shape (usually the name of a letter with that shape).

Characters not listed in ArabicShaping.txt have a joining type of either T (transparent—essentially all the non-spacing marks and invisible formatting characters) or U (non-joining, basically everything else).

DerivedJoiningType.txt repeats information from ArabicShaping.txt, but organizes it by joining type rather than by code point value. DerivedJoining-Group.txt does the same thing for joining groups.

It's important to note that the information from ArabicShaping.txt is *informative,* not normative. It represents a minimal set of information necessary to produce legible Arabic. Implementations can, and often do, go to more trouble and produce better-looking text. For more information on Arabic and Syriac, see Chapter 8.

Two invisible formatting characters that affect the joining behavior of the surrounding text are given the Join_Control property in PropList.txt.

East Asian Width

Just as Middle Eastern typography introduces interesting rendering challenges, so does East Asian typography. In the latter, lines of text often run vertically from the top of the page to the bottom.

Traditionally, Chinese characters (and, often, the characters used with them) are effectively monospaced: All the characters fit inside the same-size box (which is usually, but not always, square). When Western text is mixed with Asian text, decisions have to be made about how to lay out the mixture. Western letters can be blown up to fill an entire display cell or can be left as their normal proportionally spaced selves. Similarly, sometimes multiple Asian characters are placed together in a single cell to represent an abbreviation.

Originally, no special distinction between the two behaviors was enshrined in the Asian encoding standards, but over time one evolved. The JIS X 0201 and 0208 standards both include the Latin alphabet and the Katakana characters, so encoding schemes based on both, such as SHIFT-JIS, wound up encoding these characters twice: once as single-byte values and again as double-byte values (i.e., pairs of 8-bit code units). Over time, the single-byte codes came to represent half-width (*hankaku*) glyphs, which are either proportionally spaced or sized to fill half a standard display cell, and the double-byte codes came to represent full-width (*zenkaku*) glyphs, which fill a whole display cell.

Some characters in Unicode are specifically categorized as half-width or full-width, but most are either implicitly one or the other or have ambiguous semantics. The EastAsianWidth.txt file nails down all these semantics by giving each character one of the following codes:

F   Explicitly full-width (has "FULLWIDTH" in its name)

H   Explicitly half-width (has "HALFWIDTH" in its name)

W   Implicitly full-width

Na Implicitly half-width

A   Ambiguous; generally half-width, but full-width in an East Asian context

N   Neutral; never occurs in East Asian typography; treated the same as Na

This information is also in DerivedEastAsianWidth.txt, which lists everything in order by width category rather than by code point value. For more information on the East Asian Width property, see Chapter 10.

Line-Breaking Property

Another integral part of the process of rendering text is breaking up long passages of text into lines. The Unicode standard also specifies how a line-breaking process should treat the various characters. This information is found in

LineBreak.txt, which includes both normative and informative line-breaking categories. The normative categories are as follows:

BK Forces a line break.

CR Carriage return. Same as BK, except when followed by LF.

LF Line feed. Same as BK, but causes CR to behave differently. (The CR-LF combination we all know and love from DOS thus gets treated as a single line terminator, not two.)

CM Combining mark. Never a break before; otherwise transparent.

SG High surrogate. No break before a low surrogate.

SP Space. Generally, a break is allowed after a series of spaces.

ZW Zero-width space. Generally, the same as SP.

GL Non-breaking ("glue"). Never a break before or after.

CB Contingent break opportunity. Breaks depend on information outside the text stream.

The informative properties give a good default line-breaking behavior. Implementations are also free to do a better (or more language-specific) job if they want to go to more trouble.

As with the other properties, a DerivedLineBreak.txt file gives the same information as LineBreak.txt, but is organized by category rather than by code point value.

For more information on line breaking, including information on the other categories, see Chapter 16.

■ NORMALIZATION-RELATED PROPERTIES

We have already looked at the Unicode normalization forms and the way in which Unicode normalization works. Much of the Unicode Character Database is given over to this important topic, so we'll take a closer look at the normalization-related properties here. For more information on decomposition and normalization, refer to Chapter 4. For in-depth information on implementing Unicode normalization, see Chapter 14.

Decomposition

As we saw earlier, many Unicode characters are said to "decompose." That is, they're considered equivalent to (and, generally speaking, less preferable than) other Unicode characters or sequences of other Unicode characters. For those characters that decompose, the UnicodeData.txt file gives their decomposition.

For canonical composites, the decomposition is either a single Unicode code point value (a singleton decomposition) or two Unicode code point values, the first of which may itself have a canonical decomposition (a strategy to save space and to help implementations that also want to save space). To get the full canonical decomposition for a character requires performing the decomposition recursively until you arrive at a sequence of non-decomposing characters.

Compatibility decompositions, by comparison, can be any number of characters long. That's because the intermediate forms necessary to have every decomposition be two characters long don't always exist.

The same field in UnicodeData.txt is used for both canonical and compatibility decompositions, as a single character can have only one or the other, not both. The decomposition is preceded with a tag to specify what kind it is.

Decomposition Type

The decomposition in UnicodeData.txt for each character is optionally preceded by a tag that specified the type of the decomposition. If the tag is missing, it's a canonical decomposition. If the tag is present, it's a compatibility decomposition and the tag is intended to give you an idea of what type of information would be lost if you converted the character to its compatibility decomposition. The tags are as follows:

- **<font>** identifies a compatibility composite that's equal to its compatibility decomposition plus some additional font or styling information (for example, a script or black-letter variant of some letter used as a symbol).
- **<noBreak>** identifies a variant of a space or hyphen that prevents line breaks. A no-break variant is the same as its compatibility decomposition

with U+2060 WORD JOINER both before and after it. (U+2060 isn't included in the decomposition, however.)

- `<initial>`, `<medial>`, `<final>`, and `<isolated>` are used with the presentation forms of the Arabic letters to identify the particular glyph for the letter that the presentation form is intended to represent.

- `<circle>` identifies characters that are equivalent to their compatibility decomposition with a circle drawn around it. The same effect can be achieved (for single characters) by following the character with U+20DD COMBINING ENCLOSING CIRCLE, but this character isn't included in the decomposition.

- `<super>` and `<sub>` mark characters that are the same as their compatibility decompositions drawn as superscripts or subscripts.

- `<vertical>` is used to identify presentation forms for various punctuation marks used with East Asian text. These presentation forms are equivalent to the glyphs that are used for their compatibility mappings in vertical text (they're roughly equivalent to the horizontal forms rotated 90 degrees).

- `<wide>` marks full-width (zenkaku) variants of various Latin characters used in East Asian text.

- `<narrow>` identifies half-width (hankaku) variants of various Japanese characters used in abbreviations.

- `<small>` identifies small variants of various ASCII punctuation marks and symbols sometimes used in Chinese text.

- `<square>` indicates that the character is equivalent to the characters in its compatibility decomposition arranged in a single square East Asian display cell. It's used for various abbreviations used in East Asian text.

- `<fraction>` identifies the "vulgar fractions," single code points representing fractions, which can all be represented using U+2044 FRACTION SLASH (which *is* included in these characters' decompositions).

- `<compat>` precedes all compatibility decompositions that don't fit into one of the other categories.

The decomposition types are informative and somewhat approximate. A DerivedDecompositionType.txt file organizes the Unicode characters according to their decomposition type (if they decompose).

Combining Class

The combining class is a number that says how a combining character interacts typographically with the character to which it attaches. It is used primarily to arrange a series of combining characters into canonical order.

All non-combining characters have a combining class of 0. A fair number of combining marks also have a combining class of 0, which indicates that the mark combines typographically with its base character in a way that should prevent reordering of any marks attached to the same character. For example, the enclosing marks have a combining class of 0. Any combining marks that follow the enclosing mark shouldn't be reordered to appear before the enclosing mark in storage, as whether they appear before or after the enclosing mark in storage controls whether they're drawn inside the enclosing mark.

Here's a quick breakdown of the combining classes:

0	Non-combining characters, or characters that surround or become part of the base character
1	Marks that attach to the interior of their base characters, or overlay them
7–199	Various marks with language- or script-specific joining behavior
200–216	Marks that attach to their base characters in various positions
218–232	Marks that are drawn in a specific spot relative to their base characters but don't touch them
233–234	Marks that appear above or below two base characters in a row
240	The iota subscript used in ancient Greek

Figure 5.2 shows how the more general combining classes are arranged.

A DerivedCombiningClass.txt file organizes the characters by combining class rather than by code point value.

Composition Exclusion List

The CompositionExclusions.txt file contains the composition exclusion list for Unicode Normalized Form C. Form C favors composed forms over decomposed

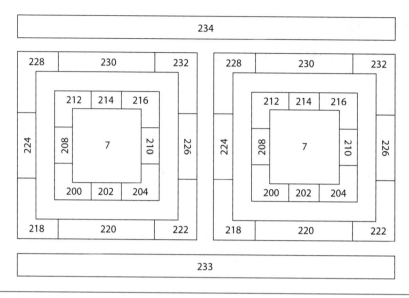

Figure 5.2 Organization of the combining classes

forms for characters that can be represented either way. This file lists canonical composites that can't appear in text normalized for Form C.

Why would you exclude certain canonical composites from Normalized Form C? There are four main reasons:

- **Script-specific exclusions.** For some writing systems, the more common way of representing the character is with the decomposed form, and converting to the composed form doesn't actually help anyone.
- **Singleton decompositions.** Some characters have a single-character canonical decomposition. In these cases, the "composite" form is just an equivalent character that was given a separate code point value for compatibility. The "decomposed" form is the form that should almost always be used.
- **Non-starter decompositions.** The composite character has a decomposition whose first character doesn't have a combining class of 0—that is, it's a composite combining character. What we really want to do with

these characters is incorporate them into a composite form that includes the base character. A composite combining mark is still a combining mark, and, given that the idea behind Form C (in general) is to eliminate combining marks when possible, composing things into composite combining marks doesn't help.

- **Post-composition version characters.** The most important category consists of canonical composites added to Unicode after Unicode 3.0. Normalized Form C is defined to use only canonical composites from Unicode 3.0 for backward compatibility purposes. If you didn't exclude new canonical composites, you could take a file in Unicode 3.0 (or an earlier version), convert it to Normalized Form C, and change the file's Unicode version. If the file was produced by a program that understood only Unicode 3.0, converting it to Form C could make the file (or at least certain characters in the file) unreadable to the program that produced it. To get around this problem, Normalized Form C can't convert to canonical composites that are added to future versions of Unicode, known as "post-composition version characters."

The Unicode 3.1 version of CompositionExclusions.txt contains 13 post-composition version characters. They are all precomposed versions of the musical symbols in the new Musical Symbols block. (All of the characters in these characters' decompositions are also new for Unicode 3.1, so it probably would have been safe not to put them in the composition exclusion list, but it's important to uphold the rules anyway.)

Normalization Test File

NormalizationTest.txt provides a fairly exhaustive set of test cases for implementations of Unicode normalization. It gives sequences of Unicode characters, along with what you should get when you convert each sequence to the four Unicode normalized forms. It can be used (in fact, it *should* be used) to test normalization implementations for conformance. We look at this file in much more detail in Chapter 14.

Derived Normalization Properties

The DerivedNormalizationProperties.txt file contains several categories that can be used to optimize normalization implementations:

- The **Full_Composition_Exclusion** category (called Comp_Ex in versions of Unicode before 3.2) includes characters that can't occur in any of the normalized Unicode forms.

- The **NFD_NO** category lists characters that can't occur in Normalized Form D. If you're normalizing to Form D, you can leave characters alone until you hit a Full_Composition_Exclusion or NFD_NO character.

- The **NFC_NO** category lists characters that can't occur in Normalized Form C. If you're normalizing to Form C, you can leave characters alone until you hit a Full_Composition_Exclusion or NFC_NO character.

- The **NFC_MAYBE** category lists characters that usually don't occur in Normalized Form C. If you're normalizing to Form C and hit an NFC_MAYBE character, you may have to check context to determine if you have to do anything.

- The **NFKD_NO** category lists characters that can't occur in Normalized Form KD.

- The **NFKC_NO** and **NFKC_MAYBE** categories are analogous to NFC_NO and NFC_MAYBE, respectively, for Normalized Form KC.

- The **Expands_On_NFD** category lists characters that turn into more than one character when converted to Normalized Form D.

- The **Expands_On_NFC** category lists characters that turn into more than one character when converted to Normalized Form C.

- The **Expands_On_NFKD** category lists characters that turn into more than one character when converted to Normalized Form KD.

- The **Expands_On_NFKC** category lists characters that turn into more than one character when converted to Normalized Form KC.

- The **FNC** category lists characters for which you get a different result if you convert them to Normalized Form KC than if you first case-fold them (using the mappings in CaseFolding.txt) and *then* map them to

Normalized Form KC. For each character, the mapping straight from the original character to the case-folded Normalization Form KC version is also included, allowing you to fast-path these two conversions.

All of these categories can be (and, in fact, were) derived from the actual normalizations in UnicodeData.txt. You can use them in a normalization implementation to avoid doing unnecessary work.

Grapheme Cluster–Related Properties

Unicode 3.2 introduces a few new properties intended to nail down how text is parsed into grapheme clusters:

- **Grapheme_Base** includes all characters that aren't in one of the other categories. Grapheme_Base characters are grapheme clusters unto themselves unless connected to other characters with Grapheme_Extend or Grapheme_Link characters.
- **Grapheme_Extend** includes all combining marks and a few other characters that go in the same grapheme cluster as the character that precedes them.
- **Grapheme_Link** includes Indic viramas and the combining grapheme joiner, which cause the characters that precede and follow them to belong to the same grapheme cluster.

■ Unihan.txt

Finally, there's the Unihan.txt file. One of the most important scripts in Unicode is the Chinese characters (also called the Han characters or CJK Ideographs). Unicode 3.1 includes more than 70,000 Han characters, and these characters have additional properties beyond those assigned to the other Unicode characters.

Chief among these properties are mappings to various source standards. Unicode defines the meanings of the various Han characters by specifying exactly where they came from. This approach also lets you see just which characters from which source standards were unified together in Unicode. All of these mappings, plus a lot of other useful data, are found in Unihan.txt.

For each Han character, the Unihan.txt file gives at least some of the following pieces of information:

- Mappings to codes for the same character in a huge number of national and vendor character encoding standards from various Asian countries
- Mappings to entries for the character in a wide variety of dictionaries
- Mappings between equivalent Simplified Chinese and Traditional Chinese characters
- Mappings between other variant forms of the same character
- Pronunciations of the character in various languages
- An English definition of the character
- The character's stroke count

For more information on the Han characters and Han unification, see Chapter 10.

6

Unicode Storage and Serialization Formats

$\mathcal{A}$s we saw earlier, the Unicode standard comprises a single, unified coded character set containing characters from most of the world's writing systems. The past few chapters—indeed, most of this book—have focused on the coded character set. Unicode also comprises three encoding forms and seven encoding schemes, and a number of other encoding forms and schemes aren't actually part of the Unicode standard but are nevertheless frequently used with it.

The encoding forms and schemes are where the rubber meets the road with Unicode. The coded character set takes each character and places it in a three-dimensional encoding space consisting of seventeen 256×256 planes. The position of a character in this space—its *code point value*—is given as a four- to six-digit hex value ranging from zero to 0x10FFFF, a 21-bit value.

The Unicode character encoding forms (or storage formats) take the abstract code point values and map them to bit patterns in memory (code units). The Unicode character encoding schemes (or serialization formats) take the code units in memory and map them to serialized bytes in a serial, byte-oriented medium such as a disk file or a network connection. Collectively, these different encoding forms and schemes are called the Unicode Transformation Formats (UTFs).

The mappings from abstract code point values to serialized bytes are sometimes straightforward and sometimes more complex. The various storage and serialization formats exist because, depending on the application, you may want to make different trade-offs between issues such as compactness, backward compatibility, and encoding complexity. In this chapter, we'll introduce them. In Chapter 14, we'll consider their implementation.

■ A HISTORICAL NOTE

Much of the terminology surrounding the presentation of Unicode in bits is relatively new, going back only a few years in Unicode's history. Indeed, some of the concepts we discuss here were originally called by different names.

When it was first designed, Unicode was a fixed-length, 16-bit standard. The abstract encoding space was 16 bits wide (a single 256×256 plane), and one character encoding form existed—a straightforward mapping of 16-bit code points to 16-bit unsigned integers in memory. The single official encoding scheme prefixed a special sentinel value to the front of the Unicode file to allow systems to auto-detect the underlying byte order of the system that created the file.

Early in the life of the standard, it became clear that a special encoding system based on Unicode but tailored for backward compatibility with ASCII was important to have. This encoding went through several names and incarnations before coming to be called UTF-8. The term "UTF" (Unicode Transformation Format) reflected the fact that the encoding was an algorithmic transformation you could perform on the 16-bit Unicode values.

By the time Unicode 2.0 came out, it was clear that an encoding space with only 65,536 cells wasn't going to be big enough. The "surrogate mechanism" was then invented. It reserved 2,048 positions in the encoding space and specified that they were to be used in pairs: one from the 1,024 "high surrogate" values followed by one from the 1,024 "low surrogate" values. The surrogates were meaningless in themselves, but *pairs* of surrogates would be used to represent more characters.

The ISO 10646 standard had started with a 31-bit encoding space—32,768 256×256 planes. It had two encoding forms:

- UCS-4, which mapped the 31-bit abstract code point values to 32-bit unsigned integers in memory (the extra bit—the sign bit—was always off, allowing a UCS-4 value to be stored in either signed or unsigned integer types with no change in numeric semantics)
- UCS-2, which allowed plane 0 to be represented with a 16-bit serialized value simply by lopping off the top two zero bytes of the abstract code point value

Unicode 2.0 with the surrogate mechanism made it possible for Unicode to cover the first 17 planes of the ISO 10646 encoding space: plane 0 with a simple Unicode code point, and planes 1 through 16 with surrogate pairs. Originally, this strategy wasn't thought of as extending Unicode to a 21-bit encoding space. Rather, some characters were just represented with two code points. Ultimately, the mapping from surrogate pairs to planes 1 through 16 of the ISO 10646 encoding space, and the abstract code point values from ISO 10646, took hold in Unicode parlance, where they were called "Unicode scalar values."

The surrogate mechanism was adopted into the ISO 10646 standard as UTF-16. By the time Unicode 3.0 came out, Unicode was being described as having a 21-bit encoding space, and UTF-16 was put on an equal footing with UTF-8 as alternative ways to represent the 21-bit abstract Unicode values in bits. The "Unicode scalar value" became the "code point value" (a code point was now 21 bits wide instead of 16 bits wide) and the term "code unit" was coined to refer to the 16-bit units from UTF-16 (or the bytes of UTF-8). A third form, UTF-32, was later added to Unicode as a counterpart to UCS-4 from the ISO 10646 standard, and several new serialization formats were introduced. Meanwhile, WG2 agreed to limit ISO 10646 to the same 21-bit encoding space Unicode was using, leading to today's situation.

The discussion that follows will refer back to this history when it's important or when older terms may still be in common use.

▪ **UTF-32**

The simplest (and newest) of the Unicode encoding forms is UTF-32, which was first defined in Unicode Standard Annex #19 (now officially part of Unicode 3.1). To go from the 21-bit abstract code point value to UTF-32, you simply zero-pad the value out to 32 bits.

UTF-32 exists for three basic reasons:

1. It's the Unicode standard's counterpart to UCS-4, the four-byte format from ISO 10646.
2. It provides a way to represent every Unicode code point value with a single code unit, which can make for simpler implementations.
3. It can be useful as an in-memory format on systems with a 32-bit word length. Some systems either don't give you a way to access individual bytes of a 32-bit word or impose a performance penalty for doing so. If memory is cheap, you can gain performance by storing text internally as UTF-32.

In the past, UTF-32 and UCS-4 didn't refer to the same thing. Originally, UCS-4 mapped ISO 10646's 31-bit encoding space to a 32-bit value, and UTF-32 mapped Unicode's 21-bit encoding space to a 32-bit value. In other words, the values from 0x110000 to 0x7FFFFFFF were legal UCS-4 code unit values but not legal UTF-32 code unit values (values of 0x80000000 and higher were illegal in both encodings).

Today, ISO 10646 conceptually has a 31-bit encoding space. WG2, the group behind ISO 10646, has, however, agreed to restrict actual allocation of code point values to characters to just the first seventeen planes, making UCS-4 and UTF-32 functionally identical from this point forward.

The big downside to UTF-32, of course, is that it wastes a lot of space. Eleven bits in every code unit are always zero and effectively wasted. In fact, because the vast majority of actual text makes use only of characters from the BMP, 16 bits of the code unit are effectively wasted almost all the time.[1] Also,

---

1. Theoretically, you could save some of that space by using 24-bit code units, but this approach has never been seriously suggested because no machine architecture can comfortably handle 24-bit values except by padding them out to 32 bits. A 24-bit encoding would effectively be limited to use as a serialization format, and there are more compact ways to represent Unicode in serialized data.

you don't generally gain a lot in implementation efficiency, because a single character as the user sees it might still be represented internally with a combining character sequence. That is, even with UTF-32, you may have to deal with single "characters" that the user sees being represented with multiple code units (the fact that Unicode considers each of these units to be a "character" isn't generally all that helpful).

■ UTF-16 AND THE SURROGATE MECHANISM

That brings us to UTF-16. UTF-16 is the oldest Unicode encoding form, although its name goes back only a few years.

UTF-16 maps the 21-bit abstract code point values to sequences of 16-bit code units. For code point values in the BMP, which represent the vast majority of characters in any typical written document, this is a straightforward mapping. You just lop the five zero bits off the top, as shown in Figure 6.1.

For characters from the supplementary planes, the transformation is more complicated. To represent supplementary-plane characters, Unicode sets aside 2,048 code point values in the BMP. These code point values will never be assigned to actual characters, which frees up their corresponding 16-bit code unit values to be used for the supplementary-plane characters.

The reserved code point values run from U+D8000 to U+DFFF. This range is called the "surrogate range," and code unit values in this range are called "surrogates." The name has some history behind it. Originally, the surrogates

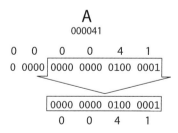

Figure 6.1 UTF-16 mapping for BMP characters

were thought of as full-fledged code point values that "stood in" or "acted as surrogates" for supplementary-plane characters. Now they're just reserved code point values.

The surrogate range is divided in half. The range from U+D800 to U+DBFF contains the "high surrogates," and the range from U+DC00 to U+DFFF contains the "low surrogates." A supplementary-plane character is represented with a single code unit value from the high-surrogate range, followed by a single code unit value from the low-surrogate range (creating a "surrogate pair"). Unpaired or out-of-order surrogates are illegal and don't represent anything.

The mapping from a supplementary-plane character to a surrogate pair is rather complicated. First, you subtract 0x10000 from the original code point value to get a 20-bit value. You then split the result into two 10-bit sequences. The first 10-bit sequence becomes the lower 10 bits of the high-surrogate value, and the second 10-bit sequence becomes the lower 10 bits of the low-surrogate value. For U+E0041 TAG LATIN CAPITAL LETTER A, that mapping looks like Figure 6.2. Thus U+E0041 turns into 0xDB40 0xDC41 when converted to UTF-16.

Some people have objected to the surrogate mechanism as a corruption of the original Unicode ideal, which was to have a *fixed-length* 16-bit encoding. They're right, of course, that a compromise had to be made here. They're wrong, however, in thinking that this strategy opens up the whole can of worms that usually comes with variable-length encoding schemes.

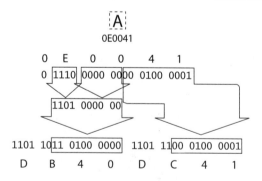

Figure 6.2 UTF-16 mapping for supplementary-plane characters

In a typical variable-length encoding, you can't tell anything by looking at a single code unit (which is usually a byte). That byte may be a character unto itself, the second byte of a two-byte character, or in some cases the first byte of a two-byte character. You could tell whether you were actually at the beginning of a character only by looking at context. If you lost a byte of the text in transmission, it could throw off the reading process, making it see the rest of the text as random garbage.

UTF-16 gets around this problem by using distinct ranges of values to represent one-unit characters, first units of two-unit characters, and second units of two-unit characters. A high-surrogate value can *only* be the first unit of a two-unit character, a low-surrogate value can *only* be the second unit of a two-unit character, and a nonsurrogate value can *only* be a single-unit character. If you ever see an unpaired surrogate, it's an error, but the only character corrupted because of this error is the character for which the surrogate represented half; the surrounding text remains intact.

ISO 10646 specifies an encoding form called UCS-2, which also uses 16-bit code units. It's important to note that UCS-2 is *not* the same thing as UTF-16. The difference relates to the surrogate mechanism. UCS-2 can represent only BMP characters, every code point is represented with a single code unit, and the code units from U+D800 to U+DFFF aren't used. Supplementary-plane characters simply can't be represented using UCS-2. In other words, UTF-16 is UCS-2 plus the surrogate mechanism. (Prior to Unicode 3.1, there were no characters in the supplementary planes, so many Unicode implementations didn't actually support the surrogate mechanism; you'll sometimes see these versions characterized as "supporting UCS-2"—a euphemistic way of saying they don't handle surrogate pairs.)

Some developers object to the additional code complexity involved in supporting UTF-16 as a representation format, but this issue shouldn't generally be all that big a deal. Code points outside the BMP are used for relatively rare characters. Mostly, the non-BMP range will contain characters for historical (i.e., dead) languages, specialized sets of symbols, and very specialized control signals. Except for scholarly documents in certain fields, non-BMP characters will never occur, or will occur only extremely rarely. Even in such specialized documents, they'll generally show up only in examples and other places where they'll be the minority of the text.

The one major exception involves the CJK ideographs, which are living characters used to write living (and, in fact, thriving) languages. Even here, however, the most common characters (tens of thousands of them) are encoded in the BMP. Most ideographic text should make only occasional forays outside the BMP to get the characters they need. The issue that will most likely require frequent trips outside the BMP is certain people's names, as the naming of children is the single biggest source of newly coined ideographs. Even here, however, someone's name appears far less often in a document about him or her than the number of times other words occur.

Another thing to keep in mind is that most of the processing required to handle surrogate pairs in memory is also required to support combining character sequences. Certain operations require a little more support to handle surrogate pairs, but for the most part, systems that correctly handle combining character sequences should also work properly with surrogate pairs.

■ ENDIAN-NESS AND THE BYTE ORDER MARK

Most experienced programmers are familiar with the concept of byte order, or "endian-ness." Most personal computer architectures of today evolved from old machine architectures that had an 8-bit word length. While their modern counterparts have longer word lengths, they still allow access to individual 8-bit fragments of a word. In other words, successive memory-address values refer to successive 8-bit fragments of words, not successive whole words. A 32-bit word on most modern machines thus takes up four memory locations.

How a 32-bit value is distributed across four 8-bit memory locations (or how a 16-bit value is distributed across two 8-bit memory locations) varies from machine architecture to machine architecture. That is, if you write 0xDEADBEEF into memory location 0, you're actually writing values into memory locations 0, 1, 2, and 3. Some machines, such as the PowerPC and SPARC families of processors, store the most significant byte of the word in the lowest-numbered memory location—that is, memory location 0 would contain 0xDE, and memory location 3 would contain 0xEF. These architectures are said to be **big-endian**. Other machines, such as the Intel x86/Pentium family of processors, store the most-significant byte of the word in the *highest-*

numbered memory location—that is, memory location 0 would contain 0xEF and memory location 3 would contain 0xDE. These architectures are said to be **little-endian**.

When a program is operating in memory, endian-ness isn't important. In our example, if you write a 32-bit value (say, 0xDEADBEEF) to memory location 0, you just do it, and it's of no concern to you which memory location contains which byte. Later, when you read the value from memory location 0 back, it is 0xDEADBEEF, just as you wrote it—again without your needing to be aware of which bytes were stored in which specific memory locations. Those memory locations will always be treated in a consistent manner. They will always be accessed by the same processor or at least shared by multiple processors that all share the same architecture. You get into trouble only in those rare instances when you treat memory locations 0 to 3 as a single 32-bit value and then later treat them as something else (e.g., four 8-bit values or two 16-bit values).

Endian-ness becomes an issue when you attempt to transfer data from a single computer's memory to some other location, such as another computer or a storage device. Writing data to the disk or sending it over a communications link of some kind requires *serializing* it—that is, writing it out as a series of values of the same size. Again, because the smallest "word" size on most modern machines is eight bits, this means writing and reading the data as a sequence of bytes.

This process, of course, requires taking all of the units that are longer than 8 bits and breaking them up into series of bytes. You must therefore make a decision as to which order you're going to write the bytes in when you break up a larger value. General practice is to go in order from lowest-numbered memory location to highest-numbered memory location. Thus, if the same computer both writes something to the disk and reads it from the disk, or if two computers of the same processor architecture share a file over a network, endian-ness isn't an issue. If processors of *different* architectures share data over a network, or if you share data on a removable medium between machines of different architectures, then you can run into serious trouble—unless, of course, you've made some kind of an agreement beforehand on the serialized format's byte order or provided some way for the reading process to detect it.

Unicode does both of these things. It defines two encoding schemes based on UTF-16: UTF-16BE and UTF-16LE, which are, respectively, the big-endian and little-endian versions of UTF-16. As this distinction is meaningless in memory, the in-memory representation is just called UTF-16. UTF-16BE and UTF-16LE are used only to refer to UTF-16 text in some kind of serialized format, such as a disk file.

The name "UTF-16" can also be used to refer to serialized UTF-16, giving you a third encoding scheme. Unicode provides a mechanism for automatically detecting the endian-ness of serialized UTF-16 text whose endian-ness isn't announced by the enclosing protocol. This mechanism is called the **byte order mark** (BOM). ("BOM" is pronounced "bomb," not "bee-oh-em," so [WARNING: lame humor follows] be careful discussing Unicode serialization while passing through airport security checkpoints.)

The code point U+FEFF is designated as the Unicode byte order mark. Its byte-swapped counterpart, 0xFFFE, on the other hand, is not a legal Unicode value. Thus, if a file you're reading contains any 0xFFFEs, either it's not Unicode text or it's the wrong endian-ness and you need to byte-swap the incoming character codes to get real Unicode. The writing process would include BOMs to allow this detection to happen on the receiving end.

The convention is to start a Unicode text file (or a transmission including Unicode text) with a BOM whenever no external mechanism is available to specify its endian-ness. A file or transmission tagged as "UTF-16" rather than "UTF-16BE" or "UTF-16LE" would, therefore, be expected to begin with a BOM. (The other formats could also begin with a BOM, but the BOM would be redundant.) If it doesn't, the convention is to assume it's UTF-16BE.

Because the BOM helps to announce the endian-ness of a Unicode text file, it can also be useful for telling whether a text file is a Unicode file in the first place or for telling the difference between versions of Unicode. You can find more information on how this process works in the section "Detecting Unicode Storage Formats" later in this chapter.

You need to be careful when using the BOM, however, because it has a double meaning. In Unicode 1.0, the code point U+FEFF had only the single meaning. It was a byte order mark and only a byte order mark. In normal Unicode text processing, it was simply a no-op.

Beginning in Unicode 2.0, however, the code point U+FEFF also acquired the semantic "zero-width non-breaking space" (ZWNBSP). A ZWNBSP is used to "glue" two characters together. It has no visual representation, but will prevent a text processor that supports it from breaking a line between the characters on either side of the ZWNBSP. You might use it, for example, in the word "e-commerce" to keep "e-" from becoming stranded on a line by itself, or to keep a Chinese phrase together on one line (Chinese text can usually have line breaks in the middle of words and phrases). When a ZWNBSP occurs between two characters that naturally stick together on a single line (e.g., the letters in any English word), it has no effect.

Of course, if the ZWNBSP occurs at the beginning of a document, it's basically a no-op because there's nothing to "glue" the first character to. But if you concatenate two Unicode text files together using something like the UNIX utility cat, however, you may inadvertently glue the last character of the first file to the first character of the second file.

Because of this problem, the double meaning of U+FEFF quickly came to be seen as a mistake. Starting in Unicode 3.2, the "zero-width non-breaking space" meaning of U+FEFF has been deprecated. Despite the name (which unfortunately can't change), U+FEFF goes back to being only a byte order mark. A new character, U+2060 WORD JOINER, has been introduced in Unicode 3.2 to take over the task of "gluing" two words together on a single line. Conforming Unicode implementations are now allowed to convert U+FEFF ZERO WIDTH NO-BREAK SPACE to U+2060 WORD JOINER.

Of course, you run into the endian-ness problem in UTF-32 as well. Today, three character encoding schemes are also based on UTF-32: UTF-32BE, UTF-32LE, and tagged UTF-32. They work the same way as their UTF-16-based counterparts.

■ UTF-8

UTF-8 is the 8-bit Unicode encoding form. It was designed to allow Unicode to be used in places that support only 8-bit character encodings. A Unicode code point is represented using a sequence of anywhere from one to four 8-bit code units.

One vitally important property of UTF-8 is that it's 100 percent backward compatible with ASCII. That is, valid 7-bit ASCII text is also valid UTF-8 text. As a consequence UTF-8 can be used in any environment that supports 8-bit ASCII-derived encodings, and that environment will be able to correctly

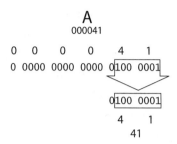

Figure 6.3   UTF-8 mapping for values from U+0000 to U+007F

interpret and display the 7-bit ASCII characters. (The characters represented by byte values where the most significant bit is set, of course, aren't backward compatible—they have a different representation in UTF-8 than they do in the legacy encodings.)

Unicode code point values from U+0000 to U+007F are mapped to UTF-8 in a very straightforward manner, as shown in Figure 6.3. You simply isolate the last seven bits and zero-pad it out to eight bits.

Code point values from U+0080 to U+07FF take two bytes, as shown in Figure 6.4. The last six bits, plus 0x80, become the second byte, and the next five bits, plus 0xC0, become the first byte.

Code point values from U+0800 to U+FFFF (the rest of the BMP) turn into three-byte sequences, as shown in Figure 6.5. The first four bits, plus 0xE0, be-

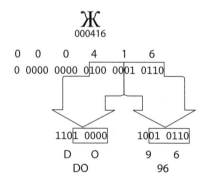

Figure 6.4   UTF-8 mapping for values from U+0080 to U+07FF

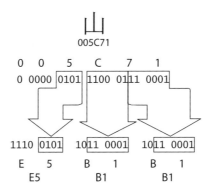

Figure 6.5   UTF-8 mapping for values from U+0800 to U+FFFF

come the first byte. The next six bits, plus 0x80, become the second byte. The last six bits, plus 0x80, become the last byte.

Finally, the code points in planes 1 through 16 (the non-BMP characters) turn into four-byte sequences, as shown in Figure 6.6. The first three bits, plus 0xF0, become the first byte. Each of the other three bytes consists of the next six bits from the original code point, plus 0x80.

This mapping can extend all the way out to cover the entire 31-bit ISO 10646 range, using five- and six-byte sequences. This fact is mostly of historical interest (and used to explain old UTF-8 implementations) now that WG2 has committed to never put any characters into planes 18 and higher.

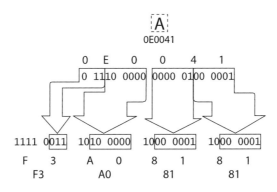

Figure 6.6   UTF-8 mapping for supplemantary-plane characters

Like UTF-16, UTF-8 avoids many of the problems with other multibyte encodings by ensuring that different ranges of values are used in different positions in the character:

00–7F	Single-byte character
80–BF	Trailing byte
C0–DF	Leading byte of two-byte character
E0–EF	Leading byte of three-byte character
F0–F7	Leading byte of four-byte character
F8–FB	Illegal (formerly leading byte of five-byte character)
FC–FD	Illegal (formerly leading byte of six-byte character)
FE–FF	Illegal

The only ambiguous thing here is the trailing byte. You can tell a byte is a trailing byte, but you can't tell which byte of the character it is, or how many bytes the character is. Because of UTF-8's design, however, you never have to scan forward or back more than three bytes to find out.

One side effect of UTF-8's design is that many code points can have more than one potential representation in UTF-8. For example, U+0041 could be represented not only as 0x41, but also as 0xC1 0x81 or 0xE0 0x81 0x81. The standard stipulates that the shortest possible representation for any code point is the only legal one. Prior to Unicode 3.1, it was legal for UTF-8 implementations to *interpret* these "non-shortest form" byte sequences. This possibility created a potential security hole, so Unicode 3.1 tightened the definition to disallow *both* interpretation and generation of nonshortest form sequences.

Another version of "non-shortest form" UTF-8 also needs to be recognized: representation of supplementary-plane characters using six-byte sequences. For example, instead of representing U+E0041 in UTF-8 as 0xF3 0xA0 0x81 0x81, as in the example above, you could conceivably represent it as 0xED 0xAD 0x80 0xED 0xB1 0x81. That is what you get if you convert it first to UTF-16, producing 0xDB40 0xDC41, and then convert the two surrogate code units to UTF-8.

Even Unicode 3.1's tightening of the UTF-8 definition still allowed this problem to occur. As with other non-shortest form sequences, it was illegal to produce such byte sequences, but legal to interpret them. Unicode 3.2 closes this loophole: UTF-8 sequences representing code point values in the surrogate range (U+D800 to U+DFFF) are now completely illegal. That is, any three-byte UTF-8 sequence whose first byte is 0xED and whose second byte is anything from 0xA0 to 0xBF is illegal.

As conversion of code points to UTF-8 results in a sequence of bytes, UTF-8 is effectively a character encoding scheme unto itself, and not just a character encoding form.

▪ CESU-8

Draft Unicode Technical Report #26 proposes an encoding scheme with the rather unwieldy name of "Compatibility Encoding Scheme for UTF-16: 8-bit," or "CESU-8" for short. CESU-8 is a variant of UTF-8 that treats the BMP characters in the same way as UTF-8 does, but deals with the supplementary-plane characters differently. In CESU-8, supplementary-plane characters are represented with six-byte sequences instead of four-byte sequences. In other words, the six-byte representation of supplementary-plane characters that is now illegal in UTF-8 is the *preferred* representation of these characters in CESU-8.

CESU-8 is what you get if you convert a sequence of Unicode code point values to UTF-16 and then convert the UTF-16 code units to UTF-8 code units as if they were code points. Supplementary-plane characters are turned into pairs of three-byte sequences, where each three-byte sequence represents a surrogate. For example, U+E0041 TAG LATIN CAPITAL LETTER A, which is 0xDB40 0xDC41 in UTF-16 and 0xF3 0xA0 0x81 0x81 in UTF-8, is 0xED 0xAD 0x80 0xED 0xB1 0x81 in CESU-8.

CESU-8 is what you get if your program uses UTF-16 as its internal representation format and its conversion to UTF-8 doesn't know about surrogate pairs (either because it was written before the surrogate mechanism was devised or because it was written by someone who assumed character allocations would never appear in the supplementary planes). It's safe to say this format will not be accepted as an official part of the standard, but it might get blessed as a technical report as a way of documenting the internal behavior of a lot of existing systems.

■ UTF-EBCDIC

One of the main applications of UTF-8 is to allow the use of Unicode text in systems that were designed for ASCII text. This is why regular ASCII text is also legal UTF-8. UTF-8 isn't the first international character encoding to be in some way backward compatible with ASCII—quite a few encodings for various languages are backward compatible with ASCII in the same way and for the same reason.

The other 8-bit encoding for Latin text that has huge bodies of text encoded in it is EBCDIC, IBM's Extended Binary-Coded Decimal Information Code. A lot of legacy data is encoded in EBCDIC, and many legacy systems are designed to assume that textual data are encoded in EBCDIC. UTF-EBCDIC (sometimes called UTF-8-EBCDIC), much like UTF-8, is designed to allow the use of Unicode in environments originally designed for EBCDIC.

EBCDIC isn't just ASCII with the characters listed in a different order; it includes characters that don't appear in ASCII and leaves out characters that ASCII includes. Classical EBCDIC used an 8-bit byte but encoded only 109 characters, leaving "holes" in the encoding space. Later versions of EBCDIC filled in the "holes," extending EBCDIC to a full 256-character encoding. Just as some variant versions of 8-bit ASCII that put different characters into the space above 0x7F, so too different variants of EBCDIC fill in the "holes" with different characters.

A set of 65 control signals and 82 printing characters are common to all current variants of EBCDIC, distributed across the 8-bit encoding space. UTF-EBCDIC aims to preserve these values, using the remaining values to encode the rest of the Unicode characters as multibyte combinations. It does so via a two-step process that makes use of an intermediate format called UTF-8-Mod or I8.

I8 is similar to UTF-8, except that the transformation to I8 preserves not only all of the values from 0x00 to 0x7F as single-byte sequences, but also the values from 0x80 to 0x9F (the "C1 controls" from the Latin-1 character set). This range covers the EBCDIC control characters as well as the printing characters that EBCDIC and ASCII have in common. It then proceeds in UTF-8 style to encode the other Unicode code points as multibyte sequences. Like UTF-8, I8 is designed so that the leading byte of a multibyte sequence indicates how many bytes appear in the sequence. Completely distinct ranges of byte values are used for single-byte characters, leading bytes of multibyte sequences, and trailing bytes of multibyte sequences. Because I8 preserves a greater range of values as single-byte sequences, the remaining Unicode characters may map to sequences of as many as five bytes. (In UTF-8, characters in the BMP mapped to a maximum of three bytes, with the non-BMP range taking four bytes; in UTF-EBCDIC, characters in the BMP may map to a maximum of four bytes, and non-BMP characters may map to either four- or five-byte sequences.)

The mapping from I8 to UTF-EBCDIC involves a simple and reversible table lookup: The single-byte values are mapped to the values that the corresponding characters have in EBCDIC, and the bytes of the multibyte characters are mapped into the remaining spaces. The resulting text can be handled properly by most processes expecting to see regular EBCDIC text.

Unlike with UTF-8, you can't tell by doing simple bit masking whether an individual byte of a UTF-EBCDIC sequence is a character unto itself or part of a multibyte sequence. Because you *can* tell this from looking at an I8 sequence, and because you can get from I8 to UTF-EBCDIC with a simple table lookup, you can also use a simple table lookup to identify the leading, trailing, and stand-alone bytes in a UTF-EBCDIC sequence.

I8, by the way, is an intermediate representation only, and not a character encoding form unto itself. Also, UTF-EBCDIC is suitable for use only in homogeneous EBCDIC-based systems and not for general interchange. In particular, you can't use UTF-EBCDIC in an ASCII or UTF-8-based environment.

Because UTF-EBCDIC is designed only for internal use on EBCDIC-based systems and not for interchange, it's not an official part of the Unicode standard. It's published as Technical Report #16 as a way of officially documenting the practice for people writing code for EBCDIC-based systems.

UTF-7

You might run across some other, less common, Unicode transformation formats. The most common of these formats is UTF-7, which was designed for use in 7-bit ASCII environments that can't handle 8-bit characters. In particular, the original version of the Simple Mail Transfer Protocol (SMTP), which is still in common use, wouldn't work with 8-bit character values and required this approach.

UTF-7 works by using a scheme similar to the numeric-character reference scheme employed in HTML and XML. Most of the ASCII characters are just themselves, but a few are used to signal sequences of characters that specify otherwise unrepresentable Unicode values. Thus, unlike the other Unicode transformation formats, UTF-7 is a stateful encoding, with values whose interpretation depends on context. By way of analogy, consider the "<" sequence in HTML. To tell whether the "l" is a real letter l, you have to scan both directions to see if it occurs between a & and an a ;. Trailing bytes in UTF-8 could be thought of as "stateful" because you can't tell specifically which position they occupy in the sequence, but you know they're trailing bytes, and the number of characters that you must examine to find the beginning of the sequence is bounded.

UTF-7 represents the letters A through Z and a through z, the digits 0 through 9, certain punctuation marks (in particular, ",()'-./:?", plus, optionally, some other characters), and the space, tab, carriage return, and line feed the same way they're represented in ASCII. The other Unicode characters are represented using a variant of the Base64 encoding. That is, the + character signals the beginning of a sequence of Base64 text. A sequence of Base64 ends when a non-Base64 character is encountered. The − character can be used to force a switch out of Base64. UTF-7 uses a modified version of Base64 that avoids using the = character, because this character has a special meaning in some of the places where UTF-7 was intended to be used.

UTF-7 was never part of the Unicode standard and was never published as a Unicode Technical Report, although it was published by the Internet Engineering Task Force as RFC 2152 (and earlier as RFC 1642). These days, it's pretty much been supplanted by regular Base64, MIME, and various other protocols. For more on using Unicode in Internet mail, see Chapter 17.

▪ STANDARD COMPRESSION SCHEME FOR UNICODE

One of the major reasons for resistance to Unicode when it first came out was the idea of text files taking up twice as much room as before to store the same amount of actual information. For languages such as Chinese and Japanese that were already using two bytes per character, this issue wasn't a problem. Nevertheless, the idea of using two bytes per character for the Latin alphabet was anathema to a lot of people.

The concern is certainly legitimate: The same document takes up twice as much space on a disk and twice as long to send over a communications link. A database column containing text takes up twice as much disk space. In an era of slow file downloads, for example, the idea of waiting twice as long to download an e-mail message is unpalatable when the process already takes too long. The idea that processing speed, transmission speed across networks, and disk space all increase so rapidly that "it won't be a problem in a couple years" always seemed to ring hollow. Just because you have more disk space doesn't mean you want to waste it.

Of course, processing speed, disk space, and even modem speeds have now reached such levels that sending, receiving, and storing text aren't that big a deal. Even long text documents don't take up much room. The bandwidth problems we're running up against today don't have anything to do with sending text back and forth—they relate to transferring graphics, sound, and video files. Today the size premium that Unicode imposes doesn't seem too onerous, although it certainly did ten years ago when Unicode was getting its start.

This problem *is* still a big deal when you have really large concentrations of text in one place. If you're General Motors and must keep track of millions of parts, doubling the size of the "Description" field in your part database will have a major impact. If you're a wire service and send an endless stream of news stories out over the wire to your subscribers, doubling the size of your news stories will have a huge impact.

The Unicode standard has always remained silent on this issue, saying that compression was a "higher-level protocol" and that existing compression algorithms could effectively take care of this problem. True enough, although using Lempel-Ziv-Welch compression or something similar to compress simple text files seems like overkill and introduces a noticeable hassle. If you're simply trying to reach the same level of efficiency you had when you were using a single-byte encoding and to do so in a way that makes it simple to compress and decompress text, the standard compression algorithms don't offer a lot of relief.

Many people started using UTF-8 for this purpose. It's easy enough to compress and decompress data, and UTF-8 represents ASCII text with the same efficiency as ASCII. Besides, it's less work to retrofit a system to use UTF-8 than to go whole-hog with UTF-16 or UTF-32.

The last justification is certainly valid and is one reason why UTF-8 will always be with us. Indeed, UTF-8 is likely to remain the most popular way of exchanging Unicode data between two entities in a heterogeneous environment. But UTF-8 does impose a small penalty on Latin-1 text. In languages such as Spanish and French that use a lot of accented letters, the fact that an accented letter takes two bytes in UTF-8 and only one in Latin-1 begins to make a noticeable difference.

UTF-8 also doesn't help speakers of non-Latin languages. Greek, for example, takes two bytes per character in UTF-8 but only one byte in a native Greek encoding. Worse yet, Japanese, Chinese, and Korean, which generally take two bytes per character in their native legacy encodings, take *three* bytes per character to represent in UTF-8! Finally, some languages, such as Thai, take only one byte per character in their native legacy encodings but take three bytes in UTF-8.

The bottom line is that using UTF-8 for compression is a very Eurocentric (even English-centric) thing to do. For English, UTF-8 has the same storage efficiency as the legacy encoding, and twice the efficiency of UTF-16; for most other European languages, it imposes perhaps a 15 percent penalty over the legacy encoding. Even so, that's still better than the 100 percent penalty that UTF-16 imposes. For Greek, Cyrillic, Hebrew, Arabic, and a few other languages, UTF-8 and UTF-16 impose the same penalty over the native encoding. For Japanese and Chinese, UTF-16 imposes little or no storage penalty, but UTF-8 imposes a 50 percent penalty. And for Thai, UTF-16 imposes a 100 percent penalty over the legacy encoding, but UTF-8 imposes a 200 percent penalty over the native encoding! Thus, unless you know you'll always be restricted to working in just the languages where UTF-8 gives you good efficiency, UTF-8 isn't effective as a means of saving space.

Earlier we saw how going from ASCII to UTF-16 would really hurt you if you were a wire service sending out thousands of news stories and other information every day. In fact, a wire service, Reuters, first put forth a solution to the problem. This simple and efficient compression scheme for Unicode was the forerunner of what is now known as the Standard Compression Scheme for Unicode (SCSU).

SCSU is a relatively simple compression scheme designed specifically for Unicode text. It takes advantage of the properties of Unicode text to achieve its efficiencies, and it produces results that are generally comparable in size to the legacy encodings. Text in SCSU can be compressed with a general-purpose compression scheme such as LZW to achieve even greater compression ratios (in fact, LZW will generally do a better job on SCSU-encoded Unicode than on regular UTF-16 or UTF-8).

Note that SCSU is a file format, not an algorithm. It lends itself to a multitude of compression algorithms that can trade off compression speed versus compactness in different ways. The algorithm for decompressing SCSU, on the other hand, remains the same and is simple and straightforward (JPEG and MPEG compression are designed around the same principle: one simple way to decompress, lots of different ways to compress).

SCSU is a stateful encoding, meaning that it has "modes." You can't jump into the middle of an SCSU-compressed file and tell what you're looking at without potentially reviewing the file all the way back to the beginning. For this reason, SCSU is generally suitable as an interchange or storage format, but not well-suited to internal processing.

SCSU has two basic modes: single-byte mode and Unicode mode. In single-byte mode, the ASCII printing characters and the most common ASCII control characters are represented as themselves. Thus most ASCII text files (those that use only the most common control characters) are interpretable as SCSU.

The byte values from 0x80 to 0xFF, as usual, are where most of the magic happens. Unlike in Latin-1 and most other encodings, where they have a fixed interpretation, and unlike in UTF-8, where they have no meaning by themselves but are used in variable-length combinations to form characters, the values from 0x80 to 0xFF have variable interpretations in SCSU. Their default interpretation is the same as in Latin-1, so most Latin-1 text files are interpretable as SCSU (remember that Latin-1 is *not* interpretable as UTF-8).

Remember, however, that only the most common ASCII control characters are represented unchanged. The compression algorithm uses the others for various things. One set of control characters is employed to control the interpretation of the values from 0x80 to 0xFF. In all cases, these values represent a contiguous range of 128 characters from somewhere in the Unicode encoding range. This range is called a "window," and the default window is the Latin-1 range. Several predefined windows cover other interesting ranges, such as the Cyrillic window and the Hebrew window. You can represent text that all falls within one 128-character range of Unicode characters simply by including one control character in the stream to set the appropriate window and then using the values from 0x80 to 0xFF to represent the characters in that window.

If the Unicode text being encoded spans more than one window (the ASCII window doesn't count, because it's always accessible), you can intersperse more control codes to shift the window back and forth. There are also "quote" control characters that shift the window only for the very next character instead of for all following characters.

SCSU also lets you define windows. Thus, if the characters you need to encode aren't in any of the predefined windows, you can define a window that does cover them and have characters that take you to it.

Of course, some scripts, with the Han characters being the most notable example, span a much larger range than 128 characters. The window-shifting scheme would be unwieldy in such cases, which is why SCSU has a Unicode mode. If you include a control character that shifts into Unicode mode, the bytes that follow are interpreted as big-endian UTF-16 (a range of byte values are used as control codes in Unicode mode to allow you to shift back into byte mode). Another code shifts into Unicode mode for a single Unicode character, rather than for all following text.

It is relatively easy to implement a decoder for this system, which allows for considerable discretion in the design of encoders. A simple encoder might simply shift to Unicode mode at the beginning of the text stream and pass the rest of the text through unchanged, taking care to insert appropriate escape characters if the input text includes the tag values that SCSU uses in Unicode mode. Alternatively, the encoder might pass through Latin-1 characters unchanged and insert the quote-single-Unicode-character tag before each non-Latin-1 character in the input stream. A sophisticated encoder, on the other hand, might make extensive use of all of the features of the encoding, combined with lots of lookahead when examining the input stream, to achieve very high levels of compression.

A good SCSU encoder should be able to produce results for most text that are similar in size to the same text encoded in the common legacy formats.

SCSU-encoded text will almost always offer a significant savings over regular UTF-16 or UTF-8 text, and should almost never (with a well-designed encoder) impose a penalty of more than a few bytes.

For more on implementing SCSU, see Chapter 14.

▦ BOCU

An interesting alternative to SCSU for Unicode compression was proposed in a recent paper on IBM's DeveloperWorks Web site.[2] Called "Binary Ordered Compression for Unicode (BOCU), it provides compression ratios comparable to SCSU, but with a number of interesting advantages. Chief among them is that a set of Unicode strings encoded in BOCU sorts in the same order as the unencoded strings would, making it useful for encoding short snippets of text in environments where the sort order is still important (think database applications). The algorithm is also a lot simpler than SCSU.

The basic idea with BOCU is that, instead of independently transforming each code point to a sequence of bytes using some fixed mapping, you transform each code point into a sequence of bytes by subtracting it from the preceding code point in the text and encoding the *difference* as a series of bytes. BOCU arranges things so that differences of plus or minus 0x3F or less are represented with single bytes, differences of plus or minus 0x40 to 0x2F3F are represented with two-byte sequences, and larger differences are represented with three-byte sequences. The lead bytes of these sequences are then arranged in such a way as to preserve the relative sorting order of unencoded strings.

Imagine that, instead of just subtracting the current character from the preceding character, you adjust the value from which you subtract to appear in the middle of its Unicode block and consider a little more context than just the immediately preceding character. You can then arrive at an encoding that's almost as efficient as SCSU (and in some cases, more so).

Variants of BOCU are used internally in parts of the International Components for Unicode, the popular Unicode support library. It's unclear whether

---

2. Mark Davis and Markus Scherer, "Binary-Ordered Compression for Unicode," IBM Developer-Works, `http://www-106.ibm.com/developerworks/unicode/library/u-binary.html`.

this scheme will catch on to a greater extent, but it's an interesting idea worth thinking about if you need the things BOCU can give you.

■ DETECTING UNICODE STORAGE FORMATS

The Unicode 2.0 standard, in its discussion of the byte order mark, described how it could be used not just to tell whether a Unicode file was the proper endian-ness, but whether it was a Unicode file at all. The idea is that the sequence 0xFE 0xFF (in Latin-1, a lowercase y with a diaeresis followed by the lowercase Icelandic letter "thorn") would basically never be the first two characters of a normal ASCII/Latin-1 document. Therefore, you could look at something you knew was a text file and tell what it was: If the first two bytes were 0xFE 0xFF, it was Unicode; if the bytes were 0xFF 0xFE, it was byte-swapped Unicode; and if the bytes were anything else, it was whatever the default encoding for the system was.

As Unicode transformation formats have proliferated, so too has the idea of using the byte order mark at the beginning of the file as a way of identifying them. The current chart looks like this:

If the File Starts with	The File Contains
0xFE 0xFF	UTF-16
0xFF 0xFE	byte-swapped UTF-16
0x00 0x00 0xFE 0xFF	UTF-32
0xFF 0xFE 0x00 0x00	byte-swapped UTF-32
0xEF 0xBB 0xBF	UTF-8
0xDD 0x73 0x73 0x73	UTF-EBCDIC
0x0E 0xFE 0xFF	SCSU (recommended; others are possible)
anything else	non-Unicode or untagged Unicode

The basic rule here is simple: If there's any other way to specify (or tell) which format some piece of text is in, don't rely on the byte order mark. If the byte order mark isn't there, then you're stuck. You don't know what the file is. If the byte order mark *is* there, a remote possibility remains that the file's in some other format and just happens to start with those bytes. (For example, is a file that starts with 0x0000 0xFEFF a UTF-32 file starting with a byte order mark or a UTF-16 file starting with a null character and a zero-width non-breaking space?)

In other words, you should use some means other than looking at the text itself to identify the encoding. Designing a system, for example, that uses ".txt" as the filename extension for all Unicode text files and then looks for the BOM to tell whether it's UTF-16, UTF-8, or ASCII isn't terribly bulletproof. Instead, you should use different extensions (or different types, if you're using a typed file system), allow only one or two types, rely on the user to tell you, or take some other step.

If you adopt some kind of protocol that *requires* the presence of the byte order mark, you're effectively specifying a higher-level protocol for identifying the character encoding. In other words, the file isn't really a Unicode text file anymore; it's in a format that contains text in some Unicode format, preceded by a tag identifying the format (to handle the BOM correctly, you've pretty much got to treat it this way). Various higher-level protocols are already available (XML, for example) that do this just as well.

The basic philosophy to follow in most situations is to treat the different Unicode transformation formats as entirely distinct character encodings or code pages, no more related than Latin-1 and Latin-2. The byte order mark works only for telling apart different forms of Unicode; something like XML allows you to distinguish these forms of Unicode from other encoding schemes as well. Process text internally in one format (for example, UTF-16 in the native byte order) and treat incoming data in all other formats—whether different flavors of Unicode or different encodings altogether—as a code-conversion problem.

Unicode in Depth

A Guided Tour of the
Character Repertoire

7

Scripts of Europe

*H*aving taken a look at the overall architecture of Unicode and the various aspects of the Unicode standard that are relevant no matter what you're doing with it, it's time to take a closer look at the details. The next six chapters will be a guided tour through the Unicode character repertoire, highlighting characters with special properties and examining the specifics of how Unicode is used to represent various languages.

Unicode is organized into blocks, with each block representing characters from a specific writing system, or script. In each of the following chapters, we'll look at collections of scripts with similar properties. First, we'll look at the issues they have in common with one another. Then, we'll look at the unique characteristics of each individual script. Along the way, we'll stop to discuss any characters with special properties you may have to know about.

Part II will concentrate mostly on the characters that make up "words" in the various languages (i.e., letters, syllables, ideographs, vowel points, diacritical marks, tone marks, and so forth), but will also include a chapter that deals with digits, punctuation, symbols, and so forth. We'll also highlight interesting digits, punctuation marks, and symbols that belong to specific scripts as we go through the individual scripts.

■ THE WESTERN ALPHABETIC SCRIPTS

One of the reasons computer technology flourished so much in the United States (and, later, Europe) before it caught on in other places might have to do with the European system of writing (this is not, of course, to discount all of the other reasons, such as economic factors, World War II, and so on). Compared to many other writing systems, the Latin alphabet is simple and lends itself well both to mechanical means of reproduction and to various types of automated analysis.

The classic Latin alphabet, as used to write English, is pretty simple. It contains only 26 letters, a very manageable number, and very few typographic complications. The letters represent both consonant and vowel sounds, unlike in most other writing systems, and they lay out very simply, marching from left to right across the page, one after another. The letters don't change shape depending on the letters around them, they don't change order depending on context, they don't combine together into ligatures, and they don't carry complex systems of marks with them to indicate meaning. Words are always separated with spaces, making it easy to detect word boundaries.

Of course, not all of these things are true all the time, and there was a time in history when each of them was false. All of the writing systems used in the West and Middle East evolved out of the Phoenician alphabet, which was written from right to left and didn't have vowels. The Greek alphabet was the first one to assign real letters to vowel sounds, and the Latin alphabet picked it up from there. Originally, the Greek alphabet was also written from right to left, but a form of writing called **boustrophedon** later developed. In boustrophedon, lines of text alternated direction: One line would run from right to left, then the next line would run from left to right, then the next line from right to left again, and so on in zigzag fashion down the page. Gradually, this system died out and all lines were written from left to right. Boustrophedon was generally seen just in Greek writing, but some early examples of Etruscan and Latin writing also use it, so it's not completely unheard-of for Latin-alphabet text to be written right to left.

Spaces between words also weren't always used. They don't appear to have become common practice until around the eighth century or so. You see spaces in some earlier writing and sometimes dots between words, but you very frequently see earlier writing where the words all run together and you have to know the language to know the word boundaries.

There are also plenty of cases in which the shapes of the letters can change depending on context. In handwritten (cursive) English text, for example, the letters don't all join the same way, giving rise to variations in the shapes of the letters. For example, at least in the way I learned to write, the letters b and o join to the succeeding letter above the baseline, rather than at the baseline. This changes the shape of the next letter slightly to account for the higher joiner. Consider the following example:

cannon

Note how the shape of the letter n changes: The a joins to the n along the baseline (and the first n joins to the second n along the baseline). But the o joins to the n above the baseline.

There are other cases where the letters change shape. In boustrophedon, the shape of a letter on a right-to-left line was the mirror image of its shape on a left-to-right line, enabling the reader to tell easily the direction of a given line of text. As recently as 200 years ago, the letter s had two forms: one that was used at the end of a word and one that was used at the beginning or in the middle of a word (in fact, this is still true in the Greek alphabet). In modern ornamental typefaces, you'll still see special versions of certain characters that are intended to be used at the ends of words.

Of course, in good typography, letters still sometimes combine into ligatures. We mentioned the fi and fl ligatures earlier in this book. In older writing, ae and oe ligatures were also common, and other forms, such as ct and st, still happen in ornamental typefaces.

As for systems of marks, you do occasionally see diacritical marks on letters in English words (such as in the word "naïve"), although they're almost never required to understand the text (we still recognize "naive"). This isn't true in most other languages that use the Latin alphabet, but in almost all of them (Vietnamese being the big exception), the number of letter–mark combinations is pretty small.

The point is not that the various more complex typographical effects *never* happen in English or other languages using the Latin alphabet, but rather that they're not *required.* Modern English text is perfectly legible with absolutely no typographic interaction between characters, no diacritical marks, and strict left-to-right ordering. In fact, you can go further: you can eliminate the one wrinkle unique to the Greek and Latin family of scripts—uppercase and lowercase forms—and you can even make all the characters the same width so that they line up as if they were written on graph paper. The text will still be perfectly legible. For example,

```
ANY SUFFICIENTLY ADVANCED TECHNOLOGY IS INDISTINGUISHABLE FROM MAGIC.
```

may not look as nice as

Any sufficiently advanced technology is indistinguishable from magic.

but no one who reads English would look at it and have trouble figuring out what it says. With many other writing systems, this isn't true.

These characteristics lend themselves well to mechanical processing, making it possible, for example, to build a typewriter for the Latin alphabet. The Arabic, Devanagari, and Chinese writing systems, in contrast, don't lend themselves at all well to being written with a typewriter.

This chapter covers the main writing systems for the languages of Europe: the Latin, Greek, Cyrillic, Armenian, and Georgian alphabets, along with the International Phonetic Alphabet. These writing systems share the following characteristics: simple left-to-right line layout, minimal (or no) typographic interaction between characters, minimal (or no) use of diacritical marks, and spaces between words. Most are descended in some way from the Greek alphabet. In addition, this chapter covers the collections of diacritical marks used with these (and some other) writing systems.

■ THE LATIN ALPHABET

As this text is an English-language book directed primarily toward an English-speaking audience, and as the bulk of text stored in computer systems today is in English or other European languages, the logical place to begin our tour of the Unicode character repertoire is with the Latin alphabet. The Latin alphabet is so named, of course, because it was originally used to write Latin (it's also frequently called the Roman alphabet because it was developed by the ancient Romans). The Latin alphabet evolved from the Etruscan alphabet, which in turn evolved from the Greek alphabet. Later, some letters that weren't used in Etruscan were borrowed straight into the Latin alphabet from the Greek alphabet. The Latin alphabet acquired the form we're familiar with sometime around the first century B.C. It originally had 23 letters:

A B C D E F G H I K L M N O P Q R S T V X Y Z

In fact, Y and Z were late additions that were used only for words borrowed from Greek. The letters I and V were used as both consonants and vowels, and J and U were just variant forms of I and V. The letter W was a special ornamental ligature that was used when two V's appeared next to each other. It wasn't until the Renaissance that I and U became consistently used as vowels and J, V, and W as consonants. That gave us the 26-letter Latin alphabet with which we're so familiar today:

A B C D E F G H I J K L M N O P Q R S T U V W X Y Z

The lowercase versions of the letters date back to about the third or fourth century A.D., but were originally just variant forms of the capital letters. Capital and small letters were being used simultaneously the way they are now somewhere around the eighth century.

The Latin alphabet spread throughout Europe first with the growth of the Roman Empire and later with the expansion of the Roman Catholic Church. In more recent times, it has also been applied to a wide variety of non-European languages. Today, the Latin alphabet is used to write more different spoken languages than any other single writing system.

Because ASCII is the most common character encoding scheme used in computers today and forms the basis for so many other encoding systems, the designers of Unicode decided to adopt the ASCII character repertoire directly into Unicode unchanged. Not only do the characters appear in Unicode in the same order, but they even have the same numeric code point values (zero-extended out to

21 bits, of course). In this way, converting between ASCII and UTF-16 or UTF-32 is a simple matter of zero-padding out to the appropriate length or truncating to eight bits, and converting between ASCII and UTF-8 is a no-op.

ASCII includes 52 letters: the uppercase and lowercase versions of the 26 Latin letters. Unfortunately, only two modern languages use the original Latin alphabet with no additional letters: English and Dutch. Even English historically had other letters in its alphabet.

With a couple of notable exceptions, no single language that uses the Latin alphabet adds more than a handful of extra letters. However, they don't all add the *same* extra letters (and many languages don't use all 26 letters of the basic Latin alphabet, either).

For instance, Spanish, Italian, Portuguese, French, and many other languages use accent marks on some vowels to clarify pronunciation or distinguish between two similar words (or forms of the same word). So, in addition to the 26 regular letters, you need the five vowels with acute and grave accents: á, é, í, ó, ú, à, è, ì, ò, ù.

French and Portuguese also use the circumflex accent, giving us five more letters: â, ê, î, ô, û. German, French, Portuguese, and a number of other languages use the diaeresis, adding six more letters: ä, ë, ï, ö, ü, ÿ. (You may think of the ¨ symbol as an "umlaut." The terms "umlaut" and "diaeresis" usually refer to the same mark—a double dot—used to mean different things. The Unicode standard chose to use "diaeresis" as a generic name for the double dot.)

Most of the forms we've just discussed may not technically rise to the definition of "different letters." In most languages that use these marks, they're just considered marks that get applied to the letters: é is seen by French speakers as "e with an acute accent," for example. Unicode supports this type of thinking through the use of combining character sequences: A character code represents the acute accent and can be used in conjunction with the other letters. However, because it's more convenient for most kinds of processing, character encoding standards typically dedicate a new code point value to the accented forms of the various letters. Unicode allows this practice in most cases, for backward compatibility.

Then there are additional characters that really *do* count as different letters in various languages. The letters ä and ö, for example, are thought of as marked forms of a and o by German speakers, but as entirely different letters by Swedish speakers. In addition, German adds the letter ß ("ess-zed" or "sharp s," originally a ligature of ss or sz) to its alphabet. Danish, Swedish, and Norwegian add the letter å. Danish and Norwegian also add the letter ø. French adds the letters ç and œ. Icelandic adds æ (which also appears in Norwegian), ý, þ, and ð. The last two characters, called "thorn" and "edh," were also used in Old English. Portuguese adds ã and õ, and Spanish adds ñ.

As you go further beyond the Western European languages, or back into historical writing systems, or look at phonetic notations, the number of new letters and variants begins to increase much more quickly. The Unicode standard includes 819 Latin letters. We'll take a quick look at all of them.

The Latin-1 Characters

Unicode didn't actually adopt the ASCII characters directly in unchanged, as was stated earlier. Rather, it adopted in the characters from the ISO 8859-1 standard unchanged. ISO 8859-1 incorporated the 128 ASCII characters unchanged and added 128 more. Unicode preserves all 256 of these characters in their original order and with their original numeric code point values (zero-padded to 21 bits). You can convert between ISO 8859-1 and UTF-16 or UTF-32 by zero-padding to the appropriate number of bits or truncating to eight bits. (Conversion between Latin-1 and UTF-8 is, unfortunately, more complicated.)

ISO 8859-1 is the most well known of the ISO 8859 family of character encoding standards first put together by the European Computer Manufacturers' Association (ECMA) in the mid-1980s. ISO 8859 is a family of 14 encoding standards that together provide a way to encode the characters of every (or at least almost every) language used in Europe. Each ISO 8859 standard is a superset of the ASCII standard: The 7-bit values from 0x00 to 0x7F represent the same characters they do in ASCII. The standards vary in their treatment of the other 128 values—the ones from 0x80 to 0xFF. Of the 14 standards in the ISO 8859 family, 10 are variations of the Latin alphabet (the other 4 are Greek, Cyrillic, Arabic, and Hebrew). These are commonly referred to as "Latin-1," "Latin-2," "Latin-3," and so on through "Latin-10." ISO 8859-1, also known as Latin-1, covers the languages of Western Europe. It's probably the most widespread 8-bit ASCII-based encoding standard, and it was the original base encoding for the HTML standard and various other Internet standards.

The Latin-1 standard was designed to cover the main Western European languages: English, French, Italian, Spanish, Portuguese, German, Dutch, Swedish, Danish, Norwegian, Icelandic, and Finnish. It includes all the extra letters discussed in the previous section—á, à, â, ä, ã, å, æ, ç, ð, é, è, ê, ë, í, ì, î, ï, ñ, ó, ò, ô, ö, õ, ø, ß, þ, ú, ù, û, ü, ý, and ÿ—except for œ. Except for ß, which doesn't have an uppercase form, and ÿ, Latin-1 provides both uppercase and lowercase versions of all these letters.

The Latin Extended A Block

There's considerable overlap between the character repertoires of the other ISO 8859 encodings, and none of them seemed to be used often enough to justify keeping their arrangements intact in Unicode in the same way that ISO 8859-1's arrangement was. The letters from the ISO Latin-2, Latin-3, Latin-4, and Latin-5 (8859-2, 8859-3, 8859-4, and 8859-9, respectively) that didn't also appear in Latin-1 were combined together into Unicode's Latin Extended A block, which extends from U+0100 to U+017F. Duplicates and nonletters (in addition to characters that were already included in the Latin-1 block) were removed, and the remaining letters were arranged in alphabetical order. Unlike in the ASCII and Latin-1 blocks, case pairs are adjacent, rather than being arranged into two separate series, one for lowercase letters and one for uppercase letters.

In addition to the letters from the Latin-2, Latin-3, Latin-4, and Latin-5 standards, the designers of Unicode added other related letters that are used in the various European languages. These include some overlooked characters from French (œ) and Finnish (š and ž), and a few others.

The Latin Extended A block brings to the party most of the additional letters necessary to write Croatian (ć, č, đ, š, ž), Czech (č, ď, ě, ň, ř, š, ť, ů, ž), Esperanto (ĉ, ĝ, ĥ, ĵ, ŝ, ŭ), Estonian (š, ž), French (œ, Ÿ), Finnish (š, ž), Greenlandic (ĩ, κ, ũ), Hungarian (ő,ű), Latin (ā, ă, ē, ĕ, ī, ĭ, ō, ŏ, ū, ŭ), Latvian (ā, ē, ġ, ī, ķ, ļ, ņ, ō, ŗ, ū), Lithuanian (ą, ė, ę, į, ū, ų), Maltese (ċ, ġ, ħ, ż), Polish (ą, ć, ę, ł, ń, ś, ź, ż), Romanian (ă, ş, ţ), Sami (đ, ŋ, ŧ), Slovak (č, ď, ĺ, ň, ŕ, š, ť, ž), Slovenian (č, ď, ž), Turkish (ğ, ı, İ, ş), Welsh (ŵ, ŷ), and many other languages.

Some other characters that aren't strictly necessary are also included. There is a single code (U+0149) representing n preceded by an apostrophe ('n) that's intended for Afrikaans, but this character is better represented by two separate code points: one for the apostrophe and one for the n (U+02BC U+006E). In Catalan, a centered dot is often placed between two l's (i.e., l·l) to indicate they should be given the *l* sound instead of the *y* or *ly* sound that a double l normally has in Spanish and Catalan. The Latin Extended A block includes a single code point (U+013F and U+0140) representing an l followed by a centered dot (l·): this, too, is better represented using two code points (for example, U+006C U+00B7). Finally, a single code point representing i followed by j (ij; U+0132 and U+0133) is provided for use in Dutch, because these two letters often form a ligature in Dutch. In practice, it's better to just use the regular i and j with a font that automatically forms the ligature. These characters are drawn from the ISO 6937 standard, a character encoding standard for videotext applications that never caught on in the computer world.

Also included is a code point (U+017F) representing the "long s" (ſ), an alternate glyph for the lowercase s. Until fairly recently, this glyph was used at the beginning or in the middle of a word, and what we now know as the lowercase s was used only at the end of a word. In handwritten text, this glyph just looks like an elongated s (ʃ). This form is still used as a character in the International Phonetic Alphabet (the integral sign in mathematics is basically this same glyph). In printing, however, the bottom of the s was cut off, with a serif added, making it look like an f without the crossbar (or, in some fonts, an f with only part of the crossbar). This style was in effect during the American Revolution, which is why you see things like "Prefident" and "Congrefs" in the Constitution and Declaration of Independence. The long s is still used in the Fraktur typefaces often used to print German. Technically, it is a compatibility character, and one should represent the letter s using its normal code point value and rely on the rendering engine or font to select the right glyph. Occasionally (such as in writing this paragraph), this code point value is useful when you specifically want this glyph.

It's worth taking a second to look at one character in the Latin Extended A block. Consider for a moment U+0110 LATIN CAPITAL LETTER D WITH STROKE, Đ. It looks exactly like U+00D0 LATIN CAPITAL LETTER ETH, and, for that matter, like U+0189 LATIN CAPITAL LETTER AFRICAN D. Even though these three characters look exactly the same and never occur in the same language, they're not unified into a single code point value. That's because they have very different uses, and because their lowercase forms are very different. The lowercase form of U+0110 is U+0111, which looks like this: đ. The lowercase form of U+00D0 is U+00F0, which looks like this: ð. The lowercase form of U+0189 is U+0256, which looks like this: ɖ.

Another character in the Latin Extended A block that deserves a close look is the letter ı, U+0131 LATIN SMALL LETTER DOTLESS I, which is used in Turkish and Azeri (when Azeri is written with the Latin alphabet). Despite its name, this letter isn't really an i at all, but a completely different vowel. The fact that the new vowel's glyph was created by dropping the dot from the lowercase i poses a bit of a problem when it comes to deciding what the uppercase forms of these two letters should be. Logically, what we normally think of as the uppercase I, which doesn't have a dot, becomes the uppercase ı in Turkish or Azeri. To distinguish it, the uppercase form of i has a dot in these two languages: İ. This form is represented in Unicode as U+0130 LATIN CAPITAL LETTER I WITH DOT ABOVE.

This choice poses a problem when mapping between uppercase and lowercase, because now you need to know the language. In every language except Turkish and Azeri, i maps to I when going from lowercase to uppercase; in Turkish and Azeri, i maps to İ. In every language except these two, I maps to i when going from uppercase to lowercase; in Turkish and Azeri, I maps to ı. It could be argued that it would make more sense to just have U+0049 LATIN CAPITAL LETTER I have a different glyph (i.e., İ) in Turkish and Azeri and introduce two new codes that always represent the uppercase and lowercase forms of the letter ı. Nevertheless, the ISO 8859 encodings opted for the alternative case-mapping behavior, and Unicode does it the same way out of respect for existing practice.

The Latin Extended B Block

Things start to get more exotic, and arguably somewhat more disorganized, with the Latin Extended B block. Latin Extended B, which extends from U+0180 to U+024F, contains a large variety of miscellaneous Latin letters that come from many different sources. They include not only more letter–diacritic combinations, but also several letters with multiple diacritics, letters with interesting typographic changes (such as upside-down or mirror-image letters or letters with elongated strokes), and entirely new letters (some borrowed in or adapted from other alphabets, some old letters that have fallen into disuse, and some totally new coinages).

Among the characters in this block are letters used to write African and Native American languages (such as U+0181, Ɓ; U+0188, ƈ; U+0194, ɣ; U+01B7, ʒ); less common European languages, including the Celtic languages covered by the ISO 8859-14 (Latin-8) standard; archaic characters formerly used to write certain languages, including such Old English characters as wynn (ƿ) and yogh (ʒ); letters used in transcribing text in languages that don't normally use the Latin alphabet; and phonetic symbols that aren't part of the current International Phonetic Alphabet.

Unicode's designers tried to keep this section in alphabetical order and to keep case pairs together, but this block has become arranged into several alphabetical series, reflecting groups of letters added at different times. Sometimes case pairs have wound up widely separated, as sometimes a character added at one time for one purpose where it doesn't have a case partner turns out to also be used for another purpose where it does have a case partner. For example, many characters were originally added as part of the International Phonetic Alphabet, which is always lowercase, but are also used in the normal writing of some languages, where they have uppercase counterparts. In these situations, the lowercase version of the letter appears in the IPA block (see page 226) and the uppercase version resides in this block.

Among the characters in this section are the characters used in the Pinyin system of transcribing Chinese into Latin letters; characters for Zhuang (the largest non-Chinese language spoken in China—it's actually related to Thai); less common Slovenian, Croatian, and Romanian letters; letters for Livonian (a rapidly dying minority language spoken in Latvia and related to Estonian); and some of the letters necessary for Vietnamese (this block rounds out the basic Vietnamese alphabet—with the characters in this block, plus the ones in the previous blocks, you can write Vietnamese, needing the combining marks only to add tone marks to the vowels).

A few characters in this block deserve a closer look. From U+01C4 to U+01CC and from U+01F1 to U+01F3 are the Croatian digraphs. Serbo-Croatian is written using both the Latin and Cyrillic alphabets: The Serbs and Montenegrins use the Cyrillic alphabet, and the Croats and Bosnian Muslims use the Latin alphabet, although most Serbo-Croatian speakers can read both alphabets.

Serbo-Croatian spelling is standardized so that there's a simple one-to-one mapping between the letters in the Serbian (i.e., Cyrillic) alphabet and the Croatian (i.e., Latin) alphabet. Because of this correspondence, converting from the Serbian spelling of a word to the Croatian spelling is a simple affair.

One thing that complicates matters is that three of the letters in the Serbian alphabet map to pairs of letters in the Croatian alphabet: the letter Џ becomes dž, the letter Љ becomes lj, and the letter Њ becomes nj. Of course, a computer finds it simpler to switch between the Serbian and Croatian alphabets if the letter pairs in the Croatian alphabet are represented using a single code point, which was done in some vendor standards. For compatibility, single code points representing these letter pairs (or "digraphs") are also included in the Latin Extended B block, although it's generally better to use the separate letters instead.

Each of these letter pairs comes in three flavors:

- One with two capital letters (the "uppercase" version), which is intended to be used when all of the letters in the word are capitalized
- One with two small letters
- One with the first letter capitalized and the second letter small (the "title-case" version), intended to be used when only the first letter of the word is capitalized.

Both the full-uppercase and titlecase versions of the letter map to the uppercase version in the Serbian alphabet. (Interestingly, the ij digraph in the Latin Extended A block, used in Dutch, doesn't have a titlecase version. It doesn't need one because when it appears at the beginning of a word, both the I and the J are actually capitalized, as in "IJssel Meer.")

Another interesting letter is U+01C3, or !. No, this isn't an exclamation point; it's a letter. It represents the retroflex click, the sound you make by pushing your tongue against the back of your upper gums and pulling it away quickly. It's a letter (and a sound) in several African languages. This is an example of how the principle of unification is applied: This character has exactly the same glyph as the exclamation point, but completely different semantics leading to its being treated differently by various processes operating on text (as a letter rather than as a punctuation mark). Because Unicode encodes semantics rather than appearance, these two uses aren't unified into a single code point value.

This example also demonstrates one of the pitfalls you can run into using Unicode: Because the characters look the same, it's very likely that some users, depending on the software they're using, will type the exclamation point where they really mean to type the retroflex-click character. Thus processes operating on the text may need to detect and account for this erroneous use of the exclamation point. Numerous groups of Unicode characters potentially have this problem.

The Latin Extended Additional Block

The Latin Extended Additional block can be considered a block of compatibility characters, so it was positioned at the end of the General Scripts Area, rather than with the other Latin blocks at the beginning. It contains a bunch of extra accented forms of the Latin letters that are used in various languages. These characters resulted from the merger with ISO 10646, and, except for the ones that obviously come from ISO 8859-14, no records were kept on their original sources.

There aren't any characters in this block that can't be represented using a combining character sequence—new Latin characters that *can't* be represented using a combining character sequence are added to the end of the Latin Extended B block instead. Thus, none of the characters in the Latin Extended Additional block is strictly necessary. They're here for compatibility with existing standards or to make life easier for implementations that can't support combining character sequences.

The Latin Extended Additional block is arranged into two alphabetical series with case pairs adjacent to each other. The first series contains a miscellany of accented Latin letters. The second series is dedicated specifically to Vietnamese. All of the basic letters of the Vietnamese alphabet (a ă â b c d đ e ê g h i k l m n o ô ơ p q r s t u ư v x y) are encoded in the other Latin blocks, but to put tone marks on the vowels, you have to use combining character sequences. Vietnamese is a tonal language—the way in which a word is said, what English speakers think of as intonation, is part of the pronunciation in

Vietnamese and many other Asian languages. Different intonations on the same syllable actually make different words. Tone marks are used to distinguish between intonations. Vietnamese uses five tone marks, all of which are attached to the vowel: ấ ầ ẩ ẫ ậ. The Latin Extended Additional block includes all of the Vietnamese vowels with each of the tone marks applied to them.

The International Phonetic Alphabet

The International Phonetic Alphabet (IPA) is an internationally recognized system of symbols for notating the sound of human speech. Real alphabets are basically phonetic in character, but tend over time to acquire nonphonetic properties—the pronunciation of a word changes over time, but its spelling doesn't. Although the phonetic dimension may be lost or obscured, the spelling may still tell you something about the meaning or etymology of the word in question. IPA doesn't mess with any of this history; it's simply a system for linguists, speech pathologists, dialogue coaches, and others interested in the mechanics or sound of speech to accurately notate how somebody says something.

IPA was first developed in 1886 and has undergone many revisions since then. It's based on the Latin alphabet, but includes lots of modified forms of letters. Sometimes, glyphs that would normally be thought of as simply typographic variants of the same letter, such as a and ɑ, are different symbols in IPA, representing different sounds. There generally isn't a systematic connection between the shapes of the characters in IPA and the sounds they represent, other than that the symbol for a particular sound is usually based on the shape of some Latin letter that has that particular sound or a similar sound. As a consequence, lots of symbols may be based on the same letter. Sometimes these are variant type styles, sometimes the letter is reversed or turned upside-down, and sometimes the basic shape of the letter is altered. For example, a stroke may be elongated or a tail or hook of some kind added. Some Greek letters are also borrowed into the IPA.

IPA isn't a completely exact method of notating speech sounds. One of the guiding principles behind it was that if you had a collection of similar sounds, they'd be given different symbols only if some language treated them as different sounds. For example, consider the aspirated and unaspirated versions of the *t* sound. Both sounds are formed by pressing your tongue against the back of your upper jaw, applying some air pressure from your diaphragm, and then let-ting the air escape by pulling the tongue away. The aspirated form allows some extra air to escape, producing a more explosive sound. The *t* at the beginning of *toy* is an aspirated *t*, while the *t* in *stamp* is an unaspirated *t*. English doesn't make a distinction between these sounds; English speakers use one in certain places, such as at the beginnings of words, and the other in other places, but consider both to be the same sound. Quite a few other languages have both of these sounds and consider them to be different sounds, represented with differ-ent letters, so the IPA gives them different symbols. Because the IPA covers so many languages, this practice yields symbols that allow us to make a useful dis-tinction between the initial *t* in most English words, which is aspirated, and the initial *t* in most Italian words, which isn't, even though both languages consider themselves to have just one *t* sound.[1]

These types of distinctions aren't always available in IPA, leading to the use of all kinds of auxiliary marks to help clarify various distinctions. Specialized symbols for things such as disordered speech are also used by specialized users. The bottom line is that there are dozens of ways of transcribing the same utter-ance using IPA, and which one is used depends on who's doing the transcribing and why.

In Unicode, many of the IPA characters are encoded in the various Latin blocks or in the Greek blocks. Some are simply unadorned Latin letters, and others are variants that were already being used as letters is some language. Unicode doesn't make a distinction between regular letters and IPA symbols, just as it doesn't make a distinction between IPA symbols and other kinds of symbols. For example, it doesn't distinguish between the esh character— the elongated s used to represent the *sh* sound in *sheep* (ʃ)—and the integral sign, which looks just like it (this character is different from the long s we discussed earlier, which has the same shape in handwritten writing, but a different shape when printed, ſ). Thus Unicode does not provide an IPA block containing all the IPA characters. Instead, an IPA Extensions block, running from U+0250 to

---

1. This is perhaps not exactly the best of examples: The IPA doesn't really have different sym-bols for these two sounds. It's got one symbol—not too surprisingly, the letter t—for the "un-voiced alveolar plosive." It then adds a second symbol—a superscript h—to show aspiration. So the *t* sound at the beginning of *toy* is actually represented in IPA with two symbols: tʰ.

U+02AF, contains just the IPA symbols that hadn't already been encoded somewhere else.

IPA is a caseless script—effectively, all IPA characters are lowercase. Even where the capital form of a letter is used to make some kind of phonemic distinction with the lowercase form, a small-cap form (a version of the capital letter altered to fit the normal dimensions of a lowercase letter) is always used. At various times, IPA characters used in transcription have become part of the normal alphabet for writing some language (this has happened with a number of African languages, for example). In these instances, the IPA character picks up an uppercase form when it passes into common usage. Because the uppercase forms aren't really IPA characters, they're encoded in the Latin Extended B block rather than with their "mates" in the IPA Extensions block. The Unicode standard includes cross-references for these case pairs.

Because the IPA characters are unified with the normal Latin and Greek letters, it doesn't make a lot of sense to give the IPA Extensions block an ordering based on the characters' pronunciations. Instead, they're arranged in rough alphabetical order according to the regular Latin letters they most closely resemble. As with the Latin Extended B block, the IPA Extensions block includes several alphabetic series for historical reasons.

One essential feature of IPA is the use of diacritical marks and other markings to clarify the meanings of the primary "letter" symbols. These extra marks aren't encoded into the IPA Extensions block either. Instead, they're kept with the other diacritical marks in the Combining Diacritical Marks and Spacing Modifier Letters blocks, which are discussed in the next section.

■ DIACRITICAL MARKS

One of the principles underlying Unicode is the idea of dynamic composition—you can represent the marked form of a letter using two code points: one representing the letter, followed by another one representing the mark. Quite a few of the letters in the Latin blocks are marked forms—base letters with some kind of mark applied. All of these characters can be represented using two code points. To make this possible, Unicode includes a whole block of characters—the Combining Diacritical Marks block, which runs from U+0300 to U+036F.

The characters in this block are special because they specifically have combining semantics. They always modify the character that precedes them in storage. As a consequence, these characters are generally not considered alone, except for the purpose of figuring out that they have combining semantics. Instead, the combination of a combining mark and the character it follows are to be treated as a *single character* by any code processing the text. This single character has the combined semantics of its two constituent characters and is called a *combining character sequence.* More than one combining mark can be applied to the same character—all members of a sequence of combining marks are considered to combine with the character that precedes the first combining mark. If several marks in the sequence are supposed to attach to the same part of the base character, the one that occurs first in storage is the one drawn closest to the base character, with the others radiating outward.

Technically, combining marks aren't "characters" at all. Instead, they're code points that modify the semantics of other characters in some prescribed way. But it's simpler to just call them "characters" like everything else. For an exhaustive treatment of combining character sequences, see Chapter 4.

Combining marks are scattered throughout the Unicode standard. Generally speaking, combining marks used with only one particular script are included in that script's encoding block. The Combining Diacritical Marks block encodes combining marks that are used primarily with the Latin alphabet or with IPA, as well as combining marks that are commonly used with multiple scripts.

The great thing about combining character sequences is that they allow you to encode characters that hadn't been previously foreseen by Unicode's designers, and that they can cut down on the number of code point values needed to usefully encode some script. A huge variety of marked Latin letters were given their own code point values, but still others that are used in real languages must be represented using combining character sequences (and more will arise over time, as the need to maintain the stability of Normalized Form C makes new precomposed characters a lot less useful). The combining marks also allow a certain amount of "future-proofing" against new letter–mark combinations that might be coined in transcriptions of languages not previously transcribed.

The downside of combining character sequences is that they can complicate handling of Unicode text. They enable a single character to be represented using multiple code points, which complicates processes such as counting the number of characters in a field or document. Also, because every letter–mark combination that gets its own code point value is considered simply an alternative representation of the multiple-code-point representation, Unicode implementations generally have to be prepared to see a particular letter–mark combination encoded either way and to treat both versions as being the same.

Of course, one simple way of dealing with this problem is to decline to support the combining marks and combining character sequences. This choice is perfectly legal and, at least with the Latin alphabet, can be done with little loss of functionality, because most of the letter–mark combinations in common use are also given single-code-point representations. The ISO 10646 standard, which is code-point-for-code-point compatible with the Unicode standard, actually defines three implementation levels, indicating an implementation's support for combining character sequences. A Level 1 implementation supports only precomposed characters; a Level 2 implementation supports only the Indic vowel signs (see Chapter 9); and a Level 3 implementation supports both the precomposed characters and all of the combining characters. Thus one way of dealing with the combining character problem is to declare your software a Level 1 implementation of ISO 10646. Unfortunately, this option really isn't feasible with a lot of scripts other than the Latin alphabet, as they often provide no way of representing certain important letter–mark combinations other than combining character sequences (the Arabic alphabet is one example).

For the Latin letters, at least, an implementation can also support the combining marks without requiring special font technology by mapping the text to Normalized Form C before passing characters through to the font engine. Thus, if you have a font that has a glyph for the single-code-point representation of é, you can still draw é even when it's represented using two code points.

Of course, the "right" thing to do is to have a font engine that understands the combining character sequences and does the right thing automatically. It's important to note that this choice isn't always as straightforward as it might first appear. Rendering a combining character sequence isn't always a simple matter of taking a glyph representing the letter and a glyph representing the mark and drawing them positioned appropriately next to each other. Sometimes it's more complicated.

The Unicode standard specifically calls out a few examples. For instance, several Eastern European languages use a caron or hacek (basically, a little v) over some of their consonants (č, š, ž), but this doesn't work well when applied to a character with an ascender, such as a d or an l. In these cases, the caron can extend up outside of its own line and collide with the previous line of text. You can get inconsistent and ugly line spacing trying to avoid this problem. One solution is to move the caron to one side to get it out of the way, but the most popular solution is to turn it into an apostrophe and move it to the side. Thus, when you combine U+0064 LATIN SMALL LETTER D (d) with U+030C COMBINING CARON (ˇ), you get this: ď. It's important to note that this character isn't the same thing as d followed by an apostrophe, and the two shouldn't compare as equal. This could potentially create a problem if the user types the letter d followed by an apostrophe, although this situation probably wouldn't happen with a user using an appropriate keyboard for the language.

Interesting things also happen with the marks that attach to the underside of a letter, such as the cedilla (¸) and ogonek (˛). These marks change shape and morph into various types of hooks and things depending on the font or the language. They may also attach to various parts of the letter depending on where they find a good place to attach.

In particular, the cedilla will often be drawn as a comma underneath the letter. This approach is especially common with letters such as k or n where there's no good spot for the cedilla to attach, but also occurs with letters such as s and t in some languages. Whether the form with the cedilla or the form with the comma is used depends heavily on the language and on the design of a particular font. Unicode provides some explicit characters with a comma below the letter instead of a cedilla, but their use is generally discouraged. In the same way, using combining character sequences with U+0326 COMBINING COMMA BELOW instead of U+0327 COMBINING CEDILLA in languages where the cedilla can be drawn either way might cause problems. You could end up with the same glyph represented in two different and incompatible ways internally without extra work to account for the difference. However, properly designed input methods should generally prevent such problems.

An especially interesting phenomenon happens when the lowercase g is combined with a cedilla, as happens in Latvian. Because of the descender on the g, there's no room to draw the cedilla under the g without it crashing into the next line of text, so most fonts actually draw it *on top of* the g as an upside-down comma (ģ). In this case, a mark that normally attaches to the bottom of the letter moves to the top. The U+0312 COMBINING TURNED COMMA ABOVE combining mark can be used to produce this glyph. Without extra Latvian-specific code that treats a combining character sequence using this mark as being the same as a combining character sequence using the cedilla, you can have different and incompatible representations for the same glyph.

The lowercase i also has interesting behavior. Generally, the dot on the i disappears when a diacritical mark is drawn on top of it: í, ï, î. If you were to apply a diacritical mark to the Turkish dotless i (ı), you'd get the same appearance but a different semantic (and unequal representations). In particular, if you take U+0131 LATIN SMALL LETTER DOTLESS I and follow it with U+0307 COMBINING DOT ABOVE, you don't get the regular lowercase i. You get something that looks just like it, but it's actually the Turkish ı with a "dot" diacritical mark on top. (Fortunately, you never see diacritical marks used with this letter in practice, so this isn't a big problem.)

In some languages, the dot on the i actually sticks around when an accent or other mark is applied. Fonts for languages where this situation arises, such as Lithuanian, might produce this effect, but the representation can be forced by explicitly using U+0307 COMBINING DOT ABOVE. (This choice gives rise, by the way, to a set of special case-conversion rules for Lithuanian that take care of adding and removing U+0307 as needed.)

Some of the combining marks actually overlay the letter to which they're applied. Examples include U+0335 COMBINING SHORT STROKE OVERLAY and U+0337 COMBINING SHORT SOLIDUS OVERLAY. Exactly where these marks are drawn depends on the letter. A stroke might be drawn across the middle of an l, but across the vertical stroke of a d above its bowl.

The precomposed forms of letters with overlay marks, such as ø, ł, or đ, don't decompose to representations using the combining marks. Thus we have another case where you can get similar-looking glyphs with incompatible representations. In practice, this shouldn't be a problem, as, for example, a Danish keyboard implementation would produce the proper representation of the letter ø and you wouldn't have to worry about the other representation that might look the same.

Interesting things can sometimes happen when multiple combining marks are applied to the same letter. In Vietnamese, for example, a few vowels have circumflexes. When a tone mark is also applied to one of these letters, it appears *next to,* rather than on top of, the circumflex. The grave accent appears to the left of the circumflex (ằ), and the acute accent and hook appear to the right of the circumflex (ấ, ẩ). The grave and acute accents actually touch the circumflex in many fonts. This breaks the general rule stating that multiple accents should stack. These examples are Vietnamese-specific, and other examples where multiple accent marks combine typographically in interesting ways are also language-specific. Once again, however, they're cases where more work than simple accent stacking might be necessary to properly display multiple combining marks. (The decomposed representation for the Vietnamese vowels always has the tone mark coming last.)

Another interesting note concerns the double-acute combinations in Hungarian (ő, ű). While each of these letters looks like it has two acute accents above it, you *don't* get these glyphs by combining the base letter with two successive combining acute accents. The double acute is a separate combining mark and isn't the same as two single acutes.

Another issue relates to what happens to accent marks on capital letters. You can encounter the problem of the accent sticking up above the character stream and crashing into the previous line of text. Different typefaces handle this issue in different ways: by making the base letter shorter, by making sure the line spacing is wide enough to accommodate any accents, by altering the accent in some way (in some German fonts, for example, the two dots of the umlaut may appear on either side of an A or O), or by omitting the accent on capital letters. The last solution is fairly common in French typography and may lead to situations where accents in the character storage don't actually appear in the rendered text.

All of the preceding examples generally qualify as language-specific and should be dealt with properly by software or fonts designed specifically for text in that language. There's no guarantee, however, that generalized Unicode software (in particular, fonts designed to display any Unicode character) will do everything right for every possible language Unicode can be used to represent.

Just because a Unicode implementation supports combining character sequences doesn't mean that it will properly draw *every possible* combining character sequence, or even every possible sequence involving characters it says it supports. Some are nonsensical, or at least extremely unusual, and there's no guarantee (and no requirement) that some of the language-specific tricks discussed here will always work. The designers of Unicode have thought of all the potential problems, but when it comes to actual implementations, your mileage may vary.

Isolated Combining Marks

What if you *want* to show the combining diacritical marks in isolation? What if you're writing a book like this one and you want to talk about the marks without attaching them to letters? The Unicode convention is to attach them to a space. In other words, if you want to see ´ by itself, you can represent it as U+0020 SPACE followed by U+0301 COMBINING ACUTE ACCENT. (Actually, the space is the "official" way of representing an isolated combining mark, but certain other characters will work, too. Control characters and paragraph separators will also work, because you can't attach combining marks to them.)

This strategy does not account for the various diacritical marks that are encoded in the ASCII and Latin-1 blocks. They include U+005E CIRCUMFLEX ACCENT (^), U+005F LOW LINE (_), U+0060 GRAVE ACCENT (`), U+007E TILDE (~), U+00A8 DIAERESIS (¨), U+00AF MACRON (-), U+00B4 ACUTE ACCENT (´), and U+00B8 CEDILLA (¸), as well as a bunch of other characters that do double duty as regular punctuation and diacritical marks. Whether these characters should have combining semantics is ambiguous. In some older teletype systems, they did. Some of them functioned as dead-key characters—after imprinting one of these characters, the carriage wouldn't advance. This meant you could get, for example, ä by sending the umlaut followed by the letter a. On all teletype machines, you could make any character become a combining character by following it with a backspace. The backspace would back the carriage up to the position of the character to which you wanted to add the mark (or back to the mark to which you wanted to add a character). However, this usage died out with the advent of the VDT, and these characters lost their combining semantics.

The designers of Unicode opted to explicitly give all these characters *noncombining* semantics. That is, the characters from Latin-1 have a compatibility decomposition to a space and the combining form of the same mark. (The ones from ASCII don't, so that ASCII text isn't affected by Unicode normalization.)

Some of the characters in the ASCII and Latin-1 block did double duty as diacritical marks and other things. For example, the tilde (~), originally intended as a diacritical mark, has also been used as a swung dash and as a mathematical operator (it's a logical-not operator in some programming languages, for example), and the glyph that's used for this code point value is often centered in the line rather than raised. The caret (^) has similarly done double duty as a circumflex accent and other things, including a mathematical operator (in various programming languages, it's either a bitwise-exclusive-or operator or an exponentiation operator). The degree sign at position U+00B0 (°) has done double duty as the ring in å. For all of these cases and a few others, the Spacing Modifier Letters block includes clones that have unambiguous semantics— they're only diacritical marks and always have noncombining semantics.

Spacing Modifier Letters

One class of diacritical marks includes marks that appear to the right of the characters they modify instead of above, below, or through them. Instead of treating these as combining marks, Unicode treats them as ordinary characters—they have noncombining semantics. Because they modify the pronunciation or other properties of letters and are therefore used in the middle of words, Unicode classifies them as "letters" and assigns them to the "modifier letter" (Lm) general character category. These characters are grouped together in the Spacing Modifier Letters block, which runs from U+02B0 to U+02FF.

Most of the characters in this block come from the IPA or from some other phonetic-transcription system. Some are just superscript letters, such as the superscript h for aspiration or the superscript j for palatalization. Other types of marks exist as well: marks for noting accented syllables, long vowels, glottal stops, tones, and so on. As mentioned in the previous section, this block also includes clones of various characters from the other blocks that did double duty as diacritical marks. These clones are always diacritical marks and always have noncombining semantics.

Two characters in this block deserve special mention. One is the rhotic hook (U+02DE, ˞). This character basically represents the *r* sound in words like *car*, *fear*, and *purr*. The *r* sound in these words isn't really a separate sound, but a modification to the vowel. This feature is called rhotacization, and it's represented in the IPA by attaching this little pigtail thing (the rhotic hook) to the right-hand side of the symbol representing the vowel (the American pronunciation of *pear* in IPA is pɝ).

Unlike the other characters in the Spacing Modifier Letters block, the rhotic hook doesn't merely appear after the character it modifies; it *attaches to it*. The shape of the character changes to include the pigtail. Because it attaches to the right-hand side of the letter (i.e., the trailing edge in left-to-right layout), it's not considered to have combining semantics. A character is considered a combining character only if it attaches to some side of the base character other than the trailing edge in its primary layout direction. If it attaches to the trailing edge in the primary layout direction (the right-hand side in left-to-right text), it's merely considered to form a ligature with the character it follows. This is a subtle (and, in my humble opinion, rather meaningless) distinction, but it's important and we'll see lots of examples of it when we look at the Indic scripts in a few chapters.

The second character that bears a closer look is U+02BC MODIFIER LETTER APOSTROPHE. Yes, this is our old friend the apostrophe. Unicode includes a whole mess of characters that look like the apostrophe, but this one is the real thing. It is used for lots of things. In IPA, for example, it represents the ejective consonants, which are formed by closing your throat and using just the air in your mouth. Most of the rest of the time, it represents the glottal stop. (The glottal stop is a break in the sound caused by momentarily closing your glottis, the back of your throat. It's best thought of as the "sound" between the "uh"s in "uh-uh".) This is how it's used, for example, in "Hawai'i."

This character isn't a single quotation mark, however. Unicode has a whole host of other characters for quotation marks, as discussed in Chapter 12. It also isn't the apostrophe used in contractions like "ma'am" or "isn't." This character is generally considered a punctuation mark, rather than a letter. You use the closing-single-quote character to represent this apostrophe as well.

It's also worth calling attention to the "tone letters" in the Spacing Modifier Letters block. The IPA has five special characters for representing five distinguishable levels of tone in tonal languages: ˥, ˦, ˧, ˨, ˩. The IPA also specifies a bunch of forms for representing tonal contours (e.g., rising, falling, falling then rising). These aren't given separate codes in Unicode, but instead are treated as ligatures. If you follow a low-tone character (˩) with a high-tone character (˥) in storage, for example, the two code points are supposed to be drawn as a single rising-tone character (˩). Exactly how the various level-tone characters should be combined to create various contour-tone characters isn't rigorously defined in the Unicode standard. Of course, these forms aren't all laid out in the IPA charts, either; they're ad hoc forms whose generation is more or less self-explanatory.

◾ THE GREEK ALPHABET

The Greek alphabet is the ancestor of both the Latin and Cyrillic alphabets. It was first developed around 700 B.C. and had largely acquired its present form by about 400 B.C. Prior to 400 B.C., a number of regional variants of the Greek alphabet existed. The Latin alphabet evolved from one of these, which explains why some of the Latin letters look different from their modern Greek counterparts. By 400 B.C., all Greek-speaking peoples had standardized on a single version of the alphabet, which has come down to us more or less intact.[2]

The Greek alphabet was originally written right to left or boustrophedon, but by 500 B.C. was always written left to right. As with the Latin alphabet, the lowercase letters were more recent developments, appearing somewhere around A.D. 800. Diacritical marks and spaces developed around the same time, but took a long time to become standardized.

As anyone who's ever pledged a fraternity knows, the Greek alphabet has 24 letters, in both uppercase and lowercase (Figure 7.1). As in the Latin alphabet, the letters of the Greek alphabet don't generally form ligatures and generally don't change their shape depending on context. The one major exception is the lowercase sigma, which has a different shape (σ) at the beginning or middle of the word than it does at the end of a word (ς).[3]

---

2. My sources for most of the historical information on the Greek alphabet, and on how it works, are Leslie Threatte, "The Greek Alphabet," in *The World's Writing Systems,* Peter T. Daniels and William Bright, eds., Oxford: Oxford University Press, 1995, pp. 271–280, and Robert K. Rittner, "The Coptic Alphabet," op. cit., pp. 287–290.

3. In some Greek writing styles, the small letter sigma has only one form, and it doesn't look like either of these.

Α Β Γ Δ Ε Ζ Η Θ Ι Κ Λ Μ Ν Ξ Ο Π Ρ Σ Τ Υ Φ Χ Ψ Ω

α β γ δ ε ζ η θ ι κ λ μ ν ξ ο π ρ σ τ υ φ χ ψ ω

Figure 7.1   The Greek alphabet

The Greek alphabet used to have 28 letters; four are now obsolete: stigma (Ϛ), digamma (Ϝ), koppa (Ϙ), and sampi (Ϡ). For a long time after these letters fell into disuse, however, the Greeks continued to use the letters of their alphabet as digits. The first nine letters of the alphabet represented the values from 1 to 9, the next nine letters represented the multiples of 10 from 10 to 90, and the third nine letters represented multiples of 100 from 100 to 900. Because you needed 27 different letters to represent the numbers up to 999, digamma, koppa, and sampi continued to be used in numerals long after they ceased to be used as letters. (A prime mark, ´, appeared after a sequence of letters used as a numeral to distinguish it from a word.) Today the Greeks use the same digits we use, but you still see the old alphabetic numbers used in numbered lists and outlines.

A number of diacritical marks are used with the Greek alphabet. There were three accent marks: the **oxia**, or acute accent (ά), the **varia**, or grave accent (ὰ), and the **perispomeni**, or circumflex accent (ᾶ). (As this example shows, the perispomeni often looks like a tilde rather than a circumflex.) Researchers think these marks originally indicated variations of tone, but this usage died out a very long time ago, and they have generally persisted just as historical quirks of spelling. Modern scholars generally treat the acute and circumflex accents as stress accents and ignore the grave accent. Graphically these symbols are somewhat different from their counterparts used with the Latin letters—the acute and grave accents are generally drawn with a much steeper angle than is used with Latin letters, and the perispomeni appears, depending on font design, as a circumflex, tilde, or inverted breve.

The two "breathing marks" evolved to represent the *h* sound. In some locations, the letter eta (H) was a consonant and represented the *h* sound; in other places, this letter was used as a long E. The latter usage eventually won out, leaving no symbol to represent the *h* sound.

The *h* sound appeared only at the beginning of a word, and only at the beginnings of words that began with vowels. A mark that looks like a comma ('), the **psili** or "smooth-breathing mark," was used to indicate the absence of an *h* sound, and another mark that looks like a reversed comma, the **dasia** or "rough-breathing mark" ('), was used to indicate the presence of the *h* sound. In transliterating ancient texts, the rough-breathing mark is transliterated as the letter h, and the smooth-breathing mark is ignored. As with the accent marks, the breathings persist as historical quirks of spelling—the initial *h* sound has long since disappeared from modern Greek pronunciation.

In the early 1970s, a system of spelling known as "monotonic Greek" developed that dispensed with the unused diacritical marks (the old system is now known as "polytonic Greek"). The acute accent, called a **tonos** (which just means "accent") is now used to mark stressed syllables, and the other accents and breathing marks have been discarded. This system has been widespread in Greek typography since the late 1970s, and was officially adopted by the Greek government for teaching in the schools in 1982.

Another mark, the **koronis**, which looks just like the smooth-breathing mark (i.e., like an apostrophe), was used in ancient Greek to indicate the elision of two vowels across a word boundary. This mark also isn't used anymore.

The diaeresis (also called the **dialytika** or **trema**) is used in Greek the same way it's sometimes used in English: to indicate that two vowels in a row are to be treated as separate vowels (i.e., with a syllable division between them) rather than as a diphthong. To use an example from English, you'll sometimes see "cooperate" spelled with a diaeresis on the second o: coöperate. The diaeresis indicates that the first four letters are pronounced as two syllables, rather than as a single syllable rhyming with "loop." This kind of thing is optional (and rather rare) in English, but mandatory in Greek.

Given all of these different marks, you'd often see Greek vowels with multiple marks. If a vowel has both a breathing mark and an acute or a grave accent, the breathing mark appears to the left of the accent (ὖ). An acute or grave accent with a diaeresis appears above the diaeresis or between the dots of the diaeresis (ΰ). The circumflex accent always appears above the other marks (ῦ). When the marks occur on a diphthong, the convention is for the marks to appear on the second vowel rather than the first. When applied to capital letters, the marks appear to the letter's left rather than over it.

Finally, there's the curious case of the iota subscript, or **ypogegrammeni**. Beginning in the thirteenth century, scribes began writing the three diphthongs αι (ai), ηι (ei), and ωι (oi), with the iota *under,* rather than following, the other vowel: ᾳ, ῃ, ῳ. This practice has stuck for writing ancient texts, but isn't used in modern Greek. The iota subscript was used only when both letters would be lowercase. When the first letter is capitalized, the iota moves to its customary place to the *right* of the other letter: the "iota-adscript" or **prosgegrammeni** (Αι, Ηι, Ωι). When all letters in a word are capitalized, the iota turns into a regular iota (AI, HI, ΩI).

Punctuation in modern Greek is basically the same as for the languages using the Latin alphabet, with two main exceptions. First, the Greek question mark (or **erotimatiko**) looks like a Latin semicolon (;). Second, the Greek colon or semicolon (the **ano teleia**) is a single centered dot (·).

The Greek Block

In Unicode, most of the characters needed to write modern monotonic Greek are encoded in the Greek block, which runs from U+0370 to U+03FF. This block is based on the ISO Greek standard (ISO 8859-7), which is almost identical to the Greek national standard. The characters that occur in ISO 8859-7 occur in Unicode in the same relative positions, facilitating conversion between the two standards. The Greek block in Unicode has been augmented with some additional characters, and a few characters from the ISO standard have been unified with characters in other Unicode blocks.

Modern Greek uses punctuation and digits from the ASCII and Latin-1 blocks as well as combining diacritical marks from the Combining Diacritical Marks block. As with the Latin blocks, the Greek block includes a few diacritical marks, and the Unicode standard declares the diacritical marks in the Greek block to have noncombining semantics. The combining versions of these marks are in the Combining Diacritical Marks block. The oxia and varia are represented using the regular acute and grave accent characters, the dialytika with the regular diaeresis character, and the psili and dasia are represented using the regular combining-comma-above and combining-reversed-comma-above characters.

The perispomeni isn't unified with any other existing combining marks. Because its form can be either a circumflex accent or a tilde, it didn't make sense to unify it with either. The koronis and the ypogegrammeni have their own code point values in the Combining Diacritical Marks block as well. Finally, the Combining Diacritical Marks block includes a combined **dialytika-tonos** character whose use is now discouraged. Today, we use the separate acute accent and diaeresis combining characters.

The Greek block also includes numeral signs and the Greek question mark and semicolon. The question mark and semicolon characters are here for historical reasons—they're now considered equivalent to the regular semicolon character, U+003B, and the middle-dot character, U+00B7.

The Greek block contains not only the basic uppercase and lowercase Greek letters, but also precomposed forms of the vowels with the tonos and dialytika marks. Keeping with existing practice, the initial/medial and final forms of the lowercase sigma are given separate code point values, even though this choice violates the general rule about unifying glyphic variants. It would be reasonable to have a system always use just one of these codes in storage and draw the correct glyph based on context, but the forms are encoded separately for backward compatibility with existing encodings and to maintain consistency with existing practice. For this reason, code that maps from uppercase to lowercase has to take into account the different forms of the lowercase sigma.

The Unicode Greek block adds the obsolete Greek letters and some alternate forms of the modern Greek letters. Normally, these alternate forms would be considered glyphic variants and the form used in any font would be up to the font designer. Some of these alternate forms, however, are used specifically as symbols rather than letters and so are encoded separately for that purpose (these characters all have "SYMBOL" in their names). Interestingly, these symbols are encoded in the Greek block rather than in one of the symbol blocks. Finally, the Greek block includes letters from the Coptic alphabet (discussed later).

Ancient polytonic Greek can be represented using combining character sequences, although algorithms that map characters from lowercase to uppercase have to be careful with text that uses the combining form of the ypogegrammeni. The combining ypogegrammeni should be drawn as a prosgegrammeni (iota adscript) when combined with a capital letter, and text that maps to all uppercase characters needs to convert the combining ypogegrammeni into a regular capital letter iota.

When representing polytonic Greek using combining character sequences, the dialytika should go first in the sequence if one is present, then the breathing mark, then any accent marks, and finally the ypogegrammeni if present. (This is another set of cases involving language-specific variation of the normal Unicode accent-stacking behaviors; this order of marks produces the correct Greek-specific visual arrangement of the marks.)

The Greek Extended Block

Like the Latin Extended Additional block, the Greek Extended block, which runs from U+1F00 to U+1FFF, includes precomposed forms for all of the vowel–mark combinations needed to write ancient polytonic Greek. It also includes forms of the vowels with macrons and breves, which are sometimes used in Greek poetry.

The block includes both the iota-subscript and iota-adscript versions of the ancient diphthongs that use the iota subscript. The iota-adscript forms are considered to be titlecase letters. The full-uppercase version is two separate letters: the base letter and the iota.

The Greek Extended block also includes a bunch of isolated diacritical marks and combinations of diacritical marks with no letter under them. Like the ones in the main Greek block, these characters have noncombining semantics. After all, the whole purpose of the characters in the Greek Extended block is to avoid using combining character sequences.

As with the Latin Extended Additional block, every character in the Greek Extended block can be represented using a combining character sequence; the characters in this block are here only for compatibility. If new Greek characters are added that can't be represented using combining character sequences, they'll be added to the main Greek block, not to this one.

The Coptic Alphabet

The Coptic alphabet was the last system used to write ancient Egyptian, and it survives as the script for liturgical materials in the Coptic Orthodox church. The Egyptians adopted the Greek alphabet for their language, supplementing it with letters from the older Demotic script when needed to represent sounds for which the Greek alphabet didn't have letters.

Although the Coptic alphabet is based on the Greek alphabet, the letterforms often differ from their forms in the modern Greek alphabet. For example, the sigma (or "semma") in the Coptic alphabet looks like the Latin letter C (or the Cyrillic letter s) rather than the Greek letter sigma.

Coptic was written left to right, and didn't use diacritical marks. The lone exception is a horizontal bar over syllables that don't have a vowel.

The designers of Unicode unified the Coptic and Greek alphabets. The Greek block includes code point values for the Coptic letters that aren't also in the Greek alphabet, and you use the same codes for the letters they have in common as you use to represent Greek. Because the Coptic letters look different, however, you have to use a font specifically designed for Coptic rather than a normal Greek font or a full-blown Unicode font that includes glyphs for all Unicode characters.

Thus, to write a document that uses both Coptic and Greek, you more or less have to use a styled-text format based on Unicode; with Unicode plain text, something (or someone) would have to understand the text to know which font to use for each character. If you use a styled-text format, you can indicate the font changes or attach language markings that a rendering process can use to choose proper fonts. (Although this situation is highly specialized, it's been put forth as an argument for adding a language-tagging facility to Unicode plain text; more important applications involve the use of the Han ideographs. More on this later.)

There's a growing consensus that unifying Greek and Coptic was a mistake. As a result, there's a good chance they'll be disunified in a future version of Unicode.

■ THE CYRILLIC ALPHABET

Tradition says that the Cyrillic alphabet was invented by St. Cyril and St. Methodius in the early 860s in preparation for a mission expedition from Constantinople to the Slavic people in Moravia. The idea was to create an alphabet for writing the liturgical texts in the native Slavic language.[4] There's no evidence of any written Slavic prior to 860 or so.

---

4. My sources for information on the Cyrillic alphabet are Paul Cubberley, "The Slavic Alphabets," in *The World's Writing Systems,* pp. 346–355, and Bernard Comrie, "Adaptations of the Cyrillic Alphabet," op. cit., pp. 700–726.

One problem with this account is that there were actually *two* alphabets created around that time for writing the Slavic languages: Glagolitic and Cyrillic. No one seems to know for sure the origin of either alphabet. It seems clear that what we now know as the Cyrillic alphabet is derived from the Greek alphabet, with extra letterforms for the sounds found in the Slavic languages that aren't also found in Greek. It's unclear where these additional letterforms originated. Several theories have been advanced to explain them, none completely convincing.

The Glagolitic alphabet, on the other hand, has the same letters as the Old Cyrillic alphabet but completely different letterforms for them—letterforms that don't seem to have an obvious origin. Paul Cubberley, in his article in *The World's Writing Systems,* theorizes that the Glagolitic alphabet is loosely based on early cursive Greek and was probably developed by the Slavs in the decades leading up to 860; St. Cyril formalized this alphabet, coined new letters for the non-Greek sounds, and spread it throughout the Slavic world. What we now know as the Cyrillic alphabet (both names came into use long after the alphabets themselves) seems to have arisen after the Glagolitic alphabet. Cubberley theorizes that it was created by Cyril's followers in Bulgaria in the 890s from the "more dignified" uncial (printed) Greek alphabet, with the non-Greek letters adapted from the Glagolitic alphabet. Some of the letterforms in what we now know as the Glagolitic alphabet appear to be later back-formations from the Cyrillic alphabet that happened during the period where both scripts were in use in the same place.

Over time, the Cyrillic alphabet seems to have won out in popularity over the Glagolitic alphabet. The Glagolitic alphabet persisted until the nineteenth century in the Slavic areas under the influence of the Roman Catholic church before finally giving way to the Latin alphabet. The Cyrillic alphabet gradually came to predominate in the Slavic regions under the influence of the Byzantine church, spreading with the spread of the Russian Empire and, later, the USSR.

Unlike the Greek alphabet, which was standardized early among the various Greek-speaking peoples, the Cyrillic alphabet was never really standardized. It had various redundant letters and competing letterforms. A first attempt at spelling reform happened under Peter the Great in 1708 with the creation of a "civil script" intended specifically for the writing of secular texts. Some later changes were proposed by the Academy of Sciences in 1735 and 1738. What we now know as the Cyrillic alphabet, the modern Russian alphabet, was standardized (and further reformed) by the Bolshevik regime in 1918. This alphabet spread to the various countries under the control of the Soviet Union, with changes being made to accommodate the different languages.

The modern Russian alphabet has 33 letters (Figure 7.2). As in the Latin and Greek alphabets, the letters come in uppercase/lowercase pairs, there are both roman and italic versions of the script, spaces are used between words, and text is written from left to right. Modern languages using the Cyrillic alphabet employ the same punctuation marks as are normally used with the Latin alphabet. Although the letters of the Cyrillic alphabet (like the letters of the Greek alphabet) were once used as numerals, today the same numerals used with the Latin alphabet are used with the Cyrillic alphabet.

The Russian alphabet includes two interesting letters: the "hard sign" (ъ) and the "soft sign" (ь). These letters really don't function like most "letters"; instead, they function more like diacritical marks. Instead of representing distinct phonemes, they modify the pronunciation of the letters around them.

To understand how the hard and soft signs work, it helps to understand **palatalization**, one feature of Russian pronunciation that surfaces in spelling. To an American English speaker, the easiest way to understand palatalization is to think of it as the addition of a *y* sound. A palatalized consonant ends with the tongue moving as if you will follow it with the *y* sound. Consider the way many people pronounce the word "Tuesday": It's best approximated as "tyoozday." But the *y* isn't really given its full value; it isn't pronounced "tee-oozday." Instead, the *y* is swallowed up into the *t* sound. Many English speakers turn this sound into a *ch* sound, pronouncing the word as "choozday," but if you don't do that, the sound at the beginning of "Tuesday" is a palatalized *t*. Likewise, the scraping sound at the beginning of "Houston" the way most people pronounce it is a palatalized *h*.

АБВГДЕЖЗИЙКЛМНОПРСТУФХЦЧШЩЪЫЬЭЮЯ

абвгдежзийклмнопрстуфхцчшщъыьэюя

Figure 7.2 The modern Russian alphabet

Russian has a whole bunch of palatalized consonants, and they're generally represented using the same letters as their non-palatalized counterparts. The distinction between the two is generally made in one of two ways.

The first way is through the use of the vowels. A palatalized vowel is a vowel with the *y* sound attached to the front of it; for example, the palatalized version of *ah* would be *yah*. The Russian alphabet has ten vowels in five pairs: а/я (*a/ya*), э/е (*e/ye*), ы/и (roughly *i/yi*, but really и has what we'd call the *ee* sound and ы has a darker *i* sound not found in English), о/ё (*o/yo*), and у/ю (*u/yu*). (Actually, ё and э are relatively rare in Russian spelling—the *e* and *yo* sounds are usually also represented by the letter е.)

The palatalized versions of the vowels are used to indicate an initial *y* sound ("Yeltsin" is spelled "Елцин") or a *y* sound between two vowels ("Dostoyevsky" is spelled "Достоевский"). When it follows a consonant, however, the palatalized version of the vowel actually indicates that the *consonant* is palatalized. The soft sign (ь) is used to indicate that a consonant is palatalized when the consonant is followed by another consonant or occurs at the end of the word.

Normally, the hard sign (ъ) isn't needed; the absence of the soft sign or the use of a non-palatalized vowel indicates the absence of palatalization. The hard sign is used now only before a palatalized vowel to indicate that the vowel, not the consonant that precedes it, is palatalized (i.e., the hard sign indicates the presence of the full *y* sound between the consonant and the vowel, rather than a change in the pronunciation of the consonant).

Diacritical marks aren't generally used with the Russian alphabet, with two major exceptions. First, a breve over the letter i (й) indicates it has the *y* sound in a diphthong (for example, "Sergei" is spelled "Сергей"). This is called the "short i" in Russian and is generally considered a separate letter of the alphabet. Second, a diaeresis over the letter е is sometimes used to indicate it has the *yo* sound (ё), but this generally happens only in pedagogical texts and in rare cases where two words with different pronunciations would otherwise look the same. Most of the time, for example, "Pyotr" is spelled "Петр" rather than "Пётр."

Like the Latin alphabet, the Cyrillic alphabet is used for writing a whole host of languages, mostly Slavic languages and the languages of various minority peoples from the former Soviet Union. In addition, Mongolian can be written either in its native script or using the Cyrillic alphabet (for more on Mongolian, see Chapter 11). Also like the Latin alphabet, the Cyrillic alphabet is a little different for every language that uses it. Most languages that use the Latin alphabet, at least among the European languages, generally just add diacritical marks to the existing letters to cover their own sounds. The languages that use the Cyrillic alphabet, however, are much more likely to add whole new letterforms to the alphabet, and different languages with the same sounds are much more likely to represent them in different ways.

The variation is noticeable even among the Slavic languages that use the Cyrillic alphabet. Belarusian basically uses the same alphabet that Russian does, with the addition of a "short u" (ў) to represent the *w* sound, but the letter I looks different: Instead of using the Russian I shape (и), it looks like the Latin letter I. (Interestingly, the short i still looks like the Russian short i.) The Ukrainian alphabet uses *both* versions of the letter I, and adds a rounded E (є). The Bulgarian alphabet uses the same letters as the Russian alphabet, but treats the Russian hard sign (ъ) as a regular vowel ("Bulgaria," for example, is spelled България).

The Serbian alphabet deviates further from this model. It drops the hard and soft signs and the palatalized vowels from the Russian alphabet and adds some new letters to represent palatalized consonants: Љ, Њ, Ђ, Џ, and Ћ. It also adds the letter J, which is used for the *y* sound in front of a vowel, rather than using a different vowel letter, as is done in Russian (for example, the Russians spell "Yugoslavia" as Югославия, but the Yugoslavs spell it as Југославија). The Macedonian alphabet takes the same basic approach as the Serbian alphabet, but uses different letter shapes for some of the letters: Ђ is rendered as Ѓ in Macedonian, and Ћ is rendered as Ќ. The Macedonian alphabet also adds another new letter: S, which doesn't represent the *s* sound, but rather the *dz* sound.

Once you leave the confines of the Slavic languages, all bets are off. The Cyrillic alphabet is used to write more than 50 non-Slavic languages, and each one adds a few new letter shapes and/or accented versions of the basic Russian letters. As with the Slavic languages, even languages from the same language family having the same basic repertoires of sounds will often use completely different letterforms to represent them.

The Cyrillic Block

The Unicode Cyrillic block runs from U+0400 to U+04FF. The first part of this block, the range from U+0400 to U+045F, is based on the ISO Cyrillic standard (ISO 8859-5). The characters in this range have the same relative positions as they do in the ISO standard, facilitating conversion between ISO 8859-5 and Unicode. This range includes all the characters necessary to write Russian, Bulgarian, Belarusian, Macedonian, Serbian, and (except for one missing character) Ukrainian.

The characters from the ISO standard are supplemented with a whole host of additional characters. The range from U+0460 to U+0489 contains the characters from the Old Cyrillic alphabet that have dropped out of the modern alphabet. It allows the writing of historical texts and liturgical texts in Old Church Slavonic. (Note that the shapes of some letters in the modern Cyrillic alphabet are different from their shapes in the Old Cyrillic alphabet, but that they've been unified anyway. You need to use a special Old Cyrillic font to get the right shapes for all the letters.) This range also includes some diacritical marks that were used with Old Cyrillic but have fallen into disuse (and can't be unified with the marks in the Combining Diacritical Marks block).

The rest of the Cyrillic block contains letters needed for the various non-Slavic languages that use the Cyrillic alphabet. It's broken roughly into two ranges: a range of unique letter shapes, and a range of precomposed letter–mark combinations that can also be represented using combining character sequences. The Unicode standard doesn't provide an official list of the languages this range is intended to cover, but does include the one missing Ukrainian letter and the following additional languages: Abkhasian, Altay, Avar, Azerbaijani, Bashkir, Chukchi, Chuvash, Kabardian, Kazakh, Khakassian, Khanty, Khirgiz, Kildin Sami, Komi, Mari, Moldavian, Mongolian, Nenets, Tatar, Tajik, Turkmen, Uzbek, and Yakut. A number of these languages, especially in the wake of the fall of the Soviet Union, are also written with other alphabets.

One interesting character worth looking at is the palochka, which also looks like the letter I. It differs from the Belarusian I in two regards:

1. It doesn't occur in uppercase and lowercase flavors; it always looks like an uppercase I.

2. It's not really a letter, but a diacritical mark. The palochka is used in a number of languages to represent the glottal stop (the way an apostrophe is in the Latin alphabet) or to turn a preceding consonant into an ejective consonant (the way an apostrophe does in the IPA).

A few other notes about the Cyrillic alphabet:

- A few languages borrow additional letterforms from the Latin alphabet; the Unicode standard makes specific mention of the letters Q and W being used in Kurdish. The Unicode Technical Committee has resisted adding these letters to the Cyrillic block, insisting that the right way to handle this situation and others like it is to use the code point values in the Latin blocks to represent these letters.
- Many alphabet changes have occurred in some of the languages that use the Cyrillic alphabet. The Unicode Cyrillic block encodes only the modern letters used in these languages, not the forms which have become obsolete.

The Cyrillic Supplementary Block

Unicode 3.2 adds a new Cyrillic Supplementary block, running from U+0500 to U+052F, which adds a bunch of letters for writing the Komi language.

▪ THE ARMENIAN ALPHABET

The Armenian alphabet is said to have been invented by St. Mesrop in 407.[5] Like the Greek alphabet, it's a one-language alphabet; it's basically used just for writing Armenian. It originally had 36 letters, but two more letters were later added. The order of the letters basically follows the order of the Greek alphabet, and some evidence suggests that the Armenian alphabet is based on the

---

5. Information in this section is drawn from Avedis K. Sanjian, "The Armenian Alphabet," in *The World's Writing Systems,* pp. 356–363, with a few things coming from Akira Nakanishi, *Writing Systems of the World,* Tokyo: Charles E. Tuttle Co., 1980, pp. 24–25.

Greek alphabet, but the shapes of the letters are wildly different. A number of different sources have been suggested for the letterforms; one theory is that they originate in some cursive Greek form, with the letters for Armenian sounds not found in Greek being supplied by Mesrop.

Aside from the addition of the extra letters, the Armenian alphabet has remained essentially unchanged since its invention, although a few different typographical styles exist. Like the other alphabets we've looked at in this chapter, the Armenian alphabet is written from left to right, with spaces between words, and the letters occur in uppercase/lowercase pairs. The Armenian alphabet is shown in Figure 7.3.

Depending on the type style, certain pairs of Armenian letters form ligatures. Nakanishi mentions that the letters ե (ech, pronounced *e*) and ւ (yiwn, pronounced *u* or *v*) usually combine together into և (pronounced *ev*), as in the Armenian spelling of Yerevan, the capital of Armenia: Երևան.

Combining diacritical marks aren't used with Armenian letters. Although a few diacritical marks are used in Armenian, they don't combine. Rather, they're written *after* the letter they modify, as a superscript. The same happens with certain characters, such as the emphasis mark and question mark, that might be better thought of as punctuation marks than diacritical marks. Armenian uses a few punctuation marks from the other blocks, but has its own period and comma, along with a few other characters.

Like the other alphabets we've considered, the letters of the Armenian alphabet were also used as digits for a long period of time. This practice died out in the nineteenth century, and today European numerals are used.

The Armenian block in Unicode, which runs from U+0530 to U+058F, contains the Armenian letters in uppercase and lowercase versions, plus the various punctuation and diacritical marks peculiar to Armenian. The ech-yiwn ligature (և) also has a code point value in the Armenian block for compatibil-

Ա Բ Գ Դ Ե Զ Է Ը Թ Ժ Ի Լ Խ Ծ Կ Հ Ձ Ղ Ճ Մ Յ Ն Շ Ո Չ Պ Ջ Ռ Ս Վ
Տ Ր Ց Ւ Փ Ք Օ Ֆ

ա բ գ դ ե զ է ը թ ժ ի լ խ ծ կ հ ձ ղ ճ մ յ ն շ ո չ պ ջ ռ ս վ
տ ր ց ւ փ ք օ ֆ

Figure 7.3 The Armenian alphabet

ity. Five other Armenian ligatures are included in the Alphabetical Presentation Forms block for compatibility (see Chapter 12).

One character, U+058A ARMENIAN HYPHEN (‿), deserves special mention. It works the same way as U+00AD SOFT HYPHEN. That is, it's used in Armenian text to mark legal positions where a word may be hyphenated at the end of a line. It's invisible unless it occurs at the end of a line. (For more information on the soft hyphen characters, see Chapter 12.)

▪ THE GEORGIAN ALPHABET

The Georgian alphabet, like the Armenian alphabet, is essentially a one-language alphabet, being used just to write Georgian (although it once was used to write Abkhasian). A number of different traditions explain the origin of the Georgian alphabet (including an Armenian tradition attributing it to St. Mesrop, who is said to have invented the Armenian alphabet), but none seems to have much currency.[6] The first example of Georgian writing dates from 430. The Georgian alphabet seems to be based, at least in its ordering and general characteristics, on the Greek alphabet, although the letterforms appear to have been independent inventions.

A number of different versions of the Georgian alphabet have been used. The oldest is called **asomtavruli** ("capital letters"). Another form, called **nuskhuri**, developed in the ninth century. The two forms were used in religious texts, originally freely intermixed, but later with nuskhuri predominating and asomtavruli taking on the role of capital letters. This style was known as **khutsuri**, or "ecclesiastical writing," and was used in liturgical texts. Today, it's mostly died out, although it's still used occasionally in liturgical settings.

Modern Georgian writing, or **mkhedruli** ("soldier's writing"), developed in the tenth century from nuskhuri. Unlike khutsuri, it's caseless: There are no uppercase or lowercase forms. Effectively, all the letters are lowercase. Like the lowercase letters in the Latin, Greek, Cyrillic, and Armenian alphabets, the letters generally stay within what English printers call the "x-height" (the vertical

---

6. My sources for this section are Dee Ann Holisky, "The Georgian Alphabet," in *The World's Writing Systems,* pp. 364–369, supplemented by Nakanishi, pp. 22–23.

space defined by the height of the lowercase "x"), with various letters having ascenders, descenders, or both. Some display fonts for Georgian get rid of the ascenders and descenders and make all the letters the height of a letter with an ascender, which makes them look like capital letters; these fonts are used primarily for titles and headlines. They're not true capital letters, however. A Georgian linguist named Akaki Shanidze made an attempt to reintroduce the asomtavruli into modern Georgian writing as capital letters, but it didn't catch on.

The Georgian alphabet has stayed relatively unchanged since the tenth century, although there have been a few reform movements. In a reform of the alphabet in the 1860s, several characters were added to the alphabet and five letters corresponding to obsolete sounds were removed. The modern mkhedruli alphabet consists of 38 letters, as shown in Figure 7.4.

As in the other alphabets examined in this chapter, Georgian is written from left to right with spaces between the words. Diacritical marks are not used, and the letters don't interact typographically. For the most part, Georgian uses the same punctuation as is used with the Latin alphabet, with the exception of the period, which generally looks like the Armenian period. As with the other alphabets, at one time the letters of the Georgian alphabet were used as digits, but this practice has died out in favor of the European numerals.

The Georgian block in Unicode extends from U+10A0 to U+10FF. It contains two series of letters: a series of asomtavruli and a series of mkhedruli. The nuskhuri have been unified with the mkhedruli; as a result, you need to use a special font to write in Old Georgian that provides the correct letterforms for the unified letters. The asomtavruli letters are categorized as uppercase letters by the standard, and the mkhedruli are categorized as lowercase letters. Algorithms for converting between cases should generally leave the mkhedruli alone instead of converting them to the asomtavruli. (Unicode doesn't define case mappings between the asomtavruli and the mkhedruli; you want to do that only if you're operating on Old Georgian rather than modern Georgian.)

ა ბ გ დ ე ვ ზ თ ი კ ლ მ ნ ო პ ჟ რ ს ტ უ ფ ქ ღ ყ შ ჩ ც ძ წ ჭ ხ ჯ ჰ

Figure 7.4 The Georgian alphabet

The Georgian block includes only one punctuation mark: the Georgian paragraph mark, which appears at the ends of paragraphs. The Georgian period has been unified with the Armenian period; you should use the Armenian period (U+0589) in Georgian text.

8

Scripts of the Middle East

ost of the alphabetic writing systems descend from the ancient Phoenician alphabet, but they do so along several different lines of descent. In the last chapter, we looked at a collection of scripts that all descended from the ancient Greek alphabet (although the relationship between the Greek alphabet and the Armenian and Georgian alphabets seems to be more distant and speculative, these two alphabets do share many common characteristics with the ancient Greek alphabet).

In this chapter, we'll look at a group of scripts that descended down a different line: from the ancient Aramaic alphabet. These scripts have several important things in common, many of which distinguish them from the scripts we looked at in the last chapter:

- They're written from right to left, instead of from left to right like most other scripts.
- They're uncased. Instead of including two sets of letterforms, one used most of the time and the other used at the beginning of sentences and proper names and for emphasis, as the European scripts do, each of these scripts has only one set of letterforms (in fact, only the European scripts are cased).

- The letters of these alphabets generally represent only consonant sounds. Most vowel sounds are either not represented at all and are filled in mentally by the reader (th qvlnt f wrtng Nglsh lk ths), or are represented by applying various kinds of marks to the letters representing the consonants.
- Like the European scripts, the Middle Eastern scripts use spaces between words.

The four scripts in this group that have encodings in the Unicode standard are Hebrew, Arabic, Syriac, and Thaana.

In addition to sharing the common characteristics listed above, the Arabic and Syriac scripts have another important characteristic in common: The letters are cursively connected, the way handwritten English often is, even when they're printed. This means that the shapes of the letters can differ radically (much more radically than in handwritten English, actually) depending on the letters around them.

▪ BIDIRECTIONAL TEXT LAYOUT

By far the most important thing the scripts of the Middle East have in common (at least from the point of view of computer programmers trying to figure out how to draw them on a computer screen and represent them in memory) is that they're written from right to left rather than from left to right. By itself, this arrangement isn't difficult to do on a computer, but if you mix text written using one of these alphabets with text written using one of the alphabets described in Chapter 7, figuring out how to position all the letters correctly relative to each other can become a rather complicated affair. Because you can end up with a line of text with individual snippets of text on the line running in two different directions, these four scripts are often referred to as "bidirectional" scripts. Computer programmers who deal with these scripts often usually abbreviate this term to "bi-di."[1]

---

1. I've seen numerous different spellings for this term, although it's always pronounced "bye-dye." "BIDI" seems to be fairly common, but to me it always looks like it's pronounced "biddy," so I'll standardize on "bi-di" here.

You don't even have to mix text in different languages to get into bidirectional text layout. In all of these languages, even though letters and words are written from right to left, numerals are written from left to right. Thus text in these languages that contains *numbers* is bidirectional, not just text in these languages containing foreign words or expressions. Because of this fact, the right-to-left scripts can correctly be thought of as bidirectional in and of themselves, not just when they are mixed with other scripts.

Let's take a look at just how this layout works. Consider the Hebrew expression *mazel tov,* which means "congratulations." (It translates literally as "good luck," but is used in the same way English speakers use the word "congratulations," not the way we'd use "good luck.") If you wrote "congratulations" in English, would look like this:

congratulations

In Hebrew, the same thing would look like this:[2]

מזל טוב

The first letter is the one farthest to the right. Just as English starts each line of text flush against the left-hand margin, Hebrew starts each line flush against the right-hand margin.

Notice that the *first* letter is against the right-hand margin. These letters transliterate as *mazel tov.* The letter Mem (מ), representing the *m* sound, is farthest to the right, followed, moving to the left, by Zayin (ז, *z*), Lamed (ל, *l*), a space, Tet (ט, *t*), Vav (ו, *o*), and finally Bet (ב, *v*).

How do you represent this mixture in memory? Well, the straightforward way to do is to place for the first letter first in the backing store:

```
U+05DE HEBREW LETTER MEM (מ)
U+05D6 HEBREW LETTER ZAYIN (ז)
U+05DC HEBREW LETTER LAMED (ל)
U+0020 SPACE
```

---

2. Many thanks to John Raley and Yair Sarig for their help translating the Hebrew examples in this chapter.

U+05D8 HEBREW LETTER TET (ט)
U+05D5 HEBREW LETTER VAV (ו)
U+05D1 HEBREW LETTER BET (ב)

By now, you're probably getting rather impatient. After all, this is so simple as to almost go without saying. It starts to get interesting, however, when you mix Hebrew text with, say, English text:

Avram said מזל טוב and smiled.

Notice that the Hebrew expression looks exactly the same when it's mixed with the English: The מ still goes farthest to the right, with the other letters extending to the left after it. The same thing happens when English is embedded into Hebrew:

אברהם אמר congratulations ותייד.

The same thing happens when you have a number in a Hebrew sentence:

יש לי 23 ילדים.

The number in this sentence is twenty-three; it's written the same way it would be in English.

You can even have these things embedded multiple levels deep:

Avram said "יש לי 23 ילדים." and smiled.

Because this example is basically an English sentence, the prevailing writing direction is left to right (1) and the sentence is justified against the left-hand margin. The Hebrew sentence reads from right to left (2). Even within the Hebrew sentence, however, the number reads from left to right (3):

Avram said "יש לי 23 ילדים." and smiled.

This means that the eye traces a sort of zigzag motion as it reads the following sentence:

Avram said "יש לי 23 ילדים." and smiled.

Now things get interesting. When you mix directions on the same line of text, there's no longer an obvious way of ordering the characters in storage. There are two basic approaches to how a sentence such as

Avram said מזל טוב and smiled.

should be represented in memory. The first approach is to store the characters in **logical order**, the order in which the characters are typed, spoken, and read:

```
U+0073 LATIN SMALL LETTER S
U+0061 LATIN SMALL LETTER A
U+0069 LATIN SMALL LETTER I
U+0064 LATIN SMALL LETTER D
U+0020 SPACE
U+05DE HEBREW LETTER MEM
U+05D6 HEBREW LETTER ZAYIN
U+05DC HEBREW LETTER LAMED
U+0020 SPACE
U+05D8 HEBREW LETTER TET
U+05D5 HEBREW LETTER VAV
U+05D1 HEBREW LETTER BET
U+0020 SPACE
U+0061 LATIN SMALL LETTER A
U+006E LATIN SMALL LETTER N
U+0064 LATIN SMALL LETTER D
```

If you store the characters this way, it places the onus on the text-rendering process (the code that draws characters on the screen) to switch the letters around on display so that they are arranged correctly. The code that accepts the text as input, on the other hand, doesn't need to do anything special: Each character, as it's typed, is simply appended to the end of the stored characters in memory.

The second approach is, somewhat paradoxically, called visual order: The characters are stored in memory in the order in which the eye encounters them if it simply scans in a straight line from one end of the line to the other. This can be done with either a right-to-left bias or a left-to-right bias (both exist in the real world). That approach leads to the following ordering (with a left-to-right bias):

```
U+0073  LATIN SMALL LETTER S
U+0061  LATIN SMALL LETTER A
U+0069  LATIN SMALL LETTER I
U+0064  LATIN SMALL LETTER D
U+0020  SPACE
U+05D1  HEBREW LETTER BET
U+05D5  HEBREW LETTER VAV
U+05D8  HEBREW LETTER TET
U+0020  SPACE
U+05DC  HEBREW LETTER LAMED
U+05D6  HEBREW LETTER ZAYIN
U+05DE  HEBREW LETTER MEM
U+0020  SPACE
U+0061  LATIN SMALL LETTER A
U+006E  LATIN SMALL LETTER N
U+0064  LATIN SMALL LETTER D
```

In this example, the Latin letters occur in the same relative order that they did in the previous example, but the Hebrew letters are reversed. If you store the characters in this way, a text-rendering process can be fairly straightforward: The characters are just drawn in succession from left to right. The onus is now on the code that accepts keyboard input, which has to rearrange the characters into the correct order as they're typed. (The simplest system of all just treats everything as unidirectional text, which puts the onus on the user to type the Hebrew text backward. This approach is suitable, perhaps, for putting together examples in books like this one, but not for doing actual Hebrew text editing.)

Visual order is easier for the rendering engine, but poses serious difficulties for most other processes. You can really store only individual lines of text in visual order—if you store a whole paragraph that way, it becomes incredibly difficult to divide into lines. Also, simple operations such as putting a paragraph break into the middle of an existing paragraph (in the middle of the backward text) suddenly become ambiguous. Although visual-order systems do still exist, they're generally older systems based on older technology. All modern Hebrew encodings, including Unicode, use logical order. (The same goes for Arabic, although visual order was always less prevalent on Arabic systems.)

Unicode goes the other logical-order encodings one better by very rigorously and precisely specifying exactly how the logically ordered characters should be arranged on the screen. That topic is the subject of the next section.

■ THE UNICODE BIDIRECTIONAL LAYOUT ALGORITHM

The Unicode bidirectional text layout algorithm (or "bi-di algorithm," as it is most commonly called) is possibly the most complicated and difficult-to-understand aspect of the Unicode standard, but it's also a vital one. The idea is that with Unicode giving one the ability to represent text in multiple languages as simply as one can represent text in a single language, you'll see more mixed-language text. You therefore have to make sure that any sequence of characters is interpreted in the same way (and has the same appearance, ignoring differences in things like font design) in all systems that claim to implement the standard. If the Unicode standard didn't specify exactly what order the characters should be drawn in when you have mixed-directionality text in a Unicode document, then the same document could look different on different systems, and the differences wouldn't be merely cosmetic—they'd actually affect the sense or legibility of the document.

Unfortunately, the business of laying out bidirectional text can get rather wild. Most of the complicated cases won't occur very often in real-world documents, but again, everything has to be specified rigorously for the standard to work right. As it turns out, the first version of the Unicode bi-di algorithm, which appeared in Unicode 2.0, wasn't specified rigorously enough—holes were discovered as people began trying to write actual implementations of it.

The Unicode 3.0 standard includes a more rigorous specification, and updated versions have also been published as Unicode Standard Annex #9. UAX #9 also includes two reference implementations of the algorithm, one in Java and one in C.

This book will not try to cover every last detail of the Unicode bi-di algorithm here; you can refer to the Unicode Standard and UAX #9 for that. Instead, it will attempt to capture the effect that the Unicode bi-di algorithm is supposed to produce and not worry about the details of how you actually produce it.

Inherent Directionality

Let's start with the basics. The Unicode bi-di algorithm is based on the concept of **inherent directionality**; that is, each character in the standard is tagged with a value that says how it behaves when laid out on a horizontal line with other characters. Those characters that Unicode classifies as "letters" (a general category that includes all characters that make up "words," including not only actual letters, but also syllables, ideographs, and noncombining diacritical marks) are classified as either left-to-right characters or right-to-left characters.

If you have two or more left-to-right characters in a row in storage, they are always to be displayed, no matter what, so that each character is drawn to the left of all the characters on the same line that follow it in storage and to the right of all characters on the same line that precede it in storage. In other words,

```
U+0041 LATIN CAPITAL LETTER A
U+0042 LATIN CAPITAL LETTER B
U+0043 LATIN CAPITAL LETTER C
```

will always be drawn as

ABC

regardless of what's going on around those characters (provided they're being drawn on the same line, of course). Right-to-left characters work in the reverse: If you have two or more right-to-left characters in a row in storage, they are always to be displayed, no matter what, so that each character is drawn to the *right* of all the characters that follow it in storage and to the *left* of all characters that precede it (again, assuming they come out on the same line). In other words,

```
U+05D0 HEBREW LETTER ALEF (א)
U+05D1 HEBREW LETTER BET (ב)
U+05D2 HEBREW LETTER GIMEL (ג)
```

will always be drawn as

אבג

regardless of what's going on around them.

What happens when you have a left-to-right character and a right-to-left character next to each other in memory depends on context. First, the characters are organized into **directional runs**, sequences of characters having the same directionality. Within the runs, the characters are displayed as shown above, which means that the characters on either side of the run boundary in memory will very likely not be drawn adjacent to each other. To see how this idea works in practice, let's say you concatenate the two sequences we just looked at together into a single sequence:

```
U+0041 LATIN CAPITAL LETTER A
U+0042 LATIN CAPITAL LETTER B
U+0043 LATIN CAPITAL LETTER C
U+05D0 HEBREW LETTER ALEF
U+05D1 HEBREW LETTER BET
U+05D2 HEBREW LETTER GIMEL
```

This can be drawn as either

ABCגבא

or

גבאABC

Which of these two arrangements is correct depends on context. If the paragraph consists of just these six characters, which arrangement is correct depends on whether the paragraph is considered a Hebrew paragraph or an English paragraph; this choice is usually specified using a higher-level protocol such as out-of-band style information. In the absence of a higher-level protocol, the first character of the paragraph determines it, in which case the first arrangement would win out, because the paragraph starts with a left-to-right letter (there are ways of overriding this behavior even in plain text—we'll get to them later).

The interesting thing to note about both examples is that the characters on either side of the run boundary in storage, C and alef, aren't drawn next to each other in either arrangement. Drawing these two characters next to each other would violate the rule about how the characters within a directional run are to be arranged.

Combining marks remain largely unaffected by this ordering. A combining mark doesn't have any directionality of its own; it always combines with the character that precedes it in storage, and it takes on the directionality of the character it attaches to. Suppose we throw a couple of combining marks into the previous mix:

```
U+0041 LATIN CAPITAL LETTER A
U+030A COMBINING RING ABOVE
U+0042 LATIN CAPITAL LETTER B
U+0043 LATIN CAPITAL LETTER C
U+05D0 HEBREW LETTER ALEF
U+05D1 HEBREW LETTER BET
U+05BC HEBREW POINT DAGESH OR MAPIQ
U+05D2 HEBREW LETTER GIMEL
```

These marks don't break up the directional runs, and the directionality doesn't affect which character they attach to, or how they attach to that character. The ring attaches to the A, and the dagesh (a dot which appears in the middle of the character) attaches to the bet:

ÅBCࢰࢰ

In other words, combining character sequences are treated as units for the purposes of laying out a line of bidirectional text. Control characters and other characters that have no visual presentation (except for a few we'll consider soon) are similarly transparent to the algorithm (i.e., the algorithm functions as though they're not there).

Neutrals

So much for the easy part. Now consider what happens if you have spaces. Consider the example sentence we used earlier:

Avram said מזל טוב and smiled.

The spaces in "Avram said" and "and smiled" are the same code point value (U+0020) as the space in "מזל טוב" and the spaces at the boundaries between the English and the Hebrew. The space is said to have **neutral directionality**, as do a bunch of punctuation marks. The designers of Unicode didn't want to have two sets of spaces and punctuation marks that were the same except that one set was supposed to be used for left-to-right characters and the other set for right-to-left characters. Instead, they created one set of spaces and punctuation, all of which have neutral directionality.

So what does that mean? Very simply, if a neutral character is flanked on both sides by characters of the same directionality, it takes on the directionality of the surrounding characters. In fact, if a sequence of neutral characters is flanked on both sides by characters of the same directionality, they all take on that directionality. For example, the sequence

```
U+0041 LATIN CAPITAL LETTER A
U+002E FULL STOP
U+0020 SPACE
U+0042 LATIN CAPITAL LETTER B
U+05D0 HEBREW LETTER ALEF
U+002E FULL STOP
U+0020 SPACE
U+05D1 HEBREW LETTER BET
```

would get drawn like this:

A. Bב .א

If a conflict arises—that is, if a neutral is flanked by characters of opposite directionality—then the overall directionality of the paragraph wins. So if you have the sequence

```
U+0041 LATIN CAPITAL LETTER A
U+0042 LATIN CAPITAL LETTER B
U+0020 SPACE
U+05D0 HEBREW LETTER ALEF
U+05D1 HEBREW LETTER BET
```

the space takes on the directionality of the A and B (because the A is the first thing in the paragraph). The space therefore goes to the right of the B, between the English letters and the Hebrew letters:

AB בא

Interestingly, if the overall paragraph direction had been specified as right-to-left, the space would still appear in the same place. That's because it would take on the directionality of the Hebrew letters, causing it to appear to the right of the א as part of the run of Hebrew letters:

בא AB

Numbers

Numbers complicate things a bit. Consider the following example:

Avram said ".יש לי 23 ילדים״

The number is twenty-three, written just as it would be in English. It's flanked by two snippets of Hebrew text: יש לי and ילדים. The sequence to the right, "יש לי", occurs in storage (and was typed) before the sequence to the left ("ילדים"). That is, the two snippets, together with the "23," constitute a single Hebrew sentence ("I have 23 children"),

יש לי 23 ילדים.

and are ordered accordingly.

Contrast that with the following example:

The first two books of the Bible are בראשית and שמות.

It has the same superficial structure as the other example: three pieces of English text interspersed with two pieces of Hebrew text. But here the *leftmost* Hebrew word, "בראשית" (*bereshith*, the Hebrew name for Genesis) occurs first in memory, and the rightmost Hebrew word (שמות, or *shemoth*, the Hebrew name for Exodus) occurs second in memory.

The difference arises because "and" and "23" are treated differently by the bi-di algorithm. The word "and" is treated as part of the outer English sentence, breaking the Hebrew up into two independent units. The "23," because it's a number, is treated as part of the inner Hebrew sentence, even though its individual characters run from left to right. Both Hebrew snippets are therefore treated as part of the same Hebrew sentence, rather than as independent Hebrew words. Because of this effect, digits are said to have **weak directionality**, while letters are said to have **strong directionality**.

Certain characters that often appear with, or as part of, numbers, such as commas, periods, dashes, and currency and math symbols, also receive special treatment. If they occur within a number (or, for some of them, before or after a number), they are treated as part of the number; otherwise, they are treated as neutrals.

Also, numbers are special only within right-to-left text. If a number occurs inside a sequence of normal left-to-right text, it is simply treated as part of that sequence.

The Left-to-Right and Right-to-Left Marks

The basic bi-di algorithm won't give you perfect results with every possible sentence you can contrive. For example, consider the sentence we looked at earlier:

Avram said "יש לי 23 ילדים." and smiled.

Notice the period at the end of the Hebrew sentence. The period is a neutral character, like the quotation mark and space that follow it. According to the Unicode bi-di algorithm, because these three characters have a left-to-right character on one side and a right-to-left character on the other side, they should take on the overall directionality of the paragraph. So the sentence should look like this:

Avram said "יש לי 23 ילדים‏." and smiled.

In other words, with the default behavior, the period would show up at the *beginning* of the Hebrew sentence, instead of at the end where it belongs. In styled text, you could use styling information to control the positioning of the period, but we need a way to make it appear in the right place even in plain text. The solution is two special Unicode characters:

```
U+200E LEFT-TO-RIGHT MARK
U+200F RIGHT-TO-LEFT MARK
```

These two characters have one primary purpose: to control the positioning of characters of neutral directionality in bidirectional text. They don't have any visual presentation of their own, and they don't affect other text processes, such as comparing strings or splitting a run of text into words. The Unicode bi-di algorithm, however, sees them as strong left-to-right and right-to-left characters.This interpretation makes them useful for two things. First, they help in controlling the directionality of neutral characters, which is what we need here. Thus, if you insert a right-to-left mark into our sentence between the period and the closing quotation mark,

Avram said "יש לי 23 ילדים‏.⃞" and smiled.

the period appears in the right place. The right-to-left mark (shown as "RLM" in the example) is a strong right-to-left character just like the Hebrew letters. Because the period is now flanked by right-to-left characters, it is treated as a right-to-left character and appears in its proper place at the end of the sentence. (The "RLM" is there just to show where the right-to-left mark goes; it's actually invisible.)

Second, the left-to-right and right-to-left marks help in controlling the overall directionality of a paragraph. In the absence of a higher-level protocol, the directionality of a paragraph matches the directionality of the first character (of strong directionality) in the paragraph. This result is usually the right answer, but not always. Consider this sentence:

מזל טוב is Hebrew for "congratulations."

The first character in this paragraph is the Hebrew letter mem (מ), which is a strong right-to-left character. Its inclusion at the beginning of the sentence means that the computer will give the paragraph right-to-left directionality. In effect, it will treat this sentence as a Hebrew sentence with some embedded English, even though it's clearly an English sentence with some embedded Hebrew. What you'll actually see is this:

".is Hebrew for "congratulations מזל טוב

If you stick a left-to-right mark at the beginning of the sentence, *it* becomes the first character in the paragraph with strong directionality. It's a left-to-right character, so the paragraph is treated as a left-to-right paragraph, even though it begins with a Hebrew letter, producing the arrangement we want. (Again, because the left-to-right mark is invisible, its presence doesn't do anything except affect the arrangement of the other characters.)

The Explicit Override Characters

Unicode provides a few other invisible formatting characters that can be used to control bidirectional layout. In some situations, you want to explicitly override the inherent directionality of a Unicode character. For example, imagine that you have part numbers that include both English and Hebrew letters, along with digits, and you want to suppress the reordering that would normally happen. The left-to-right override (U+202D) and right-to-left override (U+202E) characters force all of the characters that follow them to be treated as strong left-to-right and strong right-to-left characters, respectively. The pop-directional-formatting character (U+202C) cancels the effect of the other two, returning the bi-di algorithm to its normal operation. For example, we saw earlier that the sequence

```
U+0041 LATIN CAPITAL LETTER A
U+0042 LATIN CAPITAL LETTER B
```

```
U+0043 LATIN CAPITAL LETTER C
U+05D0 HEBREW LETTER ALEF
U+05D1 HEBREW LETTER BET
U+05D2 HEBREW LETTER GIMEL
```

is drawn like this:

אבגABC

But if we insert the proper override characters

```
U+0041 LATIN CAPITAL LETTER A
U+0042 LATIN CAPITAL LETTER B
U+0043 LATIN CAPITAL LETTER C
U+202D LEFT-TO-RIGHT OVERRIDE
U+05D0 HEBREW LETTER ALEF
U+05D1 HEBREW LETTER BET
U+05D2 HEBREW LETTER GIMEL
U+202C POP DIRECTIONAL FORMATTING
```

you get this instead:

ABCאבג

The Explicit Embedding Characters

Sometimes you wind up with multiple levels of embedding when mixing languages. For example, consider the following sentence:

"The first two books of the Bible are בראשית and שמות." אברהם אמר

Here, you've got a Hebrew sentence with an English sentence embedded in it as a quotation, and then you've got some Hebrew words embedded in the English sentence. You can get this kind of effect with numbers in right-to-left text without doing anything special, but you can't do it with this kind of text. With the basic bi-di algorithm, you get the following result:

"שמות. and בראשית The first two books of the Bible are" אברהם אמר

The two Hebrew words in the English sentence are treated as part of the Hebrew sentence instead, breaking the English sentence up into two separate English snippets. Unicode provides two more invisible formatting characters to allow you to obtain the desired effect: the left-to-right embedding (U+202A) and the right-to-left embedding (U+202B) characters. The pop-directional-format character (U+202C) is also used to terminate the effects of these two characters.

If you precede the English sentence with U+202A LEFT-TO-RIGHT EMBEDDING and follow it with U+202C POP DIRECTIONAL FORMAT, these characters force the Hebrew words to be treated as part of the English sentence, producing the desired effect.

Mirroring Characters

Several neutral characters—parentheses and brackets chief among them—not only take on the directionality of the characters around them, but also have a different glyph shape depending on their directionality. For example, consider the following examples:

Avram (the neighbor) asked for my help.

אברהם (השכן) ביקש את עזרתי.

In both cases, the parenthesis at the beginning of the parenthetical expression is represented by U+0028 LEFT PARENTHESIS, even though it looks one way [(] in the English sentence and a different way [)] in the Hebrew sentence. The same goes for the parenthesis at the other end of the parenthetical expression. (The name "LEFT PARENTHESIS" is an unfortunate side effect of the unification of Unicode with ISO 10646, which used that name.) In other words, the code point value U+0028 encodes the semantic "parenthesis at the beginning of a parenthetical expression," not the glyph shape (.

The Unicode standard includes several dozen characters with the mirroring property, mostly various types of parentheses, brackets, and math symbols. Many of these, such as the parentheses and brackets, occur in mirror-image pairs that can (in most fonts) simply exchange glyph shapes when they occur in right-to-left text. Others don't occur in mirror-image pairs. Fonts containing these characters have to include alternate glyphs that can be used in a right-to-left context.

Line and Paragraph Boundaries

It's important to note that bidirectional reordering takes place on a line-by-line basis. Consider our original example:

Avram said מזל טוב and smiled.

If this text is split across two lines with the line break occurring in the middle of the Hebrew expression such that only one of the Hebrew words can appear on the first line, it'll be the *first* Hebrew word, the one to the right, even though this makes the words appear to come in a different order than when the whole sentence is on one line. That is, when the sentence is split across two lines, you get

Avram said מזל

טוב and smiled.

and not

Avram said טוב

מזל and smiled.

In other words, bidirectional reordering takes place *after* the text has been broken up into lines.

Also, the effects of bidirectional reordering are limited in scope to a single paragraph. The Unicode bi-di algorithm never has to consider more than a single paragraph at a time. Paragraph separators also automatically cancel the effect of any directional-override or directional-embedding characters.

■ BIDIRECTIONAL TEXT IN A TEXT-EDITING ENVIRONMENT

Bidirectional text poses a few challenging problems for text-editing applications. Consider our earlier example:

ABCאבג

This is represented in memory as follows:

```
U+0041 LATIN CAPITAL LETTER A
U+0042 LATIN CAPITAL LETTER B
U+0043 LATIN CAPITAL LETTER C
U+05D0 HEBREW LETTER ALEF
U+05D1 HEBREW LETTER BET
U+05D2 HEBREW LETTER GIMEL
```

Let's say you click to place the insertion point here:

$$\textbf{ABC}\textbf{גב}\textbf{א}$$

This position is ambiguous. It can be between the letter C and the letter א, or it can be at the end of the string, after the letter ג. The same is true if you put the insertion point here:

$$\textbf{ABC}\textbf{גבא}|$$

This spot can be either of the same two positions. So if you put the insertion point in either of these spots and start typing, where should the new characters go?

Getting the right answer in this case can be tricky. One solution is to put the newly typed character at whatever position in storage will cause it to appear at the visual position where the user clicked. For instance, if you click here

$$\textbf{ABC}\textbf{גב}\textbf{א}$$

and type an English letter, it goes at the end of the English letters, before the Hebrew. But if you type a Hebrew letter, it goes at the end, after the other Hebrew letters. On the other hand, if you click here

$$\textbf{ABC}\textbf{גבא}|$$

the opposite happens. If you type an English letter, it goes at the end, after the Hebrew; if you type a Hebrew letter, it goes at the beginning of the Hebrew letters.

Most text editors actually handle this problem in the opposite way, which is easier to implement. That is, they identify each visual position with a particular position in the character storage, and draw *two* insertion points on the screen to show the two possible places in the text where newly typed characters might appear:

$$\text{ABC}\,\text{אבכ}$$

This example shows the position in the storage between the English and Hebrew letters. The leftward tick on the first insertion point shows that a new English letter would go there, and the rightward tick on the second insertion point shows that a new Hebrew letter would go there.

Selection highlighting can pose similar challenges. Consider this example:

Avram said מזל טוב and smiled.

If you drag from here

Avram said מזל טוב and smiled.

to here

Avram said טוב מזל and smiled.

it can mean two different things. In many applications, this gesture will select a contiguous range of characters in storage, starting where you clicked and ending where you released. This produces a visually discontiguous selection:

Avram said טוב מזל and smiled.

This approach, called **logical selection**, is a little simpler to handle in code because we're always dealing with logically continuous ranges of text. It's more complicated to draw, however, and can be jarring for users who aren't used to it. The opposite approach, **visual selection**, selects a visually contiguous piece of text,

Avram said טוב מזל and smiled.

even though this choice represents two separate and distinct ranges of text in the character storage. This result looks more natural, but requires a lot more behind-the-scenes juggling on the part of the text editor.

Let's see what effect the two selection types have on a copy-and-paste operation. Imagine you make that selection gesture on an editor that uses logical selection:

Avram said מזל טוב and smiled.

You've selected a logically continuous range of text. If you pick Cut from the Edit menu, you now have this:

Avram טוב and smiled.

If you immediately choose Paste from the Edit menu, you should see your original text again. This is simple to do: The insertion point marks the spot in the storage where you deleted the text, and it gets inserted in one logical lump, with the bi-di algorithm reordering things to look like they did before. Now suppose you did the same selection gesture on an editor that supported visual selection:

Avram said טוב מזל and smiled.

You pick Cut from the Edit menu and get this:

Avram מזל and smiled.

Again, if you immediately choose Paste, you should see the original text again. In the same way, if you pasted the text into any other spot in the document, the result should keep the appearance that the text had when you originally selected it. To put the text back the way it was in one paste operation requires the program to keep the two pieces of text you originally selected separate and to paste them into *two separate places* in storage such that they'll be drawn next to each other on the screen at the specified position. This approach can require some interesting behind-the-scenes juggling. For more on the issue of dealing with bidirectional text in a text editing environment and on implementing the bi-di algorithm, see Chapter 16.

With this primer on bidirectional text layout under our belts, we are now ready to look at the individual alphabets in Unicode that require it.

■ THE HEBREW ALPHABET

What we now know as the Hebrew alphabet dates back to about the second century B.C., and has come down through the years more or less unchanged.[3] It evolved from the Aramaic alphabet, which in turn grew out of the Phoenician alphabet. An earlier Hebrew alphabet dated back to about the ninth century B.C., but it gradually died out as the ancient Israelites were dominated by a succession of Aramaic-speaking groups, including the Assyrians, Babylonians, and Persians. When the Holy Land was conquered by the Greeks, the Hebrew language made a comeback and a new alphabet for it was developed from the Aramaic alphabet. The modern Hebrew alphabet is often called "square Hebrew" to distinguish it from the more rounded form of the older Hebrew alphabet, which continued to be used by the Samaritans up to relatively recent times.

Like the Phoenician alphabet from which it ultimately derived, the Hebrew alphabet consists of 22 letters, all consonants (Figure 8.1). Because the Hebrew alphabet, like all the alphabets discussed in this chapter, is written from right to left, the first letter of the alphabet, alef (א), is farthest to the right.

The letters of the Hebrew alphabet don't generally interact typographically. Although there are no uppercase and lowercase forms, five of the letters have different shapes when they appear at the end of a word: כ becomes ך, מ becomes ם, נ becomes ן, פ becomes ף, and צ becomes ץ.

אבגדהוזחטיכלמנסעפצקרשת

Figure 8.1   The Hebrew alphabet

---

3. My source for information on the Hebrew alphabet is Richard L. Goerwitz, "The Jewish Scripts," in *The World's Writing Systems*, pp. 487–498.

The fact that the Hebrew alphabet has no vowels came to be a problem as, over time, pronunciation diverged from spelling and variant pronunciations developed. Some of the consonants were eventually pressed into double duty as vowels in certain contexts and certain positions within words. But as detail-perfect interpretation of Biblical texts became more and more important, a more precise system was needed. Because the original consonants were considered so important in Biblical texts, the solution developed didn't involve the creation of new letters; instead, a system of **points**, various marks drawn above, below, and sometimes inside the consonants, outside the normal line of text, evolved. The first pointing systems evolved around A.D. 600, and the modern system of points was standardized by about 1200.

Three categories of points exist. The first includes diacritical marks that change the sound of a consonant. The most important of these is the **dagesh**, a dot drawn inside a Hebrew letterform. Exactly what the dagesh means depends on the letter with which it's being used, but it most often gives a letter a stopped sound where it would normally have a more liquid sound. The letter bet (בּ), for example, is pronounced like *b* when it's written with a dagesh (בּ), but is closer to a *v* without it. The **rafe**, a line above the letter, is used less often, and has the opposite effect. בֿ is pronounced like *v*. The Hebrew letter shin (ש) can be pronounced as either *s* or *sh*. Sometimes a dot is drawn over the letter to indicate which pronunciation it has: If the dot is drawn over the rightmost tine of the shin (שׁ), it's pronounced *sh;* if it's drawn over the leftmost tine (שׂ), it's pronounced *s*.

The second category includes the vowel points. There are eleven points that are used to indicate the vowel sounds that follow a consonant. With one exception, they're all drawn under the letter:

The **sheva**, a pair of vertically arranged dots under a letter, is used to indicate the absence of a vowel sound following that letter:

בְ

The vowel points are generally not used in modern Hebrew, except when their absence is ambiguous, in learning materials, and in Biblical and other liturgical texts. In other words, Hebrew normally looks something like this:

הדו ליהוה כי-טוב: כי לעולם חסדו

As this text is a Bible verse (Psalm 107:1, to be exact), however, it's usually written like this:

הֹדוּ לַיהֹנָה כִּי-טֹוב: כִּי לְעֹולָם חַסְדֹּו

The third category of points is the **cantillation marks**, an elaborate system of marks originally used to indicate accent and stress, and therefore also as punctuation. These points now generally appear only in Biblical and liturgical texts, where they are used to indicate accent and intonation when a text is chanted.

Diacritical marks (such as the dagesh) and vowel points generally are drawn on different parts of a letter, but either may be drawn on the same side of a letter as certain cantillation marks. The rules for how the various marks are positioned relative to each other when multiple marks are attached to the same letter can get rather complicated.

The Hebrew alphabet is used not only for writing Hebrew, but for writing some other languages spoken by the Jews of the Diaspora, especially Yiddish and Ladino. Certain letter–point combinations are more common in these languages, and sometimes these languages add extra diacritical marks beyond those used for Hebrew.

In addition, certain pairs of Hebrew letters are treated as distinct letters with their own phonetic values, in a manner similar to the way the double l (ll) is treated as a separate letter having the *y* sound in Spanish. In particular, three double-letter combinations—יי, וו, and וי—are used in Yiddish and some other languages as additional letters. That is, in these languages, וו isn't just two וs in a row, but a whole different letter.

As with many of the other alphabets we've looked at, the letters of the Hebrew alphabet were once used to write numbers as well (the system is a little more complicated than other alphabetical number systems). Today, the regular "European" numerals are used, although the old alphabetic numbering system continues to be used for item numbers in numbered lists. Modern Hebrew also uses European punctuation now—the old native Hebrew punctuation's use is restricted to Biblical and liturgical texts.

The Hebrew Block

The Unicode Hebrew block, which runs from U+0590 to U+05FF, contains all the marks necessary to write Hebrew. In addition to the 22 basic letters, the word-final forms of the five letters that have word-final forms are given their own separate code points. This practice seems to violate the normal Unicode rule about not encoding glyphic variants, but is in keeping with the practice in other Hebrew encodings. In fact, sometimes the word-final forms of these letters aren't actually used at the ends of words—this happens with many borrowed foreign words, for example. As a result, the choice of which form of the letter to use becomes a matter of spelling; you *can't* have the rendering software automatically pick the proper glyph.

The letters have the same relative ordering in Unicode as they do in the ISO Hebrew standard (ISO 8859-8), but the ISO standard doesn't include the points.

The Unicode Hebrew block also includes all of the various points and cantillation marks, encoded as combining marks. The three letter pairs that are treated as separate letters in Yiddish are also given single code points in the Hebrew block. The dots that distinguish the two versions of ש are encoded in this block as well. What they look like when attached to other letters isn't defined by the standard; the standard specifically calls this practice "an error." Unlike in the Latin or Greek alphabets, where accented forms of letters are usually represented with their own code point values, Hebrew includes too many letter–mark combinations for this approach to be feasible.

A few pointed Hebrew letters, mainly used in Yiddish, are encoded in the Alphabetic Presentation Forms block (see Chapter 12). Pointed Hebrew letters are almost always represented using combining character sequences, even in non-Unicode encodings, and these presentation forms are rarely supported in software and fonts.

■ THE ARABIC ALPHABET

The Arabic alphabet, like the Hebrew alphabet, evolved from the ancient Aramaic alphabet, but developed quite a bit later. The first inscriptions using the Arabic alphabet date from the fourth century A.D.[4] Unlike the Hebrew alphabet, the Arabic alphabet developed from a cursive form of the Aramaic alphabet, where the letters are connected and words are written without lifting the pen. As the letters became more connected, they also started to look more the same, eventually evolving into 14 families of similarly shaped letters in a 28-letter alphabet. Marks used to differentiate between letters with the same shape were developed sometime during the seventh century; the patterns of dots used for this purpose today date to the ninth century. Even though they look like diacritical marks, they're not: They're integral parts of the letters.

The Arabic alphabet has 28 letters, as shown in Figure 8.2. As in the Hebrew alphabet, the letters in the Arabic alphabet are all consonants, although three of them do double duty as long vowels. The short vowels (and occasionally the long vowels) aren't normally written; when they are, however, these marks are written above and below the normal sequence of consonantal letters. You generally see the vowels only in the Koran or other liturgical texts, in teaching materials, in cases where a word might otherwise be misread, and for decorative purposes in signs, titles, and calligraphy. There is also an elaborate system of cantillation marks and other markings that are used exclusively in Koranic texts.

In addition to the vowel signs, Arabic includes a couple of other marks. The **hamza** (ء) is used to indicate a glottal stop, usually in combination with one of the long-vowel letters (for example, ا + ء produces أ). Depending on the letters involved, the hamza can appear either above or below the letter to which it's ap-

ا ب ت ث ج ح خ د ذ ر ز س ش ص ض ط ظ ع غ ف ق ك ل م ن ه و ي

Figure 8.2 The Arabic alphabet

4. My sources for this section are Thomas Bauer, "Arabic Writing," in *The World's Writing Systems,* pp. 559–568, and Thomas Milo, "Creating Solutions for Arabic: A Case Study," in *Proceedings of the Seventeenth International Unicode Conference,* September 6, 2000, session TB3.

plied. The long vowels with the hamza are sometimes treated as different letters, because the presence or absence of the hamza is often a matter of spelling.

More rarely, you'll see the **madda**, a curved horizontal stroke, used with the letter alef, one of the long vowels, to indicate a glottal stop followed by the vowel sound (آ, which is shorthand for اا). Another mark, the **shadda** (ّ), is used to mark **consonant gemination**, which is basically the doubling of a consonant sound. (To understand consonant gemination, think about the way most Americans say the word "fourteen": most of us say "fort-teen," pronouncing a distinct *t* sound at the end of "fort" and another distinct *t* sound at the beginning of "teen," rather than "for-teen." The letter t is a geminated consonant.)

In addition, two Arabic letters take special shapes under certain circumstances and sometimes are considered separate letters. The letter alef (ا) is sometimes written as ى at the end of a word. This form is called the **alef maksura**. It looks like the letter yeh (ي), except that it lacks the dots (the letter yeh also loses its dots, but keeps its identity, when it's combined with the hamza: ئ). The letter teh (ت) takes a special form (ة) at the end of a word when it represents the feminine ending. This form is called the **teh marbuta**.

The Arabic alphabet is used for many languages besides Arabic. Because of the importance of the Koran in Islam, and the doctrine that the Koran (written in Arabic using Arabic letters) is eternal and uncreated, the Arabic alphabet is used almost everywhere throughout the Muslim world. Some of these places have also adopted the Arabic language; many others have adopted only the Arabic alphabet to write their own language. (This phenomenon, of course, isn't unusual: The Latin alphabet basically followed the influence of the Roman Catholic church, the Greek and Cyrillic alphabets followed the influence of the Greek Orthodox church, and the Hebrew alphabet followed the spread of Judaism.) At one time, in fact, the Arabic alphabet was used everywhere in the Muslim world. The few places where it isn't now are the results of political forces (the Latin alphabet being imposed by the Ataturk regime in Turkey, for example, or the former Soviet Union imposing the Cyrillic alphabet on the Muslim people within its borders).

As with the other alphabets used for multiple languages, many letters have been added to the Arabic language to adapt it for those other languages. These new letters tend to take the shapes of existing Arabic letters. They wind up being differentiated in a number of ways: the use of dots or other marks, the use of miniaturized versions of other letters as diacritics, differences in the way the letters join to their neighbors, or variant shapes of the same letter in Arabic turning into distinct letters in some other languages.

Perhaps the biggest thing that sets the Arabic alphabet apart from the other alphabets we've examined so far is its cursive nature. Generally speaking, the letters in a word all connect to their neighbors, turning a single word into one continuous pen stroke (often with dots and other marks around it), much like in standard handwritten English. Much more than in handwritten English, however, the letters change shape greatly depending on the letters around them.

The flowing nature and high elasticity of the letters of the Arabic alphabet mean that it lends itself particularly well to calligraphy. Because depictions of people and animals aren't allowed inside Muslim mosques, calligraphy has long been the primary form of Muslim religious art, and Arabic calligraphy can be extraordinarily beautiful. Many different calligraphic styles have been developed for writing Arabic.

One thing all of these styles share in common is that a letter tends to join to the letter that follows it either on the left-hand side or on the bottom. In handwritten Arabic, individual words tend to slope down and to the left, frequently overlapping the words on either side:

This means that in handwritten Arabic, spaces between words aren't really necessary. It also makes printing Arabic quite difficult and involved.

This practice also means that when Arabic text is justified against both margins, extra space on the line isn't taken up by widening the spaces between words, as it is in the other languages we've looked at so far. Instead, words can be elongated or shortened by using different forms of the various letters, or by inserting extenders called **kashidas** or **tatweels**, such as the long one in the preceding example.

The various ways that the letters can combine can also make it a fairly complicated affair to determine where the dots, vowels, and other marks that may accompany the letters go:

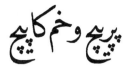

In modern times, simplified versions of the Arabic alphabet that are easier to print have developed. Most modern printed Arabic, especially that generated using computers, uses a simplified version of the Arabic alphabet that gives each letter up to four shapes. The four shapes are designed so that all the letters connect along a common baseline. Because the baseline is horizontal rather than slanted, spaces *are* used between words.

For example, the letter heh looks like this by itself:

Three of them in a row look like this:

ههه

Likewise, the letter sheen looks like this when it stands alone:

ش

The long bowl on the left goes away when it connects with a neighboring letter. Three sheens in a row look like this:

ششش

This is a good example of how some sequences of Arabic letters can turn into wiggly lines without the dots there to help discern the letters. In handwritten or better-printed Arabic, the shapes of the various humps can vary to help differentiate the letters, but this distinction is lost in simplified printed Arabic.

The four letter shapes are usually called **initial**, **medial**, **final**, and **independent**, but these names are somewhat misleading. They tend to suggest that the initial and final forms are used only at the beginnings and ends of words, with the medial form used elsewhere and the independent form used only in one-letter words or when talking about a letter by itself. In reality, some letters don't have all four forms, leading to breaks in the middle of a word. The letter alef (ا), for example, doesn't connect to the letter that follows it, so the initial form, rather than the medial form, of a letter is used when it follows alef. For example, despite the breaks in the line, this is all one word:

الأفـغـانــي

Even in simplified Arabic, special cases arise. The letter lam (ل) and the letter alef (ا) would look like this together if their normal initial and final forms were used:

ال

In actual practice, they don't join that way. Instead of forming a U shape, the two vertical strokes cross each other, forming a loop at the bottom:

لا

If the lam is joined to another character on its right, however, you don't get the loop. Instead of forming a U shape, you get a somewhat more zigzaggy form:

ﻼ

These two combinations are often called the **lam-alef ligatures**. They are required, even in simplified Arabic printing. The U shape never happens.

In simplified Arabic printing, the kashida, normally a curved line, becomes a straight line, so as to harmonize better with the letters that surround it.

This style of Arabic printing loses some of the grace and legibility of the more traditional forms, as shown here:

فلكحلهم

simplified connected script

فلكحلهم

authentic compound

Nevertheless, it's still completely legible to Arabic speakers, and a lot simpler to deal with in computerized or mechanized systems. Even in languages such as Urdu and Farsi that have traditionally used the more ornate Nastaliq form of the Arabic alphabet, the simplified letterforms are often used today.

At least in some places, Arabic doesn't use the so-called Arabic numerals ("1234567890"). Instead, *real* Arabic numerals (Arabs call these "Hindi numerals," because they originated in India, even though the Indian forms are different yet again) look like this:

١ ٢ ٣ ٤ ٥ ٦ ٧ ٨ ٩ ٠

Interestingly, even though Arabic writing runs from right to left, numbers, even when written with the native Arabic numerals, run from left to right. For example, 1,234.56 looks like this:

١'٢٣٤,٥٦

There are actually two forms of native Arabic digits. The following forms are used in Farsi:

١ ٢ ٣ ۴ ۵ ۶ ٧ ٨ ٩ ٠

The Arabic Block

The Unicode Arabic block, which runs from U+0600 to U+06FF, is based on the international standard Arabic encoding, ISO 8859-6, which is in turn based on an encoding developed by the Arab Organization for Standardization and Metrology (ASMO). The characters they share in common have the same relative positions in both encodings. A couple of the long vowels with the hamza and madda are encoded as precomposed forms, but the hamza and madda, as well as the vowel marks, are encoded as combining marks. The normal Arabic usage, like the normal Hebrew usage, is to use combining character sequences to represent the marked letters. Not counting the marked forms, each letter has a single code point value—it's up to the text rendering process to decide which glyph to draw for each letter. The teh marbuta and alef maksura, whose use is a matter of spelling and which are therefore not mere contextual forms, get their own code point values. The kashida also gets a code point value, although you should generally rely on the rendering software to insert kashidas, rather than putting them into the encoded text.

Although Arabic punctuation is generally unified with the normal Latin punctuation marks, some of the marks have such different shapes in Arabic that they're given their own code point values in this block. The Arabic block also contains two complete series of Arabic digits: one set for the versions used with Arabic and one set for the versions used with Urdu and Farsi. Even though some of the digits have the same shapes, Unicode provides two separate series of digits to simplify number formatting algorithms (the algorithms that convert numeric values to their textual representations).

Unicode rounds out the Arabic block with a selection of Koranic annotation marks and a wide selection of additional letters and punctuation marks used to write various non-Arabic languages using the Arabic alphabet. The Unicode standard doesn't give a complete list of supported languages, but they include Adighe, Baluchi, Berber, Dargwa, Hausa, Kashmiri, Kazakh, Kirghiz, Kurdish, Lahnda, Malay, Pashto, Persian (Farsi), Sindhi, Uighur, and Urdu.

Joiners and Non-joiners

Two Unicode characters deserve special mention here: U+200C ZERO WIDTH NON-JOINER and U+200D ZERO WIDTH JOINER. Like the directionality-control characters we looked at earlier in this chapter, these characters are invisible and remain transparent to most processes that operate on Unicode text. They're used for only one thing: They control cursive joining. The zero-width non-joiner breaks the cursive connection between two letters that would otherwise connect. In other words

```
U+0644 ARABIC LETTER LAM
U+0647 ARABIC LETTER HEH
U+062C ARABIC LETTER JEEM
```

looks like this:

If you add in the non-joiner,

```
U+0644 ARABIC LETTER LAM
U+200C ZERO WIDTH NON-JOINER
U+0647 ARABIC LETTER HEH
U+200C ZERO WIDTH NON-JOINER
U+062C ARABIC LETTER JEEM
```

the letters break apart, giving you this:

جہل

This is useful not only for putting together examples in books such as this one, but also for representing text in some languages. In Farsi, for example, the plural suffix isn't connected to the word it modifies.

The zero-width joiner does the opposite: It forces a cursive connection where one wouldn't normally occur. In other words, if you take

```
U+0647 ARABIC LETTER HEH
```

which by itself normally looks like

ه

and put a zero-width joiner on each side, you get the medial form:

The zero-width joiner and non-joiner can be used together to break up a ligature without breaking up a cursive connection. For example,

```
U+0644 ARABIC LETTER LAM
U+0627 ARABIC LETTER ALEF
```

normally looks like this:

لا

If you stick the zero-width non-joiner between them,

```
U+0644 ARABIC LETTER LAM
U+200C ZERO WIDTH NON-JOINER
U+0627 ARABIC LETTER ALEF
```

it breaks up both the ligature and the cursive connection:

لا

If you wanted the letters to connect but not to form the ligature (say, to produce the example above showing how these two letters *don't* connect), you'd surround the non-joiner with joiners:

```
U+0644 ARABIC LETTER LAM
U+200D ZERO WIDTH JOINER
U+200C ZERO WIDTH NON-JOINER
U+200D ZERO WIDTH JOINER
U+0627 ARABIC LETTER ALEF
```

The joiner next to each letter causes the letter to take its cursively connecting form. Because the letters aren't next to each other anymore, however, they don't form the ligature:

لا

The Arabic Presentation Forms B Block

The Arabic Presentation Forms B block, which runs from U+FE70 to U+FEFE, includes codes for the contextual forms of the Arabic letters used in simplified Arabic printing. That is, separate code point values are provided for the initial, medial, final, and independent forms of the letter beh, for example. There are also code point values representing the various forms of the lam-alef ligature.

With a font that includes the glyphs for all of these code point values, a system can implement a rudimentary form of Arabic cursive joining. That is, the system can map the canonical versions of the Arabic letters from the main Arabic block to the glyphs using these code point values.

The algorithm is a little more complicated than simply mapping to the initial-form glyph when the letter is at the beginning of the word, the final-form glyph when the letter is at the end of the word, and so on. Some letters never join on certain sides. For example, the alef never connects to the letter that follows it. The Unicode standard classifies all Arabic letters into categories based on whether they only connect with letters on the left (left-joining), whether they only connect with letters on the right (right-joining), whether they connect with letters on both sides (dual-joining), or don't connect with anything (non-joining). The glyph-selection algorithm can use these categories to help figure out which glyphs to use. For example, if a dual-joining letter is preceded by a left-joining or dual-joining letter and followed by a right-joining or dual-joining letter, you'd use the medial-form glyph to represent it. If a dual-joining letter is followed by a right-joining or dual-joining letter, but preceded by a *right*-joining letter, you'd use the initial form. To see how this process works, consider our earlier example:

لهـج

All three letters are dual-joining letters. Because the letter heh in the middle, a dual-joining letter, is flanked by two dual-joining letters, we use the medial form to represent it. Lam is a dual-joining letter, but we use the initial form because it has a letter on only one side. We use the final form of jeem for the same reason.

If you substituted alef for lam, you get this:

اهـج

Alef is a right-joining letter, which means we use the initial form of heh instead of the medial form. Because alef doesn't have a letter on its right-hand side here, we use the independent form of alef.

The ArabicShaping.txt file in the Unicode Character Database contains the classifications of the letters that enable this algorithm to work right. Simple Arabic cursive shaping is discussed in more detail in Chapter 16.

The Arabic Presentation Forms A Block

The Arabic Presentation Forms A block, which runs from U+FC00 to U+FDFF, contains a bunch of Arabic ligatures. That is, it includes single code point values representing various combinations of two or three Arabic letters. In addition, this block specifies a bunch of contextual forms of letter–diacritic combinations and phrase ligatures (entire phrases encoded as single glyphs with single code point values). These characters are provided to ensure compatibility with some existing systems, but are very rarely used. The primary idea is to produce more authentic-looking Arabic rendering by providing a wider selection of glyphs than you get with the normal four contextual forms of each letter. Because of the fluidity of the Arabic alphabet, however, a ligature-based approach doesn't work very well: The number of ligatures necessary to draw things right can grow exponentially, as each letter's shape potentially depends on the shapes of the letters on each side—something you can't really do at the ligature boundaries. Depending on the design of a font, some of the ligatures might be relevant, but there's probably no single font for which all of them would be relevant. Generally speaking, fonts that do something more than the simple Arabic shaping described in the preceding section don't use the code point values in the Arabic Presentation Forms A block—they use internal glyph codes that don't correspond to Unicode code points.

Two characters in this block—U+FD3E ORNATE LEFT PARENTHESIS and U+FD3F ORNATE RIGHT PARENTHESIS—are not compatibility characters. As their names suggest, they represent more ornate parentheses that are sometimes used in Arabic as alternatives to the regular parentheses.

■ THE SYRIAC ALPHABET

The Syriac language is a member of the Aramaic family of languages that is spoken by a variety of minority communities—mostly Christian—throughout the Middle East.[5] It's the principal liturgical language and also serves as the

---

5. My sources for the section on Syriac are Peter T. Daniels and Robert D. Hoberman, "Aramaic Scripts for Aramaic Languages," in *The World's Writing Systems,* pp. 499–510, and the very detailed linguistic and historical information in the Syriac block description of the Unicode standard itself, pp. 199–205.

vernacular for many members of these communities. Its alphabet is also used to write modern Aramaic, and many Syriac-speaking communities use the Syriac alphabet for writing other languages, particularly Arabic (Arabic written using the Syriac alphabet is called **Garshuni**.) A theological schism among the Syrian Christians in the fifth century led to a bifurcation of the language: there are two dialects of Syriac: Eastern and Western. The Eastern and Western communities have different, though related, writing styles.

The origins of the Syriac alphabet are unclear, but it clearly belongs to the same family of scripts that includes the Arabic and Hebrew alphabets. The alphabet has the same 22 letters as the Hebrew alphabet, and many of these letters have very similar forms to the forms they have in Hebrew, although Syriac letters are connected like Arabic letters. Like Hebrew and Arabic, Syriac is written from right to left. The oldest manuscript using the Syriac alphabet that has been dated dates from A.D. 411.

Owing to the split between the Syrian Christian communities, several different styles of the Syriac alphabet evolved, and the shapes of many of the letters vary significantly between the styles. The oldest style is the Estrangelo. The 22 letters of the alphabet look like this in the Estrangelo style:

ܐܒܓܕܗܘܙܚܛܝܟܠܡܢܣܥܦܨܩܪܫܬ

After the split, the styles diverged into the Serto,

ܐܒܓܕܗܘܙܚܛܝܟܠܡܢܣܥܦܨܩܪܫܬ

and the Nestorian,

ܐܒܓܕܗܘܙܚܛܝܟܠܡܢܣܥܦܨܩܪܫܬ

Today, all three type styles are used in both the Eastern and Western communities, although certain type styles continue to be favored by various communities.

As in the Arabic and Hebrew alphabets, the Syriac letters are all consonants, although several do double duty as vowels in certain contexts. As in Arabic, some of the letterforms are similar enough that the practice of using dots in various places to differentiate them developed early on.

As in Arabic and Hebrew, fully vocalized text is represented in Syriac by supplementing the basic consonantal writing with various types of vowel points. Unlike in Arabic and Hebrew, however, it's more common, especially in modern Aramaic, for the points to be included than omitted.

Because of the split in the Syrian Christian communities, two different systems of vowel points are used. The older of the two puts dots in various places to indicate the vowel sounds; this system is used exclusively in Eastern Syriac texts. The more recent system, attributed to Jacob of Edessa, uses marks based on the shapes of the Greek vowels. Western Syriac texts use a combination of this pointing system and the earlier version used by the Eastern communities. In addition, Garshuni uses the Arabic vowel signs instead of the Syriac ones. A very complicated system of diacritical marks is also used with Syriac letters to mark various pronunciation and grammatical differences.

Historical Syriac scripts employ a unique system of punctuation, but in modern Syriac and Aramaic texts, the same punctuation marks used with Arabic are generally seen. As with most other alphabets, numbers were historically written using the letters of the alphabet—when sequences of letters were used as numerals, they were marked with a barbell-shaped line above them:[6]

Today, this mark is occasionally used to mark abbreviations and contractions. In modern texts, the European digits are now used for numbers, just as they are with the Hebrew alphabet.

Syriac writing, like Arabic writing, is written cursively, with the letters connected together and spaces between the words. Properly rendering cursive Syriac shares many of the problems associated with properly rendering cursive Arabic, but systems can do a credible job using a process much like that frequently used to render Arabic: Each letter has a maximum of four glyphs, and the selection of a glyph depends on whether the letter joins to the letter preceding it, the letter following it, both, or neither. Like the Arabic alphabet, the Syriac alphabet contains a number of letters that only join to the letter that

---

6. This example is taken from the Unicode standard, p. 200.

precedes them, meaning that a glyph-selection algorithm must use the same types of combining classes that are used with simple Arabic rendering schemes. The Syriac letter alaph actually has *five* contextual glyph forms, so the rules for Syriac are a little more complicated. There is also a set of obligatory ligatures similar to the lam-alef ligatures in Arabic, although the actual set employed in practice depends on the type style.

The Syriac Block

The Unicode Syriac block runs from U+0700 to U+074F. The type styles all use the same basic letters, so the letters are encoded once and you get one type style or another by selecting different fonts. Because both the dot and the Greek-letter forms of the vowel points are used together in Western Syriac texts, they're encoded separately in this block, rather than being unified.

The block contains a few extra letters beyond the basic 22. They include a few letters used in Garshuni, two variant forms of the letter semkath (ـڡ and ـڧ) that are used in the same texts in different spelling situations, a ligature that's treated like a separate letter in some languages, and a special letter with ambiguous semantics. The letters dalath and rish (ܕ and ܖ) differ only in the placement of the dot. Some early manuscripts don't use the dot and thus don't differentiate between the two, so Unicode includes a code point value (ܖ) that can be used for either letter.

The Syriac block also includes a wide selection of diacritical marks used with Syriac. A bunch of Syriac diacritical marks are unified with the general-purpose marks in the Combining Diacritical marks block; the Unicode standard gives a complete table of the marks from this block that are used with Syriac.

In addition, the Syriac block includes the historical punctuation marks used with Syriac. The modern punctuation marks are unified with those in the Arabic and Latin blocks.

The Syriac block contains one special invisible formatting character: the Syriac Abbreviation Mark. This character is used to represent the barbell-shaped mark that's used to mark numbers and abbreviations. It has no visual presentation of its own and is transparent to all text-processing algorithms, but marks the starting point of the abbreviation bar. The Syriac Abbreviation Mark precedes the first character that goes under the abbreviation bar, and the abbreviation bar extends from there to the end of the word. For example,

which means "on the 15th" (the bar is over the two letters being used as the digits in "15"),[7] is represented like this:

```
U+0712 SYRIAC LETTER BETH
U+070F SYRIAC ABBREVIATION MARK
U+071D SYRIAC LETTER YUDH
U+0717 SYRIAC LETTER HE
```

The cursive-joining algorithm used with Syriac is essentially the same as the one used with Arabic, but includes a few modifications to deal with various Syriac peculiarities—for example, the letter alaph (ܐ) has five contextual forms instead of four. The ArabicShaping.txt file in the Unicode Character Database includes joining-class designations for the Syriac letters. The Unicode standard also gives a table of ligatures used with the various Syriac type styles.

Unicode doesn't include compatibility code point values representing the various glyph shapes of the Syriac letters as it does with Arabic. A simple Syriac shaping mechanism (one that doesn't use the facilities in the advanced font technologies) would, therefore, have to assign the various contextual forms to Private Use code point values.

■ **THE THAANA SCRIPT**

Thaana is the name of the alphabet used to write Dhivehi, the language of the Republic of the Maldives, a group of islands in the Indian Ocean south of India.[8] Dhivehi is related to Sinhala, and the oldest examples of written Dhivehi,

---

7. This example also comes from the Unicode standard, p. 200.

8. My source for the section on Thaana is James W. Gair and Bruce D. Cain, "Dhivehi Writing," in *The World's Writing Systems,* pp. 564–568, supplemented with a couple of tidbits from Nakanishi, pp. 38–39.

dating from around 1200, are written in a script called Evela, based on the Sinhala script of the time (for more on Sinhala, see Chapter 9). The current script, the Gabuli Tana, or simply "Thaana," developed in the seventeenth century under the influence of the Arabic alphabet. Its alphabet has 24 letters, as shown in Figure 8.3.

Interestingly, the first nine letters of the alphabet are derived not from the Arabic letters, but rather from the Arabic *numerals.* The next nine are based on the Telugu numerals (see Chapter 9). The last six letters evolved out of Arabic letters.

The Thaana script is written from right to left, like Arabic, Hebrew, and Syriac. As in Hebrew, the letters aren't cursively connected; spaces are used between words. As in Arabic and Hebrew, the letters represent consonants, with vowels (or the absence thereof) represented through the use of diacritical marks written above or below the letters. There are 10 vowel signs, or **fili**, here shown on the second letter of the alphabet, shaviani (ﺭ):

ﻮ   ﻮ   ﻮ   ﻮ   ﻮ   ﻮ   ﻮ   ﻮ   ﻮ   ﻮ

An eleventh "vowel sign," the **sukun**, represents the *absence* of a vowel:

ﻮ

One of the letters, **alifu** (ﺍ), similarly represents the *absence* of a consonant sound. It is used as the base letter for word-initial vowels and vowels that follow other vowels. (Interestingly, it isn't the first letter in the alphabet, like the corresponding letter in the other three alphabets we've looked at in this chapter.) Alifu with sukun (ﺍ)—that is, the null consonant with the null vowel attached to it—is used to represent the glottal stop.

Figure 8.3 The Thaana script

Unlike in Arabic and Hebrew, the vowel marks are compulsory. You never see Thaana writing without the vowel signs.

In addition to the basic alphabet, 14 extra letters, all based on the regular letters with extra dots attached, are used for writing Arabic loanwords. There's a history of writing Arabic loanwords using the Arabic alphabet, but this practice is beginning to die out.

Numbers in Thaana are written using either European or native Arabic numerals, with European numerals being somewhat more common. The Arabic decimal-point and thousands-separator characters are employed in numerals regardless of whether European or Arabic digits are used.

The same punctuation is used with Thaana now as is used with Arabic. An older practice calls for using a period where we would normally expect a comma (between phrases) and two periods where we would otherwise use one period (at the end of a sentence).

The Thaana Block

The Unicode Thaana block extends from U+0780 to U+07BF. It includes the 24 basic letters, the additional 14 letters used for Arabic, the 10 fili, and the sukun. Thaana punctuation is unified with the punctuation marks in the Arabic and Latin blocks, and Thaana also uses the digits from the ASCII or Arabic blocks.

9

Scripts of India and Southeast Asia

*I*n this chapter, we'll look at the third major group of writing systems, usually referred to as the Indic group. It is the biggest single group of scripts in Unicode, comprising a whopping 19 scripts. Fortunately, they have a lot in common.

The geographic area covered by the Indic scripts extends from Pakistan in the west to Cambodia and Laos in the east, and from Tibet in the north to Sri Lanka in the south.[1] Several different language groups are represented in this area, although the writing systems are all related.

Just as the European alphabetic scripts are all more or less descended from Greek and the Middle Eastern bidirectional scripts are all more or less descended from Aramaic, the Indic scripts are all derived from the ancient Brahmi script, which dates from the middle of the third century. In the succeeding centuries, it spread across most of southern Asia, gradually developing different forms along the way. The Brahmi script is said to have spawned more than 200 different scripts. The scripts we examine in this chapter were more or less frozen into place as printing caught on in India in the eighteenth and nineteenth centuries.

---

1. My sources for the information in this introductory section are Colin P. Masica, "South Asia: Coexistence of Scripts," in *The World's Writing Systems,* pp. 773–776; Richard G. Salomon, "Brahmi and Kharoshthi" and the accompanying section heading, op. cit., pp. 371–383; the introduction to Chapter 9 of the Unicode standard, pp. 209–210; and a few bits from Nakanishi, pp. 45–47.

The origins of the Brahmi script are rather unclear. Some schools of thought suggest that it developed from the early Semitic scripts, probably Phoenician or Aramaic; others propose that it was an indigenous Indian development. Although evidence isn't totally conclusive, considerable circumstantial evidence indicates that Brahmi did evolve in some way from a Semitic source, probably Aramaic, although the Indic scripts and the Middle Eastern scripts are pretty distant cousins now.

The diversity of scripts in South Asia seems to stem at least in part from the desire of the different ethnic groups to differentiate themselves from one another, particularly within India, in the absence of either international boundaries or major geographical features to separate them. A language, and thus the people who spoke it, was considered "major" if it had its own writing system. The religions that predominated in this part of the world (with some important exceptions) depended much more heavily on oral tradition than on written tradition, the opposite of the religious groups in the other parts of the world. As a result, the imperative to keep a writing system stable so that scriptures would remain legible and have an unambiguous interpretation wasn't really there to countervail the tendency to diversify the scripts.

Perhaps the most interesting example of diversification of scripts involves Hindi and Urdu. Urdu, the main language of Pakistan, is written using the Arabic alphabet (see Chapter 8). Hindi, one of the main languages of India and a very close cousin of Urdu, is written using the Devanagari script, which we'll look at in this chapter. In fact, Hindi and Urdu are so closely related that the difference in scripts is one of the main things that differentiates them.

Instead of literature and religion being the main things that drove the development of writing in this part of the world, administration and commerce seem to have been the major factors (although the scholars, priests, and literati were quick to take advantage of its emergence as well). Even today, the bias in much of South Asia is toward spoken rather than written communication.

This chapter covers nineteen scripts from the Indic family:

- Devanagari, used for classical Sanskrit and modern Hindi, Marathi, and Nepali, plus many less common languages, is used in most of northern India and in Nepal.
- Bengali, used for writing Bengali, Assamese, and a number of less prevalent languages, is used in eastern India and Bangladesh.

- Gurmukhi is used for writing the Punjabi language spoken in the Punjab in northern India.
- Gujarati is used for writing Gujarati, the language of Gujarat in western India.
- Oriya is used to write Oriya, the language of Orissa in eastern India.
- Tamil is used to write Tamil, spoken in southern India and Singapore.
- Telugu is used to write Telugu, spoken in southern India.
- Kannada is used to write Kannada (or Kanarese), also spoken in southern India.
- Malayalam is used to write Malayalam, spoken in Kerala in southern India.
- Sinhala is used to write Sinhala (or Sinhalese), the main language of Sri Lanka.
- Thai is used to write Thai, the language of Thailand.
- Lao is used to write Lao, the language of Laos.
- Khmer is used to write Cambodian, the language of Cambodia.
- Myanmar is used to write Burmese, the language of Burma.
- Tibetan is used to write Tibetan, the language of Tibet and Bhutan.
- Tagalog isn't used anymore, but was once used to write the Tagalog language spoken in the Philippines, as well as a few other Filipino languages.
- Hanunóo is used to write the language of the Hanunóo people on the island of Mindoro in the Philippines.
- Buhid is used to write the language of the Buhid people on the island of Mindoro in the Philippines.
- Tagbanwa is used to write the language of the Tagbanwa people on the island of Palawan in the Philippines.

A fair amount of variation characterizes the Indic scripts, but they generally share a number of important characteristics:

- All are written from left to right.
- All are uncased: The letters of each come in only one flavor.
- Most, but not all, use spaces between words.
- Each script has its own set of numerals, although some sets have been supplanted by the European numerals.

▪ All of these writing systems fall somewhere between alphabetic and syllabic. A single "character" represents a whole syllable, but it has constituent parts that consistently represent the same phonemes from syllable
to syllable. This system is related to that used for the Middle Eastern languages. That is, a basic character represents the combination of a consonant sound and a basic vowel sound. You change the vowel sound by
attaching various marks to the basic character. If a syllable has more
than one initial consonant, the basic characters for the consonant sounds
involved usually combine together into a **conjunct consonant**. (Sometimes the basic consonant shapes don't combine, but instead a mark
called a **virama**, or "killer," is attached to the first one to indicate the absence of the basic vowel sound.)

Without further ado, we'll delve into the characteristics of the individual
scripts. In the section on Devanagari, we'll explore in detail just how this formation of syllable clusters works, and then we'll highlight only the differences
between Devanagari and the other scripts in the subsequent sections.

▪ DEVANAGARI

The Nagari or Devanagari script (pronounced "deh-vuh-NAH-guh-ree," not
"duh-vah-nuh-GAH-ree") is used across a wide swath of northern and western
India and Nepal.[2] It's used to write classical Sanskrit and modern Hindi,
Marathi, and Nepali, as well as a large number of less common languages (the
Unicode standard lists Awadhi, Bagheli, Bhatneri, Bhili, Bihari, Braj Bhasha,
Chhattisgarhi, Garhwali, Gondi, Harauti, Ho, Jaipuri, Kachchhi, Kanauji,
Konkani, Kului, Kumaoni, Kurku, Kurukh, Marwari, Mundari, Newari, Palpa,
and Santali). It developed from the northern variety of the Brahmi script and
reached its current form somewhere around the twelfth century.

Devanagari, like the other writing systems in this chapter, is basically phonetic, with some kind of mark for each sound. These marks can combine in

---

2. Most of this material is taken directly from Chapter 9 of the Unicode standard, pp. 211–223,
but some is taken from William Bright, "The Devanagari Script," in *The World's Writing Systems,* pp. 384–390, and from Nakanishi, pp. 48–49.

complex and interesting ways. The word *purti*, which means "to provide," for example, looks like this:[3]

The box marked "1" surrounds the "p," the "2" marks the "u," "3" and "4" together mark the "r" (we'll see later why there are two numbers on this mark), "5" marks the "t," and "6" marks the "i."

The best way to think about Devanagari writing is to understand it as consisting of clusters of characters, each cluster representing a vowel sound, optionally preceded by a sequence of consonant sounds (the Unicode standard refers to these clusters as **orthographic syllables**). A cluster is roughly analogous to a syllable, but the two concepts don't correspond exactly. A consonant sound that's spoken at the end of a syllable is actually written at the beginning of the cluster representing the next syllable. An Indic orthographic syllable is one kind of grapheme cluster, according to Unicode 3.2.

Devanagari includes 34 basic consonant characters, as shown in Figure 9.1. Every character has a horizontal line, called the **headstroke**, running across the top, and the character basically "hangs" from the headstroke. The headstrokes of the letters in a word all connect together into a single horizontal line. When they're writing on lined paper, Indians use the lines of the paper as the headstrokes of the letters (when writing quickly on lined paper, they often

क ख ग घ ङ च छ ज झ ञ ट ठ ड ढ ण त
थ द ध न प फ ब भ म य र ल व श ष स ह

Figure 9.1 Devanagari consonants

---

3. The picture is taken from the Unicode standard, p. 14.

leave the headstrokes off the letters altogether). Each consonant also has a vertical stroke on the right-hand side (or sometimes in the center) that marks the core of the syllable, called the **stem**.

One interesting consequence of the connected headstrokes is that the "baseline" of Devanagari writing is the headstroke. Text of different point sizes is lined up so the headstrokes all connect:

$$क\ क\ क$$

When Devanagari is combined on the same line of text as Latin, or text in some other writing system where the baseline is under the characters, the text-rendering process (or the user) must perform some interesting adjustments to make the line come out looking good. This step is especially necessary if the point sizes on the line vary.

Unlike all of the other writing systems we've looked at so far, however, these symbols don't merely represent consonant sounds. Instead, they're said to carry an **inherent vowel sound**; in other words, they represent syllables. In Devanagari, the inherent vowel is a, so the symbol

$$क$$

represents the syllable *ka*. (It is actually pronounced more like *kuh*.)

To change the vowel, you add an extra sign to the consonant symbol called a **dependent vowel** or **matra**. Although some of the dependent vowels look more like letters, they behave more like diacritical marks. Some dependent vowels attach to the right-hand side of the consonant and just look like "the next letter" in the character stream; one, however, attaches to the left-hand side, giving the appearance that the characters have been reordered from the order in which they were typed. Several dependent vowel signs attach to the bottom of the consonant, others attach to the top, and some vowels that appear to one side of the consonant also overhang it on top.

There are 14 dependent vowel signs, shown in Figure 9.2 attached to the letter ka.

The sound of the dependent vowel replaces the consonant's inherent vowel sound. For example, ka plus i gives you ki:

$$क\ +\ ि\ =\ कि$$

का कि की कु कू कृ कॄ कँ कॅ के कै कॉ कॉ को कौ

Figure 9.2 Dependent vowel signs attached to the letter ka

There are also 14 *independent* vowel characters. The dependent vowel signs are basically abbreviated forms of the independent vowels. They are used for vowel sounds that occur at the beginnings of words or follow other vowel sounds. Figure 9.3 shows the independent and dependent vowels.

You can also cancel the consonant's inherent vowel sound by adding a mark called a *virama*. Thus, the following represents the sound *k* by itself:

$$क्$$

If you just write the characters sa and ta next to each other,

$$सत$$

you get "sata." If you put a virama on the sa,

$$स्त$$

you get sta.

Actually, you don't see the virama often. Instead, when two consonants appear next to each other without an intervening vowel sound, they usually combine to form a *conjunct consonant*. The virama does show up on the character representing the final consonant in words that end with a consonant sound. (Actually, Hindi spelling isn't always phonetic; often, the word is spelled as though

Independent vowels

अ आ इ ई उ ऊ ऋ ऌ एँ एँ ए ऐ आँ ऑ ओ औ

Dependent vowels

ा ि ी ु ू ृ ॢ ॅ ॆ ॊ ॉ ॉ ो ौ

Figure 9.3 Devanagari vowels

it ends with a consonant's inherent vowel, but the inherent vowel sound isn't actually spoken.)

The exact form of a conjunct consonant depends on which consonants are joining together. Sometimes they stack on top of each other:

$$क \;+\; क \;=\; क्क$$

Often the first consonant (the one without the vowel, referred to as the "dead" consonant) loses the stem and attaches to the next consonant, as in our sta example:

$$स \;+\; त \;=\; स् \;+\; त \;=\; स्त$$

The consonant symbol without its stem is called a **half-form**.

Sometimes, the two characters combine to form a new glyph that doesn't obviously resemble either of the characters that make it up:

$$क \;+\; ष \;=\; क्ष$$

The character र, representing the *r* sound, combines with other consonants in even more exotic ways. When *r* is the first sound in a conjunct consonant, it appears as a hook on top of the second character, above the syllable's stem:

$$र \;+\; प \;=\; र्प$$

This hook is called a **repha**.

When *r* is the second sound in a conjunct consonant, it appears as a chevron underneath the second character:

$$घ \;+\; र \;=\; घ्र$$

Sometimes, the chevron representing the *r* sound combines graphically with the character it's supposed to appear under:

$$क \;+\; र \;=\; क्र$$

In addition, र may combine with a dependent vowel attached to it:

$$र + \underset{\smile}{} = रु$$

$$र + \underset{\smile}{} = रू$$

More complex combinations can also occur. If *three* consonant sounds occur in a row, you might have two half-form consonants preceding the main consonant:

$$स + क + ल = स् + क् + ल = स्क्ल$$

If the first two characters in the conjunct consonant would normally form a ligature, that ligature may turn into a half-form that combines with the third character:

$$क + ष + य = क्ष + य = क्ष् + य = क्ष्य$$

Sometimes, all three characters will form a ligature:

$$स + त + र = स + त्र = स्त्र$$

There's also one case of a nonstandard half-form. The half-form of र sometimes looks like this: ⌐. It is called the "eyelash ra."

$$र + न = ⌐ + न = ⌐न$$

When a conjunct consonant combines with a dependent vowel, strict rules dictate where the dependent vowel goes. If it attaches to the top or bottom of the consonant, it goes over or under the syllable's stem:

$$स्त्र + \grave{} = स्त्रे$$

If the dependent vowel attaches to the left-hand side of the consonant, it attaches to the extreme left of the conjunct consonant:

$$स्त्र + ि = स्त्रि$$

This can get a little weird when, for example, a top-joining vowel sign attaches to a conjunct consonant with a repha:

$$ \text{कं} \; + \; \grave{} \; = \; \text{कॅं} $$

Most of the preceding examples are taken directly from Chapter 9 of the Unicode standard. This chapter gives a rigorous set of minimal rendering rules for Devanagari that cover all of the things we've looked at here.

Exactly which conjunct consonant forms you get when—that is, whether you use a ligature, a half-form, or just the nominal forms with viramas—depends on various factors, such as language, spelling, and font design. Depending on these things, you might see "kssa" look like this

क्ष

or this

क्ष

or this

क्ष

Any of these forms may be correct based on the rules of the script. The choice is purely one of font design.

A few marks are used with the Devanagari characters. The **nukta**, a dot below the basic character, is used to modify the sounds of some consonants, widening the available selection of sounds that can be represented to cover all the sounds in modern Hindi. The **candrabindu** (ँ) and **anusvara** (ं) are used to indicate nasalization. The **visarga** (ः) represents the *h* sound.

Two punctuation marks are used with traditional texts: the **danda** (।), which functions more or less like a period, and the **double danda** (॥), which marks the end of a stanza in traditional texts. With modern texts, European punctuation is usually used.

As with all of the Indic writing systems, a distinctive set of digits is used for writing numbers:

० १ २ ३ ४ ५ ६ ७ ८ ९

The Devanagari Block

The Unicode Devanagari block runs from U+0900 to U+097F. It's based on the Indian national standard, the Indian Script Code for Information Interchange (ISCII). The ISCII standard includes separate encodings for Devanagari, Bengali, Gurmukhi, Gujarati, Oriya, Tamil, Telugu, Kannada, and Malayalam, switching between them with escape sequences. All of these encodings share the same structure, just as the various scripts do. The same code point value in each code page represents the same basic sound. For example, the value 0xB3 represents the ka character in each of the various scripts, making transliteration between them simple.

The corresponding blocks in Unicode are all the same size, and the characters have the same positions within these blocks (and thus the same relative ordering) that they do in the ISCII standard, again facilitating transliteration between them. The Unicode blocks are based on the 1988 version of ISCII. Although ISCII has since been revised, putting it slightly out of sync with Unicode, converting between Unicode and ISCII remains pretty simple.

Unicode supplements the ISCII characters with several more characters. As much as possible, Unicode follows the rule of coding characters that correspond between the related scripts in the same positions in each of their blocks.

Unicode also follows the characters-not-glyphs rule religiously with regard to the Indic scripts. Each character is given a single code point value, even though it can have many shapes.

The nominal consonants, complete with their inherent vowels, are given single code point values in Unicode. Thus, ka is represented as a single code point. That is, the sequence

```
U+0915 DEVANAGARI LETTER KA
```

shows up like this:

क

A dependent vowel code is used to change the vowel of a syllable. Thus, ko is encoded like this

```
U+0915 DEVANAGARI LETTER KA
U+094B DEVANAGARI VOWEL SIGN O
```

and looks like this:

को

The characters are stored in logical order, the order in which they're typed and pronounced. Thus, ki, which looks like this

कि

is still encoded like this

```
U+0915 DEVANAGARI LETTER KA
U+093F DEVANAGARI VOWEL SIGN I
```

even though the vowel sign appears to the left of the consonant.

Conjunct-consonant combinations are represented using U+094D DE-VANAGARI SIGN VIRAMA after the nominal consonant characters, even when the virama doesn't actually appear in the rendered text. For example,

क्ष

is represented as

```
U+0915 DEVANAGARI LETTER KA
U+094D DEVANAGARI SIGN VIRAMA
U+0937 DEVANAGARI LETTER SSA
```

The sequence

स्त

is represented as follows:

```
U+0938 DEVANAGARI LETTER SA
U+094D DEVANAGARI SIGN VIRAMA
U+0924 DEVANAGARI LETTER TA
```

Conjunct consonants involving three consonant sounds require a virama after both of the first two sounds. For example,

स्त्र

is represented as

```
U+0938 DEVANAGARI LETTER SA
U+094D DEVANAGARI SIGN VIRAMA
U+0924 DEVANAGARI LETTER TA
U+094D DEVANAGARI SIGN VIRAMA
U+0930 DEVANAGARI LETTER RA
```

The zero-width joiner and non-joiner characters we looked at in Chapter 8 can be used to control the display of conjunct consonants. As we saw earlier, the sequence

```
U+0915 DEVANAGARI LETTER KA
U+094D DEVANAGARI SIGN VIRAMA
U+0937 DEVANAGARI LETTER SSA
```

is usually rendered as follows:

क्ष

The zero-width non-joiner can be used to split the conjunct consonant, causing it to appear as two nominal consonants with a virama on the first one. In other words,

```
U+0915 DEVANAGARI LETTER KA
U+094D DEVANAGARI SIGN VIRAMA
U+200C ZERO WIDTH NON-JOINER
U+0937 DEVANAGARI LETTER SSA
```

is rendered as follows:

क्ष

You can surround the non-joiner with joiners to split up the ligature but keep the conjunct-consonant rendering. This approach causes the syllable to be drawn using a half-form for ka:

```
U+0915 DEVANAGARI LETTER KA
U+094D DEVANAGARI SIGN VIRAMA
U+200D ZERO WIDTH JOINER
U+200C ZERO WIDTH NON-JOINER
U+200D ZERO WIDTH JOINER
U+0937 DEVANAGARI LETTER SSA
```

This sequence is rendered as follows:

क्ष

When a consonant with a nukta is represented as a combining character sequence (a couple of precomposed consonant–nukta combinations are encoded), the nukta follows the consonant immediately, in the manner of all other Unicode combining marks. The candrabindu and anusvara, on the other hand, apply to a whole syllable. They follow the whole syllable in memory.

To tie things together, then, the word "Hindi" would be typed and encoded like this

```
U+0939 DEVANAGARI LETTER HA
U+093F DEVANAGARI VOWEL SIGN I
U+0928 DAVANAGARI LETTER NA
U+094D DAVANAGARI SIGN VIRAMA
U+0926 DEVANAGARI LETTER DA
U+0940 DAVANAGARI VOWEL SIGN II
```

and would look like this:

हिन्दी

This breaks down into two syllable clusters. The first is hi:

हि

The ha (ह) combines with the i sign, which attaches on the left. The second cluster is ndii:

न्दी

The na (न) turns into a half-form, which attaches to the da (द) on the left. The ii vowel (ी) then attaches to the combined consonant on the right. The virama doesn't appear as a separate glyph; instead, it simply tells the system to combine the na and da into a conjunct consonant.

The example we opened the chapter with, *purti,* is encoded like this

```
U+092A DEVANAGARI LETTER PA
U+0942 DEVANAGARI VOWEL SIGN UU
U+0930 DAVANAGARI LETTER RA
U+094D DEVANAGARI SIGN VIRAMA
U+0924 DEVANAGARI LETTER TA
U+093F DEVANAGARI VOWEL SIGN I
```

and looks like this:

पूर्ति

It breaks down into two clusters. The first is puu:

पू

The uu sign (ू) attaches to the bottom of the pa (प). The second cluster is rti:

र्ति

The ra (र) turns into a repha and attaches to the top of the ta (त). The i vowel (ि) then attaches to the left-hand side of the combined consonant. Again, the virama doesn't show up as a glyph, but just tells the text renderer to treat ra and ta as a conjunct consonant.

Here's a more complex example:

आपत्ति

The word is "apatti," which means "danger." Again, it'd be represented in Unicode like this:

```
U+0906 DEVANAGARI LETTER AA
U+092A DEVANAGARI LETTER PA
U+0924 DEVANAGARI LETTER TA
U+094D DEVANAGARI SIGN VIRAMA
U+0924 DEVANAGARI LETTER TA
U+093F DEVANAGARI VOWEL SIGN I
```

This word breaks down into three clusters. The first two are just single letters. We start with an independent vowel, representing the initial *a* sound:

आ

Then there's the letter pa, representing the *p* sound:

प

Finally, the last cluster contains the other letters:

ति

The virama causes the two ta's to combine together into a single glyph: the second ta merely turns into a small spike sticking out of the first one. The final i then joins to the left side of the cluster.

Note that the clusters don't correspond directly to spoken syllables. "Hindi," for example, is spoken "hin-di," but written as "hi-ndi."

■ BENGALI

The Bengali, or Bangla, script is a close cousin of Devanagari and bears a close resemblance to it. As in Devanagari, the characters have a horizontal headstroke that connects from character to character in a continuous horizontal line. Also as in Devanagari, a vertical stem marks the core of each syllable.

The Bengali script is used in Bangladesh and northeastern India to write not only Bengali, but also Assamese, Daphla, Garo, Hallam, Khasi, Manipuri,

Mizo, Munda, Naga, Rian, and Santali. It has 32 consonants, 12 independent vowels, and 12 dependent vowels (Figure 9.4).

One interesting difference between Bengali and Devanagari is that Bengali has two **split vowels**. These vowel signs consist of two glyphs, written on either side of the consonant character. The last two dependent vowels in Figure 9.4 are split vowels.

The Bengali virama looks like this (attached to ক):

কৃ

The Bengali anusvara looks like this: ং. The Bengali candrabindu looks like this: ঁ. The Bengali visarga looks like this: ঃ.

Bengali forms conjunct consonants in the same way as Devanagari does, with many of the conjunct consonants having similar forms. The special ways in which the consonant representing the *r* sound combines with other consonants also apply in Bengali, although the shapes are a little different.

The Bengali digits look like this:

০ ১ ২ ৩ ৪ ৫ ৬ ৭ ৮ ৯

In addition to the regular digits, a series of special characters is used to write fractions and a few currency symbols are available. The **isshar** (৺) is used to write the name of God.

Consonants

ক খ গ ঘ ঙ চ ছ জ ঝ ঞ ট ঠ ড ঢ ণ ত

থ দ ধ ন প ফ ব ভ ম য র ল শ ষ স হ

Independent vowels

অ আ ই ঈ উ ঊ ঋ ৯ এ ঐ ও ঔ

Dependent vowels (attached to the letter ka, (ক)

কা কি কী কু কূ কৃ কৄ কে কৈ কো কৌ

Figure 9.4 Bengali consonants and vowels

The word "Hindi" written using Bengali characters looks like this:

হিন্দী

The Bengali Block

The Bengali block in Unicode runs from U+0980 to U+09FF. Like the Devanagari block, it follows the ISCII order, which means that corresponding characters in the two blocks are found at corresponding positions within their blocks.

The split vowels can be represented in Unicode as either single code points or pairs of code points, one representing the left-hand glyph and the other representing the right-hand glyph. The representation that uses one code point is preferable, but has a compatibility decomposition to the two-code-point representation. (When two code points are used for a split vowel, both appear in memory after the consonant.)

▪ GURMUKHI

The Gurmukhi, or Punjabi, script is used to write the Punjabi language of the Punjab region of northern India.[4] It evolved from the now-obsolete Lahnda script, of which someone once said, "It is convenient, with only one fault; it is seldom legible to anyone except the original writer."[5] A revision was undertaken under the second Guru of the Sikhs, Guru Angad, in the sixteenth century, producing the modern Gurmukhi script. The name *Gurmukhi* attests to this effort: It means "from the mouth of the Guru."

Gurmukhi resembles Devanagari. As in Devanagari, the characters hang from a continuous horizontal line, although the vertical stem that characterizes most Devanagari consonants isn't as frequent in Gurmukhi. Gurmukhi has 33 basic consonants, 10 independent vowels, and 9 dependent vowels (Figure 9.5).

---

4. My sources for information on Gurmukhi are Harjeet Singh Gill, "The Gurmukhi Script," in *The World's Writing Systems,* pp. 395–398, and Nakanishi, pp. 50–51.

5. The quote is from Nakanishi, p. 50, but doesn't carry an attribution there.

Consonants

ਸ ਸ਼ ਹ ਕ ਖ ਗ ਘ ਙ ਚ ਛ ਜ ਝ ਞ ਟ ਠ ਡ ਢ

ਣ ਤ ਥ ਦ ਧ ਨ ਪ ਫ ਬ ਭ ਮ ਯ ਰ ਲ ਲ਼ ਵ

Independent vowels

ਅ ਆ ਇ ਈ ਉ ਊ ਏ ਐ ਓ ਔ

Dependent vowels (shown attached to ਕ)

ਕਾ ਕਿ ਕੀ ਕੁ ਕੂ ਕੇ ਕੈ ਕੋ ਕੌ

Figure 9.5   Gurmukhi consonants and vowels

The independent vowels aren't completely separate forms as they are in Devanagari and Bengali. Instead, three "vowel-bearers" are provided for the three classes of vowels, and the regular dependent vowel signs are attached to them (as in the other scripts, the consonants carry an inherent *a*).

Conjunct consonants aren't as common in Gurmukhi as they are in Devanagari and Bengali. The symbols ਹ, ਰ, and ਵ are attached to the other consonant in the cluster as subscripts when they appear as the second consonant in the cluster:

$$ \text{ਪ} + \text{ਰ} = \text{ਪ੍ਰ} $$

The character ਯ takes an abbreviated form when it appears as the second consonant in the cluster:

$$ \text{ਦ} + \text{ਯ} = \text{ਦ੍ਯ} $$

Generally, other consonant combinations use an explicit virama (੍). Gurmukhi spelling isn't always phonetic; in many cases, the virama is simply understood and not written.

For comparison, this is the word "Hindi" written in Gurmukhi characters:

$$ \text{ਹਿਨ੍ਦੀ} $$

A few extra marks are used with Gurmukhi characters. The **bindi** (◌) and **tippi** (◌̊) indicate nasalization; they're roughly analogous to the anusvara and candrabindu in Devanagari. A special sign, the **addak** (◌̆), indicates the doubling of a consonant sound. Like the other scripts, Gurmukhi also uses a nukta (a dot below) as a diacritic with some consonants to allow for more consonant sounds.

Punjabi is a tonal language, but Gurmukhi doesn't include any special characters to represent tone. Instead, some of the consonant letters do double duty as tone indicators.

There is also a unique set of Gurmukhi digits:

$$੦ ੧ ੨ ੩ ੪ ੫ ੬ ੭ ੮ ੯$$

The Gurmukhi Block

The Gurmukhi block in Unicode runs from U+0A00 to U+0A7F and follows the same ISCII order as the Devanagari and Bengali blocks, with analogous characters in analogous positions in all three blocks. The additional consonants used in Punjabi, which are the regular consonants with nuktas added, also get their own code point values in this block; they have canonical decompositions to the consonant-nukta forms.

The Gurmukhi block includes codes for the unadorned vowel-bearers, meaning an independent vowel could be represented using a vowel-bearer and a dependent vowel sign. This approach isn't recommended, however, as Unicode doesn't include a decomposition from the regular independent-vowel representation to the representation including the vowel-bearer.

■ GUJARATI

The Gujarati script is used to write the Gujarati and Kacchi languages of the Gujarat region of western India.[6] The earliest known document using Gujarati

---

6. My source for Gujarati is P. J. Mistry, "Gujarati Writing," in *The World's Writing Systems,* pp. 391–398.

characters dates from 1592. Gujarati is the most closely related of the Northern Brahmi-derived scripts to Devanagari. Most of the letterforms are quite similar, but the script at first appears strikingly different from Devanagari (and the other scripts we've looked at so far) because the characters lack the horizontal headstroke connecting the letters of a word (a line of Gujarati type of different sizes still has the letters aligned at the top, however).

Gujarati has 34 consonants, which carry an inherent *a* (Figure 9.6). It also has 13 independent vowels and 13 dependent vowels. The independent vowel forms are used only at the beginnings of words or when they follow other vowels. The rest of the time, the dependent vowels, which attach themselves to the consonants, are used.

Successive consonants form conjuncts, as they do in Devanagari, generally in the same ways as they do in Devanagari, right down to the special forms of the symbol for the *r* sound. The virama generally isn't used in Gujarati, except when this script is used to write Sanskrit. Instead, if the last consonant in a word doesn't carry a vowel sign, it's merely understood not to carry the inherent *a*.

The same diacritics, the nukta, anusvara, candrabindu, and visarga, are used in Gujarati. There's also a unique set of Gujarati digits:

૦ ૧ ૨ ૩ ૪ ૫ ૬ ૭ ૮ ૯

Consonants

ક ખ ગ ઘ ઙ ચ છ જ ઝ ઞ ટ ઠ ડ ઢ ણ ત થ
દ ધ ન પ ફ બ ભ મ ય ર લ ળ વ શ ષ સ હ

Independent vowels

અ આ ઇ ઈ ઉ ઊ ઋ ઍ એ ઐ ઑ ઓ ઔ

Dependent vowels (shown attached to ક)

કા કિ કી કુ કૂ કૃ કૄ કૅ કે કૈ કૉ કો કૌ

Figure 9.6 Gujarati consonants and vowels

For comparison with the other scripts, this is "Hindi," written in Gujarati characters:

હિન્દી

The Gujarati Block

The Unicode Gujarati block runs from U+0A80 to U+0AFF. As with Devanagari, Bengali, and Gurmukhi, the characters are arranged in the ISCII order.

Like Bengali, Gujarati has split vowel signs. The Gujarati split vowels consist of a component that appears above the consonant and a component that appears after it. In each case, the individual components of the split vowel are also used by themselves to represent other vowels. The split vowel could be represented using the two code point values for the two components on systems that can't handle true split vowels. Because there's no decomposition from the official form to the two-code-point form, this practice isn't recommended.

■ ORIYA

The Oriya (pronounced "OH-ree-uh," not "oh-REE-uh") script is related to the other northern Brahmi scripts we've already considered, although its appearance varies more. It's used to write the Oriya language of the Orissa region of eastern India, as well as several minority languages spoken in the same region, such as Khondi and Santali.

The distinguishing feature of Oriya letters is the *curved* headstroke instead of the straight horizontal headstroke of Devanagari, Bengali, and Gurmukhi. Oriya has 33 consonants, 12 independent vowels, and 10 dependent vowels (Figure 9.7). As with the other scripts, Oriya consonants carry an inherent *a* sound, and the other vowels are represented as diacritical marks when they follow a consonant.

Oriya also has conjunct consonants, and they take many forms. In addition, the dependent vowel signs often form ligatures with the consonants to which they join, giving rise to a very wide variety of Oriya letterforms.

Consonants

କ ଖ ଗ ଘ ଙ ଚ ଛ ଜ ଝ ଞ ଟ ଠ ଡ ଢ ଣ ତ ଥ
ଦ ଧ ନ ପ ଫ ବ ଭ ମ ଯ ର ଲ ଳ ଶ ଷ ସ ହ

Independent vowels

ଅ ଆ ଇ ଈ ଉ ଊ ଋ ଌ ଏ ଐ ଓ ଔ

Dependent vowels (shown attached to କ)

କା କି କୀ କୁ କୂ କୃ କେ କୈ କୋ କୌ

Figure 9.7 Oriya consonants and vowels

Here's "Hindi" written using Oriya characters:

ହିନ୍ଦୀ

The same diacritical marks are used with Oriya as are used with Bengali. Oriya also has a set of distinctive digits:

୦ ୧ ୨ ୩ ୪ ୫ ୬ ୭ ୮ ୯

The Oriya Block

The Oriya block in Unicode runs from U+0B00 to U+0B7F. Like the other ISCII-derived blocks, it follows the ISCII order.

Like some other scripts discussed in this chapter, Oriya has split vowels, including one with components that appear to the left, to the right, *and* above the consonant. Unicode includes two characters, U+0B56 ORIYA AI LENGTH MARK and U+0B57 ORIYA AU LENGTH MARK, for the pieces of the split vowels that aren't dependent vowels themselves (au is the vowel sign with three components; the au length mark comprises both the top and right-hand components). All of the split vowels have canonical decompositions to their pieces and so can be represented using either single code points or pairs of code points.

■ TAMIL

The scripts we've looked at so far—Devanagari, Bengali, Gurmukhi, Gujarati, and Oriya—form the North Brahmi group of scripts. Next, we turn to the South Brahmi scripts, which descend from the ancient Brahmi script along a line that diverged fairly early from the North Brahmi scripts. This group includes the Tamil, Telugu, Kannada, Malayalam, and Sinhala scripts. With the exception of Sinhala, the main languages these scripts are used to write belong to the Dravidian language group, which is completely unrelated to the Indic language group to which the others belong—their adoption of the same basic writing system as the Indic languages stems from their geographic proximity, and they have some differences from the North Brahmi scripts that reflect the differences in their underlying languages.

The Tamil script (rhymes with "camel," not "Camille") is used to write the Tamil language of the Tamil Nadu region of southern India, in addition to several minority languages, including Badaga.[7] It follows the same basic structure as the other Indic scripts. Tamil has fewer sounds, so the Tamil script has fewer characters than the others. It includes 22 consonants, 12 independent vowels, and 11 dependent vowels (Figure 9.8). As with the other scripts, the independent vowels are used at the beginnings of words, but they are also sometimes used within a word to represent an especially prolonged vowel sound. Most of the time, however, the dependent vowel signs are used when the vowel sound follows a consonant.

As with many of the other scripts, it's worth noticing that several of the dependent vowel signs are drawn to the *left* of their consonants. Three of them have components that appear on *both sides* of the consonant.

As with the other scripts, only 11 dependent vowel signs are used because the consonant characters have an inherent *a* sound. The absence of the inherent vowel is represented using a virama, which takes a different form than in the other scripts:

ப்

---

7. Most of the information on Tamil comes straight out of the Unicode standard, but has been supplemented by information from Sanford B. Steever, "Tamil Writing," in *The World's Writing Systems*, pp. 426–430.

Consonants

க ங ச ஜ ஞ ட ண த ந ன ப ம ய ர ற ல ள ழ வ ஷ ஸ ஹ

Independent vowels

அ ஆ இ ஈ உ ஊ எ ஏ ஐ ஒ ஓ ஔ

Dependent vowels (shown attached to ப)

பா பி பீ பு பூ பெ பே பை பொ போ பௌ

Figure 9.8 Tamil consonants and vowels

One important thing that sets Tamil apart from the other writing systems we've looked at so far in this chapter is that it generally doesn't use conjunct consonants. Instead, the normal consonant forms are used, and the virama is actually visible. One exception to this rule exists: When க is followed by ஷ, instead of getting this

$$\text{கஷ}$$

you get this:

$$\text{க்ஷ}$$

This form behaves like conjunct consonants in the other Indian scripts, but it's the only conjunct consonant in Tamil.

The fact that the Tamil script doesn't have conjunct consonants doesn't mean that Tamil letters don't form ligatures. The ligatures are formed between consonants and vowels, however, rather than between successive consonants. Tamil actually has a considerable number of consonant–vowel ligatures. A few examples follow:

$$\text{ண} + \text{ா} = \text{ணா}$$
$$\text{ன} + \text{ா} = \text{னா}$$

$$ஹ + ொ = ஹொ$$

$$ட + ி = டி$$

$$ல + ி = லி$$

$$ல + ீ = லீ$$

$$க + ு = கு$$

$$க + ூ = கூ$$

$$ஜ + ு = ஜு$$

$$ஜ + ூ = ஜூ$$

There are also two forms of the vowel ெ, which changes shape in front of certain consonants (it is a left-joining vowel):

$$க + ெ = கெ$$

but

$$ண + ெ = ணெ$$

Like the other scripts in this chapter, Tamil includes a unique set of digits:

$$க உ ங ச ரு சூ எ அ கூ$$

However, these characters don't form a normal set of decimal digits used with positional Arabic notation. Instead, they're used with multiplicative notation in conjunction with signs for 10 (ய்), 100 (ர), and 1,000 (சூ):

$$ங = 3$$

$$ய்ங = 13$$

$$ங ய் = 30$$

$$ங ய் ங = 33$$

This system of numeration is actually nearly obsolete; European numerals are generally used now.

The Tamil Block

Like the other ISCII-derived blocks, the Unicode Tamil block (U+0B80 to U+0BFF) follows the ISCII order. The three split vowels all have canonical decompositions to their constituent parts. The right-hand side of ஔ, which isn't used as a vowel sign by itself, is encoded as U+0BD7 TAMIL AU LENGTH MARK.

■ TELUGU

The Telugu script (pronounced "TELL-a-goo," not "te-LOO-goo") is used to write the Telugu language of the Andhra Pradesh region of India, as well as minority languages such as Gondi and Lambadi. It follows the same basic structure as the other Indic scripts, and the letters are characterized by a chevron-shaped headstroke.[8]

Telugu includes 35 consonants, 14 independent vowels, and 13 dependent vowels (Figure 9.9). As always, the independent vowels are used only at the beginnings of words. In the middles of words, the dependent vowel signs are used.

As always, the consonants carry an inherent *a* sound. It can be canceled using a virama:

$$క్$$

Multiple consonant sounds with no intervening vowel sounds are usually represented using conjunct-consonant forms instead. Generally, the second consonant is written as a subscript under the first consonant:

$$ప + ర = ప్ర$$
$$ద + ద = ద్ద$$

---

8. Most of the examples in this section are taken from Nakanishi, pp. 60–61.

Consonants

క ఖ గ ఘ ఙ చ ఛ జ ఝ ఞ ట ఠ డ ఢ ణ త థ ద ధ న ప ఫ బ భ
మ య ర ఱ ల ళ వ శ ష స హ

Independent vowels

అ ఆ ఇ ఈ ఉ ఊ ఋ ౡ ఎ ఏ ఐ ఒ ఓ ఔ

Dependent vowels (shown attached to క)

కా కి కీ కు కూ కృ కౄ కె కే కై కొ కో కౌ

Figure 9.9   Telugu consonants and vowels

Sometimes they take other forms:

$$క + క = క్క$$
$$న + త + ర = న్త్ర$$

Notice that the consonants generally lose their headstrokes when they appear in combination. This also generally happens when they're combined with a dependent vowel sign.

Like the other scripts, Telugu has its own set of digits:

౦ ౧ ౨ ౩ ౪ ౫ ౬ ౭ ౮ ౯

The Telugu Block

Like the other ISCII-derived blocks, the Unicode Telugu block (U+0C00 to U+0C7F) follows the ISCII order. It includes one split vowel, although the component parts appear above and below the consonant. The bottom-joining part is encoded separately as U+TELUGU AI LENGTH MARK, and the split vowel has a canonical decomposition that includes this character.

■ KANNADA

The Kannada script (pronounced "KAH-nuh-dah," not "ka-NAH-da") is used to write the Kannada, or Kanarese, language of the Karnataka region of southern India, as well as minority languages such as Tulu. It is very closely related to the Telugu script. Both are derived from the Old Kannada script, but diverged around 1500, with the two different forms being hardened into place by the advent of printing in the nineteenth century.[9]

The basic letterforms of Kannada are extremely similar to those of Telugu, with the main difference being the shape of the headstroke. Like Telugu, Kannada has 35 consonants, 14 independent vowels, and 13 dependent vowels (Figure 9.10). The shapes of the dependent vowels differ from those of their Telugu counterparts, however.

Kannada forms conjunct consonants in the same basic way as Telugu, and some of the dependent vowel signs form ligatures with certain consonants, just as they do in Telugu.

One interesting wrinkle of Kannada that's different from Telugu is the behavior of ರ, which represents the *r* sound (which takes irregular forms in so many of the other Indic scripts). When this character is the *first* character in a conjunct consonant, it changes shape and appears *after* the rest of the consonants

kaa = ಕ + ೂ = ಕಾ

kraa = ಕ + ರ + ೂ = ಕ್ರಾ

rkaa = ರ + ಕ + ೂ = ಕಾ

Consonants

ಕ ಖ ಗ ಘ ಙ ಚ ಛ ಜ ಝ ಞ ಟ ಠ ಡ ಢ ಣ ತ ಥ ದ
ಧ ನ ಪ ಫ ಬ ಭ ಮ ಯ ರ ಱ ಲ ಳ ವ ಶ ಷ ಸ ಹ

Independent vowels

ಅ ಆ ಇ ಈ ಉ ಊ ಋ ಌ ಎ ಏ ಐ ಒ ಓ ಔ

Dependent vowels (shown attached to ಕ)

ಕಾ ಕಿ ಕೀ ಕು ಕೂ ಕೃ ಕೄ ಕೆ ಕೇ ಕೈ ಕೊ ಕೋ ಕೌ

Figure 9.10 Kannada consonants and vowels

---

9. This information comes from William Bright, "Kannada and Telugu Writing," in *The World's Writing Systems,* pp. 413–419.

Like the other scripts we've looked at, Kannada uses a unique set of digits:

○ ೧ ೨ ೩ ೪ ೫ ೬ ೭ ೮ ೯

The Kannada Block

The Unicode Kannada block runs from U+0C80 to U+0CFF and follows the ISCII order. Several split vowels have canonical decompositions to pairs of vowels. The Kannada block has two special code point values that represent the right-hand components of the split vowels.

The Kannada block includes one misnamed character. U+0CDE KANNADA LETTER FA should have been called KANNADA LETTER LLLA. Because the Unicode standard never renames a character, however, we're stuck with the wrong name. Fortunately, this obsolete character is used only in historical writings.

■ MALAYALAM

The Malayalam script (pronounced "MAH-luh-yah-lum," not "muh-LAY-uh-lahm") is used to write the Malayalam language, spoken in the Kerala region of southern India.[10] Malayalam shares structure with the other Indic scripts. It has 36 consonants and 14 independent vowels (Figure 9.11). As in the other scripts we've looked at so far, the consonants carry an inherent *a*. The other vowel sounds are attached to the consonants by means of the 12 dependent vowel signs.

The letterforms are similar to those of Tamil. Unlike Tamil, however, Malayalam has a large set of conjunct-consonant forms. The virama is used to cancel the vowel sound on consonants at the ends of words:

ma + ◌്

---

10. Some information comes from K. P. Mohanan, "Malayalam Writing," in *The World's Writing Systems,* pp. 420–425.

Consonants

ക ഖ ഗ ഘ ങ ച ഛ ജ ഝ ഞ ട ഠ ഡ ഢ ണ ത ഥ ദ ധ
ന പ ഫ ബ ഭ മ യ ര റ ല ള ഴ വ ശ ഷ സ ഹ

Independent vowels

അ ആ ഇ ഈ ഉ ഊ ഋ ൠ എ ഏ ഐ ഒ ഓ ഔ

Dependent vowels (shown attached to ക)

കാ കി കീ കു കൂ കൃ കെ കേ കൈ കൊ കോ കൗ

Figure 9.11 Malayalam consonants and vowels

In many cases, even the virama forms a ligature with its consonant:

$$യ + \bigcirc^\upsilon = യ^\upsilon$$

but

$$ക + \bigcirc^\upsilon = ക്$$
$$ണ + \bigcirc^\upsilon = ൺ$$
$$ഉ + \bigcirc^\upsilon = ഉ$$

The anusvara ($^\upsilon$) is used to represent the *m* sound at the end of a syllable, instead of using a conjunct-consonant form.

A script reform movement in the 1970s and 1980s produced a simplified version of the script with fewer conjunct forms and the modification of the vowel signs that appear below the letters so that the script is easier to print, consisting of a series of independent glyphs that can be written linearly. However, this version never completely caught on, giving rise to several hybrid printing styles that use the simplified forms for some things and the traditional forms for others. As a result, the appearance of the same piece of Malayalam text can vary fairly significantly depending on font design.

Unlike in the other scripts described so far in this chapter, spaces aren't always used between words in Malayalam. Some documents do so, but others run sequences of words together without spaces and use spaces only between phrases.

As in the other scripts, there is a set of Malayalam-specific digits:

൦ ൧ ൨ ൩ ൪ ൫ ൬ ൭ ൮ ൯

The Malayalam Block

The Unicode Malayalam block runs from U+0D00 to U+0D7F. It follows the ISCII order and the same encoding principles as the other scripts described previously in this chapter. The choice between traditional and simplified rendering is purely a matter of font design and not reflected in the encoding. It is possible to break up a conjunct consonant and use the virama forms of the consonants by using the zero-width non-joiner (see the "Devanagari" section earlier in this chapter for more information).

■ SINHALA

The Sinhala script is used to write the Sinhala (or Sinhalese) language of Sri Lanka; it is also used in Sri Lanka to write Sanskrit and Pali. Although Sinhala is an Indic language, the Sinhala script belongs to the South Brahmi family of scripts used to write the Dravidian languages.[11] It follows the same general structure as the other Indic scripts, with a set of 41 consonants and separate sets of dependent and independent vowels (Figure 9.12). Of the consonants, only 22 are used to write regular Sinhala. The others are used to write loanwords, or to write Pali or Sanskrit. Likewise, there are 18 independent vowels, but only 12 of them are used to write native Sinhala words. The independent vowels are

---

11. Information in this section comes from James W. Gair, "Sinhala Writing," in *The World's Writing Systems,* pp. 408–412, and from Nakanishi, pp. 66–67.

Consonants

ක බ ග ස ඩ ධ ඟ ව ජ ඥ ඤ ඦ ඥ ඦ ඨ ඪ ඩ ඬ ණ ඬ ත ථ ද ධ

න ඳ ප ඵ බ භ ම ඹ ය ර ල ව ශ ෂ ස හ ළ

Independent vowels

අ ආ ඇ ඈ ඉ ඊ උ ඌ ඍ ඎ එ ඒ ඓ ඔ ඕ ඖ

Dependent vowels (shown attached to ක)

කා කැ කෑ කි කී කු කූ කෘ කෙ කේ කෛ කො

කෝ කෞ කං

Figure 9.12 Sinhala consonants and vowels

---

used only at the beginnings of words. After consonants, vowel sounds are represented using the 17 dependent vowel signs.

As with the other scripts, the consonants carry an inherent *a* sound, which can be canceled using the virama (called **al-lakuna** in Sinhala):

$$ ක්‍ $$

The anusvara (°) is used in Sinhala not only to indicate nasalization, but in modern spelling to indicate an actual *n* sound at the end of a syllable.

Like many of the other Indic scripts, Sinhala has a fairly complex system of conjunct consonants, and many of the dependent vowel signs form ligatures with certain consonants. These include special forms of the *r* consonant when it appears at the beginning or end of a conjunct-consonant cluster, similar to the forms used in Devanagari and some of the other North Brahmi scripts.

In traditional texts, spaces were not used between words, and the only punctuation used was the **kunddaliya** (༺༻), which was used where English uses a period. In modern writing, spaces are placed between words and European punctuation is used. There is also a traditional set of Sinhala digits, although these, too, have passed into obsolescence. Today, European digits are used. Some modern printing practices eschew many of the conjunct-consonant clusters in favor of forms explicitly using the al-lakuna.

The Sinhala Block

The Unicode Sinhala block runs from U+0D80 to U+0DFF. It does *not* follow the ISCII order, partly because the ISCII standard doesn't include a code page for Sinhala and partly because Sinhala includes a lot of sounds (and, thus, letters) that aren't present in any of the Indian scripts. The basic setup of the block is the same: anusvara and visarga first, followed by independent vowels, consonants, dependent vowels, and punctuation. Unlike in the ISCII-derived blocks, the al-lakuna (virama) precedes the dependent vowels, rather than following them.

The same basic encoding principles used for the ISCII-derived scripts are used by Unicode for encoding Sinhala. That is, the character codes encode characters, not glyphs, so no special code point values are required for the conjunct ligatures or contextual forms of the vowels. The characters are stored in logical order, as they are pronounced, meaning vowel signs always follow their consonants, even when they're drawn to their left. The code point values for the consonant characters include the inherent *a* sound; the al-lakuna is used to cancel the inherent vowel and signal the formation of conjunct-consonant clusters (when conjunct-consonant clusters are formed, the al-lakuna will not show up as a separate glyph, even though it's typed and stored). The joiner and non-joiner characters can be used to control the formation of ligatures and consonant conjuncts.

Consonant forms carrying a nukta are used for writing Tamil with the Sinhala script; these forms aren't separately encoded. Interestingly, the Sinhala block doesn't include a code point value for the nukta. The Unicode standard points out this omission, but doesn't say what to do about it. As each of the other Indic blocks includes its own nukta, it's unclear which one to use with Sinhala—if, indeed, any of them is appropriate. The actual answer will depend on individual implementations and fonts. The Unicode Sinhala block includes a code point value for the kunddaliya, even though it's not used in modern writing, but doesn't include code point values for the Sinhala digits.

■ THAI

The next four scripts described in this chapter are used in Southeast Asia to write various Asian languages. All of these scripts descend from the South Brahmi forms, but show greater diversification, reflecting the wider variety of languages represented.

The Thai script is used to write the Thai language of Thailand.[12] The Thai and Lao scripts both have their roots in a script developed in 1283 by King Ramkhamhaeng of Sukhothai. They had diverged into separate scripts, with different spelling rules, by the sixteenth century.

Thai has a whopping 46 consonants (Figure 9.13), but only 21 consonant sounds. The extra letters represent sounds that aren't distinguished anymore in modern pronunciation, but still carry etymological information and are used to distinguish tone.

Thai doesn't have independent vowel signs like the other Indic scripts. Instead, the letter อ, which represents the glottal stop, is used with the dependent vowel signs to write an initial vowel sound. Thai consonants are generally considered to carry an inherent *o* sound, with the other vowel sounds represented with the 21 dependent vowel signs.

Consonants

ก ข ข ค ค ฆ ง จ ฉ ช ซ ฌ ญ ฎ ฏ ฐ ฑ ฒ ณ ด ต ถ ท ธ น บ ป ผ
ฝ พ ฟ ภ ม ย ร ฤ ล ฦ ว ศ ษ ส ห ฬ อ ฮ

Dependent vowels (shown attached to อ)

อะ อ้ อา อิ อี อึ อื อุ อู เอะ เอ เอ็ แอะ แอ โอะ โอ เอาะ อำ ใอ ไอ เอา

Figure 9.13 Thai consonants and dependent vowels

12. The information in this section and the section on the Lao script comes from Anthony Diller, "Thai and Lao Writing," in *The World's Writing Systems,* pp. 457–466, with some additional information coming from Nakanishi, pp. 76–79.

Thai, like many Asian languages, is a tonal language. Different consonants carry different inherent tones, but there's a set of four tone marks as well:

$$\text{อ่ อ้ อ๊ อ๋}$$

When a consonant has both a dependent vowel sign and a tone mark on it, the tone mark moves up and becomes smaller to make room for the vowel sign:

$$\text{อ}$$

Thai doesn't have conjunct consonants. A virama (อ) is used to cancel the inherent vowel when the Thai script is used to write Pali, but normal Thai doesn't use a virama. Instead, successive consonants are juxtaposed, and you have to know when to pronounce the inherent vowel and when not to. The omission of the virama isn't a big deal, as Thai spelling in general isn't phonetic. Only three sounds can occur at the end of a syllable, but most of the letters can be used in this position, for example. Sometimes extra letters appear at the end of a word that aren't pronounced; sometimes the **thanthakhat** (ฺ) is written over a silent letter to indicate that it's silent.

Two special symbols are used like letters in the middle of words. The **maiyamok** (ๆ) is used to represent repetition of the syllable that precedes it. The **paiyannoi** (ฯ) is used to indicate elision of letters from long words or phrases. The sequence ฯลฯ means "et cetera."

Thai also includes some special punctuation marks. The **fongman** (๏) is used in the same way as a bullet in English to mark items in lists, or at the beginnings of verses or paragraphs. The **angkhankhu** (๚) is used at the ends of long segments of text, with the sequence ๚ะ marking the end of an even longer segment of text, such as a verse in poetry. The **khomut** (๛) may follow this sequence at the end of a paragraph or document.

Spaces don't generally separate words in Thai text (although space is sometimes added between words when necessary to justify text between the margins). Instead, spaces are used between phrases or sentences, where you might use a comma or period in English.

Finally, there's a set of Thai digits:

$$\text{๐ ๑ ๒ ๓ ๔ ๕ ๖ ๗ ๘ ๙}$$

The Thai Block

The Unicode Thai block runs from U+0E00 to U+0E7F. It's based on TIS 620, the Thai national standard.

Unicode encodes Thai in a radically different manner from how it encodes the other Indic scripts. In particular, to maintain compatibility with existing usage and the Thai national standard, the Thai block breaks the logical-order rule. Like many of the other Indic scripts, Thai has left-joining and split vowels. But unlike in those scripts, in Thai, a left-joining vowel *precedes* the consonant it modifies in storage (top- and bottom-joining vowels follow their consonants in storage). Split vowels are represented using two separate code point values— one each for the left-hand and right-hand components of the split vowel. When a consonant has both a top- or bottom-joining vowel and a tone mark, the tone mark follows the vowel in memory.

Even though spaces aren't generally used between words in Thai, when text wraps from one line onto the next, the split must happen on a word boundary. This parsing can be done automatically by the text-rendering software, or U+200B ZERO WIDTH SPACE, which has no visual presentation, can be used to tell the text-rendering software where it's safe to break the lines. In justified text, the zero-width space might actually widen to be visible.

■ LAO

The Lao script is used to write the Lao (or Laotian) language of Laos. It's very closely related to the Thai script, with both having evolved from the script invented by King Ramkhamhaeng in 1283. The letterforms are very similar, although Lao includes a lot fewer letters. The Lao script has 27 consonants, no independent vowels, and 18 dependent vowels (Figure 9.14).

Lao uses a tonal system similar to that employed for Thai. It relies mostly on different combinations of letters to indicate tone, but supplements them with four tone marks:

Consonants

ກ ຂ ຄ ງ ຈ ຊ ຍ ດ ຕ ຖ ທ ນ ບ ປ ຜ ຝ ພ ຟ ມ ຍ ຮ ວ

ວ ສ ຫ ອ ຮ

Dependent vowels (shown attached to ອ)

ະ ິ າ ຳ ີ ຶ ື ຸ ູ ົ ເອ ແອ ໂອ ໄອ ໃອ

Figure 9.14 Lao consonants and dependent vowels

Lao, like Thai, includes multiple consonants with the same sound but different inherent tones. Some consonants that don't have counterparts with the opposite tone are written with ຫ, which is silent but changes the tone. Sometimes, this letter forms a ligature with the letter carrying the actual consonant sound:

$$ຫ + ນ = ໜ$$

$$ຫ + ມ = ໝ$$

The symbol ຼ is used to represent the *l* or *r* sound (the letter ລ) when it occurs after another consonant:

$$ພ + ລ = ພຼ$$

These forms are the only remaining remnants of an earlier system of conjunct consonants. Other than these forms, Lao is written like Thai: The characters for successive consonant sounds are juxtaposed, with the reader understanding when the inherent *o* is not pronounced. Like Thai, Lao doesn't use a virama. It also doesn't generally use spaces between words, placing them instead where English normally uses a comma.

Lao, like Thai, provides an ellipsis character (ຯ) and a repetition character (ໆ). There is also a distinctive set of Lao digits:

໐ ໑ ໒ ໓ ໔ ໕ ໖ ໗ ໘ ໙

Although both the languages and writing systems are similar, the Laotian government instituted a set of spelling reforms in the 1960s, with the result being a divergence in spelling between Lao and Thai. Thai spelling preserves etymological details at the expense of phonetics. Lao spelling is phonetic at the expense of etymology.

With the exception of the conjunct-consonant forms, all of the letters in the Lao script have direct counterparts in the Thai script, making the two scripts freely convertible (at least when used to write Lao, as Thai has more letters). A sizable Lao-speaking minority in Thailand generally uses the Thai script to write their language.

The Lao Block

Because the Thai and Lao scripts are so closely related and convertible, the Unicode Lao block (U+0E80 to U+0EFF) is organized with the characters in the same relative positions within their block as the analogous characters in the Thai block. Lao follows the same encoding principles as Thai, with characters being stored in visual order rather than logical order. Thus, left-joining vowel signs precede their consonants in memory, even though they're spoken after the consonants. Split vowels are represented using two separate character codes: one, representing the left-joining part of the vowel, precedes the consonant in memory, and the other, representing the right-joining part of the vowel, follows it. The subscript version of ຊ is represented using a separate character code from the full-size version and is treated as a combining mark. The two ligatures (ຫນ and ຫມ) also receive separate code point values, although they have compatibility decompositions back to the original letters.

▪ KHMER

The Khmer script is used to write the Khmer, or Cambodian, language of Cambodia. This script goes back to about the sixth century.[13] Khmer shares the

---

13. My sources for this section are Eric Schiller, "Khmer Writing," in *The World's Writing Systems,* pp. 467–473, and Nakanishi, pp. 74–75.

same general design as the other Indic scripts. There are 35 consonants and 17 independent vowels (Figure 9.15).

The Khmer consonants have an inherent vowel, but they don't all have the *same* inherent vowel. There are 13 "first series" consonants, which carry an inherent *a:*

ក ខ ច ឆ ដ ឋ ត ថ ប ផ ត ស ហ ឡ អ

The rest of the consonants belong to the "second series" and carry an inherent *o:*

គ យ ង ជ ឈ ញ ឌ ឍ ណ ទ ធ ន ព ភ ម យ រ ល វ ឲ

There are also 12 dependent vowel signs. There isn't an independent vowel character for every possible vowel sound, because not all vowel sounds can occur at the beginning of a word). The dependent vowels represent different sounds depending on whether they're used with a first-series or second-series consonant. Sometimes it's necessary to put a second-series vowel sound on a first-series consonant, or vice versa. Diacritical marks are used to do this: The **muusikatoan** (") converts a second-series consonant to a first-series consonant, and the **triisap** (˜) converts a first-series consonant to a second-series consonant.

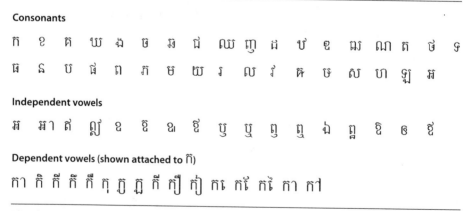

Consonants

ក ខ គ ឃ ង ច ឆ ជ ឈ ញ ដ ឋ ឌ ឍ ណ ត ថ ទ
ធ ន ប ផ ព ភ ម យ រ ល វ ស ហ ឡ អ

Independent vowels

អ អា ឥ ឦ ឧ ឩ ឪ ឫ ឬ ឭ ឮ ឯ ឰ ឱ ឲ

Dependent vowels (shown attached to ក)

កា កិ កី កឹ កឺ កុ កូ កួ កើ កឿ កៀ កេ កែ កៃ កោ កៅ

Figure 9.15 Khmer consonants and vowels

Like most of the other Indic scripts, Khmer does have conjunct consonants. Normally, the second consonant in a pair is written as a subscript under the first one:

$$ ក + ក = ក្ក $$

Sometimes the subscript has an ascender that sticks up to the right of the main consonant:

$$ ដ + យ = ដ្យ $$

Occasionally, the subscript has a completely different form from its normal form:

$$ ន + ទ = ន្ទ $$

The letter representing the *r* sound (រ), when used as a subscript, picks up an ascender that sticks up to the *left* of the main consonant:

$$ ក + រ = ក្រ $$

The r character thus appears to *precede* the main consonant even though its sound *follows* it (this is analogous to the left-joining dependent vowels).

The vowel-shifter characters muusikatoan (˝) and triisap (˜) can change shape in certain circumstances. If the consonant has an ascender that sticks up into the space that these characters normally occupy, or if a vowel sign is found in that position, the character takes a different shape and moves *under* the consonant:

$$ ស + ˝ + ˜ = ស៊ី $$

The **nikahit** (°) represents nasalization, the **reahmuk** (ះ) represents a final glottal stop, and the **bantoc** (՚) shortens the preceding vowel.

Like Thai and Lao, Khmer is written without spaces between words; instead, spaces are used more or less where English would use a comma. The **khan** (។) is used at the ends of sentences or groups of sentences. The **bariyoosan** (៕) marks the end of a section.

There is also a distinctive set of Khmer digits:

០ ១ ២ ៣ ៤ ៥ ៦ ៧ ៨ ៩

The Khmer Block

The Unicode Khmer block runs from U+1780 to U+17FF. It includes not only the regular Khmer letters, but also a series of rare letters and symbols used only in transcribing Sanskrit and Pali. It includes a wide selection of punctuation marks as well.

The encoding principle is the same as that employed with the Indic scripts (and different from Thai and Lao): The vowel signs always follow the consonants, even when the consonant glyph appears before or around the consonant. Conjunct consonants are formed by using U+17D2 KHMER SIGN COENG, the Khmer analogue to the Indic virama. This code point value has no visual presentation (the glyph shown in the Unicode standard is arbitrary); it functions merely to signal the formation of a conjunct consonant. Even though the following (subscript) form of r appears to the left of the preceding consonant, it's still represented in memory following the main consonant (and the **coeng**).

If a syllable includes a series-shifter, it follows all the consonants in the cluster and precedes the vowel. Any other marks on the cluster come last.

■ MYANMAR

The Myanmar script, which is used to write Burmese, the language of Burma, dates back to the early twelfth century. It is descended from the Mon script, which ultimately derives from the South Brahmi scripts.[14] As with the other scripts in this chapter, it follows the same basic structure as the other Indic scripts. There are 34 consonants and 7 dependent vowel signs, each of which represents a combination of a vowel and a tone (Figure 9.16).

---

14. My sources for Myanmar are Julian K. Wheatley, "Burmese Writing," in *The World's Writing Systems,* pp. 450–456, and Nakanishi, pp. 72–73.

Consonants

က ခ ဂ ဃ င စ ဆ ဇ ဈ ည ဋ ဌ ဍ ဎ ဏ တ ထ ဒ ဓ န ပ

ဖ ဗ ဘ မ ယ ရ လ ဝ သ ဟ ဠ အ

Dependent vowels (shown attached to အ)

အာ အိ အီ အု အူ ေအ အဲ

Figure 9.16 Myanmar consonants and vowels

The letter အ is a neutral consonant that is used to represent independent vowel sounds. The script also includes a few independent vowel signs, used generally in Indian loanwords.

The dependent vowel sign ာ takes a different shape when its normal shape would cause the consonant–vowel combination to be confused with another consonant:

$$ပ + ာ = ပါ$$

Myanmar has conjunct consonants. Most of the time, the second consonant is written as a subscript under the first one:

$$မ + မ = မ္မ$$

The consonants (ယ, ရ, ဝ, and ဟ), representing the *y, r, w,* and *h* sounds, respectively, take special diacritic forms when they're used in conjuncts:

$$ခ + ယ = ချ$$
$$မ + ရ = မြ$$
$$မ + ဝ = မွ$$
$$ဟ + င = ၍$$

These characters can also participate in three-consonant clusters:

$$ဟ + မ + ရ = မြှ$$

The anusvara (°) and visarga (ঃ) from the Indic languages, along with a subscript dot (ₒ), are used as tone marks. A virama, or "killer" (ᷮ), cancels a consonant's inherent *a* sound when a word ends with a consonant sound and occasionally in the middle of words.

Burmese is written with spaces between phrases rather than words. For punctuation, the danda (၊) and double danda (။), corresponding roughly to the semicolon and period, are borrowed from the Indic languages.

There is also a unique set of Myanmar digits:

၀ ၁ ၂ ၃ ၄ ၅ ၆ ၇ ၈ ၉

The Myanmar Block

The Unicode Myanmar block (U+1000 to U+109F) follows the same basic principles as the other Indic blocks: The dependent vowel signs always follow their consonants in memory, even when the vowel is drawn to the left of the consonant; each letter gets only one code point value, even if its shape changes depending on context; and conjunct consonants are formed by placing the virama between the consonants. The zero-width non-joiner can be used to break up a conjunct in the middle of a word and force the virama to be visible.

Unlike the other Indic blocks, the Myanmar block doesn't include precomposed code point values for the split vowels. All Myanmar split vowels are made up of the glyphs for two other vowels (or one or two vowels plus a tone mark). These are always represented in Unicode by using the code point values for the individual pieces, both of which follow the consonant in memory.

▪ TIBETAN

The Tibetan script is used not only to write Tibetan as spoken in Tibet, but also the Dzongkha language spoken in Bhutan. Sanskrit is also transcribed into Tibetan characters. The earliest examples of Tibetan writing date to the eighth and ninth centuries.[15] Tradition holds that the Tibetan script was created in the

---

15. The information in the section on Tibetan comes from the lengthy character block description in the Unicode standard, pp. 240–248; Leonard W. J. van der Kuijp, "The Tibetan Script and Derivatives," in *The World's Writing Systems,* pp. 431–436; and Nakanishi, pp. 88–89.

sixth century by a man named Thumi Sambhota, a member of a delegation sent
to India by the king of Tibet to study Buddhism and the Indian languages.

Tibetan, like Chinese, is a monosyllabic language, so the principles of Indic
writing are modified a bit to deal with Tibetan pronunciation. Still, the basic
principles remain the same. There are 30 consonants (Figure 9.17). Tibetan has
one independent vowel, representing the same inherent *a* sound the consonants
all have. The other vowel sounds are represented by using the four dependent
vowel signs applied to this letter.

Additional consonant and vowel characters are used in loanwords and
transliterated Sanskrit.

A Tibetan syllable has single core consonant, or "radical," which may combine with additional consonant characters. Only the core consonant has the inherent *a*. Some combinations of consonants stack on top of one another. The
consonants ར, ལ, and ས adopt an abbreviated shape when they appear above
certain other consonants:

$$ར + ཀ = རྐ$$

The consonants ཡ, ལ, ར, ཝ, and ཟ adopt an abbreviated shape when they
appear below certain other consonants:

$$ཀ + ལ = ཀླ$$

$$ཀ + ཡ = ཀྱ$$

$$ཀ + ར = ཀྲ$$

$$ཀ + ཝ = ཀྭ$$

Consonants

ཀ ཁ ག ང ཅ ཆ ཇ ཉ ཏ ཐ ད ན པ ཕ བ མ ཙ ཚ ཛ ཞ ཟ འ ཡ ར ལ ཤ ས ཧ ཨ

Independent vowel

ཨ

Dependent vowels (shown attached to ཨ**)**

ཨི ཨུ ཨེ ཨོ

Figure 9.17 Tibetan consonants and vowels

Some consonants go before a consonant stack, others go after it. A consonant after the main consonant of the syllable might represent a word-final consonant rather than part of the stack, in which case the vowel signs go on the consonant before it. If the main consonant of the syllable keeps its inherent *a* (i.e., it doesn't have a vowel sign), another consonant after it is treated as a syllable-ending consonant. If it's not supposed to be treated in this way—that is, if the syllable ends with the inherent *a* sound—the syllable will end with ᩝ. For example,

དག་

is *dag,* but

དགཨ་

is *dga.*

A syllable can consist of as many as four consonants in a row, with the main consonant optionally being a consonant stack. In most such words, the majority of the letters are actually silent; this reflects the fact that Tibetan spelling hasn't changed in centuries.

Syllables (words, basically) are separated from one another with dots called **tshegs**, which are aligned along the baseline like periods in English text. Tibetan is written hanging from the baseline, like Devanagari, rather than sitting on it, like English, so the tsheg appears on the upper-right shoulder of the last character in the syllable. When text is justified between margins, extra tshegs are added at the end of the line to pad it out to the margin.

The rules for how consonant stacks form are very regular for Tibetan, but a much wider variety of conjuncts can be formed in Sanskrit and other languages written using Tibetan characters. A complex system of abbreviation is also used in Tibetan writing that can break most of the normal character-joining rules.

Tibetan is normally written without spaces, although the tsheg serves the same basic purpose. A wide variety of punctuation marks are used with Tibetan, the most important of which are the **shad** (।) and the **nyis shad** (॥), which derive from the Devanagari danda and double danda, respectively. They're very roughly equivalent to the comma and period: The shad marks the end of an expression, and the *nyis shad* marks a change in topic.

There is also a unique set of Tibetan digits:

$$0 \quad ？ \quad ？ \quad ？ \quad ？ \quad ？ \quad ？ \quad ？ \quad ？ \quad ？$$

The Tibetan Block

The Unicode Tibetan block is quite large, running from U+0F00 to U+0FFF. In addition to the basic Tibetan letters, it includes extra letters used for transliterating certain languages and a large set of punctuation marks, cantillation marks, and astrological signs.

The Tibetan block follows a radically different encoding practice from the other Indic blocks. Instead of using a virama character to signal the formation of conjunct consonants, each consonant is encoded twice: The first series of code point values is used for consonants when they appear by themselves or at the top of a conjunct stack, and the second series is used for consonants that appear in a conjunct stack anywhere but at the top. Only certain combinations are legal in Tibetan, but all the consonants are encoded this way to allow for non-Tibetan conjuncts, such as those found in Sanskrit. Thus, ཀྲ (kra), which would be encoded like this in Devanagari (and most of the other Indic scripts)

```
U+0915 DEVANAGARI LETTER KA
U+094D DEVANAGARI SIGN VIRAMA
U+0930 DEVANAGARI LETTER RA
```

is encoded like this in Tibetan:

```
U+0F40 TIBETAN LETTER KA
U+0FB2 TIBETAN SUBJOINED LETTER RA
```

Because the letter ར can change shape when it appears at the top of a conjunct stack, something you don't necessarily want in some non-Tibetan languages, Unicode includes a separate code point value, U+0F6A TIBETAN LETTER FIXED-FORM RA, to represent a ར that always keeps its full size and shape. Likewise, because ར, ཝ, and ཡ change shape when they appear at the bottom of a conjunct stack, Unicode provides separate code point values—U+0FBA TIBETAN SUBJOINED LETTER FIXED-FORM WA, U+0FBB TIBETAN SUBJOINED LETTER FIXED-FORM YA, and U+0FBC TIBETAN SUB-JOINED LETTER FIXED-FORM RA—that also keep their normal shape no matter what. These alternate code point values should never be used in encoding native Tibetan.

▪ THE PHILIPPINE SCRIPTS

Unicode 3.2 adds four additional scripts to write various languages of the Philippines. These four scripts are sandwiched into a comparatively small area of the Unicode encoding space, running from U+1700 to U+177F.[16]

The four Philippine scripts are related to each other, probably descending from a common ancestor. They're clearly related to the Southeast Asian scripts, and probably came to the Philippines from Southeast Asia by way of Indonesia, possibly as late as the fourteenth century. The Tagalog script fell into disuse in the 1700s under European colonization, and was superseded by the Latin alphabet. The other three scripts—Hanunóo, Buhid, and Tagbanwa—are still used today, but to varying degrees. Hanunóo remains relatively popular, used most often (interestingly enough) to write love poetry. Buhid and Tagbanwa are less often used.

The four Philippine scripts all have a similar structure. Each has 3 independent vowels and 12 to 14 consonants (Figure 9.18).

As with most of the other Indic scripts, the consonants all carry an inherent *a* sound, and the vowel sound can be changed through the addition of a vowel mark. There are only two dependent vowel marks in the Philippine scripts (there are more vowel sounds, as each vowel mark represents more than one sound). In each script, the two marks are the same (depending on the script, a dot, dash, or chevron). Whether the vowel mark is drawn above or below the consonant determines which sound it represents.

---

16. Most of the small amount of information on the Philippine scripts here comes from section 9.16 of PDUTR #28, supplemented by some material from Joel C. Kuipers and Ray McDermott, "Insular Southeast Asian Scripts," *The World's Writing Systems,* pp. 474–484.

	Consonants																Vowels		
Tagalog	ⲭ	ろ	ꞇ	ⲭ	ⲭ	ꝫ	ⲭ	◯	ⲭ	ⲭ		ꝫ	ꝫ	ꝫ	◡		V	ⲭ	3
Hammóo	♃	ⲭ	ⲭ	W	ⲭ	ⲭ	ⲭ	7	ⲭ	ⲭ	–	ⲭ	ⲭ	ⲭ	V		V	ⲭ	3
Buhid	ⲭ	ⲭ	ⲭ	W	ⲭ	T	V	フ	ⲭ	ⲭ	–	ⲭ	ⲭ	ⲭ	L		V	V	7
Tagbanwa	X	ⲭ	ⲭ	ⲭ	ⲭ	T	ⲭ	◯	ⲭ	ⲭ		ⲭ	G	ⲭ			V	V	ⲭ

Figure 9.18   Philippine consonants and vowels

In all four languages, syllables have a consonant-vowel-consonant format. Most of the time, syllable-ending consonants are not written, although virama-like marks do appear in Tagalog and Hanunóo. The Hanunóo virama (called the **pamudpod**) is used somewhat more often. In both Tagalog and Hanunóo, the virama is always visible; the consonants do not form conjuncts. In Hanunóo and Buhid, however, certain consonant–vowel combinations form ligatures.

The Philippine scripts are generally written from left to right, as the other Indic scripts are. You may also see them written *from bottom to top*, with the lines running from left to right. This system seems to be a by-product of the instruments typically used to write these scripts.

Punctuation marks similar to the danda and double danda in Devanagari are used with all four scripts.

In Unicode, the four scripts are encoded in four successive blocks in the range from U+1700 to U+177F. The Tagalog block runs from U+1700 to U+171F, the Hanunóo block from U+1720 to U+173F, the Buhid block from U+1740 to U+175F, and the Tagbanwa block from U+1760 to U+177F. Characters that correspond between the scripts are encoded at analogous positions in their respective blocks. The punctuation marks are encoded once for all four scripts, in the Hanunóo block.

10

Scripts of East Asia

$\mathcal{N}$ow we come to the last of the four major groups of modern scripts. This last group comprises the East Asian scripts. In particular, it covers the various writing systems used to write Chinese, Japanese, Korean, and (prior to the 1920s) Vietnamese. These scripts are often referred to collectively as the CJK scripts (for "Chinese, Japanese, and Korean"), or sometimes the CJKV scripts (for "Chinese, Japanese, Korean, and Vietnamese").

This group of scripts is fundamentally different from the others. Recall that all of the European alphabetic scripts either descended from the Greek alphabet or arose under its influence. All of the bi-di scripts of the Middle East either descended from the ancient Aramaic alphabet or arose under its influence. The Indic scripts used in southern Asia descended from the ancient Brahmi script. The Brahmi script is generally thought to have its roots in the Aramaic alphabet, and the Greek and Aramaic alphabets are both direct descendants of the ancient Phoenician alphabet. Thus the Phoenician alphabet can properly be thought of as the ancestor of all the writing systems we've examined so far.

Not so with the CJK scripts. All of these scripts either descended from or arose under the influence of the Chinese characters. The Chinese characters have no known antecedent. They're not known to have evolved from anyone else's writing system. Just as the ancient Phoenician alphabet (actually its earlier ancestors) arose spontaneously in Mesopotamia with no outside influence, the Chinese characters arose spontaneously in China with no outside influence.

So the writing systems of East Asia are related to one another, but they're not related to any of the other scripts we've looked at. They share some unique characteristics:

- The Chinese characters are used in almost every one of these systems. Unlike the other scripts, where the characters stand for sounds, Chinese characters stand for whole words or ideas,[1] so there are orders of magnitude more Chinese characters than there are characters in any of the other writing systems—they number in the tens of thousands. Needless to say, the individual characters can get quite complex. Moreover, multiple variant forms of many Chinese characters exist, and new Chinese characters are constantly being coined.

- All of the CJK languages, except for Yi, use phonetic characters to supplement the Chinese characters. The importance of these systems varies with the language—the Chinese phonetic system is rarely used, the Korean phonetic system is used almost exclusively, and the Japanese phonetic systems fall somewhere in the middle. The modern Yi script is completely phonetic and doesn't actually use the Chinese characters, but nevertheless arose under their influence.

- These writing systems use characters that are all the same size and shape (that is, the characters are designed to fit into a square, and successive characters in a passage of text fit into the same-size squares). The characters do not interact typographically—they don't change shape depending on context, they don't connect, and they don't form ligatures. Each character stands alone. A page of CJK text often looks like the characters were laid out on graph paper.

- The writing systems are traditionally written vertically. That is, the characters in a line of text start at the top of the page and work their way down, with lines of text starting on the right-hand side of the page and working their way to the left. Under the influence of Western writing and

---

1. Not entirely true, but a decent approximation for now (and, in fact, the approximation that leads to their being called "ideographs"). Bear with me, and we'll get into the meat of the matter in the next section.

Western printing and computing equipment, however, all of these scripts are now also written like the Latin alphabet: on horizontal lines running from left to right and progressing from the top to the bottom of the page. Occasionally, short snippets of text, such as newspaper headlines, are also written from right to left.

- Spaces are not used between words (in fact, the question of what constitutes a "word" in Chinese writing can be somewhat complicated), except sometimes in Korean.

- Many of these writing systems make occasional use of a system of interlinear annotation (i.e., notes between lines of text) to clarify the pronunciation or meaning of unfamiliar characters.

■ THE HAN CHARACTERS

Because the Chinese characters form the cornerstone, in one way or another, of all the scripts we'll be talking about, we'll look at them first.

The Chinese characters are called **hanzi** in Mandarin Chinese, **kanji** in Japanese, **hanja** in Korean, and **chu Han** in Vietnamese. All of these expressions mean "Han characters," the term we'll use for them here. *Han*, from the Han Dynasty, is used to refer to traditional Chinese culture. In other words, in Asia, "Han" more or less means "Chinese."

The Han characters have a very ancient history.[2] The earliest examples of Chinese writing date back to about 1200 B.C. The Han characters used today are directly descended from these early examples. The shapes of the characters have changed over time, and many more characters have been added, but the general principles underlying the system have remained constant through more than three millennia.

The Han characters are variously referred to as "ideographs," "logographs," and "pictographs," all of which are sort of right and sort of wrong. "Ideographs,"

---

2. My sources for information on the Han characters are William G. Boltz, "Early Chinese Writing," in *The World's Writing Systems,* pp. 191–199; Victor H. Mair, "Modern Chinese Writing," op. cit., pp. 200–208; Ken Lunde, *CJKV Information Processing* (Cambridge: O'Reilly, 1999), pp. 27–65; and Nakanishi, pp. 82–87.

the term used in the Unicode standard, implies that the characters simply stand for things and concepts and not for sounds. In practice, this is more or less true, especially for non-Chinese speakers. For Classical Chinese (and, to a lesser degree, for modern Chinese languages such as Mandarin), however, the Han characters also have a strong phonetic function. "Logographs" implies that the characters stand for words. Again, this concept is close enough, although the simple "syllable = word = character" idea that many have of Chinese doesn't always hold in practice. Polysyllabic words in Chinese are usually written with multiple characters, so it may be more accurate to think of the characters as "syllabographs." "Pictographs" is just plain too simplistic. It implies that all the Han characters are little pictures of the things they represent. Some may have started out that way, and many of the simplest characters still work in that way, but for most characters, the truth is more complicated.

Western writing and Chinese writing probably started out in more or less the same way. Writing wasn't invented to tell stories; it was invented to keep records.[3] Say you have ten sheep and three head of cattle, and you want to make a record of how many pieces of livestock you have. On some handy object, maybe a leaf or a piece of bark or a piece of clay, you draw a little picture of a sheep and follow it with ten scratch marks and a little picture of a bull and follow it with three scratch marks:

Now suppose you want to record a business transaction. You give your neighbor Joe three of your sheep in exchange for two of his cattle. You might draw something like this:

---

3. See, for example, Georges Ifrah (trans. David Bellos, E. F. Harding, Sophie Wood, and Ian Monk), *The Universal History of Numbers* (New York: Wiley, 2000), p. 77ff.

Here we have the basics of pictographic writing. The simplest Han characters are pictographs just like this:

人	**man**
木	**tree**
山	**mountain**
川	**river**
口	**mouth**

Of course, some of them you have to use your imagination with a little more than others:

女	**woman**
日	**sun**
月	**moon**

As often happens, the pictographs tend to become simpler and more stylized over time, looking less and less like the things they represent. The straight lines in the "sun" and "moon" characters, for example, reflect the fact that the tools these characters were originally written with didn't do circles well.

In many cases, it's fairly simple to come up with a picture to describe an abstract concept, giving rise to characters that can properly be called "ideographs":

上   **up**
下   **down**
中   **middle**
一   **one**
二   **two**
三   **three**

You can also do variations on a single character to mean different things. For example, if you add an extra stroke to the "tree" character, you get "root":

本   **root**

You can also use characters to mean one of several related concepts. For example, the "sun" and "moon" characters also represent "day" and "month." The character for "root" also means "origin."

Then you can combine characters. For example, take two trees and put them next to each other,

林

and you get the character for "woods." Add another tree,

森

and you get the character for "forest." Put "sun" and "moon" together,

明

and you get the character for "bright."

So far we haven't talked about how the Han characters can be used to represent sounds; all the discussion as revolved around the semantic values of the characters—that is, how they are used to represent things or concepts. To understand how phonetics become involved, consider this example:

These three pictures represent the word "carpenter." To get "carpenter," you just take the names of the three objects and string them together: you have a picture of a car, a picture of a pen, and a picture of a tear running down someone's cheek. This, as you probably know, is called a **rebus**, and examples abound. A favorite old chestnut is

<u>STAND</u>
I

which means "I understand" (that is, "I" under "stand"). Rebuses involving only the names of the letters and numbers abound on personalized license plates these days. Another oldie but goodie is

OU812

which, of course, means "Oh, you ate one, too?" and was the title of an old Van Halen album (yeah, I'm really dating myself here).

If we follow the "rebus principle," we see that a Han character can be used not only for the word the character originally meant to symbolize, and not just other words with similar or related meanings, but also for words that *sound like* the original word. For example, consider the character

This character means "king." No, there's nothing about it that really leaps out at you and says "king." Instead, it provides another example of the stylization these shapes undergo over time. The original version of this character looks like

a human figure standing on a line. This doesn't really say "king," either (maybe the line is a carpet or dais), but it's closer.

But we digress. The word for "king" in Chinese is "wang." Given this fact, you could use this character for other words that are pronounced the same way. For example, the same character can be used to mean "to go toward," which is also pronounced "wang" (but with a different intonation). There's no semantic or etymological connection between the two words; they just happen to be pronounced similarly. Because we have a character for "wang" meaning "king," we can also use it for "wang" meaning "to go toward," which doesn't lend itself well to inventing an ideograph.

Another example is this character:

$$貝$$

It originally meant "cowrie shell" (which were once used as currency) and was pronounced "bei." This character also came to be used to represent the word "bai," which meant "defeat."

Between using a character to represent a group of semantically related words (such as "root" and "origin") and using a character to represent a group of words with similar pronunciations, you can greatly increase the expressive power of these characters. It was at this point that the development of Chinese writing took off in a different direction from the direction the development of Western writing took. The Phoenicians took existing pictographs and began using them to represent their initial sounds. (This development is kind of like the "Alpha, Bravo, Charlie" system used by the U.S. military for spelling out words.) For example, the word *beth* meant "house" and was represented by a little picture of a house. Over time, the character came to represent the "b" sound at the beginning of "beth," instead of the whole word "beth" or the concept of "house," and its shape also gradually changed to look less like a house (or anything else). This process eventually led to the Phoenician alphabet (and the picture of a house eventually evolved into the Latin letter B and practically every other alphabetic letter representing the "b" sound).

Chinese writing occasionally made feints in the same direction, but the Han characters never lost their semantic and etymological baggage. The characters, right down to modern times, have always represented both sounds and ideas.

Of course, if you're continually making the characters do double, triple, or quadruple duty, you're introducing ambiguity into the system. Up to a point, you can use context to determine which of several different words is intended for a particular character in a particular spot, but it gets unwieldy after a while.

The system that evolved with the Han characters involved using an extra character to resolve the ambiguity. If we go back to our "cowrie shell" example, we could set apart the "defeat" meaning by adding another character that clarified the meaning. The character chosen was

which means "strike" and is pronounced *pu*. Combine the two of them together and you get this:

The figure on the left represents the sound *bei*, and the figure on the right represents the concept of "strike." Put them together and you get "bai," or "defeat."

The same thing can also work in the other direction. Consider the character

口

which normally means "mouth" and is pronounced *kou*. It also came to represent the word "ming," which means "to call out." This time, you have a semantic similarity with a difference in pronunciation. To resolve the ambiguity, you add the character

which means "brighten" and is also pronounced *ming*. The result,

名

includes two components: one representing the sound *ming* and a second representing the concept "mouth." Together they represent the word "ming" meaning "to call out."

This process is actually recursive. You can now take the compound character and do the same thing with it. So we take our new compound character representing the word "ming" and meaning "to call out" and use it to represent yet *another* word that's pronounced *ming*, this time meaning "inscription (as on a bronze vessel)."

To set it apart from the meaning "to call out," you add another component:

which means "metal." Add it to the other two,

and you get a unique character meaning "inscription."

This process can theoretically continue ad infinitum. In practice, the characters generally become unreadable if they have more than five or six components. Characters with more than five or six components are quite rare.

The Han characters work in this way. As you might imagine, this system gives rise to a few interesting problems. First, what's to keep different people from coming up with totally different characters for the same words? Two people might follow the same basic rules, but use different component characters, leading to different, but both perfectly valid, characters for the same word. Who decides which one wins?

This problem is akin to the problem of standardizing spelling of words across a population that uses an alphabetic script, and the solution is the same: Publish a dictionary. (Of course, this solution works best if you're a powerful emperor and can force people to follow the dictionary's prescriptions.) The first known dictionary of Han characters was compiled by Xu Shen in about A.D. 100, and it had the effect (over time, anyway) of standardizing on one way of writing each word. Xu Shen's dictionary, the *Shuo wen jie zi,* contained 9,353 characters. It began by dividing them into unit characters (those that couldn't be broken down into component parts) and compound characters (those that could). With the compound characters, Xu Shen put together a list of 540 component elements, at least one of which occurred in each compound character. These component elements were called **radicals**, and one of them was classified as the main radical in every compound character. This strategy imposed a hierarchy on the component parts of a compound character, which helped to standardize the characters for each word and to ensure that the system that had developed by that time—using components that represent both sound and meaning—would remain the standard way of writing Chinese words.

By the early eighteenth century, the number of characters had grown to almost 50,000, and the Kangxi emperor commissioned a new dictionary, the *Kangxi Zidian.* Completed in 1716, it contained 47,021 characters. The Kangxi dictionary, like the many others before it, preserved the basic classification of characters based on radicals first seen in the *Shuo wen jie zi,* but despite the huge growth in the number of characters, was able to classify them all using just 214 radicals. Unlike the *Shuo wen jie zi,* the Kangxi dictionary organized characters within each radical group according to the number of additional pen strokes they contained beyond those used to write the radical.

The Kangxi dictionary remains the definitive authority for classical Chinese literature, and its system of 214 radicals continues to be used today to classify Chinese characters. In fact, this system of radicals is used in the radical–stroke index in the Unicode standard itself. (This system of organizing the characters by radicals and strokes works pretty well; even a non-Chinese speaker such as yours truly was able to find most characters in the Unicode radical–stroke index with only a modicum of effort.)

One of the beauties of the Han characters is that because they represent words, and by extension ideas, the same text can (with proper education, of course) be read and written by speakers of many different languages. (Of course, the farther the spoken language gets from classical Chinese, the less help the phonetic cues in the characters provide.) In a phonetic writing system, someone who doesn't speak a particular language but uses the same script can still look at the writing and have at least a vague idea of how the words are pronounced, albeit probably little or no idea what they mean. With the Han characters, someone can look at something other than his or her native language written using the Han characters and get a vague idea of what it says, but have little or no idea of how it's pronounced. It's interesting to compare the situations of China and India on these grounds. Both are vast countries populated by hundreds of millions of people of many different ethnic groups speaking many different languages. In India, even relatively closely related languages are frequently written with their own scripts. By contrast, in China (with a number of important exceptions such as Inner Mongolia and Tibet), all of the different spoken languages use the same written language.

Of course, standard written Chinese consists of characters based on either Classical Chinese pronunciation or modern Mandarin pronunciation, and the characters are arranged according to Mandarin grammar. Thus speakers of other Chinese languages, such as Cantonese, are effectively reading and writing a different language from the one they speak. There *are* Han characters specific to Cantonese and other Chinese languages, but until recently, no comprehensive attempt has been made to put them into any encoding standards. This situation began to change with Unicode 3.1, which includes many Cantonese-specific characters, but much remains to be done.)

Just as the various Indian scripts spread outside India, the Han characters have come to be used outside China. The Han characters formed the first writing systems used in both Japan and Korea, although both have since supplemented the Han characters with their own scripts. Until recently, the Han characters were also used in Vietnam. In all of these places, people also coined new characters using the same techniques employed to construct the original ones (but presumably according to Japanese or Korean pronunciation). In fact, the Vietnamese developed a whole system of characters, the **chu Nom**, for writing Vietnamese. These characters look and behave like Chinese characters, but are indigenous and were used instead of the traditional Chinese characters. The Japanese and Koreans didn't go this far, but rather used their own characters along with the traditional Chinese characters.

This diversity points to one of the other great things about the Han characters—the system is very malleable, and it's easy to coin new characters for new words. For this reason, the number of Han characters has grown steadily over the years. Table 10.1 shows the numbers of characters in various Chinese dictionaries down through the years.

Because of this flexibility, it's proper to think of the Han characters as an open-ended writing system. It's impossible to say just how many Han characters exist, because some occur so rarely and new ones are constantly being invented.

Of course, not everyone knows every character—that would clearly be impossible. Rather, 2,400 characters is generally considered the lower limit for ba-

Table 10.1 Growth of Chinese Characters

Year (A.D.)	Number of Chinese Characters
100	9,353
227–239	11,520
480	18,150
543	22,726
751	26,194
1066	31,319
1615	33,179
1716	47,021
1919	44,908
1969	49,888
1986	56,000
1994	85,000

sic literacy, with most educated people having a working repertoire of 4,000 to 5,000 and some especially literate people up to 8,000. Studies have repeatedly shown that 1,000 characters cover 90 percent of written Chinese, 2,400 cover 99 percent, 3,800 cover 99.9 percent, 5,200 cover 99.99 percent, and 6,600 characters cover 99.999 percent of written Chinese. Thus, the vast majority of Chinese characters are extremely rare, including many so rare that neither their pronunciation nor their meaning is known—only their shape. Some may have been used only once or twice in all of history.[4] Unfortunately, many of these characters do occur, however sporadically, in modern writing and it must be possible to represent (and thus input and print) them.

It's worth pointing out that this situation is fairly analogous to that involving words in English. The average English speaker has a working vocabulary

---

4. My source for this information is the Mair article in *The World's Writing Systems,* pp. 200–201.

roughly equivalent to the number of characters the average literate Chinese reader has in his or her working vocabulary. New characters are also invented at roughly the same rate as new English words emerge. No one regularly uses *all* the words in *Webster's Third*, and even though two people may have vocabularies of about the same size, they won't share all the same words.

▪ VARIANT FORMS OF HAN CHARACTERS

Of course, despite efforts at standardization, variant forms of the characters do creep in over time. This tends to happen most often with more complicated characters: People come up with quicker and less complicated ways of writing them, and some of these catch on and come into widespread use. Which forms become popular tends to vary either according to a particular writer's preference or, more often, according to regional convention.

As an extreme example, there are at least six variant forms of the character for "sword" in Japanese:

劍 劍 剱 劔 劎 釖

More important, however, are national variants. Over time, some characters have developed different forms in Japan and Korea than they have in China, for example. In the preceding example, the first character is a Japanese-specific variant of the second character.

Particularly notable is the difference between Traditional Chinese and Simplified Chinese. In the 1950s, the Mao government in the People's Republic of China undertook a systematic effort to simplify written Chinese. Among the outcomes of this effort were the Pinyin system of writing Chinese words with Latin letters and new versions of several thousand Han characters, many of which were so drastically simplified as to be unrecognizable given only their original forms.

Today, the new forms are generally used in the People's Republic of China, and the old forms continue to be used in Taiwan. The term "Simplified Chinese" has come to refer to Chinese as written in mainland China, and "Traditional Chinese" has come to refer to Chinese as written in Taiwan. The difference between Simplified and Traditional Chinese now goes beyond merely using characters with different shapes; the choice of which ideographs to use in the first place also tends to differ between the locales. The traditional forms of the characters are also typically used in Hong Kong and among Chinese outside China, while the simplified forms of the characters tend to be used in Singapore.

Japan and Korea have their own forms, which sometimes match the Traditional Chinese forms, sometimes match the Simplified Chinese forms, and often are completely different. As a consequence, the same basic character can have as many as four shapes, depending on the place where it's being used (the line between saying this and saying that the four different places have different, but historically related, characters for expressing the same concept is actually quite thin).

Table 10.2 gives some examples of characters with variant forms in Traditional Chinese, Simplified Chinese, and Japanese.

The mapping between Simplified and Traditional Chinese isn't always straightforward. In many cases, the language reformers mandated the *same* simplified character for several different words that originally had *different* traditional characters. For example, all of the Traditional Chinese characters

干 幹 乾 榦

have the same representation in Simplified Chinese:

干

The four Traditional Chinese characters have very different meanings, but their pronunciations are all variations on "gan." Here, rather than simplifying the more complicated characters, the reformers simply fell back on rebus writing.[5]

Korean-specific variants are more difficult to find. Generally, the Korean forms of the Han characters follow the Traditional Chinese forms, but Korean

---

5. This example is taken from Jack Halpern, "The Pitfalls and Complexities of Chinese to Chinese Conversion," an undated white paper published by the CJK Dictionary Publishing Society.

Table 10.2 Variant Forms of Han Characters

Gloss	Traditional Chinese	Simplified Chinese	Japanese
broad	廣	广	広
country	國	国	国
infant	兒	儿	児
east	東	东	東
open	開	开	開
see	見	见	見
picture	畫	画	画
old	舊	旧	旧
not/without	無	无	無
deficient/vacancy	缺	缺	欠
hall	廳	厅	庁
surround/enclose	圍	围	囲
abundant	豐	丰	豊

font-design principles (things such as stroke length and termination) tend to follow Japanese font-design principles rather than Chinese ones.

■ HAN CHARACTERS IN UNICODE

Unicode includes a truly huge number of Han characters: 70,195 different characters are included in Unicode 3.1. The Han character set in Unicode represents a massive effort put forth by a lot of East Asian–language experts over a long period of time.

Unlike with most of the other modern scripts encoded in Unicode, there's no set number of Han characters.[6] They number well into the tens of thousands, but no definitive listing of *all* of them exists. Not only are new characters created frequently, but numerous characters appear perhaps once or twice in all East Asian writing. Some of these forms might just be idiosyncratic ways of writing more common characters, but some are new coinages created for an ad hoc purpose in some piece of writing (often called "nonce forms"). Also, Chinese dictionaries contain some characters whose pronunciations and meanings have been lost.

The idea of official character sets goes back well before the introduction of information technology into the Han-character–using world. Not only are sets of characters collected in dictionaries, but governmental entities publish official lists of characters that are to be taught in school to all children or that restrict the set of characters that can be used in official government documents. This process is more or less akin to U.S. states publishing vocabulary lists containing words that every child at certain grade levels should know.

These lists form the basis of the various encoding standards employed in the various Han-character–using countries, but all of the character encoding standards go beyond these lists of basic characters to include rarer characters. Each of the main locales using the Han characters—the People's Republic of China, Taiwan, Japan, North and South Korea, Vietnam, Hong Kong, and Singapore—has developed its own sets of character-encoding standards, generally for that country's own use.

Unicode uses many of these standards as the basis for its collection of Han characters. The CJK Unified Ideographs area, the main body of Han characters in Unicode, is based on no fewer than 18 source standards, containing approximately 121,000 characters in total. Even so, the CJK Unified Ideographs area contains only 20,902 characters.

How is this discrepancy possible? Consider the various ISO 8859 standards. Together, the first 10 parts of ISO 8859 comprise 1,920 printing characters. This number is misleading, however, because each part of ISO 8859 contains the ASCII characters (in fact, the extended Latin encodings included

---

6. Most of the information in this section comes either from the Unicode standard, pp. 258–267, or from Lunde, pp. 66–137.

in ISO 8859 also contain considerable overlap). Thus, 960 characters of that 1,920-character total represent 10 copies of the 96 ASCII characters. Unicode encodes them only once.

In the same way, considerable overlap exists between the 18 source standards on which the CJK Unified Ideographs block is based. Unfortunately, determining just which characters are duplicates and which aren't isn't completely straightforward.

Unicode's designers followed several rules in deciding which characters were duplicates and could therefore be weeded out (or "unified"):

- If one encoding standard that went into the original set of Han characters (the ones designated as "primary source standards" by the committee) encodes two characters separately, then Unicode does as well, even if they would otherwise have been unified. This Source Separation Rule is analogous to the round-trip rule used in most of the rest of the Unicode standard. For characters added to Unicode more recently, the Source Separation Rule is not followed—round-trip compatibility is guaranteed only for the original primary source standard (the same is true for some more recent source standards used in other parts of Unicode). The different versions of the "sword" character we looked at earlier are encoded separately in the JIS X 0208 standard, which is a primary source standard, and so are also encoded separately in Unicode.
- If two characters look similar but have distinct meanings and etymologies, they aren't unified. This guideline is called the Noncognate Rule.

For example, this character, which means "earth,"

$$土$$

looks a lot like this one:

$$土$$

The second character is completely unrelated to the first character, however. It means "warrior" or "scholar." Both characters get their own code point values in Unicode.

For characters that *are* related historically and have similar shapes, closer examination is required to decide whether to unify them. The basic principle is that if the characters have the same "abstract shape"—that is, if the differences between them can be attributed merely to differences in typeface design—they can be unified. Otherwise, they're considered distinct forms.

To figure out whether the differences between two characters are merely typeface-design differences, the characters are decomposed into their constituent parts. If they have different numbers of components, or if the components are arranged differently, the characters are not unified. For example, these two characters have different numbers of components:[7]

$$崖 \neq 厓$$

These two characters have the same components, but are arranged differently:

$$峰 \neq 峯$$

If corresponding components in the two characters have different structures or are based on different radicals, the characters are not unified. For example, these two characters have one corresponding component that has a different structure in the two characters:

$$拡 \neq 擴$$

These two characters are similar, but are based on different radicals:

$$祕 \neq 秘$$

This leaves us with relatively minor differences, such as stroke overshoot,

$$雪 \approx 雪$$
$$鉅 \approx 鉅$$

---

7. The following set of examples is taken from the Unicode standard, p. 265.

stroke initiation and termination,

$$朱 ≈ 朱$$
$$父 ≈ 父$$

and stroke angle:

$$埀 ≈ 埀$$
$$八 ≈ 八$$

These differences (and thus the preceding pairs of characters) *are* considered differences in typeface design, so these pairs of characters *are* unified in Unicode.

One result is that, for the most part, the Simplified and Traditional Chinese versions of most characters are encoded separately in Unicode, as are the Japanese variants when they're different. Even so, sometimes this step didn't happen because the shapes were close enough to be unified, but different typeface designs are still preferred in different locales. For example, the Traditional Chinese character for "bone,"

$$骨$$

looks like this in Simplified Chinese:

$$骨$$

The differences between the two were small enough for them to be unified. In these cases, the choice of typeface is considered outside the scope of Unicode, just as the choice of typeface is outside its scope with the other scripts in Unicode (such as when historical and modern versions of letters are unified even when they have different shapes—for example, Old Cyrillic and modern Cyrillic letters).

The rigorous application of these principles resulted in the Unified Han Repertoire, the collection of Han characters in Unicode (nicknamed "Unihan"). In this way, the 110,000 characters in the original 18 source standards were boiled down to the 20,902 characters in the original Unihan collection (the original collection of characters in the CJK Unified Ideographs area was called the Unified Repertoire and Ordering, or URO). The same principles have also been applied to the collections of characters that were added after the original version of Unicode.

One other interesting problem had to be solved: the ordering of the characters. Unicode's designers didn't want to specifically follow the ordering of any of the source standards, as this choice would appear to favor one country over the others. They opted instead for a culturally neutral ordering based on the ordering of the Kangxi dictionary. This source is regarded as authoritative in all the countries that use the Han characters and contains most of the characters in Unicode. For characters that don't appear in the Kangxi dictionary, three other dictionaries (one each for Japanese, Chinese, and Korean) were used. The character in question was located in one of these dictionaries and placed in the Unicode order after the nearest character in that dictionary that was also in the Kangxi dictionary.

The CJK Unified Ideographs Area

The CJK Unified Ideographs area runs from U+4E00 to U+9FAF. The original set of Han characters in Unicode, it contains 20,902 characters drawn from 18 source standards. The source standards are divided into groups that are given letters: the G source consists of seven national standards from mainland China; the T source consists of three sections from the Taiwanese national standard; the J source consists of two Japanese national standards, and the K source consists of two Korean national standards. Eight additional sources that aren't official national standards and are collected from all the locales constitute the U source, but characters that exist only in the U source aren't included in this block.

The CJK Unified Ideographs Extension A Area

The CJK Unified Ideographs Extension A area runs from U+3400 to U+4DBF. It adds 6,582 characters drawn from 13 more sources. These include three extra G-source standards (plus extra characters from some of the original sources);

six additional T-source standards (basically, the rest of the Taiwanese national standard, which is huge); another J-source standard; two more K-source standards; two Vietnamese standards (the V source); and a bunch of supplemental (U source) materials (again, characters *only* in the U source don't actually go in this area). This collection follows the same unification and ordering rules as the original Unihan collection (except without the Source Separation Rule), but is encoded separately because it came along after the other collection had already been encoded. Extension A was added in Unicode 3.0.

The CJK Unified Ideographs Extension B Area

Unicode 3.1 opened up the non-BMP space for colonization, and the Ideographic Rapporteur Group, the group responsible for maintaining the Unihan collections, took to it with a vengeance. Plane 2, the Supplementary Ideographic Plane (SIP), now contains 42,711 Han characters. These make up the CJK Unified Ideographs Extension B area (sometimes called Vertical Extension B), which runs from U+20000 to U+2A6D6.

The characters are drawn from 20 new source standards: eight new G-source standards, most of which are dictionaries instead of character-interchange standards (the KangXi dictionary was one of them); a collection of characters used in Hong Kong (the H source), five new T-source standards (characters added to the Taiwanese national standard in its most recent incarnation); two new J-source standards; a new K-source standard; and three new V-source standards. Extension B doesn't add any U sources (supplemental works consulted by the IRG but not formally submitted by any of the member countries).

Most of the characters in Extension B are quite rare. This area is also where new characters from non-Mandarin languages go; it contains a lot of Cantonese-specific characters, many of which you see in common things such as Hong Kong place names.

The CJK Compatibility Ideographs Block

The CJK Compatibility Ideographs block runs from U+F900 to U+FAFF. The South Korean national standard, KS X 1001 (originally KS C 5601), includes duplicate encodings for many Han characters that have multiple pronunciations in Korean (the Unicode standard likens this system to having a separate code point value for each different pronunciation of the letter a). These characters are pure duplicates: They look identical and have the same meaning; they just have variant pronunciations. Because KS X 1001 is a primary source standard, the Source Separation Rule dictates that Unicode also had to give these characters multiple code point values. The designers of Unicode compromised, giving them separate code point values, but putting them into a walled-off zone, the CJK Compatibility Ideographs area, rather than interspersing them with the other Han characters in the main Unihan area. They did the same thing with duplicate characters that were inadvertently included in a few other source standards. All of these characters have *canonical*—not compatibility—decompositions to the original characters in the CJK Unified Ideographs area.

Twelve characters in this block *aren't* duplicates and can be considered part of the main Unihan collection. They're found here rather than in the main Unihan block because they were drawn from the supplemental sources (the U source) and not the national standards. These characters don't decompose and aren't compatibility characters, despite the name of the block.

The CJK Compatibility Ideographs Supplement Block

The SIP also contains the CJK Compatibility Ideographs Supplement block, which runs from U+2F800 to U+2FA1D. These characters are duplicates, but were added to maintain round-trip compatibility with the most recent version of CNS 11643, the Taiwanese national standard. They have canonical decompositions to characters in the main Unihan area.

The Kangxi Radicals Block

The Kangxi Radicals block, which runs from U+2F00 to U+2FDF, contains the 214 radicals used in the Kangxi dictionary to classify the Han characters. Most of these radicals can also be used as ideographs, so they are already encoded in the main Unihan block. The characters here aren't Han characters; they're just radicals and shouldn't be used as Han characters. Unicode classifies them as symbols rather than letters to emphasize this fact. All of these characters have compatibility decompositions to the ideographs that consist of just the radical.

The CJK Radicals Supplement Block

The set of radicals used to classify characters varies from dictionary to dictionary. Some radicals have variant shapes depending on the character that includes them (or a different shape in Simplified Chinese than in Traditional Chinese). The CJK Radicals Supplement block, which runs from U+2E80 to U+2EFF, includes many of these supplemental radicals and supplemental shapes.

■ IDEOGRAPHIC DESCRIPTION SEQUENCES

With more than 70,000 characters, it hardly seems likely that any more would be necessary. In fact, the Han characters are an open-ended set, with more being created every day (a common source, for example, is proud parents wanting to give their children unique names). As if that trend weren't enough, not all of the variant forms of the characters have separate encodings. When big differences exist, they do; as we saw earlier, however, smaller differences that can be attributed to font design are unified. The problem is that many situations involve definite regional preferences for particular font designs, meaning that it can sometimes be difficult to get precisely the glyph you want, even when the character is encoded. Unicode provides a couple of ways to deal with these problems.[8]

Let's start by looking at a rare glyph for which we might need these techniques. Consider this character:

---

8. Most of the material in this section is drawn from John H. Jenkins, "New Ideographs in Unicode 3.0 and Beyond," *Proceedings of the Fifteenth International Unicode Conference,* session C15, September 1, 1999. In particular, all of the examples in this section are taken from that source.

It is an archaic form of the character

乾

which means "dry." This passage from the writings of Mengzi, the Second Sage of Confucianism, uses it:[9]

犧牲既成，粢盛既潔，祭祀以時；
然而旱乾水溢，則變置社稷。

A modern edition would use the modern glyph, but a scholar seeking an accurate transcription of the original text might need an accurate way to represent the ancient glyph. Unicode provides a number of ways to deal with this issue.[10]

The oldest and simplest solution is the geta mark (U+3013), which looks like this: ▆. Japanese printers use this mark to reserve space on the line for a character they can't print. Using it, the passage above would look like this:

犧牲既成，粢盛既潔，祭祀以時；
然而旱▆水溢，則變置社稷。

The geta mark gives you a visual tip-off that the passage includes a character that can't be rendered, but it doesn't tell you anything about that character.

---

9. Jenkins supplies this English translation for the excerpt, attributing it to D.C. Lau: "When the sacrificial animals are sleek, the offerings are clean, and the sacrifices are observed at due times, and yet floods and droughts come, then the altars should be replaced."

10. Actually, this character *is* encoded in Unicode, in the new CJK Unified Ideographs Extension B area, so this example may not be the best choice. Nevertheless, the character was added in Unicode 3.1, so if you are dealing with a Unicode 3.0 or earlier implementation, or don't have a font that actually contains this character, you might still have to use the techniques described here.

Unicode 3.0 introduces a refinement of this idea that offers a little more information. It's called the ideographic variation indicator (U+303F):

$$\not\equiv$$

The idea is to use this mark in conjunction with some character that *is* encoded in Unicode. You precede that character with the ideographic variation indicator to say that the character you *really* want is somehow related to the character following the ideographic variation mark. It might be a glyphic variant of that character, look kind of like it, mean the same thing, or whatever. If we use it in our example, it has the following appearance:

犧牲既成，粢盛既潔，祭祀以時；
然而旱⧣乾水溢，則變置社稷。

This approach may not be a whole lot better than using the geta mark, but at least it provides some information about what's really desired. You could, of course, simply use the substitute glyph; in this example, the meaning of the passage would still be clear. The ideographic variation indicator, however, gives a visual signal that it isn't the glyph you really wanted to use.

Unicode 3.0 also introduced a much richer way of getting across which character you mean when it isn't available. The **ideographic description sequence**, makes use of the characters in the Ideographic Description Characters block (U+2FF0 to U+2FFF). The basic idea behind ideographic description sequences is simple: Most Han characters are simply combinations of two or more other Han characters. You could get at least a decent approximation of the character you want by using the characters that make it up along with some kind of character indicating how they are combined. The ideographic description characters fulfill that role of indicating how other ideographs are joined together.

For example, suppose you want to combine the character

井

which means "well," with the character

蛙

which means "frog," to produce a "frog in a well" character:[11]

井
蛙

You could use the character U+2FF1 IDEOGRAPHIC DESCRIPTION CHARACTER ABOVE TO BELOW (⿱) to indicate that you want to stack the other two characters on top of each other, yielding something that looks like this:

⿱井蛙

Perhaps it is not the most beautiful sequence of characters ever designed, but it does a good job of saying what you mean.

More complicated sequences are also possible. You could, for example, break down the "frog" character even further, because "frog" is made up of individual characters meaning "insect" and "pointed jade" (this is obviously the phonetic). Either of these sequences could also be used to describe our "frog in a well" character:

This example shows that the ideographic description characters are recursive. The basic rule is that you start an ideographic description sequence with an ideographic description character, and then follow that character with the two (or three) characters that are to be composed, in order from left to right (or top to bottom). These characters may be regular Han characters, radicals, or ideographic description sequences themselves.

---

11. "Like a frog at the bottom of a well" is a common expression in Chinese for a narrow-minded person, which is the source of this example.

This process can go to fairly wild extremes. Let's return to the old character from the Mengzi example. It can be described like this:

⿰⿱⿲⿳ 日 日 工 日 丂 乞

Crystal clear, huh? This example points up one of the problems with ideographic description sequences. They're designed to be machine-readable, and some human readability is sacrificed in the process. The sequence can be parsed like this:

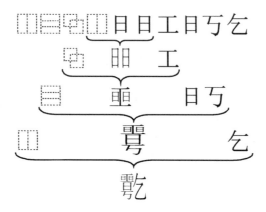

Of course, this parsing takes a bit of work on the reader's part. It also gets kind of messy when you place such a sequence into actual text:

犧牲既成，粢盛既潔，祭祀以時；然而旱⿰⿱⿲⿳ 日 日 工 日 丂 乞 水溢，則變置社稷。

Of course, what you *really* want is for a sufficiently sophisticated text-rendering engine to give you the following result when it sees that sequence:

犧牲既成，粢盛既潔，祭祀以時；然而旱𪳍水溢，則變置社稷。

Unicode gives implementations the freedom to follow this path if they want. Note, however, that this ability isn't *required* of systems that know about the ideographic description characters. It's perfectly legal for an implementation to draw them as regular visible glyphs, as in the preceding example. (It is *not* legal to make them invisible and just show the Han characters on which they operate.) The idea is that these characters *describe* a missing character, not that they *represent* that character. They're more akin to the phrase "an e with an acute accent over it" than they are to the sequence U+006E U+0301.

Part of the reason for this relationship is that they remain merely approximate descriptions of what is intended. For example, the character

can be described like this:

It might also theoretically be represented like this:

The "water" character (水) usually adopts an abbreviated shape (氵) when it's used as part of another character, but the possibility always exists that it shouldn't do that in your particular case. There's no way to say which option you mean using the facilities that Unicode gives you.

It's important to remember that ideographic description sequences are explicitly *not* combining character sequences. The ideographic description characters are classified as symbols, rather than as combining marks or formatting characters. Multiple methods of describing the same character using ideographic description sequences are possible and are explicitly *not* equivalent. If you use an ideographic description sequence to describe a character that's actually encoded in Unicode, it's explicitly not equivalent to that character. An ambitious Unicode implementation can parse an ideographic description sequence and attempt to render the character it describes, but this behavior isn't required.

Ideographic description sequences are basically intended as a way of representing some character until it's officially encoded in Unicode.

To make life easier on implementations that want to parse ideographic description sequences and try to display the characters they describe, the Unicode standard prescribes a grammar for their use. It also specifies that an individual ideographic description sequence may be no longer than 16 characters, may contain no more than 6 Han characters or radicals in a row with no intervening ideographic description characters (to minimize how far back a process examining the text from a random spot in the middle has to scan to figure out whether it's in an ideographic description sequence), and should be the shortest possible sequence that will adequately describe the character. Breaking these rules, using ideographic description characters in ways other than specified by their grammar, or using them in conjunction with characters other than the Han characters and radicals all have undefined effects.

Other methods of dealing with alternate glyphs for already-encoded characters have been proposed and may eventually be added to Unicode. Right now, the preferred way to specify a particular glyph for an encoded character is to use a higher-level protocol to specify a font. You can also use the plane 14 tagging characters (see Chapter 12) to help a system interpreting plain text pick an appropriate font. Some systems might employ a heuristic method to examine the characters themselves with no tagging or out-of-band information to pick appropriate glyphs (the basic idea is something like, "If there's kana nearby, treat it as Japanese; if there's hangul nearby, treat it as Korean; and so on"). This type of algorithm can be fooled, however.

Some people have suggested using the Unicode 3.2 variation-selector mechanism as a method of selecting variant forms of the Han characters. This strategy might cut down on future encodings of characters that are widely acknowledged to be variants of each other. There aren't any variation-selector/Han-character combinations in Unicode 3.2, but the IRG is working on standardizing some for later Unicode versions.

■ BOPOMOFO

The Han characters always have both phonetic and semantic values, but sometimes it's necessary to use characters that have a purely phonetic purpose. The

National Phonetic Alphabet (Zhuyin Zimu, or Zhuyin for short; also called Chu Yin and Guoyin) was invented in 1911 for this purpose, as part of a general literacy campaign in China after the fall of the Manchu regime. This alphabet is nicknamed "Bopomofo," which is the names of the first four letters run together into one word.

Bopomofo includes 21 consonants, 16 vowels, and 4 tone marks (Figure 10.1). The characters are either written on a horizontal line from left to right or on a vertical line from top to bottom, just like the Han characters. They are written in pronunciation order and don't interact typographically. The tone marks generally occur after the syllables to which they apply (in vertical text, they sometimes occupy a column of their own to the right of the main characters).

Bopomofo characters are rarely used alone; instead they're generally used to annotate regular Chinese text with pronunciations. (For more information on how this process works, see the "Ruby" section later in this chapter.) You generally see them in children's books or other educational materials.

The Bopomofo Block

The Unicode Bopomofo block, running from U+3100 to U+312F, contains the basic set of Bopomofo characters used to write Mandarin, plus three characters used to write non-Mandarin dialects. The tone marks are unified with Western accent marks in the Spacing Modifier Letters block.

Consonants

ㄅㄆㄇㄈㄉㄊㄋㄌㄍㄎㄏㄐㄑㄒㄓㄔㄕㄖㄗㄘㄙ

Vowels

ㄚㄛㄜㄝㄞㄟㄠㄡㄢㄣㄤㄥㄦ

Tone marks

ˉ ˊ ˇ ˋ

Figure 10.1 Bopomofo characters

The Bopomofo Extended Block

The Bopomofo Extended block, running from U+31A0 to U+31BF (there wasn't enough room to put these characters in the same block as the other Bopomofo characters), contains less universally recognized Bopomofo characters used to write various non-Mandarin Chinese languages. A few additional tone marks are unified with characters in the Spacing Modifier Letters block.

▪ JAPANESE

Japanese may have the most complicated writing system of any language spoken today. It's written in a combination of three complete scripts, sometimes supplemented with Latin letters and various other marks.[12]

The history of written Japanese dates back to the third century, when the Han characters were first used to write Japanese (in Japanese, the Han characters are called kanji). Japanese isn't linguistically related to Chinese (although it contains a lot of words borrowed from Chinese), so the Han characters never worked as well for Japanese. Most of the phonetic cues in the Han characters don't help in Japanese (one estimate holds that only 25 percent of the commonly used kanji characters contain useful clues to their Japanese pronunciations). Furthermore, while Chinese is generally monosyllabic and noninflecting (or at least has far fewer polysyllabic words than most other languages, including Japanese and Korean), Japanese is polysyllabic and has a fairly complex inflectional system. Writing Japanese exclusively with kanji generally means that the grammatical endings on words aren't written and must be supplied by the reader, or that they have to be represented using kanji with the right pronunciations, which can be confusing (especially given that almost all kanji have at least two pronunciations in Japanese).

Eventually a standardized set of kanji came to be used for writing the grammatical endings and for other types of phonetic representation. These characters came to be known as the *man'yogana* ("Chinese characters used

---

12. My sources for the section on Japanese are Janet Shibamoto Smith, "Japanese Writing," in *The World's Writing Systems,* pp. 209–217; Lunde, pp. 42–47; and Nakanishi, pp. 94–95.

phonetically to write Japanese"), and their shapes gradually became more sim-plified and differentiated from their shapes when used as regular kanji. This process culminated in the two modern Japanese syllabic scripts: Hiragana and Katakana (collectively called Kana), which were officially standardized by the Japanese government in 1900. The Hiragana were derived from more cursive, calligraphic forms of the original characters, while the Katakana were very simplified variants of the non-cursive forms of the characters.[13]

Both forms of Kana are "pure syllabaries"; that is, each Kana character repre-sents an entire syllable of spoken Japanese. Unlike so-called "alphasyllabaries," such as Hangul, Kana characters can't be broken down into component parts that represent the individual sounds in the syllable.

The more cursive form, Hiragana, is generally used to write native Japanese words and grammatical endings. There are 48 basic Hiragana characters (Fig-ure 10.2). (The characters ゐ and ゑ are rarely used nowadays.)

	–	K	S	T	N	H	M	Y	R	W
A	あ	か	さ	た	な	は	ま	や	ら	わ
I	い	き	し	ち	に	ひ	み		り	ゐ
U	う	く	す	つ	ぬ	ふ	む	ゆ	る	
E	え	け	せ	て	ね	へ	め		れ	ゑ
O	お	こ	そ	と	の	ほ	も	よ	ろ	を
N	ん									

Figure 10.2 Basic Hiragana characters

---

13. Lunde provides a very interesting table (pp. 46–47) showing which Kana characters derived from which kanji.

Each character (with the exception of あ, い, う, え, お, and ん) represents the combination of an initial consonant sound and a vowel sound. The vowels by themselves are represented by あ, い, う, え, and お and are used not just at the beginnings of words but as the second characters in diphthongs. Only one syllable-final consonant exists, and it's represented by ん.[14] Thus, the system isn't a 100 percent perfect syllabary—a number of syllables are actually represented using more than one Hiragana character.

Not all of the characters have the pronunciation shown in Figure 10.2. For example, つ is pronounced *tsu*, ち is pronounced *chi*, ふ is pronounced *fu*, and し is pronounced *shi*. The character ん is pronounced *m* before *b* and *p* sounds.

In addition to the basic sounds shown in Figure 10.2, diacritical marks are used to widen the palette of available sounds. Two strokes on the upper-right shoulder of the character, called **nigori** or **dakuten**, are used with certain characters to turn their initial consonant sound from an unvoiced sound into a voiced sound. For example, さ (*sa*) becomes *za* when the dakuten is added (ざ). The characters in the h-series (i.e., は, ひ, ふ, へ, and ほ) are special: A small circle on the upper-right shoulder, called **maru** or **handakuten**, gives them an initial *p* sound. The dakuten gives them an initial *b* sound. That is, は is pronounced *ha*, ぱ is pronounced *pa*, and ば is pronounced *ba*. Finally, the dakuten can be added to う to get *vu* (ゔ). These combinations of basic Hiragana characters and diacritical marks give us another 25 syllables (Figure 10.3).

Smaller versions of some of the Hiragana characters are also used more or less like diacritics. For example, Japanese has palatalized syllables (syllables with a *y* sound between the consonant and the vowel). These are represented using a basic character representing the initial consonant and the *i* sound, followed by a small version of や, ゆ, or よ representing the *y* sound and the final vowel. For example, *nya* is represented with に (*ni*) followed by a smaller version of や (*ya*): にゃ. The one other case of two initial consonants, *kwa,* is represented similarly: く (*ku*) plus a small version of わ (*wa*): くゎ. This gives us another 36 possible combinations (Figure 10.4).

---

14. Actually, Japanese speakers think of this character as a syllable unto itself.

	G	Z	D	B	P	V
A	が	ざ	だ	ば	ぱ	
I	ぎ	じ	ぢ	び	ぴ	
U	ぐ	ず	づ	ぶ	ぷ	ゔ
E	げ	ぜ	で	べ	ぺ	
O	ご	ぞ	ど	ぼ	ぽ	

Figure 10.3 Hiragana character/diacritical mark combinations

The small version of つ is used to indicate consonant gemination (i.e., the doubling or prolonging of a consonant sound). Thus, べつど is "betsudo," but べっど is "beddo" (which means "bed," and is normally written in Katakana).

The small versions of the bare vowels (あ, い, う, え, and お) are used with certain characters for borrowed sounds, although this happens much more frequently in Katakana. Generally, the resulting syllable is a combination of the initial consonant sound from the main character and the vowel sound denoted by the small character. For example, ふぁ is *fa* and とぅ is *tu*.

	K	S	T	N	H	M	R	G	Z	D	B	P
YA	きゃ	しゃ	ちゃ	にゃ	ひゃ	みゃ	りゃ	ぎゃ	じゃ	ぢゃ	びゃ	ぴゃ
YU	きゅ	しゅ	ちゅ	にゅ	ひゅ	みゅ	りゅ	ぎゅ	じゅ	ぢゅ	びゅ	ぴゅ
YO	きょ	しょ	ちょ	にょ	ひょ	みょ	りょ	ぎょ	じょ	ぢょ	びょ	ぴょ

Figure 10.4 Hiragana palatalized syllables

Long vowel sounds are usually represented by using two of the regular vowel characters in a row. For example, ā is written as あ あ. The one exception is ō, which is written お う.

When Hiragana is written vertically, the character 〱 is occasionally used to indicate that the preceding two characters are to be repeated. Adding the dakuten changes the initial consonant on the repeated sequence to a voiced consonant. The sequence

て
ん
〲

is pronounced *tenden*. Notice, by the way, that the repeat mark takes up two display cells, visually indicating that it's repeating two characters.

Katakana, the more angular form of Kana, is used for foreign words and onomatopoeia. Sometimes, native Japanese words are written in Katakana for emphasis or to indicate euphemism or irony (in other words, using Katakana for a word that's normally written in kanji or Hiragana is similar to putting quotation marks around an English word that's not actually part of a quotation). Katakana works almost exactly the same way as Hiragana. It includes 48 basic characters (Figure 10.5). (Again, the characters ヰ and ヱ are rarely used nowadays.)

Dakuten and handakuten work exactly the same way with Katakana (Figure 10.6). A few additional syllables are possible, however.

Smaller versions of certain Katakana characters also work the same way as their Hiragana counterparts (Figures 10.7 and 10.8).

Long vowels are generally represented in Katakana using a dash ("choon") instead of a doubled vowel. That is, ā is written as ア ー rather than ア ア.

With Katakana, the 〳 mark is occasionally used to indicate repetition. Unlike the Hiragana repetition mark, the Katakana repetition mark repeats only the last character. For example, コ 〳 is *koko*.

Like Chinese, Japanese is traditionally written in vertical columns that run from the right-hand side of the page to the left-hand side, but it's becoming

	–	K	S	T	N	H	M	Y	R	W
A	ア	カ	サ	タ	ナ	ハ	マ	ヤ	ラ	ワ
I	イ	キ	シ	チ	ニ	ヒ	ミ		リ	ヰ
U	ウ	ク	ス	ツ	ヌ	フ	ム	ユ	ル	
E	エ	ケ	セ	テ	ネ	ヘ	メ		レ	ヱ
O	オ	コ	ソ	ト	ノ	ホ	モ	ヨ	ロ	ヲ
N	ン									

Figure 10.5 Basic Katakana characters

more common to see Japanese written in horizontal lines with the same reading order as English. Spaces are not used between words, although word boundaries are usually detectable due to the mixture of scripts and inclusion of punctuation in most Japanese text. Japanese text is not word-wrapped: Certain punctuation

	G	Z	D	B	P	V
A	ガ	ザ	ダ	バ	パ	ヷ
I	ギ	ジ	ヂ	ビ	ピ	ヸ
U	グ	ズ	ヅ	ブ	プ	ヴ
E	ゲ	ゼ	デ	ベ	ペ	ヹ
O	ゴ	ゾ	ド	ボ	ポ	ヺ

Figure 10.6 Katakana character/diacritical mark combinations

	K	S	T	N	H	M	R	G	Z	D	B	P
YA	キャ	シャ	チャ	ニャ	ヒャ	ミャ	リャ	ギャ	ジャ	ヂャ	ビャ	ピャ
YU	キュ	シュ	チュ	ニュ	ヒュ	ミュ	リュ	ギュ	ジュ	ヂュ	ビュ	ピュ
YO	キョ	ショ	チョ	ニョ	ヒョ	ミョ	リョ	ギョ	ジョ	ヂョ	ビョ	ピョ

Figure 10.7 Katakana palatalized syllables

marks can't appear at the beginning of a line and others can't occur at the end of a line, but basically line breaks can occur anywhere, including the middles of words. Latin letters are used for certain foreign words and expressions, and numbers are written using both kanji and Western numerals, depending on context.

If you put all these writing systems together, you get something that looks like this:[15]

私は、U.S. オリンピック選手の積極的な態度に感動した。

ベッド = *beddo*

フ ァ = *fa*

ト ゥ = *tu*

ヂェット = *jetto*

Figure 10.8 Small Katakana combinations

---

15. Huge thanks to Koji Kodama for his help putting this example together.

These characters break down as follows:

Original text	Pronunciation	Meaning	Script
私	*Watakushi* (or *watashi*)	I	Kanji
は	*Wa*	Pronoun-to-context connector	Hiragana
U.S.	*Yuu esu*	U.S.	Romaji
オリンピック	*Orinpikku*	Olympic	Katakana
選手	*Senshu*	Athlete(s) [or player(s)]	Kanji
の	*No*	Possessive connector (connects "positive attitude" to "athletes")	Hiragana
積極的	*Sekkyoku-teki*	Positive (mental)	Kanji
な	*Na*	Adjective connector	Hiragana
態度	*Taido*	Attitude (or manner)	Kanji
に	*Ni*	By (or at)	Hiragana
感動	*Kandou*	Deeply moved (emotionally)	Kanji
した	*Shita*	Tense marker ("was")	Hiragana

Put it all together and you get the following: "I was deeply moved by the positive attitude of the U.S. Olympic athletes."

The Hiragana Block

The Unicode Hiragana block runs from U+3040 to U+309F. The basic syllables, the syllables with dakuten and handakuten, and the small versions of the syllables all get individual code point values. In addition, the dakuten is encoded as U+3099 COMBINING KATAKANA-HIRAGANA VOICED SOUND MARK and the handakuten as U+309A COMBINING KATAKANA-HIRAGANA SEMI-VOICED SOUND MARK. These are regular Unicode combining characters, and the syllables that use them have canonical decompositions to their unadorned forms and the combining marks. Standard practice in native Japanese encoding standards is to use the precomposed versions of the characters, however. The analogous characters in Japanese encodings don't have combining semantics, so Unicode also has noncombining versions of these characters.

The Hiragana repetition marks are encoded in this block as U+309D HIRAGANA ITERATION MARK and U+309E HIRAGANA VOICED ITERATION MARK. A special version of the Hiragana repetition mark for use in vertical text is encoded in the CJK Symbols and Punctuation block as U+3031 VERTICAL KANA REPEAT MARK. (A clone with the dakuten is encoded at U+3032; because this character normally takes up two display cells, the upper and lower halves are encoded at U+3033, U+3034, and U+3035.)

The Katakana Block

The Unicode Katakana block runs from U+30A0 to U+30FF and encodes the Katakana characters in the same relative positions as the Hiragana characters are encoded in the Hiragana block, along with a few extra characters that don't have counterparts in Hiragana. The combining voiced and semi-voiced sound marks from the Hiragana block are also used with Katakana, and the appropriate characters employ them in their canonical decompositions. The choon mark is encoded as U+30FC KATAKANA-HIRAGANA PROLONGED SOUND MARK. The Katakana repetition marks are included here as well, as is a centered dot that is used to separate words in a sequence of foreign words written in Katakana.

The Katakana Phonetic Extensions Block

Unicode 3.2 adds a new Katakana Phonetic Extensions block running from U+31F0 to U+31FF. It contains more "small" Katakana characters used for phonetic transcription of Ainu and some other languages.

The Kanbun Block

The Kanbun block (U+3190 to U+319F) contains a small set of characters that are used in Japanese editions of classical Chinese texts to indicate the Japanese reading order. These small versions of ideographs are typically written as annotations to the side of a line of vertically arranged Chinese text. All of these characters have compatibility mappings to regular Han characters, because they're just smaller versions of them used as annotations.

▪ KOREAN

Like Japanese, the Han characters (called hanja in Korean) were originally used to write Korean, with the oldest example dating to about 414.[16] Korean, which is distantly related to Japanese[17] but not to Chinese or the other Asian languages, isn't really any better suited to writing with hanja than Japanese is, and various phonetic systems similar to Japanese Kana were devised to supplement the Han characters. Several of these systems are obsolete, but one of them—Hangul—has become the main writing system used for modern Korean. Interestingly, even though Hangul was invented in 1446, the Chinese characters persisted as the preferred method of writing Korean until the beginning of the twentieth century; Hangul was accorded a kind of second-class status as the writing of the uneducated. Since Korea was liberated from Japan in 1945, however, Hangul has risen steadily in importance and the Han characters have increasingly fallen into disuse. In North Korea today, Hangul is used almost exclusively, although a small set of hanja is taught in school. In South Korea, hanja are still used, but they tend to make up a small minority of the characters in most modern texts.

Hangul (also spelled Hankul or Hangeul, and called by a variety of other names, including [before 1910] *changum, enmun,* or *kwukmun,* or [in North Korea] *chosengul* or *wuli kulcha*) was invented in 1446 by the sage King Sejong. Although it bears a superficial resemblance to the Han characters (probably not accidentally) and borrows some concepts from other writing systems, it's more of a pure invention than something that grew organically from other origins, as almost every other writing system we've looked at did. The design is based on sound linguistic principles, and it's quite well suited to the writing of Korean.

---

16. The material on Hangul comes from Ross King, "Korean Writing," in *The World's Writing Systems,* pp. 218–227.

17. At least according to some linguists; there's a lot of controversy on this point.

Hangul is basically an alphabetic script, consisting of letters called **jamo**, which represent both consonant and vowel sounds. Unlike in the Middle Eastern and Southeast Asian scripts, the vowels are neither left out nor written as marks that attach to the consonants; they're independent characters in their own right like the vowels in the Latin, Greek, and Cyrillic alphabets. Instead of being written sequentially like letters in Western alphabets are, Hangul jamo are arranged into blocks representing whole syllables. The blocks fit into square display cells, like the Han characters, and somewhat resemble them. There have been proposals to write the jamo sequentially on a line of text, but this idea has never caught on. Even though it requires more different pieces of movable type, the arrangement into syllable blocks makes more efficient use of space and is (arguably, at least) more efficient to read.

There are five basic consonant characters, whose shapes originally were designed to resemble the positions of the speech organs while making the sounds. ㄴ, which represented the *n* sound, represented the tip of the tongue against the roof of the mouth, as it would be to produce the *n* sound (imagine the speaker facing to the left). ㅅ, which represented the *s* sound, represented the tip of the tongue against the back of the teeth. ㄱ represented the *k* sound, pronounced with the back of the tongue against the roof of the mouth. ㅁ represented the lips together, as necessary for the *m* sound, and ㅇ represented the open mouth, as necessary for the *h* sound (even though this letter is either silent now or used to represent the *ng* sound). The other consonants were then organized into families according to the basic ones, with extra strokes added (Figure 10.9).

The construction of the vowels isn't quite as concrete: Three basic shapes—the horizontal line, representing earth; the dot, representing the heavens; and the vertical line, representing humans—were used in various combinations to represent the vowels. (The dot has since morphed into a short stroke.) These also combine in various ways to form diphthongs (Figure 10.10).

A syllable consists of an initial consonant, a vowel, and, optionally, a final consonant. If the vowel is based on a vertical line, the initial consonant goes to its left. If the vowel is based on a horizontal line, the initial consonant goes above it. If the vowel is a combination of vertical and horizontal strokes, the initial consonant goes in the upper-left corner. The final consonant, if present,

Consonants

ㄱ k	ㄴ n	ㅅ s	ㅁ m	ㅇ ng
	ㄷ t	ㅈ c	ㅂ p	
ㅋ kh	ㅌ th	ㅊ ch	ㅍ ph	ㅎ h
ㄲ kk	ㄸ tt	ㅆ ss	ㅃ pp	
		ㅉ cc		
	ㄹ l			

Vowels

ㅣ i	ㅡ u	ㅜ wu
ㅔ ey	ㅓ e	ㅗ o
ㅐ ay		ㅏ a

Figure 10.9 Korean consonant and vowel families

	ㅢ uy	ㅟ wuy
		ㅚ oy
		ㅠ ywu
ㅖ yey	ㅕ ye	ㅛ yo
ㅒ yay		ㅑ ya
ㅞ wey	ㅝ we	
ㅙ way		ㅘ wa

Figure 10.10 Korean diphthongs

goes underneath the initial consonant and the vowel. Syllables beginning with a vowel sound use ㅇ as their initial consonant (it's silent at the beginning of a syllable). Certain combinations of final consonants can go at the end of a syllable; the first sound goes to the left of the second. Thus, the reading order within a syllable block is left to right, top to bottom:

ㅂ (*p*) + ㅏ (*a*) = 바 (*pa*)

ㅂ (*p*) + ㅏ (*a*) + ㅁ (*m*) = 밤 (*pam*)

ㅅ (*s*) + ㅗ (*o*) = 소 (*so*)

ㅅ (*s*) + ㅗ (*o*) + ㄴ (*n*) = 손 (*son*)

ㅇ (silent) + ㅏ (*a*) = 아 (*a*)

ㅇ (silent) + ㅘ (*wa*) = 와 (*wa*)

ㅇ (silent) + ㅏ (*a*) + ㅇ (*ng*) = 앙 (*ang*)

ㅂ (*p*) + ㅏ (*a*) + ㄹ (*l*) + ㅂ (*p*) + ㄷ (*t*) + ㅏ (*a*) = 밟다 (*palpta*)

ㅇ (silent) + ㅣ (*i*) + ㄹ (*l*) + ㄱ (*k*) + ㄷ (*t*) + ㅏ (*a*) = 읽다 (*ilkta*)

Like Chinese and Japanese, Korean is traditionally written in vertical columns running from right to left across the page, but horizontal writing is becoming more common, especially in North Korea. In South Korea, Hangul is mixed with hanja; Hangul is used exclusively in North Korea. Spaces are frequently, but not always, used between words. When spaces are not used between words, lines can be broken anywhere (except for certain punctuation marks). When spaces are used, line boundaries must come between words, as in Western writing. There are no native Korean numerals—numbers are written using Han characters or Western numerals.

The Hangul Jamo Block

There are two basic ways of representing Hangul in Unicode: Unique code point values can be given to each possible syllable block, or unique code point values can be given to the individual jamo, which are then used in combination to build up syllable blocks. The designers of Unicode opted to have it both ways.

The Hangul Jamo block, which runs from U+1100 to U+11FF, gives a code point value to each jamo. The basic approach is based on the Johab encoding from the Korean national standards. The Johab encoding classifies the jamo into three categories: initial consonants (or **choseong**), vowels (**jungseong**), and final consonants (**jongseong**). There are 19 possible initial consonants, 21 possible vowels and vowel combinations, and 27 possible final consonants and combinations of final consonants. Each receives its own code point value. In Johab, each of these categories gets a unique 5-bit combination, which are then concatenated, with a 1 bit on the front, to form a 16-bit character code; in Unicode, each jamo combination is given a full 16-bit code point value.

This approach means that a jamo that can appear either at the beginning or the end of a syllable has a different code point value depending on its position within the syllable. It also means that combinations of vowel or consonant jamo get their own code point values. In this way, every syllable can be represented using a sequence of three jamo (for those that consist of only two jamo, invisible "filler" characters are provided).

Unicode doesn't define decompositions for any of the jamo, even those that are made up of combinations of smaller jamo. This position is consistent with standard Korean encodings and with the way Koreans think of the jamo. The characters in this block have combining semantics: A sequence of initial-consonant, vowel, final-consonant represents a single syllable block, rather than three isolated jamo. The standard defines any arbitrary sequence of initial consonants, followed by any arbitrary sequence of vowels, followed by any arbitrary sequence of final consonants, to be a single combining character sequence representing one syllable, although any sequence consisting of something other than exactly one of each category is considered to be malformed.

In addition to the 67 modern Hangul jamo, the Hangul Jamo block includes several ancient jamo that aren't used in modern Korean. It also provides two invisible "filler" characters that can be used to make each syllable consist of three code points, even when it doesn't contain three jamo.

The Hangul Compatibility Jamo Block

The Hangul Compatibility Jamo block, which runs from U+3130 to U+318F, contains duplicates of the characters from the Hangul Jamo block. These characters are intended to represent individual jamo, rather than being used in combination to represent whole syllables (that is, they don't have combining semantics like the characters in the Hangul Jamo block). This block doesn't make a distinction between initial and final consonants, as the characters aren't intended to be used in combination.

All of the characters in this block have compatibility decompositions to characters in the regular Hangul Jamo block. This choice has an interesting side effect: The compatibility jamo don't conjoin, but the regular jamo do. For example, if you convert a passage of compatibility jamo to Normalized Form KD or KC, they combine into syllables. The conjoining jamo can be prevented from clustering together by inserting non-Korean characters (the zero-width space works nicely for this purpose).

The Hangul Syllables Area

The Korean Johab encoding allows for an encoding of every possible combination of the 67 modern jamo, even though only about 2,500 actually occur in written Korean. This gives a grand total of 11,172 possible syllables. Although the characters in the Hangul Jamo block work in the same way as those in the Korean Johab encoding, a single syllable takes up six bytes in Unicode, but only two bytes in Johab. Unicode, as of Unicode 2.0, also provides a unique 16-bit code point value for each of the 11,172 syllables representable using Johab. These occupy the Hangul Syllables area, which runs from U+AC00 to U+D7FF. The ordering is the same as Johab, but the relative positions are different. Johab contains holes, while the Unicode Hangul Syllables area keeps all the characters contiguous, squeezing out the holes.

Unicode defines a syllable represented using a code point value from this area to be equivalent to the same syllable represented using three code point values from the Hangul Jamo block. In effect, even though the Unicode Character Database doesn't spell them all out, the characters in this block all have canonical decompositions to sequences of characters from the Hangul Jamo block. The Hangul Jamo block and the Hangul Syllables area are arranged in such a way that converting from one representation to the other can be done algorithmically (rather than requiring a translation table of some kind).

The Hangul Syllables area contains combinations of only the 67 modern jamo. Syllables using the archaic jamo must be represented using sequences of characters from the Hangul Jamo block.

■ HALF-WIDTH AND FULL-WIDTH CHARACTERS

Now that we've taken a look at the characters involved and how they work, we can go back and look a little more closely at some of the interesting issues involved in dealing with East Asian characters.

You'll often hear the terms "half-width" and "full-width" (or their Japanese equivalents, **hankaku** and **zenkaku**) used in conjunction with various characters. These terms have their origin in the variable-width character encoding standards used for most East Asian languages. Japanese variable-length encodings such as SHIFT-JIS or EUC-JP included the characters from both the JIS X 0201 and JIS X 0208 standards. These standards overlap, resulting in several characters with two different encodings: a one-byte version and a two-byte version. This collection included the ASCII characters and a basic set of Katakana.

The double encoding of these collections of characters prompted many implementations to draw a distinction in how they should be displayed. In a monospaced East Asian typeface, all of the regular East Asian characters (kanji, Kana, Bopomofo, Hangul, and so on) fit into a square design space: They are as wide as they are high. The foreign characters (in particular, the Latin letters, digits, and punctuation) would be sized to take up half of a display cell: They are half as wide as they are high. This system came to be identified with the encoding length: One-byte characters occupied half a display cell, and two-byte characters occupied a full display cell. For those characters that had both one-byte and two-byte encodings, the two-byte version would fit into a single display cell, and the one-byte version would fit two to a display cell. For the Latin letters, the two-byte versions were shown using glyphs that were stretched horizontally and surrounded with extra whitespace. For the

Katakana characters, the one-byte versions would be squooshed horizontally to fit in half of a display cell. (The original encodings of half-width Katakana included only the basic 48 characters; distinctions between regular and small kana were lost, and the dakuten and handakuten were treated as separate spacing marks that appeared in their own half-width display cells after the characters they modified.)

Even in these days of proportional fonts and sophisticated typesetting, the distinction between half-width and full-width occasionally remains a useful one. East Asian word-processing software, for example, still systematically treats full-width and half-width characters differently for the purposes of line breaking and line layout.

To retain backward compatibility with the various East Asian character encoding standards that give certain characters redundant one- and two-byte encodings, Unicode does the same for these characters. It segregates the redundant versions into a separate block located within the Compatibility Zone (discussed later in this chapter). These are the only characters in the Unicode standard that are officially designated as either "half-width" or "full-width."

Unicode Standard Annex #11, "East Asian Width," extends these definitions to the entire Unicode character repertoire, so that applications that treat "half-width" and "full-width" characters differently will know how to treat every character in Unicode. It does so by classifying the Unicode characters into six categories. An application resolves these six categories down to two broad categories, "narrow" and "wide," depending on context. The six categories are described below:

- Fullwidth (F). These characters in the Compatibility Zone have "FULL-WIDTH" in their names and are always treated as "wide."
- Halfwidth (H). These characters in the Compatibility Zone have "HALFWIDTH" in their names and are always treated as "narrow."
- Wide (W). This category includes those characters that have counterparts in the H category (the regular Katakana), plus all the other East Asian characters: Han, Hangul, Hiragana, Katakana, Bopomofo, all of the symbols that are designed for use in East Asian typography (or taken exclusively from East Asian encoding standards), and so on. These characters, of course, are always treated as "wide."

- Narrow (Na). These characters have counterparts in the F category. Basically, they include the ASCII characters. They're obviously always treated as "narrow."

- Ambiguous (A). These characters have two-byte encodings in the legacy East Asian encodings and thus are usually treated by East Asian systems as "full-width," but are treated by other systems in the same way as Latin characters are. This category includes the Cyrillic and Greek alphabets, plus some math symbols. These characters are treated as either "wide" or "narrow" depending on context. In an East Asian context, they're "wide"; otherwise, they're "narrow." (UAX #11 doesn't really define what an "East Asian context" means, leaving that up to implementation; the basic idea is that an "East Asian context" would be a document or other piece of text consisting predominantly of East Asian characters, or a piece of text set using an East Asian font, even for the Western characters.)

- Neutral. This category includes all characters that don't occur in any East Asian legacy character encoding standards and, by extension, don't occur in East Asian typography. Officially, they're neither "wide" nor "narrow," but for all practical purposes they can be treated as "narrow." This category includes the Arabic and Devanagari alphabets.

Combining marks don't have an East Asian width property at all. Instead, they take on the East Asian width property of the characters to which they're applied, just as they take on most of the other properties of those characters.

The East Asian width properties of all Unicode characters are given in the EastAsianWidth.txt file in the Unicode Character Database (see Chapter 5).

The classification of characters as "half-width" or "full-width" (or, as UAX #11 puts it, "wide" or "narrow") categories doesn't mean that these characters are always typeset this way. Purely monospaced typefaces aren't used any more in East Asian typesetting than they are in Western typesetting. Although the Han characters (and the characters that are used with them, such as Bopomofo, Kana, and Hangul) are generally all set in the same-size display cells,[18] punctuation and

---

18. These cells aren't always square, by the way. Newspapers, for example, often use fonts with rectangular display cells to fit more text on a page.

symbols often aren't. Latin letters and digits are usually set using proportional typefaces as well, and various justification techniques are used in different situations to ensure that, even when most of the characters are the same size, you don't get that "graph paper" look. Furthermore, some proportional fonts do use different-sized display cells for certain Han and Han-related characters. For an extensive treatment of these issues, see Chapter 7 of Ken Lunde's *CJKV Information Processing*.

The Half-width and Full-width Forms Block

Unicode's Half-width and Full-width Forms block, which runs from U+FF00 to U+FFEF, is the dumping ground for all characters that have redundant one- and two-byte encodings in legacy East Asian encoding standards. The characters in this block have compatibility mappings to characters elsewhere in the standard. They include full-width versions of the ASCII printing characters, half-width versions of the basic Katakana characters, half-width versions of the modern Hangul jamo, half-width versions of certain symbols and punctuation marks, and full-width versions of several currency symbols.

■ VERTICAL TEXT LAYOUT

As mentioned repeatedly throughout this chapter, East Asian text is traditionally written vertically, with characters proceeding in a line from the top of the page to the bottom, and with lines of text proceeding from the right-hand side of the page to the left. Books in Chinese or Japanese, like books in right-to-left languages such as Hebrew, appear to English speakers to be bound on the wrong side: They begin at what we normally think of as the back.[19]

Thanks to Western influence and the inability of early computer systems to handle vertical text, most East Asian languages are now also written horizontally, with characters running from left to right and lines running from top to

---

19. This section and the next section rely heavily on Lunde, pp. 336–386.

bottom, as in English text.[20] The main East Asian characters don't really behave any differently when they're arranged horizontally as opposed to vertically, but many other characters do. Consider this example:[21]

良治は、「僕には二十三にんの子供がいる」と言って、笑った。

This text is basically the same example from our discussion of the bi-di algorithm translated into Japanese: "Ryoji said, 'I have 23 children,' and smiled." Here is what it looks like laid out vertically:

良治は、「僕には二十三にんの子供がいる」と言って、笑った。

Notice what happened to the Japanese quotation marks (「」). In the vertical text, they were rotated 90 degrees clockwise. This happens with a lot of punctuation marks: Parentheses, ellipses, dashes, and so forth are all rotated. Some undergo additional transformations. A more subtle transformation can be observed if you look closely at the period and comma (。、). Their shapes stay the same, but they occupy different positions relative to the other characters. In horizontal text, the period and comma appear in the lower-left corner of the display cell, like a Western period. In vertical text, however, they appear in the upper-right corner. Various other characters, such as the small Kana in Japanese, keep their shapes but are drawn in different parts of their display cells depending on the directionality of the surrounding text.

Except for a few characters in the Compatibility Zone (see Chapter 12), Unicode adheres to the characters-not-glyphs rule for those characters whose glyphs change depending on the directionality of the surrounding text. An

20. Right-to-left writing also happens. Nakanishi (p. 114) gives an interesting example of a single newspaper page from Taiwan containing Chinese text written vertically, left to right, and right to left.

21. Many thanks to Koji Kodama for his help translating the vertical-text examples.

implementation that supports vertical text must be smart enough to make the appropriate glyph selections when drawing vertical text.

In some cases, exactly how the character is transformed depends on the locale. The colon (:), for example, looks the same in horizontal Japanese and Chinese text. In Japanese vertical text, it turns sideways. In Chinese vertical text, it remains upright but becomes smaller and moves to the upper-right corner of its display cell:

Chinese	**Japanese**
良	良
治	治
は:	は:

Unicode doesn't give separate code point values to these language-specific transformations, just as it doesn't assign separate code point values to language-specific variants of certain Han characters. The assumption is that you'll use a font designed for the language in which you're writing, and that the font will be selected either manually by the user and specified using a higher-level protocol, or automatically by the system based on analysis of the text (or, in a pinch, use of the language-tagging characters).

Things get even more fun when you start mixing non-Asian text with Asian text. Suppose, for example, that we used Western digits for the "23" in our previous example:

良治は、「僕には23にんの子供がいる」と言って、笑った。

When you write this text vertically, you can treat the "23" in three ways. First, you can keep the digits upright and stack them vertically:

良治は、「僕には23にんの子供がいる」と言って、笑った。

Second, you can rotate the number 90 degrees clockwise:

良治は、「僕には23にんの子供がいる」と言って、笑った。

Third, you can keep the "23" upright and put the digits side-by-side in a single vertical display cell:

良治は、「僕には23にんの子供がいる」と言って、笑った。

The third approach (referred to in Japanese as **tate-chu-yoko**, or "horizontal in vertical") is generally reserved for abbreviations and other very short snippets of text. You'll see it used with native characters as well. For example, month names are written in Japanese with a Western numeral and the "moon" character in a single display cell (10月). Some abbreviations consist of as many as four or five characters stuck into a single display cell (キロメートル). The second approach, rotating the horizontal text, works best for long snippets of foreign text.

Because Unicode allows for mixing of languages that were much more difficult to mix before the creation of this standard, such as Arabic and Japanese, you also run into the possibility of mixing right-to-left text with vertical text. No hard-and-fast rules explain how to do this. Generally—especially with Arabic—you would rotate the text. It makes sense to keep the overall top-to-bottom writing direction, so you'd probably rotate right-to-left text 90 degrees counterclockwise:

良治は、「בני דוד」と言って、笑った。

Of course, you could also mix left-to-right, right-to-left, *and* vertical text in the same document. In this case, you'd probably rotate all of the horizontal text in the same direction (probably 90 degrees clockwise) and use the Unicode bi-di algorithm to lay out the individual pieces of the horizontal text relative to each other. The right-to-left text would then read from the bottom of the page up when you rotated the page.

良治は、「The first two books of the Bible are בראשית and שמות」と言って、笑った。

Unicode doesn't set forth any specific rules for mixing vertical and horizontal text. The correct behavior depends on the situation. (It's unclear that any word-processing system today can even handle all of these examples.)

■ RUBY

Even native speakers of the languages that use the Han characters don't know *all* of them. Consequently, in East Asian typography (especially Japanese), annotation techniques are often used to help readers deal with unfamiliar characters. The most common of these techniques is something called **interlinear annotation** or, in Japanese, **ruby** or **furigana**.[22]

---

22. Ken Lunde, the Japanese text-processing expert whose book provided much of the information in this chapter, has a daughter named Ruby, which somehow seems quite appropriate.

With this approach, you adorn a character with one or more smaller characters that clarify its meaning or, more commonly, its pronunciation. In Japanese, you might see an unusual kanji character adorned with a few small Hiragana characters that give the Kanji character's pronunciation. The annotations go above the character being annotated in horizontal text, and (generally) to the right in vertical text. The effect is something like this, using English:

SLO-buh-dahn   mi-LO-she-vitch
Slobodan Milosevic was defeated by

VOY-slav   ko-SHTOO-nit-sa
Vojislav Kostunica in the Yugoslav

general election.

Ruby occurs relatively rarely in most text, but frequently in children's books or books written for non-native speakers learning the language. It's most common in Japanese, but also occurs in Chinese and Korean.

The Interlinear Annotation Characters

Ruby is one of those issues generally best left to a higher-level protocol. Nevertheless, Unicode includes some very rudimentary support for ruby for those situations where it absolutely has to be exchanged using plain text. (The interlinear annotation characters can also be useful as an internal implementation detail, giving implementations a way to store the annotations along with the actual text without getting the two mixed up.) Three characters in the Specials block are used to represent ruby:

```
U+FFF9 INTERLINEAR ANNOTATION ANCHOR
U+FFFA INTERLINEAR ANNOTATION SEPARATOR
U+FFFB INTERLINEAR ANNOTATION TERMINATOR
```

U+FFF9 marks the beginning of a piece of text that is to be annotated. U+FFFA marks the end of the piece of text to be annotated and the beginning of the annotation. U+FFFB marks the end of the annotation. The preceding example would be represented as follows (with the anchor, separator, and terminator characters represented by [A], [S], and [T], respectively):

[A]Slobodan[S]SLO-buh-dahn[T] [A]Milosevic[S]mi-LO-she-vitch[T] was defeated by [A]Vojislav[S]VOY-slav[T] [A]Kostunica[S]ko-SHTOO-nit-sa[T] in the Yugoslav general election.

Unicode doesn't give you any way to control how exactly the ruby will be laid out. It also stipulates that paragraph separators can't occur inside annotations. A paragraph separator inside an annotation terminates the annotation.

You can attach more than one annotation to a piece of annotated text by separating the annotations with extra instances of U+FFFA INTERLINEAR ANNOTATION SEPARATOR.

Generally, you want annotations to be significant only when you're laying out or otherwise rendering text; for other operations, such as sorting and line breaking, you want them to be transparent. Most applications can, therefore, safely ignore all three annotation characters, plus all characters that occur between U+FFFA and U+FFFB (or between U+FFFA and the end of a paragraph). Typically, unless you know you're interchanging text with something that definitely understands these characters, they, along with any annotations, should be filtered out.

■ Yɪ

Before we leave East Asia, let's take a quick look at one more writing system. The Yi (or Lolo or Nuo-su) people are one of the largest minority groups in China. Most live in various parts of southwestern China, but they're scattered all over southeastern Asia as well. The Yi language is related to Tibetan and Burmese and is written with its own script, called, not surprisingly, the Yi script, but sometimes known as Cuan or Wei.[23]

---

23. My sources for this section are the Unicode standard and Dingxu Shi, "The Yi Script," in *The World's Writing Systems,* pp. 239–243.

Classical Yi is an ideographic script, like the Chinese characters. Although it probably arose under the influence of the Han characters, it's not directly related to them; the characters have a notably different look from Han characters. The earliest examples of Yi writing date back about 500 years, although linguists suspect its real history may go back as far as 5,000 years. An estimated 8,000 to 10,000 different characters appear in the surviving examples of classical Yi writing. Because the Yi have been scattered geographically, the same characters look quite different from group to group; no real standardization has occurred.

In the 1970s, in an effort to increase literacy in Yi, a new writing system for Yi was developed. It takes some of the old Yi ideographs and removes their semantic value, creating a purely phonetic script. Like the Japanese Kana scripts, modern Yi writing is a pure syllabary: Each character represents a whole syllable, and the characters can't be broken down into smaller components representing the original sounds (as, for example, Korean Hangul syllables can).

There are many more possible Yi syllables than there are Japanese syllables, so the Yi syllabary is considerably larger than the Japanese syllabaries. Each Yi syllable consists of an optional initial consonant and a vowel. There are 44 initial consonants and 10 vowels, giving 440 possible syllables. Each syllable can have four tones, so each syllable has four different symbols, one for each tone. Thus 1,760 syllables are possible in Yi. Of course, not all of these syllables actually exist in Yi: The standard Yi syllabary actually has 1,165 characters. (By comparison, more than 11,000 Hangul syllables are possible in Korean, but only 2,500 or so actually occur.)

The characters representing the various Yi syllables don't have anything in common (they're derived from earlier ideographic characters with those sounds), with one exception: each syllable has *three* unique characters. The fourth, middle-rising, tone is written by using the character for the middle-high tone and putting an arch (an inverted breve) over it. Thus there are actually 819 unique Yi characters; the rest are duplicates with the arch over them. For example, here are the four characters for the syllable *pi*; they represent that syllable with, respectively, the high, middle-high, low-falling, and middle-rising tones:

Yi is written horizontally, from left to right.

The Yi Syllables Block

Currently, Unicode encodes only the modern Yi syllabary, not the classical Yi ideographic script. The Unicode Yi Syllables block runs from U+A000 to U+A48F and is based on the Chinese national standard for Yi, GB 13134-91. It contains separate code point values for each of the 1,165 syllables. The characters representing syllables with the middle-rising tone have their own code point values. Even though they're the same as the characters representing the syllables with the middle-high tone with an added arch, they *don't* decompose and *can't* be represented with combining character sequences. Unlike the Han characters and the Hangul syllables, each Yi syllable has an assigned name rather than an algorithmic name. Each name is an approximation of the syllable's sound, with an extra character added to the end to indicate the tone. The four characters shown in the previous example, for instance, have the following code point values and names:

```
U+A038 YI SYLLABLE PIT
U+A03A YI SYLLABLE PI
U+A03B YI SYLLABLE PIP
U+A039 YI SYLLABLE PIX
```

The Yi Radicals Block

The Yi Radicals block (U+A490 to U+A4CF) contains a group of radicals that function similarly to the radicals in the Han characters. The Yi syllables are classified into categories according to certain visual elements (radicals) they share in common, and these radicals are used to facilitate lookup in dictionaries. This block contains 50 radicals.

11

Scripts from Other Parts of the World

$\mathcal{S}$o far in Part II, we've taken an in-depth look at the four major script groups still in use around the world today. To recap:

- In Chapter 7, we looked at the five European alphabetic scripts, which are descended from the ancient Phoenician alphabet by way of the ancient Greek alphabet. These scripts are all alphabetic in nature, consist of uppercase/lowercase pairs, are written from left to right, and use spaces between words. There is little or no typographic interaction between characters in the printed forms of these scripts, but most scripts make moderate to heavy use of combining diacritical marks. These scripts are employed throughout Europe and other parts of the world colonized by the Europeans.

- In Chapter 8, we examined the four Middle Eastern scripts, which are descended from the ancient Phoenician alphabet by way of the ancient Aramaic alphabet. These scripts are consonantal in nature, generally using letters for consonant sounds and writing most vowel sounds, if at all, with combining marks above or below the consonants. They're written from right to left. Two scripts, Arabic and Syriac, are cursive, with the characters in a word generally being connected and with the shapes of the letters varying greatly depending on the surrounding letters.

These scripts are used in the Middle East (i.e., southwestern Asia and northeastern Africa) and throughout the Muslim and Jewish worlds.

- In Chapter 9, we considered the 19 Indic scripts, which are descended from the ancient Brahmi script, which in turn is probably descended from the ancient Phoenician alphabet by way of the Aramaic alphabet. These scripts are alphasyllabic in nature, with individual characters for consonant and vowel sounds reordering, reshaping, and combining in interesting ways to form clusters representing syllables. They're written from left to right. Most, but not all, place spaces between words. These scripts are used throughout south and southeastern Asia.

- In Chapter 10, we looked at the Han characters, which have an independent history going back more than 3,000 years. They're ideographic or logographic in nature, number in the tens of thousands, include numerous regional and historic variants of some characters, and are an open-ended set to which new characters continue to be added. They're supplemented in various ways by three other scripts, two syllabic (Japanese and Yi) and one alphabetic (Korean). These scripts are traditionally written vertically, but can also be written from left to right. Spaces are *not* used between words (except in Korean), and the characters generally don't interact typographically. These scripts are used in East Asia.

All in all, we've looked at 32 different writing systems. Along the way, you may have noticed something interesting: We've looked at writing systems only in Europe and Asia. What about the other continents?

The Europeans colonized Africa, Australia, and the Americas. As a result of their emigration, European languages (along with Arabic in northern Africa) have come to be spoken on those continents, and their writing systems (especially the Latin alphabet) have emerged as the chief writing systems used in those places. Among the indigenous languages used in most of those places, most of those that are still spoken either don't have a written language or historically didn't, and now have a recently developed written language based on one of the European scripts (usually the Latin alphabet). Some exceptions exist, however.

In this chapter, we'll discuss the four major exceptions. These scripts don't fit well into any of the other categories we've examined to this point, although some of them are related to the others. Three of the four are indigenous to areas outside Europe and Asia.

■ MONGOLIAN

The exception is the Mongolian alphabet, which is (not surprisingly) used in Mongolia. Mongolian is written using this alphabet in Inner Mongolia (the Mongolian district in China). In Outer Mongolia (the Mongolian People's Republic), Mongolian was written using the Cyrillic alphabet for much of the twentieth century, but the Mongolian alphabet was restored by law in 1992. Unlike with other biscriptal languages, such as Serbo-Croatian, no direct one-to-one mapping exists between the two versions of written Mongolian; spelling of words in the two scripts is independent.

The Mongolian alphabet is, at best, only very distantly related to the other Asian and Southeast Asian scripts; it's actually a cousin of the Arabic alphabet. It has been used in Mongolia since the early thirteenth century, when it evolved from the old Uighur script, which in turn evolved from the ancient Aramaic alphabet. (Modern Uighur is written using the Arabic alphabet.)

Like Arabic, Mongolian letters are cursively connected and change their shape depending on the surrounding letters. A couple of important differences are noted, however:

- The Mongolian script is fully alphabetic, using full-fledged letters for both vowels and consonants, instead of using combining diacritical marks for vowel sounds.
- The Mongolian script (like the ancient Uighur script before it) is written *vertically*. Letters proceed from the top of the page to the bottom, and lines of text proceed from left to right (unlike the East Asian scripts, where lines proceed from right to left). The effect is similar to taking a page of Arabic writing and rotating it 90 degrees counterclockwise. In fact, this is probably how the difference arose: Right-handers often write Arabic vertically in lines that go from left to right across the page, even though it's read horizontally, to keep from smudging the page. It's not a big leap from writing with the page held like this to reading it that way as well.

The Mongolian alphabet has 35 letters (Figure 11.1). The figure includes the same letterforms as are used in the Unicode code charts—generally the initial or independent form of the letter. Some letters have the same initial forms,

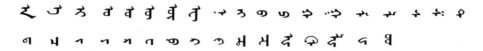

Figure 11.1 Mongolian alphabet

so some other form of the letter is used, ensuring that they all appear differently in Figure 11.1.

The Mongolian alphabet is used to write a few other languages, including Todo, Sibe, and Manchu. The Mongolians also use their alphabet for religious and classical texts in Sanskrit and Tibetan; extra letters are added to accommodate each of these languages.

As in Arabic, the letters of the Mongolian alphabet change shape depending on their context. Most letters have initial, medial, and final forms. Some letters have similar appearances, with the initial form of one letter serving as the medial form of another, or the final form of one letter being the initial form of another. Context and the principle of vowel harmony, which specifies which combinations of letters in a word are legal, permit the differentiation of similar-looking characters. Certain pairs of letters also form ligatures.

The shaping rules for Mongolian are actually more complicated than those for Arabic. Some letters take on special shapes in certain contexts, which can't always be determined algorithmically. Sometimes the correct shape for a letter is something other than the default choice, and the exact shape to use is a matter of spelling (i.e., different in that position depending on the actual word). Some letters have as many as 10 different contextual glyph shapes.

Spaces are used between words in Mongolian, but whitespace also appears within some words. Many words consist of a stem word with one or more suffixes attached to it; these suffixes are separated from the basic word with a small space. Sometimes the presence of the space causes the letters on either side of it to take on special shapes. Also, sometimes when the letters ﻭ (a) or ﻭ (e) appear at the end of the word, they're separated from the rest of the word with a break in the continuity of the cursive stroke; this break usually affects the shape of the preceding letter.

Like many writing systems, Mongolian includes its own period (ᢀ), comma (ᢀ), colon (ᢀ), and so forth. A special symbol (❖) is used to mark the end of a chapter or a text. In Todo, hyphenation is indicated with a small hyphen at the *beginning* of the line containing the second half of the divided word, rather than with a hyphen at the end of the line containing the first half, as in English.

Mongolian also has a unique set of digits:

○ ⊂⊃ ⊋ ⊋ ⊂� ⊋ ⊋ ⊋ ⊋

No hard-and-fast rules govern what happens when Mongolian text is combined with text written in other scripts. If words from normally horizontal scripts are included in the middle of a Mongolian text, they're generally rotated 90 degrees clockwise, as they would be in Chinese or Japanese (right-to-left scripts are rotated 90 degrees counterclockwise, to preserve the top-to-bottom ordering, unless the included excerpt consists of a mixture of left-to-right and right-to-left text). If a few snippets of Mongolian are included in a generally left-to-right text, the Mongolian that can be rotated 90 degrees counterclockwise, preserving the left-to-right reading order of the text. This approach generally works only with short excerpts, as the relative order of successive lines of Mongolian text would be backward in such cases. (For long blocked quotes using the Mongolian script, it would be preferable to preserve the vertical directionality.)

The Mongolian Block

The Unicode Mongolian block runs from U+1800 to U+18AF. It includes not only the basic Mongolian alphabet, but also extensions necessary for Todo, Sibe, Manchu, Sanskrit, and Tibetan; the digits; and various Mongolian- and Todo-specific punctuation marks.

As it does for other scripts that have contextual glyph shaping as one of their basic features, Unicode encodes only the letters themselves, not the individual glyphs. There's no "presentation forms" block containing code point values for the individual glyph shapes for the Mongolian letters.

The Mongolian block does include a few special formatting characters: The three characters U+180B, U+180C, and U+180D, MONGOLIAN FREE VARIATION SELECTOR ONE, TWO, and THREE, are used to affect the contextual shaping of the letters. They apply in the situations where a letter has a special shape only in certain positions or words and you can't get the correct shape by using the zero-width joiner and non-joiner (which work the same way on Mongolian as they do on Arabic). The free variation selectors have no visible representation themselves. Rather, they serve as signals to the text-rendering process, indicating that it should use an alternate glyph for the preceding letter. The three free variation selectors allow for as many as three alternative glyphs for each letter. The characters have no effect when they follow something other than a Mongolian letter.

U+180E MONGOLIAN VOWEL SEPARATOR is similar in function to the free variation selectors, but is intended specifically to be used before word-final ⵊ and ⵌ. Unlike the free variation selectors, it does have a visual presentation: a thin space. It also causes the preceding character to take on a special shape.

U+202F NARROW NO-BREAK SPACE has a special function in Mongolian. It's used for those situations where suffixes are set off from the base word with a small space. This character counts as part of the word; it's used for word-internal space. It can also cause special choices of contextual glyph selection.

The narrow no-break space works differently in Mongolian than the regular non-breaking space (U+00A0) does. The regular no-break space is a normal-size space rather than a narrow one, so it's unsuitable for use as a word-internal space in Mongolian. It also doesn't cause any special Mongolian glyph selection to happen. Although it can glue two words together on the same line, it shouldn't be used for the word-internal spaces.

Special mention should also be made of U+1806 MONGOLIAN TODO SOFT HYPHEN. It works much like the regular soft hyphen (see Chapter 12). That is, it marks a legal hyphenation position in a Todo word and remains invisible unless the word is actually hyphenated there, but it appears at the beginning of the second line rather than at the end of the first line.

When Unicode 3.0 was published, the definition of the Mongolian block was incomplete. In particular, it lacked full information on the Mongolian shaping rules, especially the definition of exactly which glyphs were created by use of the free variation selectors in conjunction with each of the letters. The book anticipated publication of the full Mongolian shaping rules as a Unicode Standard Annex and mentions a special committee made up of experts from China, Mongolia, and other interested parties similar to the Ideographic Rapporteur Group that is working on this document. As of February 2002, that annex had not yet appeared on the Unicode Web site, even in draft form. The updated information was also not included in UAX #27, Unicode 3.1, so apparently the definition of Mongolian is still incomplete in Unicode 3.1.

Unicode 3.2 provides a little more information. The new Standardized Variants.html file in the Unicode Character Database, which shows which combinations of regular characters and the new variation selectors are legal and which glyph shapes they represent, also includes a complete list of legal combinations of Mongolian letters and Mongolian variation selectors, along with the glyph shapes *they* represent.

ETHIOPIC

The Ethiopic script was originally developed to write the Ge'ez language spoken in ancient Ethiopia. Today Ge'ez is limited to liturgical use, but its writing system is also used to write several different modern languages spoken in Ethiopia and Eritrea, including Amharic, Oromo, Tigre, and Tigrinya.[1]

Ge'ez and Amharic are southern Semitic languages, cousins of Arabic and Hebrew. The writing system also has a Semitic origin, being more distantly related to the Arabic and Hebrew alphabets. It doesn't actually descend from the Phoenician alphabet, like so many other modern scripts, but it shares a common ancestor with the Phoenician alphabet.[2] The Ethiopic script was adapted from an earlier script, the Sabean script, which was used for Sabean, another southern Semitic language. A distinct writing system for Ge'ez developed sometime in the early fourth century. Several letters have since been added to represent sounds in Amharic that are not found in Ge'ez (the added characters can frequently be identified by a barbell-shaped stroke at the top of the character—compare ሀ and ኸ, for example).

---

1. My sources for the section on Ethiopic are Getatchew Haile, "Ethiopic Writing," in *The World's Writing Systems,* pp. 569–576, as well as the Unicode standard, pp. 284–286, and Nakanishi, pp. 102–103.

2. See the chart on p. 89 of *The World's Writing Systems.*

Originally, Ethiopic was a consonantal script, like Hebrew and Arabic, with letters representing only consonant sounds. The basic Amharic consonantal alphabet has 33 letters:

ሀ ለ ሐ መ ሠ ረ ሰ ሸ ቀ በ ተ ቸ ኀ ነ ኘ አ ከ ኸ ወ ዐ ዘ ዠ የ ደ ጀ ገ ጠ ጨ ጰ ጸ ፀ ፈ ፐ

This alphabet was fairly quickly deemed unsuitable for Ge'ez, and a system of vowel marks was developed to supplement the basic consonantal script. Unlike in Hebrew and Arabic, where the vowel sounds are represented (if at all) with various dots placed near and around the basic letter, the Ethiopic consonants sprouted various appendages to represent the vowels, which became mandatory. There are seven vowel sounds, so the script includes seven combinations of base consonant and vowel mark. Here's a typical example, on the basic letter qaf:

ቀ ቁ ቂ ቃ ቄ ቅ ቆ

A few consonants also have labialized forms, where a *w* sound is interpolated between the main consonant sound and the main vowel sound. The consonant sprouts extra appendages to represent these combinations:

ቄ ቈ ቊ ቋ ቈ

The formation of some of these consonant–vowel combinations can be irregular. Sometimes the character sprouts a leg to provide a place for the vowel mark to attach:

ወ ዉ ዊ ዋ ዌ ው ዎ

The marks for some vowels aren't always consistent, however. Compare, for example, these three versions of lawe,

ሌ ል ሎ

with the corresponding versions of hawt:

ሔ ሕ ሖ

Because of this variation in the basic forms, the Ethiopic script is currently considered to be a syllabary, with each character representing a combination of consonant and vowel sounds (sometimes with the interpolated *w*). The syllabary is normally shown as a 43 by 8 matrix: 43 consonants (including 10 extra consonants for writing languages other than Amharic) and 8 vowels. This matrix yields 344 possible characters, although the number actually used is smaller (not every syllable exists in the languages represented).

Ethiopic is written from left to right, and the syllable characters don't interact typographically. Traditionally, a colon-like mark (፡) was used to separate words, but the ordinary Western space is now becoming common. Other punctuation consists of the word-space character with other marks added to it: ። is a period, ፣ is a comma, ፤ is a semicolon, and ፧ is a question mark, for example.

Ethiopic has its own system of writing numbers. It uses an additive-multiplicative system similar to that employed in Chinese, rather than Western positional notation (for more information, see Chapter 12). The basic number characters, representing the numbers from 1 to 10 and 100, are shown here:

፩ ፪ ፫ ፬ ፭ ፮ ፯ ፰ ፱ ፲ ፻

The Ethiopic Block

The Ethiopic block (U+1200 to U+137F) separately encodes all of the syllables. It arranges them in the traditional consonant–vowel matrix, leaving gaps for combinations of sounds that don't have corresponding characters. The Ethiopic syllables don't decompose; despite their historical relationship, they're treated as separate, independent characters in Unicode. This block also contains the Ethiopic wordspace characters and the other punctuation marks, as well as a complete set of Ethiopic numerals.

■ CHEROKEE

Unlike all of the other scripts we've examined so far, the Cherokee script doesn't have a long history. It was invented in 1821 by Sequoyah, a monolingual Cherokee. It was quickly picked up by the Cherokee nation in general, having spread as early as 1824.[3] Sequoyah apparently got the idea from seeing written English, then invented his script based on the same general idea. The modern forms of many of the characters resemble Latin, Greek, or Cyrillic letters and Arabic digits, although no relationship exists between the sounds of the characters in Cherokee and the sounds of similar-looking characters in other scripts. (Sequoyah's original letterforms are said to have been unique, but the forms were later modified by missionaries to look more like European letters in an effort to make the language easier to print.)

The Cherokee script is a syllabary, with 85 characters representing various combinations of 13 basic consonants and 6 vowels (Figure 11.2). These 85 characters actually represent a far wider selection of actual sounds, as can be seen by the fact that multiple characters appear in certain cells of the chart in Figure 11.2, representing variants of the basic consonant sounds in those syllables. (Other cells have similar variant sounds, but they're represented with the same character.) With a few exceptions (often involving ♂Ꮖ, which represents the *s* sound without a vowel), successive consonant sounds with no intervening vowel sounds are written using an arbitrary syllable with the right consonant sound—the vowel sound is understood to be silent.

Cherokee is written from left to right, with Western punctuation and spaces between words. In handwritten Cherokee, words are sometimes separated by raised dots. Cherokee writing is basically caseless, but some printed materials in Cherokee use larger forms of the syllables in a way analogous to capital letters in English. The Cherokee syllables don't interact typographically and aren't used with combining diacritical marks.

Sequoyah also invented a Cherokee numeration system, but it never caught on. Today, numbers are either written out in words or with regular Western digits.

The Cherokee Block

The Unicode Cherokee block runs from U+13A0 to U+13FF. It just contains the basic Cherokee syllables. Normal Western spaces, numerals, and punctua-

---

3. My source is Janine Scancarelli, "Cherokee Writing," in *The World's Writing Systems,* pp. 587–592.

Figure 11.2 Cherokee syllabary

tion are used with these characters. Unicode treats Cherokee as uncased. As a result, it doesn't include separate code point values for the larger versions of the letters used in some printed Cherokee materials; these must be represented using out-of-band styling information.

■ CANADIAN ABORIGINAL SYLLABLES

The Canadian aboriginal syllabary is used to write various Native American languages in Canada.[4] It was invented in 1841 by the Wesleyan missionary

4. My source is John D. Nichols, "The Cree Syllabary," in *The World's Writing Systems,* pp. 599–611.

James Evans to write Cree and Ojibwe, and the letterforms were based on a form of British shorthand. The characters generally represent syllables (combinations of an initial consonant and a vowel), but additional characters are used to represent syllable-initial vowels and syllable-final consonants. The basic Cree syllabary consists of 63 characters (Figure 11.3).

The vowels alone are represented with triangles pointing in various directions. The syllables are represented with various other character shapes, with the orientation specifying the vowel sound. Small superscripted forms of the various syllables are generally used to represent syllable-final consonant sounds.

This script spread fairly rapidly among the Native American communities in Canada. Today, it's used to write a variety of languages in the Algonquian, Inuktitut, and Athapascan families. For example, the script is used to write Eastern and Western Algonquian, Cree, Ojibwe, Naskapi, Inuktitut, Inuktun, Athapascan, Chipewyan, and Carrier.

As the script was adopted by each new group, it was modified as necessary to suit that language, with various new characters being added and dots and other marks being applied to many of the original characters. As a result, virtually every language using this writing system has its own version with its own characters and its own character-to-sound mapping. Generally speaking, the spelling of the various languages isn't standardized, and some writers may omit certain dots and marks used with the characters.

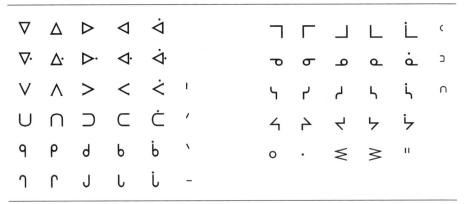

Figure 11.3 Cree syllabary

The Canadian syllables are written from left to right, spaces are used between words, and (with one exception) English punctuation marks are used. The exception is the period, which looks like this: ×.

The Unified Canadian Aboriginal Syllabics Block

The Unified Canadian Aboriginal Syllabics block (U+1400 to U+167F) contains all of the characters needed for the languages that are written with scripts based on the original Cree syllabary. The unification is based on glyph shape: If the same syllable has a different glyph in different languages, the versions are encoded separately. If different languages use the same shape for different sounds, they're still unified. The basic idea is to allow the mixture of different Canadian aboriginal languages in the same document without forcing a change of fonts.

Many of the characters in this block consist of a basic letterform with added dots or other marks. These characters don't decompose—they're treated as fully independent first-class syllables rather than as combinations of a basic character and one or more marks.

The Canadian aboriginal period and the chi sign (✕), used to write the name of Christ in some texts, are also included in this block.

■ HISTORICAL SCRIPTS

We've now rounded out the set of 36 modern scripts encoded in Unicode. With the characters in these blocks, all of the modern written languages in common business or official use can be represented. Certainly, other modern scripts are in use and could be encoded (and most eventually will be). Nevertheless, the current Unicode set is sufficient to write at least one language written by practically every literate person on Earth.

Many more writing systems have fallen into disuse but still appear in scholarly literature. In many cases, communities of hobbyists also use these scripts. Unicode 3.1 includes encodings for five such scripts, and we'll take a brief look at each of them next.

Runic

The Runic script was used in various parts of Europe from the first century to the nineteenth century.[5] Its origins are uncertain, but the earliest inscriptions using runes were found in Denmark and Germany. The traditional Runic alphabet (or "futhark," a name derived from the sounds of the first six letters) consisted of 24 letters (Figure 11.4).

The use of runes spread north and west into Scandinavia and the British Isles. As it reached new peoples, changes occurred both in the alphabet itself (addition and removal of letters, changes in their sounds) and in the shapes of the individual letters. In Scandinavia, for example, the alphabet was shortened to 16 letters. In Britain, it was extended to 28 letters.

Runic was a full alphabetic script, with letters for both consonant and vowel sounds. Like many early writing systems, the writing direction varied. Some inscriptions were written from left to right, some from right to left, and some in alternating directions (boustrophedon). Spaces weren't used between words, but sometimes words were separated by dots. Certain pairs of letters form ligatures in certain inscriptions.

The Runic block in Unicode (U+16A0 to U+16FF) contains 75 letters. Letters with common historical origins are generally unified (a few exceptions exist, notably the "long branch" and "short twig" runes), even when their shapes differ significantly. For this reason, a user must use a font designed especially for the particular variety of Runic to be represented. The Unicode Runic block also includes a few Runic punctuation marks whose exact meaning is unknown, and a few special runes that were only used for writing numbers.

ᚠ ᚢ ᚦ ᚨ ᚱ ᚲ ᚷ ᚹ ᚺ ᚾ ᛁ ᛃ ᛄ ᛈ

ᛉ ᛊ ᛏ ᛒ ᛖ ᛗ ᛚ ᛜ ᛝ ᛟ

Figure 11.4 Runic alphabet

---

5. The material from the Unicode standard is supplemented by material from Ralph W. V. Elliott, "The Runic Script," *The World's Writing Systems,* pp. 333–339.

One interesting quirk of the Runic block is that the name of each character is actually the concatenation of *several* names for the character, in cases where the same character was used in different places and times and had different names. This nomenclature helps figure out which character you want when it's been unified with several other characters that had different names.

Ogham

Ogham (pronounced "Ohm") was used in the fifth and sixth centuries for inscriptions on stone in early Irish (the surviving examples are generally territory markers and tombstones).[6] Its origins remain uncertain, but there's some consensus that Ogham was inspired by the Latin script. It's alphabetic in character, with characters for both consonants and vowels. There are 20 basic marks, organized into four groups of five (Figure 11.5).

These characters originally consisted of a series of notches cut along the edge of the stone. The first group would be cut in the stone along one face, the second group would appear along the other face, the third group would cross both faces, and the fourth group would comprise notches just in the edge between the faces. Inscriptions would begin on the lower-left corner of the stone and continue up the left side, along the top, and down the right side. There was no punctuation or word division.

In later periods, Ogham was also written on paper. In that case, a central line would often be used to symbolize the edge of the stone (hence the forms shown in Figure 11.5). Six additional letters ("forfeda") were added during this time. The normal left-to-right writing direction is typically used when writing Ogham on paper, and spaces are more common, at least in scholarly work.

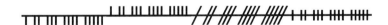

Figure 11.5   Ogham characters

---

6. The material from the Unicode standard is supplemented with material from Damian McManus, "Ogham," *The World's Writing Systems,* pp. 340–345.

The Unicode Ogham block runs from U+1680 to U+169F and includes the 26 Ogham letters, plus a space character consisting of the center line with no marks crossing it (in fonts that don't use the center line, it looks the same as a regular space) and "feather marks," chevron-like marks that indicate the beginning and end of a text.

Old Italic

The Latin alphabet evolved from the ancient Etruscan alphabet, which was derived from an ancient form of the Greek alphabet. Many related alphabets used around Italy in that same period derived from the same version of the Greek alphabet. They may be thought of as siblings of the Etruscan alphabet.

The Unicode Old Italic block, which runs from U+10300 to U+1032F in the SMP (i.e., plane 1), is a unification of these various Etruscan-related alphabets used in Italy beginning in roughly the eighth century B.C. In particular, the Etruscan, Umbrian, North and South Picene, Faliscan, Sabellian, Oscan, Volscian, Elimian, Sicanian, and Siculan alphabets are unified into the Old Italic block. (Various other alphabets from that area and time period, such as Gallic, Venetic, Rhaetic, and Messapic, belong to different families and remain unencoded in Unicode 3.1.) The unified letters are related historically and phonetically, but don't necessarily look the same in each of the unified alphabets. Use of a font customized for the particular alphabet you want to represent is therefore required.

These alphabets were generally written from right to left, with boustrophedon sometimes occurring. Modern scholarly usage generally turns them around and writes them from left to right (the better to include glosses and transcriptions in modern Latin letters). For this reason, Unicode encodes them as strict left-to-right characters. The directional-override characters can be used to display these characters in their original directionality; rendering engines should use mirror-image glyphs when these characters are written from right to left.

None of these alphabets used punctuation or spaces between words, although in later usage dots sometimes appeared between words. Unicode doesn't include special codes for these dots, unifying them instead with similar symbols elsewhere in the standard. The Old Italic numbering system was not well attested, but some numeral characters are included in this block; they work like Roman numerals.

Gothic

The language of the Goths, from a now-extinct branch of the Germanic languages, has come down to us only in very few examples. Nevertheless, this script is important to scholars because of the historical importance of the Goths and its status as a representative of a now-extinct branch of a major language group.[7] The few examples of written Gothic appear in a distinctive script that tradition holds was invented by the Gothic bishop Wulfila in the late fourth century, primarily to allow for a translation of the Bible into Gothic. Indeed, almost all examples of written Gothic are Bible fragments, and these fragments are important for Biblical scholarship. Many sources have been proposed for Wulfila's script—it probably derived at least partially, if not completely, from the Greek alphabet.

The Gothic alphabet has 27 letters (Figure 11.6). Two of these (𐍁 and 𐍊), as far as we know, were used only for writing numerals. The letter 𐌹 is written with a diaeresis (𐌹̈) when it occurs at the beginning of a word or at certain grammatically significant positions within a word. Contractions are written with a bar over the word (𐍇̄𐌿̄𐍃̄, *xus*, was the abbreviation for "Christ," for example).

As with many ancient alphabets, the letters were also used to write numbers. Two letters, as far as we know, were used only for this purpose. Numerals were set off with a dot on either side (·𐍁𐌴·) or with lines above and below (𐍁̲̄𐌴̲̄).

Gothic was written from left to right. Spaces were not used between words, but spaces, centered dots, and colons were all used between phrases and for emphasis.

𐌰 𐌱 𐌲 𐌳 𐌴 𐌵 𐌶 𐌷 𐌸 𐌹 𐌺 𐌻 𐌼 𐌽 𐌾 𐌿
𐍀 𐍁 𐍂 𐍃 𐍄 𐍅 𐍆 𐍇 𐍈 𐍉 𐍊

Figure 11.6 Gothic alphabet

7. The information from the Unicode standard is supplemented by Ernst Ebbinghaus, "The Gothic Alphabet," *The World's Writing Systems*, pp. 290–293.

The Unicode Gothic block runs from U+10330 to U+1034F in the SMP and contains only the 27 Gothic letters. **ϳ̈** is represented using the code point for **J** (U+10339), followed by U+0308 COMBINING DIAERESIS. Similarly, U+0305 COMBINING OVERLINE is used for the bar that indicates contractions. Numerals are set off using either U+00B7 MIDDLE DOT before and after, or with a combination of U+0304 COMBINING MACRON and U+0331 COMBINING MACRON BELOW attached to each character. The normal space, middle-dot, and colon characters are used for phrase division and emphasis.

Deseret

Unlike the other historical scripts in the current version of Unicode, all of which are of considerable antiquity, the Deseret alphabet is a modern invention. It was developed in the 1850s at the University of Deseret, now the University of Utah, and promoted by the Church of Jesus Christ of Latter-Day Saints (the Mormons).[8] The word *Deseret* comes from the Book of Mormon, which defined it to mean "honeybee." (The beehive was used as a symbol of cooperative industry by the early Mormons, who named the region where they were settling "Deseret.")

Interestingly, the Deseret alphabet was invented for the writing of *English,* not some exotic language spoken only historically or by some small group of people. The idea was to provide a completely phonetic way of writing English in an effort to make it easier for Mormon immigrants from Europe to learn English. It was heavily promoted by Brigham Young over a period of some 15 years, but never really caught on. On the other hand, it's never completely died out—there is still interest among some Mormons, and some new materials continue to be published from time to time using this alphabet.

The Deseret alphabet has 38 letters: 16 vowels and diphthongs, and 22 consonants (Figure 11.7). The letters are written from left to right, spaces are used between words, punctuation and numerals are the same as in English, and no diacritical marks or other complex typography are required. The letters come in capital/small pairs, but they differ only in size, not in shape.

---

8. The information from the Unicode standard is supplemented by John H. Jenkins, "Adding Historical Scripts to Unicode," *Multilingual Computing and Technology,* September 2000.

Vowels and diphthongs

Ə (long *i*)   Ɛ (long *e*)   Ə (long *a*)   Ɵ (long *ah*)   O (long *o*)   Ф (long *oo*)

† (short *i*)   ⅃ (short *e*)   ◁ (short *a*)   ◀ (short *ah*)   ⊦ (short *o*)   ٩ (short *oo*)

♁ (*ay*)   Ə (*ow*)   Ш (*wu*)   Ѱ (*yee*)

Consonants

Ψ (*h*)   ⅂ (*pee*)   Ⴚ (*bee*)   ꓷ (*tee*)   ꓷ (*dee*)   C (*chee*)   ꝅ (*jee*)   Ⴍ (*kay*)

Ⴚ (*gay*)   ⊦ (*ef*)   Ⴔ (*vee*)   L (*eth*)   Ɣ (*thee*)   ℁ (*es*)   6 (*zee*)   Ꭰ (*esh*)

S (*zhee*)   Ψ (*er*)   Ꮮ (*el*)   Ɔ (*em*)   Ꜧ (*en*)   Ꞑ (*eng*)

Figure 11.7 Deseret alphabet

One interesting quirk of Deseret writing is that when the name of a letter is pronounced in the same way as an actual word, that word can be written using only that letter: For example, ♁ (*ay*) is used for "I," Ⴚ (*bee*) is used for "be" and "bee," and Ɣ (*thee*) is used for "the" and "thee."

Here's an example of some actual English written with Deseret letters:[9]

> Ⴔoꜱⴍoⴕ ◁Ꜧⴇ ℁⅃ⴚⅬꜧ Ѱ†ⴕ6 ⅂ⴍⴇ Ə⅃ⴕ ⅂◀ѰⅬⴕ6 ⴚⴕⴇꓷ ⅂ⴇⴕⅬ ◁Ꜧ Ɣ†℁ ⴍ◁Ꜧꓷⴕꜧⴕꜧꓷ ⴇ
>
> Ꜧⴇ ꜧⅬꓷⅬꜧ, ⴍⴕꜧ℁ⴇⴚⴇ †Ꜧ LⅬⴇⴕⴕ◁Ꜧⴇ ◁Ꜧⴇ ⴇ⅃ⴇⴚⴍⴇⅬꓷⴇ ꓷⴍ Ɣ ◁ⴕⅎⅬ⅂ⴕ†ꓷⅬꜧꜧ Ѱ◁ꓷ ⴍL
>
> Ɔꓷꜧ ◀ⴕ ⴍⴕⴇⴚꓷⅬꓷⴇ ⴇⴍⅬ⅂L.

I'll leave it to the reader to decode what it says. Hint: The author of these words is on the five-dollar bill.

The Unicode Deseret block runs from U+10400 to U+1044F in the SMP and contains uppercase and lowercase forms of the 38 Deseret letters. Because the punctuation and numerals are the same as English, and diacritics aren't used, no other characters are encoded in this block.

---

9. Many thanks to John Jenkins for providing me with this example.

12

Numbers, Punctuation, Symbols, and Specials

*I*t's been a long trip, but we've finally covered all of the writing systems in Unicode 3.2. But we're not done yet with our guided tour of the character repertoire. At this point, we've looked at the characters in Unicode that are used to write words—the letters, syllables, ideographs, diacritical marks, and so on that are used to write the languages of the world. In this chapter, we'll look at everything else:

- Characters used to write numeric values, and the characters used with them
- Punctuation marks
- Special Unicode characters and noncharacter code point values, including control characters, invisible formatting characters, noncharacters, and other characters with special properties
- Symbols
- Miscellaneous characters, such as the dingbats, the box-drawing characters, and the geometric shapes.

We've checked out some of these characters as we've gone through the writing systems, mainly the ones that are used only with particular scripts. In this chapter, we'll look at those characters briefly again in the context of a more comprehensive treatment of their character categories.

■ NUMBERS

Written numbers are probably older than written words, and it's just as important to have characters for the writing of numeric values as it is to have characters for the writing of words. Unicode includes lots of digit and numeral characters, as well as many characters that do double duty as digits or numerals and as something else (usually letters or ideographs). In this section, we'll look at all of them.

Western Positional Notation

The numeration system we use in the United States and Europe is called positional, or place-value, notation. To write decimal numbers, positional notation makes use of nine basic "digit" characters that represent not only the values from one to nine, but also those values times the various powers of 10. The exact value of a digit (i.e., which power of 10 you multiply by) is determined by the digit's position within the numeral. The rightmost digit in an integer keeps its nominal value, and each succeeding digit to the left has its nominal value multiplied by a higher power of 10. A special placeholder digit, called a "zero," is used to mark digit positions that aren't used, so that the meanings of the surrounding digits are unambiguous.

The positional system of numeration and the shapes of the characters we use as digits have their origins in India somewhere around the fifth century A.D.[1] In the West, the characters are commonly called "Arabic numerals" because the Europeans got this system of numeration from the Arabs. (As if this nomenclature weren't confusing enough, the Arabs call their numerals "Hindi numerals" because they got them from the Indians.)

Although almost every system using positional notation uses digits derived from the original Indian ones, the shapes have diverged quite a bit in the inter-

---

1. Ifrah, p. 420.

vening centuries. Unicode includes 16 sets of decimal digits. Each set of digits is used to make up numerals in the same way as our familiar Western digits are. In some countries, both the Western digits and the native digits are used. Unicode encodes each set of digits in the block for the script that uses those digits (the Western digits are in the ASCII block), and in every case it puts them in a contiguous block arranged in ascending order from 0 to 9. Number-formatting code (i.e., code that converts a number from its internal representation into characters for display to the user) can thus be adapted to use a locale's native digits rather than the European digits simply by telling it which code point to use for 0—the others follow automatically.

Table 12.1 lists the various sets of decimal digits in Unicode.

Some other characters in Unicode have the "decimal digit" property, but they're either presentation forms, or the series isn't complete because a different system of numeration is used. Typically, the zero is missing and there are additional characters for 10, 100, and so on.

Alphabetic Numerals

Many cultures, most notably the Greeks and Hebrews, have used the letters of their alphabets as digits as well as letters. Typically, the first nine letters of the alphabet represent the values 1 to 9, the next nine letters represent the multiples of 10 from 10 to 90, the third group represents the multiples of 100 from 100 to 900, and so on. In some languages, such as Greek and Gothic, some of the letters eventually fell into disuse as letters but continued to be used as digits. In Hebrew, the alphabet had only 24 letters, so 700, 800, and 900 had to be written using combinations of characters. In most languages that used letters to write numbers, some special mark was used to distinguish numerals from words.

None of the cultures that used alphabetic notation for writing numbers still does, except sometimes for tasks such as list numbering or dates (similar to when we might use Roman numerals). Unicode, in keeping with its principle of unification, designates the regular letters as doing double duty as digits when alphabetic notation is used. In all cases, letters that came to be used only as digits as well as the special distinguishing marks used to mark sequences of letters as numerals instead of words are also encoded.

Table 12.1 Unicode Decimal Digits

European	U+0030	1 2 3 4 5 6 7 8 9 0
Western Arabic	U+0660	١ ٢ ٣ ٤ ٥ ٦ ٧ ٨ ٩ ٠
Eastern Arabic	U+06F0	۱ ۲ ۳ ۴ ۵ ۶ ۷ ۸ ۹ ۰
Devanagari	U+0966	१ २ ३ ४ ५ ६ ७ ८ ९ ०
Bengali	U+09E6	১ ২ ৩ ৪ ৫ ৬ ৭ ৮ ৯ ০
Gurmukhi	U+0A66	੧ ੨ ੩ ੪ ੫ ੬ ੭ ੮ ੯ ੦
Gujarati	U+0AE6	૧ ૨ ૩ ૪ ૫ ૬ ૭ ૮ ૯ ૦
Oriya	U+0B66	୧ ୨ ୩ ୪ ୫ ୬ ୭ ୮ ୯ ୦
Telugu	U+0C66	౧ ౨ ౩ ౪ ౫ ౬ ౭ ౮ ౯ ౦
Kannada	U+0CE6	೧ ೨ ೩ ೪ ೫ ೬ ೭ ೮ ೯ ೦
Malayalam	U+0D66	൧ ൨ ൩ ൪ ൫ ൬ ൭ ൮ ൯ ൦
Thai	U+0E50	๑ ๒ ๓ ๔ ๕ ๖ ๗ ๘ ๙ ๐
Lao	U+0ED0	໑ ໒ ໓ ໔ ໕ ໖ ໗ ໘ ໙ ໐
Tibetan	U+0F20	༡ ༢ ༣ ༤ ༥ ༦ ༧ ༨ ༩ ༠
Myanmar	U+1040	၁ ၂ ၃ ၄ ၅ ၆ ၇ ၈ ၉ ၀
Khmer	U+17E0	១ ២ ៣ ៤ ៥ ៦ ៧ ៨ ៩ ០
Mongolian	U+1810	᠑ ᠒ ᠓ ᠔ ᠕ ᠖ ᠗ ᠘ ᠙ ᠐

Roman Numerals

Just as we're all familiar with Arabic numerals, we're all familiar with Roman numerals, where the letters I, V, X, L, C, D, and M are used in combination to represent numeric values. Roman numerals used an additive notation, with the values of the characters being added up to get the value of the whole numeral (XVIII = 10 + 5 + 1 + 1 + 1 = 18). (The subtractive notation that causes IV to be interpreted as 4 was a later development, and doesn't really change the basic nature of the notation). The I, V, and X characters probably evolved from early methods of representing numeric values by making notches or scratch marks in things—similar methods exist in lots of ancient cultures.

The basic way of representing Roman numerals in Unicode is the same as for representing alphabetic notation: to use the normal Latin-letter characters. There's no need for special I, V, X, or other characters for writing Roman numerals. Exceptions do occur, however.

The M for 1,000 was a fairly late development; before it appeared, the symbol ⅭⅠↃ was used in Roman numerals to represent 1,000. You could represent higher powers of 10 by adding concentric circles. For example, ⅭⅭⅠↃↃ represents 10,000. You cut these symbols in half to represent half the value. For example, Ⅾ represents 5,000, and this is also why D represents 500. Unicode includes code point values for these three characters in the Number Forms block at U+2180, U+2182, and U+2181, respectively.

In more recent centuries, you'll see the symbols for the large numbers represented using whole characters. In situations where printers didn't have type for the special characters, they'd fake them using C, I, and an upside-down C: ⅭⅠↃ would be written as CIↃ and ⅭⅭⅠↃↃ as CCIↃↃ. The upside-down C is in the Number Forms block at U+2183.

A more modern practice represents large numbers using bars over the traditional letters. A bar over a letter multiplies its value by 1,000: $\overline{X}$, for example, represents 10,000. You can use U+0305 COMBINING OVERLINE to do this.

Finally, even though Unicode doesn't need special code point values for the other Roman numerals, it has them. This is a legacy issue. Several Japanese and Chinese character encoding standards, for instance, have code point values for the Roman numerals (they're useful for such things as making a whole Roman numeral show up in a single display cell in vertical text), and Unicode adopts them to ensure full round-trip compatibility with these standards. For this reason, the

Unicode Number Forms block includes two sets of Roman numerals, representing the values from 1 to 12, plus 50, 100, 500, and 1,000. One series uses capital letters and the other uses small letters. Thus you can represent "VIII" either with four code points, for the letters V, I, I, and I, or with a single code point, U+2167, representing the concept "Roman numeral 8." These characters occupy the range U+2160 to U+217F in the Number Forms block, and all of them have compatibility decompositions to sequences of regular letters.

Han Characters as Numerals

Certain Han characters represent basic numeric values and are combined using an additive-multiplicative system to write the other numeric values. Table 12.2 shows the basic characters representing the numbers from 1 to 9. These characters are used in conjunction with characters that represent various powers of 10, also shown in Table 12.2.

The additive-multiplicative principle is fairly simple: If one of the basic-number characters appears before a power-of-10 character, their values are multiplied together. If it appears after it, their values are added together. So you get this:

$$二 = 2$$

$$十 = 10$$

$$十二 = 12$$

$$二十 = 20$$

$$二十二 = 22$$

$$二百二十二 = 222$$

Table 12.2 Han Characters as Numerals

一	二	三	四	五	六	七	八	九
1	2	3	4	5	6	7	8	9

十	百	千	万	億	兆
10	100	1,000	10,000	100,000,000	1,000,000,000,000

For values larger than 10,000, a new character is provided for every power of 10,000 instead of every power of 10. This system is analogous to how in English, for values exceeding 1,000, you introduce a new word for every power of 1,000 instead of every power of 10. Just as 123,456 is "one hundred twenty-three thousand four hundred fifty-six," so 1,234,567 in Han characters is

百二十三万四千五百六十七

The last part is simple, representing 4,567 with pairs of characters for 4,000, 500, and 60, and a single character for 7:

四千五百六十七

The first part follows the same principle for 123 (a single character for 100, a pair of characters for 20, and a single character for 3) and follows this sequence with the character for 10,000, which multiplies the whole sequence by 10,000. Thus, this sequence represents 1,230,000:

百二十三万

Other Han characters are also used in special situations to represent numbers, particularly in accounting. Suppose that somewhere in the amount on a check you have

二

representing 2. You add another stroke to it to get 3:

三

In fact, you can add two additional strokes to get 5:

五

For this reason, alternate characters that can't be altered just by adding a couple strokes are used on checks or in other places where it's necessary to deter counterfeiting. Exactly which characters are substituted varies from region to region, but Table 12.3 provides a fairly complete selection.

Another Han character is sometimes used to represent the value 0:

零

Sometimes, you'll also see the Han characters used with Western positional notation. In these situations, a special zero character is used. For example, 1,203 would normally be written

千二百三

but you may occasionally see it written using positional notation:

一二〇三

All of the characters shown above are regular Han characters in the CJK Unified Ideographs block, where some have other meanings and some are used exclusively for writing numbers. The one exception is 〇, which is in the CJK Symbols and Punctuation block.

Also in the CJK Symbols and Punctuation block are the "Hangzhou-style" numerals. They come to Unicode via a number of East Asian encoding standards,

Table 12.3   Han Accounting Numeral Characters

一	二	三	四	五	六	七	八	九	十	百	千	万
1	2	3	4	5	6	7	8	9	10	100	1,000	10,000
壹	貳	參	肆	伍	陸	柒	捌	玖	拾	佰	仟	萬
壱	贰	叁			陆					陌		
弌	弐	叄										
	弍	弎										

Source: Unicode standard, p. 97.

but their provenance is rather cloudy. Some are similar to the "regular" Han characters for numbers, but based on vertical lines instead of horizontal lines:

一	二	三	乂	㆐	亠	二	三	夕	十	卄	卅
1	2	3	4	5	6	7	8	9	10	20	30

They appear to be another set of "commercial" numerals, used by shopkeepers in parts of China (and maybe also Japan) to mark prices.[2]

Finally, the Japanese and Koreans, and less frequently the Chinese, also use the Western digit characters to write numbers.

Other Numeration Systems

Tamil uses the same additive-multiplicative system used with the Han characters. The characters for 1 through 9 are

௧ ௨ ௩ ௪ ௫ ௬ ௭ ௮ ௯

and the following characters represent 10, 100, and 1,000, respectively:

௰ ௱ ௲

This system appears to be dying out in favor of Western numerals.

Ethiopic uses a system that's a hybrid of the additive system underlying Greek and Hebrew alphabetic notation and the additive-multiplicative system used in Japanese and Chinese. The following nine characters represent the values from 1 to 9:

፩ ፪ ፫ ፬ ፭ ፮ ፯ ፰ ፱

---

2. My information here comes from Thomas Emerson, "On the 'Hangzhou-Style Numerals in ISO/IEC 10646-1," a white paper published by Basis Technology. Emerson cites the source encodings for these characters, his best information as to what they're used for, and goes on to say that the term "Hangzhou" isn't attested in any source he could find. He proposes the term "Suzhou," which was attested in a number of sources, instead. (Thanks to Tom for forwarding his paper to me.)

The following nine characters represent the multiples of 10 from 10 to 90:

The other values from 1 to 99 are represented using pairs of these characters. The value 100 is represented with this character:

Multiples of 100 are represented by putting pairs of the other characters before the. Thus 1,234 is written like this:

The same pattern is followed for values over 10,000: Each power of 100 is represented using an appropriate number of characters. Thus, 123,456 is

A few languages also have special ways of writing fractions. Bengali includes several special characters for writing the numerator of a fraction (╱, ᶹ, ᶻ, l, and ᴎ, representing 1, 2, 3, 4, and one less than the denominator) and one special character for writing the denominator (°, representing a denominator of 16).

Tibetan has special characters representing halves. Each is a regular Tibetan digit with a hook that subtracts ½ from its value: For example,

is the Tibetan digit 3, and

represents 2½ (or "half three").

Numeric Presentation Forms

Unicode also includes many numeric presentation forms. These are all compatibility characters, included for round-trip compatibility with some national or vendor standard, and most have compatibility decompositions. Most represent a number with some sort of styling added, but some are simply single-code-point representations of a sequence of characters. (These latter combinations generally come from various East Asian encoding standards, where they're used for tasks such as list numbering in which all the digits and punctuation should appear in a single display cell in vertical text.)

Superscripts and Subscripts   Unicode includes superscript and subscript versions of all the digits, as well as some math operators and the letter n (as in "2^n"). The superscripted versions of 1, 2, and 3 are found in the Latin-1 block at U+00B9, U+00B2, and U+00B3, respectively, and the other characters are located in the Superscripts and Subscripts block, which ranges from U+2070 to U+209F.

Circled   Unicode includes versions of the numbers 1 through 20 with circles around them in the range U+2460 to U+2473 in the Enclosed Alphanumerics block. Several other versions of the numbers from 1 to 10 (sans serif versions with circles around them, and black circles with white serifed and sans serif numbers on them) are in the Dingbats block from U+2776 to U+2793. The Han characters for 1 to 10 with circles around them are encoded in the Enclosed CJK Letters and Months block from U+3280 to U+3289.

Parenthesized   Unicode includes single code point values representing the numbers from 1 to 20 surrounded with parentheses in the Enclosed Alphanumerics block from U+2474 to U+2487.

With a Period   Unicode includes single code point values representing the numbers from 1 to 20 followed by a period. These are also in the Enclosed Alphanumerics block, from U+2488 to U+249B.

Fractions   Unicode has several single code point values representing fractions (the "vulgar fractions"). The fractions ½, ¼, and ¾ are in the Latin-1 block at

U+00BC, U+00BD, and U+00BE, respectively. Several more, for the thirds, fifths, sixths, and eighths, are found in the Number Forms block from U+2153 to U+215E. The Number Forms block also includes a single code point value representing just the numerator 1 and the slash (⅟, U+215F). It can be used with the subscript digits to make other fractions.

National and Nominal Digit Shapes

The ISO 8859-6 standard didn't have enough room to encode both the Western digits and the native Arabic digits, so it had the code points in the ASCII range that normally represent the Western digits do double duty and represent both the Western digits and the native Arabic digits. When transcoding from this encoding to Unicode, you're not guaranteed, for example, that U+0032 represents "2"; it might actually represent "٢", depending on the source material. The original version of ISO 10646 included two characters, U+206E NATIONAL DIGIT SHAPES and U+206F NOMINAL DIGIT SHAPES. These invisible formatting characters would control whether the digits in the ASCII block were rendered with their normal glyph shapes or with the local (usually Arabic) glyph shapes. These characters came into Unicode with the merger with 10646.

In Unicode 3.0, these characters were deprecated. The preferred approach to this problem relies on the process that converts from 8859-6 to Unicode to be smart enough to know whether to convert 0x30 through 0x39 to U+0030 through U+0039 or to U+0660 through U+0669. The digit characters in the ASCII block should now always be treated as representing the European digit shapes.

■ PUNCTUATION

The other thing you need for a writing system to be complete (generally speaking—there are exceptions) is punctuation. As with all of the other character categories, Unicode includes a wide variety of punctuation marks, some specific only to one writing system and some common to several systems. As we've seen, script-specific punctuation marks are scattered throughout the Unicode encoding range. Also, two encoding blocks are reserved exclusively for punctuation marks. We'll take a brief look at the whole universe of Unicode punctuation and then study a few of the more interesting cases more closely.

Script-Specific Punctuation

A lot of punctuation marks have been scattered throughout the Unicode encoding range. Some, mainly those in the ASCII and Latin-1 blocks, are where they are for historical or compatibility reasons; most of the others are specific to one or two writing systems and are kept in the same block as the other characters in that script. Most punctuation marks are used to delimit ranges of text in various ways. Table 12.4 shows most of these marks. The rows show the block containing the marks (which generally corresponds to the scripts with which they're used). The columns attempt to categorize the marks according to the amount of text they delimit. The first column contains marks that are used within words or in place of words (abbreviation or elision marks, "etc." or "and" signs, and so on). The second column contains marks that are used between words. The third column contains marks that are used between groups of words (e.g., phrases or list items). The fourth column contains marks that are used between sentences (or roughly equivalent groupings of words). The fifth column contains marks that are used between groups of sentences (e.g., paragraphs or topics). The last column contains marks that generally appear at the beginning or end of an entire text.

Many marks don't fit well into this taxonomy (parentheses and quotation marks, for instance). We'll look at most of these later in this section.

The General Punctuation Block

The General Punctuation block, running from U+2000 to U+206F, is just what its name suggests: It contains punctuation marks that are intended to be used with many different scripts. For historical reasons, most of the most common punctuation marks, such as the period, comma, question mark, exclamation point, and so on are actually in the ASCII block. The General Punctuation block tends to contain more specialized or less ambiguous versions of characters that appear in the ASCII block and a miscellany of less common marks. In particular, it contains a large collection of spaces, dashes, quotation marks, dot

Table 12.4 Unicode Punctuation Marks

	<word	word	>word	sentence	>sentence	text
ASCII	' &	/ -	, ; :	. ! ?		
Latin-1	‐ ·			¡ ¿		
Greek			·	;		
Armenian	՝ ՚	֊	՛	՝ ՞ ։		
Hebrew	׳ ״					
Arabic			، ؛	؟		
Syriac	÷	··	· ·. .· ·.	· ؛ .·	·.· :	
Devanagari	०		।	॥		
Sinhala			෴			

Table 12.4 Unicode Punctuation Marks, *continued*

	<word	word	>word	sentence	>sentence	text
Thai			◉		ᵉᴶᴶ	Cᴖᴖ
Tibetan		ᴛ	ꜱ	｜	ꜱ	ꝰ
		ᴛ	˚	｜	‖	ꝰ
				｜	‖	ꝰ
						ꝰ
Myanmar			｜	‖		
Georgian					∴	
Ethiopic		꞉	꞉	꞉꞉	꞉꞉꞉	
			꞉	꞉		
			꞉			
			꞉			
Canadian Aboriginal				×		
Ogham						＞
						＜
Khmer	ꞓ		˳	ꞓ	ꞓ	ꞓ
	ꞓꞓꞓ		⊙			
	ꞓ					

Table continued on next page

Table 12.4   Unicode Punctuation Marks, *continued*

	<word	word	>word	sentence	>sentence	text
Mongolian	⁝ ⁝ ᠁ ┃ ┙		᠂ ᠈ ᠊	᠅ ᠃		᠎ ⁘
CJK		〜 〰	、		○	

leaders, and bullets, as well as various other marks and symbols. It also contains most of Unicode's special invisible formatting characters.

The CJK Symbols and Punctuation Block

The CJK Symbols and Punctuation block, which runs from U+3000 to U+303F, is analogous to the General Punctuation block, but contains various marks drawn from various East Asian encodings and specific to East Asian text. These include the period and comma used with CJK characters; a space that's sized correctly for use with CJK characters; parentheses, dashes, and quotation marks; Kana repetition marks; tone marks; miscellaneous signs and symbols; and the Ideographic Variation Indicator, which we looked at in Chapter 10.

Spaces

Now let's examine some of the more interesting and important categories of characters in Unicode. Unicode specifies a number of groups of characters with similar appearances and semantics, and it's worth the effort to take a closer look at these and understand just what their differences are.

The basic space character in Unicode, used for representing the spaces between these words, is U+0020 SPACE, Unicode's equivalent to the ASCII space character. Other space characters differ from the regular space in width only. In rough order from widest to narrowest, the fixed-width Unicode spaces are as follows:

- U+2003 EM SPACE, also known as the "em quad," is a space one em wide. An em is a unit of horizontal space on a line of type that is exactly as wide as the font in use is high. So a space one em wide (the em quad) is square, at least in most fonts. The term "em" comes from the fact that in old Roman inscriptions the capital letter M was square, so the em quad is the width of the capital letter M (in most modern fonts, the capital M actually isn't an em wide, but the name has stuck). The term "quad" reflects the fact that the space is square. U+2001 EM QUAD was a mistaken duplicate encoding of the same thing and now has a singleton canonical decomposition to this character.
- U+3000 IDEOGRAPHIC SPACE is a space that's the same width as the Han characters. In most fonts, the Han characters occupy a square space, so it can be thought of as equivalent to the em quad, but intended for use in Japanese, Chinese, and Korean text. Unlike the em quad, which has a fixed width, the ideographic space can vary in width in justified text.
- U+2002 EN SPACE, also known as the "en quad," is a space one-half of an em wide. In other words, it defines a space one-half as wide as it is high. Two en quads make an em quad. The term "en" probably comes from the idea that the en is the width of the capital letter N, but even in old Roman inscriptions the letter N probably was never half the width of the letter M. U+2000 EN QUAD, another mistaken double encoding, has a singleton canonical decomposition to this character.
- U+2007 FIGURE SPACE is a space that's the same width as the digits in a typeface whose digits are all the same width. It's useful for lining up figures in columns, as the normal space is usually narrower than the digits.
- U+2004 THREE-PER-EM SPACE is a space that's one-third of an em in width, or one-third as wide as it is high. Three three-per-em spaces (or "three-em spaces" for short) make an em quad.
- U+2005 FOUR-PER-EM SPACE is a space that's one-fourth of an em in width, or one-fourth as wide as it is high. Four four-per-em spaces (or "four-em spaces" for short) make an em quad.

- U+2006 SIX-PER-EM SPACE is a space that's one-sixth of an em in width, or six times higher than it is wide. Six six-per-em spaces (or "six-em spaces") make an em quad.
- U+2009 THIN SPACE is more analogous to the regular U+0020 SPACE in that it doesn't have a set width. It's narrower than the regular space, but can vary in width like the regular space when it's used in justified text.
- U+205F MEDIUM MATHEMATICAL SPACE (new in Unicode 3.2) is a thin space for mathematical typesetting, defined to be four-eighteenths of an em wide.
- U+2008 PUNCTUATION SPACE is defined to be the same width as the period. Like the figure space, it's used for lining up columns of numbers.
- U+200A HAIR SPACE is the narrowest space of all. In most fonts, it's only a point or so wide.
- U+200B ZERO WIDTH SPACE is a space that takes up no horizontal space at all. The name is an oxymoron (a "space" that doesn't take up any space?). The zero-width space, despite its name, is more properly thought of as an invisible formatting character. It's used to mark word boundaries in text without actually causing a visible break. For instance, Thai is written without spaces between words (spaces in Thai are used in a manner roughly analogous to commas in English), but you're supposed to respect the word boundaries when laying Thai text out on a line (unlike in Japanese text, it's not acceptable to break a line of Thai text in the middle of a word). One way to deal with this problem is to put zero-width spaces in the text to mark the word boundaries. Word-wrapping will then do the right thing, but you won't see any spaces between the words.

Where does the normal space we all know and love fit into this classification? Unlike most of the space characters listed above, U+0020 SPACE can vary in width as necessary to produce properly justified text. The base width before any adjustments are applied varies from font to font, but is usually the same size as the three-per-em or four-per-em space.

Unicode also defines a class of so-called non-breaking spaces. The nonbreaking characters in Unicode (they're not all spaces) behave normally except that code that wraps lines of text isn't allowed to put the characters on either side of the non-breaking character on different lines. In other words, the non-breaking characters are used to keep other characters together on one line of text. Unicode has four non-breaking spaces:

- U+00A0 NO-BREAK SPACE (often abbreviated "NBSP") is the basic non-breaking space. It's the same width as the regular space (U+0020) and similarly can vary in width in justified text. Unlike the regular space, however, it doesn't mark a word boundary for the purposes of word-wrapping. In fact, it specifically prevents word-wrapping. For example, in some languages (e.g., French), the space is used as the thousands separator in large numbers instead of a period or comma, but you don't want the number split across two lines. Also, in some languages, certain punctuation marks are separated by a space from the words they follow. In French again, there's usually a space between the last word of a question and the question mark, unlike in English, where the question mark appears right next to the last word of the question. Again, you don't want the question mark to appear at the beginning of the next line. Sophisticated word-wrapping algorithms will handle this issue correctly, but you can use the NBSP to get the correct effect with naive word-wrapping algorithms. Because of the NBSP's use as a thousands separator in French and some other languages, the Unicode bi-di algorithm treats it as a number separator.
- U+202F NARROW NO-BREAK SPACE is roughly analogous to the thin space in the way that the regular NBSP is analogous to the regular space. It's narrower than a regular space, may or may not be variable-width depending on the language and font, and doesn't mark a word boundary. In Mongolian, this character is used to separate grammatical particles from their stem words while keeping them semantically part of the same word. (In Mongolian, this character also causes special shaping behavior, but this effect isn't seen with any other script.)
- U+FEFF ZERO WIDTH NO-BREAK SPACE is also not technically a space, despite its name. In Unicode 2.x, 3.0, and 3.1, it was an invisible formatting character used to control word-wrapping. Starting in Unicode 3.2, this use has been deprecated. Use U+2060 WORD JOINER instead.

- U+2060 WORD JOINER is the new zero-width non-breaking space. It "glues" the two characters on either side of it together, forcing them to appear on the same line. Any character can be turned into a non-breaking character by putting U+2060 before and after it.

You could also consider U+180E MONGOLIAN VOWEL SEPARATOR to be a Unicode non-breaking space, but its use is restricted to Mongolian. In other contexts, it's either ignored or treated as being the same as U+202F NARROW NO-BREAK SPACE. In Mongolian, however, it causes special shaping behavior when it precedes certain letters.

Dashes and Hyphens

Unicode specifies a wide variety of dashes and hyphens. The original ASCII character (0x2D) did triple duty as a hyphen, dash, and minus sign. As ASCII was originally used mostly on computer terminals and teletype machines where everything was monospaced and these three things looked the same anyway, this choice wasn't a big deal originally. In real typesetting, these characters look and act differently, and it helps tremendously if the different appearances and semantics have different code point values.

The ASCII hyphen was retained at its same position in Unicode as U+002D HYPHEN-MINUS and continues to have ambiguous semantics. Several unambiguous characters have been added to replace it (although U+002D remains the most commonly used):

- U+2010 HYPHEN is the hyphen character (-). This character is used in hyphenated English words and phrases, such as "day-to-day." In most typefaces, you get the same glyph for U+002D HYPHEN-MINUS and U+2010 HYPHEN, but this is the preferred representation for that glyph.
- U+2013 EN DASH is a dash that is an en (i.e., half of an em) wide (–). It's used for things like separating ranges of values ("1921–1991").
- U+2012 FIGURE DASH has the same ambiguous semantics as U+002D HYPHEN-MINUS and, like U+002D, appears in Unicode to ensure compatibility with older standards. It's defined to have the same width

as the digits in fonts where the digits are all the same width (in many fonts, it's the same as the en dash).

- U+2212 MINUS SIGN is the minus sign, used to indicate subtraction or negative numbers ("–23" or "75 – 27 = 48"). This character usually has the same glyph as the en dash, but it behaves differently. In particular, most word-wrapping algorithms will wrap words on a hyphen or dash, but not on a minus sign. The rule of thumb should be to use U+2013 when it's acceptable to break the line after it (such as when it's used to separate the numbers in a range) and U+2212 when it's not (such as in "–23").

- U+2014 EM DASH is a dash that's an em wide (—). In other words, the length of the dash is the same as the height of the font. The em dash is often used in English to indicate a break in continuity or to set off a parenthetical expression ("Bill would—if *I* had anything to say about it—be in a lot of trouble right now").

- U+2015 HORIZONTAL BAR (also known as the "quotation dash") is an even wider dash (——) used in some older typographical styles to set off quotations.

A few dash characters have special behaviors:

- U+00AD SOFT HYPHEN functions in a manner analogous to the zero-width space—it's used to indicate to a word-wrapping algorithm places where it's acceptable to hyphenate a word. A word-wrapping routine can treat it in the same way as any other dash or hyphen for the purposes of figuring out where to break a line, but it remains invisible unless it actually appears at the end of a line. At the end of a line (i.e., when the word containing it actually needs to be hyphenated), it has the same glyph as the regular hyphen (U+2010).

- U+2011 NON-BREAKING HYPHEN functions in a manner analogous to the non-breaking space and opposite to the regular and soft hyphens: You use it when you want a hyphen in a word but you want the entire hyphenated word or expression to remain on the same line. A word-wrapping routine isn't allowed to break lines on either side of the non-breaking hyphen. Again, the glyph is the same as U+2010.

There are also a few language-specific hyphen characters:

- U+058A ARMENIAN HYPHEN (֊) is just what its name suggests: It works the same way in Armenian as the regular hyphen works in English, but has an Armenian-specific appearance.
- U+1806 MONGOLIAN TODO SOFT HYPHEN (᠆) is used when Todo is written using the Mongolian alphabet (it's a vertical line because the Mongolian script is written vertically). It works in the same way as the regular soft hyphen, except that when a line is broken at the hyphen position, the hyphen itself appears at the *beginning* of the line *after* the break, as opposed to Western hyphens, which always appear at the *end* of the line *before* the break.
- U+301C WAVE DASH and U+3030 WAVY DASH are dashes used in Japanese. When Japanese text is laid out vertically, these two characters rotate.

Some other characters are horizontal lines that are occasionally confused with the dash characters. Notable among them is U+30FC KATAKANA-HIRAGANA PROLONGED SOUND MARK. You'll occasionally run across Japanese text that uses one of the dash characters for the Katakana length mark instead of U+30FC.

You also periodically encounter a "swung" dash ("~"). This character isn't specifically encoded in Unicode, but because U+007E TILDE generally isn't used as a tilde anymore (in the old days of teletype machines, this character would be used in conjunction with the backspace character to form "ñ", for example), today most fonts use a glyph that's vertically centered, rather than one that's raised above the font's x-height, for U+007E TILDE. Thus, this character can be thought of as the Unicode swung dash character. (Theoretically, you could use the CJK wave dash, but the metrics are usually wrong for use with Western characters and it's rarely included in Western fonts.)

Quotation Marks, Apostrophes, and Similar-Looking Characters

Quotation Marks   Even though most languages that use the Latin alphabet use the same marks for such things as the period, comma, question mark, and exclamation point, they all seem to use different marks for quotation marks. The situation with quotation marks in Unicode is rather complicated and ambiguous.

For starters, there's U+0022 QUOTATION MARK, the character that's familiar to all of us from typewriter keyboards (and, later on, computer keyboards). It's used for both opening and closing quotation marks, so its glyph shape is a compromise. It usually looks like this:

"

Like the "hyphen-minus" character, this character has ambiguous semantics both because all of the semantics corresponded to a single key on a typewriter keyboard and because of ASCII's limited encoding space. We're all used to seeing this mark from older computer-generated or typewritten material. With the advent of laser printers and computer-generated typography, however, we'd generally prefer to see the quotation marks the way we write them or the way they've always appeared in printed material:

"English"

Unicode provides unambiguous code point values for these characters; U+201C LEFT DOUBLE QUOTATION MARK and U+201D RIGHT DOUBLE QUOTATION MARK. Most modern word processors now map the U+0022 character you get from the keyboard to either U+201C or U+201D depending on context, a feature that can work quite well. Of course, it doesn't always work well, leading to stupidities such the upside-down apostrophe in "the '60s" that you see all too often.

French and a number of other languages use completely different-looking quotation marks. Instead of the comma-shaped quotation marks employed in English, French and a number of other languages use chevron-shaped quotation marks known in French as **guillemets**:

« Français »

The guillemets were included in the Latin-1 standard and thus appear in the Latin-1 block as U+00AB LEFT-POINTING DOUBLE ANGLE QUOTATION

MARK and U+00BB RIGHT-POINTING DOUBLE ANGLE QUOTATION
MARK.

Now matters get more interesting. These same marks don't mean the same
thing in all languages. For example, in German, U+201C is the *closing* quotation mark rather than the opening quotation mark. A quotation is usually punctuated like this in German:

„Deutsch"

The German opening double-quote mark is included as U+201E DOUBLE
LOW-9 QUOTATION MARK. (The "9" refers to the fact that the marks look
like little 9s.) The single-quote version of this character has the same glyph
form as the comma—systems should be careful not to use the comma for a single quote.

You'll also sometimes see the guillemets used with German text. In German they point *toward* the quoted material, rather than away from it as in
French:

»Deutsch«

Swedish and some other Scandinavian languages sidestep the problem of
paired quotation marks altogether, using the same character for both the opening and closing quotation mark. Depending on typographic style, they use either the guillemets or (more commonly) the curly quote marks. You get the
same effect either way:

"svenska" or »svenska»

Numerous other linguistic and regional variants in quotation mark usage
are possible, but you get the basic idea. The practical upshot is that while quotation mark characters come in pairs, exactly *which* pair is used depends on language. Likewise, whether a given character (with a few exceptions) is an
opening or closing quote also depends on language.

Unicode deals with this issue by encoding each glyph shape only once and
declaring that different languages should use different code point values for

their quotation marks, rather than just having abstract "opening quotation mark" and "closing quotation mark" code point values that are associated with different glyph shapes depending on language. This kind of goes against the "characters, not glyphs" rule, but it eases confusion in most situations. Encoding the abstract semantics and depending on some outside process to pick the right glyphs in this case would have led to different fonts being necessary for each language that uses (for example) the Latin alphabet, just because their quotation mark characters look different. Alternatively, it might have required language tagging along with the regular abstract characters to get the right glyph shapes. Unicode's designers have gone for this kind of approach when an *entire alphabet* is semantically the same but different font styles are preferred in different languages, but doing it for *just the quotation mark characters* is kind of ridiculous.

This leads to a problem: Quotation marks are inherently paired punctuation, like parentheses, but which character serves as which member of the pair depends on language. For this reason, the quotation marks generally can't be put into the regular Ps and Pe (starting and ending punctuation) general categories.[3] Beginning in Unicode 2.1, two new categories, Pi and Pf (for "initial-quote punctuation" and "final-quote punctuation," respectively) were created expressly for these characters, and the quotation marks were dropped rather arbitrarily into one bucket or the other. The idea is that a process that cares about paired punctuation would know the language used for the text and be able to map Pi and Pf to Ps and Pe in an appropriate manner for that language.

The initial-quote category consists of the following marks:

« U+00AB LEFT-POINTING DOUBLE ANGLE QUOTATION MARK

' U+2018 LEFT SINGLE QUOTATION MARK

' U+201B SINGLE HIGH-REVERSED-9 QUOTATION MARK

" U+201C LEFT DOUBLE QUOTATION MARK

" U+201F DOUBLE HIGH-REVERSED-9 QUOTATION MARK

‹ U+2039 SINGLE LEFT-POINTING ANGLE QUOTATION MARK

---

3. There are a few exceptions to this rule: The low-9 marks used in German and some other languages always appear at the beginning of a quotation, for example.

The final-quote category consists of the following marks:

» U+00BB RIGHT-POINTING DOUBLE ANGLE QUOTATION MARK

’ U+2019 RIGHT SINGLE QUOTATION MARK

” U+201D RIGHT DOUBLE QUOTATION MARK

› U+203A SINGLE RIGHT-POINTING ANGLE QUOTATION MARK

Two marks always appear at the beginning of a quote and thus appear in the normal "starting punctuation" category:

‚ U+201A SINGLE LOW-9 QUOTATION MARK

„ U+201E DOUBLE LOW-9 QUOTATION MARK

East Asian Quotation Marks   Unicode includes three pairs of quotation mark characters used in East Asian languages (Table 12.5). Within these pairs, the glyph shape *does* vary depending on context. The brackets turn sideways when used with vertical text:[4]

⌐

宇

内

⌐

Table 12.5   East Asian Quotation Marks

⌈ U+300C LEFT CORNER BRACKET	⌋ U+300D RIGHT CORNER BRACKET
⌈ U+300E LEFT WHITE CORNER BRACKET	⌋ U+300F RIGHT WHITE CORNER BRACKET
‟ U+301D REVERSED DOUBLE PRIME QUOTATION MARK	„ U+301F LOW DOUBLE PRIME QUOTATION MARK

---

4. This example and the one that follows are taken from the Unicode standard, p. 153.

The "double-prime" quotation marks may either point toward or away from the quoted text depending on font design:

〝宇内〟 or 〟宇内〝

They'll also change direction and move to different quadrants of their display cells when used with vertical text. Another character, U+301E DOUBLE PRIME QUOTATION MARK, is used only when Western text is quoted inside East Asian text; it's not used with East Asian quotations.

Single Quotes and the Apostrophe   The single-quote character in ASCII was even more overloaded than the double-quote character. The same code point value, 0x27, was used for both the opening and closing single quotes, the apostrophe, the acute accent, the prime mark, and occasionally other things. It's normally rendered with a direction-neutral glyph like the one used for the double quote:

'

Sometimes you'll see it rendered with a left-slanted or curly glyph on the assumption that 0x60, the grave accent character, would be used as the opening single quote. As with the double quote, these characters and their original numeric values have been adopted into Unicode with their original muddled semantics, and extra characters with unambiguous semantics have been added. We've already discussed how quotation marks work, and the rules apply equally to single and double quotes. Most languages will alternate between double and single quotes for quotes within quotes. Different languages have different preferences for whether single or double quotes should be used for the outermost pair or quotation marks. In British usage, for example, single quotes are usually used for the outermost pair instead of the double quotes you typically see in American usage.

Another problem arises with the apostrophe, which has exactly the same glyph as the (English) closing single quote. In many languages, and in Latin-alphabet transcriptions of many languages that don't use the Latin alphabet, an apostrophe is used as a letter, typically to represent the glottal stop, as in

"Hawai'i." In particular, the Arabic letter alef and its counterparts in languages such as Hebrew are usually written with an apostrophe when transliterated into Latin letters.

Unicode draws a distinction between the apostrophe being used as a letter, where U+02BC MODIFIER LETTER APOSTROPHE is the preferred representation, and the apostrophe being used as a punctuation mark, where U+2019 RIGHT SINGLE QUOTATION MARK is the preferred representation. In other words, Unicode doesn't distinguish between this usage of the apostrophe and the single quotation mark. Both characters have the same glyph shape, but may be treated differently by some text-analysis processes (such as word-wrapping).

As with the double quotes, a single key usually generates U+0027, and the system automatically maps it to U+2018 or U+2019 as appropriate. This mapping is another argument for not having a separate character code for the apostrophe—keyboards would probably still generate the right-single-quote character code. For this reason, U+2019 will probably show up in a lot of places where the truly appropriate character code is U+02BC. This is just one example where code that operates on Unicode text probably can't assume everything is represented the way it should be.

Modifier Letters   In addition to U+02BC, the Spacing Modifier Letters block includes a number of other apostrophe-like characters. U+02BB MODIFIER LETTER TURNED COMMA has the same glyph shape as U+2018 LEFT SINGLE QUOTATION MARK, and U+02BD MODIFIER LETTER REVERSED COMMA has the same glyph shape as U+201B SINGLE HIGH REVERSED-9 QUOTATION MARK. The same rule applies here: The modifier letter characters are appropriate when the glyph is used as a letter or diacritical mark, and the quotation mark characters are appropriate when the glyph is used as a quotation mark (or other punctuation mark).

Other Apostrophe-like Characters   Further adding to the confusion, Unicode includes a whole host of other characters that look much like apostrophes or quotation marks but have distinct semantics. Usually, they also have distinct, but often subtly so, glyph shapes, but not always.

The half-ring characters in the Spacing Modifier Letters block, for example, are very similar to the apostrophe and reversed apostrophe. There are the various acute accent and grave accent characters in the ASCII and Spacing Modifier Letters blocks. There are the prime, double prime, reversed prime, and related characters in both the Spacing Modifier Letters block, where they're used as diacritical marks, and the General Punctuation block, where they're used as math or logical symbols or as abbreviations for "feet," "inches," "minutes," and "seconds." There are language-specific marks, such as the Armenian half-ring and apostrophe, which look like the characters in the Spacing Modifier Letters block, and the Hebrew geresh and gershayim marks, which look like the prime and double-prime marks.

These marks are generally extensively cross-referenced in the Unicode standard, and it's fairly apparent which of the various similar-looking marks apply if you look in the Unicode standard. Unfortunately, real life doesn't always match theory. You'll very often see some code point value used in a spot where some other code point value is more appropriate. A number of reasons explain this tendency. Sometimes the wrong character is used because only one of several similar-looking characters is available on the keyboard. Sometimes the problem occurs because fonts support only one code point value. Sometimes the wrong character is used in a legacy encoding where more appropriate character codes aren't available and appropriate adjustments aren't made when converting to Unicode. On some occasions, this is a flaw in the conversion algorithm, and other times it's because Unicode draws a semantic distinction that the original source encoding didn't draw.

The sad consequence is that code that operates on Unicode text can't always assume that the correct code point value has been used to represent some mark; often, a code point value representing a similar-looking character has been used instead. In particular, many characters look like apostrophes and quotation marks and are often represented with U+0022 and U+0027 even in Unicode. This mistake also happens with many other groups of characters, however (see the later section on line-breaking conventions, for example). One can hope that this situation will improve as Unicode use becomes more widespread, but there'll probably never be anything close to 100 percent purity in use of Unicode code point values.

Paired Punctuation

In addition to the quotation marks, some other punctuation marks in Unicode come in pairs. Most are various types of parentheses and brackets, and most are used in a variety of languages and thus are encoded in the ASCII and General Punctuation blocks. Table 12.6 provides a complete list of the non-quotation paired punctuation marks.

Table 12.6 Non-quotation Paired Punctuation Marks

(U+0028	) U+0029	PARENTHESIS
[U+005B	] U+005D	SQUARE BRACKET
{ U+007B	} U+007D	CURLY BRACKET
U+0F3A	U+0F3B	TIBETAN GUG RTAGS
U+0F3C	U+0F3D	TIBETAN ANG KHANG
U+169B	U+169C	OGHAM FEATHER MARK
U+2045	U+2046	SQUARE BRACKET WITH QUILL
⟨ U+2329	⟩ U+232A	ANGLE BRACKET
〈 U+3008	〉 U+3009	ANGLE BRACKET
《 U+300A	》 U+300B	DOUBLE ANGLE BRACKET
【 U+3010	】 U+3011	LENTICULAR BRACKET
〔 U+3014	〕 U+3015	TORTOISE SHELL BRACKET
〖 U+3016	〗 U+3017	WHITE LENTICULAR BRACKET
〘 U+3018	〙 U+3019	WHITE TORTOISE SHELL BRACKET
〚 U+301A	〛 U+301B	WHITE SQUARE BRACKET
﴾ U+FD3E	﴿ U+FD3F	ORNATE PARENTHESIS

The two Tibetan pairs of characters function like parentheses. The Ogham feather marks generally bracket a whole text. The brackets in the U+3000 block originally come from CJK encodings and are intended specifically for use with CJK text. The "ornate parentheses" are intended for use specifically with Arabic—they're in the Arabic Presentation Forms A block even though they're neither presentation forms nor compatibility characters.

Dot Leaders

The em and en dashes and the curly quotation marks and apostrophes are leading examples of instances where the way we type something and the way it's printed in quality typography differ. Another notable exception is the ellipsis. Three periods in a row generally don't come out spaced right, so a "typographer's ellipsis," a single piece of type with three periods that are spaced correctly, is provided. In Unicode, this character is U+2026 HORIZONTAL ELLIPSIS. (The "horizontal" distinguishes it from the vertical and diagonal ellipses, which are used sometimes to abbreviate matrices and appear in the Mathematical Operators block.)

You'll also see other numbers of periods used in a row for various other purposes, such as lines of dots in tables of contents. Unicode includes U+2025 TWO DOT LEADER, which has two periods, and U+2024 ONE DOT LEADER, which has only one period. The one-dot leader looks exactly the same as the regular period, but when a bunch of them are used in a row, they space optimally.

These three characters all have compatibility mappings to series of regular periods of appropriate length.

Bullets and Dots

Unicode includes a bunch of centered dots for various purposes. Many of these characters are designed as list bullets. The canonical bullet is U+2022 BULLET (•), but the General Punctuation block also includes the following specially shaped bullets:

- U+2023 TRIANGULAR BULLET (‣)
- U+2043 HYPHEN BULLET (⁃)

- U+204C BLACK LEFTWARDS BULLET (◄)
- U+204D BLACK RIGHTWARDS BULLET (►)

The following language-specific characters are typically used in their respective languages as list bullets:

- U+0E4F THAI CHARACTER FONGMAN (๏)
- U+0F09 TIBETAN MARK BSKUR YIG MGO (༉)
- U+17D9 KHMER SIGN PHNAEK MUAN (៙)

In addition, many characters from the Dingbats and Geometric Shapes blocks are often used as bullets.

A number of other centered-dot characters have distinct semantics but similar appearances:

- U+000B7 MIDDLE DOT has multiple semantics, but one of the main ones is as the dot that's used in Catalan between a pair of l's to indicate that this pair should be pronounced distinctly rather than treated as a single letter and pronounced like *ly*.
- U+2219 BULLET OPERATOR is a mathematical operator that looks like a bullet.
- U+22C5 DOT OPERATOR is a mathematical operator used to indicate multiplication.
- U+2027 HYPHENATION POINT is a centered dot used in dictionaries to indicate places within a word where it may be hyphenated.

▪ SPECIAL CHARACTERS

Not every Unicode code point value represents something most people would actually call a "character." Some Unicode code point values have no glyph shape at all, but exist solely to influence the behavior of some process operating on the surrounding text. In addition to the "control characters" with which we're all familiar from ASCII, Unicode includes "characters" whose purpose is to influence line breaking, glyph selection, bidirectional text layout, and various other text processes.

Line and Paragraph Separators

Arguably the most important special characters in Unicode are those used to mark a line or paragraph division. Unfortunately, the situation in Unicode with regard to line and paragraph divisions is rather complicated.

Two ASCII characters deal with line breaks: LF, or Line Feed (0x0A), and CR (0x0D), or Carriage Return. On a teletype machine, an LF would cause the platen roller to move forward one line without moving the carriage, and a CR would return the carriage to the beginning of the line without advancing the platen roller. Starting a new line of text, as you would on a manual typewriter by hitting the carriage-return lever and pushing the carriage all the way back, or on an electric typewriter by hitting the carriage-return key, required two signals: a CR and an LF. You could use CRs by themselves to perform overprinting effects, such as underlining or adding accents (BS, or Backspace, was also used for these purposes), but LF without CR wasn't terribly useful.

The carriage-return/line-feed combination (CRLF) is still used as the end-of-line signal in most DOS and Windows applications, but other platforms have diverged from this practice. Since LF doesn't really do anything interesting without CR, you can interpret it as carrying an implicit CR and signaling a new line all by itself. Most UNIX and UNIX-derived systems (including the Java programming language) do so. The Macintosh platform, on the other hand, went in the opposite direction. Noting that the "carriage return" button on a typewriter both returns the carriage and advances the platen, it gave the CR character the same semantic—it effectively carries an implicit LF and signals the beginning of a line all by itself.

To complicate matters even further, the EBCDIC encoding has a specific "new line" character (NL, either 0x15 or 0x25 depending on the system), and the ISO 6429 standard, which defines the control characters used with many other encoding standards (including the ISO 8859 family), adopted it into the C1 space as 0x85. Some EBCDIC and 6429-based systems use NL as their new-line signal, although this practice is rarer than using CR, LF, or CRLF.

As if matters weren't bad enough, different applications treat the platform-specific new-line sequences in different ways, regardless of which specific character codes are involved. Originally, as the name suggests, the new-line sequences signaled the beginning of a new line of text, analogous to hitting the carriage-return key on a typewriter. Many applications, especially simple text editors, still use the new-line sequences in this way. The standard Internet mail protocols also use new-line sequences between lines of an e-mail message, even though most e-mail programs don't require you to type a new-line sequence at the end of each line (they wrap the lines automatically and supply the extra new-line sequences at transmission time).

With the advent of word processing software and other programs that wrap lines automatically, having a special character to signal the beginning of a new line became superfluous. Instead, these programs generally treated the new-line sequence as a new-paragraph signal.

Complicating things even *more,* some word processing programs allow explicit line divisions within a paragraph. Because they already used the regular new-line sequence to signal a new *paragraph,* they had to invent a *new* character to signal an explicit line break within a paragraph. Microsoft Word uses the ASCII VT (Vertical Tab, 0x0B) for this purpose, but this choice is even less standardized than the regular new-line sequences.

The problem is relevant because Unicode includes all the characters from the ASCII and ISO 8859-1 standards in their original relative positions. It therefore includes all the characters that are used to signal line and paragraph divisions in these encodings and inherits their ambiguous meanings.

To solve this problem, Unicode includes two new characters in the General Punctuation block, U+2028 LINE SEPARATOR and U+2029 PARAGRAPH SEPARATOR (often abbreviated as LS and PS, respectively), which have unambiguous semantics. Unfortunately, most systems that use Unicode persist in using the old characters to signal line and paragraph boundaries. The Java programming language, for example, follows the UNIX convention and uses the LF character (in Unicode, it is U+000A LINE FEED) as its new-line sequence. This character is output at the end of the line when you call `System.out.println()`, for example; it's the character represented by \n. Similarly, Windows NT and the other Unicode-based versions of Windows continue to follow the old DOS convention of using CRLF at the ends of lines or paragraphs.

As a consequence, software that operates on Unicode text must be prepared to deal with *any* new-line convention. It should always interpret LS as a line separator and PS as a paragraph separator, but it should also treat CR, LF, CRLF, and NL in Unicode text the same as either LS or PS depending on the application (generally, you'd treat them all the same as PS except in program editors and a few other specialized applications).

For code that doesn't know whether the legacy new-line sequences should be treated as LS or PS (library code, for example), it should make the safest assumption. The boundary-finding code in Java, for example, treats CR, LF, and CRLF the same as PS when looking for character or word boundaries (where they're really only whitespace). It treats them the same as LS when looking for sentence boundaries (where a new-line sequence might be the end of a paragraph or just whitespace, but where the end of a paragraph generally includes punctuation that tips you off to the end of a sentence).

Character encoding conversion is also complicated by the new-line mess. When going to Unicode from some other encoding, if you know whether the platform new-line sequence is being used in the source text to represent line breaks or paragraph breaks, you can map the platform new-line sequence to LS or PS. If you don't, you can either just map to PS and hope you didn't get it wrong, or leave the characters alone and depend on the process that will render the text to do something with the text to interpret the new-line sequences correctly.

Converting *to* another encoding from Unicode is similarly complicated. You can simply leave CR, LF, and NL alone, which at least doesn't mess them up any more than they're already messed up, but you must still handle LS and PS. Assuming you know the platform on which you're running, the simplest course of action—unless you know the ultimate destination of the text—is to map both PS and LS to the platform new-line sequence. (It may be a good idea to map any other new-line sequences in the text to the platform sequence as well.) If you don't know the platform, you're stuck. You could play the odds and convert LS and PS to LF or CRLF, but you may well get it wrong.

This issue is sufficiently complicated that the Unicode Consortium issued a Unicode Standard Annex (UAX #13) specifically to discuss these issues and nail down some recommendations. This section parrots back most of UAX #13.

Segment and Page Separators

Related to the issue of line and paragraph separators are the issues of page and segment separators. Fortunately, they don't involve the same level of ambiguity as do line and paragraph separators.

Consider the page separator. The ASCII FF (Form Feed, 0x0C) character originally signaled the teletype or printer to eject the page and begin a new one. This character is the natural choice for signaling the beginning of a new page, and, in fact, it's almost universally used for this purpose. Because Unicode includes all of the ASCII control characters, this character is encoded as U+000C FORM FEED, and it's considered the correct character to use for this purpose even in Unicode. A page break is also a line break, so processing code that deals with explicit line breaks should generally treat FF as having all the semantics of LS, plus the additional semantic of signaling an explicit page break. FF shouldn't be altered in conversion.

Other breaks occur within a single line, usually to line up individual pieces of text in columns. In ASCII text, the TAB or HT (Horizontal Tab, 0x09) character is used for this purpose, analogous to the Tab key on a typewriter. Again, there isn't any ambiguity here, so the analogous Unicode character (U+0009 HORIZONTAL TABULATION) means the same thing in Unicode.

The ASCII standard includes a number of other control characters for use in structured text. For example, the FS, GS, RS, and US (File Separator, Group Separator, Record Separator, and Unit Separator, respectively) characters were once used to delimit different-sized units of structured text. These characters are rarely used nowadays, although their analogues do exist in Unicode. Today, in very simple structured-text documents, TAB is used as a field separator and the platform new-line sequence is used as a record separator. More sophisticated structured-text interchange is usually considered the province of a higher-level protocol, rather than the job of the character encoding. The higher-level protocol of choice for this kind of operation is currently XML, which uses markup tags as field and record delimiters.

Control Characters

Unicode adopts all of the control characters from the ISO 6429 standard. These occur in two blocks: the C0 block, which contains the original ASCII control characters, and the C1 block, an analogous encoding area in the 0x80–0xFF range containing an extra 32 control codes. Because Unicode is designed to be freely convertible to ISO 8859-1 (Latin-1, which includes all the ASCII characters and is based on ISO 6429), it also has all the same control characters. The Unicode standard doesn't formally assign any semantics to these characters, but they're generally agreed to have the same interpretations as they do in their original source standards. In particular, U+0009 HORIZONTAL TABULATION and U+000C FORM FEED are the tab and page-break characters of choice in Unicode. Unicode's designers didn't see a reason to encode "official" Unicode characters with these semantics.

In addition to U+0009 and U+000C, you'll frequently see U+000A LINE FEED, U+000D CARRIAGE RETURN, and U+000B VERTICAL TABULATION in Unicode text, even though U+2028 LINE SEPARATOR and U+2029 PARAGRAPH SEPARATOR are the officially sanctioned characters representing line and paragraph breaks. See the earlier section on line and paragraph separators for more information on their use.

Characters That Control Word Wrapping

It's a little misleading to call this section "Characters That Control Word-Wrapping" because almost every character in Unicode has an effect on word-wrapping. For example, the line and paragraph separators always cause a line break, and the spaces, hyphens, and dashes always produce a place in the text where a line break can happen. Other characters affect word-wrapping in more complicated, language-defined ways. We'll examine this subject in great depth in Chapter 16.

For now, note that there are a couple of special characters designed solely to affect word-wrapping. We looked at them earlier in the section on spaces, but it's worth considering them briefly here.

U+200B ZERO WIDTH SPACE (ZWSP) isn't really a space at all, but an invisible formatting character that indicates to a word-wrapping process that it's acceptable to break a line between the two characters on either side of it. As an example, suppose you have the following sentence:

I work at
SuperMegaGiantCorp.

The margins are just a little too tight for "SuperMegaGiantCorp." to fit on the same line as the rest of the sentence, leaving a big white gap at the beginning of the first line. Maybe it would be okay to split "SuperMegaGiantCorp." at the capital letters. You could do so by inserting ZWSP before each of the capital letters. Then you'd get

I work at SuperMegaGiant Corp.

which includes a reasonable amount of text on the first line. Now if the text changed or the margins were widened, you'd get this:

I work at SuperMegaGiantCorp.

When it all fit on one line, you'd still see "SuperMegaGiantCorp." without any spaces.

Of course, you wouldn't see this kind of thing in English very much, but in other languages it happens frequently. In Thai, for example, spaces aren't used between words, but word-wrapping should honor word boundaries. Most Thai word processors employ sophisticated language-sensitive word-wrapping processes to figure out where the word boundaries are, but they sometimes guess wrong. You can use the ZWSP character as a hint to the word-wrapping process as to where the word boundaries exist.

In English, such as in our example, you would probably want "Super-MegaGiantCorp." to be hyphenated. Related to the ZWSP is U+00AD SOFT HYPHEN (SHY). Like ZWSP, it normally functions as an invisible formatting character that indicates to the word-wrapping routine where a line break is acceptable. The difference is that it tells the word-wrapping routine that if it actually puts a line break at that position, it should precede it with a hyphen. In other words, this invisible formatting character indicates places where it's okay to hyphenate a word. As with ZWSP in Thai, you might be working with a word processor that hyphenates words automatically. If the hyphenation process hyphenates some word incorrectly (for example, a proper name that's not in its dictionary, such as "SuperMegaGiantCorp."), you can use SHY as a hint to indicate where the right places are. In our example, if the margins are wide enough, you see the sentence the way it looks in the previous example. If the margins are smaller, you get the following:

I work at SuperMegaGiant-Corp.

U+1806 MONGOLIAN TODO SOFT HYPHEN works the same way with Mongolian text. See the previous section on dashes and hyphens for a discussion of this character.

You may also want the reverse behavior. Unicode generally says that spaces and dashes indicate legal places to break a line, but sometimes you don't want that behavior. In French, for example, spaces are used to separate powers of 1,000 in large numbers. Suppose you have the following sentence (we'll pretend it's in French):

You owe me 100 000 000 €.

If the margins were tighter, you might get this instead:

You owe me 100 000 000 €.

Of course, you don't want the number to be split across two lines. In fact, you probably want the currency symbol to appear on the same line as the number as well. U+2060 WORD JOINER (WJ), like its cousin ZWSP, isn't really a space, but an invisible formatting character that tells word-wrapping routines that it's *not* acceptable to put a line break between the two characters on either side. It's often called the "glue" character because it "glues" two characters together and forces them to appear on the same line. If you put a WJ character after each real space in the number above, the same example would wrap like this:

You owe me
100 000 000 €.

The number and the currency symbol that follows it are all kept together on a single line.

In versions of Unicode prior to Unicode 3.2, the "glue" function was represented with U+FEFF ZERO WIDTH NO-BREAK SPACE (ZWNBSP), which also did double duty as the Unicode byte order mark. This usage is one of those "seemed like a good idea at the time" things. The semantics would seem to be unambiguous: At the beginning of a file, U+FEFF is a BOM; anywhere else, it's a ZWNBSP. Of course, a particular U+FEFF might shift meanings when you concatenated two files together or extracted characters from the middle of a file. Unicode 3.2 deprecated the ZWNBSP meaning of U+FEFF, returning it to just a byte order mark.

Most of the time, word-wrapping routines treat spaces and hyphens as marking legal break positions—the behavior you're trying to suppress by using WJ. For this reason, Unicode includes special space and hyphen characters that also have non-breaking semantics. U+00A0 NO-BREAK SPACE (NBSP) and U+2011 NON-BREAKING HYPHEN look and act exactly the same as their regular counterparts U+0020 SPACE and U+2010 HYPHEN, but they also suppress line breaks both before and after themselves. That is, using NBSP produces the same effect as putting WJ on either side of a regular space—it glues together the space and the characters before and after it.

In addition to the regular no-break space, U+202F NARROW NO-BREAK SPACE and U+2077 FIGURE SPACE have non-breaking semantics. U+0F0C TIBETAN MARK DELIMITER TSHEG BSTAR, a non-breaking version of the Tibetan tsheg mark, is used between words and normally indicates a legal line-break position.

Characters That Control Glyph Selection

Unicode includes several invisible formatting characters that control glyph selection and character shaping.

The Joiner and Non-joiner   The two most important of these characters are U+200C ZERO WIDTH NON-JOINER (ZWNJ) and U+200D ZERO WIDTH JOINER (ZWJ). The purpose of the non-joiner is to break a connection between two characters that would otherwise be connected. To take a trivial example:

```
U+0066 LATIN SMALL LETTER F
U+0069 LATIN SMALL LETTER I
```

would normally be rendered like this:

fi

If you insert ZWNJ,

```
U+0066 LATIN SMALL LETTER F
U+200C ZERO WIDTH NON-JOINER
U+0069 LATIN SMALL LETTER I
```

you get this instead:

fi

ZWNJ breaks up both cursive connections and ligatures. For example, in Arabic,

```
U+0644 ARABIC LETTER LAM
U+0647 ARABIC LETTER HEH
U+062C ARABIC LETTER JEEM
```

normally looks like this:

لهج

If you add in the non-joiner,

```
U+0644 ARABIC LETTER LAM
U+200C ZERO WIDTH NON-JOINER
```

U+0647 ARABIC LETTER HEH
U+200C ZERO WIDTH NON-JOINER
U+062C ARABIC LETTER JEEM

the letters break apart, giving you this:

جەل

In the Indic scripts, ZWNJ can be used to break up conjunct consonants, forcing the explicit virama form. For example, the sequence

U+0915 DEVANAGARI LETTER KA
U+094D DEVANAGARI SIGN VIRAMA
U+0937 DEVANAGARI LETTER SSA

is normally rendered as a conjunct consonant:

क्ष

If you stick ZWNJ into the sequence,

U+0915 DEVANAGARI LETTER KA
U+094D DEVANAGARI SIGN VIRAMA
U+200C ZERO WIDTH NON-JOINER
U+0937 DEVANAGARI LETTER SSA

the conjunct is broken, and the virama becomes visible:

क्ष

The zero-width joiner has the opposite effect: It creates cursive connections where they wouldn't otherwise exist. Its behavior, however, is a little more complicated than that of ZWNJ. ZWJ doesn't actually work on pairs of characters. Rather, it independently affects the characters on either side of it, both of which may not necessarily change shape based on context. In other words, if you put ZWJ between two characters A and B, the rendering engine (assuming properly designed fonts and so forth) will use the right-joining version of A, if there is one, and the left-joining version of B, if there is one. If A has a right-joining form and B has a left-joining form, they appear cursively connected. If only one of them has the appropriate form, it still takes it on even though no cursive connection is created. Of course, if *neither* character connects cursively, ZWJ has no effect.

For example, the character

```
U+0647 ARABIC LETTER HEH
```

normally looks like this:

ه

If you precede it with the ZWJ,

```
U+200D ZERO WIDTH JOINER
U+0647 ARABIC LETTER HEH
```

you get the final form of the character:

ﻪ

If you follow it with ZWJ,

```
U+0647 ARABIC LETTER HEH
U+200D ZERO WIDTH JOINER
```

you get the initial form:

ﻫ

If you flank it with ZWJs,

```
U+200D ZERO WIDTH JOINER
U+0647 ARABIC LETTER HEH
U+200D ZERO WIDTH JOINER
```

you get the medial form:

$$ﻬ$$

This is true no matter what the character on the other side of the joiner is; the characters on either side of the joiner effectively join to the joiner, not to each other. For example, there's no left-joining form of alef, so the sequence

```
U+0627 ARABIC LETTER ALEF
U+0647 ARABIC LETTER HEH
```

would normally be drawn with both characters' independent forms:

$$ﻫا$$

If you put ZWJ between them,

```
U+0627 ARABIC LETTER ALEF
U+200D ZERO WIDTH JOINER
U+0647 ARABIC LETTER HEH
```

it forces the final (i.e., right-joining) form of heh to be used, even though it can't actually join to the alef (which has no left-joining form):

$$ﻪا$$

An exception to this normal rule about ZWJ affecting the characters on either side independently is noted: If the characters on either side can form a ligature, ZWJ creates this ligature. If it's a mandatory ligature, ZWJ is superfluous. If it's an optional ligature, you can use ZWJ, rather than out-of-band styling information, to create it.

For example, many Latin-alphabet fonts (especially italic fonts) include an optional ligature for the letters c and t. The sequence

```
U+0063 LATIN SMALL LETTER C
U+0074 LATIN SMALL LETTER T
```

would normally be rendered like this:

$$ct$$

If you put ZWJ between the letters

```
U+0063 LATIN SMALL LETTER C
U+200D ZERO WIDTH JOINER
U+0074 LATIN SMALL LETTER T
```

you might get this instead:

$$ct$$

Some pairs of characters can take an intermediate form between fully joined and fully broken apart. For example, two adjacent characters might either form a ligature, join cursively without forming a ligature, or just be drawn independently. To get the middle form (joining cursively without forming a ligature), you use both ZWJ and ZWNJ. You use ZWNJ to break up the ligature and then flank it with ZWJs to force the use of the cursively joining versions of the characters. Consider the Arabic letters lam and alef. Represented in their normal way,

```
U+0644 ARABIC LETTER LAM
U+0627 ARABIC LETTER ALEF
```

they form a ligature:

$$ﻻ$$

If you put ZWNJ between them,

```
U+0644 ARABIC LETTER LAM
U+200C ZERO WIDTH NON-JOINER
U+0627 ARABIC LETTER ALEF
```

the ligature breaks apart and you get the independent forms of both letters:

 lJ

If you surround the ZWNJ with ZWJs, however,

```
U+0644 ARABIC LETTER LAM
U+200D ZERO WIDTH JOINER
U+200C ZERO WIDTH NON-JOINER
U+200D ZERO WIDTH JOINER
U+0627 ARABIC LETTER ALEF
```

the characters join together without forming the ligature:

lJ

Both joiners are required, because each independently affects one of the letters (each joiner effectively joins its letter to the non-joiner, which keeps them from forming the ligature). If you have only one joiner,

```
U+0644 ARABIC LETTER LAM
U+200D ZERO WIDTH JOINER
U+200C ZERO WIDTH NON-JOINER
U+0627 ARABIC LETTER ALEF
```

you still get the independent form on one of the letters:

lJ

A similar effect can be seen in Devanagari and some other Indic scripts. Two consonants that normally form a conjunct,

```
U+0915 DEVANAGARI LETTER KA
U+094D DEVANAGARI SIGN VIRAMA
U+0937 DEVANAGARI LETTER SSA
```

क्ष

are rendered independently with an explicit virama if ZWNJ is used:

```
U+0915 DEVANAGARI LETTER KA
U+094D DEVANAGARI SIGN VIRAMA
U+200C ZERO WIDTH NON-JOINER
U+0937 DEVANAGARI LETTER SSA
```

क्‌ष

If you surround the ZWNJ with ZWJs, you actually get the *half-form* of ka instead of the explicit virama:

```
U+0915 DEVANAGARI LETTER KA
U+094D DEVANAGARI SIGN VIRAMA
U+200D ZERO WIDTH JOINER
U+200C ZERO WIDTH NON-JOINER
U+200D ZERO WIDTH JOINER
U+0937 DEVANAGARI LETTER SSA
```

क्ष

Like the other formatting characters discussed in this section, the joiner and non-joiner have no appearances of their own, and they don't affect any process on the text except for glyph selection. As far as other processes on the text (e.g., searching, sorting, line breaking) are concerned, ZWJ and ZWNJ are transparent.

Variation Selectors   Unicode 3.2 adds 16 new characters that affect glyph selection: the characters in the new Variation Selectors block, which runs from U+FE00 to U+FE0F. For certain characters, you can follow the character with a variation selector. The variation selector acts as a "hint" to the rendering processing that you want the preceding character to be drawn with a particular glyph. The variation selectors never have appearances of their own, and they remain transparent to all other processes that operate on Unicode text.

The variation selectors apply to items such as math symbols, where 90 percent of the time, two similar glyphs (for example, the $\geq$ sign with either a

horizontal "equals" line or an "equals" line parallel to the lower half of the >) are just variants of the same character. Sometimes, however, writers use the two versions to mean different things. In situations where the glyph shape matters, you might follow ≥ with U+FE00 VARIATION SELECTOR-1 to indicate you want the version with the slanted line, or with U+FE01 VARIATION SELECTOR-2 to indicate that you want the horizontal line. If you don't use either variation selector, it means you don't care which glyph is used, and the font or the rendering process is free to use whichever one it wants.)[5]

Starting in Unicode 3.2, the Unicode Character Database includes a new file, StandardizedVariants.html, which lists which combinations of a normal character and a variation selector are legal, and which glyphs they represent. You cannot use unassigned combinations for your purposes. Instead, as with unassigned code point values, all unassigned variation selector combinations are reserved for future standardization. If a variation selector follows a character that isn't listed in StandardizedVariants.html as taking a variation selector, the variation selector simply has no effect. There are no "private-use" variation selectors, although you could designate some of the regular private-use characters to work that way if you wanted.

Nonrendering processes typically treat variation selectors as combining characters with a combining class of 0, which gives the correct behavior most of the time with no special-casing code. This does mean, however, that variation selectors must always be used with noncombining, noncomposite characters (you'll never see a variation selector used to select acute accents with different angles, for example).

In addition to the 16 generic variation selectors, three variation selectors appear in the Mongolian block. They work exactly in the same way (including having the variants listed in StandardizedVariants.html), except that their use is restricted to Mongolian. This organization is a historical quirk: The Mongolian variation selectors were added in Unicode 3.0, before the generic variation selectors.

---

5. This isn't the best example: The version of ≥ with the slanted line is actually one of the new math symbols in Unicode 3.2.

The Grapheme Joiner

Unicode 3.2 adds another interesting character, U+034F COMBINING GRAPHEME JOINER. Like the variation selectors, it's treated as a combining character and has no visible presentation. With one important exception, it doesn't affect the way text is rendered.

The grapheme joiner is more or less analogous to the word joiner. Instead of suppressing word breaks, however, it suppresses a grapheme cluster break, "gluing" the grapheme clusters on either side together into a single grapheme cluster. The entire sequence is, therefore, treated as a unit for such operations as cursor movement, searching, and sorting. In cases where a word-wrapping process must wrap on character boundaries rather than word boundaries, it also suppresses a line break.

In Unicode 3.2, enclosing marks are defined to enclose everything up to the most recent grapheme cluster boundary. The grapheme joiner can, therefore, be used to cause an enclosing mark to surround more text than it might otherwise. For example, the sequence

```
U+0031 DIGIT ONE
U+0032 DIGIT TWO
U+20DD COMBINING ENCLOSING CIRCLE
```

is drawn like this:

1②

The 1 and the 2 are separate grapheme clusters, so the circle surrounds only the 2. If you put a grapheme joiner between them,

```
U+0031 DIGIT ONE
U+034F COMBINING GRAPHEME JOINER
U+0032 DIGIT TWO
U+20DD COMBINING ENCLOSING CIRCLE
```

you get this:

⑫

The grapheme joiner "glues" the 1 and the 2 together into a single grapheme cluster, causing the circle to surround both of them.

For more information on grapheme clusters and the grapheme joiner, see Chapter 4.

Bidirectional Formatting Characters

Unicode includes seven characters whose purpose is to control bidirectional reordering:

```
U+200E LEFT-TO-RIGHT MARK
2+200F RIGHT-TO-LEFT MARK
U+202A LEFT-TO-RIGHT EMBEDDING
U+202B RIGHT-TO-LEFT EMBEDDING
U+202D LEFT-TO-RIGHT OVERRIDE
U+202E RIGHT-TO-LEFT OVERRIDE
U+202C POP DIRECTIONAL FORMATTING
```

Chapter 8 provides an in-depth treatment of these characters, so there's no point in repeating the entire discussion here. Here's a brief recap:

- The left-to-right mark (LRM) and right-to-left mark (RLM) have no visual appearance, but look to the Unicode bi-di algorithm like strong left-to-right and strong right-to-left characters, respectively. These characters affect the interpretation of characters with weak or neutral directionality that appear in ambiguous positions in the text.
- The left-to-right and right-to-left override characters (LRO and RLO) cause all of the characters between themselves and the next PDF (or another override or embedding character) to be treated by the bi-di algorithm as characters with strong directionality in the direction specified, no matter their natural directionality.
- The left-to-right and right-to-left embedding characters (LRE and RLE), like LRO and RLO, are used with the PDF to delimit a range of text, but they cause the enclosed run of text to be *embedded* within the surrounding text. For example, if you have a Hebrew quotation in an English sentence, but the Hebrew quotation includes an English word, you can use

LRE to cause the English word to be treated as part of the Hebrew quotation rather than as part of the enclosing English sentence (which would cause the Hebrew parts of the quotation to appear out of order).

- The pop-directional-formatting character (PDF) terminates the effect of a preceding LRO, RLO, LRE, or RLE.

Like the other formatting characters discussed in this section, the bi-di formatting characters have no visual appearance of their own and are transparent to all processes operating on the text except for bidirectional reordering.

Deprecated Characters

The General Punctuation block includes six more invisible formatting characters that were deprecated in Unicode 3.0. These characters shouldn't be used anymore, but since characters can't be removed from the Unicode standard, they're still there. The Unicode Consortium strongly discourages users from using these characters, and it strongly discourages developers implementing the Unicode standard from supporting them. For completeness, here's a quick explanation of what they were originally intended to do:

- U+206A INHIBIT SYMMETRIC SWAPPING turns off mirroring. Normally, characters such as the parentheses have a different glyph depending on whether they appear in left-to-right text or right-to-left text. The starting parenthesis appears as (in left-to-right text but as) in right-to-left text, maintaining its semantic identity as the starting parenthesis regardless of text direction. U+206A turns off this behavior, causing the mirrored characters to take on their left-to-right glyphs even when they appear in right-to-left text. U+206B ACTIVATE SYMMETRIC SWAPPING turns mirroring back on, returning things to the default state.

  This ability was included to provide backward compatibility with older standards that didn't have the concept of mirrored characters. When converting from such a standard to Unicode, the conversion process should be smart enough to understand the bi-di state and exchange the code point values for the mirroring characters instead of trying to turn mirroring on and off.

- U+206D ACTIVATE ARABIC FORM SHAPING causes the same glyph-selection process that's used for the Arabic letters in the U+0600 block to be used with the characters in the Arabic Presentation Forms blocks. In other words, all of the different presentation forms of the letter heh in the presentation forms blocks are treated the same as the nominal version of heh in the Arabic block. That is, their glyph shapes are determined by context, rather than always being the glyph shapes specified in the Unicode standard. U+206C INHIBIT ARABIC FORM SHAPING turns this behavior off, returning to the default state where the Arabic presentation forms always have their specified glyph shapes.

  These codes came into Unicode in the 10646 merger. They shouldn't be used; if you want contextual glyph selection, use the nominal forms of the Arabic letters instead of the presentation forms.

- U+206E NATIONAL DIGIT SHAPES causes the Unicode code point values from U+0030 to U+0039 to take on the glyph shapes for the digits in the script of the surrounding text. For example, in Arabic text, U+206E causes U+0031, U+0032, U+0033 to appear as ١, ٢, ٣ instead of 1, 2, 3. U+2006F NOMINAL DIGIT SHAPES returns things to their default state, where the digits in the ASCII block are always drawn as European digits.

  This character was included to ensure compatibility with ISO 8859-6, which called for the ASCII digit codes to represent both the European digits and the Arabic digits depending on context. Code converting to Unicode from ISO 8859-6 should be smart enough to map the ASCII digit characters to the appropriate code point values in the Arabic block when they should appear as the Arabic digits.

Interlinear Annotation

In Chinese and Japanese text, you'll periodically see characters adorned with little annotations between the lines of text. Usually, these annotations are intended to clarify the pronunciation of unfamiliar characters. In Japanese, this practice is called *furigana* or *ruby*.

Text containing interlinear annotations is normally considered to be structured text, in the same way that text containing sidebars or footnotes would be structured text. Typically, Unicode would represent the characters in the annotations themselves. A higher-level protocol, such as HTML or XML, would then associate the annotation with the annotated text and specify where the text of the annotation would appear in the document.

Occasionally it's necessary to include the annotations in otherwise plain, unstructured text. For this reason Unicode includes characters for interlinear annotation:

- U+FFF9 INTERLINEAR ANNOTATION ANCHOR marks the beginning of a piece of text that has an annotation.
- U+FFFA INTERLINEAR ANNOTATION SEPARATOR marks the end of a piece of text that has an annotation and the beginning of the annotation itself. A piece of text might have multiple annotations, in which case the annotations are separated from one another with additional U+FFFA characters.
- U+FFFB INTERLINEAR ANNOTATION TERMINATOR marks the end of the annotation and the resumption of the main text.

Chapter 10 provides a full treatment of interlinear annotations, complete with examples.

The Object Replacement Character

Fully styled text may include nontext elements, such as pictures or other embedded elements. How such elements are included in a document is the province of a higher-level protocol, but Unicode includes one character intended to simplify matters.

In a markup language such as HTML, embedded elements are included via appropriate pieces of markup text (such as the <img> tag) in appropriate places in the text. In many word processors and similar programs, however, the nontext information resides in a separate data structure from the text itself and is associated with it by means of a **run-array** mechanism, a data structure that associates ranges of text with records of styling information (for example, it includes records that say, in effect, "characters 5 through 10 are in boldface"). Embedded elements are usually stored in the style records in the run array.

Unlike normal styling information, embedded elements aren't really associated with a character; rather, they are associated with a position *between* two characters, something a normal run-array mechanism doesn't handle very well. Unicode provides U+FFFC OBJECT REPLACEMENT CHARACTER to help out with this operation. In most styled-text situations, this character is invisible and transparent to operations on the text. Even so, it provides a spot in the text with which to associate embedded elements. In this way, an embedded element such as a picture can be stored in a style record and the run array can associate a character in the text with it.

In plain Unicode text, U+FFFC can be used to mark the spot where a picture or other embedded element had once been or is to be placed.

The General Substitution Character

U+FFFD REPLACEMENT CHARACTER is used to represent characters that aren't representable in Unicode. If you're converting text from some legacy encoding to Unicode and the text includes characters for which Unicode lacks code point values, you convert those characters to U+FFFD. This character provides a way to indicate in the text that information has been lost in the translation. There's no standardized visual representation for this character—indeed, it doesn't have to have any visual representation—but ◆ is the glyph shown in the Unicode standard and is frequently used.

The ASCII SUB character (U+001A SUBSTITUTE in Unicode) is often used in ASCII-based encodings for the same purpose. Even though this character also exists in Unicode, it shouldn't be used to provide this function in Unicode text.

Because the designers of Unicode used most of the other encoding standards as sources for characters, it will rarely be necessary to convert something to U+FFFD. Until Unicode 3.0, you would generally see this character used for CJK ideographs that weren't yet included in Unicode. Unicode 3.0 added more specialized character codes for representing otherwise unrepresentable CJK ideographs. They include the geta mark (U+3013), which functions like U+FFFD and marks the position of an unknown ideograph (but which has a standard visual representation); the ideographic variation indicator (U+303E), which is used in conjunction with a character that *is* representable to say "a character kind of like this one"; and the ideographic description characters, which provide a whole grammar for describing an otherwise unencoded character. For a full treatment of these characters, see Chapter 10.

Tagging Characters

One long-standing point of controversy in Unicode has been the doubling up of certain blocks of characters to represent multiple languages where the characters have historical relationships but distinct glyph shapes. Such pairs include Greek and Coptic; modern and old Cyrillic; Traditional Chinese, Simplified Chinese, Japanese, and Korean; and (possibly) Arabic and Urdu. To get the correct appearance for the characters in these ranges, you need some additional out-of-band information either specifying the font to be used or the language of the text.

Various processes operating on the text might also work differently depending on language. Spell-checking and hyphenation are obvious examples, but many others are possible.

The position of the Unicode Consortium on issues such as specifying the language of a range of text is that it's the proper province of a higher-level protocol, such as HTML or MIME, and such information doesn't belong in plain text. In rare situations, however, language tagging might be useful even in plain text.

Unicode 3.1 introduces a method of putting language tags into Unicode text. The tagging mechanism can be extended to support other types of tagging, but only language tagging is supported at the moment.

Many of the members of the Unicode Technical Committee approved this concept while holding their noses, and the Unicode tagging characters come with all sorts of warnings and caveats about their use. The bottom line is that if you can use some other mechanism to add language tags to your text, do so. If you can get by without language tags, do so. Only if you absolutely must have language tags in Unicode plain text should you use the Unicode tag characters—and even then you should be careful.

The tagging characters appear in plane 14, the Supplementary Special-Purpose Plane. The 95 main tagging characters correspond to the 95 printing characters of ASCII and occupy the same relative positions in plane 14 that the

ASCII characters occupy in plane 0, from U+E0020 to U+E007E. For example, if U+0041 is LATIN CAPITAL LETTER A, then U+E0041 is TAG LATIN CAPITAL LETTER A.

A tag consists of a string of ASCII text in a syntax defined by some external protocol and spelled using the tag characters rather than the ASCII characters. A tag is preceded by an identifier character that indicates what kind of tag it is. Currently, one tag identifier character is available: U+E0001 LANGUAGE TAG. Eventually, others might be defined.

The nice thing about this arrangement is that processes that don't care about the tags can ignore them with a very simple range check. You also don't need a special character code to terminate a tag, because the first non-tag character in the text stream terminates the tag.

For language tags, the syntax is an RFC 3066 language identifier: a two-letter language code as defined by ISO 639, optionally followed by a hyphen and a two-letter region or country code as defined by ISO 3166. You can also have user-defined language tags beginning with "x-".

For example, you might precede a section of Japanese text with the following:

```
U+E0001 LANGUAGE TAG
U+E006A TAG LATIN SMALL LETTER J
U+E0061 TAG LATIN SMALL LETTER A
U+E002D TAG HYPHEN-MINUS
U+E006A TAG LATIN SMALL LETTER J
U+E0070 TAG LATIN SMALL LETTER P
```

This sequence, of course, is "ja-jp" spelled out with tag characters and preceded with the language tag identifier. All text following this tag is tagged as being in Japanese. Of course, nothing guarantees that the tag is right—you could easily have Spanish text tagged as French, for example.

A language tag stays in scope until you reach the end of the text ("the end of the text" being an application-defined concept), see another language tag, or reach U+E007F CANCEL TAG. U+E007F in isolation cancels all tags in scope at that point. U+E0001 U+E007F cancels just the language tag in effect. (Right now, there's no difference because language tags are the only kinds of tags defined, but this situation may change in the future.) Language tags don't nest.

If other tag types are defined in the future, tags of different types will be totally independent. Except for U+E007F canceling all tagged text in scope (a feature allowed to permit concatenation of files without tags bleeding into one another), the scope of one kind of tag doesn't affect the scope of any other kind of tag that may also be in effect.

A Unicode implementation is permitted to ignore any tags, but implementations should try not to corrupt the tags by, for example, inserting regular characters into the middle of a tag. Tag-aware applications should, however, be prepared to deal with just such a problem in some reasonable way. Unicode 3.1 prescribes that malformed language tags should be treated the same as CANCEL TAG by conforming applications—text after a malformed tag is simply considered untagged.

Because language tags are stateful, they pose a problem for interpretation. If you care about the language tag in effect at some point in the text, you might have to scan backward from that point for an indefinite distance to find the appropriate language tag. A good policy is to read the file sequentially when it's loaded into your program, strip out all language tags, and put the information into an out-of-band data structure such as a style run array.

The Unicode standard doesn't require conforming applications that care about the tags to do anything special with tagged text other than interpreting the text. In particular, conforming implementations don't have to do anything different with text that's tagged as being in some language than they would do with the same text if it were untagged. They're *permitted* to treat tagged text differently, of course, but this treatment isn't *required*.

Noncharacters

Unicode includes a number of code point values that are not considered to be legal characters. These values are described next:

- **U+FFFF.** Having this code point value not be a character does two things. First, it allows you to use an `unsigned short` in C++ (or corresponding type in other programming languages) for Unicode characters and still be able to loop over the entire range with a loop that will terminate. If U+FFFF was a legal character, a naive loop would loop forever unless a larger data type were used for the loop variable or the code included some extra shenanigans to keep track of how many times you've seen a particular value, such as 0. Second, defining U+FFFF in this way provides a noncharacter value that can be used for end-of-file or other sentinel values by processes operating on Unicode text without forcing them to resort to using a larger-than-otherwise-necessary data type for the characters. (Despite this feature, the relevant Java I/O routines return `int`—go figure.)

- **U+FFFE.** The byte-swapped version of this code point value is U+FEFF, the Unicode byte order mark. Having U+FFFE not be a legal character makes it possible to identify UTF-16 or UTF-32 text with the wrong byte ordering.

- **U+xxFFFE and U+xxFFFF.** The counterparts to U+FFFE and U+FFFF in all of the supplementary planes are also set aside as noncharacters. This organization is a holdover from the early design of ISO 10646, when it was expected that the individual planes would be used independently of one another (i.e., the UCS-2 representation could be used for planes other than the BMP when, for example, the text consisted entirely of Han characters).

- **U+FDD0 to U+FDEF.** These code point values in the BMP were set aside starting in Unicode 3.1. The idea was to give implementations a few more noncharacter values that they could use for internal purposes (without worrying that these values would later be assigned to actual characters). For example, a regular-expression parser might use code point values in this range to represent special characters such as * and |.

The noncharacter code point values should never occur in Unicode text for interchange, and it's not acceptable to treat them as characters—they're not just extensions of the Private Use Area. Rather, these values are expressly reserved for internal application use in situations where you need values that don't represent characters (such as sentinel values).

■ SYMBOLS USED WITH NUMBERS

Of course, Unicode includes a vast collection of signs and symbols. We'll examine these characters in two separate sections. This section deals with those symbols that are used with numbers or in mathematical expressions.

Numeric Punctuation

Many of the cultures that use Arabic positional notation employ punctuation marks in numerals. For example, Americans use the period to separate the integral part of the number from the fractional part of the number; in large numbers, we use a comma every three digits to help make the numeral easier to read. Many other cultures also use punctuation marks for these purposes, but they rely on different punctuation marks. In much of Europe, for example, a comma is used as the decimal-point character, and various characters from the period (Germany) to the space (France) to the apostrophe (Switzerland) are used as thousands separators.

Almost all of these cultures do share one thing in common: They use regular punctuation marks for these purposes. Unicode follows this pattern and doesn't separately encode special numeric punctuation characters. There's no "decimal point" character in Unicode, for example; the regular period or comma code point values are used as decimal points.

The lone exception is Arabic, which has special numeric punctuation. With native Arabic digits, you use U+066B ARABIC DECIMAL SEPARATOR and U+066C ARABIC THOUSANDS SEPARATOR. For example, 1,234.56 looks like this when written with Arabic digits:

$$١'٢٣٤,٥٦$$

Currency Symbols

Unicode includes a wide variety of currency symbols. Most reside in the Currency Symbols block, which runs from U+20A0 to U+20CF. Notably, the euro sign (€) is in this block, at U+20AC. U+20A0 EURO-CURRENCY SIGN is a historical character that's different from the modern euro sign, so be careful not to confuse them!

A number of other currency symbols, including many of the most common, aren't in the Currency Symbols block for one reason or another (Table 12.7).

U+00A4 CURRENCY SIGN is a holdover from the international version of the ISO 646 standard. Rather than enshrine the dollar sign (or any other country's currency symbol) at 0x24 (where ASCII put the dollar sign), ISO 646 declared it to be a national-use character and put this character, which

Table 12.7   Currency Symbols Found Outside the Currency Symbols Block

Character	Code Point Value	Units
$	U+0024	Dollars (many countries), plus some other units
¢	U+00A2	Cents (U.S.)
£	U+00A3	British pounds
¤	U+00A4	*(see note in text)*
¥	U+00A5	Japanese yen
ƒ	U+0192	Dutch guilder
৲	U+09F2	Bengali rupees
৳	U+09F3	Bengali rupees
฿	U+0E3F	Thai baht
៛	U+17DB	Khmer riels

isn't actually used anywhere as a currency symbol, in that position as the default. The later International Reference Version of ISO 646 restored the dollar sign as the default character for 0x24, and ISO 8859-1 set aside another code point value, 0xA4, for the generic currency symbol. It comes into Unicode by way of ISO 8859-1. Although this character still isn't used as an official currency symbol anywhere, it is occasionally used as a "generic" currency symbol (the Java currency formatting APIs, for example, use it to mark the position of a currency symbol in a formatted number).

Unit Markers

Many characters are used with numerals to specify a measurement unit. Much of the time, the unit is simply an abbreviation in letters (such as "mm"), but there are a lot of special unit symbols as well. Among them are the following:

- **In the ASCII block:** # [pounds, number] (U+0023), % [percent] (U+0025)
- **In the Latin-1 block:** ° [degrees] (U+00B0)

- **In the Arabic block:** ٪ [Arabic percent sign; used with native Arabic digits] (U+066A)
- **In the General Punctuation block:** ‰ [per thousand] (U+2030), ‱ [per ten thousand] (U+2031), ′ [minutes, feet] (U+2032), ″ [seconds, inches] (U+2033)
- **The Letterlike Symbols block** (U+2100 to U+214F) includes many characters that are symbols for various units and mathematical constants. Most of the characters in this block are regular letters with various stylistic variants applied to them. In a few cases, they're clones of regular letters, but are categorized as symbols. In the case of the few clones of Hebrew letters encoded in this block, the symbols are also strong left-to-right characters.
- **The CJK Compatibility block** (U+3300 to U+33FF) consists almost entirely of unit symbols used in East Asian typography. They comprise Latin letters or digits, Katakana or kanji characters, or combinations thereof arranged to fit in a standard East Asian character cell. For example, both of the following characters are used in vertical Japanese typography as a "kilometer" symbol (the one on the left is the word "kilometer" written in Katakana):

キロメ／ートル km

Math Symbols

Unicode provides a whole mess of mathematical symbols. The greatest concentration of them appears in the Mathematical Operators block, which runs from U+2200 to U+22FF. Many math symbols are also unified into the Arrows and Geometric Shapes blocks. A fair amount of unification has taken place within the Mathematical Operators block itself. When a particular glyph shape has multiple meanings, they're all unified as a single Unicode character. When a symbol with a single semantic has several variant (but similar) glyph shapes, they're unified into a single code point value.

Further increasing the number of possible math symbols, the Combining Diacritical Marks for Symbols block, running from U+20D0 to U+20FF, contains combining marks that are used specifically with various symbols to change their meaning. Some of the characters in the regular Combining Diacritical Marks block, such as U+0338 COMBINING LONG SOLIDUS OVERLAY, are also frequently used with symbols.

There are a few math symbols in the Letterlike Symbols block as well. In addition, a number of math symbols reside in other Unicode blocks:

- **In the ASCII block:** + (U+002B), < (U+003C), = (U+003D), > (U+003E), | [absolute value] (U+007C) [The hyphen/minus, slash, and tilde characters are often used as math operators, but have counterparts in the Mathematical Operators block that are specifically intended for mathematical use.]
- **In the Latin-1 block:** ¬ [not sign] (U+00AC), ± (U+00B1), ÷ (U+00F7) [The centered dot character at U+00D7 is also often used as a math operator, but has a more appropriate counterpart in the Mathematical Operators block.]
- **In the General Punctuation block:** ‖ (U+2016) [norm of a matrix], plus the various prime marks from U+2032 to U+2037
- **In the Miscellaneous Technical block:** ⌈ ⌉ ⌊ ⌋ (U+2308 to U+230B)

Unicode 3.2 adds a whopping 591 new math symbols, a product of the STIX (Scientific and Technical Information Exchange) project, an effort by a consortium of experts from the American Mathematical Society, the American Physical Society, and a number of mathematical textbook publishers.[6] Their work resulted in five new blocks being created in the Unicode encoding space:

- The **Miscellaneous Mathematical Symbols–A** (U+27C0 to U+27EF) and **Miscellaneous Mathematical Symbols–B** (U+2980 to U+29FF) blocks contain a wide variety of operators, symbols, and delimiters. Of particular note are the brackets that are disunified from similar-looking counterparts in the CJK Miscellaneous Area. The CJK brackets should be used as punctuation in East Asian text and have the "wide" East Asian width property. This property may create funny spacing in mathematical text, so new brackets specifically for mathematical use have been added.

---

6. As always with comments about Unicode 3.2, which was still in beta when this book went into production, the details may have shifted a bit by the time you read this.

- The **Supplemental Arrows–A** (U+27F0 to U+27FF) and **Supplemental Arrows–B** (U+2900 to U+297F) blocks contain new arrows and arrow-like symbols used as math operators. Of note here are a few arrows that are longer versions of arrows in the regular Arrows block. The longer arrows actually have different semantics from their shorter counterparts and can appear in the same expressions.
- The **Supplemental Mathematical Operators block** (U+2A00 to U+2AFF) contains more mathematical operators.

Together, these five blocks, along with the math symbols already in Unicode 3.1, cover almost everything that's in reasonably common use as math symbols. Of course, math symbols are like Chinese characters: New ones are constantly being coined. If one researcher invents a symbol just for his or her own use, that's generally not grounds to encode it (it's a "nonce form" and can be handled with Private Use Area code point values). If the new symbol catches on in the larger mathematical community, however, it becomes a candidate for future encoding.

Unicode 3.2 adds a number of "Symbol pieces" to the Miscellaneous Technical block (joining a few that were already there). These items include things like the upper and lower halves of brackets, braces, parentheses, integral signs, summation and product signs, and so forth, as well as extenders that can be used to lengthen them. These pieces are used to put together extra-large (or at least extra-tall) versions of characters, such as brackets to enclose arrays and vectors that are several lines long. Sometimes they are pressed into service as independent symbols in their own right. As a general rule, the symbol pieces shouldn't appear in interchange text, but they are handy as internal implementation details for drawing extra-large math symbols.

Finally, the General Punctuation block includes several special characters for mathematical use. U+2044 FRACTION SLASH can be used with regular digit characters to form typographically correct fractions. For example, the sequence

```
U+0035 DIGIT FIVE
U+2044 FRACTION SLASH
U+0038 DIGIT EIGHT
```

should be rendered like this:

$$\frac{5}{8}$$

The basic behavior calls for any unbroken string of digits before the fraction slash to be treated as the numerator and any unbroken string of digits after it to be treated as the denominator. If you want to have an integer before the fraction, you can use the zero-width space. For example,

```
U+0031 DIGIT ONE
U+200B ZERO WIDTH SPACE
U+0031 DIGIT ONE
U+2044 FRACTION SLASH
U+0034 DIGIT FOUR
```

should be rendered as

$$1\frac{1}{4}$$

Unicode 3.2 adds some new "invisible operators" to the General Punctuation block as well. They include U+2061 INVISIBLE TIMES, U+2062 FUNCTION APPLICATION, and U+2063 INVISIBLE SEPARATOR. None of these characters has a visible presentation; they exist simply to make life easier for code that's parsing a mathematical expression represented in Unicode. Consider this expression:

$$\mathbf{A}_{ij}$$

It could either be the jth element in the ith row of A, a two-dimensional matrix, or the i-times-jth element of A, a one-dimensional vector. You could put U+2063 INVISIBLE SEPARATOR between i and j to let the parser know you mean the first meaning, and U+2061 INVISIBLE TIMES between them to indicate you mean the second meaning. Similarly, if you have

$$f(x+y)$$

it could be either the application of function f to the sum of x and y, or the variable f times the sum of x and y. Again, you could use U+2062 FUNCTION AP-

PLICATION to indicate the first meaning and U+2061 INVISIBLE TIMES to indicate the second.

In all of these cases, the invisible operator isn't visible in the rendered expression, although it might cause a sufficiently sophisticated math renderer to space things a little differently.

These issues and more are covered in Proposed Draft Unicode Technical Report #25, "Unicode Support for Mathematics," which will probably be a real Technical Report by the time you read this book. It goes into great detail on the various math symbols in Unicode, proper design of fonts for mathematical use, and tips for the design of Unicode-based mathematical-typesetting software. Among the more interesting parts of PDUTR #25 are a list of proposed new character properties to help mathematical typesetters parse Unicode text (which might be adopted into future versions of the standard) and an interesting and detailed proposal for using plain Unicode text to express structured mathematical expressions, a method that is potentially both more concise and more readable than either MathML or T_EX.

Mathematical Alphanumeric Symbols

Unicode 3.1 added the Mathematical Alphanumeric Symbols block (U+1D400 to U+1D7FF in the SMP). Like the Letterlike Symbols block, it contains clones of letters and digits enhanced with various stylistic variations. Unlike the Letterlike Symbols block, the new block systematically encodes every combination of a prescribed set of characters and a prescribed set of stylistic variations (except those that are already encoded in the Letterlike Symbols block, for which corresponding holes have been left in the Mathematical Alphanumeric Symbols block). Also, unlike the characters in the Letterlike Symbols block, the characters in the Mathematical Alphanumeric Symbols block don't generally have well-established semantics.

The idea behind this block is that the characters can appear as symbols in mathematical equations and that the different styles of the same letter are actually *different* symbols meaning different things and can appear in the same equation. Using normal styled-text markup for this kind of thing can be both clumsy and heavyweight, and some text-processing operations might treat the letters in the equation as real letters. The characters in this block are unambiguously to be treated as *symbols*. Because they have different code point values, a search for, say, a bold **h** won't accidentally find an italic *h*. You also don't want a case-mapping routine to accidentally convert the symbols from one case to another (which would turn them into completely different symbols). If you transmit the equation as plain text, you wouldn't want both *h* and **h**—obviously meaning different things—to turn into a regular h, which might mean yet a third thing in addition to blurring the original distinction between **h** and *h*.

A classic example involves the Hamiltonian formula:[7]

$$\mathcal{H} = \int d\tau (\varepsilon E^2 + \mu H^2)$$

If you convert this equation to plain text and lose the distinction between the *H*s, you get a simple integral equation over the variable *H*:

$$H = \int d\tau (\varepsilon E^2 + \mu H^2)$$

Note that it's *not* acceptable to use the characters in the Mathematical Alphanumeric Symbols block to fake styled text in a plain-text environment. That's not what these characters are designed for, and that's part of the reason why they're classified as symbols rather than letters.

■ OTHER SYMBOLS AND MISCELLANEOUS CHARACTERS

Finally (puff puff puff), Unicode encodes a raft of characters that don't readily fit into any of the other categories. These include both nonmathematical symbols and other types of characters.

Musical Notation

Unicode 3.1 adds the new Byzantine Musical Symbols block (U+1D000 to U+1D0FF) and Musical Symbols block (U+1D100 to U+1D1FF), which include various musical symbols. Full-blown Western musical notation is often considered to be the most comprehensive and complex written language ever

---

7. This example is lifted straight from the text of UAX #27.

devised, and Unicode doesn't attempt to provide the means to fully specify a musical score. In particular, the specification of pitch is left to a higher-level protocol, as are most of the more complex music-related layout issues.

Unicode does provide a complete set of symbols that can be used by a higher-level protocol for representing musical notation. In plain text, these symbols can be used just as simple symbols and are useful for writing *about* music.

Some characters in the Musical Symbols block require special treatment even in plain text. To achieve flexibility in the selection of noteheads, for example, notes are built out of pieces that are treated as combining character sequences. Precomposed characters are provided for the most common cases. For example, a simple eighth note

can be represented as a single character:

```
U+1D160 MUSICAL SYMBOL EIGHTH NOTE
```

This character has a canonical decomposition:

```
U+1D158 MUSICAL SYMBOL NOTEHEAD BLACK
U+1D165 MUSICAL SYMBOL COMBINING STEM
U+1D16E MUSICAL SYMBOL COMBINING FLAG-1
```

Likewise, Unicode encodes a set of combining marks for the common articulation marks and for augmentation dots. Thus we can make our eighth note into a dotted eighth note and add an accent to it

by adding the appropriate combining characters:

```
U+1D160 MUSICAL SYMBOL EIGHTH NOTE
U+1D16D MUSICAL SYMBOL COMBINING AUGMENTATION DOT
U+1D17B MUSICAL SYMBOL COMBINING ACCENT
```

The Musical Symbols block includes several invisible formatting characters that, in combination with the musical symbols, signal the beginnings and ends of beamed groups of notes, slurs, ties, and phrase marks. For example, the sequence

```
U+1D173 MUSICAL SYMBOL BEGIN BEAM
U+1D160 MUSICAL SYMBOL EIGHTH NOTE
U+1D161 MUSICAL SYMBOL SIXTEENTH NOTE
U+1D175 MUSICAL SYMBOL BEGIN TIE
U+1D161 MUSICAL SYMBOL SIXTEENTH NOTE
U+1D174 MUSICAL SYMBOL END BEAM
U+1D173 MUSICAL SYMBOL BEGIN BEAM
U+1D161 MUSICAL SYMBOL SIXTEENTH NOTE
U+1D176 MUSICAL SYMBOL END TIE
U+1D161 MUSICAL SYMBOL SIXTEENTH NOTE
U+1D160 MUSICAL SYMBOL EIGHTH NOTE
U+1D174 MUSICAL SYMBOL END BEAM
```

would be rendered like this by a sufficiently sophisticated rendering engine:

The Byzantine Musical Symbols block encodes the symbols used by the Eastern Orthodox Church (especially the Greek Orthodox Church) for writing hymns and other liturgical music. In plain text, all of these symbols can just be treated as regular spacing symbols. Music-notation software, however, can use them as primitives for building up Byzantine musical notation.

Braille

Unicode 3.0 added the Braille Patterns block (U+2800 to U+28FF), which encoded the 256 possible eight-dot Braille patterns. Generally speaking, Braille can be thought of as a font variant of a regular script in Unicode, and text in Braille can be represented in Unicode using the regular code point values for the characters being represented in Braille. Many different standards for representing writing in Braille exist, however, and they're all different. Furthermore, it often takes more than one Braille character to write one regular character, making translation into Braille very complicated. This block is intended to allow an abstract representation of the dot patterns themselves, without worrying about the actual characters that they represent. In certain situations, the ability to represent the abstract dot patterns saves systems from having to do extra round-trip conversions back to standards that assign actual meaning to the dot patterns. Most of the time, these characters are used in internal representations; users would typically deal with text represented using the normal Unicode characters, and an internal process would convert the normal Unicode characters to the characters in this block for output on a Braille printing device. Alternatively, a Braille input device would generate the abstract characters in this block, which would then be converted by a separate process into the appropriate regular Unicode characters for the language that the user speaks.

Other Symbols

Other symbols blocks in Unicode include the following:

- The Letterlike Symbols block (U+2100 to U+214F) includes a collection of symbols that either are clones of regular letters with some special stylistic variant applied or are special combinations of multiple letters. Some are mathematical symbols (the Riemann integral [$\mathcal{R}$], the Weierstrass elliptic function [$\wp$]), some represent constants (the Planck constant [h], the first transfinite cardinal [$\aleph$]), some represent units of measure (degrees Fahrenheit [°F], ohms [Ω], angstrom units [Å]), and some are just abbreviations (care-of [℅], trademark [™], versicle [℣]).
- The Arrows block (U+2190 to U+21FF) includes various arrows. Most are mathematical or technical symbols of one kind or another, but all arrowlike symbols have been collected into this one block. Multiple semantics with the same glyph shape have been unified.
- The Miscellaneous Technical block (U+2300 to U+23FF) encompasses a variety of symbols that didn't fit into any of the other blocks. They include keycap symbols used in computer manuals, a complete set of functional symbols from the programming language APL, and symbols from other technical disciplines.

- The Control Pictures block (U+2400 to U+243F) includes glyphs that provide visible representations for the various ASCII control characters (plus two different visible representations for the space).

- The Optical Character Recognition block (U+2440 to U+245F) includes symbols from the OCR-A character set that don't correspond to regular ASCII characters, as well as the MICR (magnetic-ink character recognition) characters that are used to delimit the numbers on the bottom of a check.

- The Miscellaneous Symbols block (U+2600 to U+26FF) collects non-technical symbols that didn't fit anywhere else. They include such things as weather symbols, astrological symbols, chess pieces, playing-card suits, die faces, I-Ching trigrams, and recycling symbols.

Presentation Forms

Several blocks in Unicode gather together special presentation forms of characters whose normal encoding appears elsewhere in the standard. These characters generally exist solely for round-trip compatibility with some legacy encoding standard. Among the blocks are the following:

- The Superscripts and Subscripts block (U+2070 to U+209F) consists of digits and mathematical symbols in superscripted or subscripted form (some superscripts and subscripts are also encoded in the Latin-1 block).

- The Number Forms block (U+2150 to U+218F) consists of various pre-composed fractions and Roman numerals.

- The Enclosed Alphanumerics block (U+2460 to U+24FF) consists of letters and numbers with circles around them, with parentheses around them, or with periods after them.

- The Hangul Compatibility Jamo block (U+3130 to U+318F) contains non-conjoining clones of the characters in the regular Hangul Jamo block.

- The Enclosed CJK Letters and Months block (U+3200 to U+327F) contains CJK characters with circles or parentheses around them, plus precomposed symbols for the 12 months in Japanese.

- The CJK Compatibility block (U+3300 to U+33FF) contains a wide variety of abbreviations arranged so as to fit in single CJK character cells.

- The CJK Compatibility Ideographs block (U+F900 to U+FA5F) contains clones of characters in the CJK Unified Ideographs block. Most of these characters come from the Korean KS X 1001 standard and are identical to their counterparts in the CJK Unified Ideographs block. KS X 1001 had duplicate encodings for some Han characters that had more than one Korean pronunciation—each pronunciation received its own code point value. A number of other characters that received mistaken double encodings in other East Asian standards for other reasons also reside in this block. The characters in this block are included here solely to ensure round-trip compatibility with their original source standards—they would have been unified with their counterparts in the Unihan block otherwise.

- The Alphabetic Presentation Forms block (U+FB00 to U+FB4F) contains some common Latin and Armenian ligatures, as well as precomposed Hebrew-letter-with-point combinations used in Yiddish.

- The Arabic Presentation Forms A block (U+FB50 to U+FDFF) contains precomposed Arabic ligatures that are virtually never used.

- The Combining Half Marks block (U+FE20 to U+FE2F) contains clones of the double diacritics (diacritics that appear over two characters) from the Combining Diacritical Marks block. The clones in the Combining Half Marks block have been split in half. To represent a double diacritic over two letters using the half marks, you follow the first letter with the first half of the desired mark and then follow the second letter with the second half of the desired mark. The use of these characters is discouraged.

- The CJK Compatibility Forms block (U+FE30 to U+FE4F) contains clones of various CJK punctuation marks rotated sideways. Normally, in vertical text you use the regular punctuation marks and the rendering engine automatically turns them sideways; these characters always represent the glyphs used in vertical text for those punctuation marks.

- The Small Form Variants block (U+FE50 to U+FE6F) contains small versions of the ASCII symbols. They are included to ensure round-trip compatibility with the Taiwanese CNS 11643 standard.

- The Arabic Presentation Forms B block (U+FE70 to U+FEFF) contains characters representing the contextual glyphs used for the Arabic letters (e.g., the initial form of heh). Unlike the regular Arabic letters, these characters represent specific glyph shapes and aren't subject to contextual glyph selection. Some rendering engines use these characters for rendering the regular Arabic letters, and they can also be used to represent specific glyphs in text that discusses the Arabic letters. The byte order mark/zero-width no-break space is also encoded in this block.

- The Halfwidth and Fullwidth Forms block (U+FF00 to U+FFEF) contains full-width variants of the ASCII characters and half-width variables of selected CJK characters.

Miscellaneous Characters

Unicode also includes the following blocks of miscellaneous characters:

- The Box Drawing block (U+2500 to U+257F) contains characters that can be used to "draw" lines on a character-oriented display. This block is derived from the box-drawing characters in the IBM PC code pages that were used to draw Windows-like user interfaces in old DOS programs, and from a similar collection of box-drawing characters in the Japanese JIS standards.

- The Block Elements block (U+2580 to U+259F) contains glyphs that represent different fractions of a monospaced display cell being colored in. These characters also come from the old DOS and terminal code pages.

- The Geometric Shapes block (U+25A0 to U+25FF) contains geometric shapes. Some are used as symbols or bullets of various kinds, and they come from a variety of sources.

- The Dingbats block (U+2700 to U+27BF) contains the characters in the Zapf Dingbats typeface. Because this typeface has been included on so many laser printers, these characters (pictures, bullets, arrows, enclosed numbers, and so on) have become something of a de facto standard, and the Unicode designers decided they deserved unique code point values in Unicode.

And that concludes our guided tour of the Unicode character repertoire! Starting in Chapter 13, we'll examine how Unicode text is actually handled in software.

Unicode in Action

Implementing and Using the
Unicode Standard

13

Techniques and Data Structures for Handling Unicode Text

We've come a long way. We've looked at the general characteristics of Unicode, the Unicode encoding forms, combining character sequences and normalization forms, and the various properties in the Unicode Character Database. We've taken a long tour through the Unicode character repertoire, looking at the unique requirements of the various writing systems, including such things as bidirectional character reordering, Indic consonant clusters, diacritical stacking, and the interesting challenges associated with representing the Han characters. Now we've finally gotten to the point where we can talk about actually doing things with Unicode text.

In Part III, we'll delve into the mechanics of performing various processes on Unicode text. We'll discover how you search and sort Unicode text, perform transformations on Unicode text (including converting to other character sets, converting between encoding forms, performing Unicode normalization, mapping between cases, performing various equivalence transformations, and carrying out more generalized transformations), and draw Unicode text on the screen. We'll also see how Unicode is used on the Internet, and we'll assess the Unicode support provided in several operating systems and programming languages.

Most of the time, you don't need to know the nitty-gritty details of how to perform operations on Unicode text; the most common operations have already been coded for you and exist in a variety of operating systems and third-party libraries. You just need to know where to find the support and how to use it. Chapter 17 will also touch on this. If you're not in the business of implementing pieces of the Unicode standard, you may just want to read that chapter.

Sometimes, you might need to do things with Unicode text that aren't supported by the libraries at your disposal. This chapter will give you the ammunition to deal with your particular situation and provide a grounding in the techniques that are used in the commercial libraries to perform the more common operations on Unicode text.

■ USEFUL DATA STRUCTURES

In this chapter, we'll look at a series of useful data structures and techniques for manipulating Unicode text. Most operations on Unicode text boil down to one or more of the following:

- Testing a character for membership in some collection of characters
- Mapping from a single character to another single character, or to some other type of value
- Mapping from a variable-length sequence of characters to a single character (or, more commonly, some other single value)
- Mapping from a single character (or other type of value) to a variable-length sequence of characters (or other values)
- Mapping from a variable-length sequence of characters or values to another variable-length sequence of characters or values

More simply put, you may need to do one-to-one, one-to-many, many-to-one, or many-to-many mappings, with the universe of possible Unicode characters being the set on either side (or both sides) of the relation, and with mixes of different-length sequences and different repetition characteristics appearing in the sets. We'll look at a variety of data structures designed to solve such problems.[1]

---

1. Except where otherwise noted, the techniques described in this chapter are either from Mark Davis, "Bits of Unicode," *Proceedings of the Eighteenth International Unicode Conference,* session B11, April 27, 2001, or from my own research. "Bits of Unicode," along with Mark Davis's other papers, can be found at http://www.macchiato.com.

TESTING FOR MEMBERSHIP IN A CLASS

A very common operation, and one that can't always be handled by out-of-the-box software, is testing a character for membership in a particular category of characters. For those categories that are defined by the Unicode standard, such as lowercase letters or combining diacritical marks, the standard Unicode libraries almost always provide relevant APIs. In addition, many APIs provide functions to perform character-class-membership queries that are specific to their environment—for example, the Java class libraries provide methods for testing whether a character is legal in a Java identifier.

If the test you're seeking is available in an API library at your disposal (such as testing whether a character is a letter, digit, or whitespace character), you're usually best off using that library's functions. In some situations, however, the category or categories of characters may be specific to your application and not match the predefined categories set up by the designers of the APIs you're using. Consider the following scenarios:

- You're interested in whitespace characters, but want to include not just the Unicode space-separator characters, but also the line separator, paragraph separator, and the ASCII horizontal tab, vertical tab, line-feed, form-feed, and carriage-return characters.
- You're interested in letters, but only in certain scripts (say, Latin, Greek, Cyrillic, Arabic, and Hebrew, but not Armenian, Georgian, Syriac, Thaana, or any of the Indic characters).
- You're interested in Indic vowel signs only.
- You're filtering out any character whose use in XML files is discouraged, and you don't have access to an API that will handle this task for you.
- You're interested in valid filename or identifier characters, and your application or system defines this set in some way other than the Unicode standard. (A personal favorite example is the Dylan programming language, where identifiers may consist of not only letters and digits, but also many special characters, including !, &, *, <, >, |, ^, $, %, @, _, -, +, ~, ?, /, and =.)
- You're defining a grammar (e.g., a programming-language grammar) and the categories of characters that are significant to the grammar don't line up exactly with the Unicode categories. (A particularly interesting

example involves scanning natural-language text for linguistic boundaries, something we'll talk about in depth in Chapter 16.)

- You're interested in only the subset of Unicode characters that have equivalents in some other standard (only the Han characters in the Tongyong Hanzi, only the Hangul syllables in the KS X 1001 standard, only the Unicode characters that aren't considered "compatibility characters" according to some appropriate definition, only the Unicode characters that can be displayed with a certain font, and so on).

In all of these cases, you need a way to check an arbitrary character to see whether it is included in the set of interest (or, if you're interested in multiple sets, which particular set includes the character).

You can pursue a number of options to carry out this task. If the category is relatively close to one of the Unicode categories (or the union of several), you might use a standard API to check for membership in that category and then just special-case the exceptions in code. For instance, you could do the whitespace check with something like the following code in Java:

```java
public static boolean isWhitespace(char c) {
    // true for anything in the Zs category
    if (Character.getType(c) == Character.SPACE_SEPARATOR)
      return true;

    // true also for any of the following:
    switch (c) {
      case '\u2028':      // line separator
      case '\u2029':      // paragraph separator
      case '\n':          // line feed
      case '\t':          // tab
      case '\f':          // form feed
      case '\r':          // carriage return
      case '\u000b':      // vertical tab
        return true;

      // everything else is a non-whitespace character
      default:
        return false;
    }
}
```

This, of course, is kind of an unnecessary example, as Character. isWhitespace() accomplishes essentially the same thing. Nevertheless, it's useful for illustrative purposes.

For some sets of characters, this approach is sufficient, but it can be kind of clunky and it doesn't perform well for complicated categories. There are other simple alternatives, too. If the characters all form one or two contiguous ranges, you can do a simple range check:

```
public static boolean isASCIILetter(char c) {
    if (c >= 'A' && c <= 'Z')
      return true;
    else if (c >= 'a' && c <= 'z')
      return true;
    else
      return false;
}
```

Unfortunately, this solution also doesn't scale well.

If the characters in which you're interested all fall within, say, the ASCII block, you could use a range check followed by a simple array or bitmap lookup:

```
public static boolean isASCIIConsonant(char c) {
    if (c > 0x7f)
      return false;
    else
      return consonantFlags[c];
}
```

```
private static boolean[] consonantFlags = {
    false, false, false, false, false, false, false, false,
    false, false, false, false, false, false, false, false,
    false, false, false, false, false, false, false, false,
    false, false, false, false, false, false, false, false,
    false, false, false, false, false, false, false, false,
    false, false, false, false, false, false, false, false,
    false, false, false, false, false, false, false, false,
    false, false, false, false, false, false, false, false,
```

```
      false,  false,  true,   true,   true,   false,  true,   true,
      true,   false,  true,   true,   true,   true,   true,   false,
      true,   true,   true,   true,   true,   false,  true,   true,
      true,   true,   true,   false,  false,  false,  false,  false,
      false,  false,  true,   true,   true,   false,  true,   true,
      true,   false,  true,   true,   true,   true,   true,   false,
      true,   true,   true,   true,   true,   false,  true,   true,
      true,   true,   true,   false,  false,  false,  false,  false
};
```

Arrays and bitmaps become unwieldy quite rapidly if the characters cover more than a small subset of the Unicode characters.

The Inversion List

A nice, elegant solution for representing any arbitrary set of Unicode characters is the **inversion list**. It's a simple array, but instead of having an entry for each Unicode character or simply listing all the Unicode characters that belong to the category, the entries define *ranges* of Unicode characters.

An inversion list works as follows: The first entry in the array is the first (that is, the lowest) code point value that's in the category. The second entry in the array is the first code point value that's higher than the first entry and *not* in the set. The third entry is the first code point value that's higher than the second entry and *is* in the set, and so on. Each even-numbered entry represents the lowest code point value in a contiguous range of code point values that are in the set, and each odd-numbered entry represents the lowest code point value in a contiguous range of code point values that are *not* in the set.

The set of basic Latin letters would be represented like this:

U+0041 ('A')
U+005B ('[')
U+0061 ('a')
U+007B ('{')

Here, the first entry represents the first character in the set (the capital letter A). The set then consists of all characters with code point values between that one and the next entry (the opening square bracket). The second entry (the opening square bracket) is the beginning of a range of characters that isn't in the set. That range is terminated by the third entry (the small letter a), which marks the beginning of the next range. *That* range is terminated by the fourth entry (the opening curly brace), which marks the beginning of a range of code point values that isn't included in the set. This range extends to the top of the Unicode range, so the last character before this range (the small letter z) is the character with the highest code point value that's included in the set.

Conceptually, this idea can be depicted as follows:

Here, the brackets represent the beginnings of ranges (the entries in the table), and the shaded ranges are included in the set.

Testing a character for membership in the set is a simple matter of binary-searching the list for the character. That is, you code the binary search so that if the desired character isn't specifically mentioned, you end on the highest code point value less than the character. If you end on an even-numbered entry, the character is in the set. If you end on an odd-numbered entry, the character is not in the set.

The following Java code illustrates this algorithm:

```java
public static boolean charInSet(char c, char[] set) {
    int low = 0;
    int high = set.length;
    while (low < high) {
      int mid = (low + high) / 2;
      if (c >= set[mid])
        low = mid + 1;
      else if (c < set[mid])
        high = mid;
    }

    int pos = high - 1;

    return (pos & 1) == 0;
}
```

Armed with this new routine, we can recast our `isASCIIConsonant()` example using a much shorter table:

```
public static boolean isASCIIConsonant(char c) {
    return charInSet(c, asciiConsonants);
}


private static char[] asciiConsonants = {
    'B', 'E', 'F', 'I', 'J', 'O', 'P', 'U', 'V', '[',
    'b', 'e', 'f', 'i', 'j', 'o', 'p', 'u', 'v', '{'
};
```

An empty array represents the null set. An array with a single entry containing U+0000 represents the set containing all Unicode characters. A set containing a single character would (generally) be a two-element array where element 0 is the code point value that character and element 1 is that value plus one.

Performing Set Operations on Inversion Lists

One neat thing about this representation is that set operations on inversion lists are relatively simple to perform. A set inversion is especially simple: If the first entry in the array is U+0000, you remove it; otherwise, you add it:

```
public static char[] invertSet(char[] set) {
    if (set.length == 0 || set[0] != '\u0000') {
      char[] result = new char[set.length + 1];
      result[0] = '\u0000';
      System.arraycopy(set, 0, result, 1, set.length);
      return result;
    }
    else {
      char[] result = new char[set.length - 1];
      System.arraycopy(set, 1, result, 0, result.length);
      return result;
    }
}
```

TESTING FOR MEMBERSHIP IN A CLASS

Union and intersection are somewhat more interesting, but still fairly simple operations. To find the union of two sets, you proceed in the same way as you would to merge two sorted lists of numbers (as in a merge sort, for example). Instead of writing every entry you visit to the output, however, you write only some of them.

To decide which entries to write, you keep a running count. You start the count at 0, increment it every time you visit an even-numbered entry (i.e., the beginning of a range), and decrement it every time you visit an odd-numbered entry (i.e., the end of a range). If a particular value causes you either to increment the running count away from 0 or decrement it to 0, you write it to the output.

Suppose, for example, you have two sets: one containing the letters from A to G and M to S, and one containing the letters from E to J and U to X. The running counts would be calculated as follows:

The union of the two sets should contain all letters where the running count is greater than zero. When you see A, for example, the running count is incremented to 1 and you write A to the result set. When you see E, the running count is incremented to 2 and you don't write anything. When you see H, the running count is decremented to 1 and you still don't write anything. When you see K, however, the count is decremented to 0, which causes you to write K to the result set.

You must watch for an important wrinkle here: what to do if the entries from the two lists are equal. Suppose, for example, you have two sets: one containing the letters from A to E, and one containing the letters from F to K:

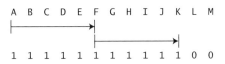

The letter F occurs in both sets: as the endpoint of the first set (the first character after the range it contains) and as the starting point of the other set. When merging the two arrays, you will therefore come across a situation where you're looking at two Fs. If both are even-numbered entries or both are odd-numbered entries, you can process them in any order: Only one of them will decrement the running count to 0 or increment it away from 0, and it doesn't matter which one.

If, as in our example, one is an odd-numbered entry and the other is an even-numbered entry, you have a problem. If you process the odd-numbered entry first, you might decrement the count to zero and then immediately increment the count away from zero again. In our example, this action would cause F to be written to the result set twice. The result then consists of two ranges: the range from A to E and the range from F to K. We still find the right answer, but the result wastes space. What you really want is a single range, running from A to K. Processing the even-numbered entry first will correctly coalesce the two ranges into a single range and prevent the Fs from being written to the result set.

Here's what the union function looks like in Java:

```java
public static char[] union(char[] a, char[] b) {
    char[] tempResult = new char[a.length + b.length];
    int pA = 0;
    int pB = 0;
    int pResult = 0;
    int count = 0;
    char c;
    int p;

    // go through the two sets as though you're merging them
    while (pA < a.length && pB < b.length) {

        // if the lower entry is in the first array, or if the
        // entries are equal and this one's the start of a range,
        // consider the entry from the first array next
        if (a[pA] < b[pB] || (a[pA] == b[pB] && (pA & 1) == 0)) {
            p = pA;
            c = a[pA++];
        }
```

```
  // otherwise, consider the entry from the second array next
  else {
    p = pB;
    c = b[pB++];
  }

  // if the entry is the start of a range (i.e., an even-numbered
  // entry), increment the running count. If the count was zero
  // before incrementing, also write the entry to the result
  // set.
  if ((p & 1) == 0) {
    if (count == 0)
      tempResult[pResult++] = c;
    ++count;
  }

  // if the entry is the end of a range (i.e., an odd-numbered
  // entry), decrement the running count. If this makes the
  // count zero, also write the entry to the result set.
  else {
    --count;
    if (count == 0)
      tempResult[pResult++] = c;
  }
}

// figure out how big the result should really be
int length = pResult;

// if we stopped in the middle of a range, decrement the count
// before figuring out whether there are extra entries to write
if ((pA != a.length && (pA & 1) == 1)
      || (pB != b.length && (pB & 1) == 1))
  --count;

// if, after the adjustment, the count is 0, then all
// entries from the set we haven't exhausted also go into
// the result
if (count == 0)
  length += (a.length - pA) + (b.length - pB);
```

```
    // copy the results into the actual result array (they may
    // include the excess from the array we hadn't finished
    // examining)
    char[] result = new char[length];
    System.arraycopy(tempResult, 0, result, 0, pResult);
    if (count == 0) {
        // only one of these two calls will do anything
        System.arraycopy(a, pA, result, pResult, a.length - pA);
        System.arraycopy(b, pB, result, pResult, b.length - pB);
    }
    return result;
}
```

The preceding code contains an optimization: Rather than continue through the loop until we've exhausted both input sets, we drop out of the loop as soon as we've exhausted one of them. This approach avoids some extra checks in the first `if` statement to account for the possibility that one of the input lists is exhausted and speeds up that loop. If, after dropping out of the loop, our running count is greater than 0, the result set ends with an even-numbered entry and every larger value is included in the set; we can safely ignore the entries we haven't examined yet. If, on the other hand, the running count *is* 0, we can just copy all of the entries we haven't looked at yet directly into the result.

The code to perform an intersection is identical to the code for performing the union, except for the following differences:

- Instead of writing a value to the output when the count is incremented away from 0 or decremented to 0, you write a value to the output when the count is incremented to 2 or decremented away from 2.
- If the entries from the two input sets are equal, you process the *odd-numbered* entry (i.e., decrement the running count) first.
- In the optimization at the end, instead of copying the extra entries from the nonexhausted list into the result when the count is 0, you do so when the count is 2.

Other operations can be built up from the primitives described previously. A set difference is simply an inversion followed by an intersection. To add a single character, first turn it into an inversion list (to make *c* into an inversion list, create a two-element array consisting of *c* followed by *c* + 1) and then take the union of the new set and the set to which you're adding. To remove a single character, turn that character into an inversion list and do a set difference. Optimized implementations of these operations are certainly possible, but are left as an exercise.

Inversion lists have a number of desirable characteristics. Chief among them is their compactness. The entire set of ideographic characters in Unicode (as defined in PropList.txt) can be represented as follows:

```
{ 0x3006, 0x3008, 0x3021, 0x302A, 0x3038, 0x303B, 0x3400, 0x4DB6,
  0x4E00, 0x9FA6, 0xF900, 0xFA2E, 0x20000, 0x2A6D7, 0x2F800, 0x2FA1D }
```

That's a pretty compact way to represent a list of 71,503 characters.

Similarly, the entire set of Latin letters (ignoring IPA characters and full-width variants) compresses to the following:

```
{ 0x0041, 0x005B, 0x0061, 0x007B, 0x00C0, 0x00D7, 0x00D8, 0x00F7,
  0x00F8, 0x0220, 0x0222, 0x0234, 0x1E00, 0x1E9C, 0x1EA0, 0x1EFA }
```

Again, 662 characters compress to 16 entries.

Inversion lists are also relatively fast to search and easy to modify. Unfortunately, they do have some drawbacks. First, searching such a list is fairly quick, unless you're doing a lot of searches in succession, as you might in a very tight loop while iterating over a long string. In this case, you need a data structure that's truly optimized for fast lookup. We'll look at just such a beast later in this chapter.

Second, because they don't operate on groups of characters, inversion lists can operate on the full Unicode range only if they store their code point values as UTF-32 units. Thus a Unicode 3.1-compatible inversion list in Java has to be an array of int, not an array of char, as in the previous example code. Also, you may have to perform conversions from UTF-16 to UTF-32 before you can do a lookup. In Java, for example, strings are sequences of UTF-16 code units; if you encounter a surrogate pair, you must convert it to a single UTF-32 code unit before you can look it up in an inversion list. This requirement can make inversion lists less than ideal and force the use of an alternative data structure that can handle variable-length sequences of code units and thus work on UTF-16 in its native form.

Finally, the benefit of the compression disappears if you have long stretches of code point values that alternate between being in the set and not being in the set. For example, an inversion list representing the set of capital letters in the Latin Extended A block would look like this:

```
{ 0x0100, 0x0101, 0x0102, 0x0103, 0x0104, 0x0105, ... }
```

If the inversion list is being used in only a transient manner (say, to derive character categories for a parser), this limitation may be acceptable. For longer-lived lists of characters, alternative representations can provide better compression.

■ MAPPING SINGLE CHARACTERS TO OTHER VALUES

Testing a character for membership in a class is really just a special case of mapping from a single character to a single value—in essence, you're mapping from a character (or, more accurately, a code unit) to a Boolean value. Most of the time, however, you want to map to something with more possible values than a Boolean value. For example, instead of checking whether a character is a member of some class, you may want to perform one operation to see which of several mutually exclusive classes a given character belongs to (as opposed to checking each category one by one for the character, as you might have to do if the categories overlapped). There are plenty of other uses for this kind of thing: mapping characters from uppercase to lowercase or to a case-independent representation;[2] looking up a character's combining class, bi-di category, or numeric value; or (sometimes) converting from Unicode to some other encoding standard.

Inversion Maps

One possible approach is to use an **inversion map**. An inversion map is an extension of an inversion list. With a regular inversion list, the value being

---

2. Actually, this isn't always a one-to-one operation, but we'll ignore that for the time being.

mapped to is implicit: Even-numbered entries represent ranges of characters that map to "true," and odd-numbered entries represent ranges of characters that map to "false."

You can extend this mapping by storing a separate parallel array that contains the values to which you want to map. Each entry in the main list contains the first code unit in a range of code units that map to the same output value. The range extends until the beginning of the next range (i.e., the code unit value in the next entry), and the value to which all the characters map is stored in the corresponding entry in the parallel array.

For example, the character categories for the characters in the ASCII range could be represented in two parallel arrays:

```
U+0000            Cc (control character)
U+0020            Zs (space separator)
U+0021 (!)        Po (other punctuation)
U+0024 ($)        Sc (currency symbol)
U+0025 (%)        Po (other punctuation)
U+0028 (()        Ps (starting punctuation)
U+0029 ())        Pe (ending punctuation)
U+002A (*)        Po (other punctuation)
U+002B (+)        Sm (math symbol)
U+002C (,)        Po (other punctuation)
U+002D (-)        Pd (dash punctuation)
U+002E (.)        Po (other punctuation)
U+0030 (0)        Nd (decimal-digit number)
U+003A (:)        Po (other punctuation)
U+003C (<)        Sm (math symbol)
U+003F (?)        Po (other punctuation)
U+0041 (A)        Lu (uppercase letter)
U+005B ([)        Ps (starting punctuation)
U+005C (\)        Po (other punctuation)
U+005D (])        Pe (ending punctuation)
U+005E (^)        Sk (modifier symbol)
U+005F (_)        Pc (connector punctuation)
U+0060 (`)        Sk (modifier symbol)
U+0061 (a)        Ll (lowercase letter)
U+007B ({)        Ps (starting punctuation)
U+007C (|)        Sm (math symbol)
```

```
U+007D (})              Pe (ending punctuation)
U+007E (~)              Sm (math symbol)
U+007F                  Cc (control character)
```

It's rather ugly because the punctuation marks and symbols in the ASCII range are scattered across several Unicode categories. Nevertheless, it manages to compress a single 128-element array into a pair of 29-element arrays.

The Compact Array

The inversion map works fairly well for a lot of tasks, but if you must perform frequent lookups in the table, this approach isn't the most effective option. If the compression leads to a list containing only a few entries, lookup is pretty fast, and the speed of lookup degrades fairly gradually as the list gets longer. Even so, there's no escaping the fact that it's faster to go straight to the entry you want than to binary-search the array for it (even if that, in turn, is much faster than a linear search), and that constant-time lookup performance is (generally speaking) better than O(log n) performance. If you're doing a lot of lookups in a very tight loop, as you will when working with a large body of text (e.g., Unicode normalization, conversion between Unicode and some other encoding, glyph selection for rendering, bidirectional reordering, searching and sorting), this difference can become quite large. Just how large, of course, depends on what you're doing—both the number of lookups required by the algorithm and the nature of the table of data make a big difference.

A regular array—the reasonable way to do most of these operations on single-byte non-Unicode text—would be prohibitively huge when you're operating on Unicode text. With Unicode 3.0 and earlier, you'd need an array with 65,536 entries (assuming you don't have to worry about the private-use code points in planes 15 and 16). With Unicode 3.1, you'd need an array with a whopping 1,114,112 entries. True, hardware is getting cheaper and more complex, and memory and storage capacities are getting bigger, but this array size is still ridiculous, especially if you need more than one lookup table.

Fortunately, a simple and elegant technique exists for compressing a 65,536- (or 1,114,112-) element array that still offers fast constant-time lookup performance. Lookup with this technique takes a little more than twice the time associated with a straight array lookup, but this speed is still blazingly fast, and it's a constant time for every item in the array. This basic technique (and various others based on it) forms the cornerstone of most of the common algorithms for manipulating Unicode text, and it's well worth understanding. This technique goes by a number of different names, but for our purposes here, we'll refer to it by the rather unimaginative name of **compact array**.

To understand how a compact array works, consider the following array:

This array has 24 elements. Obviously, there's no real need to compress a 24-element array, but it makes it easy to see what's going on. First, you (conceptually) break the array into a number of equally sized blocks. For the purposes of this example, we'll use four-element blocks, although this choice would do you no good at all in real life. Now you have something that looks like this:

If a block ends with the same set of elements that begins the next block (or if the blocks are simply the same), those elements can share the same storage. For example, the first block ends with "3 3" and the second block begins with "3 3," so you can stack them on top of each other:

The second block and the third block are identical, so you can stack them on top of each other:

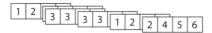

If you continue in this way, stacking adjacent blocks that have elements in common, you end up with something that looks like this:

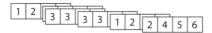

So we've compressed our original 24-element array to 11 elements. To access the elements in the array, you must use an external index that tells you where in the compressed array the beginning of each block is found. Thus the uncompressed data structure really looks like this:

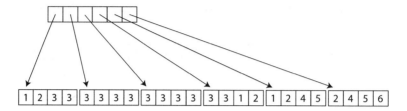

The compressed data structure really looks like this:

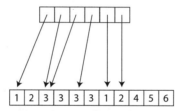

In our example array, you save 13 elements in the data array, but you need a new six-element index array, for a net savings of seven array elements. With real Unicode-based tables, the compression is generally much greater.

Looking up a character in a compact array is relatively simple. The most-significant bits of the code point give you the offset into the index array, and the least-significant bits of the code point give you the offset into the data block pointed to by the index-array entry (Figure 13.1).

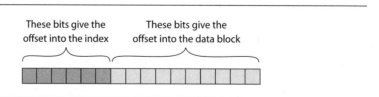

Figure 13.1   Indexing into a compact array

The code to perform a lookup into a compact array is quite simple:

```
result = data[index[c >> INDEX_SHIFT] + (c & BLOCK_MASK)];
```

In this code snippet, c is the character for which we're looking up a value, and index and data are the index and data arrays, respectively. INDEX_SHIFT is the number of bits in the character that constitute the offset into the data block (and, hence, the number of bits by which you shift the code point value to the right to get the offset into the index block). BLOCK_MASK is a mask that isolates the offset into the data block and is always equal to (1 << INDEX_SHIFT) - 1. The lookup process consists of two array lookups, a shift, an AND operation, and an addition. In fact, if you're willing to have the index array include four-byte elements (it's usually necessary for the index elements to be only two bytes), you can store actual pointers in the index array (at least in C or C++) and eliminate the addition. This lookup compiles extremely efficiently on almost all programming languages and machine architectures.

Note that the >> in the preceding example is a *logical* (i.e., zero-filling) right shift. In C, c must be of an unsigned integral type or a type that's at least a bit wider than necessary to hold the code point value, so the sign bit is always zero. In Java, this problem shouldn't occur, because char is an unsigned type, and int is bigger than necessary to hold a UTF-32 value (which is actually 21 bits wide—even a full UCS-4 value would be only 31 bits wide). If you had the code point value stored in a short, however, you'd have to remember to use the >>> operator to do the shift.

There are several important things to note about using compact arrays. First, this technique works best either on sparsely populated arrays (i.e., arrays where the vast majority of elements are 0), arrays with long stretches of identical values or long stretches of identical patterns of repeating values, and other arrays with high levels of redundancy. Fortunately, virtually all Unicode-related lookup tables either fit this profile or can be represented in a way that does meet these criteria. For example, mappings between code point values, such as conversions from Unicode to other encodings and case-mapping tables, don't lend themselves to compression unless the tables are sparsely populated, and then the populated blocks can't be coalesced. Turning these into tables of numeric offsets that are added to the input value to produce the output value may turn long stretches of different values into long stretches of the same value, permitting compression.

Second, nothing about the design of this data structure requires that the data blocks appear in the same order in the compressed data array as they did in the original uncompressed array, or that blocks that are coalesced together be adjacent in the original array. Most real-life tables achieve most of their compression from coalescing identical blocks in the original uncompressed array. The unpopulated space in a sparse array, for example, turns into a single unpopulated block in the compressed representation, even though not all of the unpopulated blocks in the original array were next to one another. (Often, part of the unpopulated block can be doubled up with the unpopulated space in one or two of the populated blocks.)

Third, it's impossible to make generalizations about the optimal value for INDEX_SHIFT. As INDEX_SHIFT gets larger, the individual blocks in the data array grow as well, but the index gets smaller. As it gets smaller, the individual blocks shrink (possibly permitting more of them to be doubled up in the compressed representation), but the index gets longer, offsetting those gains. If INDEX_SHIFT goes either to zero or to the total number of bits in the character code, you're simply performing a simple array lookup again, as either the index size or the block size goes to zero in that case. Generally, for a 16-bit code point value, values of INDEX_SHIFT between 6 and 10 work best.

Fourth, although many methods are used to compress the data in a compact array, none is particularly fast. These techniques don't work well for tables of data that change frequently at run time. Rather, they work best when the tables can be built once at run time and then used repeatedly, or, better yet, when the tables can be calculated as part of the development of the software that uses them and simply used at run time (i.e., tables that don't depend on data that's available only at run time, such as the tables of data that are defined in the Unicode standard).

Generally, the fastest method of compressing a compact array is to just pick an INDEX_SHIFT and worry about coalescing only identical blocks. More compression can be obtained by coalescing half-blocks or quarter-blocks or by examining adjacent blocks for identical heads and tails. The only way to achieve the absolutely optimal amount of compression for an arbitrary collection of data is to try every possible ordering of the blocks and examine the adjacent pairs for identical heads and tails (this effort would also involve trying all of the possible `INDEX_SHIFT` values). Most of the time, this extra effort isn't worth the trouble, and coalescing identical blocks or half-blocks (and maybe looking for identical heads and tails in blocks adjacent in the original ordering) will provide good results. Fortunately, the algorithm used to compress the data doesn't affect the algorithm used to look up values in the compressed array, nor does it affect the performance.[3]

Two-Level Compact Arrays

A simple compact array works well with UTF-16 values, but this choice leaves out all of the new characters in Unicode 3.1 (and the private-use characters in planes 15 and 16). If your application can ignore these characters, you can use a simple compact array. If you need to support the characters in the supplementary planes, however, a simple compact array doesn't work so well. When you're trying to partition a 21-bit value into two groups, you tend to end up with either very long data blocks, making compression more difficult, or very long indexes, making compression less relevant.

One approach to dealing with this problem is to use a *two-level* compact array. Instead of having a single index array, you have two such arrays. In other words, you apply the same compression techniques to the index that you apply to the data array. The first index points to a block of values in the second index, which in turn points to a block of values in the data array (Figure 13.2).

The code point value is broken into three groups instead of two. The most-significant bits give the offset into the first index, the next set of bits gives the offset into the appropriate block of the second index, and the least-significant bits give the offset of the result in the appropriate block of the data array (Figure 13.3).

Performing the lookup into a two-level compact array is a little more complicated and a little slower than the lookup for a regular compact array:

```
result = data[index2[index1[c >> INDEX1_SHIFT] + (c & INDEX2_MASK)
>> INDEX2_SHIFT] + (c & DATA_MASK)];
```

---

3. In some processor architectures and programming languages, lookup can be made a little faster if you use an `INDEX_SHIFT` of 8, but the improvement is minuscule.

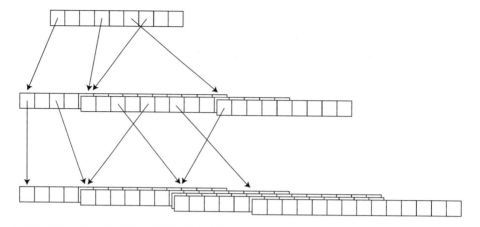

Figure 13.2 Two-level compact array

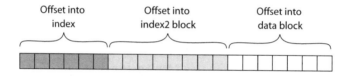

Figure 13.3 Offsets into a two-level compact array

Instead of two array lookups, a shift, a mask, and an addition, this lookup takes three array lookups, two shifts, two masks, and two additions. That is, it requires nine operations instead of five, but is still quite fast and still constant time.

■ MAPPING SINGLE CHARACTERS TO MULTIPLE VALUES

Compact arrays are still basically just that—arrays to which compression and indexing have been applied. Like regular arrays, they are best suited to storing values that are all the same size. They also work best when the values being mapped to are relatively small; a big array of 32-byte values, for example, can become quite unwieldy.

But what if you're looking up a value that is large, or could be of variable length? A couple of techniques can be used.

If the total universe of values that can be mapped to is relatively small, you can save space without imposing too huge a performance penalty by offloading the target values into a separate array (or other data structure). The target values in the compact array would just be indexes into the auxiliary array containing the values.

For large, complex data structures, you could go so far as to have the entries in the compact array's data array act as pointers to the target data structures. The major drawback is that the data array would have to hold 32-bit values, which could make it pretty big if you couldn't achieve much compression. A popular alternative is to use an auxiliary array to hold the pointers. The data elements in the compact array then need only be big enough to hold the indexes into the auxiliary array: 16 or even eight bits.

If you're mapping to string values, and especially if most of the resultant strings are short, it's often useful to store the target strings in one big array. This approach cuts down on memory-manager overhead (on most systems, every independent block of memory has some additional amount of memory, usually eight or more bytes, allocated to it as a block header that stores housekeeping information for the memory manager). The compact array can then contain offsets into the big string block or, if you're willing to have the compact array map to 32-bit values, actual pointers to the individual strings in the memory block. This technique works best in C and C++, where pointers can point into the interiors of memory blocks, where character strings are null-terminated, and where a string is just a pointer to an arbitrary run of character data.

Exception Tables

A common situation might be one where you're generally mapping to a fixed-length value, but occasionally target values are longer. Typically, this case arises when you're mapping to strings and the vast majority of the resulting strings are single characters. You can run into it, for example, doing language-sensitive case mapping, Unicode normalization, language-sensitive comparison, or mapping Unicode to a variable-length target encoding. In these cases, you should consider implementing an optimization.

In this optimization, you make the data array elements be the same size as the most common result values. Then you designate some range of the result values as sentinel values. The nonsentinel values serve as results; the sentinel values are parsed in some way to derive result values. Usually this technique means performing some mathematical transformation on them to get an offset into an auxiliary array containing the large or variable-length results.

Suppose you're mapping single Unicode characters to either characters or strings, with characters predominating. You'd set up the compact array to store characters, but set aside a range of character values as sentinel values. An obvious range to use for this purpose is the range from U+D800 to U+F800, the surrogate space and the private-use area. If you look up a character in the compact array and it's outside this range, then the character is your result. If it's inside this range, you subtract 0xD800 from it to get the offset into an auxiliary data structure holding the strings, such as the one we looked at earlier. If any of the single characters in the private-use area is a result value, you treat it as a one-character string: It appears in the auxiliary data structure with the longer strings, and the entry in the compact array is the properly munged reference to its position in the auxiliary structure.

Even if you're simply mapping single characters to single characters, this technique can prove useful. A generalized mapping to Unicode characters would have to use a data array with 32-bit elements, as some of the result characters might be supplementary-plane characters. If, as is usually the case, BMP characters dominate your result set, you can use a data array with 16-bit elements and store the supplementary characters in a separate array. You can then store the auxiliary array offsets in the compact array using the munging technique described above.

Another approach sets aside only one value in the compact array's result set to act as a sentinel value. If you get something other than this value from the compact-array lookup, it's the result. If you get the sentinel value, you repeat the lookup operation in a slower data structure that holds only the exceptional values.

Consider, for example, the Unicode bi-di categories. There are 19 of these categories, but six categories consist of only one character. If we collapse them down to a single "category," we get 14 bi-di categories. We can then represent each bi-di category as a 4-bit value. We could squish the bi-di categories for two characters into a single byte, potentially halving the size of a table of bi-di categories. Bi-di reordering code would normally have a section of code that looks up the category for each character and takes some action based on the result. If this code looked up the category and got "single character category," it could just look at the input character itself to decide what to do.

In other cases, when you get the "exceptional character" value, you'd refer to an "exception table." This slower data structure, such as a hash table or a sorted array of character–result pairs, would hold the results for the exceptional characters. You might pay a performance penalty, but you'd have to pay it for only a small and relatively infrequent subset of the characters.

We'll see numerous examples of these techniques in the chapters that follow.

◼ MAPPING MULTIPLE CHARACTERS TO OTHER VALUES

In some situations, you want to map a key that may consist of *more than one* character to some other value. If, for example, Unicode decomposition entails mapping single characters to variable-length strings, Unicode composition involves mapping variable-length strings to single characters. Even when you're consistently mapping single characters to single characters (or to some other fixed-length value), a UTF-16–based system (or a system that wants to save table space) might choose to treat supplementary-plane characters as pairs of surrogate code units, effectively treating single characters as "strings."

Like mapping single characters (or other values) to variable-length strings, mapping variable-length strings to single characters (or other values) is something we'll encounter frequently in the coming chapters. It's important, for example, for canonical composition, language-sensitive comparison, character encoding conversion, and transliteration (or input-method handling).

Exception Tables and Key Closure

There are a couple of broad methods for approaching this problem. If the vast majority of your keys are single characters and you have relatively few longer keys, you can use the exception-table approach described in the previous section. That is, you can look up a character in a compact array and either get back a real result or a sentinel value. The sentinel value tells you that the character you looked up is the first character in one or more multiple-character keys. You'll have to look at more characters to determine the answer, and you'll be doing the lookup in a separate exception table designed for multiple-character keys.

Again, you can take many different approaches in designing the exception table. The simplest is a hash table or a sorted list of key-value pairs.

Let's assume that you use a sorted list of key-value pairs. If you can set aside more than one sentinel value in your result set, you can use the sentinel value to refer directly to the zone in the exception table that contains the keys that start with the character you already looked up. Each successive character then moves forward in the exception table until you reach a sequence that isn't in the table (i.e., it does not exist as a key or as the beginning of a key). At this point, the last entry you see gives the answer, and you start over with the last character you were examining, looking it up in the main table again.

This concept can be made clearer with an example. Imagine you're implementing code to allow someone to input Russian text with a regular Latin keyboard. As you type, characters will be converted from Latin letters to their Cyrillic equivalents. A number of Cyrillic letters are normally transliterated into Latin using more than one letter. For example, consider this group of letters:[4]

с	→	s
ш	→	sh
щ	→	shch
ц	→	c
ч	→	ch

If you type an "s," we don't know whether you mean for c to appear on the screen or will type "h" next to get ш. For that matter, if you type "sh," you might mean for ш to appear on the screen or you might follow it with "ch" to get щ. If "sh," "ch," and "shch" were the only three multiple-keystroke se-

---

4. This example is taken directly from Mark Davis, "Bits of Unicode," op. cit.

quences you had to worry about, then, you'd wind up with an exception table
that looked like this:

| c => Ц |
| ch => ч |
| s => C |
| sh => Ш |
| shch => Щ |

The main compact array would contain the mappings for all other Latin letters,
but would contain pointers into this table for "s" and "c." That explains why
you need entries for "s" and "c" themselves: Their mappings can't appear in the
main table; the main table contains the signal that "s" and "c" are exceptional
characters.

If the user types "s," the main mapping table points you to line 3 of the exception table:

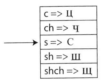

You buffer the "s" in preparation for getting more characters. Now the user
types "h," and you add this character to the buffer. The buffer now contains
"sh." You scan forward in the exception table looking for the first key that begins with "sh." It's the next entry, so now you're pointing there:

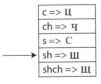

Next, the user types "a." You add it to the buffer (which now contains "sha")
and scan forward for the first entry that starts with "sha." The next entry is
"shch," which comes after "sha," so "sha" isn't in the table. You output the result

for the last key ("sh"), which gives you ш, and then you go back and look up "a" in the main lookup table. Because "a" isn't an exceptional character, you get an immediate result—a—and output that. You've now correctly mapped "sha" to "ша."

This algorithm breaks down if the user types "shca." After processing "shc," the buffer contains "shc" and you're pointing at the entry for "shch," the first entry that begins with "shc":

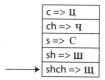

c => Ц
ch => ч
s => C
sh => Ш
→ shch => Щ

If the next letter typed is "a," you're already past where it would go in the table, so it clearly does not appear in the table. Your code would do one of two things. If it's designed to always scan forward, it will behave as though you typed "shcha," outputting the result for the current entry ("щ") and then looking up "a" again to get "ща." Alternatively, it could know you were already past the entry you were looking for and use the *last* entry that matched, giving "ш." If it uses the second approach, the code now has to be smart enough to know that *two* input characters haven't been accounted for, and it must go back and look up *both* of them in the main table.

As you see, the code has to be much more complicated to account for the cases where you have to go back and reprocess more than one character. Otherwise, you have to change the table.

Changing the table is the cleaner solution. The principle involved in changing the table is called **key closure**. The principle of key closure dictates that for every key that's represented in the exception table, every *prefix* of that key must also appear in the table. For our example, this means that if "shch" is in the table, "s," "sh," and "shc" must all occur in the table. We solve our bug by including "shc" as a key in the table:

c => Ц
ch => ч
s => C
sh => Ш
shc => ШЦ
shch => Щ

If you type "shca," then, you'll end up on the entry for "shc" when you realize "shca" isn't in the table, output шц, and go back and look up just "a," adding a to the output. You output the correct answer for that series of characters, which is шца.

Tries as Exception Tables

Modeling the exception table as a simple array of pairs of strings is easy, but it's not terribly efficient. As you walk through the table, you must keep track of all the characters you've seen before and perform a series of string comparisons to get to the right entry. If the keys and the table are both short, these operations probably won't matter much. For more complicated tables, all of the lookups can be a pain, however. You can actually change things so that each key is only one character long. To do so, you recursively apply the exception-table rule. The entry in the main table has a sentinel character indicating that this character may be the first character of a multicharacter key and referring to an exception table. You look up the *next* character from the input in the exception table. This lookup will produce either a real result or a sentinel value telling you to go to *another* exception table and look up the *next* character from the input *there*. The process continues until you land on a real result. For our Russian example, the resulting data structure looks like this:

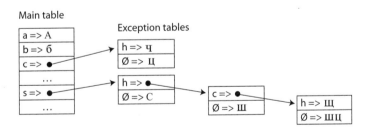

Each entry contains either a result or a reference to an exception table. If you find a reference to a new exception table, you get the next character and use it to find the entry in the next table. If you don't find the character, you end up on the ∅ entry. It tells you that the previous character was the last one in the key and that the character you're on now is the beginning of a new key. The result is the result for the key, and you go back and start the lookup over in the main table with the current character.

Suppose the input is "shca." You read the "s" and look up "s" in the main table.

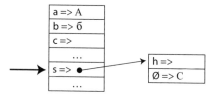

This entry would refer you to the "s" table. You read the "h" and look it up in the "s" table.

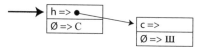

This would take you to the "sh" table. You read the "c" from the input and look it up in the "sh" table, taking you to the "shc" table.

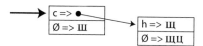

You read "a" from the input. The "shc" table doesn't have an entry for "a," so you use the "Ø" entry.

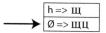

It tells you that "щц" is the output to use for "shc," and that you have to go back to the main table and look up "a" again there.

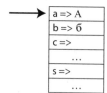

You look up "a" in the main table and get "a." Now you're done.

You have to look up a character twice only if you hit a $\varnothing$ entry. Suppose, for example, the input was "cha." You read "c" from the input, look it up in the main table, and find the reference to the "c" table. You read "h" from the input, look it up in the "c" table, and find "ч."

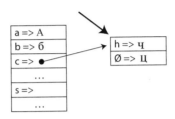

This is your output, and you've used all the characters you've seen so far. You read "a" from the input and look it up in the main table, where you find "a." This is your output. You've now read all the characters from the input and produced "ча" as your output, which is correct. Along the way, you didn't have to look up anything twice.

You can eliminate the $\varnothing$ entries, and the double lookups they cause, by simply having every exception table include an entry for each possible input character. This approach also lets you use a simple array of some kind, rather than an associative data structure—you basically use the same data structure used for the main table for the exception tables—but this array will typically get quite large.

You also don't need the $\varnothing$ entries if you don't need key closure. That is, if you never have a key that's a substring of another key, you don't need to repeat the lookup. For example, if your lookup is UTF-16–based and you find a high surrogate, it's meaningless on its own. You must look at the next code unit to know what to do. As long as malformed UTF-16 (i.e., unmatched surrogates) isn't possible, you'll never have to do a repeated lookup and you don't need the $\varnothing$ entry.

If you're experienced in text processing or if you recall your data structures class, you've already recognized that the data structure described here is a trie. A **trie** is a tree structure in which each node in the tree points directly or indirectly to the results for all keys that share a common prefix. In a character-based trie, each level of the tree corresponds to a character in the key, and the number of nodes you traverse to look up the result for a key equals the number of characters in the key. (Actually, as we saw in the previous example, if keys may be substrings of other keys, the number of nodes you visit matches the number of characters in the key plus one.) The word "trie" comes from "information re- *trie*val," but is usually pronounced "try" to distinguish it from "tree."

Many different ways of representing a trie in memory are possible. In our example, each "exception table" is a node in the trie, so the nodes are repre- sented by key–value arrays that you walk through linearly. These nodes could be split into linked lists, which turns the overall structure into a binary tree. Bi- nary trees work especially well when the data in the trie must be modified fre- quently. The array-based representation shown in the examples works more or less the same way as a binary-tree representation but is more compact and use- ful when the data in the trie won't change. An alternative that gives a faster lookup time and works well when the trie is being modified is to split each indi- vidual node into a binary tree instead of a simple linked list. This technique turns the overall structure into a **ternary tree**.

You could also expand each node outward into a regular flat array holding an entry for each possible character. This option speeds up lookup by quite a bit (at least when each node has many entries), but generally carries a fairly heavy price in terms of compactness. For a Unicode-based data structure, where each character could possibly be any of more than a million choices, it obviously isn't practical unless you come up with some kind of compaction scheme for the nodes.

Tries as the Main Lookup Table

This point returns us to the compact array. You might have noticed that the compact array is essentially a trie. You do a lookup based on part of the key, which takes you to a spot where you do another lookup based on another part of the key, and so on, until you've either used up the whole key or reached a point where the rest of the key doesn't matter (i.e., where the result will be the same no matter what the rest of the key is). Two things make the compact array dif- ferent from a more general trie:

- Every branch has the same number of levels, so you always know that the result of the first (or, for a two-level compact array, the first and second) lookup is a pointer to the next node of the trie, and that the last lookup returns a real result value.

- Because of this fact, the chunks of the key that are considered at each node lookup don't have to be the same size. Asymmetrical partitions of the character for lookup in a compact array are actually more the norm than the exception.

These considerations suggest a number of variations on the basic trie idea that might be useful in different situations.

Pruning Branches   In a normal compact array, you always do a lookup in the index array followed by a lookup in the data array. If the value of every entry in a particular block is the same, you can save space by storing that value directly into the index array and not allocating space for it in the data array. Keep in mind the following caveats about this technique:

- This technique works best for tables that have a lot of blocks that consist only of one value, but those blocks don't all contain the *same* value. If every uniform block contains the same value as the other uniform blocks (i.e., you have a sparsely populated array where each block is either all zeros or something interesting), this technique saves you (at most) one block's worth of entries in the data array.
- This technique works well when the long stretches of the same value tend to begin and end on block boundaries. If a range of the same value begins halfway into one block, spans three whole blocks, and ends three quarters of the way into another block, pruning the branches saves only about a quarter of a block's worth of space. The ends of the long stretch must still appear in the data array. You can coalesce them so that you need only as many as are in the longest segment (in our example, three-quarters of a block). Since you can do this anyway if the homogeneous blocks are included, you save only the difference between the longest stretch without homogeneous blocks (three quarters of a block) and the longest stretch with them (a whole block).

  The savings could be even less if several stretches of the same value don't begin and end on or near block boundaries. You can manage this issue by fiddling with the block size, but that can introduce other problems.
- If the result values and the pointers to blocks of the data array aren't naturally disjoint, you may have to munge them in some way to make them

disjoint or make the array elements bigger. This change could trump any savings in the number of elements.

- The lookup code must check after each lookup to see whether it's done. This check can impose a serious performance penalty unless most of your lookups occur along the pruned branches.

- Pruning of branches is rarely worth the trouble for a simple one-level compact array, unless space is at a premium and the size of the data you're trying to compress will shrink dramatically if you prune. It has more utility as the number of levels in the trie increases.

Using the Same Array for the Data and Index Values   This strategy doesn't buy you anything in a single-level compact array. In fact, if the elements in the data array are smaller than the ones in the index, it hurts performance. As with pruning of branches, it might help with multilevel lookups. In a sparsely populated, two-level compact array, for example, you could double up the zeros in the indexes with the zeros in the data array and save some space. This case might be worth the effort, but generally the win here comes with tables where you traverse a varying number of nodes depending on the key.

Basing Lookup on UTF-8 or UTF-16   If you base your lookup on UTF-16 code unit values, you can fix matters so that you can do two array lookups for most characters but perform a third lookup only when you encounter a supplementary-plane character (of course, unless you do branch pruning, you'll actually need *four* lookups when you hit a supplementary-plane character, but given their rarity in most text, this might be a good optimization).

If you do the lookup based on the UTF-8 representation, you can whittle the operations down to a single lookup when you're dealing with the ASCII characters and achieve some very nice compaction with little additional cost with the other characters (assuming, of course, that you can either guarantee well-formed UTF-8 or deal with weird results from malformed UTF-8). Because many combinations of bytes don't happen in UTF-8 text, most of the nodes in the tree won't need 256 entries in the array, so you can realize a fair amount of natural compaction (and, potentially, tree pruning). The downside is that you either have to pay attention to which byte of the character you're on, or the result values and pointer values have to be disjoint and you must pay the cost of checking whether you're done. If the text in which you're interested doesn't already appear in UTF-8, you must also waste time converting it (which probably isn't worth the trouble). If the text is already in UTF-8, this technique can be helpful with a lot of sets of data, especially if the majority of the text being processed is in the ASCII range or if you can do tree pruning on the branches dealing with Han and Hangul (i.e., get the answer after looking at only the first byte, letting you skip over the other two bytes).

Combining the Main Lookup Table with the Multicharacter Exception Table   If you're dealing with variable-length keys, it might make sense to use a unified trie structure for the entire lookup, rather than using a compact array for the first character in the key and some other data structure for the subsequent characters. This tactic can simplify your code and potentially speed it up. If all of the nodes after the root node are very sparse (i.e., you don't have many multicharacter keys or few start with the same character), however, it can waste a lot of space. If you can safely make assumptions about the input text, this combination might save space and prove feasible. And if most of the nodes are *not* sparsely populated, it can yield a big win.

▪ SINGLE VERSUS MULTIPLE TABLES

One more point is worth addressing here. If you need to perform several different mappings on Unicode characters, do you want to use a completely separate table for each mapping or use one big table for all of them?

It's obviously tough to generalize, but sometimes a big unified table will certainly save space and time relative to a bunch of smaller, more specific tables. The most common case is dealing with the Unicode character properties: Should there be a separate table for each property, or a huge table for all of them? The answer is that you can cram most of the Unicode character properties into a single table. The majority of the Unicode properties for a single character can be jammed into a single 32-bit word (the main exceptions are the canonical and compatibility decompositions, which need their own tables).

The Unicode general category can fit into five bits. As we saw earlier, the bi-di category can fit into four bits, with provisions being made for a few exceptional values. The information about whether the character is mirrored can fit into a single bit. The rest of the bits can be overloaded depending on the character's general category. For non-spacing and enclosing marks, the remaining bits can hold the character's combining class (the combining class is 0 for characters in the other categories). For characters in the "number" categories, the remaining bits can be used for the character's numeric value (some of the numeric values are fractions, and some are especially large, so a bit or two of the numeric value field must be set aside as a flag bit to indicate which format is used to encode the actual value into the other bits). For characters in the cased-letter categories, the other bits can hold the value you add or subtract from the character's code point value to obtain its equivalent in the opposite case (or in titlecase). Again, a couple of bits may need to be used as flag bits to choose between alternative representations of the case mapping.

There are, of course, many other ways of storing the data tables that are used to work with Unicode characters. Nevertheless, the ones discussed in this chapter are some of the most important and useful. In the coming chapters, we'll see how these various techniques are used to perform actual operations on Unicode characters.

14
Conversions and Transformations

*N*ow that we've taken a good look at some of the most common and useful data structures and techniques for doing things with Unicode text, we'll put them to work to do some useful things with Unicode text.

In this chapter, we'll examine conversions and transformations on pieces of Unicode text. We'll study not only conversions among the various Unicode representations and between Unicode and other encoding standards, but also two other important types of transformations on Unicode text: converting cased text between uppercase and lowercase, and transliteration, the process of converting text from one script to another that is often used as the basis for accepting Unicode text as input (especially when dealing with the Han and Hangul-based languages).

One thing you'll notice is that most operations on Unicode text can be thought of as transformations of one kind or another. Searching and sorting, for example, involves mapping from Unicode to abstract sort-key values. Rendering text on the screen involves, among other things, mapping Unicode characters to glyph codes. We'll look at these more specialized transformations and the other processes that accompany them in later chapters. For now, we concentrate on Unicode-to-Unicode mappings and Unicode-to-legacy-encoding mapping.

The data structures and techniques described in Chapter 13 form the basis of what we do here, and they will form the basis of much of what we do in the next chapters. Each of these conversions has its own special quirks, however. Each makes use of the data structures in its own unique way or supplements the more general mappings with additional, more specialized work.

▪ CONVERTING BETWEEN UNICODE ENCODING FORMS

We'll start by looking at Unicode-to-Unicode transformations. As we've seen, the Unicode standard comprises a single coded character set, but multiple encoding forms:

- UTF-32 represents each 21-bit code point value using a single 32-bit code unit.
- UTF-16 represents each 21-bit code point value using either a single 16-bit code unit (for code points in the BMP) or a pair of 16-bit code units (for code points in the supplementary planes).
- UTF-8 represents each 21-bit code point value with a single 8-bit code unit (for code points in the ASCII block), a sequence of two or three 8-bit code units (for code points in the rest of the BMP), or a sequence of four 8-bit code units (for code points in the supplementary planes).

This section discusses how you convert text between these three encoding forms. Unicode also comprises seven encoding *schemes* (or serialization formats) that take into account the byte order properties of different machine architectures. Converting between byte orderings is trivial, so we won't cover that issue here. We *will* look at implementing SCSU, a common encoding scheme that isn't officially part of the Unicode standard.

Usually, you pick one of the Unicode encoding forms for representing text in your application (or some API you've decided to use effectively makes the choice for you) and stick with it, but environments that make mixed use of multiple encoding forms are not all that uncommon. It's not unusual, for example, for an application to use one format for its internal representation (typically UTF-16, but UTF-32 is becoming more common) and another more compact (or, sometimes, more portable) UTF (typically UTF-8) in its data-file format. Alternatively, a client-server application might use one format (e.g., UTF-16) on the client side and another (perhaps UTF-32) on the server side. Another client-server application might use the same format for internal processing on both sides (again, usually UTF-16 or UTF-32) but a different, more compact format (usually UTF-8) in the communication protocol between client and server. Mixed environments like these abound.

For one concrete example, consider the Java run-time environment. The `String` and `StringBuffer` classes in Java (and the `char` primitive type) use UTF-16 to store the characters, but the Java serialization facility (the format that is written or read when you apply `writeObject()` or `readObject()` to an object that implements the `Serializable` interface) uses UTF-8 for serializing strings. The conversion to UTF-8 and back again when an object is serialized and deserialized in Java is transparent to the programmer, but it's still useful to be aware of it. In many other mixed environments, this conversion isn't transparent—you have to do it manually.

Virtually all APIs that support Unicode provide the ability to convert a stream of text from one UTF to another, so you rarely have to write this code yourself. Most systems treat one UTF as the native character format and use their normal character-code-conversion facility to convert to the others (or to the non-native endian-ness). In Java, for example, the internal character format is UTF-16 in the native endian-ness of the host processor, and conversion to all other UTFs (or UTF-16 in the opposite endian-ness) is handled through the conversion APIs in the `java.io` package (typically accessed through the `Reader` and `Writer` classes).[1]

We will discuss conversion to non-Unicode encodings later in the chapter. Even though most systems use the same API for conversion between UTFs that they use for conversion from Unicode to something else, note that the implementations are usually different. While conversion between Unicode and most non-Unicode encodings must be table-driven, conversion between UTFs is entirely algorithmic. You can take advantage of this fact to eliminate the mapping tables entirely or to cut them down greatly in size, which can also improve performance by eliminating time spent loading the table into memory. Table-loading time aside, the actual conversion can usually be made just as fast, or almost as fast, as a table-driven conversion.

---

1. The one exception is the aforementioned serialization facility, which bypasses the `java.io` code and does the conversion itself for performance reasons.

Converting Between UTF-16 and UTF-32

Conversion between UTF-16 and UTF-32 is fairly simple, as the vast majority of the characters in a typical body of text will be BMP characters, which have the same representation in both formats. Only the supplementary-plane characters, which are generally quite rare, need special treatment. You can optimize for the BMP characters and save time.

Conversion from UTF-32 to UTF-16 looks something like this in Java (just to treat all formats equally, all these examples avoid char):

```
public static short[] utf32to16(int[] in) {
    int size = in.length;
    short[] out = new short[size * 2];

    int p = 0;
    for (int i = 0; i < size; i++) {
    if (in[i] > 0xffff) {
      out[p++] = (short)((in[i] >> 10) + 0xD7C0);
      out[p++] = (short)((in[i] & 0x03FF) + 0xDC00);
    }
    else
      out[p++] = (short)in[i];
    }
    short[] result = new short[p];
    System.arraycopy(out, 0, result, 0, p);
    return result;
}
```

Pretty obvious. You check the code point value to see whether it's in the BMP and then take the appropriate action based on the result. If it's in the BMP, you just truncate it to a short. Otherwise, the UTF-32 code unit is a supplementary-plane character and we must turn it into a surrogate pair. The low surrogate is simple enough: Just mask off all but the bottom 10 bits and add 0xDC00. The high surrogate is a little trickier: You're actually cramming the top 11 bits from the UTF-32 code unit into the bottom 10 bits of the high surrogate. Out of these 11 bits, the bottom six remain unchanged. The top five bits are converted into four by treating them as an integer value and subtracting 1; this process works because 16 (or 0x10) is the highest value these five bits can have. You can add 0xD800 to the resulting 10-bit value to get the high surrogate. In the example, we shift the 11 bits we care about over to the right and add 0xD7C0. The 0xD7C0 is the combination of knocking 1 off the top five bits (subtract 0x40) and adding 0xD800 to the result.

Going back the other way is a little bit uglier because you have to check each UTF-16 code point value to make sure it's not a surrogate. There's really no good way to handle this task except by doing two comparisons. If you compare against 0xD800 first, the vast majority of the time this comparison will be true and you won't have to perform the second comparison. The values above 0xDFFF are the private use and compatibility zones, and characters in these zones are relatively infrequent.

In Java, the code is as follows:

```
public static int[] utf16to32(short[] in) {
    int size = in.length;
    int[] out = new int[size];

    int p = 0;
    int q = 0;
    while (q < size) {
        int temp = in[q++] & 0xffff;
        if (temp < 0xD800 || temp > 0xDFFF)
            out[p++] = temp;
        else {
            out[p] = (temp - 0xD7C0) << 10;
            out[p++] += in[q++] & 0x03FF;
        }
    }
    if (p == size)
        return out;
    else {
        int[] result = new int[p];
        System.arraycopy(out, 0, result, 0, p);
        return result;
    }
}
```

The actual conversion of the surrogate pair back to the UTF-32 code point value is simply the reverse of the calculations we did in the previous example. No magic here.

Of course, the preceding example is a bit oversimplified. If you can guarantee that the conversion routine will always be handed well-formed UTF-16 (that is, surrogate values occur only in high–low pairs), or if you're willing to accept slightly garbled results when you get malformed UTF-16, code will work well. Otherwise, you have to do a little more work to account for unpaired surrogates. Traditionally, unpaired surrogates are converted in the same way as non-surrogate values are, giving you something that looks like this:

```
if (temp >= 0xD800 && temp <= 0xDBFF && q < in.length
      && (in[q] & 0xffff) >= 0xDC00
      && (in[q] & 0xffff) <= 0xDFFF) {
   out[p] = (temp - 0xD7C0) << 10;
   out[p++] += in[q++] & 0x03FF;
}
else
   out[p++] = temp;
```

With slightly more complicated code, you could instead flag the error by converting unpaired surrogates into U+FFFD, the REPLACEMENT CHARACTER, which by convention is used to indicate the position of an unconvertible character in the source text; eliminate any trace of the unpaired surrogates from the output text; or throw an exception.

The extra code to ensure correctness is kind of ugly and takes a little bit more time, but you're sure you get the right answer. You have to make a trade-off here between speed and absolute correctness.

Converting Between UTF-8 and UTF-32

Going between UTF-32 and UTF-8 is more complicated because UTF-8 is a more complex encoding standard, with anywhere from one to four code units per character.[2] Here's one way of carrying out that conversion:

---

2. Earlier versions of ISO 10646 specified a version of UTF-8 that used as many as six code units per character, but more recent decisions by the committees maintaining both Unicode and ISO 10646 have declared the encoding space above U+10FFFF to be off limits. Five- and six-byte sequences are necessary only to represent values in the area that's now off-limits for encoding; therefore, five- and six-byte UTF-8 are now illegal.

```
public static byte[] utf32to8(int[] in) {
    int size = in.length;
    byte[] out = new byte[size * 4];

    int p = 0;
    for (int i = 0; i < size; i++) {
      int c = in[i];
      if (c <= 0x007F)
        out[p++] = (byte)c;
      else {
        if (c <= 0x07FF) {
          out[p++] = (byte)((c >> 6) + 0xC0);
          out[p++] = (byte)((c & 0x3F) + 0x80);
        }
        else {
          if (c <= 0xFFFF) {
            out[p++] = (byte)((c >> 12) + 0xE0);
            out[p++] = (byte)(((c >> 6) & 0x3F) + 0x80);
            out[p++] = (byte)((c & 0x3F) + 0x80);
          }
          else {
            out[p++] = (byte)((c >> 18) + 0xF0);
            out[p++] = (byte)(((c >> 12) & 0x3F) + 0x80);
            out[p++] = (byte)(((c >> 6) & 0x3F) + 0x80);
            out[p++] = (byte)((c & 0x3F) + 0x80);
          }
        }
      }
    }
    byte[] result = new byte[p];
    System.arraycopy(out, 0, result, 0, p);
    return result;
}
```

The code's a little complicated, but you can't really improve on it much in terms of performance. The one drawback with this approach is that it performs three comparisons for each character for code point values exceeding U+07FF. This group of characters includes the Han and Hangul areas and all the Indic scripts, as well as a smattering of other scripts and all of the supplementary planes. For many scripts, including most of the stuff in the supplementary planes, they occur rarely enough not to be a problem. Conversely, there's a fairly heavy price to pay for, say, whole documents in Chinese, Japanese, Hindi, or Thai.

If you're willing to take up some space for a translation table, you can turn the series of if statements into a switch statement, which effectively performs one comparison for all the code point ranges. You can do so with a 256-byte lookup table by using the leading byte of the UTF-16 code point value as an index into the table. This approach, for obvious reasons, works much better when you're going straight from UTF-16 to UTF-8. Because you must do some extra work to get from a UTF-16 surrogate pair to a four-byte UTF-8 sequence, however, you lose a little speed with the supplementary-plane characters in exchange for gaining some on the BMP characters.

Going back from UTF-8 to UTF-32 is more interesting. The obvious, straightforward approach is something like this:

```
public static int[] utf8to32(byte[] in) {
    int size = in.length;
    int[] out = new int[size];

    int p = 0;
    int q = 0;

    while (q < size) {
      int c = in[q++] & 0xff;

      if (c <= 0x7F)
        out[p++] = c;
      else if (c <= 0xDF) {
        out[p] = (int)(c & 0x1F) << 6;
        out[p++] += (int)(in[q++] & 0x3F);
      }
      else if (c <= 0xEF) {
        out[p] = (int)(c & 0x0F) << 12;
        out[p] += (int)(in[q++] & 0x3F) << 6;
        out[p++] += (int)(in[q++] & 0x3F);
      }
      else if (c <= 0xF7) {
```

```
      out[p] = (int)(c & 0x07) << 18;
      out[p] += (int)(in[q++] & 0x3F) << 12;
      out[p] += (int)(in[q++] & 0x3F) << 6;
      out[p++] += (int)(in[q++] & 0x3F);
    }
    else
      out[p] = 0xFFFD;
  }

  int[] result = new int[p];
  System.arraycopy(out, 0, result, 0, p);
  return result;
}
```

This code gets the job done and performs reasonably well. It doesn't check for malformed UTF-8 sequences (except for byte values from 0xF8 to 0xFF, which can't occur in legal UTF-8). In the presence of malformed UTF-8, this algorithm will produce garbled results, so it's acceptable only if that outcome is acceptable, or if you can guarantee that the UTF-8 fed to this algorithm is well formed.

If you're willing to pay a little extra to keep some tables around, you can make the algorithm faster and more elegant and have it handle malformed UTF-8 more gracefully. The following approach is based on a 128-byte lookup table:

```
private static final byte X = (byte)-1; // illegal lead byte
private static final byte Y = (byte)-2; // illegal trail byte
private static final byte[][] states = {
    //00 08 10 18 20 28 30 38 40 48 50 58 60 68 70 78
    // 80 88 90 98 A0 A8 B0 B8 C0 C8 D0 D8 E0 E8 F0 F8
    { 0, 0, 0, 0, 0, 0, 0, 0, 0, 0, 0, 0, 0, 0, 0, 0,
      X, X, X, X, X, X, X, X, 1, 1, 1, 1, 2, 2, 3, X },
    { Y, Y, Y, Y, Y, Y, Y, Y, Y, Y, Y, Y, Y, Y, Y, Y,
      0, 0, 0, 0, 0, 0, 0, 0, Y, Y, Y, Y, Y, Y, Y, Y },
    { Y, Y, Y, Y, Y, Y, Y, Y, Y, Y, Y, Y, Y, Y, Y, Y,
      1, 1, 1, 1, 1, 1, 1, 1, Y, Y, Y, Y, Y, Y, Y, Y },
    { Y, Y, Y, Y, Y, Y, Y, Y, Y, Y, Y, Y, Y, Y, Y, Y,
      2, 2, 2, 2, 2, 2, 2, 2, Y, Y, Y, Y, Y, Y, Y, Y }
};
private static final byte[] masks = { 0x7F, 0x1F, 0x0F, 0x07 };
```

```java
public static int[] utf8to32b(byte[] in) {
    int size = in.length;
    int[] out = new int[size];

    int p = 0;
    int q = 0;
    int state = 0;
    byte mask = 0;

    while (q < size) {
      int c = in[q++] & 0xff;

      state = states[state][c >>> 3];

      switch (state) {
        case 0:
          out[p++] += c & 0x7F;
          mask = 0;
          break;

        case 1:
        case 2:
        case 3:
          if (mask == 0)
            mask = masks[state];
          out[p] += c & mask;
          out[p] <<= 6;
          mask = (byte)0x3F;
          break;

        case Y:
          --q;
          // fall thru on purpose

        case X:
          out[p++] = 0xFFFD;
          state = 0;
          mask = 0;
          break;
    }
  }
```

```
    int[] result = new int[p];
    System.arraycopy(out, 0, result, 0, p);
    return result;
}
```

We can eliminate the chain of if statements and some of the redundant code in the first example by using a state table to keep track of your location in a multibyte character. The state table also provides a convenient way to detect malformed sequences of UTF-8. This example actually distinguishes between longer-than-normal and shorter-than-normal sequences. If it sees a leading byte when it's expecting a trailing byte (a shorter-than-normal sequence, represented by Y in the state table), it throws out the incomplete sequence it's seen until then, writes U+FFFD to the output as a placeholder for the corrupted character, and starts over with the leading byte it encountered prematurely (i.e., it treats the premature leading byte as good and the truncated sequence that precedes it as bad). If, on the other hand, it sees a trailing byte where it expects a leading byte (a longer-than-normal sequence, denoted by X in the state table), or a byte that is illegal in UTF-8, it treats the byte as an illegal sequence all by itself.

Even here, we do not protect against non-shortest-form UTF-8. An ASCII character represented with three bytes will come through just fine with either of these converters. You can actually guard against these illegal combinations without altering the basic approach by making the state table a little more complicated. We leave this task as an exercise for the reader.

As always, many variations on this basic approach are possible. For example, you can eliminate the right shift in the state table lookup by making the table bigger. You can also eliminate some of the manipulation of the mask variable (and the if statement based on it) by just looking up the mask every time, which also requires a larger table of masks. You can fetch both the mask value and the new-state value in a single array lookup by munging the values together mathematically in the table (for example, we need only six state values and the bottom three bits of every mask value are 1, so we could use the bottom three bits for the state and the rest of the value for the mask), but then you need extra code to take the two values apart.[3]

---

3. One thing to keep in mind if you try to use the code examples from this book verbatim in your code: This particular example won't compile as-is. Integer literals in Java have type int, and can't be used in an array literal of type byte[] without casts. The casts are left out here to make the table more readable.

Converting Between UTF-8 and UTF-16

Conversions between UTF-8 and UTF-16 are left as an exercise for the reader. Conceptually, you really can't get from UTF-8 to UTF-16 (or vice versa) without going through UTF-32. You can cut out some of the work that would occur if you just, for example, called the 8-to-32 function followed by the 32-to-16 function, but you can't eliminate much of it.

Implementing Unicode Compression

The Unicode compression scheme (also known as the Standard Compression Scheme for Unicode, or SCSU, which is documented in Unicode Technical Standard #6) isn't officially a Unicode Transformation Format, but sort of informally qualifies. Thus it's yet another way of translating a sequence of abstract Unicode numeric values into patterns of bits. Unlike UTF-16 and UTF-32 (and, to a lesser extent, UTF-8), SCSU isn't really suitable as an in-memory representation of Unicode because it's a stateful encoding—particular byte values mean different things depending on the bytes that have come before. This is arguably true of trailing bytes in UTF-8 or low surrogates in UTF-16, as their exact meanings depend on the preceding lead bytes or high surrogates, but two important differences arise:

- In both UTF-8 and UTF-16, leading code units, trailing code units, and single-unit characters (code units that represent a whole character by themselves) are represented by distinct numerical ranges. As a result, you can tell which category a particular code unit is in just by looking at it. In UTF-8, the leading bytes of different-length sequences also occupy different numerical ranges. You can therefore tell how long a UTF-8 sequence is supposed to be just from looking at the leading byte.

- When you do see a code unit that represents only part of a character, the number of units forward or backward you must scan to get the whole character is strictly limited. If you happen upon a nonsurrogate code unit in UTF-16 or an ASCII value in UTF-8, the code unit stands on its own. If you happen upon a surrogate in UTF-16 or a leading byte in UTF-8, you can tell from it exactly how many code units you have to scan and in which direction to get the rest of the character. If you happen upon a trailing byte in UTF-8, you have to scan backward no more than three bytes to find the beginning of the character, which will then tell you where the end of the character is located.

These two things aren't true in SCSU. A decompressor for SCSU maintains a "state" that can be changed by each byte as it's read, and the current state determines the meaning of the next byte you see (which may, in turn, change the state again). You can't drop into the middle of an SCSU byte stream and tell what's going on (i.e., correctly interpret any arbitrary byte in the stream) without potentially scanning all the way back to the beginning of the file to figure out the state. You don't *always* have to scan back to the beginning of the file, and you can often make an educated guess as to what certain bytes mean, but nothing limits your maximum lookback: You *may* have to scan all the way back to the beginning of the file.

SCSU, however, is useful as a serialization format. As you read the text into memory (or otherwise deserialize it), you decompress it, converting it into one of the other representations for use in memory. You do the opposite when writing the text back out. UTF-8 is often used for this purpose because it's backward compatible with ASCII and because the representation is more compact than UTF-16 for Latin. UTF-8 actually is *less* compact than UTF-16 for many scripts, especially the East Asian scripts. A Japanese document is 50 percent larger in UTF-8 than it is in UTF-16 (or, generally speaking, a legacy Japanese encoding). SCSU solves this problem: It's somewhat more expensive to convert to and from than UTF-8 and can't be used as an in-memory representation as UTF-8 can, but it's also backward compatible with ASCII and is more compact than (or equally as compact as) both UTF-8 and UTF-16 for all scripts. In most cases, SCSU text is almost as compact as a legacy encoding for a given script. SCSU also lends itself well to further compression with a more-general scheme such as LZW. In addition, it's backward compatible with Latin-1—not just ASCII.

The International Components for Unicode library includes conversion utilities for SCSU, but most other libraries don't. If you're not using ICU and want to use Unicode compression, you may well need to code it yourself. Here we'll look at how to do that.

SCSU allows for many different ways of encoding the same piece of Unicode text. Unlike, say, UTF-8, it doesn't prescribe one particular alternative as the "canonical representation" for a particular piece of text. Thus, even though SCSU is always decoded in the same way, Unicode text can be *encoded* in many different ways. A particular encoder can choose to optimize for speed or compactness.

The basic idea is that SCSU has two "modes," single-byte mode and double-byte mode. In single-byte mode:

- The byte values from 0x00 to 0x1F, except for 0x00, 0x09, 0x0A, and 0x0D (the ASCII null, tab, line-feed, and carriage-return characters, respectively), are "tag" bytes that control the interpretation of the other byte values.
- The byte values from 0x00 to 0x7F are used to represent the bottom 7 bits of a Unicode code point, with the upper 14 bits being determined by the decoder's state. There are eight "static windows," or ranges of 128 Unicode code point values that can be represented by these byte values. Normally they represent the characters in "static window 0," which encompasses the Unicode code point values from U+0000 to U+007F (i.e., with ASCII characters), but they can be temporarily shifted to represent one of the other seven windows.
- The byte values from 0x80 to 0xFF are also used to represent the bottom 7 bits of a Unicode code point, with the upper 14 bits being determined by the decoder's state. There are eight "dynamic windows," or ranges of 128 Unicode code point values that can be represented at any one time. Unlike the static windows, however, these eight dynamic windows can be repositioned almost anywhere in the Unicode encoding range.

In double-byte mode, the bytes are interpreted in pairs as big-endian UTF-16. The exception is that the byte values from 0xE0 to 0xF2, when in the lead-byte position (corresponding to the high-order byte of code point values in the private-use area), are generally interpreted as tag values.

The tag values do various things:

- Switch to single-byte or double-byte mode long enough to encode one Unicode code point.
- Switch to single-byte or double-byte mode indefinitely.
- Interpret just the next byte (in single-byte mode) according to some particular static or dynamic window (which changes the interpretation of all byte values in single-byte mode).
- From now until it's changed again, interpret the byte values from 0x80 to 0xFF according to some particular dynamic window. (The values from 0x00 to 0x7F are still treated as either tag values or members of static window 0—you can't indefinitely switch the values from 0x00 to 0x7F to some other static window.)
- Reposition a particular dynamic window to refer to a different range of values in the Unicode encoding space.

The initial positions of the windows mean text containing only characters from the ASCII and Latin-1 blocks has the same representation in SCSU as it does in Latin-1, unless it contains control characters other than the tab, line feed, and carriage return. (Note that this situation differs from UTF-8, where all the control characters come through without change, but the characters in the Latin-1 block turn into two-byte sequences—like the East Asian scripts, Latin-1 text is better served by SCSU than by UTF-8.) Text in many other scripts can be represented in SCSU entirely by one-byte values as well, with a single extra byte at the beginning shifting the values from 0x80 to 0xFF to the appropriate window. For rarer scripts that fit into a 128-code-point window, you need two or possibly three bytes at the front of the file, but can otherwise represent everything with a single byte per character.

Scripts that span more than 128 code point values can often still be represented fairly well with single-byte SCSU, with more tag bytes scattered throughout to shift the windows around. For those that occupy too wide a span of code point values for the shifting-window technique to work well, you can simply shift to Unicode mode—the representation then becomes simply big-endian UTF-16 with an extra byte on the front to tag it as such.

The code to perform this operation isn't too ridiculous, although it's more complicated than converting from UTF-8. Here's one fairly straightforward interpretation (in Java, albeit somewhat abbreviated):

```java
// single-byte-mode tag values:
//==============================
// shift to specified window for one byte
private static final int SQ0 = 0x01;
// SQ1-SQ6 omitted for brevity
private static final int SQ7 = 0x08;

// define a new window using extended semantics and shift to it
private static final int SDX = 0x0B;

// shift to double-byte mode for one pair of bytes
private static final int SQU = 0x0E;

// shift to double-int mode
private static final int SCU = 0x0F;

// shift to specified window
private static final int SC0 = 0x10;
// SC1-SC6 omitted for brevity
private static final int SC7 = 0x17;

// define a new window and shift to it
private static final int SD0 = 0x18;
// SD1-SD6 omitted for brevity
private static final int SD7 = 0x1F;

// double-byte-mode tag values:
//==============================
// shift to single-byte mode using specified window
private static final int UC0 = 0xE0;
// UC1-UC7 omitted for brevity

// define a new window and shift to it (and to single-byte mode)
private static final int UD0 = 0xE8;
// UD1-UD7 omitted for brevity
```

```
// quote a single Unicode character (can start with tag byte)
private static final int UQU = 0xF0;

// define a new window using extended semantics and shift to it
private static final int UDX = 0xF1;

private static final int[] staticWindows = {
    0x00, 0x00, 0x0100, 0x0300, 0x2000, 0x2080, 0x2100, 0x3000 };
private static final int[] initialDynamicWindows = {
    0x80, 0xC0, 0x0400, 0x0600, 0x0900, 0x3040, 0x30A0, 0xFF00 };
private static final int[] dynamicWindowOffsets = {
    0x0000, 0x0080, 0x0100, 0x0180, 0x0200, 0x0280, 0x0300, 0x0380,
    0x0400, 0x0480, 0x0500, 0x0580, 0x0600, 0x0680, 0x0700, 0x0780,
    // ...and so on through...
    0x3000, 0x3080, 0x3100, 0x3180, 0x3200, 0x3280, 0x3300, 0x3380,
    0xE000, 0xE080, 0xE100, 0xE180, 0xE200, 0xE280, 0xE300, 0xE380,
    // ...and so on through...
    0xFC00, 0xFC80, 0xFD00, 0xFD80, 0xFE00, 0xFE80, 0xFF00, 0xFF80,
    0x0000, 0x0000, 0x0000, 0x0000, 0x0000, 0x0000, 0x0000, 0x0000,
    // ...nine more rows of zeros...
    0x0000, 0x00C0, 0x0250, 0x0370, 0x0530, 0x3040, 0x30A0, 0xFF60
};

public static void decompressSCSU(
            InputStream in, OutputStream out)
              throws IOException {
    boolean singleByteMode = true;
    boolean nonLockingShift = false;
    boolean nonLockingUnicodeShift = false;
    int currentWindow = 0;
    int tempWindow = 0;
    int[] dynamicWindows = (int[])initialDynamicWindows.clone();

    int b = in.read();
    while (b != -1) {
      while (b != -1 && singleByteMode
          && !nonLockingUnicodeShift) {
        switch (b) {
          case SQU:
            nonLockingUnicodeShift = true;
            break;
```

```
case SCU:
  singleByteMode = false;
  break;

case SQ0: case SQ1: case SQ2: case SQ3:
case SQ4: case SQ5: case SQ6: case SQ7:
  nonLockingShift = true;
  tempWindow = b - SQ0;
  break;

case SC0: case SC1: case SC2: case SC3:
case SC4: case SC5: case SC6: case SC7:
  currentWindow = b - SC0;
  break;

case SD0: case SD1: case SD2: case SD3:
case SD4: case SD5: case SD6: case SD7:
  currentWindow = b - SD0;
  b = in.read();
  dynamicWindows[currentWindow] =
      dynamicWindowOffsets[b];
  break;

case SDX:
  int hi = in.read();
  int lo = in.read();
  currentWindow = hi >>> 5;
  dynamicWindows[currentWindow] =
      0xD800DC00 + ((hi & 0x1F) << 21)
      + ((lo & 0xF8) << 16)
      + ((lo & 0x07) << 7);
  break;

case 0x80: case 0x81: case 0x82: case 0x83:
// ...plus the other values from 0x80 to 0xff
  if (nonLockingShift) {
    writeChar(out,
          dynamicWindows[tempWindow]
          + (b - 0x80));
    nonLockingShift = false;
  }
  else
    writeChar(out,
```

```
                    dynamicWindows[currentWindow]
                    + (b - 0x80));
          break;

      default:
        if (nonLockingShift) {
          writeChar(out,
                staticWindows[tempWindow] + b);
          nonLockingShift = false;
        }
        else
          writeChar(out, b);
        break;
    }
    b = in.read();
  }

  while (b != -1 && (!singleByteMode
      || nonLockingUnicodeShift)) {
    if (nonLockingUnicodeShift || b < 0xE0 || b > 0xF0) {
      writeChar(out, (b << 8) + in.read());
      nonLockingUnicodeShift = false;
    }
    else {
      switch (b) {
        case UQU:
          nonLockingUnicodeShift = true;
          break;

        case UC0: case UC1: case UC2: case UC3:
        case UC4: case UC5: case UC6: case UC7:
          singleByteMode = true;
          currentWindow = b - UC0;
          break;

        case UD0: case UD1: case UD2: case UD3:
        case UD4: case UD5: case UD6: case UD7:
          singleByteMode = true;
          currentWindow = b - UD0;
          b = in.read();
          dynamicWindows[currentWindow] =
              dynamicWindowOffsets[b];
```

```
            case UDX:
                singleByteMode = true;
                int hi = in.read();
                int lo = in.read();
                currentWindow = hi >>> 5;
                dynamicWindows[currentWindow] =
                    0xD800DC00 + ((hi & 0x1F) << 21)
                    + ((lo & 0xF8) << 16)
                    + ((lo & 0x07) << 7);
            }
        }
        b = in.read();
    }
  }
}

private static void writeChar(OutputStream out, int c)
        throws IOException {
    if (c < 0x10000) {
      out.write(c >> 8);
      out.write(c & 0xff);
    }
    else {
      out.write(c >> 24);
      out.write((c >> 16) & 0xff);
      out.write((c >> 8) & 0xff);
      out.write(c & 0xff);
    }
}
```

The code is fairly long, but reasonably simple and efficient. This particular version writes UTF-16 to the output, as that result is what you get when you're in double-byte mode. The window-offset arrays are arrays of `int`, but their elements aren't UTF-32 code points; rather, they're either single UTF-16 code points padded out to 32 bits (pretty much the same thing) or UTF-16 surrogate pairs packed into a single `int`. The helper function `writeChar()` accounts for the second case. You could easily modify this routine to output UTF-32 instead. The window-offset arrays would then be UTF-32 values, the code that handles the SDX and UDX characters would change, and the double-byte mode would convert UTF-16 surrogate pairs into UTF-32.

The preceding example also assumes it's looking at well-formed SCSU. It will act funny or throw exceptions if the text it reads isn't well formed.

There are a bunch of ways of producing SCSU in the first place. A very simple algorithm that optimizes for Latin-1 text would look like this:

- If the character is a Latin-1 noncontrol character (or if it's tab, carriage return, or line feed) and we're in single-byte mode, just truncate it to a byte and write it to the output.
- If the character is a control character other than the ones listed above, write SQ0 to the output, followed by the character, truncated to a byte.
- If the character is not a Latin-1 character but is a BMP character, and the character after it *is* a Latin-1 character, write SQU to the output, followed by the character's big-endian UTF-16 representation.
- If the character is not a BMP character or a Latin-1 character, and neither is the following character, and we're still in single-byte mode, write SCU, shift to double-byte mode, and reprocess that character.
- If we're in double-byte mode and the character is a not a Latin-1 character or a private-use character, write its big-endian UTF-16 representation to the output.
- If we're in double-byte mode and the character is a private-use character, write UQU to the output, followed by the character's big-endian UTF-16 representation.
- If we're in double-byte mode and the character is a Latin-1 character, but the character following it is not, write its big-endian UTF-16 representation to the output.
- If we're in double-byte mode, the character is a Latin-1 character, and so is the following character, write UC0, shift back to single-byte mode, and reprocess the character.

A more complicated algorithm that tries to account for all the Unicode characters might look something like this:

- Start out in single-byte mode, with the windows set up as they would be in the initial state of the decoder.
- If the current character is an ASCII printing character, tab, line feed, or carriage return, truncate it to a byte and write it to the output.

- Otherwise, if the character fits into the current dynamic window (as defined by the last SCx written, or by the Latin-1 block if we haven't written any SCx codes), write the bottom seven bits of the code point value plus 0x80 to the output.

- Otherwise, if the character fits into a static window, or one of the currently defined dynamic windows, but the next two characters don't fit into the same window, write the appropriate SQx code to the output, followed by the appropriate byte value. If the character fit into a static window, this value is the bottom seven bits of the code point value; if it fit into a dynamic window, it's the bottom seven bits plus 0x80.

- If the current character doesn't fit into any of the currently defined dynamic or static windows, and the next two characters don't fit into the same window, write SQU to the output, followed by the character's big-endian UTF-16 representation.

- If the next three characters in a row fit into the same dynamic window, and it's not the current dynamic window but is one of the currently defined dynamic windows, write the appropriate SCx code to the output, followed by the bottom seven bits of the current character plus 0x80.

- If the next three characters in a row fit into the same window but it's not one of the currently defined dynamic windows, emit an appropriate SDx code, followed by the appropriate defining byte (or, if necessary, SDX, followed by the appropriate defining two bytes) and the bottom seven bits of the current character plus 0x80. (It's best to use some sort of "least recently used" algorithm to determine which window to redefine—a more sophisticated algorithm would also ignore ASCII printing characters in determining whether "the next three characters" fit into the same window.)

- If the next three characters in a row don't fit into the same window, write SCU to the output, switch to double-byte mode, and reprocess the current character.

- If you're in double-byte mode, write characters out in their big-endian UTF-16 representations (preceding private-use characters with UQU) for as long as you don't encounter a sequence of three or more characters that either fit into the same window or are ASCII printing characters. If you see such a sequence, write the appropriate code to switch back to single-byte mode (UCx, UDx, or UDX, with the necessary defining bytes, determined according to the same criteria used in single-byte mode), switch back to single-byte mode, and process the sequence in single-byte mode.

UNICODE NORMALIZATION

The other category of Unicode-to-Unicode transformations we need to consider is Unicode normalization. You may or may not need to care about Unicode normalization as such; often it happens as a by-product of some other process. For example, character code conversion is usually written to produce normalized Unicode text; a legacy encoding naturally converts to one normalized form or the other in most cases. (Of course, not all converters available on a particular system may produce the *same* normalized form, unless they've all been designed to do so.) Similarly, keyboard layouts and input methods can be designed to produce normalized text, usually without any extra work; again this might mean that different input methods and keyboard layouts on a given system produce *different* normalization forms, unless they were expressly designed to produce the same one.

If all of your text comes from an outside process, you may be able to depend on the process that originally produced it to use it in some normalized form. For example, the World Wide Web Consortium's early-normalization rules require that every process on the Web that produces text do so in Normalized Form C, so processes downstream of the process that produced the text (XML parsers, for example) can assume the text is already in Form C.

Finally, your application might not care whether the text is normalized. Generally, Unicode normalization provides two benefits: You can compare two strings for equality using a straight bitwise comparison, and rendering processes don't have to account for alternative representations of characters they can display. If you're already performing language-sensitive comparison rather than bitwise comparison of your strings, you don't have to carry out Unicode normalization, as language-sensitive comparison has to do normalization anyway (or take the alternate representations of a given string into account). If the rendering process can handle the alternative representations of a given string (or if you don't care), you also don't have to do Unicode normalization.

If you *do* have to perform Unicode normalization, there's a fairly high probability you'll have to code it yourself. As with Unicode compression, the International Components for Unicode provide an API for normalization, but most other Unicode-support APIs don't.

Four Unicode normalization forms exist, but only three processes need to be implemented to support them:

- **Normalized Form D:** Canonical decomposition
- **Normalized Form C:** Canonical decomposition, followed by canonical composition
- **Normalized Form KD:** Compatibility decomposition
- **Normalized Form KC:** Compatibility decomposition, followed by canonical composition

The original normalized form for Unicode was Normalized Form D, which consists of canonical decompositions. Normalized Form KD, compatibility decomposition, allows text to be mapped from characters that are provided only to ensure round-trip compatibility with some other standard to noncompatibility characters. Of course, many of the compatibility composites involve some kind of stylistic transform on the original character, so information can be lost going to Form KD.

Normalized Forms C and KC evolved more recently. In real life, many implementations prefer composed representations of characters over the decomposed representations because the composed representations are more compact and because many of the legacy encodings (most of the ISO 8859 family of encodings, for example) use composed representations. Converting to Forms C and KC involves both a decomposition and a recomposition mainly because of issues related to the order of combining marks. For example, suppose your text includes the letter a with a macron on top and a dot underneath. No code point value is assigned to this character, so you have to represent it with a combining character sequence. There *are* precomposed characters for both a-macron and a-underdot, so you could represent a-macron-underdot with either a-macron plus a combining underdot or a-underdot plus a combining macron. As it turns out, the correct representation in Normalized Form C is a-underdot plus a combining macron (because of the canonical accent order). If you have text with the other representation (a-macron plus a combining underdot), you can get to the correct representation only by fully decomposing it, reordering the accents, and *then* composing it again.

There isn't any such thing as "compatibility composition." Normalized Form KC uses compatibility decomposition as the basis for canonical composition instead of using canonical decomposition as the basis for canonical composition.

Canonical Decomposition

Canonical decomposition actually consists of two separate processes: canonical decomposition and **canonical reordering**. Canonical decomposition is the process of taking any canonical composites in the input stream and replacing them with their decomposed forms. Canonical reordering is the process of taking any combining character sequences and sorting them according to their combining classes. When you decompose a composite character, the decomposed representation will already be ordered by combining class. Canonical reordering is oriented toward getting combining character sequences *already in* the input stream—not those produced by decomposing composite characters—into canonical order.

Canonical Decomposition   Exactly two types of canonical decompositions exist: those that consist of two characters and those that consist of only one character. A character with a one-character ("singleton") decomposition is a character whose use is effectively discouraged—it's not supposed to show up in normalized Unicode text, regardless of normalization form. Two-character canonical decompositions, on the other hand, represent "real" composite characters that can be represented with combining character sequences.

In some cases, a character should decompose to a *three*-character (or longer) combining sequence (for example, ṻ should decompose to small u, combining diaeresis, combining macron). The standard is structured so that such characters decompose to a combining sequence that contains *another* composite character (in this case, to ü, combining macron). As a consequence, you may have to perform several mappings to fully decompose a character. The decompositions are set up so that the composite character is always the first character in the decomposition, and each iteration of the mapping effectively peels one mark off the end:

$$\bar{\ddot{u}}$$
$$\ddot{u} + {}^-$$
$$u + {}^{..} + {}^-$$

You can take advantage of the two-character limit in constructing a lookup table to use in decomposition. As certain supplementary-plane characters are canonical composites, you have to use either a two-level compact array or some kind of more generalized trie structure for your lookup table. The data array can consist of 32-bit values. For the two-character decompositions, the 32-bit value is the UTF-16 representations of the two characters packed into a single 32-bit value. For the singleton decompositions, the upper 16 bits are zero and the lower 16 bits are the UTF-16 representation of the character to map to.

Canonical Decomposition on Supplementary-Plane Characters   One hitch occurs in doing canonical decomposition this way: Some of the supplementary-plane characters have decompositions that include other supplementary-plane characters. In Unicode 3.1, these fall into two main categories:

- Musical symbols that decompose to sequences of other musical symbols (for example, the eighth note decomposes to a black notehead, followed by a combining stem, followed by a combining flag).
- Compatibility ideographs that map to noncompatibility ideographs in plane 2 (many compatibility ideographs in plane 2 map to ideographs in the BMP).

You can handle this issue in a couple of different ways:

- You can assume that no BMP characters include supplementary-plane characters in their decompositions (this assumption holds now and is likely to hold in the future, but might be invalidated by some future version of Unicode). You could use a single-level compact array with the packing scheme described previously to handle the BMP characters and a separate lookup table for the non-BMP characters (or a separate table for each plane). For the plane 1 characters (currently the musical symbols), your code could assume that all of the characters in the decomposition are also in plane 1 and use the same packing scheme. For the plane 2 characters, your code could assume that the decompositions are all one-character decompositions and store the decompositions using UTF-32.

- You could use a different lookup table for non-BMP characters and just have the entries be 64 bits wide, packing together two UTF-32 code units.

- You could use a unified lookup table for the whole Unicode range using the format described earlier, but use a range of sentinel values (say, 32-bit values where the top 16 bits, treated as a UTF-16 value, appear in the surrogate range) to refer to an exception table containing strings. This approach makes sense if you're storing compatibility decompositions in the same table (because you have to do so anyway—see below). If you handle matters in this way, you don't want to do the recursive lookup, though: Just have the exception table contain the full decompositions of all characters. As many of the decompositions in the musical symbols block are suffixes of other decompositions, you can actually achieve fairly decent compression.

One thing you really can't do is ignore the supplementary-plane characters. Unlike with most other processes on Unicode text, where you can pick which characters you will support, you can't pick and choose with Unicode normalization. That is, you don't have the option of normalizing some characters and leaving other characters alone. If you're producing text that will be (or may be) read by another process, and it purports to be in some normalization form, you can't cut corners. You can get away with blowing off some of the mappings only in the following cases:

- If you're normalizing for internal use and it doesn't have to be in an official normalized form
- If you're willing to output error characters or throw an exception if you encounter characters you can't handle (not really an option if you're operating on text from an outside source and purporting not to mess it up

other than to normalize it, as this isn't legal according to the Unicode standard)

- If you can guarantee that certain characters will never appear in the text you're trying to normalize

If you can't guarantee your input character repertoire, and you're sending the normalized text on to another process, you have to handle all the characters.

Canonical Decomposition on Hangul Characters   One important exception exists to the rule that canonical decompositions have only one or two characters: decomposition of Hangul syllables. Hangul syllables all have a canonical decomposition to the equivalent sequence of conjoining Hangul jamo characters, and a Hangul syllable can decompose to as many as three jamo.

The nice thing about Hangul is that you can decompose Hangul syllables algorithmically; you don't need a table lookup. Thus all you have to store in the decomposition table for Hangul is a sentinel value indicating that the character is a Hangul syllable and needs special treatment, or you can check whether the character is a Hangul syllable before doing the initial table lookup.

The code to decompose a Hangul syllable looks something like this:[4]

```
// beginning of Hangul syllables block, number of syllables
private static final char SBase = '\uAC00';
private static int SCount = 11172;


// beginning of leading consonants, number of leading consonants
private static final char LBase = '\u1100';
private static final int LCount = 19;


// beginning of vowels, number of vowels
private static final char VBase = '\u1161';
private static final int VCount = 21;


// beginning of trailing consonants, number of trailing consonants
private static final char TBase = '\u11A7';
private static final int TCount = 28;
```

---

4. This example is taken almost verbatim from the Unicode standard, pp. 54–55.

```
// number of syllables with a given initial consonant
private static final int NCount = VCount * TCount;

public static char[] decomposeHangulSyllable(char syl) {
    int sIndex = syl - SBase;
    int l = LBase + (sIndex / NCount);
    int v = VBase + (sIndex % NCount) / TCount;
    int t = TBase + (sIndex % TCount);

    if (t == TBase)
      return new char[] { (char)l, (char)v };
    else
      return new char[] { (char)l, (char)v, (char)t };
}
```

Canonical Reordering   Converting to Normalized Form D involves two conceptual passes. The first pass goes through the whole string and replaces every canonical composite with its canonical decomposition. You repeat this step until the string is made up entirely of noncomposite characters.

Once that operation is complete, you make a second pass through the string to perform canonical reordering. You go through the string and locate every sequence of two or more characters in a row that have a nonzero combining class. (This definition generally means "every sequence of combining marks," although some combining marks have combining class 0 specifically so things won't reorder around them—the enclosing marks, for example, inhibit reordering. On the other hand, all characters that *aren't* combining marks *do* have a combining class of 0.)

For each sequence of combining marks, you sort it in ascending order by combining class, being careful not to disturb the relative order of any characters in the sequence that have the *same* combining class. Only rarely would you deal with sequences of more than two or three marks, so anything more than a simple bubble or insertion sort would be overkill.

Of course, you need a lookup table that contains each character's combining class. Often, the libraries you're working with will have an API you can call to get a character's combining class. If not, you'll have to create your own lookup table. The compact array or another trie-based structure lends itself well to this task: Most characters have a combining class of zero, a number of large blocks of characters have the same (nonzero) combining class, and the combining class is a byte value. Because of its size (and relative infrequency), the combining class can easily be doubled up with other Unicode properties in a single lookup table, if you also need to look up the other properties. See Chapter 13 for more details.

Putting It All Together   You probably don't want to go through the whole string twice to convert it into Normalized Form D. In fact, normalization often occurs as part of another process (such as string comparison) where you don't really want to store the normalized string at all.

Unfortunately, you can't just consider one character at a time when doing canonical decomposition. You often have to look at multiple characters in the input to figure out what the next output should be, and you typically end up generating several output characters at once. For this reason, a character-by-character interface generally requires both input and output buffering. The following pseudocode summarizes how an object that returns the canonically decomposed version of a string one character at a time (and, in turn, gets the original string to be normalized one character at a time) might go about it:

- If the output buffer contains characters, return the first character in the output buffer, and delete it from the output buffer.
- Otherwise, do the following to replenish the output buffer:

  1. Read a character from the input. If it's not a canonical composite, write it to the output buffer. Otherwise, look up the character's canonical decomposition. If the first character of the canonical decomposition is also a canonical composite, look *that* up, and so on until the original character is fully decomposed. Write the resultant characters to the output buffer. One way to perform this step is to use an intermediate buffer. As you look up each decomposition, write the *second* character, if one exists, to the intermediate buffer. If the first character is decomposable as well, look up its decomposition and write the second character to the intermediate buffer. Repeat this process until you reach a decomposition where the first character does not have a decomposition, then write the *first* character to the buffer. At this point, you have the decomposition in the intermediate

buffer in reverse order, and you can reverse the order as you copy the characters into the output buffer.

2. Peek at the input. If the next input character has a nonzero combining class, read it from the input, decompose it following the above rules, and write the decomposed version to the output buffer. Continue in this way until you reach a character with a combining class of zero. Do *not* read this character from the input yet.

3. If the output buffer contains only one character, clear the buffer and return that character.

4. If the output buffer has more than two characters, look for a pair of adjacent characters (starting with the second and third characters) where the first character in the pair has a higher combining class than the second. If you find such a pair, exchange the two characters. Compare the new first character in the pair with the character that now immediately precedes it and exchange *them* if their combining classes are out of order. Continue in this way until you've found the appropriate place for what was originally the second character in the pair, and then continue looking for out-of-order pairs. (In other words, do an insertion sort to order the combining marks by combining class without disturbing the relative order of characters with the same combining class.)

5. Remove the first character from the output buffer and return it to the caller.

Compatibility Decomposition

Compatibility decomposition (i.e., conversion to Normalized Form KD) works just like canonical decomposition. In fact, it's a superset of canonical decomposition. For every canonical composite in the string, you replace it with its decomposition. In addition, for every *compatibility* composite in the string, you replace it with its decomposition. In fact, you may have to do both on the same character, because the canonical decompositions of some characters include compatibility composites. Repeat the replacement step until no characters are left in the string that have either a canonical or a compatibility decomposition. Finish as before, by performing canonical reordering on the whole string.

The only difference is that you decompose compatibility composites. Unlike a canonical decomposition, a compatibility decomposition may have any number of characters. This proliferation occurs because with canonical decompositions, you could guarantee that the lead character in each partially decomposed version of the character existed in the Unicode standard. That is, for every character whose full decomposition consisted of more than two characters, you could guarantee that Unicode included appropriate characters that would allow you to represent it as the combination of a single combining mark and another composite character. You don't have this guarantee with compatibility decompositions.

As a consequence, you need a way to map from a single Unicode character to a variable-length string. You can use a two-level compact array (or generalized trie) for the main lookup table and have the results be pointers into an auxiliary data structure containing the result strings.

There are a couple ways of optimizing this operation. For instance, you could have the compact array map to 16-bit values. The value would be either a single UTF-16 code unit or a pointer into the auxiliary string list (you'd probably reserve the surrogate and private-use values for use as these pointer values). Alternatively, you could have the compact array map to 32-bit values. The value could be a single UTF-16 code unit (zero-padded out to 32 bits), two UTF-16 code units, or the pointer into the auxiliary string list (again, using 32-bit values where the first 16 bits were surrogate or private-use code units).

If the compact array maps to 32-bit values, another approach would be to have the 32-bit value encode both an offset into the auxiliary string list *and a length*. The strings in the auxiliary list then wouldn't have to be null-terminated, and you could be cleverer about packing things together in that list.

As an example, consider the Roman numeral characters in the Number Forms block. They have compatibility mapping to sequences of normal letters. You could store the compatibility mappings for the numbers from I to XII (U+2160 to U+216B) with the following string:

IXIIVIII

Twenty-six characters' worth of compatibility mappings stored using just 8 characters' worth of string storage. Of course, if you're storing the one- and two-character mappings directly in the lookup table, you can lop the "I" off the front of the example and store 13 characters' worth of compatibility mappings in 7 characters' worth of storage. Still not bad.

No Unicode characters have both canonical decompositions and compatibility decompositions (at the top level—a character can have both kinds of decomposition by virtue of having a canonical decomposition that contains a compatibility composite). For this reason, you can store both types of decompositions in the same table. This approach saves room, although it means you must load all of the compatibility mappings into memory even when you're doing only canonical decomposition, which could waste time and memory. The big problem with putting both kinds of mappings in the same table is that you need a way to tell which are the canonical mappings and which are the compatibility mappings (unless, of course, you want to do only compatibility decomposition).

To solve this problem, you can perform a lookup in a different table (perhaps combining it with the lookups necessary to get a character's combining class). If, on the other hand, you use only one table, you could have separate auxiliary tables for canonical and compatibility mappings (and declare that compatibility mappings always go to the auxiliary table, even if they fit in 32 bits) or you could reserve some part of the table-lookup value as a flag that indicates whether a particular mapping is canonical or compatibility. The latter technique either makes each entry bigger or forces you to go to the auxiliary table more frequently than you otherwise might.

Canonical Composition

Normalized Forms C and KC are more recent normalized Unicode forms than Normalized Forms D and KD, which have been around as long as Unicode itself. They arose out of a need for a more compact canonical representation, and from the fact that many legacy encodings favor composite forms for character–mark combinations over combining character sequences. These forms are specified in Unicode Standard Annex #15 (which also gives Normalized Forms D and KD their current names), which was officially incorporated into version 3.1 of the Unicode standard.

Part of the reason why the older versions of Unicode preferred decomposed forms over composite forms is that normalizing to the composed forms is inherently a more complicated business than normalizing to the decomposed forms. To get to Normalized Form C or Normalized Form KC, you start by converting the text to Normalized Form D or Normalized Form KD, respectively. In other words, you start by taking apart all the composite characters already in the text. Only then can you put them all back together. Canonical ordering behavior is the driving force here. As we saw earlier in the chapter, there are two alternative ways of representing a-macron-underdot with precomposed characters: a-macron plus a combining underdot or a-underdot plus a combining macron. The a-underdot plus a combining macron is the canonical representation in Normalized Form C. If you start with a string that contains a-macron followed by a combining underdot,

$$\bar{a} + .$$

the only way you can get from that to the preferred representation is to first decompose it,

$$a + {}^{-} + .$$

perform canonical reordering on it,

$$a + . + {}^{-}$$

and *then* recompose what you can, yielding the preferred representation:

$$ạ + {}^{-}$$

Thus you start by doing canonical or compatibility decomposition and then perform canonical reordering. Only after both of these operations are complete, producing Normalized Form D or KD, do you perform the new process, canonical composition.

Canonical Composition on a Single Pair of Characters   The fun thing here is that instead of going from a single character to a pair of characters, you're going from a pair of characters to a single character. In effect, instead of having a lookup table with 1,114,112 entries, each consisting of either one or two characters, you need a lookup table with 1,114,112 *times* 1,114,112 entries. That's more than 1.24 *trillion* entries! Luckily, each entry needs to store only one character instead of a pair of characters.

Of course, only 13,038 of those entries actually have a character in them. That's how many characters have canonical decompositions in Unicode 3.1— remember, this process never generates characters that have *compatibility* decompositions. Normalized Form C will leave such characters alone if they were initially in the text. Normalized Form KC won't, but neither form will produce new ones.

Because the lookup table is so sparsely populated, it lends itself well to trie-based schemes for reducing the memory required, but there's actually an even simpler implementation approach: Use a hash table.

We know a few important things that can help us. First, canonical composition only produces canonical composites, and canonical composites always decompose to pairs of characters (except, of course, for singleton decompositions, which are explicitly excluded from canonical composition). This means we only have to consider pairs of characters. Second, all of the characters that participate in canonical composition—the characters that can be composed and the characters produced by the composition—are in the BMP. This means we're mapping pairs of 16-bit keys to a single 16-bit result.

We can combine the two characters that need to be composed into a single 32-bit key and use it to index into a hash table. Depending on the size and structure of the table, you might be able to use it as-is as a hash key, or you might have to pass it through a simple hashing function. Because the conceptual table is very sparsely populated (only 13,038 out of more than 4 billion keys map to values) and the keys that map to values are dispersed fairly well across the encoding space, it's not difficult to devise a hashing function that leads to no collisions in the hash table. Thus, the table itself can be a single array of 16-bit values. The table can be made very compact and the lookup can be made very fast.

Just as a single character can be decomposed into a sequence of three or more characters when performing canonical decomposition, so too can a sequence of three or more characters be composed into a single character when performing canonical composition. You perform this task by repeatedly applying the composition rules to pairs of characters. The details are a little trickier than for decomposition, however—we'll look at them later.

Canonical Composition on a Sequence of Hangul Jamo   You can also recompose a Hangul syllable algorithmically, although some wrinkles occur. When you canonically decompose a Hangul syllable, you end up with a very regular sequence of characters: exactly one initial consonant, exactly one vowel, and no more than one final consonant. These are the only sequences that can be recomposed.

It's legal to have multiple initial consonants or vowels or final consonants in a row in a sequence of conjoining Hangul jamo, and it's easy to see how this might happen. For example, the character U+1115 HANGUL CHOSEONG NIEUN-TIKEUT (ᄕ) could be represented with two Unicode characters: U+1102 HANGUL CHOSEONG NIEUN followed by U+1103 HANGUL CHOSEONG TIKEUT. If you broke down a Hangul syllable into individual marks in this way, you could theoretically represent a single syllable with as many as eight code point values (three initial consonants, two vowels, and three final consonants).

Unicode allows this decomposition, but does nothing to encourage it. None of the conjoining jamo characters has either a canonical or a compatibility decomposition. Instead, the jamo that consist of two or three marks (that can also be used on their own as jamo) exist on a completely equal footing with their brethren that consist only of a single mark. Nothing in Unicode will either break down U+1113 into U+1102 followed by U+1100 or combine U+1102 and U+1100 into U+1113. In practice, pathological sequences consisting of more than one of a particular kind of jamo in a row (or missing an initial consonant or vowel) don't really happen: Standard Korean keyboard layouts don't generate them, and rendering engines generally won't draw such sequences correctly.

Of course, if you're *writing* a Korean input method, a Korean character renderer, or other software designed to operate on Korean text, you very well *may* care about these "pathological" sequences and their equivalences to more "well-formed" sequences. The appropriate equivalences aren't specified by the Unicode standard, however, and mappings based on them aren't part of Unicode normalization. Unicode 1.0 had some of these mappings, but they were removed from later versions and declared to be application-specific.

A canonical-composition process operating on Hangul jamo starts by checking whether it's looking at a leading consonant/vowel or leading consonant/vowel/trailing consonant combination. If it isn't, it leaves the jamo characters alone and keeps searching for one of these combinations. (For the purposes of canonical composition, U+115F HANGUL CHOSEONG FILLER doesn't count as an initial consonant and U+1160 HANGUL JUNGSEONG FILLER doesn't count as a vowel.) If it does see a lead-vowel-trail or lead/vowel sequence, then and only then does it perform the reverse of the transformation described in the section on canonical decomposition. The code to do that composition is left as an exercise for the reader.

One other wrinkle: If a stretch of text *mixes* conjoining jamo with precomposed syllables, you'll get the right answer only if you decompose the syllables before you compose the jamo. This restriction occurs for the same reason that you have to decompose any composite characters before composing everything: If a sequence consists of a syllable that contains only a leading consonant and a vowel, followed by a trailing-consonant jamo, the trailing consonant *can* combine with the syllable to form a different syllable. You'll get this result if the original syllable had been spelled with jamo, so you have to ensure that the process also works if the first part of the syllable is spelled with an actual precomposed-syllable character.

Composition Exclusion   Unicode Standard Annex #15, which defines the normalization forms, also specifies a list of characters with canonical decompositions that *aren't* allowed in Normalized Forms C and KC. This **composition exclusion list** may become longer over time, so it's supplied in the Unicode Character Database as CompositionExclusions.txt.

Four classes of composite characters appear in the composition exclusion list:

- Characters with singleton decompositions. A character with a one-character canonical decomposition is a character that is either deprecated or discouraged in Unicode text—discouraged strongly enough so as to be prohibited in normalized Unicode text, in fact. These characters shouldn't appear in *any* normalization form, but need to be explicitly prohibited in Forms C and KC, because they are supposed to prefer canonical composites. (This is also why we know that canonical composition always works on pairs of characters: Singleton decompositions are explicitly prohibited.)

- Composite characters with a nonzero combining class. Some combining characters do break down into pairs of combining characters in Normalization Forms D and KD. For example a single code point value represents both a dialytika (diaeresis) and a tonos (acute accent) on top of a Greek letter: it decomposes to separate diaeresis and acute accent characters. That's the preferred representation in all normalization forms. Like the characters with singleton decompositions, composite characters with nonzero combining classes are effectively discouraged and shouldn't appear in normalized Unicode text.

- Script-specific exclusions. In a few scripts, for script-specific reasons, some composite characters are provided for compatibility purposes, but their preferred representation is a combining character sequence. For example, the Alphabetic Presentation Forms block includes a few pointed Hebrew letters. These particular letter–point combinations are fairly common in Yiddish or other non-Hebrew languages that use the Hebrew alphabet, but not in Hebrew or in other languages. If you normalize pointed Hebrew to Form C, you don't want the weird situation in which 90 percent of the text uses the characters in the Hebrew block (with the points being represented with their own code points), but occasional letter–point combinations are represented with these compatibility composites from the Alphabetic Presentation Forms block. As a consequence, these presentation forms are excluded.

- New characters. If version X of Unicode represents, say, x with a dot underneath by using an x plus a combining underdot character, but version X+1 of Unicode introduces a new precomposed x-underdot character, you get into trouble. Now if you take text in version X of Unicode and normalize it using a program designed for version X+1, the resulting text is no longer in version X of Unicode or readable by the program that originally produced it. To prevent this kind of problem, Normalized Forms C and KC were permanently nailed to version 3.0 of Unicode. Canonical composites added to Unicode after version 3.0 can never be produced by canonical composition. The canonical representation for these characters in *all four normalized forms* will always be the decomposed representation. For this reason, we don't have to worry about supplementary-plane characters in our canonical composition tables.[5]

You generally don't have to specifically worry about the characters in the composition exclusion list in your code at run time. The table that maps base–mark pairs to composite characters just has to be set up so as not to map anything to characters in the composition exclusion list.

Canonical Composition on a Whole String   Applying canonical composition to a string of characters is a little more complicated than applying canonical decomposition to a string of characters. This complexity arises because you have to be careful not to do anything that would mess up the ordering of the combining marks in a combining character sequence. If you start with a string that's in Normalized Form D or KD, the code would look something like this:

```
public static char[] canonCombine(char[] in) {
    char[] result = new char[in.length];
    int p = 0;
    int p2 = 1;

    // start by comparing the first and second characters in the
        string
    int i = 0;
    int j = 1;

    while (i < in.length) {
      // if both characters are of combining class 0, we're done
      // combining things with the first character. Advance
```

---

5. You don't have a stability problem if the composite character *and all the characters in its full decomposition* are introduced in the same Unicode version, as is the case with the musical symbols in Unicode 3.1. You have a stability problem only if a newly added composite character has characters in its full decomposition that were added in an earlier version of Unicode. UAX #15 doesn't make that distinction, however: All composite characters added after Unicode 3.0 are disallowed in normalized text, even if their presence wouldn't cause a stability problem.

```
    // past the combining character sequences in both
    // input and output.
    if (combClass(in[i]) == 0
        && (j == in.length || combClass(in[j] == 0)) {
      result[p] = in[i];
      p = p2;
      ++p2;
      i = j;
      ++j;
    }

    // if the second character is a combining character and it
    // can combine with the first character, combine them,
    // storing the temporary result in the input buffer,
    // and advance past the combining mark without writing it
    // to the output
    else if (combClass(in[i]) == 0 && canCombine(in[i], in[j])) {
      in[i] = combine(in[i], in[j]);
      ++j;
    }

    // if the second character is a combining character and it
    // CAN'T combine with the first, this character (and any
    // others of the same combining class) will remain in the
    // output.  Copy them to the output (keeping track of where
    // the base character is) and advance past them.
    else if (combClass(in[i]) == 0) {
      int jCombClass = combClass(in[j]);
      while (combClass(in[j]) == jCombClass)
        result[p2++] = in[j++];
    }
  }
}
}
```

This example assumes the existence of a function called combClass() that returns a character's combining class, a function called canCombine() that says whether a particular pair of characters can be combined into a single composite character, and a function called combine() that composes two characters into a single composite character. The code tries to combine each base character (character with combining class 0) with as many combining characters after it as possible, with one exception: Any characters that *can't* combine with the base character block any characters of the same combining class that follow them from combining with the base character.

You have to take this tack because two combining characters with the same combining class interact with each other typographically—their order indicates which one to draw closer to the base character. If the inner character can't combine with the base characters, you can't combine the outer one with the base character without changing their visual presentation (i.e., making the outer character show up closer to the base character than the inner character does).

Putting It All Together   Just as you can interleave canonical decomposition with canonical reordering, so too can you interleave both of these processes with canonical composition. If the string you're trying to convert to Normalized Form C is already in Form C, it is a big waste of time to convert it to Form D just so you can convert it back to Form C. You can avoid this step with the following algorithm:

- If the current character is a composite character but it's not in the composition exclusion list, and if the next character is of combining class zero, leave the current character alone.
- If the current character is a composite character, perform canonical decomposition on it and, if necessary, perform canonical reordering on the result and any subsequent combining characters. Next, perform canonical composition on the resulting sequence. (If the character that was decomposed wasn't of combining class 0, you'll have to back up until you find a character that is of combining class 0 and start both canonical reordering and canonical composition from there.)
- If the current character is *not* a composite character and the character that follows it is a combining character, perform canonical composition on this character and any combining characters that follow it.
- Otherwise, leave the current character alone.

Optimizing Unicode Normalization

The DerivedNormalizationProperties.txt file in the Unicode Character Database can be useful in optimizing your Unicode normalization code. For each

Unicode character, this file tells you whether it can occur in each of the Unicode normalized forms. You can use this to do a quick check on each character to see whether anything at all needs to be done with it. If you're converting to Normalized Form C, for example, you don't actually have to drop into the full normalization logic until you see a character with the CompEx, NFC_NO, or NFC_MAYBE property. This can save you a lot of work.

The DerivedNormalizationProperties.txt file also includes properties that tell you whether a particular character will expand to more than one character when converted to a particular normalized form. You can use this to defer allocation of extra storage space for the result string until you really need it (or to find out before you start normalizing whether or not you can do it in place).

Testing Unicode Normalization

The Unicode Character Database includes a file called NormalizationTest.txt. You use this file to determine whether your implementation of Unicode normalization is correct.

Each line of NormalizationTest.txt consists of a set of Unicode code point values written out as hex numerals (each line also has a comment with the literal characters and their names to make everything more readable). The lines are divided into five parts, or "columns," separated with semicolons. The first column is some arbitrary Unicode string, which may or may not be normalized already. The other four columns represent that string converted into Normalization Forms C, D, KC, and KD, respectively. If your implementation of normalization is correct, the following statements will be true for each line of the file:

- If you convert every sequence on the line into Normalized Form C, columns 2 and 4 shouldn't change, columns 1 and 3 should change to be the same as column 2, and column 5 should change to be the same as column 4.
- If you convert every sequence on the line into Normalized Form D, columns 3 and 5 shouldn't change, columns 1 and 2 should change to be the same as column 3, and column 4 should change to be the same as column 5.

- If you convert every sequence on the line into Normalized Form KC, column 4 shouldn't change, and the other four columns should change to be the same as it.
- If you convert every sequence on the line into Normalized Form KD, column 5 shouldn't change, and the other four columns should change to be the same as it.

The file is divided into three parts: Part 0 performs a spot check for a number of interesting characters. Part 1 carries out a character-by-character test of every Unicode character that has a decomposition (in addition to the characters listed here, you should check all the other Unicode characters to make sure they don't change when any of the normalizations are applied to them). Part 2 is a fairly elaborate test of canonical reordering.

For more information, see the file itself. The basic rule is simple, however: If your normalization code can't satisfy all of the conditions described above for every line in the file, it doesn't conform to the standard.

■ CONVERTING BETWEEN UNICODE AND OTHER STANDARDS

It would be nice if all digitally encoded text in the world were already in Unicode—but it isn't, and it never will be. Not only do innumerable pieces of encoded text and computer programs that process text predate the introduction of Unicode and will never be updated, but there are and will always be documents, computer systems, and user communities that don't and won't use Unicode. While one can hope that over time the computing public will move more and more toward using Unicode exclusively for the encoding of text, the reality is that some text will always be encoded using non-Unicode encodings, and Unicode-based systems will frequently have to contend with text encoded in these encodings.

For this reason, some sort of conversion facility will be required for almost every system that exchanges text with the outside world. Of course, virtually every Unicode-support library already includes such a conversion facility—unlike the situation with compression and normalization, you'll rarely find yourself working with a library that doesn't include some type of character encoding conversion. The important question usually isn't "Am I working with an API that provides encoding conversion?" but rather "Am I working with an API that provides the conversions I need?" or "Am I working with an API that does conversion in the way I want it done?"

If the answer is yes, or the API produces a close-enough answer that you can modify reasonably easily to get the desired answer, use it. There's no sense in going to the trouble of creating a conversion system yourself when you don't have to. But if you find you have to implement character conversion for whatever reason, read on.

Getting Conversion Information

The first issue is coming up with the information on just how you convert between a particular encoding and Unicode. For a wide variety of encoding standards, you can find the answer on the Unicode Web site. The Unicode Consortium maintains an unofficial repository of mapping tables between Unicode and a variety of national, international, and vendor encoding standards. The tables are in a simple textual format where each line consists of a sequence of bytes (shown as two-digit hex values), a tab character, and a sequence of Unicode code point values (shown as four-or-more-digit hex values).

Interestingly, Unicode Technical Report #22 proposes a richer XML-based format for describing how to convert from some encoding to Unicode and back. As of this book's writing, this format wasn't being used for the mapping tables on the Unicode Web site, but certain third-party libraries—notably the open-source International Components for Unicode—were using it. This report on character encoding conversion includes a lot of instructive information, and it's worth reading.[6]

Converting Between Unicode and Single-Byte Encodings

The mechanics of converting from a single-byte encoding to Unicode are trivially simple: Just use an array of 256 code point values. Converting back the

---

6. Much of the information in the rest of this section, and particularly the information on choosing converters and handling exceptional conditions, is drawn from UTR #22.

other way isn't much more difficult: Use some form of trie structure (if the conversion doesn't involve any supplementary-plane characters, it can be a one-level compact array). Often, you'll get better compression if the trie stores numerical offsets rather than the actual values to map to, but this choice generally won't make a difference when you're converting to a one-byte encoding.

Converting Between Unicode and Multibyte Encodings

Converting between Unicode and a multibyte encoding will generally require a trie structure of some type for conversions in both directions. If the non-Unicode encoding has both one- and two-byte code point values, it often makes sense for the Unicode-to-non-Unicode table to behave as though all of the code point values in the target encoding are two bytes long, representing one-byte code point value with an invalid leading byte value (0x00 will work in most cases), and to suppress that when emitting the resulting characters. This approach lets you always map to 16-bit values in the table and helps if you want to store numeric offsets in the table instead of actual code point values in the target encoding. With multibyte encodings, the sequence being mapped to often includes enough code point values for this technique to help your compression in the trie.

Other Types of Conversions

In a few interesting cases, you can't do simple table-based conversion but rather must do something special.

Stateful Encodings   In a stateful encoding, bytes seen earlier in the conversion process affect the interpretation of bytes seen later in the process. Here we do not refer to simple multibyte encodings, where several bytes in a row combine into a single code point, but rather situations where whole code point values are overloaded with multiple semantics. Typically, you have a bank of code point values, each of which represents two (or more) characters. Shift-in and shift-out codes in the text stream put the converter in a "mode" that specifies which of the two sets of characters that bank of code points will represent. That mode persists until the next shift-in/shift-out character.

SCSU is an example of a stateful encoding. Likewise, the old Baudot code, which used the same range of code points for letters and digits and used control codes to shift that bank back and forth, was a stateful encoding. A number of modern EBCDIC-based encodings also use this technique.

For stateful encodings, your converter will have to keep track of its mode. You'll need multiple to-Unicode conversion tables, one for each mode, or your tables must be able to store all of the overloaded values for those overloaded code point values. The from-Unicode converter will also have to keep track of the mode, with the table including information on which mode to use for the overloaded code points in the non-Unicode encodings. You would emit a mode-shift character anytime you have to emit a code point with a mode you're not currently in.

ISO 2022   ISO 2022 is a special example of a stateful encoding. This standard defines a set of common characteristics for coded character sets, but doesn't actually define a coded character set. Instead, it defines a character encoding scheme for representing characters from different coded character sets in the same text stream by making use of various escape sequences to change the meanings of characters in different parts of the encoding space. An ISO 2022 converter would generally use other converters for the actual character code conversion; it would simply interpret (or emit) the escape sequences to shift coded character sets.

Algorithmic Conversions   A few encodings allow you to do all the work with a simple mathematical transformation. The classical example is, of course, ISO 8859-1 (Latin-1). You could convert from this standard to Unicode simply by zero-padding the byte values out to 16 bits. You could convert from Unicode back to ISO 8859-1 by truncating the value back down to 8 bits (although you would probably want to do a little more work to handle exceptional conditions).

In some other encodings, Unicode preserves the relative order of the characters in the code charts. You can convert to and from Unicode by just adding or subtracting a constant (or, in the case of some ASCII-based encodings, doing a range check and adding or subtracting one of two constants depending on the result).

Transformations on Other Conversions   If you're implementing a variety of encodings, you may be able to save space for conversion tables by doubling up. For example, you might have two encodings, one of which is a superset of the other. You could use the same table for both and postprocess the conversion for the subset encoding. This technique might work, for example, with ISO 8859-1 and Microsoft code page 1252, which is a superset (but only if you ignore the C1 control-code space in ISO 8859-1). As another example, a number of encoding schemes are based on the JIS X 0208 character set, so you might use a table to convert to the abstract JIS 208 values and then algorithmically convert to the actual encoding scheme in use (for example, EUC-JP).

Consider also variants on the same conversion. For example, you may want 0x5C in a Japanese ASCII-based encoding to be treated as the yen sign, or you may want it to be treated as the backslash. Rather than having two tables that differ only in their handling of that character, you might just have a table for one variant and postprocess the result when you want the other variant.

Handling Exceptional Conditions

You must handle a number of exceptional conditions when converting between any two encodings:

- The input text is malformed. You encounter a byte or sequence of bytes that isn't supposed to occur in that encoding. For example, U+FFFF is illegal in all Unicode transformations, 0xFF should never happen in UTF-8, a high surrogate is illegal in UTF-16 unless it's followed by a low surrogate, and so forth. Many encodings, particularly the variable-length ones, have such restrictions.
- A byte or sequence of bytes is legal, but isn't assigned to a character. This scenario may indicate malformed text, or it may indicate that the text is in a newer version of the encoding than your converter is designed to handle.
- A byte or sequence of bytes is legal and assigned to a character, but the encoding you're mapping to doesn't have a representation for it.

You may want to treat all three conditions in the same way, or you may want to treat them differently. Your response may also depend on the situation (if you're writing an API library, you may want the calling code to tell you what to do). You have a number of options for dealing with exceptional conditions:

- Halt the conversion and report an error. Generally, just choking on the input isn't a good idea. If the conversion is restartable, however, this technique can be used to defer the job of handling the exception to the caller.

- Ignore the bytes from the source text stream that caused the exception. This is a popular strategy, but has the disadvantage of masking problems in the source text. The resulting text may look okay, with the user never realizing that some additional text was never converted.

- Write some kind of error character. If you're converting text to Unicode, this usually means writing U+FFFD, the replacement character, when you encounter an illegal input sequence or one you can't map. (Most encodings have an analogous character—in ASCII, 0x1A, the SUB character, serves this purpose.) Sometimes, you might want to distinguish between unmappable and illegal input sequences. You could use U+FFFF in Unicode for the illegal sequences. You have to be careful with this technique, though, because U+FFFF should never occur in well-formed Unicode. It's acceptable for internal-processing purposes, but you must be careful to convert U+FFFF to U+FFFD or to strip it out before sending the text to some other process.

- If you encounter an unmappable character when converting to Unicode (which doesn't happen very often), you can map it to a code point value in the private-use space. The beauty of this approach is that if you later convert back to the source encoding from Unicode, the characters you couldn't handle can be restored. (If you know which characters you're converting to private-use code point values, you can treat them as ordinary characters inside your application as well.)

- Write an escape sequence. If the text you're converting is in a format that supports numeric escape sequences, you can convert unmappable source code point values into escape sequences. For example, if you're converting from Unicode to ASCII and you know the destination is a Java source file, you can convert the unmappable character to a sequence of the form \u1234. If you're going to an XML file, you can convert to an XML numeric character reference (e.g., Ӓ).

- Use a fallback mapping. If the character you're mapping can't be represented in the target character set, you might convert it to something reasonably similar. For example, you might convert the curly "" quotation marks to the straight quotation marks when going to ASCII. Be careful when using fallback mappings, however: If you convert from Unicode to something else using fallback mappings, and then back to Unicode, you lose data. Sometimes this loss is acceptable, but if you need to preserve round-trip integrity, you can't use fallback mappings (or you need to flag them as such). In systems such as HTML and XML, which can correctly handle characters encoded as escape sequences, that's generally a better way to go.

  For the same reason, multiple characters in one encoding generally shouldn't map to the same character in another encoding, because this approach also loses data in a round-trip conversion. Unless the mappings are truly for alternative representations (say, Unicode characters with singleton canonical mappings to other characters), you usually want to flag all but one of them as fallback mappings.

Dealing with Differences in Encoding Philosophy

You might have to worry about some other types of transformations when converting between Unicode and something else.

Normalization Form   Usually, an encoding naturally converts to Normalized Form C or to Normalized Form D. Some will convert naturally to both (they don't include any composite characters and they don't include any combining characters—our old friend ASCII is an example). When converting from Unicode to one of these encodings, you generally want to convert to the appropriate Unicode normalized form first (or as part of the encoding conversion) to make sure that you really catch everything representable in the target encoding.

If the non-Unicode encoding doesn't naturally convert to any Unicode normalized form (i.e., it contains sequences that would convert to unnormalized Unicode text), it's generally a good policy to normalize the result after converting to Unicode.

Combining Character Sequences   Not all encodings that use combining character sequences encode them in the same way that Unicode does. If, say, you're converting to or from an encoding, such as ISO 6937, that puts the mark *before* the character to which it attaches, you have to switch the base–mark pairs as part of the conversion.

Character Order   Some older vendor encodings for Hebrew and Arabic use visual order instead of logical order to store the characters. In these cases, you have to apply the Unicode bi-di algorithm (or a reversed version of the bi-di algorithm) as part of the conversion.

Glyph Encodings   Some encodings (again, generally older vendor encodings) are glyph-based. In these encodings, different glyphs for the same character get different code point values. Converting to such an encoding involves the same kind of contextual glyph selection logic you need to render the text on the screen.

Choosing a Converter

Choosing a converter is generally straightforward, but you can get into interesting situations if the converter you want doesn't exist but one converter comes close to matching the desired one. In such situations, you can sometimes do a "best fit" mapping. You acknowledge that you might lose data, but sometimes this loss is okay as long as you know errors will occur and you don't purport to be doing the correct conversion.

The one case where things work perfectly is if the text you're reading is in encoding X, you have a converter for some encoding that's a superset of X, and you're going from X to Unicode. If the environment supports escape sequences (say, you're producing an XML file), you can do the opposite: You want to output X, you have a converter for a subset of X, and you're going from Unicode to X. Some characters that are representable in X aren't representable in the subset to which you're converting, but you don't lose data because you can convert them to escape sequences.

Line-Break Conversion

Line-break conventions (i.e., which characters signal the end of a line or paragraph) are generally specific to a particular platform or application, rather than a particular target encoding (of course, the target encoding defines which choices you have). If your converters have to operate on a cross-platform basis or are used in some other situation where you can't nail down the line-breaking conventions, you may need to do line-break conversion in a separate pass or separate out line-break conversion from the rest of the conversion logic.

■ CASE MAPPING AND CASE FOLDING

English speakers are familiar with the concept of case. Every letter in the Latin alphabet comes in two "cases": upper and lower (or capital and small). Like the Latin alphabet, the Greek, Cyrillic, and Armenian alphabets are cased, or "bicameral." (The letters in the Georgian alphabet also come in two distinct styles, which for a short time in history were treated as uppercase and lowercase, but generally aren't anymore.)

Occasionally, you will run into situations where you want to convert one letter (or a whole string) from one case to the other. Many word processors, for example, let you convert to uppercase or lowercase with a single command or a character style. On many systems, you can convert everything to uppercase or lowercase not for display, but rather to erase case distinctions when searching. In Unicode, this is done with a different process, known as **case folding**.

Unicode Technical Report #21 provides more information on performing case mappings on Unicode characters.

Case Mapping on a Single Character

It should come as no surprise to learn that you can't just convert from one case to another by adding or subtracting some constant, as you can with ASCII. After all, not all case pairs are the same distance apart. For example, the case pairs in the ASCII block are 32 code points apart, but those in the Latin Extended A block are immediately adjacent to each other.

For this reason, you have to do a table lookup. The UnicodeData.txt and SpecialCasing.txt files in the Unicode Character Database include the case mappings for all Unicode characters. You can use a one-level compact array as your case mapping table. As with code conversion, you will achieve better compression if the table holds numeric offsets rather than actual code point values.

You do, however, need an exception table for case mappings. A number of reasons explain why:

- *Titlecase.* Unicode includes a number of single code point values that represent two characters. If one of these values occurs at the beginning of a word, you need a special "titlecase" version that represents the capital version of the first letter and the lowercase version of the second letter and can be used at the beginning of a word. For the characters that have titlecase versions, you have to store *two* mappings: one to titlecase and one to the opposite case. (For all other characters, the titlecase form is the same as the uppercase form.)
- *Expansion.* Some characters turn into two characters when mapped to uppercase.
- *Context sensitivity.* Some characters map to different characters depending on where they occur in a word.
- *Language sensitivity.* Some characters have different mappings depending on the language.

The UnicodeData.txt file includes the titlecase mappings for everything. The other special mappings, for historical reasons, reside in a separate file, SpecialCasing.txt. For a complete treatment of SpecialCasing.txt, see Chapter 5. To recap here, some of the more important mappings in the SpecialCasing.txt file are as follows:

- Many characters that expand when converted to uppercase. The most important and common example is the German letter ß, which uppercases to "SS," but many others exist.
- The Greek letter sigma, which has two lowercase versions: one that occurs at the end of a word and another that occurs in the middle of a word (or when the letter sigma appears on its own as a "word").
- Mappings to deal with Lithuanian. In Lithuanian, a lowercase i or j with an accent mark over it doesn't lose the dot, as it does in other languages. In other words, a lowercase i with an acute accent normally looks like this—í—but in Lithuanian it looks like this: i̇́. You can handle this issue

with a special font for Lithuanian, but if you want to explicitly represent it this way in Unicode, you have to use combining character sequences that include an explicit U+0307 COMBINING DOT ABOVE. The case mapping code also has to be smart enough to add and remove this character as necessary.

- Language-sensitive mappings for Turkish and Azeri that deal with the letter ı, whose uppercase form is I. (The uppercase version of i becomes İ so you can tell them apart.)

One thing to keep in mind when doing case mappings is that they lose data and aren't inherently reversible. If you start with "Lucy McGillicuddy" and convert it into uppercase, you get "LUCY MCGILLICUDDY." If you now convert back to lowercase, you get "lucy mcgillicuddy." Going to title-case also doesn't get back the original string; you get "Lucy Mcgillicuddy," instead. In a word processing program or other situation in which you provide a case mapping facility to the user, you must save the original string so that you can restore it if necessary. (A simple Undo facility usually takes care of this requirement.)

Case Mapping on a String

Mapping a string from one case to another is relatively simple if you're going to uppercase or lowercase: Just apply the appropriate transformation to each character one by one. The only thing you need to keep in mind is that the string may become longer in the process. This expansion may make converting case in place impossible or force you to fall back on the single-character mappings in UnicodeData.txt, even though they're not always correct.

Going to titlecase is a little more complicated. Here, you must iterate through the string and check context. If a character is preceded by another cased character (whatever its case), convert it to lowercase. Otherwise, convert it to titlecase (which, most of the time, will be the same as converting it to uppercase).

Of course, this technique doesn't actually give you what you want every time. "Ludwig van Beethoven" would turn into "Ludwig Van Beethoven" under this transformation, again possibly making it necessary to save the original string before manipulating it. More importantly, applying the transformation to "THE CATCHER IN THE RYE" gives you "The Catcher In The Rye," when what you really want is "The Catcher in the Rye." In other words, not every word in a real title is capitalized. Getting this issue right is language-specific, as the list of words you don't capitalize varies from language to language. A simple algorithm won't worry about this problem and will just capitalize everything.

Case Folding

If you're really trying to erase case distinctions from a pair of strings you're about to compare for equality, you don't want to use the case-mapping stuff. Converting to any one case will preserve some distinctions that converting the other way will erase, and doing both conversions is a little costly (and doing it in different orders will produce *different* results).

The Unicode Character Database includes another file, CaseFolding.txt, specifically for this task. It maps the cased letters to case-independent sequences of characters. Generally, but not always, the mapping is equivalent to mapping first to uppercase, then mapping the result to lowercase.

CaseFolding.txt includes two separate sets of mappings. One set has a one-character mapping for everything. It'll generally give you the right answer, but will leave in some distinctions that you'd eliminate if you actually mapped to uppercase and then back to lowercase. The other set includes expanding mappings. It'll erase more differences, but is a little more complicated (and perhaps slower) to implement.

Once again, the Turkish letter ı causes trouble in case folding. CaseFolding.txt includes two optional mappings for dealing with this issue. If you use them, they erase any case distinction, but also erase the distinction between ı and i. If you don't use them, the case differences for i and ı aren't normalized (i.e., they and their uppercase counterparts will still compare as different).

Keep in mind that you want to use the CaseFolding.txt mappings only for *language-independent* comparisons, such as building search trees or other internal uses. If you want truly language-sensitive behavior, you need a full-blown collation facility. We'll be looking at collation in Chapter 15.

▪ TRANSLITERATION

Finally, there's **transliteration**.[7] This term generally refers to taking a piece of text written using some writing system and converting it to another writing system. It isn't the same as *translation,* which involves converting the text to a different language and changing the *words.* When text is transliterated, the words (and the language) stay the same; they're just written with different characters.

In computer text-processing circles, the word "transliteration" is used in a broader sense to refer to a broad range of algorithmic transformations on text. A facility designed to convert text from one writing system to another should be flexible enough to perform a bunch of other transformations as well.

Why is transliteration useful? Suppose you've got the following customer list:[8]

김, 국삼

김, 명희

정, 병호

たけだ, まさゆき

ますだ, よしひこ

やまもと, のぼる

Ρούτση, Άννα

Καλούδης, Χρήστος

Θεοδωράτου, Ελένη

This list will be a lot easier for an English-speaking user to understand if it appears like this instead, especially if he doesn't have Japanese, Korean, or Greek fonts installed on his computer:

Gim, Gugsam

Gim, Myeonghyi

---

7. Most of the material in this section is drawn from Mark Davis and Alan Liu, "Transliteration in ICU," *Proceedings of the 19th International Unicode Conference,* session B14, April 27, 2001, and can also be found at http://www.macchiato.com.

8. This example is taken directly from the Davis/Liu paper, op. cit.

Jeong, Byeongho

Takeda, Masayuki

Masuda, Yoshihiko

Yamamoto, Noboru

Roútsē, Ánna

Kaloúdēs, Chrêstos

Theodōrátou, Elénē

Of course, a Russian-speaking user might be more comfortable with the list transliterated into Cyrillic letters instead.

In addition to converting text into some target writing system for display, a transliteration facility is useful for a number of other types of mappings:

- Accepting keyboard input for a particular script using a keyboard designed for another script (e.g., entering Russian text using an English keyboard)
- Accepting keyboard input for Han and Hangul characters, where it takes multiple keystrokes on a conventional keyboard to enter a single character (building up a whole Hangul syllable out of several component jamo, for example, or entering Japanese or Chinese characters by entering a Romanized version of the text on an English keyboard)
- Converting text in a multiscriptal language from one script to another (e.g., converting Serbo-Croatian from Cyrillic letters to Latin letters, Japanese from Hiragana to Katakana, Chinese from Simplified Chinese characters to Traditional Chinese characters)[9]
- Case conversions
- Converting typewritten forms of certain characters to their typographically correct equivalents (for example, converting -- to —, or converting " or `` to ")

---

9. Some of the more complicated conversions, such as from Han characters to any of the phonetic scripts, or between Simplified Han and Traditional Han, often require more sophisticated logic, often involving linguistic analysis and dictionary lookup, that go beyond what a typical transliteration package can do. Conceptually, it's the same type of problem, but practically speaking, it requires different code.

- Allowing input of arbitrary Unicode characters by typing their hexadecimal code point values along with some special character
- Fixing typing and spelling mistakes on the fly (think of Microsoft Word's AutoCorrect feature, for example)
- Unicode normalization

Many of these transformations, especially the script-to-script conversions, are more complex, and require a more complicated approach, than the other conversions we've examined. Not only do you have to deal with the full generality of many-to-many mappings (where source and destination strings that are longer than a single character are the norm rather than the exception), but you also have to handle some thorny problems:

- *Context.* A particular character or sequence of characters may be mapped to some other sequence of characters only when certain sequences of characters appear before or after it. For instance, " may be mapped to " only when it's preceded by a nonletter and followed by a letter.
- *Wildcard matches.* To specify the curly-quote mapping above, you don't want to spell out every single pair of surrounding characters that cause the mapping to happen; rather, you want to specify character categories and let the engine expand them into actual pairs of characters.
- *Partial matches.* If the text on which you're operating is coming in chunks—say, from a buffered file API or from keyboard input—in some situations you may have to wait to see more characters to know which mapping to perform. For example, if you're mapping Latin letters to Cyrillic letters and have a rule that maps "s" to "c" and "sh" to "ш," if the input includes an "s" you have to wait for the next character (and see whether it is an "h") before deciding what to do with the "s" (unless you know that the "s" is the last character in the input). This effort may involve either buffering characters you're not done with yet or keeping track of which part of the input hasn't been fully mapped yet.
- *Backup.* After you perform a mapping on a piece of text, you'll generally want to start the next mapping with the first character you haven't examined yet. Sometimes, however, you may want to back up into the

result of the mapping you just performed instead. This strategy can sometimes cut down drastically on the number of rules you need to achieve some effect.

For example, consider the palatalized Katakana combinations. Your rules might say that "kyu" turns into "キュ," "kyo" turns into "キョ," "pyu" turns into "ピュ," and so on. Alternatively, one rule might state that "ky" turns into "キ~y" and another rule might state that "~yu" turns into "ュ." If x different consonants can start a palatalized syllable and y different vowels can end a palatalized syllable, you can reduce the number of mapping rules needed from x times y to x plus y using this technique. It works only if you can back up after the first mapping and consider the "~y" again when determining what to do in the second mapping.

In essence, these operations require something similar to a generalized regular-expression–based search-and-replace facility. Without going into huge amounts of detail, one solution to the problem might involve the following data structures:

- A compact array or trie that maps single characters to character categories. It is important for keeping the main lookup table small when rules involve wildcard matches.
- A generalized trie structure that maps arbitrary-length sequences of character categories to result strings in an auxiliary data structure. You probably want the system to consider rules in some defined order (ensuring, for example, that you see the rule for "sh" before you see the rule for "s"), making a ternary-tree representation less than ideal. Most likely you'd base the main mapping table on a binary tree or a generalized tree of arrays. (That is, the list of matching rules or partially matching rules could be a simple linked list or an array.)
- A results data structure, probably a single memory block containing all of the result strings. The strings could either be null-terminated or the main trie could contain pointers and lengths, possibly leading to better compaction.

The results data structure is interesting, because you store not only result strings there, but also information on which parts of the original matching sequence are context and aren't replaced and information on how far to back up into the result before starting the next matching operation. (Flags indicating which parts of the matching sequence are context could appear in the main trie as well.) The new noncharacter code point values in Unicode 3.1 come in handy in these situations, because you can use them as tokens to indicate the backup and context positions, and then just "mark up" the result string with them.

The algorithm would look something like this:

1. Look up a category for the character at the starting position.
2. Use that category to look up the character in the main trie.
3. If the character leads to another node in the trie, advance to the next character in the input and go back to step 1.
4. If the character leads to an entry in the result table, replace the noncontext part of the matching text in the input with the result text from the result table. The new starting position is located after the result text unless the result text specifies a backup position, in which case it is the new starting position. Start over at the root level of the main trie and go back to step 1.
5. If you exhaust the input text while pointing at something other than the root level of the main trie, either you have to pull in more text to figure out what to do or you're really done. In the latter case, you use the "if the next character doesn't match" rule at the current level of the main trie.

This approach may not be the most effective for really complicated mappings that require more knowledge of the language, such as mapping Simplified Chinese to Traditional Chinese. For most generalized mappings, however, it works quite well.

In Chapter 15, we'll look at more complicated operations on Unicode text, many of which also involve mappings of the type discussed in this chapter.

Searching and Sorting

$\mathcal{A}$ side from drawing it on the screen (or some other output device), the most important processes that are usually performed on text are searching and sorting. Of course, the main thing these two operations have in common is string comparison. As with the other processes we've considered, a number of interesting complications are involved in performing string comparison on Unicode strings, many of which stem from the larger repertoire of characters in Unicode. Unlike with many of the other processes, however, some of the issues that make good string comparison difficult are not at all unique to Unicode, but are issues that arise when dealing with text in any format.

Virtually every Unicode support library provides language-sensitive string comparison. Indeed, you'll rarely have to implement this feature yourself—you should usually be able to take advantage of some API that provides language-sensitive comparison. Of course, it might not do exactly what you want or support the languages in which you're interested. In such a case, you might have to write your own comparison routines. Nevertheless, it's often more a matter of learning how to specify your desired results to the API you're using. Searching, on the other hand, is something you might well need to code on your own.

At any rate, it's instructive to understand what goes into doing Unicode-compatible searching and sorting. We'll start by looking at the basics of language-sensitive string comparison, then consider the unique challenges Unicode brings to the party, and finish by discussing some additional things to keep in mind when doing actual searching or sorting.

■ THE BASICS OF LANGUAGE-SENSITIVE STRING COMPARISON

The first thing to remember is that you can't simply rely on comparison of the numeric code point values when you're comparing two strings. Unless the strings that may be compared conform to a very tightly restricted grammar, this approach will always give you the wrong answer. (The one exception occurs when the ordering and equivalences implied by the comparison routine will have no user-visible effects, but even then you must worry about some wrinkles—see "Language-Insensitive String Comparison" later in this chapter.)

This isn't just a Unicode issue. Any binary comparison will give the wrong answers with most encodings. In fact, for every encoding standard, it's probably possible to come up with a pair of strings that will compare wrong if you just use binary comparison, but it's a bigger problem with some encoding standards. The numeric order of the code point (or code unit) values in most encodings is good enough to give you a reasonably acceptable ordering for many sets of strings (for example, the letters of the Latin alphabet are encoded contiguously and in alphabetic order in most encodings), but that's usually about it.

Consider the following list of English words and names, sorted in ASCII order:

Co-Op of America
CoSelCo
Coates
Cohen
Cooper
Cooperatives United
Cosell
MacIntosh
MacPherson
Machinists Union
Macintosh

Macpherson

Van Damme

van der Waal

van den Hul

Vandenberg

If you squint hard enough, you can kind of convince yourself that this order makes sense, but it's definitely not intuitive. The spaces, punctuation, and capital letters gum things up. The order should probably look more like this:

Coates

Cohen

Cooper

Cooperatives United

Co-Op of America

CoSelCo

Cosell

Machinists Union

MacIntosh

Macintosh

MacPherson

Macpherson

Van Damme

Vandenberg

van den Hul

van der Waal

In other words, you probably just want to consider the letters, with things like capital letters and spaces being secondary considerations. Sorting by the raw ASCII code point value doesn't give you that order.

If you consider the Latin-1 encodings, things just get worse. Take the following list, for example:

archaeology

archway

    archæology
    co-operate
    coequal
    condescend
    cooperate
    coziness
    coöperate
    restore
    resume
    resurrect
    royalty
    rugby
    résumé

Again, the accent marks gum things up. The alternate spellings of "cooperate" and "archaeology" are widely scattered, and "resume" and "résumé" wind up far apart. In general, the accented forms of letters become separated from their unaccented counterparts, leading to weird results. Again, you probably expect the list to be sorted more like this:

    archaeology
    archæology
    archway
    coequal
    condescend
    cooperate
    coöperate
    co-operate
    coziness
    restore
    resume
    résumé
    resurrect
    royalty
    rugby

Latin-1 has an additional problem: It's used to encode text in many different languages, and the concept of "alphabetical order" isn't the same across all of them. For example, consider the letter ö. In English, it is just the letter o with a diaeresis mark on it. The diaeresis indicates that the o should be pronounced in a separate syllable from the vowel that precedes it, rather than forming a diphthong (such as in "coöperate"), but the letter is still the letter o and should sort the same as if it didn't have the diaeresis.

In German, the diaeresis indicates a significant change in pronunciation, but the letter is still basically an o. Just the same, depending on who's doing the sorting, ö may sort either as a variant of o or as equivalent to "oe" ("oe" being an acceptable variant spelling of ö in German).

In Swedish, ö is an entirely different letter, not just an o with a mark on it. It sorts with a number of other letters, such as å, ä and ø, at the end of the Swedish alphabet, after z.

It works the other way, too: In English, v and w are different letters. In Swedish, on the other hand, w is just a variant of v.

The upshot is that not only can't you trust the binary order of the code points, but also the actual order you use depends on the language of the text. If you're sorting a group of Latin-1 strings, the final order will be different depending on whether they're in English, Spanish, French, German, or Swedish (to name just a few). Sorting a list of Swedish names using the German or French sorting order is just as wrong as using the binary order.

This point is important. The encoding isn't necessarily aligned with the language. Many encodings can be used to encode multiple languages. Although some encodings tend to be used only with certain languages, this relationship isn't guaranteed and shouldn't be depended upon. In fact, sorting doesn't depend on the language of the strings themselves, but rather on the language *of the person reading them.* An English-speaking user will want to see a list of Swedish names (or a mixed list of Swedish and English names) sorted in English alphabetical order.

This consideration doesn't mean that you have to write a new string comparison routine for every language you might encounter. Instead, the normal approach is to use a rule-driven algorithm, where you have a generalized sorting routine and you pass it some sort of table of information explaining how to sort text in a particular language. In the simplest form, you'd map each character to an abstract weight value appropriate for the specified language and sort the strings according to the weights of their characters instead of the code point values. In reality, the mapping of characters to weights is more complicated, even in non-Unicode encodings such as Latin-1.

Multilevel Comparisons

For starters, you actually need more than one weight value. Consider the following list:

> **car**
>
> **CAT**
>
> **Cat**
>
> **cAT**
>
> **cAt**
>
> **caT**
>
> **cat**
>
> **CAVE**

You want to sort according to the letters without taking the case differences into account, so that "car" sorts before all the "cat"s and "cave" sorts after them. On the other hand, you don't want the order of the "cat"s to be determined by the whim of your sorting algorithm. The "cat"s aren't identical—you want a defined ordering of some kind. For example, maybe the capital letter should come before its small counterpart.

Your first thought might be that you can achieve this effect by interleaving the weight values for the capital and small letters. For example, you could put "C" before "c", but both of them after "b" and before "D". This approach doesn't work, however. It yields this order:

> **CAT**
>
> **CAVE**
>
> **Cat**
>
> **cAT**
>
> **cAt**

car
caT
cat

Note how "car" and "cave" wind up in the middle of the "cat"s instead of on either side of them.

To get the desired effect, you must assign each letter *two* weight values: a **primary weight** and a **secondary weight**. The primary weights are the same for the capital and small versions of each letter. For example, both "A" and "a" have a weight of 1, "B" and "b" have a weight of 2, "C" and "c" have a weight of 3, and so on. The secondary weights, on the other hand, are different for the different cases. Because you already have the primary weights to differentiate things, you can reuse the same secondary-weight values for each letter. All of the capital letters have a secondary weight of 1, and all of the small letters have a secondary weight of 2.

You use them as follows: You compare two strings using their primary weights only. If they're different, you're done. *Only if they're the same* do you compare them again using their secondary weights. This way, a primary difference later in the string still beats a secondary difference earlier in the string (e.g., "Cat" comes after "car" even though "c" comes after "C" because "r" comes before "t" and the difference between "r" and "t" is more important than the difference between "c" and "C"). This technique produces the ordering in the first example above.

To cover all languages, you generally need three or more weight values (or "levels") per character. For most languages, those characters that are considered "different letters" receive different primary weights. Versions of the same letter with different accent marks attached to it (or other variants of the letter, such as "v" and "w" in Swedish) receive different secondary weights. Versions of the same variant of the same letter with different cases receive different tertiary weights.

Again, you compare the strings first using their *primary weights only*. If they compare as equal, you break the tie by comparing them again using their secondary weights. If they're still equal, you break the tie again using their tertiary weights. If they're equal at this level, they really are equal and you either don't care about their ordering or you differentiate based on a secondary key.

You don't have to make three complete passes through the strings to compare strings in this way, of course. You can compare the weights at all levels in a single pass. The code looks something like this:

```
public static int compare(char[] a, char[] b) {
  int firstSecondaryDifference = EQUAL;
  int firstTertiaryDifference = EQUAL;
  int i = 0;

  while (i < a.length && i < b.length) {
    char cA = a[i];
    char cB = b[i];
    if (primaryWeight(cA) > primaryWeight(cB))
      return A_GREATER;
    if (primaryWeight(cB) > primaryWeight(cA))
      return B_GREATER;
    if (firstSecondaryDifference == EQUAL) {
      if (secondaryWeight(cA) > secondaryWeight(cB))
        firstSecondaryDifference = A_GREATER;
      else if (secondaryWeight(cB) > secondaryWeight(cA))
        firstSecondaryDifference = B_GREATER;
      else if (firstTertiaryDifference == EQUAL) {
        if (tertiaryWeight(cA) > tertiaryWeight(cB))
          firstTertiaryDifference = A_GREATER;
        else if (tertiaryWeight(cB) > tertiaryWeight(cA))
          firstTertiaryDifference = B_GREATER;
      }
    }
    ++i;
  }
  if (a.length > b.length)
    return A_GREATER;
  if (b.length > a.length)
    return b_GREATER;
  if (firstSecondaryDifference != EQUAL)
    return firstSecondaryDifference;
  return firstTertiaryDifference;
}
```

Ignorable Characters

Defining levels of difference doesn't by itself always give the right answer. Consider the variant spellings of "cooperate" (with some other words thrown in to clarify things):

concentrate

co-operate

cooperate

coöperate

copper

What weights do we give the hyphen to end up with this order? You cannot assign any primary weight to the hyphen that will yield the right answer (short of making the hyphen sort between "n" and "o," which will produce goofy results when the hyphen appears in other words). Instead, you should give the hyphen *no* primary weight: At the primary level, this character should simply be transparent to the sorting algorithm. In other words, the hyphen should be *ignorable* at the primary level.

The hyphen is still there, of course, and it affects the string comparison. It's just that this character doesn't become significant until we're looking for secondary differences. It's ignorable at the primary level, but not at the secondary level.

Generally, you deal with this issue by declaring some weight value as indicating "ignorable." If you encounter this value in your comparison routine, it signals you to skip the associated character. This tactic, of course, means you're no longer comparing characters in the same positions in the two strings. It makes examining all three levels in a single pass more difficult, but it's still possible. (Don't worry—it gets worse.)

Also, it doesn't make sense to treat a character as, say, ignorable at the secondary level but not at the primary level. Virtually all Unicode comparison routines declare that a character that's ignorable at any particular level is also ignorable at all more significant levels. For example, a character that's ignorable at the secondary level is automatically ignorable at the primary level; it might still be significant at the tertiary level, however.

French Accent Sorting

The unspoken assumption in every case presented so far is that differences (at the same level) earlier in the string beat differences later in the string: "bat" comes before "car" because "b" comes before "c." The fact that "r" comes before "t" doesn't count because we found a difference earlier in the string.

Consider the French words "cote" (meaning "quote" or "quantity"), "coté" ("quoted" or "evaluated"), "côté" ("side"), and "côte" ("hillside").[1] You'd normally expect them to sort like this:

cote
coté
côte
côté

The accented letters sort after their unaccented counterparts—at least in the English order for these words. In French, they sort like this:

cote
côte
coté
côté

In the first example, the two words with the unaccented "o" sort together, as do the two words with the accented "o." In the second example, the two words with the accented "e" sort together, as do the two words with the unaccented "e." The difference occurs because in French, if words differ in spelling only in the placement of accents, accent differences *later* in the string are more important than differences *earlier* in the string. That is, you start the comparison at the end and work your way back to the beginning.

In text-processing circles, this phenomenon is usually called "French accent sorting" or "French secondary order." It actually happens in some other languages (such as Estonian and Albanian), too.

---

1. Thanks to Alain LaBonté for suggesting the example.

Contracting Character Sequences

In Spanish, the digraphs "ch" and "ll" actually count as separate letters. That is, "ch" isn't a "c" followed by an "h"; it's the letter "che." In Spanish, "ch" sorts between "c" and "d", and "ll" sorts between "l" and "m." This list of Spanish words is in alphabetical order:

> **casa**
>
> **cero**
>
> **clave**
>
> **como**
>
> **Cuba**
>
> **chalupa**
>
> **charro**
>
> **chili**
>
> **donde**

In this case, a single set of weights is assigned to a *pair* of letters rather than a single letter.[2]

If you're dealing with an encoding (such as Unicode) that uses combining character sequences, you use the same approach to have an accented letter be treated as a different letter from its unaccented counterpart. For example, in Swedish, "a" comes at the beginning of the alphabet and "ä" comes toward the end of the alphabet. If "ä" is represented as "a" followed by a combining diaeresis, you have the same phenomenon: Two characters are mapped to a single set of weights that cause the combination to be ordered differently from either character individually. This phenomenon is called a **contracting character sequence**. Contracting character sequences are also essentially what Unicode 3.2 means when it discusses "language-specific grapheme clusters." For the purposes of string comparison, a contracting character sequence is the same thing

---

2. Because for a long time computer systems couldn't handle contracting character sequences, Spanish speakers have gotten used to seeing "ch" and "ll" sorted the same way they sort in English. This order is now called "modern Spanish sorting" and the version that treats "ch" and "ll" as single characters is called "traditional Spanish sorting."

as a grapheme cluster: a sequence of multiple Unicode code points that behaves as a single character during string comparison.

One interesting side effect is that the relative order of two strings can change if you append characters to the end of both or take substrings from the beginning. If a concatenation causes characters at the end of the original string to become involved in a contracting character sequence, or if taking a substring breaks up a contracting character sequence, order may change.

Expanding Characters

The reverse also happens: A single character can map to a sequence of weight values. For example, if you want "archaeology" and "archæology" to sort together, then the "æ" needs to be treated as equivalent to "a" followed by "e."

Note here that we say "equivalent" and not "the same." The strings should be considered different so that you get a defined ordering between them regardless of the sort algorithm. Normally, this issue is handled by having "æ" map not to the "a" weights followed by the "e" weights, but rather to a set of weights that has the same primary weight as "a" but a different secondary weight, followed by the "e" weights. (You don't have to do anything special with the "e" weights, as you already made things different with the first set of weights.)

Expanding characters happen a lot in German. For instance, "ß" is equivalent to "ss." You also often see it with the umlauted vowels: A vowel with an umlaut can also be spelled with the unadorned vowel followed by an "e," so "ä," "ö," and "ü" sort as though they were "ae," "oe," and "ue."

Context-Sensitive Weighting

Occasionally, a character will behave differently for comparison purposes depending on the surrounding characters. The classic example involves the long mark in Katakana. A vowel followed by a long mark is equivalent to the vowel twice in a row. For example, ア— is equivalent to アア.

In other words, if a contracting character sequence is a many-to-one mapping and an expanding character is a one-to-many mapping, this type of sequence is a many-to-many mapping. You treat each sequence involving the long mark independently: ア— maps to two sets of weights that sort with a secondary difference from アア, イ— maps to two sets of weights that sort with a secondary difference from イイ, and so on.

Putting It All Together

How do you implement this kind of string comparison ordering? You do the comparison by creating a "sort key" from each of the strings being compared. A sort key is simply a sequence of weight values. To produce it, you go through the string and look up the primary weight for each character, writing it to the sort key. Ignorable characters don't result in anything being added to the sort key, expanding characters result in multiple weights being added to the sort key, and contracting sequences result in single weights corresponding to multiple characters in the string being added to the sort key.

After you've derived the primary weights for all characters, you write a separator value to the sort key, derive the secondary weights, write another separator, and derive the tertiary weights. (If you need to do French secondary sorting, you write the secondary weights into the sort key backward.) After you've performed these operations with both strings, you have a pair of sequences of values that can be compared with traditional bitwise comparison.

The idea behind the separator character is that you pick a value that's lower than any of the actual weight values (typically you use zero and make sure your lowest weight value is 1). Then, if you're comparing two strings where one is a proper substring of the other, you'll wind up comparing the level separator of the shorter string, and not one of the secondary weights, to one of the primary weights for the longer string.

An individual weight value in a sort key is called a "sort element" or "collation element." In fact, a **collation element** is usually the concatenation of all weight values for a particular character or sequence (i.e., the primary, secondary, and tertiary weight values). Instead of pulling them apart and arranging them in sequence so that you obtain all the primary differences before the secondary and tertiary differences, a sort routine might build up a sequence of full sort keys and go through them multiple times, masking out all except a particular weight on each pass.

Generally, you don't have to create the sort keys (although they can indeed be useful; we'll look at them later). Rather, you just need to do the work to create them unit by unit until you find a difference.

Other Processes and Equivalences

You might also need to take the following issues into consideration when doing searching and sorting:

- When sorting titles, you usually don't want to consider articles such as "a" or "the" at the beginning of a string. For instance, "A Farewell to Arms" usually sorts in the F's, and "The Catcher in the Rye" usually sorts in the C's. Of course, which words you disregard when they appear at the beginning of a string vary with language.

- Strings containing numbers are often sorted as though the numbers were spelled out. For example, "9½ Weeks" would sort in the N's, and "48 Hours" would sort in the F's.

- Another choice with strings that contain numbers is to sort the number parts in numeric order so that, for example, "10th St." sorts after "1st St." and "2nd St." instead of between them.

- Sometimes you want abbreviations to be expanded so that, for example, "St. Paul" sorts before "San Diego" (or, for that matter, "Saint Tropez"), as though it had been spelled "Saint Paul." Of course, this operation can be a little tricky in many cases. In our example, "St." is also the abbreviation for "Street," so you'd need to be able to tell from context how to expand it.

- When sorting lists of people's names, you usually want to sort by the surname. This determination can be complicated, as the surname isn't always the last word in a person's name—it varies depending on language and, often, depending on the person.

- If a list includes words (people's names, for example) in different scripts, you might want to sort everything by its spelling in one script in particular. For example, you might want "Михаил Горбачев" to sort in the G's, just as if it had been spelled "Mikhail Gorbachev."

- When searching, you might want to catch variant spellings of the same word, especially the same word in different scripts—for example, Chinese using either Simplified or Traditional Han characters, or possibly even Bopomofo or pinyin; Japanese in Hiragana, Katakana, Kanji, or possibly even Romaji; Korean in either Hangul or Hanja; Serbo-Croatian in either Latin or Cyrillic; Yiddish in either Latin or Hebrew letters; Mongolian in either Cyrillic or the traditional Mongolian script.

These kinds of problems are rarely handled in the base string-comparison routine, but instead are usually done with some kind of preprocessing. For example, you might pass strings through transliteration prior to putting them through the string-comparison process, or store alternate representations that are used only for searching or sorting and not for display. A movie-title database might, for example, have an extra title field in each record that stores "Nine and a Half Weeks" as an alternate representation of "9½ Weeks," or "Catcher in the Rye" for "The Catcher in the Rye," and sort on this field instead of the regular title field.

■ LANGUAGE-SENSITIVE COMPARISON ON UNICODE TEXT

To the previously mentioned considerations, which you have to deal with regardless of which encoding standard you use to encode your characters, Unicode adds a few more interesting complications.

Unicode Normalization

Unlike in most other encoding schemes, many characters and sequences of characters have multiple legal representations in Unicode. One of the requirements of supporting Unicode is that (provided you support all of the characters involved) all representations of a character be treated as equal. Thus, whether you represent "ä" with

```
U+00E4 LATIN SMALL LETTER A WITH DIAERESIS
```

or

```
U+0061 LATIN SMALL LETTER A
U+0308 COMBINING DIAERESIS
```

it should look and behave the same way everywhere. As a consequence, a Unicode sorting facility must compare U+00E4 and U+0061 U+0308 as equal. It gets better with characters that have multiple combining marks on them. All five of the following sequences,

```
U+1ED9 LATIN SMALL LETTER O WITH CIRCUMFLEX AND DOT BELOW

U+1ECD LATIN SMALL LETTER O WITH DOT BELOW
U+0302 COMBINING CIRCUMFLEX ACCENT

U+00F4 LATIN SMALL LETTER O WITH CIRCUMFLEX
U+0323 COMBINING DOT BELOW

U+006F LATIN SMALL LETTER O
U+0302 COMBINING CIRCUMFLEX ACCENT
U+0323 COMBINING DOT BELOW

U+006F LATIN SMALL LETTER O
U+0323 COMBINING DOT BELOW
U+0302 COMBINING CIRCUMFLEX ACCENT
```

should compare as equal. (All are alternate representations for the Vietnamese letter ộ.) Of course, to do so, you convert both strings being compared into one of the Unicode normalized forms. Thus all of the above sequences are converted either to the first one in the list (in Normalized Form C) or to the last one (in Normalized Form D). In practice, Form D (fully decomposed) is the more common way to go, both because you have to go through Form D on your way to Form C (see Chapter 14) and because it's usually simpler to treat the accents independently (as characters that are ignorable at the primary level) than as part of their base letters (which might involve treating more characters as expanding characters). Unicode normalization is usually done on the fly, one character (or combining character sequence) at a time, as part of the process of mapping characters to collation elements.

The requirement that equivalent representations be treated as identical applies only to sequences that are canonically equivalent (i.e., identical when mapped to Normalized Form D). Often, it makes sense to extend this requirement to compatibility equivalents as well (i.e., sequences that are identical when mapped to Normalized Form KD but not when mapped to Normalized Form D). Because mapping a character to its compatibility decomposition may lose data, compatibly equivalent strings usually aren't treated as identical; the difference between a compatibility composite and its compatibility decomposition is typically considered a tertiary-level difference.

Korean represents an interesting exception to this rule. Both sets of Hangul characters are arranged in the correct order such that you can use straight binary comparison to sort a list of strings in Hangul and get the correct answer (of course, this technique fails if any of the strings contains non-Hangul characters). In fact, this approach is representation-independent: You get the same answer whether all of the strings use the precomposed syllables or the conjoining jamo. As a consequence, you may not have to bother with converting Hangul syllables to Normalized Form D, which can be a useful performance optimization. Of course, if some of the strings use precomposed syllables and others use conjoining jamo, or if any of the strings use a combination of precomposed syllables and conjoining jamo, then you'll obtain the correct answer only if you actually convert everything to Normalized Form D first.

Because two Unicode strings can compare as identical without actually being bit-for-bit identical, Unicode-oriented comparison algorithms often include a fourth level of comparison. If two strings are identical all the way down to the tertiary level, their binary representations may be used to impose an ordering on the strings.

Reordering

Another interesting wrinkle that Unicode brings to the party relates to Unicode's representation of Thai and Lao. Most of the Indic scripts in Unicode are stored in logical order, so that vowel marks always follow the consonants to which they attach, regardless of on which side of the consonant they are connected.

Thai and Lao, on the other hand, are stored in visual order. Top-, bottom-, and right-joining vowels follow the consonants to which they attach in the backing store, but left-joining vowels precede the consonants. Split vowels with left- and right-joining components are represented with two components. One, representing the left-joining half, precedes the consonant; the other, representing the right-joining half, follows it. The difference in encoding philosophy between Thai and Lao and the other Indic scripts reflects the difference in encoding philosophy in the national standards on which the Unicode blocks were based; changing the encoding philosophy for Thai and Lao would have made interoperability between Unicode and the national standards more difficult and gone against standard practice, so Unicode includes this inconsistency. (This is one situation where optimizing for truth and beauty would have led to fewer people using the standard.)

What makes this issue fun is that Thai and Lao still *sort* as though they were stored in logical order. (Strictly speaking, this issue isn't unique to Unicode, as the Thai national encoding standard shares it as well.) Thus, if you encounter a Thai left-joining vowel followed by a Thai consonant, you have to exchange them before mapping them to collation elements. The collation element for the consonant precedes the collation element for the vowel in the resulting sort key. In other words, this list of Thai words is in sorted order:

กก

กิก

โกก

งก

งึก

โงก

The words that begin with โ don't sort together because โ is a left-joining vowel, not a consonant, and therefore it gets considered *after* the character that follows it in the backing store (the *real* first letter in the word).

Because your mapping tables need to support many-to-many mappings anyway (this ability usually comes for free once you provide support for one-to-many and many-to-one mappings, both of which are unavoidable), you could deal with this reordering by including all of the pairs of characters that need to be exchanged as many-to-many mappings in your mapping table. There are a lot of them, however, and their inclusion would make the table very large, so most systems just handle this problem algorithmically.

A General Implementation Strategy

As you see, putting together a good general-purpose string comparison algorithm for Unicode is quite complex. At the core, you need mapping tables capable of one-to-one, one-to-many, many-to-one, and many-to-many mappings. Usually, the table is optimized for one-to-one mappings. You either use a generalized trie structure or a simpler compact array augmented with exception tables to perform the mapping. The main trie handles single characters and contracting sequences, and each maps either to a single collation element or to a spot in an auxiliary table of multiple-collation-element mappings (used for expanding characters and many-to-many mappings).

Generally speaking, all three weight values for a character can be crammed into 32 bits, so collation elements are usually 32-bit values. In most real implementations, a fourth level, corresponding to the actual binary representation of the string, is added. Because the fourth weight value in this case is the character's original hex value, it doesn't need to be stored.

You can employ either of two basic strategies for mapping raw Unicode text to collation elements. First, you can perform decomposition and reordering in a separate preprocessing step and have the mapping table just map from normalized Unicode to collation elements. Second, you can combine all of these operations into a single operation and use the mapping table for them.

Using a single table for everything can be faster, but results in a huge mapping table (it would have to deal with canonical accent reordering, so it would need separate mappings for all five representations of ộ, whereas a table that depends on normalized Unicode might need mappings for only the o, the circumflex, and the underdot). Unless you're handling a small subset of the Unicode characters, it typically makes more sense to handle decomposition and reordering in a separate step or pass.

Once you've mapped everything to collation elements, you then need to make another pass to split apart the different weight values in the collation elements (so that primary weights are compared before secondary weights, and so on) and possibly to reverse the order of the secondary weights (if you have to do

French accent sorting). Only then can you compare the sort keys to get an actual result.

To recap, language-sensitive comparison on Unicode strings proceeds in four conceptual phases:

1. Decomposition and reordering
2. Mapping normalized, reordered Unicode text to collation elements
3. Splitting the weights in the collation elements and possibly reversing the secondary weights to produce collation keys
4. Performing binary comparison on the collation keys to generate an actual result

Let's examine how this process works on a pair of sample strings, "Resume" and "résumé." The two strings start out like this:

```
Resume:  0052 0065 0073 0075 006D 0065
résumé:  0072 00E9 0073 0075 006D 00E9
```

First, you map them both to Normalized Form D:

```
Resume:  0052 0065 0073 0075 006D 0065
résumé:  0072 0065 0301 0073 0075 006D 0065 0301
```

Next, you map to collation elements (the weights are separated by periods, and the values are illustrative):

```
Resume:  [09CB.0020.0008] [08B1.0020.0002] [09F3.0020.0002]
         [0A23.0020.0002] [0977.0020.0002] [08B1.0020.0002]

résumé:  [09CB.0020.0002] [08B1.0020.0002] [0000.0032.0002]
         [09F3.0020.0002] [0A23.0020.0002] [0977.0020.0002]
         [08B1.0020.0002] [0000.0032.0002]
```

Then you split out the weights (dropping the ignorable values) to get the sort keys (we use 0000 as a level separator):

Resume: 09CB 08B1 09F3 0A23 0977 08B1 0000 0020 0020 0020 0020
0020 0020 0000 0008 0002 0002 0002 0002 0002

résumé: 09CB 08B1 09F3 0A23 0977 08B1 0000 0020 0020 0032 0020
0020 0020 0020 0032 0000 0002 0002 0002 0002 0002 0002
0002 0002

Finally, you compare them:

Resume: 09CB 08B1 09F3 0A23 0977 08B1 0000 0020 0020 **0020** 0020
0020 0020 0000 0008 0002 0002 0002 0002 0002

résumé: 09CB 08B1 09F3 0A23 0977 08B1 0000 0020 0020 **0032** 0020
0020 0020 0020 0032 0000 0002 0002 0002 0002 0002 0002
0002 0002

Notice what has happened. The strings are the same at the primary level, and you end up with two sort keys that start with the same sequence of primary weights (the zero primary weights, representing the accents, which are ignorable at the primary level, are skipped when creating the sort keys). The first difference we see is the presence of the accent on the first "é" in "résumé," which has a secondary weight of 0032. It compares higher than the secondary weight of the "s" in "Resume" (0020). Thus the strings compare as different, with "résumé" coming second. The difference between the capital "R" in "Resume" and the small "r" in "résumé" is found later in the sort key: The capital-ness of the "R" in "Resume" is represented by 0008 in the first sort key. Even though this difference appears earlier in the strings, it comes later in the sort keys, because it's a lower-priority difference.

Of course, for many strings some of these passes are no-ops. The four passes may therefore be interleaved so that a primary difference in the first character is caught early rather than after you've jumped through all of these hoops (or at least so that all four operations happen in a single pass with comparatively little use of temporary storage).

One nice thing about this flexibility is that it allows you to base an implementation on UTF-16 (or even UTF-8) directly rather than having to convert strings to UTF-32 before you can work on them. A supplementary-plane character can be represented with a UTF-16 surrogate pair and still be treated as a single character: It is simply treated as a contracting character sequence.

Another notable issue is that it usually doesn't make sense to write a string comparison routine whose behavior is hard-coded for just one particular language or group of languages. Typically, string comparison takes the form of a rule-driven library, where you can provide rules to specify the desired sort order. The Java `Collator` object, for example, takes rule strings of this form:

```
A , a < B , b < C , c < D , d < ...
```

The characters are listed in their desired order, with less-than signs indicating characters with primary differences and commas indicating tertiary differences. (Semicolons are used for secondary differences, and the ellipsis at the end indicates that the example would normally continue.) Most of the time, ordering rules are specified as deltas to a default ordering. The ampersand can be used to allow insertion of characters into the middle of the default rules. For example, the traditional Spanish sorting rules look like this:

```
& c < CH , Ch , cH , ch
& l < LL , Ll , lL , ll
& n < Ñ , ñ
```

The first line indicates that the "ch" digraph (in its different cased variations) sorts after "c" (and, by implication, before "D," the next item in the default order). The less-than sign indicates that "ch" has a primary difference from "c," which makes the "ch" digraph behave as a completely different letter. The second line inserts the "ll" digraph between "l" and "M," and the third line inserts "ñ" between "n" and "O."

With this kind of generalized comparison routine, you have essentially two choices. You can take a set of rules in a specialized meta-language like the one above and build appropriate mapping tables on the fly, or you can choose from a set of prebuilt mapping tables. The latter approach offers better speed (because you don't have to build the tables) and compression (because the developer can compress the tables at his or her leisure and then serialize the result), but diminishes flexibility. Building the tables on the fly from rules in a meta-language entails the opposite set of trade-offs. Some systems, such as the International Components for Unicode, allow for both approaches.

The Unicode Collation Algorithm

This discussion of how you'd handle language-sensitive comparison in Unicode leads nicely into our next topic. The Unicode standard defines a set of criteria for a Unicode-compatible string comparison routine called the **Unicode Collation Algorithm** (UCA).

Strictly speaking, the UCA isn't really part of the Unicode standard. You can compare strings however you want and (as long as canonically equivalent strings compare as equal) conform to the Unicode standard. The UCA is a companion standard, or a Unicode Technical Standard (UTS #10, to be exact).[3]

In the same way that Unicode is aligned with the ISO 10646 standard, the Unicode Collation Algorithm is aligned with ISO 14651, an international string-ordering standard. As with Unicode and 10646, the two standards are not identical, but implementations that conform to one generally conform to the other (or will with comparatively little work). One important difference does exist: While Unicode is *much* more restrictive than 10646, 14651 is *somewhat* more restrictive than the UCA.

The Unicode Collation Algorithm calls for these features:

- It requires at least three distinct weighting levels, but provides for the possibility of more. Most conforming implementations define a fourth level based on the original binary representations of the strings.
- It requires support for ignorable characters, contracting character sequences, expanding characters, and context-sensitive weightings.
- It strongly encourages, but doesn't require, French accent sorting. (The UCA calls this "backward levels.")

---

3. The designation "10" doesn't mean there are nine other Unicode Technical Standards—the numbering of Unicode Technical Reports, Unicode Technical Standards, and Unicode Standard Annexes is consecutive across all three types of documents, reflecting the fact that they were all once called Unicode Technical Reports.

- It provides for, but doesn't require, Thai vowel reordering.
- It provides for "alternate weighting," which we'll discuss in a minute.
- It specifies a default ordering for all Unicode characters. In the absence of tailorings (discussed next), all UCA-conformant comparison implementations must sort any given set of strings into the same order.
- It provides for "tailorings," alterations to the default order normally used to produce the correct ordering for a particular language (the default ordering can generally get things right for only one language per script; tailoring gives you the ability to get it right for other languages or customize the results for application-specific purposes). All UCA-conformant comparison implementations must, given the same set of tailorings, also sort any given set of strings into the same order.

The UCA follows the algorithm described in the previous section:

1. Convert everything to Normalized Form D.
2. Exchange Thai and Lao left-joining vowels with the characters that follow them.
3. Map everything to collation element values. This step may involve mapping single characters to multiple collation elements, mapping groups of characters to single collation elements, or mapping groups of characters to groups of collation elements in different ways than would happen if the characters were treated individually.
4. Create sort keys from the collation elements by reorganizing so that all primary weights come first (with ignorable characters omitted), followed by a separator value and all the secondary weights, followed by another separator value and all the tertiary weights, and so on.
5. Reverse the order of the secondary weights (or possibly some other level) if the tailoring you're using calls for it.
6. Compare the resulting sort keys using straight binary comparison.

One complication arises: Instead of just converting to Normalized Form D and mapping things sequentially to collation elements, you have to take one additional step. You start by looking for the longest substring that has an entry in the mapping table, but before you map it, you check after it for extra combining marks. If you find any combining marks that

- Aren't separated from the substring you're considering by a noncombining character or a combining character with a combining class of 0,
- Aren't separated from the substring you're considering by another combining mark of the same combining class, and
- When combined with the substring under consideration form a string that also has an entry in the mapping table,

you use that string instead and ignore the combining marks you were able to combine with the main character.

Why is the extra work necessary? Suppose your mapping table has a special mapping for the letter ô and you encounter the Vietnamese letter ộ in the string. In Normalized Form D, it decomposes to o, followed by the underdot, followed by the circumflex. You then map each character to a collation element independently. The rule allows you to recognize ô as a sequence with its own mapping, even with the intervening underdot. Instead of getting three collation elements (one for o, one for the underdot, and one for the circumflex), you get two: one for ô and one for the underdot.

The Default UCA Sort Order

Other than specifying a good algorithm for comparing Unicode strings, the big thing the Unicode Collation Algorithm brings to the party is a default ordering for all characters in Unicode. This ordering is spelled out in a file called all-keys.txt, which is available from the Unicode Web site. It's not part of the Unicode Character Database, as the UCA isn't officially part of the Unicode standard, but you can reach it via a link in UTS #10.

The allkeys.txt file includes a list of mappings. Each mapping consists of a Unicode code point value (or, in some cases, a sequence of Unicode code point values), followed by a semicolon, followed by one or more collation key values. The Unicode code point value sequences are given (as in all other Unicode data files) as space-delimited sequences of four-digit hex values. Each collation element is shown as a series of four period-delimited four-digit hex values in brackets. The four values represent the primary-level weight, the secondary-level weight, the tertiary-level weight, and the fourth-level weight, respectively. For example, the entry

```
0061 ; [.0861.0020.0002.0061] # LATIN SMALL LETTER A
```

indicates that the single Unicode code point value U+0061 (the small letter A, as the comment at the end of the line makes clear) maps to a single collation element. The primary weight is 0x0861, the secondary weight is 0x20, the tertiary weight is 0x02, and the fourth-level weight is 0x61 (which, not coincidentally, is the original character's raw code point value).

The contracting and expanding sequences in allkeys.txt are usually included to make sure the same thing happens with different normalization forms of the text. As an example, consider the following two entries, one of which is a contracting character sequence:

```
04D1 ; [.0B05.0020.0002.04D1] # CYRILLIC SMALL LETTER A WITH BREVE
0430 0306 ; [.0B05.0020.0002.04D1] # CYRILLIC SMALL LETTER A WITH
    BREVE
```

These entries make sure that the Cyrillic letter ̆ sorts the same way in both its composed and decomposed forms. Most of the time you can sort accented letters according to their decomposed forms—that is, you can just treat the letter and the accent mark as separate characters. In this example, however, the accent mark turns the character into a completely different letter in the languages that use it.

An expanding character's entry would look like this:

```
2474 ; [*0266.0020.0004.2474] [.0858.0020.0004.2474]
    [*0267.0020.0004.2474] # PARENTHESIZED DIGIT ONE; COMPATSEQ
```

This entry states that the character U+2474, the parenthesized digit one, sorts as though it were a regular opening parenthesis, followed by a regular digit one, followed by a regular closing parenthesis. The weights are the same as for those characters, except for the tertiary-level weight on the first collation element, which preserves the fact that U+2474 isn't canonically equivalent to "(1)" written as three characters.

The entries in allkeys.txt are listed in order by the collation elements, although this arrangement isn't required. This ordering makes it easy to see the order for sorting the characters. The basic ordering boils down as follows:

- Control and formatting characters, which are transparent to the sort algorithm (they're ignorable at all four levels)
- Various whitespace, punctuation, noncombining diacritic, and math-operator characters, plus some other symbols
- The combining diacritical marks, followed by more noncombining diacritical marks
- Currency symbols, followed by more miscellaneous symbols
- Digits and numbers, in approximate numerical order by digit (i.e., "10" comes between "1" and "2")
- Letters and syllables from the various scripts, in the following order: Latin, Greek, Cyrillic, Georgian, Armenian, Hebrew, Arabic, Syriac, Thaana, Ethiopic, Devanagari, Bengali, Gurmukhi, Gujarati, Oriya, Tamil, Telugu, Kannada, Malayalam, Sinhala, Thai, Lao, Tibetan, Myanmar, Khmer, Mongolian, Cherokee, Canadian aboriginal syllabics, Ogham, and Runic
- Hangul (The file lists only the jamo, depending on canonical decomposition to get the precomposed syllables into the same order)
- Hiragana and Katakana (interleaved).
- Bopomofo
- The Han ideographs and radicals (They're not all listed; the regular Han ideographs have weights that can be derived algorithmically.)

The entire table can't be derived algorithmically, but many pieces of it can be. This fact can be used to reduce the size of the table employed in the implementation:

- Canonical composites (including the Hangul syllables) sort according to their decompositions. Exceptions to this rule arise in situations where it will give the "wrong answer" from a linguistic standpoint. Generally in these cases, you'll see the decomposed version spelled out in the file as a contracting character sequence. (See the Cyrillic example above.)

- Compatibility composites sort according to their decompositions, but the resulting collation elements have a different tertiary weight than the decomposed version would have. The tertiary weight can be algorithmically derived from the type of the decomposition as listed in the Unicode-Data.txt file (e.g., "<font>," "<small>," or "<compat>"). This extra work imposes a definite ordering on, say, the different presentation forms for the Arabic letters.

- The Han characters have their Unicode hex values as their primary weights, and 0x20 and 0x02 as their secondary and tertiary weights. The compatibility Han characters and the Han radicals are listed in the file and sort as equivalent to various regular Han characters.

- Code point values that shouldn't appear in the data stream, such as unpaired surrogate values or the value U+FFFF, should either cause an error or be treated as completely ignorable.

- Unassigned and private-use code points are given algorithmically derived collation element values that cause them to sort after everything that's explicitly mentioned in the table. Because there's no way to achieve this effect with a single code point value, they're all treated as expanding characters. The first collation element uses the first few bits of the Unicode hex value and adds it to a constant that puts the character at the end of the sequence; the second collation element uses the rest of the bits in the character's hex value.

- The fourth-level weight can be derived algorithmically. For characters with decompositions, this weight consists of the original character value. For completely ignorable characters, it's zero. For Han and unassigned code points, it's usually 1. Generally speaking, for everything else, it's the original code point value.

- The tertiary weight can also be derived algorithmically. For compatibility composites, it is derived from the decomposition type. For characters in the general category Lu (uppercase letter), it's 0x08. For everything else, it's 0x02.

Note that the weight values themselves are not normative; you can use any weight values desired, so long as they cause things to sort in the same order as the weight values given in allkeys.txt. The weight values in the table are specifically chosen so that they don't occupy overlapping numerical ranges (which allows you to dispense with separator characters in your sort keys) and so that you don't actually need 16 bits for each weight value, as the table appears to imply. In fact, the secondary and tertiary weights can each be stored in eight bits, and the fourth-level weight can always be computed. Thus you can store a complete collation element in 32 bits.

In addition to the actual mapping entries, allkeys.txt has a heading at the top that specifies some global characteristics for the sort. These characters include the following:

- Versioning information.
- A tag that specifies how to handle characters with alternate weightings (see below).
- A tag that specifies which levels need to be reversed in the final sort key (to allow French accent sorting). This reversal never occurs in the default sort order, but the tag is included here so that you can specify tailorings using the same file format as is used for the default order.
- A tag that lists which characters are swapped with the characters that follow them before being turned into collation elements. This swap should always involve the left-joining Thai and Lao vowels, but the tag is included in the file in case future Unicode versions add more characters that need to be handled this way.

The UCA default order tends to lag a bit behind the actual Unicode version and is keyed to a particular version of Unicode. The current version of the UCA as of December 2001 is keyed to Unicode 3.1 and doesn't include mappings for the new Unicode 3.2 characters. It will produce a definite ordering for them, however, as a specific algorithm explains how to give weights to characters that aren't explicitly mentioned. The order for those characters is likely to change when a future version of the UCA explicitly mentions them (which will probably have happened by the time this book goes to press).

Alternate Weighting

You may have noticed that the collation element values in allkeys.txt begin with an extra character. A period or an asterisk always appears before the first weight value. As an example, consider the entry for the space character:

```
0020 ; [*0209.0020.0002.0020] # SPACE
```

The UCA default ordering specifies a group of characters (the ones with the asterisks) that have "alternate weightings." Depending on the situation, you might want to treat these characters as either ignorable or significant. Depending on the setting of a flag, a UCA-compliant comparison routine that implements alternate weighting (it's an optional feature) can either use the weight values from the table as-is or perform various transformations on them. You have four choices for treatment of the characters with alternate weightings:

- *Non-ignorable.* The characters have the weights listed in allkeys.txt and have primary differences with each other and with other characters. Consider the following example:

  e–mail
  e-mail
  effect
  email
  exercise

  Punctuation comes before letters, so the strings that contain the hyphens sort before the strings that don't. The variant spellings of "email" are separated. (For the purposes of this example, the longer dash is intended to represent the ASCII hyphen-minus character U+002D and the shorter hyphen the Unicode hyphen character U+2010.)

- *Ignorable* (or *blanked*, the term used in UTS #10). The character has zero as its primary, secondary, and tertiary weights and its original code point value as the fourth-level weight. This choice effectively makes the character transparent to the comparison algorithm unless it must refer to the actual code point values to break a tie. The same set of words as our previous example comes out like this:

effect
e–mail
email
e-mail
exercise

The three variants of "email" are grouped together, but the punctuation marks are transparent, and the strings' binary representations are used to break the tie. Because U+2010 (the hyphen) is greater than U+006D, the two punctuated versions of "email" come out on either side of the non-punctuated version.

- *Shifted.* This option is similar to *ignorable*. Characters with alternate weightings are treated in the same way as "ignorable," but all other characters receive a fourth-level weight of 0xFFFF. This option gives slightly better-looking results when strings compare as equal at the first three levels, ensuring that all otherwise-equal strings with an ignorable character in some position are grouped together in the sorted order, rather than being interspersed with strings that don't have an ignorable character in that position.

effect
e–mail
e-mail
email
exercise

In the preceding example, the three variants of "email" cluster together. Again, the hyphens are transparent at the first three levels, but here we have a slightly better algorithmically derived fourth level to break the tie. The shifting algorithm makes sure the two versions of "email" with the hyphens come out grouped together.

- *Shift-trimmed.* This option is the same as *shifted*, but the characters that don't have alternate mappings have a fourth-level weight of 1 (or no fourth-level weight). The effect is the same as with shifted characters, except that the strings with ignorable characters sort *after* the strings that don't have them, instead of before.

effect

email

e–mail

e-mail

exercise

The three variants of "email" come out together, but this time the two versions with the hyphen sort after the version without the hyphen.

The default sort order is set up in such a way that the primary weights for all characters that have alternate mappings come before the primary weights for all characters that don't (except, of course, those that are always ignorable at the primary level, which have a primary weight of 0 and don't need to be treated in a special way). As a consequence, no extra storage in your mapping tables is needed to indicate which characters have alternate mappings. You can look up their primary weights and check each against a constant.

Optimizations and Enhancements

A number of possible optimizations and enhancements are worth thinking about:[4]

Computing Sort Key Values   When it's possible to compute a sort key rather than to look it up in the table, you don't have to store this value in the table. As we saw, for the default Unicode ordering, you can get away without storing table entries for the Han characters, the Hangul syllables, unassigned and private-use code point values, canonical composites, and compatibility composites. In

---

4. Most of these optimizations come from the "Implementation Notes" section of UTS #10, but some are taken from Mark Davis, "Collation in ICU 1.8," *Proceedings of the 18th International Unicode Conference,* session B10, April 27, 2001. This paper can also be found at http://macchiato.com.

addition, for the default Unicode ordering, the fourth-level weights can always be computed and don't have to be stored. Except for a few rare exceptional characters, the tertiary weights can, too.[5]

Computing values rather than storing them in the table sets up a classical performance-versus-memory trade-off. Nevertheless, it's frequently worth making this trade-off in the direction of saving memory—you can use other means to improve performance.

Reducing the Size of the Weight Values   The UCA data table gives secondary weight values that are too large to be stored in eight bits, a result of the algorithm that was used to generate these weights. However, there are never 256 different secondary weight values for any particular primary weight. You can take advantage of this fact to save space by storing the secondary weights and reusing values to mean different things depending on the primary weight. Remember, if the primary weights are different, you never compare the secondary weights.

Increasing the Repertoire of Available Weight Values   The UCA assumes 16-bit values for all weights, but what if you need more than 65,536 primary weight values? This situation can happen, for example, if you're specifying an ordering for all of the Han characters in Unicode 3.1, both the ones in the BMP and the ones in plane 2. You can handle this problem by treating some of the characters as expanding characters. You set aside some range of primary key values as special. Some of the characters map to two collation elements. The first element has one of the "special" primary keys (chosen so as to get the right ordering on its own when compared with a "nonspecial" primary key), and the second element is used for disambiguation. Each "special" value thus gives you an extra 65,536 primary key values. The trick here is to ensure that all characters with a particular "special" value for the first primary key sort in the same way relative to all characters with "nonspecial" primary keys or different "special" primary keys.

---

5. This is true only of the default UCA sort ordering; language-specific tailorings will often have tertiary-level weights that can't be algorithmically derived.

To clarify how this process works, let's consider a very simple example. Suppose you need 100,000 primary key values. The first 65,535 can be made available with single collation elements having primary key values from 0000 to FFFE. The remaining 34,465 characters map to two collation elements: The first element has a primary weight of FFFF, and the second element has a value in the range 0000 to 86A0. The secondary and tertiary weights for the second collation element can actually be zero—this scenario is one situation in which a collation element can be "ignorable" at the second and third levels but not at the first.

Of course, it generally makes sense to use a more sophisticated technique. For example, you might designate all odd primary key values to be single-element values and all even values to be the leading element of a two-element value. You could then fix matters so that more common characters map to single collation elements and less common characters map to pairs of elements. This technique can also be used, of course, to give you more than 256 secondary or tertiary key values without using more than eight bits.

Dealing with Tailorings   Much of the time (probably most of the time) you will deal not with the UCA default ordering, but rather with a language-specific tailoring of the UCA default ordering. It's really painful to have a language-specific mapping table for each language that includes the parts of the UCA mapping table that didn't change. If you set up your UCA table to leave "holes" between the characters (using the technique described earlier, for instance), the tailorings can put things in the "holes." The mapping table for a tailoring then doesn't have to repeat the default UCA stuff: You can look up a collation element mapping in the tailoring's mapping table, look it up in the UCA table if you don't find it in the tailoring table, and generate it algorithmically according to UCA rules if you don't find it in the UCA table.

Optimizing the Comparison   You don't have to go through all the steps of the UCA right from the beginning of the string. Instead, you can use a binary comparison initially and drop into the UCA only when you encounter a character that's different between the strings. The potential complication is that you may hit the difference in a nonleading code point of a contracting character sequence or a code point that will be affected by normalization (such as by accent reordering). In these cases, you must back up to the beginning of the characters that need to be considered as a unit. For instance, if the difference happens on a combining character or a low surrogate, you must back up in both strings to the first noncombining character or the high surrogate. You also may have to maintain a table of characters that occur in nonleading positions in contracting character sequences (it need not include combining characters, as you can deal with them algorithmically) and back up until you reach a character that isn't in this table. Only then can you drop into the full UCA to compare the rest of the strings. Despite the complication, this optimization can actually buy you quite a bit of improvement in performance.

Avoiding Normalization   In many cases, you don't have to do any normalization. If both strings being compared are already normalized (in either Form C or Form D), you can compare them without any transformation. If you encounter a sequence of characters that isn't normalized (or a mixture of the two forms), you can drop in and do normalization then, on just that piece. This optimization requires an extra table to specify when you need to perform normalization.

Inverting Cases   Whether capital letters sort before small letters, or vice versa, is often a matter of personal preference. The UCA default order sorts small letters before capital letters. You can flip this order algorithmically for the untailored UCA default order if you're also generating the tertiary weights algorithmically. The normal rule assigns the tertiary weight 0008 to the characters in the Lu category and 0002 otherwise (with a compatibility composite, you do this check first and the result serves as one input for figuring out the tertiary weight). Just change the mapping so that you get 0008 on Ll and 0002 the rest of the time.

For tailored orderings, matters are somewhat trickier. The simplest approach is to map each character to its opposite-case counterpart when generating the tailoring table. Alternatively, you can generate the tailoring table in the normal way and then swap the resulting collation-element mappings of any case pairs after the fact.

Another approach is to leave the tables and collation element generation alone and flip the cases of the input characters as part of the normalization/reordering pass.

Reordering Scripts Sometimes you may want to retain the relative order of the characters in a particular script, but change the relative order of the different scripts. You can do so in a similar manner to how you deal with switching the cases. The simplest method is to pass a "raw" primary weight value through an extra lookup table that rearranges the primary weights according to the desired order of the scripts.

▪ LANGUAGE-INSENSITIVE STRING COMPARISON

Of course, you don't always want language-sensitive string comparison. After all, it's complicated and, no matter how much you optimize it, it'll never be as fast as binary comparison. Of course, if binary comparison gives the wrong answer, its speed doesn't matter. Sometimes, however, you don't care about linguistically correct ordering. You just want *some* kind of ordering, and the user will never see the results of that ordering.

There are two classical versions of this problem. In the first case, you care only about whether two strings are equal. If they aren't, you're not interested in which one comes first. "Equal" can also be a language-sensitive issue, but if you're dealing with non-natural-language strings (such as programming language identifiers or XML tags), it doesn't matter.

You can use straight binary comparison in this case, but only if you know (or are in a position to demand) that both input strings appear in the same normalized form. (The W3C character model, discussed in Chapter 17, requires all text to be in Normalized Form C, for example.) If you can't depend on that factor, you must perform Unicode normalization on the strings but can blow off the other work.

In the second case, you're using some kind of ordered index to speed up searching. For example, you might be building a binary tree or need a sorted list on which you can do a binary search. The most common scenario, of course, is indexed fields in a database. Here you need a well-defined order, but the exact properties of the order don't matter because the user will never see it. Again, you can use straight binary comparison, as long as you can guarantee that the strings will be in the same normalized form (or if your index can have multiple entries for strings that are supposed to be equal). In the worst case, you'll have to worry about Unicode normalization but can avoid all the other apparatus.

Of course, if you want the comparisons to be case insensitive but don't care about linguistically appropriate results (program identifiers are the classic example), you have to pass the text through a case-folding table (see Chapter 14) and compare the results rather than doing straight binary comparison on the strings. The DerivedNormalizationProperties.txt file in the Unicode Character Database provides a set of mappings that let you do case folding and normalization simultaneously. Once again, this approach allows you to avoid all the other string-comparison baggage.

There's one important thing to keep in mind when performing binary comparisons on Unicode strings: The exact binary format makes a difference. Specifically, if you sort a list of strings encoded in UTF-8 or UTF-32, the order won't be the same as you would have gotten if the strings were encoded in UTF-16. The supplementary-plane characters will sort after the BMP characters in UTF-8 and UTF-32, but between U+D7FF and U+E000 in UTF-16, because the surrogate mechanism uses values between 0xD800 and 0xDFFF to encode the supplementary-plane characters. This consideration is vitally important if you're depending on binary comparison in a mixed-UTF environment.

You have two main ways of dealing with this issue, short of using the same UTF throughout your system. The simplest technique is probably to modify the comparison routine for one UTF to replicate the ordering of the other UTF. For one UTF, you do normal binary comparison. For the other UTF, you use a modified algorithm that produces the same results as the other UTF (for example, you use a modified algorithm on UTF-16 that causes the values from U+D800 to U+DFFF to sort in a block after U+FFFF). This code is trivially easy to write and can work almost as fast as regular binary comparison.

The second way of dealing with the problem is to use a modified form of UTF-8—the CESU-8 encoding form described in DUTR #26—instead of the regular form of UTF-8. CESU-8 represents supplementary-plane characters using six-byte sequences instead of the normal four-byte sequences. The six-byte sequence is effectively the result of mapping from UTF-16 to UTF-8 using a UTF-32-to-UTF-8 converter. Each surrogate is independently converted into a three-byte UTF-8 sequence, rather than having the surrogate pair be treated as a unit and converted to a four-byte UTF-8 sequence. Note that encoding supplementary-plane characters in this way is prohibited in real UTF-8; it violates the shortest-sequence rule and can be a security violation.

The latter approach can work, with some loss of storage efficiency, as long as the outside world never sees the bowdlerized UTF-8 (or at least it's not advertised as real UTF-8). The system still needs to handle real UTF-8 coming from outside the system and to send real UTF-8 to the outside world. But sending the bowdlerized form to the outside world and advertising it as "real" UTF-8 is a Very Bad Idea. It's almost always better to fix the sorting routines.

Compressed Unicode can also be very helpful for saving space in database implementations. SCSU is great for this purpose, but because of its stateful nature, binary ordering based on SCSU will be wildly and unpredictably different from the binary order of uncompressed Unicode. An interesting alternative compression scheme for Unicode called BOCU preserves the binary ordering of the uncompressed text and might be useful for compressing text in fields that also need to be indexed. (See Chapter 6.)

■ SORTING

There's not a lot to say about sorting per se, as you can use any sorting algorithm to sort a list of Unicode strings. A number of things are worth keeping in mind, however.[6]

Collation Strength and Secondary Keys

First, it's worth thinking a little about your sort algorithm and what it does with keys that compare as equal. Sort algorithms such as the bubble and insertion sorts are *stable:* Records with identical keys will remain in the order of their original insertion after sorting the list. Fast sort algorithms such as the Quicksort and the merge sort are generally *unstable:* Records with identical keys are

---

6. Much of the material in this section comes from the Davis paper, op. cit. and from UTS #10.

not preserved in insertion order during a sort. In effect, the sort algorithms will put records with identical keys in random order.

It's important to keep this issue in mind, because the Unicode Collation Algorithm may treat many strings that aren't bit-for-bit identical as equal, and an unstable sort algorithm will arrange them randomly. Of course, if the whole record *is* the key, this probably doesn't matter, because even if the strings aren't bit-for-bit identical, they're the same for all intents and purposes (for example, they'll typically look the same when drawn on the screen).

In other cases, however, you should think about the sorting implications. If you don't want things scrambling gratuitously when, for example, you add a new item to the list, you should either define your comparison algorithm to treat strings as different if it possibly can (i.e., treat differences at all levels as significant and possibly do a bitwise comparison to break the tie if the language-sensitive comparison says the strings are equal) or fall back on a secondary key. Usually disambiguating things with a secondary key makes more sense. In fact, if you're breaking ties using a secondary key, you may want to treat only primary-level differences in your primary key as significant.

Be careful, however, because this option won't always produce the desired results. Suppose that your primary key is someone's last name and your secondary key is his or her first name. If you treat fourth-level differences in the last name as significant before going to the first name, you might end up with something like this:

van Dusen, Paul
van Dusen, Tom
vanDusen, Paul
vanDusen, Tom
Van Dusen, Paul
Van Dusen, Tom

(Okay, so it's a contrived example.) The first names are interleaved: Each variant spelling of "Van Dusen" is treated as a group in itself. The versions with the spaces wind up separated because if the space is ignorable, differences in spaces are a fourth-level difference and the case differences are a tertiary difference.

Next, suppose you decide to fix this problem by treating only primary differences in the last name as significant before going to the first name. Now the first names sort together:

van Dusen, Paul
vanDusen, Paul
Van Dusen, Paul
Van Dusen, Tom
vanDusen, Tom
van Dusen, Tom

If you're using an unstable sort algorithm, the last names come out in random order. You group by first name, but within each group, the variant spellings of the last name come out scrambled.

To get around this problem, you have to use a composite key. You might store the first and last names separately, but for sorting purposes, you consider them as a single key, concatenating the first name onto the end of the last name. *Then* you treat all differences as significant. This way, primary differences in the first name beat lower-level differences in the last name, but you still consider lower-level differences in both names if both names are equal at the primary level. This approach gives a reasonable result:

van Dusen, Paul
vanDusen, Paul
Van Dusen, Paul
van Dusen, Tom
vanDusen, Tom
Van Dusen, Tom

The "Van Dusens" are correctly grouped by first name, and they sort into the same order within each group.

Be careful what you use as a field delimiter when you're putting together composite keys. In the default UCA order, the comma, like the space, has alternate mappings. If you treat characters with alternate mappings as ignorable, as we did in the preceding example, shorter last names won't necessarily sort before longer last names of which they're substrings. You'll go to the first name prematurely, possibly giving something like this:

Van, Bill
van Dusen, Paul
Van Dusen, Paul
van Dusen, Tom
Van Dusen, Tom
Van, Steve

Here, Bill Van and Steve Van sort on either side of the Van Dusens, rather than clustering together before them, because the first letters of their first names are compared against the D in "Van Dusen." To prevent this problem, you must either tailor your sort order or pick a field delimiter that's not ignorable (and sorts before the letters). Because you're just using this composite key for internal processing and not displaying it, it doesn't much matter what you use for the field delimiter for your composite keys, so long as it produces the right results. The dollar sign fills the bill, for example.

Exposing Sort Keys

Until now, we've talked about sort keys mainly as an internal construct you use to get things to sort in the right order. You calculate them on the fly when you compare two strings. Nevertheless, it's also frequently worth the effort to keep sort keys around rather than just creating them (or, more often, partially creating them) when you do a comparison. It's relatively expensive to create a sort key. If you're doing many comparisons involving the same strings, it's much cheaper to put the sort keys together once and then do all comparisons directly on the sort keys using a simple binary comparison.

Most of the time when you compare two strings on the fly, you'll find a difference in the first few characters. Thus you have to go through all the work for only a few characters rather than for the entire string. Unless the strings you're comparing are quite similar, an on-the-fly comparison will be faster unless you're doing a *lot* of comparisons. If you're sorting a long list, do many searches on a long list, or have a lot of similar strings in the list, the balance shifts toward keeping the sort keys around. Most Unicode-aware string comparison APIs do provide a way to create a sort key from a string as well as a way to compare two strings on the fly.

There are a few things to keep in mind if you're not just going to create sort keys long enough to do a long sort, but store them in a database or file. Most importantly, it's completely meaningless to compare sort keys generated from different sort tables. For example, if you compare a sort key generated from a Spanish sort order to one generated from a German sort order, the result is meaningless, because the same weight values may mean different things in different sort orders. Suppose, for example, that a German sort order assigns primary weights of 1, 2, 3, 4, and 5 to A, B, C, D, and E, respectively. A Spanish sort order might instead assign these weights to A, B, C, CH, and D, respectively, as "ch" is a separate letter in the Spanish alphabet. You can see how comparing sort keys generated from these two sets of weights would produce goofy results.

A system that always uses the same values for the UCA default ordering and puts tailorings in the "cracks" between them will produce less goofy results, but still doesn't work perfectly. "Ch" will sort differently depending on whether it's in a string that had a Spanish sort key or one with a German sort key.

This problem falls into the "Doctor, it hurts when I do this!" category ("Then don't do that!"), but it can also arise between different versions of the same sort order—for example, going from sort keys based on the Unicode 2.1.8 version of the UCA default order to sort keys based on the Unicode 3.0 version of the UCA default order. One way to avoid it is to append a version tag to the beginning of every sort key. You can use an algorithm to generate a hash code based on the actual contents of the mapping table and then use this hash code as the version tag. It's then a simple matter to detect a version mismatch. Even if you just compare the sort keys, you'll at least wind up with a bunch of sublists, one for each collation table used to create any of the sort keys.

Minimizing Sort Key Length

The other issue that becomes important with persistent sort keys is minimizing their size. You can employ a number of strategies for minimizing sort key size.

Eliminating Level Separators   You don't have to waste space putting level separators in your sort keys if you use distinct ranges of numeric values for the primary, secondary, and tertiary weight values. This approach doesn't work for the fourth-level weights, however, so you usually need a separator there. It also tends to make some of the other optimizations more difficult.

Shrinking the Secondary and Tertiary Weights   It doesn't make sense to use a 16-bit value for the secondary and tertiary weights, as we can typically use 8-bit values for both. To make this process work, you need a level separator after the primary weights, as you may need the 8-bit values for the secondary and tertiary weights (you might be able to eliminate the one between the secondary and tertiary weights, but that saves only a byte). The level separator after the primary weights needs to be two bytes, because the primary weight values are two-byte values, unless you don't use the separator-byte value as the leading byte in a primary weight value.

Avoiding Zero   If you are using C-style zero-terminated strings to store your sort keys, you must avoid using the byte value 0 anywhere in the sort key except at the end. You can use 1 or 0x0101 as a level separator (which is why the tertiary weights in the UCA table start at 2), and your primary weight values cannot include 00 as either byte. (This restriction knocks out 512 possible primary weight values.) Avoiding 00 as either byte of a fourth-level key value is tougher—you could add one to each byte of a fourth-level key value and use two bytes to express the byte values 0xFE and 0xFF.

Run-Length Encoding   Run-length encoding doesn't really buy you much at the primary level, where there tends to be little repetition, but it can buy you a lot at the secondary and tertiary levels, which often have lots of repetition. In particular, the "neutral" tertiary weights—the ones used for uncased or unaccented characters—tend to show up frequently in most sort keys.

UTS #10 describes one way of going about this process. At each level, you take all weight values higher than the one that repeats (all values higher than 0x20 for the secondary weights, and all values higher than 0x02 for the tertiary weights) and move them to the opposite end of the byte. The highest weight value becomes 0xFF, the second-highest weight value becomes 0xFE, and so on. This technique opens up a "hole" in the middle above the value that repeats. Each value in this "hole" represents some number of repetitions of the value that repeats. For example, with the tertiary weights, 0x03 represents 02 02, 0x04 represents 02 02 02, and so on.

Actually, matters are a little more complicated. The range that represents repeating values is divided in half. For each number of repetitions of the repeating value, there are two different byte values: a "high" value and a "low" value.

As an example, suppose we're talking about the tertiary weights. The value that repeats is 0x02, and the highest tertiary weight value is 0x1F. The values 0x00 and 0x01 are represented in the normal way (in the standard UCA algorithm, 0x01 would be the level separator and 0x00 wouldn't happen). The values 0xE3 to 0xFF represent 0x03 to 0x1F, and the values from 0x03 to 0xE2 represent varying repetitions of 0x02. The sequence 02 02 can be represented by either 0x03 or 0xE2, 02 02 02 by either 0x04 or 0xE1, 02 02 02 02 by either 0x05 or 0xE0, and so on. Whether you use 0x04 or 0xE1 to represent 02 02 02 depends on the value that comes next. If it's higher than 0x02, you use 0xE1. If it's lower than 0x02, you use 0x04.

Of course, it's possible to have more repetitions of the repeating value in a row than can be represented with a single byte. You handle this situation in the obvious way: Use as many of the values representing the maximum number of repetitions as you need, followed by one more for the remainder. For example, if 0x80 is the highest "low" value representing 127 repetitions of 0x02 (you can put the partition between "high" and "low" values wherever you want), you'd represent 300 repetitions (when followed by a value lower than 0x02) of 0x02 with 0x80 0x80 0x2D.

This technique will never lead to sort keys longer than the uncompressed format, and it can often result in tremendous amounts of compression. Of course, the strings sort in the same way as the uncompressed versions, as long as everything follows the compressed format.

■ SEARCHING

The other major use for string comparison involves searching.[7] By now, it should be apparent that sequences of Unicode code points that aren't bit-for-bit

---

7. Much of the material in this section is drawn from Laura Werner, "Unicode text searching in Java," *Proceedings of the Fifteenth International Unicode Conference,* session B1, September 1, 1999.

identical should compare as equal in many situations and thus should be returned as a hit from a text searching routine. Not only do you have to deal with issues such as Unicode canonical and compatibility equivalents, but you also have to handle linguistically equivalent strings. For example, if you're searching for "cooperate," you would probably want to find "coöperate" and "co-operate" as well. By now, you've undoubtedly figured out that the best strategy is not to match Unicode code points, but rather to convert both the search key and the string being searched to collation elements and match them instead.

In fact, searching is where different levels of equivalence really come in handy. If you want to ignore case differences, for example, you can declare that anything that's equivalent down to the secondary level matches and ignore tertiary-level differences. To ignore accent variations as well, you'd treat only primary-level differences as significant and ignore both secondary-level and tertiary-level differences.

Doing so requires catching the collation process at a slightly earlier point than you do for sorting. Instead of converting the search key and the string being searched into sort keys, you stop a step earlier, while they're still sequences of collation elements. That is, you skip the step where you segregate all the weight values into separate parts of the sort key and (possibly) reverse the order of the weights at the secondary level. Instead, you catch things while all of the weights are still stored together in one numeric value. Typically, you convert the search key into a sequence of collation elements and then convert the string being searched into collation elements one character at a time while you're searching.

Ignoring secondary- or tertiary-level differences in this situation is a simple procedure. They occupy certain ranges of bits in the collation element, so you can mask out the parts of the collation element that don't interest you. In our previous examples, a 32-bit collation element was divided into a 16-bit primary weight with 8-bit secondary and tertiary weights. If you're interested in only primary differences, you could mask off the bottom 16 bits of the collation elements before doing your comparison. You also have to be careful of ignorable characters: If, after masking off the uninteresting parts, you end up with zero (or whatever value is used to signal an ignorable character), you skip that collation element without using it in the comparison.

One additional complication arises. If you find a match, it doesn't count as a match unless it begins and ends on a grapheme cluster boundary. If accent differences are important, you don't want a match if you're searching for "cote" and find "coté" in the text. If "coté" is in the text in its decomposed form, however, "cote" is a prefix of it and you'll find it, even though you shouldn't and wouldn't if "coté" was represented in memory in its precomposed form. When you find a prospective match, then, you must check whether it begins and ends on a grapheme cluster boundary. For instance, "cote" wouldn't match "coté" because the matching sequence of code point values ends in the middle of a grapheme cluster: It includes the letter e but not the accent. This is very similar to how you implement a "find whole words only" function, which we'll examine in a minute.

Depending on your API, getting the collation elements in the necessary form may be difficult (unless, of course, you have a searching API). In Java, you can use the `CollationElementIterator` class to access the collation elements. The ICU libraries for both C and Java provide a searching API on top of the `CollationElementIterator` utility.

The Boyer-Moore Algorithm

To do a simple brute-force string search in a Unicode-compatible linguistically sensitive way, all you need is sequential access to the collation elements in a string before they're split into the multiple zones of a sort key. There are, of course, better and more efficient ways to search a string for another string.

One of the classical efficient string-search algorithms was first published by Robert S. Boyer and J. Strother Moore of the University of Texas in a 1977 article in *Communications of the ACM*.[8] The Boyer-Moore algorithm takes advantage of the fact that each comparison actually tells you more than just that two characters don't match.

Let's say you're searching for the word "string" in the phrase "silly spring string."[9] In a traditional brute-force search, you'd start with the search key and

---

8. Robert S. Boyer and J. Strother Moore, "A Fast String Searching Algorithm," *Communications of the Association for Computing Machinery,* vol. 20, no. 10, pp. 762–772, 1977.

9. This example is taken from the Werner paper, op. cit.

the string being searched lined up at the first character and compare until you find a difference:

The "s"'s compare as equal, but then you fail in comparing "t" to "i." Now you slide "string" over by one character and try again:

This time, the first comparison fails ("s" against "i"), so you slide "string" over by one character and try again:

And so it goes until you finally locate "string" at the end of "silly spring string." By the time you've found it, you've performed 21 character comparisons.

There's a better way. Start as before, with the two strings lined up at their initial positions, but begin in the comparison at the *end* of the search key:

You compare "g" to the space. The result tells you that "string" doesn't occur at the first position in the phrase. You also know that the space doesn't occur at all in the search key. You therefore know that "string" can't occur starting at any of the positions up to and including the one you just checked. So you can slide the search key over six spots and try again:

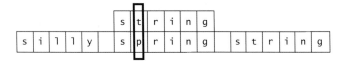

This time, you can work your way back from the end of the search key until you get to "t," which isn't equal to "p." Again you know you don't have a match at the position you're trying. Because we also know that "p" doesn't occur in our search key, we can slide over to the first position following "p":

Next, we compare "g" to "s." Again, the result tells us we don't have a match. Unlike the other characters we've looked at, however, "s" does appear in the search key, so we slide over just far enough to put the last "s" in the search key (which also happens to be the *first* "s" in the search key) at our current position and try again:

																s	t	r	i	n	g
s	i	l	l	y		s	p	r	i	n	g		s	t	r	i	n	g

This time we have a match, which took us 13 character comparisons to find.

The key to the Boyer-Moore algorithm is going through the search key first and building up a table that indicates for each character how far you can skip forward before doing the next comparison. For "string," the table would look like this:

s	5
t	4
r	3
i	2
n	1
g	0
(everything else)	6

The beauty of the Boyer-Moore algorithm is that if you repeatedly search for the same search key, you can reuse this table, which can save a lot of time.

Notice that when we compared "t" to "p," we slid over only two places, instead of the six the table would suggest, because of the matches we saw before. For each match, you deduct one from the shift value you use when you get to the mismatch.

What happens if the same character occurs more than once in the search key? The table contains the *lowest* shift value that would apply to that character. If the word was "status," for example, you'd get this table of shifts:

s	0
t	2
a	3
u	1
(everything else)	6

When you see a "t" in the string being searched, it could mean you have to shift forward either two or four characters, so you play it safe and shift forward two. Likewise, an "s" could mean you need to shift forward five characters, or it could mean you have a match, so you treat it as a potential match. The bottom line is that if you shift too far, you may miss a match. If you don't shift far enough, you may just make a few otherwise unnecessary comparisons. Thus it is wise to be conservative when populating the shift table.

For a simple byte-based encoding where you don't have to worry about issues such as expanding and contracting character sequences, this kind of search is simple. Your shift table has 256 entries, which is entirely manageable. For Unicode, a 64K table is unwieldy, and a 1MB-plus table is even more unwieldy, which would seem to make the Boyer-Moore algorithm unworkable.

Using the Boyer-Moore Algorithm with Unicode

Actually, the shift table is even larger than 1MB because you're comparing collation elements, not Unicode code points, and collation elements are 32 bits wide. A table with 4 billion elements is definitely unworkable.

Of course, the Boyer-Moore algorithm actually isn't unworkable with Unicode. The solution is one of those clever "Why didn't I think of that?" ideas. It was first discovered (and patented[10]) by Mark Davis of IBM (actually Taligent at the time of the patent). The secret lies in how you handle a character that occurs in the sort key twice: You use the shorter shift distance.

When working with Unicode, you still use a 256-element table (or any size you want—the principle is the same) and a hash function to map the collation element values into this one-byte space. You can perform the hashing in a number of ways, but the simplest technique is to isolate the low byte of the primary weight from the collation element and use that as your index into the table. More complicated hash functions can provide somewhat better distribution, but it's usually not worth the trouble.

If you have multiple collation elements with the same low byte in their primary weights, the entry in the table is the shortest shift distance for any of the collation elements that map to that table entry. As with characters that occur multiple times in the search key, this may mean you sometimes don't shift as far as possible, giving up a little performance, but you still get the right answer. In real-world use, you also don't lose much in terms of performance.

---

10. IBM has agreed to license the patented code freely. The same approach is used in ICU, which is an open-source project.

Two additional complications arise. The first is ignorable characters. If they occur in the string being searched, they don't hurt. They may mean your shift distances aren't quite big enough, but you'll still find the right answer. If they occur in the search key, on the other hand, you have to filter them out before calculating your shift distances or you risk shifting too far.

The second complication is matching up the collation elements to the characters in the original string you're searching. If you treat the shift values as how many *code point values* to move ahead, rather than how many *collation elements* to move ahead (which can be cheaper, as you can avoid mapping some characters to collation elements), you must watch out for expanding characters and adjust your shift values to account for the possibility of skipping over expanding characters.

If you go by collation elements, everything's already expanded and you don't have to worry about shifting too far. In this case, though, you have to watch out for false matches. You might find a match that starts on the second (or later) collation element of an expanding character. You'd need to do some extra bookkeeping to detect this condition.

"Whole Word" Searches

Many times you want to search a document for a string, but you want a match to count as a hit only if it is a whole word. That is, if you're searching for "age," you don't want the system to tell you it found those letters in the middle of "cabbages."

To avoid this problem, you can do one of two things: After you find a match, you can check whether both ends of the match fall on word boundaries, or you can adjust the Boyer-Moore algorithm so that it will shift forward to the next word boundary following the position specified in the shift table. In fact, you can check whether the end of the search key falls on a word boundary at the current position and know you don't have a match without doing any comparisons at all, although doing one comparison usually helps more.

But how do you tell whether a position in the text is a word boundary? Two approaches to this problem are possible: the pair-based approach and the state-machine-based approach. The pair-based approach looks at two characters and decides whether a word boundary separates them. The state-machine-based approach parses the text (or some subset of it) to find word boundaries according to a state machine. It can consider more context than just two characters and sometimes produces more accurate results (and, in fact, is required for some languages).

These strategies are also the main approaches to deciding where to insert line breaks when laying out a paragraph of text. For this reason, we will defer a full treatment of these techniques to Chapter 16, when we talk about laying out lines of text.

Even when you're not doing a "whole word" search, you have to be sure that a matching sequence begins and ends on a grapheme cluster boundary, as we saw earlier in the chapter. The same techniques that are useful for locating word boundaries are also useful for locating grapheme cluster boundaries.

■ Using Unicode with Regular Expressions

In addition to normal searching where you match a literal pattern to a document (with potentially varying degrees of looseness in what constitutes a "match"), text is often searched for text that matches a regular expression. A regular expression describes a category of related strings. Any string in that category is said to "match" the regular expression. For example, a regular expression such as

```
p[a-z]*g
```

might be used to specify a category consisting of all words that start with p and end with g. "Pig," "pug," "plug," and "piling" would all match this regular expression. If you searched a string for this regular expression, the search would stop on any of those words (or any other word that began with p and ended with g).

We will not explain how to write a regular expression engine—there are plenty of books focusing on this subject. As always, however, we have some things to think about when implementing a regular expression engine for Unicode.

Unicode Technical Report #18 gives a set of guidelines for writing a Unicode-compatible regular expression engine. It provides for three levels of Unicode compatibility:

- Level 1 is basic Unicode support, the minimal set of features necessary to make a regular expression engine usable with Unicode.
- Level 2 goes beyond Level 1 by adding in a deeper understanding of how Unicode text is structured.
- Level 3 provides complete locale sensitivity of the kind we've been studying for regular searching and sorting.

We don't have enough room to go into lots of detail on exactly what each of these levels means, but here's a brief summary. Level 1 requires or recommends the following:

- The engine must (when operating on UTF-16 text) work correctly on UTF-16 code units instead of treating them as pairs of bytes.
- The regular expression language must have some way to refer to a Unicode character by its code point value (for example, you could specify the Greek capital letter sigma with something like \u03A3). Because not all systems can display (or allow you to type) every character in the Unicode repertoire, this feature is essential.
- The language must have some way to specify Unicode categories. In an ASCII-based regular expression language, it's feasible to express "all letters" by saying "[a-zA-Z]"; as there are thousands of "letters" in Unicode (tens of thousands if you count the Han characters), this approach isn't feasible with Unicode. You need a special token that at least lets you specify groups of characters with the same Unicode general category.
- The language needs some way to remove characters from a set of characters. This ability would let you specify "all Latin consonants" by saying something like [a-z]-[aeiou]. This feature goes hand in hand with the need for specification of Unicode categories. Without it, there's no reasonable way to say things like "all currency symbols except the cent sign."
- If the engine supports case-insensitive matching, it must be smart enough to handle all the Unicode case equivalences. For Level 1 support,

single characters that map to multiple characters when uppercased don't have to be supported, but multiple mappings do. A case-insensitive match to the Greek letter sigma, for example, has to match both lower-case forms.

- If the regular expression language supports matching of line boundaries, the support must conform to the Unicode new-line guidelines, recognizing as newlines not only the various ASCII and Latin-1 characters that can be used as newlines, but also LS and PS (U+2028 and U+2029) and the CRLF sequence.

Level 2 adds the following features to Level 1:

- It must allow specification of supplementary-plane characters by code point value and must treat them as first-class characters, even if it's actually operating on UTF-16 text where they're stored as surrogate pairs.
- It must correctly match canonically equivalent strings.
- Its concept of a "character" should match a normal user's concept of a "character" (the Unicode documents refer to this concept as a "grapheme cluster"). This feature requires not counting as matches those apparent matches that don't begin and end on grapheme cluster boundaries.
- The engine should be fairly intelligent about word boundaries. In particular, it should ignore combining marks and formatting characters when examining pairs of characters to determine whether they constitute a word boundary.
- Case-insensitive matches should work correctly with characters (such as the German letter ß) that can turn into multiple characters when uppercased.

Level 3 provides fully language-sensitive support. It builds on top of the collation element stuff discussed earlier in the chapter. It's much slower than the language-insensitive approach and should generally be an option rather than a requirement.

Level 3 support involves:

- Mapping the Pi and Pf categories to Ps and Pe in a way that's appropriate for the specified locale. (This requirement means taking the ambiguity out of the way Unicode handles quotation marks.)
- Treating as a "grapheme" anything that speakers of the specified language would consider to be one. This feature means not only dealing with the generic Unicode grapheme clusters of Level 2, but also treating as "graphemes" anything specified as a contracting character sequence in the locale's sort order. In Spanish, for example, "ch" would be considered a single grapheme.
- Respecting the locale's conception of what a "word" is. For languages such as Thai or Japanese, this ability may involve some fairly sophisticated linguistic analysis.
- Allowing for locale-dependent loose matching. This feature provides the ability to allow sequences with only second- or third-level differences according to the sort order to match if desired. For example, "v" and "w" are variants of the same letter in Swedish, so a pattern containing "v" should still match a "w" in Swedish text.
- Specifying ranges according to the language's sort order, not the order of the Unicode code point values. For example, [a-ø] would have a different meaning in English (where it would match only about half the alphabet) and Swedish (where it would match the entire alphabet).

16

Rendering and Editing

$\mathcal{I}$f the second most important process performed on text is string comparison (the basis of sorting and searching), by far the most important process for text is rendering—that is, drawing it on a computer screen or printing it on a piece of paper. Much of the time it goes hand in hand with providing the user a means of entering text into the computer or editing the text once it's been entered.

Rendering and editing text are both enormously complicated subjects, and we will not go into all the gory details here. Most of the time you'll be able to take advantage of the facilities provided by your operating environment to allow you to render and edit Unicode text. Much of the complexity also isn't unique to Unicode, but rather is inherent in the various scripts that Unicode can represent and must be managed with any encoding scheme used to represent those scripts. But as with the other processes we've discussed, there are enough interesting things about rendering and editing that are unique to Unicode that make this subject worth a long look.

Three major categories of tasks must be handled when rendering text, regardless of the encoding involved, all of which become more interesting when Unicode is your encoding:

- Splitting a large body of text up into lines and paragraphs. This task can be as simple as looking for spaces in the text and breaking a line at the last space that comes before the desired right margin, but for many scripts it's much more complicated.

- Arranging the individual characters on a line of text. This task can be as simple as putting them in a single-file line running from left to right, but can become much more complicated, especially when the Unicode bi-di algorithm must be used.
- Figuring out which glyph to draw for each character. Often, this process is a simple one-to-one mapping, but for many scripts the rules for deciding which glyphs to draw for a character or series of characters are much more complicated.

In addition to these considerations, we'll take a brief look at some of the issues involved in editing Unicode text.

■ LINE BREAKING

If you're drawing more than a few words, the first thing you have to do when drawing text on the screen is to break it up into lines. Usually a text-rendering process will maintain a **line starts array** that lists the offset in the backing store of the first character of each line of rendered text. To draw a block of text, you must first build that line starts array.

Dividing a block of text up into lines generally proceeds in three conceptual phases:

1. Locate all the positions in the text where a line break *has* to go. This step divides the text into a series of blocks. For the purposes of this discussion, we'll call these blocks "paragraphs," although most word processing programs allow forced line breaks within a paragraph.
2. For each paragraph that can't fit entirely on one line, locate all the positions in that paragraph where it would be legal, according to the rules of the text's language, to break a line. (For example, it's not acceptable to break a line in the middle of an English syllable, and it's not acceptable to break a line in the middle of an English word unless you can hyphenate it.) This step divides the paragraph into a series of short units. Again, for the purposes of this discussion, we'll call these units "words," even though you can run into situations where two or more real words form a single unit for the purposes of line breaking as well as situations where a single real word breaks into multiple units for the purposes of line breaking.

3. Assemble the words into lines. The simplest and most common algorithm is to pack as many words as possible onto the first line, pack as many of the remaining words as possible onto the second line, and so on until you've assembled all of the words in the paragraph into lines. More complicated algorithms are also possible. In fact, professional typesetting software typically uses more sophisticated algorithms than the simple "maximal packing" algorithm.

As with the other processes we've examined, these three conceptual phases can be (and usually are) interleaved. It's also possible to abbreviate some of the phases; for instance, you can generally get away without finding every single word boundary in a paragraph you're dividing into lines.

For that matter, because it can be expensive to calculate the entire line starts array for a long document, you often see line starts calculated on an as-needed basis. Typically, the line starts are calculated only for the part of a document that's visible on the screen (with some slop on either side to make scrolling faster), and more line starts are calculated as more text scrolls into view.

In addition, most text-processing software will optimize the calculation of line starts so that only a minimal set of line starts are recalculated when the text is changed. (In fact, often line *lengths* are stored instead of actual line *starts,* because less updating is required.) For instance, a localized change such as the addition or deletion of a single character or word will affect only the line starts in a single paragraph. In fact, if you're using the maximal-packing algorithm, it affects only the line starts that follow the location of the change: You can start at the line of the change and recalculate line starts until you reach either a line whose starting position didn't change or the end of the paragraph. Algorithms other than the maximal-packing algorithm usually require rewrapping the whole paragraph, or propagating in *both* directions from the change, because they consider more context.

Line-Breaking Properties

Most text layout issues are language-specific (or transcend language) rather than being unique to Unicode. If the user mixes languages or scripts, however, certain issues may come up more often with Unicode than with other encoding schemes.

The most interesting step in the line-breaking process from the standpoint of dealing with Unicode is the process of boundary analysis: dividing a document up into paragraphs and dividing a paragraph up into words. As with most other processes, the Unicode standard gives both rules and guidelines for performing this analysis on Unicode text. You'll find these rules in Unicode Standard Annex #14. (I say "rules and guidelines" because some of the material in UAX #14 is normative and some is informative.)

UAX #14 outlines a set of character properties that describe how a line-breaking process should treat the characters. Some of these properties are normative; most are informative. The complete listing of which characters have which line-breaking properties appears in the file LineBreak.txt in the Unicode Character Database.

UAX #14 divides the entire Unicode repertoire into several broad categories:

- Characters that are always followed by a line break ("breaking characters")
- Characters that may never be preceded or followed by a line break ("glue characters")
- Characters that stick to the characters that precede them and are otherwise transparent to the algorithm ("combining characters")
- Spaces, which affect the treatment of other characters
- Characters whose treatment depends on context
- A few special categories

The first category, breaking characters, is the most important, and is normative. These characters force a line break to happen afterward, no matter what. You use them to divide a document up into paragraphs, as the characters in this category mark the end of a paragraph. These characters include LS, PS, and FF. LF, CR, and the CRLF combination also fall into this category, but because the CRLF combination is treated as a single breaking "character," CR and LF get their own special categories: LF behaves in the same way as the other breaking characters, and CR does as well, unless it's followed by LF. A break can never occur between CR and LF.

All of the other categories focus on how you divide up paragraphs into words for the purposes of line breaking. (Remember we're using "paragraph" and "word" to refer to units of text that are divided and assembled by a line-breaking algorithm—they usually, but not always, map to the common-sense definitions of "paragraph" and "word.") For the rest of this section, we'll use the phrase "word break" to refer to a boundary between "words" for the purposes of line breaking—that is, a "word break" is a place in the text where it's legal for a line break to happen.

Glue characters are the next most important category. A word break can never appear on either side of a glue character. These characters suppress any word breaks that would otherwise occur (that is, they "glue" characters or words together). They include the WORD JOINER, all characters with "NO-BREAK" in their name (NBSP, ZWNBSP, and so on), plus a handful of special-purpose characters that also have "gluing" semantics.

The third normative category contains the combining characters. They include not only the characters you'd expect (the combining and enclosing diacritical marks, the characters in the "Mc" and "Me" categories), but also a few other things. Specifically, the non-initial conjoining Hangul jamo (i.e., the conjoining vowels and final consonants) are members of this category, as are the Indic vowel signs. The basic idea is that all of these characters are nonleading characters in combining character sequences. For the purposes of line breaking, the entire combining sequence should be treated as a single character, with the first character in the sequence determining the sequence's behavior. Thus all of the characters in the sequence are "glued" together, and the sequence behaves as a unit.

Interestingly, the invisible formatting characters are also treated as combining characters. Of course, they're not really combining characters, but each is intended to have an effect on only one process and to remain invisible to all other processes. The easiest way to treat a character as invisible for line breaking is to treat it in the same way as a combining character. The exceptions, of course, are ZWSP and WORD JOINER, the invisible formatting characters whose whole job is to affect line breaking.

UAX #14 calls out a few other special characters for normative purposes. The zero-width space (ZWSP) always precedes a word break. Other spaces can affect the behavior of surrounding characters in interesting ways. The object replacement character relies on out-of-band information to determine how it behaves for word-breaking purposes. Surrogate pairs stick together much like other combining character sequences. (This rule shouldn't strictly be necessary, because surrogates aren't really characters. A UTF-16 surrogate pair should behave according to the rules for the character it represents.)

The other line-breaking categories are all informative and are designed, like the default Unicode Collation Algorithm ordering, to give a reasonable default behavior for every character in Unicode. Without going into detail for all the categories, they're designed to achieve the following behavior (for full details, see UAX #14 itself):

- Generally, a word break occurs after a series of spaces, although this behavior depends on the characters on either side of the run of spaces. The one exception to this rule (other than the normative behaviors we have already discussed) relates to punctuation in some languages. Punctuation marks in certain languages (for example, the question mark in French) are separated from the words that surround them with spaces on both sides:

Parlez-vous français ?

  Even though there's a space, a word break shouldn't occur between most punctuation marks and the word that precedes them.
- Generally, a word break occurs after a series of dashes or hyphens, except when they precede a numeral (in this case, a dash or hyphen might be used as a minus sign). The major exceptions are the em dash, which has a word break both before and after it, and the Mongolian hyphen, which has the word break before it instead of after.
- Word breaks don't occur in the middle of a sequence of dot-leader characters.
- Certain punctuation marks, such as periods or commas, have a word break after them except when they occur in the middle of a numeral. Other punctuation marks, such as the question and exclamation marks, always have a word break after them.
- Opening punctuation (such as the opening parenthesis) never has a word break after it, and closing punctuation never has a word break before it. As quotation marks are often ambiguous, they don't have word breaks on either side.
- In the languages that use the Han characters, what constitutes a "word" is difficult to figure out and often ambiguous, so it's acceptable to break

a line in the middle of a word. Consequently, the Han characters and the Han-like characters (i.e., Hangul, Hiragana, Katakana, Bopomofo) generally have word breaks on both sides. Some punctuation and diacritical marks (the ideographic period, small Kana, the Katakana long-vowel mark, and so on) can't occur at the beginning (or sometimes the end) of a line and "stick" to the preceding or following character as appropriate.

- Full-width presentation forms are treated in the same way as Han characters. Some other characters that don't have full-width variants (such as the Greek and Cyrillic letters) are treated as either Han characters or regular Latin letters depending on their resolved East Asian width property.
- Thai and Lao represent another interesting case. Like Japanese and Chinese, they don't use spaces (or any other mark) between words. Nevertheless, you're allowed to break lines only between actual words. This goal can be accomplished by using ZWSP, but better systems actually analyze the text to determine where the word boundaries occur. UAX #14 puts the affected characters into their own special category that indicates more information is needed to parse a run of these characters into words.

The important thing to remember here is that the category assignments are designed to give a reasonable default behavior. Sometimes (although not as often as with the UCA) tailorings are necessary to get good line-breaking behavior for a particular language. For example, the quotation mark characters have language-dependent semantics (a particular mark might be an opening quote in one language, but a closing quote in another). Their behavior can be nailed down in a language-specific tailoring. Another example is Korean, which can be written either with or without spaces between words. If it's written without spaces, Hangul syllables behave in the same way as Han characters. If it's written with spaces, they behave in the same way as Latin letters.

Implementing Boundary Analysis with Pair Tables

How do you write code to perform word boundary analysis?[1] The classical approach to this problem is to use a pair table. In its simplest incarnation, a pair

---

1. Most of the material in this section is drawn from my own paper, "Text Boundary Analysis in Java," *Proceedings of the Fourteenth International Unicode Conference,* session B2, March 24, 1999.

table is a two-dimensional array of Boolean values. For each possible pair of adjacent character categories, the table tells you whether the position between them is a word boundary. This approach, of course, is simple to implement: You use the techniques we've already examined to map each character in the pair to a category and then use the categories to look up the answer in the pair table.

A straight pair-based algorithm can be limiting, however, because it considers only two characters. For instance, you can't correctly handle sequences of combining characters with a simple pair-based algorithm, nor can you correctly handle the case where a punctuation mark is separated from the preceding word by a space (without making simplifying assumptions, anyway). Usually, the pair-based algorithm is extended to cover such situations. That is, you purposely skip over a run of combining marks or spaces and look up the characters on *either side* of the run in the pair table. Instead of Boolean values, the table contains tags that tell you things like "there's always a break here," "there's a break here only if there weren't any intervening spaces," "there's a break here only if there *were* intervening spaces," and so on. This approach is suggested by UAX #14, which gives both sample code for implementing this algorithm and a sample pair table that implements the semantics it describes.

Even this approach can break down in some sufficiently complex situations, although those situations are relatively rare.[2] You can continue to extend the pair-table algorithm to deal with the complex cases, but it requires more hard-coding and is less flexible.

To see how this process works, suppose we're implementing a drastically simplified algorithm. Our algorithm has only three character categories: letters, whitespace, and sentence-ending punctuation. A "word" is a sequence of zero or more letters, followed by a sequence of zero or more whitespace characters, followed by a sequence of zero or more sentence-ending punctuation characters, followed by a sequence of zero or more whitespace characters (the idea is to implement something that will correctly handle French punctuation). If you implement this scheme as a pair table, it looks like this:

---

2. In fact, the only ones I can think of are related to other processes that use the same algorithms (we'll look at some of them later), not line breaking.

	ltr	punct
ltr	*	
punct	X	*

Notice that we don't include the whitespace category in the pair table. It must be handled algorithmically to get the desired effect. Also notice that three things can appear in the cells: an asterisk, an X, or nothing. The asterisk means "put a break between the two characters only if there's intervening whitespace." The X means "always put a break between the two characters, intervening whitespace or not." The empty cell means "never put a break between the two characters, intervening whitespace or not."

To implement this algorithm, you need code that reads a character and takes note of its category, reads more characters until it reads a non-whitespace character and takes note of whether it saw any whitespace characters, and *then* looks up the categories of the two non-whitespace characters in the pair table. Finally, the code should use the result (and the determination of whether whitespace appeared between them) to decide whether to place the break there.

Implementing Boundary Analysis with State Machines

An alternative approach is to recognize that locating word break positions is essentially a parsing problem and to apply the traditional tools and techniques that are used for parsing text into tokens. Here, the traditional approach is to use a finite state machine.

In this approach, you still use a two-dimensional array, but this time only the columns represent character categories. Each row represents a state of the state machine. You start in some well-defined "start" state. Then, for each character, you look up its category and use the category and the current state number to determine the next state. You continue to read characters, look up categories, and look up new states until you transition to a well-defined "end" state, which indicates that the character you just read is the first character of the next "word" and you should put a word break between it and the preceding character. Then you start over in the "start" state with the first character in the next word (the character you just looked at) and do the whole thing again.

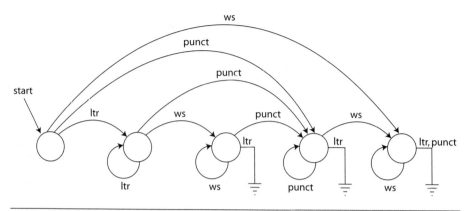

Figure 16.1   Example state transition diagram for word boundaries.

If you use a state machine to implement our example algorithm, you get a set of state transitions that look like Figure 16.1.

If you model this transition diagram as a two-dimensional array, you get the following table:

	ltr	**ws**	**punct**
start	1	4	3
1	1	2	3
2	STOP	2	3
3	STOP	4	3
4	STOP	4	STOP

Notice that we don't have to treat the handling of the whitespace as a special case now; the state transition table takes care of that task. Now you can consider however much context you need to determine a break position, and you don't have to write special-case code to handle the situations where you need to consider more than two characters.

The one thing that isn't clear from this example is what happens when you need to look at several characters after the break position to determine where the break position will go. In the current algorithm, when we transition to the "stop" state, the break position always goes before the character that caused us to reach the "stop" state. Thus you always have to be able to identify a break position after looking only at the character immediately following it.

One simple way of considering more characters after the break position is to deviate a bit from having the parser be a pure deterministic state machine. That is, you mark either each transition or each state (each state is almost always sufficient) with a flag. Instead of using your transition to the "stop" state as your indication of where to put the break, you use the flags. You start with a prospective break position at your starting point (or, in many algorithms, one character after your starting point, to avoid endless loops). Each time you enter a flagged state (or follow a flagged transition, if you go that route), you update the prospective break position to be before the character you just examined. The break goes wherever your prospective break position was located at the time you transitioned to the "stop" state. This approach lets you consider multiple characters after the break position in the relatively rare circumstances in which this step is necessary.

Of course, the marking technique isn't perfect: It always moves the mark forward, and you can, in very rare situations, run into cases where you find, after looking at more characters, that you actually need to move the break position *backward*. I have yet to encounter a real-world situation where this has happened; if you did, it would probably mean that it was time to switch to a nondeterministic state machine.

One problem with using a state-machine-based approach is that you generally must start at the beginning of the text, because the state machine assumes you're in some ground state (generally a known word boundary) when you begin. If you have to parachute into the text in the middle rather than parsing the whole thing (we'll see why this possibility is important in a minute), you need to back up from the random-access position until you find a position where you can safely start using the state machine to do the parsing without worrying about getting the wrong answer. (For pair-based approaches, you might need this ability as well, but you only have to worry about things you've already had to treat as special cases, such as the spaces in our earlier example.)

Typically you can locate the "safe place to turn around" with straight pair analysis. That is, you identify the pairs of characters that *always* have a word boundary between them and seek backward until you find one of these pairs. Occasionally, however, you might have to use a more sophisticated state-table-based approach to avoid seeking back to the beginning of the paragraph every time.

Performing Boundary Analysis Using a Dictionary

Correctly handling Thai and Lao is more difficult. These languages don't use spaces between words, but still require lines to be broken at word boundaries (as opposed to Chinese and Japanese, for example, which also don't use spaces between words but permit you to break lines almost anywhere).

The classical way of handling this problem is to use a dictionary-based algorithm. You compare the text to a list of known words and use the matching sequences to parse the text into words. This analysis is fairly complicated. The simplest approach (find the longest word that matches the beginning of the text, put a word break after it, then repeat this process for the remainder of the text until you've used up everything) doesn't work most of the time. Perhaps the first word in the text *isn't* the longest word in the dictionary that matches; it might be a shorter word that starts with the same letters. If you use the longest match, you may later encounter a sequence of letters that don't match any word in the dictionary. If you were using this algorithm on English without spaces, for example, and the sentence you were trying to parse was "themendinetonight," you'd wind up trying "theme" as your first word and discovering that it left you with something that began with "nd" as your second word.

Instead, you must find the set of words in the dictionary that enables you to use all of the characters. This strategy involves trying various sequences of words until you find one that fits. The approach is similar to a traditional maze-solving algorithm: Try each sequence of turns one at a time until you find the sequence that gets you all the way through the maze. In our example, "theme" would lead you to "nd," so you'd fall back on "them," which would eventually lead you to "eto," so you'd fall back on "the." With a few more wrong turns and backtrackings, you'd eventually end up with "the men dine tonight."

Of course, if *multiple* sequences of words match the text you're parsing, you're stuck. You must either pick one and hope for the best or use digram or trigram analysis. In the latter approach, you analyze the relative frequencies of the various two- or three-word sequences in the text to figure out which sequence of words is the most likely, which requires another table of digrams or trigrams and their frequencies.

You're also stuck if you hit a word that isn't in the dictionary, whether an uncommon word or just a typographical error. Various fallback approaches can be used here. You could assume you've seen a typo and use auxiliary information to guess what the word should have been. You can break the text up so that the longest series of letters you could parse successfully is kept and you start over with the remainder of the text after skipping an offending character. Or you could fall back on algorithmic approaches: While it isn't possible to locate *word* boundaries in Thai purely algorithmically, you can locate *syllable* boundaries algorithmically.

Of course, you don't want to use the dictionary-based approach on everything. After all, punctuation and spaces do occur in Thai text and always mark word boundaries. Generally, you use the techniques described earlier in the chapter and then fall back on the dictionary only when you encounter a sequence of two or more Thai or Lao letters in a row.

A Few More Thoughts on Boundary Analysis

It's probably evident that parsing Unicode text by looking for logical boundaries is useful for tasks other than just line breaking. It's how you could tell, for example, whether a search hit falls on word boundaries (for a "find whole words" search). It's how you know what to select when a user double-clicks or triple-clicks at some arbitrary place in the document. It's also the approach you use to count words or sentences in a document.

One important thing to keep in mind, though, is that the exact definition of "word" varies depending on how the information will be used. For double-click selection or spell checking, you might need a dictionary-based algorithm, whereas you don't for line breaking (at least in Japanese or Chinese). For "find whole words" searching, you want to exclude whitespace and punctuation from a "word," whereas you generally want to include these items for line-breaking purposes. For word counting, you might want to keep together sequences of characters (such as hyphenated phrases) that the line-breaking routine will divide up. A generalized algorithm that lets you substitute your own pair tables or state tables will let you do all these things without writing a whole new parser each time.

Performing Line Breaking

Once you've analyzed a paragraph into "words" (i.e., units of text that must be kept together on one line), how do you use that information to divide the paragraph up into lines? Many different techniques have been developed, but the most popular (probably because it's the simplest) is the maximal-packing algorithm. The basic approach here is to fit as many words as possible on the first line, then fit as many of the remaining words as possible on the second line, and so on until you reach the end of the paragraph.

One obvious way to approach this task is to interleave the process of parsing the text into words with the process of measuring it. You know how many pixels are available, so you parse into words until the total number of pixels exceeds that limit. Then you insert a line break and start over with the next word.

An alternative approach is to leap forward and then work your way back. If you're wrapping by number of characters instead of pixels (or you're working in a monospaced font where characters and pixels correlate), you can skip forward by the maximum number of characters that'll fit and then back up until you reach a word boundary. This approach can also work if you already know the widths of the text. If you have a good idea of the average width of the characters in the font, you could jump forward to the spot in the text where the end of the line would fall if every character was the average width, measure to see how close you got, and then work your way forward or backward from there, as appropriate, by parsing the text into words.

Keep in mind that you usually can't measure the text one character at a time to figure out how much text will fit on the line. This technique (generally) works for English, but for many other scripts, the characters interact typographically, so that the width of a character depends on the characters that surround it (because the glyph that will be displayed depends on the surrounding characters). Thus you have to measure text at least one word at a time. Of course, this requirement also means that you have to perform glyph mapping on the text. In fact, because this mapping may depend on rearrangement, you may also have to perform glyph rearrangement before you can break the text into lines accurately. This step can be tricky, because glyph rearrangement depends on line breaking in some scripts—you may have to perform speculative glyph rearrangement and then redo it if your assumptions turn out to be wrong.

Another point to keep in mind is that the widths of pieces of text may depend on where the line break actually goes. If the text includes the SOFT HYPHEN, which is invisible unless it occurs at the end of a line, you have to take its width into account if the break will occur after it. (If your line-breaking routine does hyphenation, you likewise have to take the width of the hyphen into account.) In fact, in some languages, such as Swedish, words have different spellings when they're hyphenated, so extra letters may be added (or deleted) before or after the hyphen in some languages.

Because of these potential complications, the usual course is to measure *all* of the text that would go on the line if the line break appeared in a certain position (with all the necessary processes happening on the text to get an accurate measurement). You pick a spot for the line break, measure the entire resulting line, decide whether it's too long or too short, skip an appropriate distance in the appropriate direction, try again, and so on until you achieve an optimally fitting line.

Hyphenation and justification are two techniques that often come into play when dividing text into lines. If you can't find a good fit, for example, you may have to hyphenate a word to achieve a better fit. Hyphenation in most languages involves the same kind of dictionary-based techniques used for regular line breaking in Thai. Other approaches may involve adding or removing interword or intercharacter spacing to get the right margin to line up better (in languages like Thai in which you don't normally have interword spacing, a justification routine may add a minimal amount of interword spacing to line up margins). Sometimes, alternate glyphs may be used for certain letters to line up text better. This tactic works particularly well in Arabic, for example, where often pairs of characters may join together in a number of different ways that yield different widths. Arabic justification also uses extender bars called *kashidas* to introduce extra space between certain pairs of letters when necessary to make a word wider.

Advanced techniques such as these are employed globally across all the lines in a paragraph to achieve optimal-looking results. For instance, a more advanced line-breaking algorithm might:

- Break in less "optimal" places to avoid leaving a single word alone on the last line of the paragraph.
- Avoid hyphenation on certain lines to eliminate "ladders" (i.e., several lines in a row that end with a hyphen).
- Deviate from maximal packing so as to keep the amount of interword or intercharacter spacing more consistent from line to line in a justified paragraph.
- Deviate from maximal packing in a way that keeps the "color" (the approximate density of the ink) consistent across the paragraph.
- Allow the text to go slightly outside the margin on either side (round characters, for example, look lined up with the margin when they actually go a little beyond the margin and don't look lined up when they actually are; this procedure is called "optical justification").

■ Line Layout

Once you've decided which words will go together on a line, the next step is to determine the order in which the characters will be arranged on that line. For the majority of scripts, this task is straightforward: The characters march in succession, one by one, from the left-hand side to the right-hand side (or, in some languages, from the top of the page to the bottom). In a couple of situations, matters get more interesting:

- The most common exception involves combining character sequences. Usually, a combining character sequence turns into a single glyph, but sometimes (especially when the text contains a lot of base–diacritic combinations) the rendering process has to draw two (or more) separate glyphs and figure out how to position them relative to each other.

Vowel and tone marks in Thai must be stacked, for example. Points in
Hebrew and Arabic need to be positioned correctly relative to the base
character (in Arabic in particular, the rules can become quite complicated in a high-quality font). This sort of layout is usually done in the
font itself, and we'll look at this issue more closely when we talk about
glyph selection.

- Indic scripts may follow complex positioning rules. Vowel marks aren't
  always positioned consistently relative to the consonant that immediately
  precedes them. If the syllable contains multiple leading consonants,
  sometimes they all come into play (left-joining vowels and the left halves
  of split vowels, for example, usually go at the extreme left of their syllables rather than merely exchanging places with the consonant to their
  left). The exact placement of viramas, rephas, and diacritical marks often depends heavily on the surrounding letters. Again, most of this positioning is usually handled by the font and will be looked at more closely
  in the next section. The one exception is left-joining vowels. On many
  systems, they're treated as separate characters and rearranged by the
  line-layout algorithm before glyph mapping.

- The big challenge in line layout, and the one to which we'll devote the
  rest of the section, is bi-di. If you're dealing with one of the right-to-left
  scripts (currently Hebrew, Arabic, Syriac, and Thaana), some complicated work goes on when these languages mix with left-to-right languages (or with numerals) on the same line. The Unicode bidirectional
  layout algorithm was designed to make sure you always get a well-defined
  ordering when scripts of different directionality are mixed on a line.

We looked at the Unicode bi-di algorithm in Chapter 8, but there we focused on the results it's designed to produce. Here we'll look a little more
closely at how to implement this behavior.

Unicode Standard Annex #9 describes the bi-di algorithm in excruciating
detail (it's also explained in Section 3.12 of the Unicode standard, but UAX #9
is more up-to-date). The bi-di algorithm works by dividing up the line into directional runs, groups of characters that all run in the same direction (left to
right or right to left). Within a directional run, the characters are laid out in the
normal, straightforward manner: The characters run one by one either from

right to left or from left to right. The big challenge comes in figuring out how to order the runs relative to each other.

To do so, the bi-di algorithm organizes the characters into **embedding levels**. Each level consists of a sequence of characters belonging strictly to that level, in one or more directional runs, and embedded levels. The items in each level are arranged relative to each other in a consistent direction (again, either left to right or right to left).

To see how this works, consider the following sentence:

Avram said מזל טוב and smiled.

It consists of three directional runs at two levels. The outermost level runs left to right and contains the two outer directional runs, "Avram said" and "and smiled," and the inner level. The inner level, which runs right to left, contains the inner directional run, "מזל טוב."

Without doing explicit embeddings, the deepest you can get is three levels: You can have a left-to-right outer level with right-to-left levels embedded within it. If a right-to-left level contains a numeral (numerals always run left to right), an inner level runs left to right. Combining character sequences in right-to-left text are generally treated as inner levels that run left to right (after the character codes have been reordered for display, the combining marks still follow the characters with which they combine). Of course, explicit embeddings can be used to get deeper levels of embedding, up to a maximum of 62 (which should be *way* more than enough for any rational piece of text).

To lay out a line, you need three buffers (actually, you can generally optimize some of them out, but bear with me for a few minutes). The first buffer contains either the characters, the glyph codes to which they map, or sequence numbers mapping positions in the display to positions in the backing store (or vice versa). We'll call it the "character buffer." The second buffer contains the resolved bi-di category for each character; we'll call it the "category buffer." The third buffer contains the resolved embedding level for each character; we'll call it the "level buffer."

The character buffer initially holds all the characters in the line in their normal (logical) Unicode order. The category buffer initially contains every character's directional category as specified by the Unicode Character Database. The level buffer initially holds either all zeros or all ones, depending on the paragraph's directionality. (The bi-di algorithm uses a convention that even-numbered levels are left-to-right levels and odd-numbered levels are right-to-left levels. Thus, if the paragraph's directionality is left-to-right, everything starts out at level 0; if right-to-left, everything starts out at 1.) The paragraph's directionality is usually specified with a property on the document or with styling information; in the absence of either, it defaults to the directionality of the first strong-directionality character in the paragraph.

Next, you take care of any explicit embeddings or overrides. They can be specified either by out-of-band styling information or by the explicit directional characters in the General Punctuation block—that is, the LRE (left-to-right embedding), LRO (left-to-right override), RLE (right-to-left embedding), and RLO (right-to-left override) characters. When you see an RLE or RLO, you increment the embedding level of all characters between it and the next matching PDF (pop directional formatting) character to the next-higher odd value. For LRE and LRO, you increment the embedding level to the next-higher even value. The sequences can nest; the incrementing happens at each nesting level.

For the override characters, you also change the entries in the category buffer for the characters between them and the next PDF (except for any additional embedding or override characters encountered). For LRO, everything between it and the next PDF (except characters embedded in a nested pair of explicit embedding/override characters) becomes L; for RLO, everything becomes R.

To see how this process works, let's look at another example. Suppose you're trying to get the following as your displayed text:

"The first two books of the Bible are בראשית and שמות.", אמד אבדהם

The algorithm begins with things looking like this (backing-store order is shown running from left to right here to make things a little easier):

```
אבדהם אמד, #"The first two books of the Bible are בראשית and שמות."#
RRRRRNRRRNN#NLLLNLLLLLLNLLLNLLLLLNLLNLLLNLLLLLNLLNRRRRRRNLLNRRRRNN#
111111111111111111111111111111111111111111111111111111111111111111
```

The first # sign is an LRE and the second one is a PDF. They cause the Hebrew words in the English sentence to be treated as part of the English sentence,

keeping the English sentence in order, rather than as part of the Hebrew sentence, which would break the English sentence into pieces and put them out of
order. After dealing with the explicit embeddings, we get this:

```
דמא סהדבא, #"The first two books of the Bible are תישאדב and תומש."#
RRRRNRRRNN#NLLLNLLLLLNLLLNLLLLLNLLNLLLNLLLLLNLLLNRRRRRRRNLLLNRRRRNN#
11111111111122222222222222222222222222222222222222222222222222222222
```

Next, you resolve weakly typed characters. This step causes combining characters to be treated the same as the base characters to which they attach, and it
causes punctuation inside numerals to be treated the same as the digits (if a numeral occurs in a left-to-right directional run, it is incorporated into that run).
Because our example doesn't have any numbers or weakly typed characters,
this pass has no effect on it.

Now you resolve neutral characters. If a neutral character has characters with
the same directionality on either side, it takes on the same directionality; otherwise, it takes on the directionality of the embedding level. At the end of this pass,
every character's entry in the category buffer is either L or R. In our example.

```
דמא סהדבא, "The first two books of the Bible are תישאדב and תומש."
RRRRRRRRRRRLLLLLLLLLLLLLLLLLLLLLLLLLLLLLLLLLLLLLLLLLRRRRRRRLLLLLRRRRLL
11111111111122222222222222222222222222222222222222222222222222222222
```

Once you've reached this point, you can go back and find the rest of the levels.
For each character whose directionality is counter to the directionality specified
by its entry in the level buffer (L characters with an odd embedding level or R
characters with an even embedding level), you increment its entry in the level
buffer. (Actually, numerals are special cases: They go up two levels when the
underlying embedding level is even.) For our example, that step gives the following result:

```
דמא סהדבא, "The first two books of the Bible are תישאדב and תומש."
RRRRRRRRRRRLLLLLLLLLLLLLLLLLLLLLLLLLLLLLLLLLLLLLLLLLRRRRRRRLLLLLRRRRLL
111111111111222222222222222222222222222222222222222233333322222333322
```

At this point, you no longer need the category buffer; its purpose is to help you
get the embedding levels right. Now you can use the embedding levels to reorder

the text. You start by locating every run of characters whose embedding level is 1 or higher and reversing their order. For our example, this step reverses the string:

"‏.אמוה dna ‏בדשיה era elbiB eht fo skoob owt tsrif ehT" ,‏אבדהם אמד"
223333322222333333322222222222222222222222222222222222222221111111111

Then you locate every run of characters whose embedding level is 2 or higher and reverse them again:

"The first two books of the Bible are‏בדאשית **and** ‏שממת‎." ,‏אבדהם אמד
222222222222222222222222222222222222222233333332222233332211111111111

And so on. For our example, you'd again reverse the runs with a level of 3:

"The first two books of the Bible are ‏בדאשית **and** ‏שממת‎." ,‏אבדהם אמד
2222222222222222222222222222222222222223333332222233332211111111111

And there you have it!

This seems like a lot of work and a lot of passes through the text, but like most of the other algorithms we've seen, it can be optimized. It's possible to go from the original text to the resolved levels in a single pass using a state-machine-based algorithm, leaving only the reordering pass as a separate pass.

The discussion here has glossed over some crucial details in the interest of brevity. For the full story, refer to UAX #9. The Unicode Web site also includes two reference implementations of the bi-di algorithm. One follows the description in UAX #9 literally, making numerous passes through the text. The other reference implementation uses a state machine to do the whole job in one pass.

Things also become more complicated when you're working in context and have to perform glyph reordering as well as line breaking and glyph selection (a paragraph of Arabic text, for example). You can't actually do the three processes in three separate passes as we're looking at them here. UAX #9 gives these recommendations:

1. For each paragraph, start by applying the bi-di algorithm to the whole paragraph, but only go far enough to figure out the embedding levels; don't actually reorder the characters.

2. Map the "reordered" characters to glyphs. This step lets you get the right results with Arabic letters and choose the right glyph for the "mirrored" characters (those that change glyph depending on their directionality).

3. Use these glyphs when measuring the text to parse it into lines, and divide it into lines.

4. *For each line,* reorder the glyphs according to their embedding levels.

5. Draw everything on the screen.

The reordering has to come *after* the line breaking, because the words that come first in the *logical* order should go before the line break. For example, if you have the sentence

Avram said מזל טוב and smiled.

and you split it into two lines so that only one of the Hebrew words can fit on the first line, you get this:

Avram said מזל

טוב and smiled.

Also keep in mind that if you're doing styled text, you can't apply the bi-di algorithm separately to each style run. The bi-di algorithm may reorder the style runs. In other words, if you underline "said" and "מזל," you should get

Avram <u>said</u> טוב <u>מזל</u> and smiled.

and not

Avram <u>said מזל</u> טוב and smiled.

■ GLYPH SELECTION AND POSITIONING

Arguably the most important part of drawing Unicode text is glyph selection and positioning. The Unicode character-glyph model (encode the semantics, not the appearance), combined with the inherent complexities of certain scripts, make rendering a complicated affair, at least for some scripts. For others, combining character sequences make things interesting.

Dealing with this issue is usually the province of font designers. Nevertheless, it's important to have some knowledge of how various font technologies work, as some support for certain scripts may also require help from the rendering engine.

Font Technologies

Let's start by considering font technologies and seeing how things are normally done in modern computerized fonts. This information will help the following discussions of particular technologies and techniques make more sense.

In a modern text-rendering system, a font is a piece of software. It works in concert with the rendering engine to draw text on an output device, such as the computer screen or a piece of paper. A typical font may supply:

- Glyph images (bitmap fonts) or glyph descriptions (outline fonts). A glyph description may stand alone or rely on other glyph descriptions to draw all or part of its glyph. (An accented-e glyph description might call out to separate descriptions for the letter e and the accent, for example.)
- One-to-one mappings between code point values in one or more character encoding standards and glyphs.
- Tables that allow for more complex many-to-many mappings between code point values and glyphs.
- Tables that allow the rendering engine to alter the default position of a glyph depending on the surrounding glyphs.
- Tables that alter the default glyph mappings based on style settings chosen by the user.

Two categories of font technologies exist: bitmap and outline fonts. In a bitmap font, each glyph is associated with a bit-oriented image; this bit image is simply copied to the screen to draw that character. Because the character has already been "rasterized" by the font designer, it's designed for a particular combination of point size and device resolution. Bitmap fonts are essentially obsolete in modern personal computers and printers, except sometimes for really small point sizes, but you still see them on PDAs and in various embedded applications (the displays on cell phones or copy machines, for example).

Outline fonts, on the other hand, are resolution independent. An outline font stores a geometric description of an ideal shape for each glyph. Each glyph description consists of zero or more ordered lists of points in an ideal coordinate space. Each ordered list of points is connected together to form a closed shape called a "loop" or "contour." (This process doesn't work quite like a child's connect-the-dots puzzle. Some points in the loop are "off-curve" points—instead of being connected into the loop, they define the shape of a curve that connects together the preceding and following points.) The loops are colored in to form the glyph. When loops intersect, rules describe which parts are colored in, which allows you to have characters with "holes" in them. The rendering engine uses the idealized description to create a bitmapped image on the fly that represents the character. Thus an outline font can represent the same characters at any size.

At small point sizes or coarse resolutions, however, the ideal coordinate space that is used to describe the glyphs begins to interact uncomfortably with the actual coordinate space where the rasterized image will be drawn. For this reason, outline fonts also include "hints" or "instructions" that are used to optimize the display at low resolutions. The instructions for each glyph define an algorithm for deforming the idealized shape in a way that fits onto the output device's coordinate system well while still honoring (as much as possible) the type designer's intent.

The first major outline-font technology in the personal-computer arena was Adobe Systems' PostScript, which first appeared on the Apple Laser-Writer printer in 1986. This was followed a number of years later by Apple's TrueType font technology. For a while after that, these two incompatible font technologies coexisted on the Mac, with PostScript being used in most printers and TrueType being used to render text on the screen. Many fonts were issued in both formats, but TrueType gradually became more popular—the highest-quality PostScript font format was closed, requiring license fees to use; Apple provided renderers that allowed TrueType fonts to be used on PostScript printers; the TrueType file format had a flexible structure that allowed for addition of extra tables, making the format more flexible and future-proof; and the internals of the TrueType format were independent of character encoding.

The deal was essentially sealed in the late 1980s when Apple agreed to license TrueType to Microsoft for use on Windows. After this, Windows and the Mac had a common, compatible font format, and Adobe was forced to open its PostScript format to avoid losing market share. Shortly thereafter, Apple updated the TrueType format to allow glyph outlines in the PostScript format.

In the early 1990s, Apple began work on TrueType GX, a more advanced font format based on TrueType that would support various more-advanced typographical features, such as those necessary for rendering the Indic scripts. TrueType GX has since evolved into Apple Advanced Typography (AAT).[3] Microsoft responded with its own advanced font format, OpenType.

Old-style TrueType fonts are compatible with both OpenType and AAT. Newer OpenType or AAT fonts are generally (though not always) minimally compatible with each other. Unless they were designed as dual-purpose fonts, however, they behave as old-style TrueType fonts on the system for which they weren't designed.

OpenType and AAT fonts contain one or more **character mapping tables** (or "cmap" tables) that map code point values in some encoding standard to internal glyph indices. A font can have multiple cmaps, allowing it to be used with more than one character encoding standard without the system having to perform code conversion before it can render text. These days, fonts from all the major font vendors include cmap tables for Unicode (specifically UTF-16). The glyph indices aren't standardized—these internal values are used only by the renderer to access the glyph outlines. Glyph indices are two-byte values, meaning a single font can never contain more than 65,536 glyphs. The cmap table maps single characters to single glyphs; more complex mappings are handled differently in OpenType and AAT.

---

3. Apple's rendering engine for AAT fonts is called Apple Type Services for Unicode Imaging, or ATSUI (pronounced "at-sooey"), which gets my vote for funniest-sounding computer-industry acronym—I always want to say "gesundheit" when someone talks about it.

Poor Man's Glyph Selection

Most Unicode-compatible systems begin by doing the stuff they can do *without* any cooperation from an underlying font engine (or from the fonts themselves). Quite a bit of Unicode can, in fact, be covered using a rendering engine (or a font) that doesn't support complex typography. With suitable fonts but no special rendering technology, you can handle:

- Latin (precomposed characters only)
- Greek (again, precomposed characters only)
- Cyrillic
- Armenian
- Georgian
- Hebrew (unpointed, assuming you apply the bi-di algorithm to the characters before you pass the characters to the renderer)
- Ethiopic
- Cherokee
- Han, Hiragana, Katakana, and Bopomofo (assuming the fonts can hold sufficient numbers of characters)
- Hangul (precomposed syllables only)
- Yi
- Canadian aboriginal syllabics

You can go a bit beyond this list by performing mappings on characters before sending them to the renderer. If you map to Normalized Form C before sending characters to the renderer, you pick up support for all combining character sequences that have equivalent precomposed forms.

You can even go a little beyond this capability, especially if you use compositions that are excluded in Normalized Form C. For example, you can't do fully pointed Hebrew in this way, but you can work with some other languages that use only a few combinations of Hebrew letters and points, such as Yiddish.

Many proportional-font technologies enable characters to overlap—that is, you can draw a character outside its designated bounding box. This technique provides some support for combining character sequences that can't be normalized to Form C; you just have the glyphs for the combining characters overhang whatever happens to precede them. Of course, if the width of the preceding character can vary, you won't get very good-looking results, but it's better than nothing. The same technique also provides rather crude support for a few more scripts, such as Thai, pointed Hebrew, or Thaana, as long as you don't encounter characters that have more than one mark on them, such as Thai consonants with a top-joining vowel *and* a tone mark.

If the font technology allows you to specify kerning pairs (pairs of characters that can be moved closer together than the default), you can use this feature to fine-tune the placement of combining marks for the characters to which they're being applied. Of course, kerning doesn't help you when marks have to be moved vertically or change shape to avoid colliding.

You can also handle one script that requires complex typography: Arabic. The minimally required contextual forms of the Arabic letters (and the minimal combinations of these forms with points) are found in the Arabic Presentation Forms B block as compatibility composites. Using the rules in the ArabicShaping.txt file from the Unicode Character Database, you can perform minimal contextual shaping. The algorithm is fairly simple:

1. Map the text to Normalized Form C.
2. Split the text into lines and apply the Unicode bi-di algorithm.
3. If you encounter U+0627 ARABIC LETTER ALEF to the immediate left of U+0644 ARABIC LETTER LAM, check the joining class of the character to the right. If it's R or N, replace the lam and alef with U+FEFB ARABIC LIGATURE LAM WITH ALEF ISOLATED FORM. If it's L or D, replace the lam and alef with U+FEFC ARABIC LIGATURE LAM WITH ALEF FINAL FORM. (In real life, this step must be extended to account for pointed forms of alef as well as the unadorned version.)
4. Go through each character on the line in visual order. Look up its joining category in ArabicShaping.txt, along with the categories of the characters on either side. Use Table 16.1 to match the abstract character from the Arabic block to an appropriate presentation form from the Arabic Presentation Forms B block.

The abbreviations in Table 16.1 should be fairly self-evident: L means the character connects to the character on its left but not the character on its right. R means the character connects to the character on its right but not the one on

Table 16.1   Matching Arabic Abstract Characters to Presentation Forms

Class to Left	Current Class	Class to Right	Presentation Form to Use
Any	N	Any	Independent
R or D	L	Any	Initial
L or N	L	Any	Independent
Any	R	L or D	Final
Any	R	R or N	Independent
L or N	D	R or N	Independent
R or D	D	R or N	Initial
L or N	D	L or D	Final
R or D	D	L or D	Medial

its left. D means the character can connect to characters on both sides (D stands for "dual-joining"). N means the character doesn't connect to anything (it stands for "non-joining"). Anything not listed in ArabicShaping.txt is, by definition, in category N.

It's theoretically possible to extend this technique to get somewhat better-looking results by also using the ligatures in the Arabic Presentation Forms A block. Unfortunately, it doesn't work very well in practice (points and other marks tend to get misplaced, for example) and very few fonts provide glyphs for these characters.

Arabic is the only script for which Unicode encodes presentation form characters for all contextual forms of each letter. Nevertheless, you can extend this technique to other scripts using special fonts and code points in the Private Use Area.

Glyph Selection and Placement in AAT

Apple Advanced Typography fonts go far beyond the basics to provide lots of advanced-typography features. Perhaps most important among the extra features in AAT fonts is the **glyph metamorphosis table**, or "mort" table, which provides the ability to do much more complex character-to-glyph mapping than is possible with the standard cmap table.[4]

The transformations in the mort table are applied after the mappings in the cmap table have been applied. One advantage of this design is that it keeps the font independent of the character encoding of the original characters: The original characters are mapped first into internal glyph indices using the cmap table, and then the resulting sequence of glyph indices can be further transformed into a *different* sequence of glyph indices (using the mort table) before being rendered.

AAT provides for two kinds of glyph transformations. Noncontextual transformations are one-to-one mappings that aren't based on surrounding characters. Instead, these mappings are based on global settings such as the internal state of the renderer. This design lets you do things such as choose between regular and old-style numerals, or between regular lowercase letters and small caps, depending on a font-feature setting. It also lets you pick different glyphs depending on whether text is being rendered vertically or horizontally (parentheses and hyphens, for example, rotate 90 degrees when used with vertical text).

More interesting are contextual transformations. AAT uses finite state machines to allow glyph selection for a particular character to be based on arbitrary amounts of context on either side. In fact, the state-machine implementation allows you to modify the text stream as it goes, which permits some fairly complex mappings. This ability not only enables you to do the kind of contextual glyph selection necessary for cursive joining in Arabic, but also lets you do things such as reordering glyphs (to deal with left-joining Indic vowel signs, for example), adding glyphs to the text stream (to deal with split Indic vowel signs represented by single code point values in the original text), and removing glyphs from the text stream (to make Indic viramas invisible, for example).

Contextual glyph transformations also support ligature formation and accent stacking in AAT. In fact, an accented letter is just a special kind of ligature

---

4. My main sources for this information were the TrueType Reference manual, available online at `http://developer.apple.com/fonts/TTRefMan/index.html`, and Dave Opstad, "Comparing GX Line Layout and OpenType Layout," `http://fonts.apple.com/WhitePapers/GXvsOTLayout.html`.

in AAT. AAT includes the concept of a **compound glyph**. A compound glyph doesn't have its own outlines, but instead uses the outlines from one or more other glyphs, possibly applying transformations to them as part of the composition process. Essentially, it calls the other glyphs as subroutines. The letter é, for example, would generally have a compound glyph: It would use the glyph for the regular letter e, plus the glyph for the acute accent, possibly repositioning the accent to appear in the right place above the e.

The major problem with this approach is that it doesn't lend itself well to arbitrary combinations of accents and base characters, especially if a single character will have several accents applied to it. If the font designer didn't think of the particular base–accent combination you want to use, figure out how the pieces should go together to draw it, and assign a glyph code to it, then an AAT font can't draw it.

AAT fonts can include a lot of other interesting goodies, as discussed next.

Kerning   Kerning is the process of fine-tuning the positioning of two characters to look better, usually by moving them closer together. Normal font spacing typically leaves a little bit of whitespace between each pair of characters, but this space can make certain pairs of characters appear to be too far apart. For example, the word "To" looks better if the crossbar of the T hangs a little over the "o," and "AVANTI" looks better if the slanted strokes of the As and V are moved a little closer together so the letters overlap. AAT kerning tables not only allow for this kind of pair-based kerning, but also support state-table-based algorithms that let you consider more than two characters at a time when deciding how to position the characters. In "cross-stream kerning," a character is moved up or down based on the surrounding characters, which can be useful for characters such as hyphens and dashes (a hyphen should be positioned higher when it's between two capital letters or two digits than when it's between two small letters, for example).

Justification and Tracking   Tracking is a global adjustment that moves all characters on a line closer together or farther apart. Justification is the process of systematically widening or narrowing a line of text using various techniques to take up a given amount of horizontal space. Both processes interact in interesting ways with the design of the typeface and with the script you're using, and AAT allows you to add special tables to a font that specify how they should affect the text rather than leaving it to the rendering process. The font designer can choose, for example, when to justify by inserting kashidas, when to justify by increasing interword spacing, when to break up ligatures, and when to do a combination of these things and in what proportions.

Baseline Adjustment   In English text, we're used to the idea of text sitting on a *baseline*. With the exception of letters like the lowercase p that have *descenders*, letters all sit on an imaginary line. If a particular line of text mixes text of different point sizes, the differently sized pieces of text line up along the baseline.

The baseline occurs in a different place in some other scripts. Han characters and their allied scripts (such as Hangul and Kana) commonly use a baseline that runs through the center of the line, so that differently sized characters are centered vertically with respect to each other. Devanagari and other Indic scripts use a "hanging baseline"; the horizontal stroke at the top of most characters stays in the same place as the point size changes.

If you mix characters that use different baselines on the same line of text, you need some way of relating the different baselines to one another so that things appear to line up correctly. AAT fonts can include a special table that includes information to facilitate this alignment.

Optical Alignment   Characters typically include a little bit of whitespace on either side so that they don't touch when drawn in a row; this extra space is called the "left-side bearing" and "right-side bearing." The extra whitespace can lead to a ragged appearance when the text is lined up along a margin, however, especially if type size varies from line to line. In addition, straight and curved strokes don't appear to line up correctly if the leftmost pixels of the curved stroke line up with the leftmost pixels of the straight stroke, requiring curved characters to be positioned slightly outside the margins. Certain punctuation marks in some scripts are also allowed to appear outside the margins. AAT fonts can include tables to facilitate this kind of positioning.

Caret Positioning   An AAT font can include tables that indicate where to draw the insertion point when it's positioned between two characters that are represented by a ligature. That feature allows you to do things such as specify a slanted caret that will appear between the characters in an italic or oblique typeface.

These abilities are just some of the special features that can be included in an AAT font. You can do many other things as well. In addition, Apple's ATSUI renderer handles a number of tasks for you automatically (the Unicode bi-di algorithm being the big one). Much more work goes into designing a good AAT font, but it leaves less work in the end for the application developer.

Glyph Selection and Placement in OpenType

OpenType has some features in common with AAT, owing to their common lineage, but some important differences as well.[5] Both share the same overall file format (but contain different tables), and both can make use of TrueType outlines. In addition, OpenType fonts can use Adobe Type I Compact Font Format (CFF) outlines. Both AAT and OpenType also support bitmap glyphs, but have different formats for them.

OpenType has a lot of the same features as AAT, but takes a completely different approach to them. For example, its approach to complex glyph selection is dramatically different. It starts the same way—characters are mapped to glyphs in a one-to-one manner via the cmap table, which is the same as the cmap table in AAT, and then additional transformations are performed on the resulting glyph indices.

In OpenType, the additional transformations are defined in a **glyph-substitution table**, or GSUB table. The GSUB table uses a different operating principle from AAT's mort table. Instead of a state-machine-based implementation, it employs a string-matching implementation. You specify a list of sequences of glyph indices and the glyph indices to which to map them. This approach offers a lot of flexibility. You can do the same kinds of noncontextual mappings that are possible in AAT, although OpenType fonts don't include a built-in concept of "font feature"; choices of glyph based on font features are left to the rendering engine.

---

5. For the section on OpenType, I relied on the OpenType font specification, found at `http://partners.adobe.com/asn/developer/opentype/`, as well as on the Opstad paper cited earlier.

There's also a lot of flexibility in the contextual mappings. You can specify literal strings to be replaced by other literal strings, or you can specify strings based on various "glyph classes" or user-defined collections of glyphs. In addition, you can specify sequences that must appear before or after the sequence to be mapped for the mapping to take place. In essence, you have something very similar to a regular-expression–matching system at your disposal for specifying glyph substitutions.

In effect, this system uses a state machine for doing glyph substitution. The big difference between it and the AAT state-machine implementation is that the latter implementation allows the glyph stream to be modified on the fly while the state machine is passing over the text. This feature makes reordering and insertion of new glyphs—both necessary for proper rendering of many Indic scripts—more difficult in OpenType. It's still possible, but it requires a prohibitively large number of entries in the GSUB table, so most OpenType fonts for Indic scripts don't bother, leaving the work of dealing properly with split vowels to the underlying rendering engine, which must preprocess the text in ways analogous to the handling of the Unicode bi-di algorithm.

One really neat thing about OpenType fonts is their handling of combining marks and accents. OpenType uses the same compound-glyph idea as AAT, because it inherits it from the TrueType outline format (CFF outlines don't have this capability). It provides a more powerful approach to accent application, however: the GDEF and GPOS tables. The GPOS table functions much like a fancier version of the TrueType kerning table (some early formats of which are supported by OpenType), but it allows adjustment of character positions in both directions. By comparison, the AAT kerning tables allow adjustment only in one direction. Better yet, the GPOS table lets you position glyphs relative to each other by mating **attachment points**, which are defined (along with some other stuff) in the GDEF table. In this way, for example, instead of saying that when you see the letter e and an acute accent next to each other, the accent should be moved to the left so many pixels and down so many pixels to ensure that it is drawn in the right place over the e, you can simply say that for all Latin-letter/top-joining-accent combinations, you should mate the top-center attachment point on the letter with the bottom-center attachment point on the accent. You then leave it to the GDEF table to specify where those points appear on the various letters and accent marks. This strategy can drastically shrink the number of entries needed in the GPOS table (and, by eliminating the need for compound glyphs, the number of glyph indices you have to waste for letter–accent combinations).

These tables can be set up in such a way that they work correctly with multiple combining marks on a single base character (including arbitrary Unicode combining character sequences). They can support the same kinds of contextual matching that's possible in the GSUB table.

OpenType font files also include tables for justification, baseline adjustment, and caret positioning that do roughly the same things as their AAT counterparts. They have a different format from the analogous tables in AAT fonts, however.

Special-Purpose Rendering Technology

Some specialized applications go outside the bounds of what normal rendering engines can do and require specialized rendering engines. For example, Unicode provides math and musical symbols, but mathematical formulas and music both require much more complex shaping and layout than normal written language does.

Another interesting case is Arabic. Because of its cursive nature, an almost endless variety of combinations of characters might have special forms (not to mention the rather complex placing of vowel points and other marks around the letters). Trying to achieve calligraphic-quality text with contextual forms and ligatures in a conventional font technology is just too complicated. To render really first-class Arabic typography requires more of an algorithmic approach. Specialized rendering engines just for Arabic exist that use special fonts and take this kind of algorithmic approach.

Compound and Virtual Fonts

In any language, you'll get the best-looking results if you render styled text and specify the font to use and the point size and style to use with it. Unicode, combined with the Internet, raises the likelihood of running into text in some language and script other than the ones you read and write. While if you don't read the text, it might not matter so much what you see, you can generally make some sense out of it (or take it to someone who *does* read it) if the text is rendered correctly. For this reason, some operating systems come with special Unicode fonts that include glyphs for all Unicode characters (or at least a sizable subset). This technique can get rather unwieldy, however.

A different approach is to use a **compound font**. Some systems give you the ability to specify an ordered list of fonts to try for text display if the document asks for an unavailable font or uses characters that aren't in that font. In this way, instead of having a huge "Unicode" font, you can have separate Greek, Hebrew, Arabic, Japanese, and other fonts. This fallback list can be thought of as a "font" on its own—it relies on other fonts to supply the actual glyphs. This technique allows you to avoid carrying huge multi-megabyte font files around to see all of Unicode and to fine-tune things to your liking (picking a preferred default font for your native language, for example, or preferring Chinese glyphs over Japanese glyphs for the Han characters).

Usually, a "last resort" font lies at the root of a compound font hierarchy. You can use it to get something more meaningful than the standard "missing" character for characters that don't appear in any of the fonts in the fallback list. The "last resort" font usually has one glyph for each Unicode character block, and that glyph is used for all characters in that block. If you don't have a Devanagari font, for example, you can at least still tell that a piece of text you can't read was in Hindi (or some other language that uses the Devanagari script).

Java and the MacOS are two examples of environments that use a virtual-font technique to handle Unicode's huge repertoire of characters.

■ SPECIAL TEXT-EDITING CONSIDERATIONS

It's worth taking a little time to look at a few issues that arise when you're writing a Unicode-compatible text-editing utility. There are a number of Unicode-specific things to keep in mind when allowing a user to edit text.

Optimizing for Editing Performance

The first issue isn't actually Unicode-specific at all, but if you don't already know about it, it's worth taking a few minutes to discuss. That's a useful technique for speeding performance during editing.

Suppose you have a 1 million character document, and you start typing at the beginning. If you've stored your text in a single contiguous block (probably with some slop space at the end so you don't have to reallocate your character storage on every keystroke), you have to slide 1 million characters up two bytes in memory with every keystroke. This performance, obviously, is unacceptably slow.

It generally makes more sense to break the document up into pieces. This way, you don't have to shove massive numbers of characters around whenever you're editing at the beginning of the document, and you don't have to allocate a new block and copy all the characters into it whenever you overflow the available storage space. This technique also lets you read a document from disk in pieces rather than all at once and, if your system is memory-constrained, page parts of the document out to disk as you're working.

Full-blown block storage can be complicated to maintain. A lot of book-keeping is associated with keeping track of which blocks are where, which text is in which block, when to split or coalesce blocks, and so on. A simpler approach that offers many of the same performance benefits involves splitting the document up into only *two* blocks. It's called **gap storage**.

To understand how gap storage works, let's start by imagining your typical memory buffer holding a piece of text. Normally the buffer will be bigger than the actual text so you have room for it to grow as the user edits. It looks something like this:

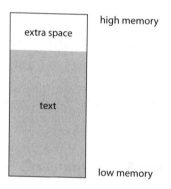

You don't necessarily have to keep the extra space at the end of your backing store. The gap technique *moves it around* as the text is edited. After an edit in the middle of the document, for example, the buffer looks like this:

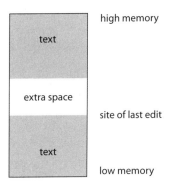

The idea here is very simple. Instead of moving all text above the edit position up or down in response to an edit, you instead reposition the gap so that it occurs immediately after the position of the edit. The edit itself, whether an insertion or a deletion, doesn't cause any more characters to move at all: it behaves just as an edit at the very end of the document would with ordinary storage.

On average, you move far fewer characters around with this technique than you would the old-fashioned way. Better yet, if you're doing the edits in response to keyboard input, where large edits happen one character at a time, you realize an even bigger win. If you type a 10-letter word at the beginning of the document, for example, the gap moves to the beginning of the document in response to the first keystroke. The other nine characters are inserted at the position of the gap and require no more moves at all! This approach can generally give you lightning-fast performance.

The bookkeeping associated with gap storage is minimal. Basically, you have to keep track of where the gap is located in the backing store and how big it is. Operations that simply retrieve text from the buffer without changing it don't generally move the gap, so you need to keep track of whether a retrieval is directed at text before or after the gap. If a retrieval of text *crosses* the gap, then you may have to do a little more work (or move the gap). Even so, the bookkeeping remains much simpler than doing the same thing with a full-fledged block storage mechanism.

Of course, if the text grows beyond the bounds of the storage buffer, you must still reallocate the storage and copy the text into the new buffer. Because moving the gap can occur as part of the process of copying the text from the old buffers to the new buffers, the incremental cost of the reallocation can be kept down. If your system is memory-constrained, you have to rely on a virtual memory subsystem to do the paging in and out.

The gap technique can prove even more beneficial with the other data structures associated with the text than for the text storage itself, such as the data structure that stores styles and other out-of-band information, or the line starts array. Let's consider style storage for a moment. Typically, style information is stored in a **run array**, a data structure that associates records of style information with positions in the text. Each entry in a style run array refers to a **style run**, a contiguous sequence of characters that have the same styling information. The entry specifies the position and length of the style run in the text and contains a pointer to another record somewhere that describes how that run of text should be drawn (or possibly contains some other information about the text).

Now think about what happens when you add a character to a style run near the beginning of the document. All of the style runs that come later in the document must have their positions updated so that they refer to the same characters they did before your addition. You can get around this problem by storing lengths instead of positions—then only the run you change needs to be updated—but it becomes more difficult to find out which styles are in effect at an arbitrary position in the text. To do so, you must start at the beginning of the run array and walk through it, accumulating run lengths until you find the run containing the targeted position.

The best approach is to store both the positions and the lengths of the runs in the run array, but you don't want to waste time updating every run in the array every time an edit happens to the document. Gap storage can be a big help here.

With run arrays, you're less interested in the performance you save by not moving entries up and down every time an edit occurs. Run arrays are usually much smaller than character arrays, and whole runs are added and deleted less frequently than they're updated. In this situation, gap storage helps you with the task of updating run positions in response to edits.

You proceed the same way as before: Each time an edit occurs, you reposition the gap in the run array so that it occurs immediately after the run that's affected by the edit. Then you merely have to update that run's length in response to the edit.

The magic happens in the repositioning. The trick is the way in which you store the run *positions*. For the runs *before* the gap, you store the positions in the normal way: relative to the *beginning* of the text. For the runs *after* the gap, you store the positions relative to the *end* of the document.

Now the position of a given run is updated only when it switches polarity. If the same style run includes several localized edits, the gap appears immediately after it and the runs after it don't have to have their positions recalculated (they're relative to the end of the document, and while the end of the document will move, their positions relative to it don't). When you make a change later in the document, the positions of the runs after your first edit are recalculated as part of moving the gap. The recalculation is simple: You just add up the lengths as you switch things.

Suppose you have the following sentence:

I am **very** happy to meet you.

It has three style runs: "I am," "**very**," and "happy to meet you." The style run array starts out looking like this:

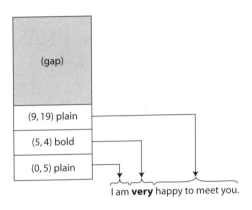

Now suppose you select "am" and delete it. The run array looks like this:

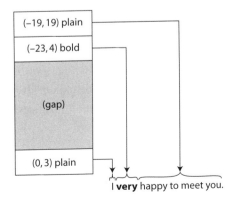

You replace "am" with "was once." The gap doesn't move, and no positions need to be recalculated. Only the length of the run you're editing changes:

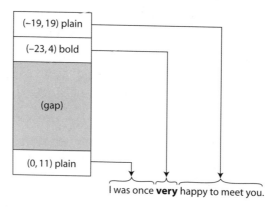

If you go to the end of the document, switch to boldface, and add "But not now!", the gap moves back to the end, and all positions are recalculated:

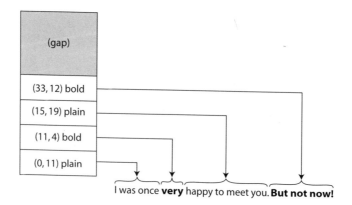

This technique can be very useful in keeping style information and other meta-data up-to-date without sacrificing performance.[6] It's also useful for doing the same kind of thing with internal tables—the line starts array, in particular.

---

6. The polarity-switching technique used with gap storage and applied to style runs is patented by IBM (the inventors are Doug Felt, John Raley, and me).

Accepting Text Input

We won't spend a lot of time dwelling on text input, but it's worth emphasizing that Unicode doesn't assume a one-to-one mapping between keystrokes and characters any more than it assumes a one-to-one mapping between characters and glyphs. Code that accepts input from the user should keep this fact in mind.

For instance, combining character sequences can cause interesting things to happen. A Vietnamese keyboard might generate the sequence U+0061 U+0323 U+0302 (representing the letter ậ) with a single keystroke. Conversely, it might produce U+1EAD (the precomposed form of the same letter) with two keystrokes; one for the basic letter and another for the tone mark, potentially in either order.

Many European keyboards have "dead keys," which cause an accent to be applied to the next character you type. Thus the two-keystrokes-to-one-character mapping happens even in European languages. Most encodings tend to favor precomposed forms, so one keystroke producing multiple characters doesn't happen as often, but it definitely does occur. In Burmese, for example, some split vowels can be represented only with combinations of two vowel signs, but the vowel might still be produced with a single keystroke. It's important to keep this issue in mind when designing an input engine.

The more complicated case happens with the Han characters, which generally require an **input method**, a process that maps keystrokes (or possibly input gestures on some other device, such as handwriting or voice input) to characters. Because so many Han characters exist, it's impractical to have a keyboard that includes every character. Thus smaller keyboards (often conventional Latin keyboards) are used, and multiple keystrokes are used to enter each character. In Japanese, for example, it's fairly common to use a normal English keyboard and enter text in romaji (the standard Latin letter representation of Japanese). As letters are typed, they appear first as Latin letters; then, as whole syllables are completed, they turn into Hiragana. When a sequence of letters corresponding to the romanization of some kanji character is completed, the text turns into that character. (Because many kanji characters have the same romanization, the process usually includes an intermediate step in which all possible Kanji characters corresponding to a given romanization are shown to the user in a menu and he or she picks one.)

Similar techniques are used for the other languages that work with Han characters. The keystrokes might represent Latin letters in some recognized romanization; they might represent characters in a phonetic system such as Kana, Bopomofo, or Hangul; or they might represent more abstract concepts such as groups of strokes. In all cases, complex mappings exist from series of keystrokes to input characters, and extra work must be done to manage the interaction between user and computer as keystrokes are assembled into characters.

If you want to support East Asian languages, you may have to deal with the input method issue, either by providing input methods or ways of writing them, or by tying into any input method support provided by the underlying operating system. Even on an American keyboard, sometimes input methods come into play, such as in implementing the "smart quotes" feature in most word processors that turns " into either " or " depending on context. A transliteration engine (see Chapter 14) generally plays a major role in input method support.

Handling Arrow Keys

Now we turn to the issue of handling selection feedback and arrow keys. Again, this process isn't always straightforward in Unicode.

Consider the handling of arrow keys, for example. What should happen when you press the right arrow key? The correct answer is *not* necessarily to move the insertion point forward by one code point value in the backing store. If, for example, the backing store contains U+0065 U+0301, the insertion point is before U+0065, and the screen shows the letter é, you don't want the insertion point to move forward by one code point. If you do, it puts you in the middle of the é, rather than past it. You either see no movement in the insertion point, it moves past the é and gives a misleading picture, or it is drawn through the middle of the é, which is ugly and potentially confusing. If the user types the letter a now, the result is eá instead of what was really meant, probably éa.

It isn't just regular combining character sequences that can cause trouble. What should happen, for example, as you arrow through "कि"? There are two marks here with a fairly clear distinction between them, but the mark on the left (ि) comes *after* the mark on the right; the mark on the left is a left-joining vowel sign. Should you be able to arrow into the middle of this kind of syllable?

What about something more complex:

This syllable consists of four code point values. The main letter, k, is represented by क. The second letter, r, is represented by a boomerang-shaped mark that is subsumed into the क, appearing here only as the spike sticking out of the bottom of the loop. In fact, to join the k and the r together in this way, you use a virama (a vowel-killer sign) after the क to cancel its inherent vowel and make it combine with the r. The virama is invisible in this particular syllable; its presence is represented by the fact that the k and r have combined into a single glyph. Finally, you have the vowel, i, which is represented by the ि mark on the left.

In the preceding example, the relationship between visual positions and positions in the backing store is very complicated. The fourth character in the backing store comes first, followed by the first character stacked on top of the third. The second character isn't visible at all.

You could have the insertion caret appear inside the syllable cluster in cluster-specific positions (AAT fonts let you do this kind of thing), but it's very complicated and difficult and may confuse the user. Most of the time, the only reasonable solution is for the arrow keys to move syllable by syllable when dealing with Indic syllable clusters in the scripts that have complicated reordering or shaping rules. Thus you may have to keep together not only regular combining character sequences, but also Indic syllables.

You also have to watch out for this issue when handling mouse clicks. You don't want a mouse click to put the insertion point in the middle of a combining character sequence any more than you want the user to arrow into it.

The bottom line is that your arrow key algorithm (not to mention your hit-testing algorithm, your selection-drawing algorithm, and possibly your line-breaking algorithm) must honor grapheme cluster boundaries. It may be able to deviate a bit from Unicode 3.2's default definition of a grapheme cluster, but it has to treat the text in logical units that make sense to the user, units that may be multiple code points in length. The parsing techniques we examined earlier in the chapter for line breaking can also be brought to bear to parse text into grapheme clusters.

On top of all this, you may encounter text that contains invisible formatting characters such as the zero-width joiner and non-joiner. You must skip these characters as well when you're handling the arrow keys, unless, of course, your editor has some sort of "show invisible characters" feature turned on. Otherwise, it simply looks like the keystroke didn't register.

An even uglier problem arises in bidirectional text. The right arrow should move you to the right whether you're in left-to-right or right-to-left text. If you're in right-to-left text, the right arrow actually moves you *backward* through the backing store.

Furthermore, interesting things happen when text of mixed directionality appears on the same line. Any boundary between directional runs can be interpreted as two positions in the backing store. For example, in the sentence

Avram said מזל טוב and smiled.

the visual position between the first set of English letters and the Hebrew snippet could either represent position 11 in the backing store (after "Avram said" and before "מזל טוב") or position 18 (after "מזל טוב" and before "and smiled"). The visual position between the Hebrew and the second English phrase can represent the same two positions. Furthermore, either logical position in the backing store can map to both visual positions on the screen. For example, if you are at position 11 and insert a Latin letter, it should appear after (i.e., to the right of) "Avram said." If you insert a Hebrew letter, it should appear before (i.e., to the right of) "מזל טוב". Thus you have to keep track of which position you mean, you have to draw both insertion point positions, and you have to do some complex gymnastics as you go through the text with the arrow keys.

As you arrow through the text from the left, for example, the insertion point goes up one by one until it gets to 11 (the ambiguous visual position). Then it jumps to position 17 (between the last two Hebrew letters) and counts down until it gets to position 12. The next right arrow (the other ambiguous visual position) is position 18, after which the positions count up again. (If you left-arrow through the text, positions 11 and 18 switch places; see Figure 16.2.)

It takes some interesting algorithms to get this effect right. They involve re-applying pieces of the Unicode bi-di algorithm on the fly as the user arrows through the text. Generally, however, you already need some kind of data struc-

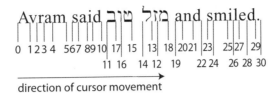

direction of cursor movement

Figure 16.2 Moving through text of mixed directionality with the arrow keys.

ture that maps positions in the backing store to the order of the characters on the screen. Typically, you must produce this mapping to draw the characters. Instead of reapplying the bi-di algorithm on the fly, it's easier to use this mapping to help determine what position in the backing store corresponds to the next visual position on screen.

Handling Discontiguous Selection

In addition to handling arrow keys, you must deal with drawing selections. We talked about this issue in Chapter 8, but it's worth repeating that if you're dealing with bidirectional text, selection drawing becomes more complicated. If a selection crosses the boundary between directional runs, a discontinuity occurs. The discontinuity can be either in the rendered feedback on screen (logical selection) or in the characters in the backing store (visual selection). For instance, if in our example sentence you click down between "Avram" and "said" and drag to the position between "מזל" and "טוב," you could either have meant to select a logically contiguous range consisting of "said" and "מזל,"

Avram said טוב מזל and smiled.

or you could have meant to select a visually contiguous range consisting of "said" and "טוב":

Avram said טוב מזל and smiled.

Logical selection is generally easier to implement despite the fact that you may have to draw several visually discontiguous highlight ranges. After all, a selection highlight that spans a line boundary may also consist of two visually discontiguous highlight ranges.

Visual selection can be a little easier on the user, but trickier to implement. This complexity doesn't arise just because you have to keep track of more than one selection range in memory. It also makes operations such as copying and pasting more difficult. For example, it seems logical that if you select some text, choose Cut from the program's Edit menu, and then change your mind and choose Paste from the Edit menu without doing anything in between, you should get back what you had originally. If you select "said" and "טוב" as we saw above, clicked Cut, and then immediately clicked Paste, you would expect to get the original sentence back again. But remember that the two selected words weren't originally contiguous in memory. The paste operation has to put them back in two logically discontiguous locations so they'll be drawn next to each other. "Said" goes between "Avram" and "מזל" in the backing store, but "טוב" goes between "מזל" and "and."

If you're not pasting at a directional boundary, the two pieces are stored contiguously in memory. The order may be different, however, because you want the stuff you copied to the Clipboard to come out in the same order as you originally saw it. For example, if you paste at the beginning of the sentence, you want to see this:

<u>said טוב</u> Avram מזל and smiled.

To achieve this effect, both "said" and "טוב" go before "Avram" in the backing store, and "said" precedes "טוב". On the other hand, if you clicked Copy instead of Cut and then pasted the duplicate words between "מזל" and "טוב", you would expect to see this:

Avram said טוב <u>said טוב</u> מזל and smiled.

The pasted text still comes out with "said" to the left of "טוב," but because you're pasting into right-to-left text now, "טוב" precedes "said" in the backing store.

Handling Multiple-Click Selection

The last interesting thing you may have to worry about is double- and triple-click handling. Generally, double-clicking selects a word and triple-clicking selects a line, paragraph, or sentence, depending on the application. You can use the same parsing techniques used for locating possible line-break positions to figure out where the selection range should begin and end in response to a multiple click.

Of course, the "word" you select with a double-click may or may not be the same thing as a "word" for the purposes of line breaking. You may or may not want to include whitespace and surrounding punctuation, for example. In languages that don't use spaces between words, such as Japanese, you might want to honor word boundaries anyway using a dictionary-based parser. Alternatively, you might want to use a heuristic that selects more text than you'll find between possible line-break positions (which usually include only one character). In Japanese, for example, a common heuristic might be to select a contiguous range of kanji followed by a contiguous range of Hiragana and any leading or trailing punctuation (if the user clicked in kanji or Hiragana), or a continuous range of Katakana (if the user clicks in Katakana). The result is usually a decent approximation of real word boundaries. (Of course, in Chinese this technique will select a whole sentence or paragraph—for Chinese, it's better to use a dictionary-based algorithm or select a single character.)

Sentence parsing can also be tricky. In English, for example, you can't be certain whether a period marks the end of a sentence or just the end of an abbreviation (you can tell when it's being used as a decimal point or URL delimiter, because it isn't followed by a space in these situations). One heuristic is to behave as though the period appears at the end of a sentence if it's followed by whitespace and the next letter after the whitespace (and any intervening punctuation such as parentheses or quotation marks) is a capital letter. If the next letter is a small letter, you're not at the end of a sentence.

Of course, this is a pretty inexact heuristic. It will choke on a person's name with a preceding title (such as "Mr. Jones"), for example. You can fine-tune the algorithm by including a list of common abbreviations that are usually followed by capitalized words (such as "Mr.," "Mrs.," "Ms.," and "Dr."), but of course this list is language-specific.

17

Unicode and Other Technologies

*M*ost of the time you don't want to *implement* the Unicode standard; you just want to *use* it. In slightly more than 10 years of existence, Unicode has racked up an impressive array of supporters. A lot of other standards depend on it, and a lot of products use it in one way or another. In this last chapter, we'll take a look at some of the places where Unicode intersects with other technologies and standards.

■ UNICODE AND THE INTERNET

Perhaps the area where Unicode will be most important over time is on the Internet. In this area, people all over the world can communicate with each other and access information. If they do so only in English, use of the Internet will be limited mostly to English-speaking countries. Instead, a growing movement calls for material on the Internet to be available in a wide variety of languages.

Of course, if you go beyond English, ASCII doesn't cut it any more as a method of representing characters. If you go outside the Western European languages, neither does Latin-1. This requirement means either designing the Internet protocols and the various pieces of software that speak them to handle many different character encoding standards, or it means Unicode. (In most cases, the actual answer is "both.")

Of course, a wide variety of standards and technologies are in use on the Internet. They were developed at different times by different people and are currently maintained by different standards bodies, so it's no wonder that they exist at different points along the adoption curve or take different approaches to integrating Unicode support. Next, we take a look at a few of the most important standards.

The W3C Character Model

The World Wide Web Consortium, or W3C for short, is an industry group responsible for many of the more important Internet standards, including XML and HTML. Its standing internationalization committee is charged with the task of looking over other W3C standards and ensuring that they don't contain biases in favor of particular languages or nationalities.

Because the W3C aims for its standards to be internationally usable, it has adopted Unicode as the standard character encoding for all of its standards that involve encoded characters. Just saying "the text will be in Unicode" doesn't go far enough, however—you still have to worry about things like versions of Unicode, encoding formats, normalization forms, and so forth. The W3C has therefore issued a document, the *Character Model for the World Wide Web,* that attempts to nail down these ancillary issues in the context of W3C standards.[1] All W3C standards published or updated after the character model was published have to follow its recommendations.

Here's a quick summary of what the W3C character model specifies:

- It demands that W3C technologies never assume one-to-one mappings between characters (in all the myriad definitions of "character"), code points, glyphs, and keystrokes. (Unicode, of course, prohibits this assumption.)
- It proposes a list of more specific terms than "character" and "string" and provides definitions for them.

---

1. The document is available at http://www.w3.org/TR/charmod. As of January 2002, the most recent working draft was dated December 20, 2001. A working draft doesn't have normative force and may change later. But the draft was in the final stages of revision, and by the time this book appears in print, the final version of this document should have been adopted and published.

- It requires that all implementations of W3C specifications treat all text as though it were encoded in Unicode, although it allows other encodings to be used.

- It requires all W3C standards either to assume all text is in UTF-8 or UTF-16 (or both, with an appropriately unambiguous way of distinguishing between the two) or to provide some mechanism for specifying the encoding used by various pieces of text. If the latter approach is used, it requires that the default be UTF-8 or UTF-16 if no encoding is explicitly specified, and it strongly recommends the use of the Internet Assigned Numbers Authority (IANA) charset identifiers for the purposes of identifying character encodings. (We'll talk more about the IANA charset identifiers in a minute.)

- It places strong restrictions on the use of Unicode private-use characters. In particular, it requires that W3C specifications neither impose semantics on any private-use code point value nor provide a mechanism for formally imposing semantics on private-use code point values. The idea is to preserve these code points' identity as private-use code point values, rather than allowing a particular protocol to usurp them for some purpose. W3C protocols have to use markup elements to identify characters that aren't in Unicode (MathML, for example, has a special `mglyph` element for specifying math symbols that aren't encoded in Unicode).

- It requires the presence of an escaping mechanism to allow the use of characters in text (such as the ampersand or less-than sign) that normally have special syntactic meaning, and to allow the representation of all Unicode characters even in documents that don't actually use Unicode as their encoding. It doesn't specify a particular format for an escape sequence (although it strongly recommends XML's `&#x1234;` format), but does require escape sequences to have an explicit end character (such as the semicolon in the XML escape sequence), allowing the code point value to have any number of digits.

- It imposes very specific normalization requirements. Processes that produce or modify text *must* produce it in Normalized Form C (escape sequences can't be used to get around this requirement—the text must *still* be in Normalized Form C even after all escape sequences are turned into real characters). Processes that receive text *must* interpret it as Normalized Form C and must *not* normalize it themselves. Processes that receive text encoded using encodings other than Unicode *must* convert it to Unicode using converters that produce Normalized Form C. The idea is to place responsibility for normalizing the text as early in the process as possible, with the processes that produce the text in the first place. Processes that merely receive text can then be lighter-weight; they don't have to do anything special to make sure variant forms of the same strings compare as equal. In fact, they're prohibited from normalizing text themselves because it would introduce a potential security hole: The text might be interpreted differently depending on the receiving process.

- It recommends discouraging or prohibiting the use of compatibility composites, but doesn't actually require (or even recommend) converting text to Normalized Form KC. (More on this issue later.)

- It defines two strings as equal only if, after converting both to the same Unicode encoding format and turning all escapes into real characters, they're code-point-for-code-point equal. (This constraint assumes they were both in Normalized Form C initially.) One important implication of this requirement is that string matching is case-sensitive.

- It recommends consistent methods of indexing particular characters in strings. In particular, it recommends indexing strings by abstract Unicode code point value (regardless of actual storage format) or, failing that, by physical code unit. It also recommends a zero-based indexing format (actually, it recommends numbering the "cracks" between the code points or units, rather than the units themselves, which works out to the same thing).

- It recommends that standards allow the use of all Unicode characters in URL references, even though only ASCII characters are actually allowed in URLs. It also specifies how the non-ASCII characters are to be converted into ASCII in real URLs. (More on this issue later.)

- It recommends that W3C standards specify a particular version of Unicode for their syntactic elements, but make an open (non-version-specific) reference to Unicode for their non-syntactic elements. It also specifies that open references always be to Unicode 3.0 or later.

Earlier drafts of the W3C character model restricted the allowable repertoire of Unicode characters to a subset of the entire Unicode repertoire (disallowing more than just the private-use characters). This restriction effectively made W3C normalization a different and more-restrictive beast than regular Unicode normalization. These requirements have since been removed from the W3C character model, but appear in a separate document, *Unicode in XML and Other Markup Languages*, published jointly by the Unicode Consortium as Unicode Technical Report #20 and by the W3C as W3C Note 15.

According to UTR #20, Unicode includes some characters whose functions are normally carried out by markup tags when Unicode is used in markup languages such as XML. UTR #20 enumerates those characters that are redundant or conflict with markup tags and explains why they shouldn't be used and what should be done instead. It discourages the use of certain invisible formatting characters and compatibility composites, but not *all* of the characters in either category. In particular:

- It discourages the use of the LS and PS characters (you should use the <p> and <br> tags instead), or specifies that they, like CR and LF, should be treated as plain whitespace rather than as actual line and paragraph delimiters.
- It discourages the bi-di embedding and override characters in favor of markup tags that do the same things.
- It discourages the use of the deprecated Unicode characters.
- It discourages the interlinear-annotation characters in favor of markup tags that do the same thing.
- It discourages the object-replacement character, which is provided for internal implementation use.
- It discourages the plane 14 language-tag characters in favor of markup tags that do the same thing.
- It does *not* discourage the other invisible formatting characters, including the non-breaking characters, the zero-width joiner and non-joiner, the zero-width space, the left-to-right and right-to-left marks, and the various language-specific formatting characters. All of these characters either occur inside words where interposing markup tags would mess things up or don't cause problems when used with markup tags.

- It lists a fairly small subset of Unicode compatibility composites that it recommends converting to Normalized Form KC and a few others that it recommends replacing with markup tags. It suggests leaving most Unicode compatibility composites alone, however, either because they have semantic differences from their decomposed versions (in particular, the styled versions of letters, which are typically used as symbols) or no current markup syntax can produce the appropriate effect (for example, the various symbols intended for use in vertical CJK text).

XML

Extensible Markup Language (XML) is a document format for expressing structured data in a simple text-based manner. An XML file consists of arbitrary textual data interspersed with "markup," text in specially defined formats that imposes structure on the data and supplies extra information about it. XML doesn't specify a particular method for representing particular kinds of data, but merely provides a generalized mechanism for representing arbitrary structured data in a flat text file. Other standards, such as XSL (Extensible Stylesheet Language), MathML (Mathematical Markup Language), XHTML (Extensible Hypertext Markup Language), and SVG (Scalable Vector Graphics) specify how XML can be used to represent different specific kinds of data.

Not surprisingly given its source, the XML standard follows the recommendations in the W3C character model: It's based on Unicode as the character encoding for the text, but discourages the use of private-use characters, most compatibility composites, and most invisible formatting characters. Numeric character references (XML's escaping mechanism) are based on abstract Unicode code point values. All of the XML syntax characters are defined in terms of their Unicode code point values. All XML parsers are required to understand both UTF-8 and UTF-16, but are permitted to understand non-Unicode encodings as well.

An XML document is assumed to be in Unicode unless it's explicitly tagged as being in some other encoding. If it's not tagged, it can be either UTF-8 or UTF-16; UTF-16 documents must begin with the byte order mark, which signals that the document is in UTF-16 and indicates the document's byte order. Text that doesn't begin with a byte order mark or an explicit character encoding declaration is assumed to be in UTF-8. If the document contains byte sequences that aren't legal in UTF-8, it's an illegal XML document.

Interestingly, the XML standard doesn't specify an encoding for the encoding declaration itself, but instead gives a method whereby the encoding of the declaration can be deduced. As the document has to start with the declaration or a byte order mark, and the declaration has to start with `<?xml`, this deduction isn't particularly difficult. If the encoding specified in the declaration does not match the actual encoding used in the document, a parser must report an error.

In all the cases where strings have to be matched in XML (matching start tags and end tags, for example, or matching attribute names and values to their declarations), the matching happens using simple binary comparison. In other words, an XML parser is required to assume the text has already been converted to Normalized Form C, and case differences are significant. One important implication of this requirement is that identifier matching is case-sensitive. For instance, `</record>` is not a legal closing tag for `<RECORD>`.

XML includes an identifier syntax similar to the ones used in programming languages. It generally follows the Unicode identifier syntax guidelines, but adds a few extra punctuation characters. The XML standard lays out explicitly which characters are considered to be "letters," "digits," "combining marks," and so on. These definitions are based on the Unicode Character Database general categories from Unicode 2.0, when the XML standard was adopted. Thus more recent "letters," such as Sinhala, Khmer, Myanmar, and the various extensions to the Han repertoire, aren't legal in XML identifiers (they *are* legal in XML character data). Most likely, the next version of the XML standard will update the repertoire of name characters to whatever version of Unicode is current at that time. Of course, documents that use the new name characters wouldn't be backward compatible with XML 1.0 documents.

XML forms the basis for many other Internet document standards, such as XHTML, CSS, XSL, SVG, MathML, and so on. All of these standards therefore inherit XML's Unicode compatibility.

HTML and HTTP

Users of the World Wide Web are, of course, familiar with Hypertext Markup Language (HTML), the markup language used for most of the styled-text documents on the Web. HTML is similar to XML (both are based on SGML), but the syntax is a lot looser, and it's been around a lot longer. The most recent version of HTML, HTML 4.1, uses Unicode as the base character set and generally follows the W3C character model. Earlier versions of HTML were based on ISO 8859-1.

Documents in HTML 4.1 can be in any encoding, much as XML documents can, with the actual encoding specified in the document. HTML doesn't have a designated place for this information as XML does, so it appears as an attribute in the <META> element in the document's header.

Recently, there's been a move toward bringing HTML into conformance with XML. That is, instead of HTML looking much like XML but having some important differences, HTML would be *based* on XML, much as other document formats such as XSL and SVG are. The result of this move is XHTML, an XML-based format that does the same things that HTML does, but with a tighter syntax. XHTML, of course, inherits XML's Unicode support.

The HTTP protocol used by Web browsers has the ability to exchange information about the encodings of the documents being shared. Because of spotty application support, however, the encoding specified in a document's HTTP header might not be the document's actual encoding (FTP and other file-sharing protocols don't have any way at all of exchanging information about document encodings). Better to rely on the information in the document itself.

URLs and Domain Names

A Uniform Resource Locator (URL) is a short text string that identifies and helps locate a particular resource on the Internet; it's sort of the Internet equivalent of a person's mailing address.[2] The syntax for URLs is very restrictive. In essence, only the uppercase and lowercase Latin letters, the Western digits, and

---

2. Technically speaking, a URL is a string that identifies a particular resource by specifying an access path—a way of reaching it, hence the term "locator." A Uniform Resource Name (URN) identifies a resource in a way that's independent of the access path. The standards community uses the term Uniform Resource Identifier (URI) as an umbrella term for both URL and URN. Informally, URL is used in a manner synonymous with URI, which is the convention used here. Also, in some documents, the "U" in all of these terms is said to mean "Universal" rather than "Uniform."

a handful of special symbol and punctuation characters are allowed in URLs, which makes it possible to transmit a URL in almost any character encoding and through almost any protocol.

The problem, of course, is that the use of just the Latin letters introduces a bias toward languages that rely on the Latin alphabet. This issue wouldn't be a big problem if URLs were simply internal identifiers, but they're not. These days, you see URLs everywhere, and they're intended to be mnemonic: You'll always see `http://www.ibm.com`, not `http://129.42.16.99`.

The URL specification explicitly provides a mechanism for escaping characters in URLs. You can use the percent sign followed by two hexadecimal digits to indicate an arbitrary byte value. The problem with this approach is that nothing specifically says what the byte values mean or how they're to be interpreted.

The industry is converging around always treating escape sequences in URLs as referring to UTF-8 code units. That is, the industry is leaning toward always interpreting `R%c3%a9sum%c3%a9.html` to mean `Résumé.html` (and always representing `Résumé.html` as `R%c3%a9sum%c3%a9.html`). If everyone agreed on this system, then you could use illegal URL characters (such as the accented é in our example) in URL references in other kinds of documents (such as HTML or XML files) and know that a universally understood method of transforming them into a legal URL existed. Web browsers or other software could do the reverse, displaying URLs that include escape sequences by using the characters the escape sequences represent (at least in the cases where they represent non-ASCII characters) and allowing you to type them in that way.

The XML standard already allows URL references to be specified this way and indicates that they must be converted to legal URLs by using the escape sequences to mean UTF-8 code units. The W3C character model will extend this practice to the other W3C standards. Various other standards are also converging on this approach.[3]

The %-escape approach, unfortunately, doesn't work for Internet domain names. These names have a more restricted syntax: Each component can con-

---

3. My information here mostly comes from the W3C Internationalization Working Group's paper, "URIs and other identifiers," found at `http://www.w3.org/International/O-URL-and-ident`.

sist only of Latin letters, Western digits, and hyphens; must begin with a letter; and must end with a letter or digit. Each individual component of a domain name can't be longer than 63 characters, and the entire domain name (including the periods between components) can't be longer than 255 characters.

Some protocols and software implementations allow you to go outside these restrictions, but doing so poses a big risk to interoperability. Many creative name-mangling schemes have been proposed for representing arbitrary Unicode strings using only legal domain-name characters. Currently, the Internet Engineering Task Force, the other major entity that maintains Internet standards, has an Internationalized Domain Names working group working on an official proposal. As of this writing, this work was ongoing, and domain names were still restricted to Latin letters.[4]

Mail and Usenet

Mail and Usenet (newsgroups) are the oldest services on the Internet, and their transfer protocols attest to that fact. While many proprietary e-mail and bulletin-board systems provide all kinds of features, the standard Internet protocols for mail and news are relatively simple and primitive.

The various mail and news protocols are all based on the Internet Engineering Task Force's Request for Comments #822 (RFC 822 for short).[5] RFC 822, which dates back to the dawn of personal computers, specifies the format for mail messages on the Internet. It defines a mail message as a series of CRLF-delimited lines of 7-bit ASCII text. RFC 822 goes on to give a detailed specification of the message header format and the address format, but does not go into any more detail as to the contents of the message body. The message body simply extends from the end of the header (delimited by a blank line) to the end of the message.

---

4. My sources here are RFC 1034, "Domain names: Concepts and Facilities," and RFC 2825, "A Tangled Web: Issues of I18N, Domain Names, and the Other Internet protocols," both found on the IETF Web site, www.ietf.org.

5. The IETF publishes many documents as "Requests for Comments." Even though many of them eventually become formal standards, they're generally still referred to by their RFC numbers rather than the new numbers assigned when they become standards. The IETF encourages this practice by setting things up so that you search for all documents by their RFC number.

RFC 822 doesn't impose a line-length limit, but many mail protocols do. In particular, the SMTP protocol imposes a 1,000-byte maximum length on each line of a message. This includes the CR and LF at the end of the line.

This format works adequately for simple text messages (at least if you speak American English), but is rather constraining. Also, it doesn't help you if you want to send things other than text in your e-mail. Over the years, various methods have been devised for sending data other than text (or in addition to text, or text in encodings other than ASCII) in the body of an RFC 822 message. The one that eventually caught on is MIME, the Multipurpose Internet Mail Extensions, the most recent version of which is documented in RFCs 2045, 2046, 2047, 2048 and 2049.

MIME adds a few extra fields to the standard RFC 822 message header that are used to say more about what's in the message body. The `MIME-version` field identifies the message as being in MIME format (and could be used to identify the version of MIME, except that there's currently only one version of MIME). The `Content-Type` field identifies the type of the message body (e.g., text, image, multipart message body, undifferentiated byte stream, application-specific binary data). The `Content-Transfer-Encoding` field specifies how the data type specified by the `Content-Type` field is encoded into lines of 7-bit ASCII characters. If the `Content-Type` starts with `multipart`, the message body is divided into multiple parts, each of which gets its own `Content-Type` and `Content-Transfer-Encoding`. This approach lets you send the same message in several alternative formats, attach binary files to a message, or include a separate message (for example, one you're forwarding) in the message body.

Many of the `Content-Types` also allow you to specify parameters. For text messages, the most important parameter is the `charset` parameter, which identifies the scheme used to encode the text. The term "charset" is a bit of a misnomer, harkening back to the days when a straightforward transformation between all coded character sets and character encoding schemes existed. Nowadays, the `charset` parameter specifies a character encoding scheme, not a coded character set.

A standard ASCII message is understood to have the following `Content-Type` declaration in its header:

```
Content-Type: text/plain; charset=US-ASCII
```

The Internet Assigned Numbers Authority (IANA), which is affiliated with the IETF (both are sister organizations under the umbrella of the Internet Society, or ISOC), is the registration authority for various Internet-related parameters, including domain names. The IANA registers `Content-Types` and `charsets`. A number of Unicode-related `charset` identifiers are registered by the IANA:

`utf-8`	UTF-8
`utf-16be`	UTF-16 in big-endian byte order
`utf-16le`	UTF-16 in little-endian byte order
`utf-16`	UTF-16 with a byte order mark to specify the byte order (if the BOM is missing, it is the same as `utf-16be`)
`scsu`	Standard Compression Scheme for Unicode

Other `charset` identifiers for Unicode are now obsolete. There aren't yet `charset` identifiers for the various flavors of UTF-32, but they will probably appear eventually.

The `Content-Transfer-Encoding` field is important because the only character encoding that can safely be included in a message and expected to make it unscathed from source to destination without encoding is ASCII. For all other encodings, the only way to ensure that the message body reaches its destination without getting messed up is to use a special transfer encoding. For text, this encoding takes the text in its native encoding (for us, Unicode) and applies an algorithmic transformation to convert it into 7-bit ASCII.

MIME specifies two ways of handling this task: quoted-printable and Base64. Quoted-printable is best for situations where most of the encoded data is readable ASCII text and you want to preserve human readability. It represents the printable ASCII characters as themselves (except for the = sign). All other byte values are represented by an = sign followed by a two-digit hexadecimal number. Thus, "Résumé" in UTF-8 comes out like this in quoted-printable:

```
R=C3=A9sum=C3=A9
```

The lowercase é, U+00E9, is 0xC3 0xA9 in UTF-8.

Because quoted-printable doesn't mangle the original ASCII characters, it's useful for messages in Latin-based scripts. You might identify a message with the following header.

```
Content-Type: text/plain; charset=utf-8
Content-Transfer-Encoding: quoted-printable
```

Quoted-printable also requires that lines be only 80 characters long (counting the CRLF). The = sign is therefore used at the end of a line to indicate that the CRLF following it was inserted by the protocol and not part of the original message (CRLF sequences that aren't preceded by = *are* part of the message).

The other format, Base64, is better for pure binary data or text where the majority of the text isn't readable as ASCII. It's also a little more robust in the face of various transformations than quoted-printable can be. If you escape only non-7-bit characters, control characters, and the = sign, for instance, a quoted-printable message can be mangled on its way through an EBCDIC-based mail gateway and may corrupt interpretation of a multipart MIME message.

In Base64, each sequence of three bytes (24 bits) is converted into four ASCII characters, with six bits of the original 24-bit sequence going to each character. Thus you need 64 characters to represent each "nibble" (hence the name). The 64 characters (the uppercase and lowercase letters, the digits, +, and /) were chosen because they're not syntax characters in anything that might appear in a MIME message and because they exist in EBCDIC and will stay intact through an EBCDIC-based gateway. (A sixty-fifth character, =, is used at the end of messages as padding.) The word "Résumé" in UTF-8 would look like this in Base64:

```
UsOpc3Vtw2k=
```

This result, of course, isn't human-readable, but it works well for cases where the majority of the text isn't initially in ASCII. A Unicode-encoded Japanese message, for example, might have the following heading:

```
Content-Type: text/plain; charset=utf-16be
Content-Transfer-Encoding: base64
```

Like quoted-printable, Base64 divides everything into 80-character lines (counting the terminating CRLFs). Because spaces and control characters aren't used in Base64, they can be filtered out on the decoding side.

Of course, the normal MIME encoding helps only with the body of a message; the header information must still be in ASCII. One piece of the MIME specification, RFC 2047, addresses this issue with an escaping scheme that can be used in certain parts of an RFC 822 header to allow non-ASCII characters. Basically, it's a shorthand form of the preceding format: You specify the encoding using a `charset` identifier, you specify the transfer encoding using B or Q, and then you have the encoded text. It looks like this:

```
Subject: =?utf-8?Q?Here's my r=C3=A9sum=C3=A9?=
```

None of these schemes is particularly beautiful, and all of them impose some overhead on the size of messages. Nevertheless, they do let you use Unicode and other encodings in protocols that weren't originally designed for them. These days, most Internet mail clients understand MIME and do the work necessary so that you see that last example the way you expect:

```
Subject: Here's my résumé
```

■ UNICODE AND PROGRAMMING LANGUAGES

Most of the more recent programming languages now either use Unicode as their base internal character encoding or have a way to let you use it if you want. Many even allow Unicode characters in the syntax of the language in addition to using it in comments and literal strings.

The Unicode Identifier Guidelines

The Unicode standard gives guidelines for how programming languages (and other protocols such as XML) that want to use the full Unicode range in their identifiers can do so.[6] The basic idea is to extend the common definition of an

---

6. See pp. 133–135 of the Unicode standard.

identifier (a letter followed by zero or more letters or digits) to the full Unicode repertoire, and to do so in a way that allows for combining character sequences and invisible formatting characters.

The guidelines say that an identifier may start with anything Unicode considers a "letter" (all characters in the general categories Lu, Ll, Lt, Lm, Lo, and Nl). Subsequent characters may be "letters," combining marks (Mc and Mn, but not Me), "digits" (Nd but not No), connector punctuation (Pc), or formatting codes (Cf). Specifications following these guidelines are encouraged to allow but ignore the formatting characters, but this behavior isn't required.

Because the characters in these categories change with each Unicode version, a specification making use of this guideline must either list all the characters or nail itself to a specific Unicode version. XML nailed itself to Unicode 2.1, for example.

Individual specifications can do whatever they want with these guidelines, including ignoring them. Following them, however, ensures that users of non-Latin scripts can construct identifier names in their native languages without any undue constraints being imposed by the systems. Most specifications that allow Unicode in identifiers follow the Unicode identifier guidelines and add additional legal characters.

Java

Sun's Java programming language has led the way in terms of Unicode support. The base `char` data type is specifically defined to be a UTF-16 code unit, not just an unsigned 16-bit integer. A Java `String` is a sequence of `char` and therefore inherits this characteristic.

One implication of this rule is that all the Java functions that operate on `String` and `char` know they're operating on UTF-16 text and can do the right thing. The case-conversion functions in Java follow the mappings in the Unicode Character Database, for example. The various character-type queries on `Character` are also based on the Unicode categories.

Non-Latin characters are also legal in Java syntax. A Java source file can be in virtually any encoding, but is translated into Unicode internally at compile time. The specific syntax characters are all ASCII characters, but non-ASCII characters are allowed not just in literal strings and comments, but also in identifiers. Java provides an escaping mechanism, the \u1234 syntax, for putting Unicode characters into a Java source file when the source file isn't in Unicode (and provides the native2ascii tool to facilitate this operation).

The Java class libraries offer an extensive array of Unicode support facilities, including character encoding conversion, language-sensitive comparison, text boundary detection, rendering, and complex input method support. There are no specific APIs for text searching, transliteration, or Java normalization, but these abilities are available in open-source libraries. The Java Collator class doesn't automatically follow the Unicode Collation Algorithm default order, but the implementation follows the UCA guidelines. The rendering and input facilities don't yet support every script in Unicode, but more scripts are added in every release. As of J2SE 1.4, the built-in text-rendering software was OpenType compatible, implemented the Unicode bi-di algorithm, and supported Hebrew, Arabic, Devanagari, and Thai, in addition to the scripts that don't require contextual shaping or bidirectional reordering.

C and C++

C and C++, being older, don't directly support Unicode. The char data type is simply defined as an integral type in C, so implementations can make it any size they want and the string-handling routines in the standard libraries can treat char data as any encoding they want. Most treat char as an 8-bit byte and use the default platform encoding (or sometimes just ASCII) as their encoding.

The wchar_t data type was added to allow for "wide" characters, such as Unicode, but doesn't necessarily help. As with char, the language specification doesn't impose any particular semantics on wchar_ts, so portable code can't depend on wchar_t data being Unicode. Worse, the C and C++ standards don't require wchar_t to be big enough to hold a UTF-16 code unit; like the other integral types, it has to be only *as big as* char, not necessarily larger.

String literals are equally problematic. A string literal preceded by "L" is an array of wchar_t, which may or may not be a Unicode string.

Some compilers and run-time libraries treat wchar_t as Unicode. If you're trying to write code that's portable to any C or C++ compiler, however, you can't depend on this interpretation. There are, of course, many Unicode support libraries available for C and C++.

There's hope however: Discussion in the C++ community is heating up around the idea of adding *real* Unicode support to the language.

Javascript and JScript

Javascript and JScript, the Web browser scripting languages from Netscape and Microsoft, respectively, are both based on the ECMA 262 standard for scripting languages. ECMA 262, or ECMAScript, also uses Unicode as its base character type in strings. The third edition of ECMA 262 nails this relationship down by specifying that string data are in UTF-16 and that the internal APIs assume Normalization Form C. It also stipulates that ECMAScript source code is Unicode and provides an escaping mechanism similar to Java's for including otherwise-untypeable Unicode characters in source code. The third edition of ECMA 262 provides for a minimal set of Unicode-compatible string manipulation APIs; the idea was to keep things small and rely on whatever Unicode support is available from the host system. Most ECMAScript implementations also provide a method of accessing the Unicode support available from the host system.

Visual Basic

The current version of Microsoft Visual Basic is Unicode-compatible. Its internal character storage mechanism is Unicode, so all strings are automatically in Unicode. The `option compare text` statement enables locale-sensitive string comparison, which is Unicode-aware. The behavior here is both case- and accent-insensitive; in other words, it ignores secondary and tertiary differences.

Perl

Unicode support in Perl is a work in progress, and has been gradually added over the lifetime of Perl 5 and reaches full maturity in the new Perl 5.8.[7] Perl uses UTF-8 as its internal encoding.

---

7. My source for this information is Jarkko Hietaniemi, "Unicode Support in Perl," found at `http://www.iki.fi/jhi/perlunicode.pod`.

The UTF-8 support in Perl has "character semantics," which means that operations that index by or match individual bytes in other encodings match whole characters (actually, Unicode code points) in UTF-8, regardless of how many bytes they take up internally. Character-type queries and other related operations follow the specifications in the Unicode Character Database. The \x character escaping syntax has been extended to allow for values above 255: \x{2028} refers to the Unicode paragraph separator, for example. For values between 128 and 255, the semantics are slightly different: \xE9 is always the byte value 0xE9 (the Latin-1 é character), and \x{E9} is the Unicode é (internally 0xC3 0xA9, the UTF-8 representation of the letter é).

A new \p token matches all characters in a particular Unicode category. For example, \p{Lu} matches any Unicode uppercase letter. Actually, the "category" mentioned here encompasses more than just the general categories from the UnicodeData.txt file: You can use the \p syntax to match characters in a given script (\p{InTibetan}), or with a particular bi-di property (\p{IsMirrored}), or many other things as well as the general categories.

Currently, the UTF-8 support in Perl doesn't interact well with the locale support in Perl. The latter facility is based on the older POSIX locale standard, which is based on the old byte-oriented character encodings. As a consequence, operations such as locale-sensitive string comparison don't work well when operating on Unicode strings. Perl also now includes libraries for code conversion, collation, and code normalization.

Perl's source files can now be in UTF-16 (with a BOM) or UTF-8 (with the use UTF8 pragma). Unicode characters can be used not only in string literals and regular expressions, but also in identifiers.

ICU

The International Components for Unicode (ICU) is an open-source project coordinated out of IBM. It consists of a broad array of utilities for Unicode support and related internationalization tasks, including character encoding conversion, language-sensitive comparison and searching, boundary detection, character property queries, case mapping, transliteration, and bidirectional reordering, with APIs in C and C++. Originally based on the already-extensive internationalization libraries in Java, it now goes beyond them to the point that a separate Java version of ICU, ICU4J, contains all the ICU features that aren't in the JDK.

▪ Unicode and Operating Systems

As with the other technologies we've looked at, the major operating systems all either have Unicode support now or are moving rapidly in the direction of adding it. Here's a quick rundown.

Microsoft Windows

Microsoft has been gradually adding Unicode support to Windows for some time now.[8] Windows XP, NT, and 2000 are built upon a Unicode base; all of the system APIs store strings as Unicode. (The same is not true of Windows 95, 98, and Me—the two operating system lines have been united in Unicode support with the introduction of the home and professional versions of Windows XP.) The file system and networking protocols are Unicode-based, too. The Windows system uses the UTF-16 encoding internally and is based on Unicode 2.1.

For backward compatibility, all of the Win32 API functions that take strings as parameters come in two flavors: a version whose name ends in "A" (for ANSI) that takes the strings in one of the traditional byte-oriented Microsoft code pages, and a version whose name ends in "W" (for "wide") that takes the strings in UTF-16.

Windows includes an extensive array of character encoding converters. It provides a wide variety of Unicode-aware functions for operations such as string comparison, boundary detection, case mapping, character-type queries, and so forth.

Finally, Windows 2000 includes a Unicode-aware text layout and display engine called Uniscribe that provides the ability to display multiscript text. It implements the Unicode bi-di algorithm and does the character shaping and accent stacking necessary to handle Arabic, Thai, Devanagari, Tamil, and Vietnamese (as well as those scripts that don't require complex shaping, such as Latin, modern Greek, Hebrew, and CJK).

---

8. My sources are various documents found on the Microsoft Web site, particularly at `http://www.microsoft.com/globaldev`.

MacOS

MacOS 9 and earlier aren't based on Unicode, but do have extensive Unicode support. Among the APIs are the following:

- The Text Encoding Conversion Manager, an extremely sophisticated and complete API for converting between various character encodings
- Apple Type Services for Unicode Imaging (ATSUI), Apple's answer to Microsoft's Uniscribe, a Unicode-compatible text-rendering engine that handles complex typography (It implements the Unicode bi-di algorithm and supports Apple Advanced Typography, where most other script-specific complex shaping behavior can be handled in individual fonts.)
- The Multilingual Text Engine (MLTE), an ATSUI-based styled-text editing utility
- The Text Services Manager, which provides Unicode-compatible input method support
- The Unicode Utilities, which provide Unicode-compatible language-sensitive comparison, language-sensitive boundary detection, and character property queries.

MacOS X includes all of these services in its Classic and Carbon APIs and offers counterparts to most of them in its Cocoa API. It includes a variable-length Unicode-based string object, CFString, in its Core Foundation services. The underlying technologies are generally Unicode-based, although not all underlying technologies, owing to their diverse origins, use the same flavors of Unicode. In general, the application programmer doesn't have to worry about this diversity, but issues do arise at the boundaries of some of the environments (or in upgrading a MacOS 9 application to run under Carbon).[9]

Varieties of UNIX

It's difficult to generalize about Unicode support in UNIX because so many different flavors of UNIX exist, each of which has a different feature set. All of the major UNIX vendors support Unicode to one degree or another.

---

9. My sources are various documentation volumes found online at `http://developer.apple.com/techpubs`.

One interesting development of the past several years has been the rise of Linux, the open-source version of UNIX. In the past few years, Linux has not only gained popularity, but won so many converts that most of the major UNIX hardware vendors have found themselves announcing support for it alongside their own proprietary versions of UNIX. This trend might have the effect of bringing more consistency, if not outright standardization, to the UNIX world.

In 1999, some Linux vendors and other supporters (including biggies such as IBM, Hewlett-Packard, and Sun) got together to form the Free Software Foundation. This industry standards body is dedicated to developing a universal specification for Linux implementations—basically, a common feature set (or group of feature sets) for Linux implementations. Implementations conforming to the Linux Standards Base (LSB) could be relied upon to have a certain set of features and APIs.

An important offshoot of the LSB effort was the Linux Internationalization Initiative, nicknamed LI18NUX, which was charged with standardizing the internationalization capabilities of Linux implementations. This group issued the Linux Globalization Specification[10] in 2000. It includes specifications for every aspect of software internationalization, from low-level character manipulation APIs to tools support, rendering support, and input method support. Among other things, the LI18NUX specification mandates support for UTF-8 across a wide variety of locales. In addition to the standard UNIX and C internationalization libraries, it requires (for the more-sophisticated implementations) the inclusion of ICU. (ICU4J is also mandated for LI18NUX-conforming Linux versions that support Java.)

■ CONCLUSION

Unicode is firmly entrenched in the software community. The software that doesn't support it now (and is still being actively maintained) eventually will. Interest in international markets and internationalized software continues to grow. Not only does Unicode solve a real problem, but it's also the only technology that solves that particular problem.

---

10. http://www.li18nux.net/docs/html/LI18NUX-2000.htm.

Unicode got where it is today through a carefully maintained balance of careful, meticulous design and political know-how. Careful attention was paid to maintaining backward compatibility and interoperability; to upholding existing practice; to making sure everything was implementable in reasonable and reasonably performing ways; to providing consistency, comprehensiveness, and elegance; and to ensuring that the needs of all prospective user communities were taken seriously and addressed. That the Unicode standard is thriving (as evidenced by the increasing attendance at each successive Unicode Conference as well as the growing number of Unicode-compatible software products) is a testament to how well these different and often conflicting objectives were balanced. It's doubly impressive when you consider just how many write-only standards now exist. Unicode is not only an idea whose time has come, but an idea's *realization* whose time has come.

And this realization is here to stay, at least as long as we continue to manipulate written language on computers.

Glossary

AAT. Abbreviation for Apple Advanced Typography.

Abstract character repertoire. A collection of characters with no reference to their encoded representation (for example, "the English alphabet").

Accent. A diacritical mark, usually modifying the sound of a vowel or indicating that a syllable has stress applied to it.

Accent stacking. The process of adjusting multiple diacritical marks applied to the same base character so that they don't collide with each other.

Accented letter. A letter with one or more accents or other diacritical marks applied to it.

Accounting numerals. Chinese characters that are used in place of the "normal" Chinese numerals for accounting and commercial purposes, generally because they're more difficult to alter.

Acute accent. A slanted line drawn over a vowel, usually to indicate primary stress or to change the sound of the vowel in some way.

Addak. A sign used in Gurmukhi to indicate consonant gemination.

Additive notation. A system for writing numerals in which the numeric value is derived by adding together the numeric values of all individual characters in the numeral.

Additive-multiplicative notation. A system for writing numerals in which the numeric values of some characters are added together and the numeric values of other characters are multiplied together (generally the order of the characters tells you whether to add or multiply).

Alef maksura. A special form of the Arabic letter alef sometimes used at the end of a word.

Alifu. The name for the null-consonant character in Thaana.

Al-lakuna. The Sinhala virama.

allkeys.txt. The data file giving the default weights of all Unicode characters for the Unicode Collation Algorithm.

Alphabet. A writing system in which the individual characters represent individual sounds (phonemes) in the language. A "pure" alphabet uses letters to represent both consonant and vowel sounds.

Alphabetic. The property applied to all letters in alphabetic writing systems.

Alphasyllabic (alphasyllabary). A writing system with characteristics of both alphabets and syllabaries. An alphasyllabary typically consists of complex marks representing syllables, but which can be decomposed into individual marks (which may change order or shape) representing the individual sounds.

Alternate weighting. A property assigned to certain characters in the Unicode Collation Algorithm. These characters have several possible sort weights that are user-selectable when a comparison is performed.

American National Standards Institute. One of the main standards-setting bodies in the United States; the United States national body in ISO.

American Standards Association. The former name of the American National Standards Institute.

Angkhankhu. A Thai punctuation mark used to mark the ends of long segments of text.

Ano teleia. A bullet-like character used as a semicolon in Greek.

ANSI. Abbreviation for American National Standards Institute.

ANSI X3.4-1967. The official standard number of ASCII.

Anusvara. A character used in Devanagari and some other Indic scripts to indicate nasalization or an *n* or *m* sound at the end of a syllable.

Apple Advanced Typography. Apple's advanced TrueType-derived font format.

Arabic form shaping. Another term for contextual shaping when applied to Arabic. It is used with deprecated formatting characters that control whether contextual shaping is applied to the Arabic presentation form characters.

Arabic numerals. (1) The common name for the digit characters used in English and other Western languages. Also known as "European digits" or "Western digits." These digits are *not* generally used with Arabic. (2) One of two sets of digits normally used with Arabic. They are *not* the same as the "Arabic numerals" used with English and the European languages.

Arabic-Indic numerals. The Unicode term for the native digit characters used with Arabic and other languages that use the Arabic alphabet.

ArabicShaping.txt. A file in the Unicode Character Database that specifies a minimal set of rules for performing Arabic and Syriac contextual shaping.

Array. A data structure in which the individual elements are stored contiguously in a single block of memory.

Articulation mark. A mark applied to a musical note to indicate how it should be articulated.

ASA. Abbreviation for American Standards Association; the former name of ANSI.

Ascender. The part of a character that rises above the font's x-height (such as the vertical stroke on the lowercase letter b).

ASCII. American Standard Code for Information Interchange. A character encoding developed from early telegraphy codes in the early 1960s that remains the most widespread character encoding standard used in data processing. ASCII encodes the 26 letters of the English alphabet, plus the Western digits and a small selection of punctuation marks and symbols. It is a subset of a wide variety of other encodings.

ASCII_Hex_Digit. A property assigned to those Unicode characters that can be used as digits in hexadecimal numerals and are also in ASCII. (The uppercase and lowercase letters A through F, plus the digits 0 through 9.)

Asomtavruli. A style of Georgian writing predominantly used in ecclesiastical texts and sometimes as capital letters.

Aspiration. Letting extra air escape the mouth in the pronunciation of a letter. The difference between the *t* at the beginning of "toy" (an aspirated *t*) and the *t* in "stamp" (an unaspirated *t*).

ATSUI. Apple Type Services for Unicode Imaging. Apple's advanced text-rendering technology.

Attachment point. A location in a glyph shape in an outline font where a mark can be applied. An accent can be positioned correctly relative to different base characters by mating its attachment point to a particular attachment point on the base character.

Augmentation dot. A dot that, when applied to a musical note, lengthens the note by half its normal value.

Backing store. The area of memory containing the text that's being displayed (or otherwise manipulated).

Backspace. (1) A control character in a telegraphy code that indicates that the print head should move back one character position, or the direct descendants of a control code with this original use. (2) The key on a keyboard that deletes the character before the insertion point.

Backward level. A level in a multilevel string comparison algorithm where differences later in the string are more significant than differences earlier in the string.

Bank. One of two or more alternate collections of characters that can be represented by the same numeric values in an encoding scheme (used particularly with older telegraphy codes such as the Baudot code). Special control characters are used to switch between banks.

Bantoc. A Khmer character that shortens the preceding vowel.

Bariyoosan. A Khmer punctuation mark used to mark the end of a section.

Base character. A character to which a diacritical mark can be applied.

Base64. A transfer encoding syntax that represents arbitrary binary data using only 65 printing characters that exist in almost all 7-bit encodings.

Baseline. An imaginary line against which all characters on a line of text are aligned. When text from different fonts or different type sizes is mixed on a line, the characters all line up along the baseline.

Baseline adjustment. The process of properly lining up text from scripts that use different baselines on a single line of text. (For instance, letters in Western scripts sit on the baseline, whereas letters in most Indic scripts hang from the baseline. When Western and Indic writing is mixed on a single line of text, the baseline of one script has to be adjusted upward or downward to make the text appear to line up properly.)

Basic Multilingual Plane. The official name of plane 0 of Unicode and ISO 10646. The plane where the characters in all modern scripts are located.

Baudot. Emile Baudot, who invented a "printing telegraph," the immediate predecessor of the teletype machine.

Baudot code. (1) The method of representing characters used with Baudot's printing telegraph. (2) A number of other telegraph codes that shared a similar 5-bit, stateful structure.

BCD. (1) A method of representing numeric quantities using binary digits that preserves the ability to do decimal arithmetic on it. (2) Alternate name for BCDIC.

BCDIC. An in-memory character representation on early IBM computers based on the punched-card codes of the day. Four bits of the 6-bit code were used to indicate the location of a punch in the rows 0 to 9, and the other two bits were used to indicate punches in the zone rows.

Beam. A line that connects together a group of musical notes (usually all notes that occur in a single beat).

BEL. A control code that, in old telegraphy codes, caused a bell to ring (or some other audible signal to happen) on the receiving end of the communication link.

Bicameral script. A script with two sets of letters: uppercase and lowercase.

Bi-di. (1) Bidirectional text layout. (2) A collective term for the scripts that require bidirectional text layout.

Bi-di algorithm. Bidirectional text layout algorithm.

Bi-di category. A property assigned to a character to indicate its directionality.

Bidi_Control. A character property applied to the invisible formatting characters that can be used to alter the default behavior of the bi-di algorithm.

BidiMirroring.txt. A file in the Unicode Character Database that links together characters with mirror-image glyphs. This file can be used to implement a rudimentary version of mirroring.

Bidirectional text layout. The process of arranging characters of mixed directionality on a single line of text.

Bidirectional text layout algorithm. The part of the Unicode standard that defines how characters of mixed directionality should be arranged on a single line of text.

Big5. An industry-developed character encoding standard for Traditional Chinese commonly used in Taiwan.

Big-endian. (1) A serialization format that sends and receives multiple-byte values with the most significant byte first. (2) A processor architecture that stores the most significant byte of a multibyte value lowest in memory.

Binary comparison. The process of comparing two strings by performing a simple numeric comparison of the individual code point values until a difference is discovered.

Binary tree. A linked data structure consisting of individual nodes that are arranged in a hierarchy and where each node points to no more than two other nodes.

Bindi. The Gurmukhi anusvara.

Bit map. (1) An array of Boolean values, usually packed together so that each Boolean value is represented by a single bit. (2) A series of bytes representing a visual image where each bit determines whether a particular pixel is lit.

Bitmap font. A font where the glyph images are represented as bitmaps that can be copied directly into the display buffer.

Bitmapped display. A display device that is controlled by a bitmap in memory, where the bitmap specifies which pixels are to be lit.

Bitwise comparison. Alternate term for binary comparison.

Blanked. An alternate-weighting mode in the Unicode Collation Algorithm where all characters with alternate weights are treated as ignorable.

Block. A contiguous range of code point values in the Unicode encoding space set aside for a particular purpose (e.g., the Greek block contains characters used in Greek).

Block storage. A storage scheme for a long range of contiguous information (such as a text document) that stores it by dividing it up into a number of separate blocks in memory.

Blocks.txt. A file in the Unicode Character Database that gives the boundaries of the different "blocks" of the Unicode encoding space.

BMP. Abbreviation for Basic Multilingual Plane.

BOCU. Byte-Order Preserving Compression for Unicode. A Unicode compression scheme that will produce the same sort order when strings are compared with binary comparison as the raw UTF-8 or UTF-32 text.

BOM. Abbreviation for byte order mark.

Bottom-joining vowel. An Indic vowel sign that is drawn below the consonant it modifies.

Boundary analysis. The process of analyzing a piece of text for boundaries between linguistic units such as words or sentences. Line breaking and double-click detection are two processes that perform boundary analysis.

Boustrophedon. Text where successive lines are written with alternating directionality (i.e., a left-to-right line is followed by a right-to-left line, which is followed by a left-to-right line, and so on). Used in ancient Greek and a few other ancient writing systems.

Box-drawing character. A character representing a straight line, an angle, or some other piece of a box. A succession of box-drawing characters are used to draw lines and boxes on character-oriented display devices.

Boyer-Moore algorithm. A fast text-searching algorithm that takes advantage of the mix of characters in the search key to skip over positions in the text being searched where a match can't start.

Breathing mark. One of two marks used in polytonic Greek to indicate the presence and absence of a *h* sound at the beginning of a word or syllable.

Breve. A U-shaped diacritical mark, typically used to indicate the absence of stress on a particular syllable.

Byte order. The order in which the individual bytes of a multibyte value are stored in memory or sent over a communication link.

Byte order mark. The Unicode code point value that, by convention, can be used at the beginning of a Unicode text file to indicate its byte order or to announce the Unicode character encoding scheme being used in that file.

C0. In an ISO 2022-based encoding, the range of code point values from 0x00 to 0x1F set aside for control characters, or the set of control characters allocated to this range. In most ISO 2022-based encodings, the C0 set consists of the ASCII control characters.

C1. In an ISO 2022-based encoding, the range of code point values from 0x80 to 0x9F set aside for control characters, or the set of control characters allocated to this range (and represented using escape sequences in a 7-bit encoding).

Candrabindu. A mark used in Devanagari and some other Indic scripts to indicate nasalization.

Canonical accent ordering. Alternate term for canonical reordering.

Canonical composite. A Unicode character whose canonical decomposition is different from the character itself (i.e., a Unicode character representing a character that can also be represented with a combining character sequence).

Canonical decomposition. The preferred method of representing a particular character in Normalized Form D. For most characters, it is the same as the character itself, but for characters that can also be represented with combining character sequences (i.e., canonical composites), the equivalent combining character sequence (or, if the same character can be represented with more than one combining character sequence, the equivalent sequence with the combining marks in canonical order).

Canonical order. For a given collection of Unicode combining marks applied to a base character, the order in which they are to be arranged in normalized Unicode text.

Canonical reordering. The process of putting a sequence of Unicode combining marks into canonical order.

Canonical representation. For a character that has multiple representations in Unicode, the representation that must be used in some Unicode normalized form.

Canonically equivalent. Two strings that are identical when converted to Normalized Form D.

Cantillation mark. A mark used in Hebrew and some other scripts to indicate accent and stress, especially for chanting in a liturgical context.

Capital. Alternate term for uppercase.

Caret. A mark used to indicate a position in text where more text is to be inserted. Also used as an alternate term for insertion point.

Caron. A v-shaped diacritical mark drawn over some letters to alter their pronunciation.

Case folding. The process of converting a piece of text to a case-independent representation, usually done as part of comparing it to another piece of text when case differences between the two aren't significant.

Case mapping. The process of converting a cased letter (or series of cased letters) to a particular case.

Cased letter. A letter with different uppercase and lowercase forms.

CaseFolding.txt. A file in the Unicode Character Database containing mappings that can be used to perform case folding on a piece of Unicode text.

Case-insensitive comparison. The process of comparing two strings in such a way as to treat differences in case as insignificant (e.g., "hello", "Hello", and "HELLO" all compare as equal).

Cc. The abbreviation used in the UnicodeData.txt file to identify characters as belonging to the "control character" general category.

CCCII. Chinese Character Code for Information Interchange. A Taiwanese industry-developed encoding standard.

CCITT. Consultative Committee for International Telephone and Telegraph. A European standards body that sets standards for the telecommunications industry.

Cedilla. A hook- or comma-shaped mark that attaches to the bottom of some consonants to change their pronunciation.

CESU-8. Compatibility Encoding Scheme for UTF-16, 8-bit. A character encoding form for Unicode similar to UTF-8, but differing in its treatment of supplementary-plane characters. Supplementary-plane characters are represented as though they are converted first to UTF-16 and then the UTF-16 surrogates are converted directly to UTF-8.

Cf. The abbreviation used in the UnicodeData.txt file to denote a character with the "formatting character" general category.

CGJ. Abbreviation for combining grapheme joiner.

Character. (1) The minimal unit of writing in some writing system (see grapheme). (2) Any of a collection of marks having the same semantics and generally considered to be the same by ordinary users of a writing system; the abstract concept of which a glyph is a concrete representation (compare *glyph*.) (3) The entity represented by a Unicode code point (or by a code point in some other encoding).

Character code. Alternate term for code point.

Character encoding form. A mapping from code points to code units. The way in which code points in a coded character set are represented in memory. The intermediate layer between a coded character set and a character encoding scheme in the Unicode character encoding model.

Character encoding scheme. A mapping from code point units to bytes. The way in which code point values in a coded character set are represented in a serialized medium such as a disk file or communication link.

Character generator chip. The device that maps from code point values to lit pixels on the screen in a character-oriented display device.

Character mapping table. The table in a TrueType-based font that maps from code point values to glyph indexes.

Character-oriented display. A display device that is controlled by a range of code point values in memory, using a character generator chip to map from the code point values to the groups of lit pixels on the screen.

Character repertoire. See *abstract character repertoire*.

Character set. Usually used as a synonym for coded character set or abstract character repertoire.

CharMapML. Character Mapping Markup Language. An XML-based format for describing mappings between encoding standards.

charset. The parameter used in a number of IETF standards to specify the character representation used. A `charset` is equivalent to a character encoding scheme.

Chinese character. One of the characters originally used for writing Classical Chinese and now used for a variety of languages, including Japanese and Korean.

Choon. The dash-like character used with Katakana characters to indicate prolongation of a vowel sound.

Choseong. A Hangul jamo character representing the initial consonant sound of a syllable.

Chu Han. Vietnamese name for a Chinese character.

Chu Nom. The characters used to write Vietnamese prior to the twentieth century. The Chu Nom characters are constructed according to the same principles that guided the construction of the Chinese characters, but are specific to Vietnamese.

Circumflex accent. A mark similar to an upside-down V drawn above certain vowels to change their sounds.

CJK. Chinese, Japanese, and Korean.

CJK Joint Research Group. The group that originally developed the unified Han repertoire in Unicode. The forerunner of the Ideographic Rapporteur Group.

CJK Miscellaneous Area. The area of the Unicode encoding space running from U+2E80 to U+33FF and containing various characters used with the Han characters in various languages. It includes punctuation, symbols, and various phonetic writing systems used in conjunction with Han characters.

CJKV Unified Ideographs area. The area of the Unicode encoding space containing the Han characters.

CJK-JRG. Abbreviation for CJK Joint Research Group.

CJKV. Chinese, Japanese, Korean, and Vietnamese.

CL area. The area in an ISO 2022-based encoding running from 0x00 to 0x1F and set aside for control characters. In most ISO 2022-based encodings, the ASCII control characters are assigned to the CL area.

Closing punctuation. Alternate name for ending punctuation.

cmap table. Abbreviation for character mapping table.

Cn. The abbreviation used in the UnicodeData.txt file for noncharacter code point.

CNS 11643. The official encoding standard of the Taiwanese government.

Co. The abbreviation used in the UnicodeData.txt file for private-use character.

Code chart. A chart that shows the mappings from characters to code point values in a character encoding standard.

Code page. Alternative name for coded character set.

Code point. (1) An abstract numeric value representing a character. (2) In Unicode 2.0, what is now called a code unit.

Code point value. One of the values that a code point can have.

Code set. In Extended UNIX Code, one of the four coded character sets you can switch between.

Code unit. A fixed-length numeric value representing a code point (or part of a code point) in memory. A code point may map to a single code unit, or to a sequence of code units.

Coded character set. A mapping of characters to code point values.

Code-switching scheme. A character encoding scheme that allows the representation of more than one coded character set, usually through the use of control characters or escape sequences to switch from one coded character set to another.

Coeng. The Khmer virama.

Collation. Another term for language-sensitive string comparison.

Collation element. A collection of weight values for a particular character or contracting character sequence based on a particular sort order.

Collation key. A sequence of weight values for a string based on a particular order. The weights are ordered in such a way that binary comparison of collation keys produces the same result as language-sensitive comparison of the original strings.

Collation strength. In language-sensitive comparison, the level of differences that are significant.

Combining character. A character that combines typographically in some way with the preceding character. Combining characters are generally accents, vowel signs, or other diacritical marks.

Combining character sequence. A sequence of Unicode code points that together represent a single character, usually a letter with one or more marks (such as vowels or diacritical marks) applied.

Combining class. A number from 0 to 255 assigned to every character in Unicode (noncombining characters all have a combining class of 0) and used to arrange the characters in a combining character sequence into canonical order.

Combining grapheme joiner. A character that can combine two grapheme clusters together into a single grapheme cluster.

Combining half mark. A combining character representing half of a double diacritic.

Combining mark. A mark, usually a diacritical mark, that attaches to the character that precedes it in the backing store.

Combining spacing mark. A combining mark that occupies space on the baseline.

Commercial numerals. Alternate term for accounting numerals.

Comp_Ex. Old name for Full_Composition_Exclusion.

Compact array. A data structure that can be used to represent an array containing repetitive patterns of values in a compact manner that preserves speed of lookup.

Compatibility Area. The section of the Unicode encoding space dedicated primarily to compatibility characters.

Compatibility character. A character encoded in Unicode solely for round-trip compatibility with some source standard. Many, but not all, compatibility characters are also composite characters.

Compatibility composite. A character whose compatibility decomposition differs from its canonical decomposition; a compatibility character with a preferred representation in Unicode.

Compatibility decomposition. A mapping from a compatibility composite to a preferred representation consisting of one or more noncompatibility characters. The main difference between a compatibility decomposition and a canonical decomposition is that a canonical decomposition is exactly equivalent to the original character; a compatibility decomposition, on the other hand, may lose data (usually formatting data).

Composite character. A character whose canonical or compatibility decomposition is different from the character itself.

Composite key. A key for sorting a record that is constructed from two or more other fields in the record.

Composition. The process of replacing a combining character sequence (or part of a combining character sequence) with a canonical composite character.

Composition exclusion list. The list of canonical composites that may not appear in any of the Unicode normalized forms.

CompositionExclusions.txt. The file in the Unicode Character Database that contains the composition exclusion list.

Compound font. A virtual font that draws on more than one other font for the actual glyph shapes.

Compound glyph. A glyph description in an outline font that doesn't contain actual outlines, but instead combines two or more other glyph descriptions.

Conform. To meet all the requirements set forth in a standard.

Conjoining Hangul jamo. Unicode code points representing Hangul jamo that are meant to be used in sequences to represent Hangul syllables.

Conjunct consonant. The glyph or glyphs representing a series of consonants with no intervening vowel sounds in an Indic script. The characters may combine into a ligature or may remain as separate glyphs. Most of the characters have different glyphs from the glyphs they have in isolation, and the viramas that connect the characters together aren't visible.

Connector punctuation. A punctuation mark that causes the words on either side to join together into a single word.

Consonant conjunct. See *conjunct consonant*.

Consonant gemination. The doubling or prolonging of a consonant sound (e.g., the *t* sound in "fourteen" as spoken by most Americans).

Consonant stack. A vertical stack of two or more glyphs representing consonants without intervening vowel sounds in Tibetan. The Tibetan analogue to the conjunct consonant in other Indic scripts.

Consonantal. Used to describe an alphabet in which the letters represent only consonants and in which vowel sounds are represented by applying diacritical marks to the consonants. (In most consonantal scripts, some vowel sounds are represented with letters, but these letters are also used as consonants.)

Content-transfer-encoding. The entry in a MIME message header specifying the transfer encoding syntax with which the message's content is encoded.

Content-type. The entry in a MIME message header specifying the type of data that the message (or message part) contains.

Context-sensitive weighting. A situation in language-sensitive comparison in which a particular character has a different set of weights depending on the surrounding characters. It is usually treated as a combination of a contracting character sequence and an expanding character.

Contextual shaping. The process by which the glyph to use to represent a given character is chosen based on the surrounding characters.

Contour. Alternate term for loop.

Contracting character sequence. A sequence of code point values that map to a single collation element.

Control character. (1) Alternate term for control code. (2) The Unicode general category consisting of the Unicode counterparts to the C0 and C1 code point values in the ISO 2022 standard.

Control code. A single code point representing a control function.

Control function. A sequence of one or more code points that don't represent characters, but instead affect the interpreting process in some way (e.g., managing the communication protocol, delimiting fields in structured data, telling the receiving equipment to do something). A control function consisting of a single code point is called a control code or control character. A control function consisting of a sequence of code points is called an escape sequence.

Control picture. A visible glyph used to represent a control character.

Control point. Alternate term for off-curve point.

CR. Carriage return. A control character that tells the receiving equipment to return the print head to the home position. On some systems (notably the Macintosh), it is the new-line function.

CR area. The range of code point values from 0x80 to 0x9F in an ISO 2022-based encoding, reserved for control characters.

CRLF sequence. A code point value representing the CR function followed by a code point value representing the LF function. The combination of these two code point values in a row is treated as the new-line function by some systems (notably DOS and Windows).

Cs. The abbreviation used in the UnicodeData.txt file for surrogate character.

Currency symbol. A symbol that precedes or follows a numeral to indicate that it represents a currency value.

Cursive. Written characters that generally join together into a single unbroken line.

Cursive joining. Contextual shaping that causes a succession of characters to be drawn connected together into a single unbroken line.

Dagesh. A dot drawn inside a Hebrew letter to change its pronunciation, generally from a more liquid sound (such as *v*) to a stopped sound (such as *b*).

Dakuten. Two small strokes added to the shoulder of a Kana character to change the syllable's consonant sound to a voiced consonant.

Danda. A vertical stroke used as punctuation with many Indic scripts. It functions more or less like a period.

Dash. A property assigned to characters in the "dash punctuation" category that are dashes rather than hyphens.

Dash punctuation. A category of characters that includes hyphens and dashes.

Dasia. The Greek "rough breathing mark," which was used to indicate the presence of an initial *h* sound at the beginning of a word that starts with a vowel.

Dead key. A key that generates a character (usually a diacritical mark) but doesn't advance the print head or carriage to the next character position.

Decimal-digit number. A category of characters that includes all characters that are normally used as decimal digits in place-value notation.

Decimal-digit value. A property assigned to characters in the "decimal digit number" category that specifies the numeric value the character represents when used as a decimal digit.

Decomposition. (1) A property assigned to a character that specifies a sequence of one or more characters that is equivalent to that character.

Usually the decomposition is either the character itself, a combining character sequence (when the character can also be represented using a combining character sequence), or some kind of preferred representation of the character. A canonical decomposition is strictly equivalent to the character; a compatibility decomposition may lose some data (usually formatting). (2) The process of replacing a character with its decomposition or of converting an entire string to Normalized Form D or KD.

Decomposition type. (1) An indication of whether a particular decomposition is canonical or compatibility. (2) A classification applied to compatibility decompositions that attempts to capture any information lost by replacing the character with its decomposition.

Default ignorable code point. A character (or unassigned code point value) that should be ignored by default by a process that doesn't know how to deal with it specifically. This property is generally provided to specify code point values that a font should treat as invisible (i.e., not draw) instead of handling by drawing a "missing" glyph.

DEL. A control function in ASCII and older telegraphy codes that either is ignored by the receiving equipment or tells the receiving equipment to ignore the preceding character. Typically represented by an all-bits-on signal. (The character is derived from the practice of erasing an error in a paper-tape representation of a piece of text by punching out all the holes in the row with the error.)

Dependent vowel. In Indic scripts, a mark that, when applied to a consonant character, changes its inherent vowel to some other vowel sound.

Deprecated. (1) Strongly discouraged from use. Character assignments can't be removed from Unicode, so if a character was encoded in error, it's deprecated. (2) A character property assigned to characters that are deprecated.

Derived data file. A file in the Unicode Character Database whose contents can be derived from data in other files in the database (or from rules in the standard itself).

Derived property. A property whose members can be determined from other properties rather than by merely listing all the members.

DerivedAge.txt. A file in the Unicode Character Database that tells when each character was added to the standard.

DerivedBidiClass.txt. A file in the Unicode Character Database that lists the characters belonging to each of the bi-di categories.

DerivedBinaryProperties.txt. A file in the Unicode Character Database that lists the characters belonging to each of the binary properties (i.e., the properties that have only two values). Currently, the only property listed in this file is the "mirrored" property.

DerivedCombiningClass.txt. A file in the Unicode Character Database that lists the characters in each of the combining classes.

DerivedCoreProperties.txt. A file in the Unicode Character Database that lists characters with various properties. The properties can usually be derived from other properties in UnicodeData.txt and PropList.txt.

DerivedDecompositionType.txt. A file in the Unicode Character Database that lists the composite characters with each of the decomposition types.

DerivedJoiningGroup.txt. A file in the Unicode Character Database that classifies the Arabic and Syriac letters according to their basic shapes.

DerivedJoiningType.txt. A file in the Unicode Character Database that classifies the Arabic and Syriac letters according to how they can join to their neighbors.

DerivedLineBreak.txt. A file in the Unicode Character Database that lists the characters with each of the line-break properties.

DerivedNormalizationProperties.txt. A file in the Unicode Character Database that lists groups of characters with similar behavior under normalization—for example, characters that can't appear in some normalization form, characters that can appear only in certain normalization forms, characters that turn into more than one character when converted to certain normalization forms, and so on.

DerivedNumericType.txt. A file in the Unicode Character Database that groups the various Unicode numeric characters together according to how they can be used to represent numbers.

DerivedNumericValues.txt. A file in the Unicode Character Database that lists all characters that can represent each numeric value.

DerivedProperties.html. A file in the Unicode Character Database that gives information on all derived data files in the database.

Descender. The part of a character that extends below the baseline.

Diacritic. (1) A mark that is added to a letter or other character to change its pronunciation or meaning in some way. (2) A property assigned to all Unicode characters that are used as diacritics.

Diaeresis. (1) Pronouncing a vowel as part of a new syllable rather than as part of a diphthong. (2) A mark (usually a double dot) applied to a letter to indicate diaeresis.

Dialytika. Greek name for diaeresis.

Dialytika-tonos. A single character representing both a dialytika and a tonos applied to the same letter.

Digit. A single character in a numeral written with place-value notation.

Digit value. A property applied to any character that can be used as a digit, specifying the numeric value it represents when used as a digit.

Digraph. (1) A pair of characters used together to represent a single sound. (2) A Unicode code point representing two characters.

Dingbat. A special symbol, usually used decoratively, especially a character from the Zapf Dingbats font found on most laser printers.

Diphthong. (1) Two vowel sounds pronounced consecutively and sliding into one another. (2) A pair of vowels used together to represent a single sound, whether or not that sound is actually a diphthong.

Directional run. A sequence of consecutive characters with the same resolved directionality.

Directionality. A property that specifies the order in which consecutive characters are arranged on a line of text (and the way in which consecutive lines are arranged on a page). For example, a series of characters with left-to-right directionality are arranged on a line such that the first character in memory appears farthest to the left, with the succeeding characters progressing toward the right. A character may have strong directionality, weak directionality, or neutral directionality.

Discontiguous selection. (1) A selection in a text-editing application that includes two or more ranges of characters that aren't contiguous in memory. (2) A selection in a text-editing application that includes two or more ranges of characters that aren't contiguous on the screen.

Display cell. (1) In a monospaced font, the space occupied by a single character. (2) In East Asian typography, the space occupied by a single Chinese character.

Disunify. To take two different meanings or glyph shapes represented by a single code point value and assign different code point values to them. The different uses of the ASCII hyphen character (i.e., hyphen, dash, minus sign) are *disunified* in Unicode.

Dot leader. (1) A sequence of dots spaced at equal intervals and used to help lead the eye between two separated pieces of text (such as a chapter name and page number in a table of contents). (2) A single character consisting of one or more dots intended to be used repeatedly in sequence to form a dot leader.

Double danda. A punctuation mark consisting of two vertical strokes used with many Indic scripts. A double danda usually marks the end of a larger run of text, such as a paragraph or stanza, than is ended with a single danda.

Double diacritic. A diacritical mark that applies to a sequence of two characters.

Draft Unicode Technical Report. A Unicode Technical Report that hasn't achieved final approval yet, but whose content has generally been agreed on in principle. Unicode Technical Reports carry no normative force while still in draft form.

Dual-joining letter. An Arabic or Syriac letter that is capable of connecting cursively to letters on either side.

DUTR. Abbreviation for Draft Unicode Technical Report.

DUTR #26. A Draft Unicode Technical Report defining CESU-8, a UTF-8-like encoding scheme used for compatibility on some systems.

Dynamic composition. The principle of being able to represent a character with a sequence of code points representing its constituent parts.

Early normalization. The principle set forth by the W3C that text must be produced in normalized form by the process that produces it (and kept that way by any process that modifies it). This requirement allows processes that only receive and interpret text to assume it's in normalized form.

East Asian width. A property assigned to a character that specifies how many display cells it takes up in East Asian typography.

EastAsianWidth.txt. A file in the Unicode Character Database that gives the East Asian width property for each character.

EBCDIC. Extended Binary Coded Decimal Information Code. A family of encoding standards used on some IBM computers that evolved from BCDIC, which itself evolved from earlier punched-card codes. The original version of EBCDIC added two bits to the 6-bit BCDIC, making it possible to represent a wider variety of punch patterns than was possible with BCDIC.

Ech-yiwn ligature. The ligature that is often formed when the Armenian letters ech and yiwn occur together.

ECMA. A pan-European standards-setting body specializing in information technology standards. ECMA is an ISO member body. The letters formerly stood for European Computer Manufacturers' Association.

ECMA-6. The original international-standard version of ASCII. It became ISO 646.

ECMA-35. The standard that became ISO 2022.

ECMA-94. The standard that became ISO 8859-1.

ECMAScript. A standard specifying a core syntax and set of libraries for scripting languages. Netscape's Javascript and Microsoft's JScript, as well as some other scripting languages, are based on the ECMAScript model.

Editing. The process of using a piece of software to interactively change or compose a piece of text.

Elision character. A character used to indicate the absence of several other characters. The apostrophe is often used as an elision character in English.

Ellipsis character. (1) A character, such as the series of periods used in English, that is used to indicate the absence of one or more words. (2) Elision character.

Em. A unit of measurement along a line of text that is equivalent to the height of the line.

Em dash. A dash that is one em wide, used in English to indicate a break in continuity or to set off a parenthetical expression.

Em quad. A space that is one em wide.

Em space. Alternate term for em quad.

Embedding level. A number assigned to characters by the Unicode bi-di algorithm that governs how successive directional runs are arranged on a line relative to one another.

En. Half of an em.

En dash. A dash that is one en wide, used in English to separate ranges of numbers or as a minus sign.

En quad. A space that is one en wide.

En space. Alternate term for en quad.

Enclosing mark. A combining mark that surrounds the character (or grapheme cluster) to which it is applied.

Encoding form. See *character encoding form.*

Encoding scheme. See *character encoding scheme.*

Encoding space. The range of possible code point values for a coded character set, often represented as a two- or three-dimensional array of cells containing characters. The size of an encoding space is often derived from the size in bits of the code point values. The phrases "8-bit encoding space" and "16×16 encoding space" are both synonymous with "256-character encoding space."

Encoding standard. A standard that specifies a coded character set, character encoding form, character encoding scheme, or some combination of the above.

Endian-ness. Alternate term for byte order.

Ending punctuation. A category of characters that serve to mark the end of some range of text (such as a parenthetical expression or a quotation).

Erotimatiko. The semicolon-like mark used in Greek as a question mark.

Escape sequence. (1) A sequence of more than one code point value representing a control function (traditionally, the ASCII ESC character was used as the first character of an escape sequence). (2) A sequence of more than one code point value used to represent a single code point in a programming language or other structured text format (e.g., \u1234 in Java).

Estrangelo. The oldest style of writing the Syriac letters.

EUC. Abbreviation for Extended UNIX Code.

EUC-CN. A version of Extended UNIX Code with code sets drawn from mainland Chinese encoding standards.

EUC-JP. A version of Extended UNIX Code with code sets drawn from Japanese encoding standards.

EUC-KR. A version of Extended UNIX Code with code sets drawn from Korean encoding standards.

EUC-TW. A version of Extended UNIX Code with code sets drawn from Taiwanese encoding standards.

Exception table. An auxiliary data structure used to store records that won't fit in the main data structure, or cases where the rules specified in the main structure don't hold. A data structure that needs to store mappings for character sequences might use a main table that holds single-character mappings and points into one or more exception tables that hold the multiple-character mappings. A data structure that groups characters into categories for some process might consist of a main table that maps entire Unicode general categories to its categories and an exception table that contains category mappings for characters whose mappings don't match those for their Unicode category.

Expanding character. A character that maps to more than one collation element.

Expands_On_NFC. A derived property containing all characters that turn into multiple characters when converted to Normalized Form C.

Expands_On_NFD. A derived property containing all characters that turn into multiple characters when converted to Normalized Form D.

Expands_On_NFKC. A derived property containing all characters that turn into multiple characters when converted to Normalized Form KC.

Expands_On_NFKD. A derived property containing all characters that turn into multiple characters when converted to Normalized Form KD.

Explicit embedding character. A character that forces the characters after it to be placed at a new embedding level.

Explicit override character. A character that overrides the inherent directionality of the characters after it.

Extended ASCII. Any of a large number of 8-bit encoding standards whose first 128 code point assignments are identical to those in ASCII, particularly ISO 8859-1.

Extended UNIX Code. A code-switching scheme that allows for the representation of as many as four coded character sets: One is represented with code point values in the G0 space, one with code point values in the G1 space, and the other two with code point values from the G1 space preceded by special "introducer" characters.

Extender (property in PropList.txt). A property assigned to characters that lengthen—graphically or phonetically—the characters or words they follow.

Eyelash ra. A special half-form of the Devanagari letter ra used in certain conjunct consonants.

Fancy text. Alternate term for rich text.

Feather mark. A mark used in Ogham to mark the beginning and ending of a piece of text.

FF. Form feed. A control character that tells the receiving equipment to advance the platen to the beginning of the next page.

FIELDATA. A telegraphy code developed by the U.S. Army that is one of ASCII's most important antecedents.

FIGS. A control character that would cause the receiving equipment to interpret succeeding code points as digits or punctuation instead of letters.

Fili. The Thaana vowel signs.

Final form. (1) The glyph shape that a character takes on when it appears at the end of a word. (2) In Arabic and Syriac, the glyph shape that a character takes on when it appears before a character that doesn't join to the preceding character.

Final-quote punctuation. A category assigned to half of the quotation mark characters in Unicode. Whether the characters in this category are actually closing quotation marks or are instead opening quotation marks depends on the language of the text.

First-series consonants. The Khmer consonants that carry an inherent *a* sound.

FNC. A derived property that gives a mapping from a character to a case-folded representation in Normalized Form C.

Fongman. A character used as a list bullet in Thai.

Font. (1) A collection of glyphs with a common typographical design. Several fonts may make up a typeface. (2) A computer program or set of tables that, in conjunction with a text-rendering process, can draw the glyphs in a particular font.

Forfeda. Extra letters added to the Ogham alphabet after it began to be written on paper.

Format effector. Early term for a control character.

Formatting character. The category assigned to Unicode characters that have no visual presentation of their own, but that exist to alter the way some process operating on the text treats the surrounding characters.

Fourth-level difference. In a multilevel comparison, a difference between fourth-level weights.

Fourth-level weight. In a multilevel comparison, the fourth weight value assigned to a character or contracting character sequence. In the Unicode Collation Algorithm, the fourth-level weight is the character's actual code point value or is algorithmically derived from the character's code point value.

Fraction slash. A special slash character that causes surrounding sequences of digits to combine together into a fraction. If you put a normal slash between 1 and 2, you get "1/2"; if you put a fraction slash between them, you get "½".

French accent sorting. Alternate name for French secondary.

French secondary. Treating the secondary level of a multilevel sort as a backward level. So called because it's required to sort French properly.

FTP. File Transfer Protocol. A protocol used for sending files over the Internet.

Full_Composition_Exclusion. A derived property assigned to characters that can't occur in any of the Unicode normalized forms.

Full-width. Used to describe characters that take up a full display cell in East Asian typography. Unicode draws a distinction between characters that are explicitly full-width (i.e., have "FULLWIDTH" in their names) and those that are implicitly full-width (such as the Han characters).

Furigana. Alternate term for ruby.

Futhark. The name for a Runic alphabet.

G source. The collective name for sources of ideographs submitted to the IRG by the Chinese national body.

G0. The range of the ISO 2022 encoding space running from 0x20 to 0x7F and set aside for printing characters. 0x20 is always the space and 0x7F is always the DEL character, leaving 94 code point values available for other characters. The term also refers to the set of characters encoded in this space. In most ISO 2022-based encodings, the G0 set of characters is the ASCII printing characters.

G1. The range of the ISO 2022 encoding space running from 0xA0 to 0xFF and set aside for printing characters. The term also refers to one of three alternate sets of characters encoded in this space (G2 and G3 are the others).

Gakushu Kanji. A list of characters that all Japanese learn in elementary school.

Gap storage. A method of storing a large amount of contiguous data, such as the characters in a document being edited, that can greatly improve the performance of processes, such as interactive text editors, that manipulate the data. The basic principle is that the memory block is larger than the data, giving it room to grow before a new block must be allocated, and the extra memory in the block is stored at the position of the last change rather than at the end of the block, minimizing the number of characters that must be moved when changes occur.

Garshuni. Arabic written using the Syriac alphabet.

GB 2312. The main Chinese national standard for character encoding.

Gemination. See *consonant gemination*.

General category. A property given to every Unicode character that classifies it according to its general purpose.

General Scripts Area. The area of the BMP running from U+0000 to U+1FFF and containing the characters for the modern non-CJK writing systems.

Geta mark. A mark sometimes used in Japanese typography to take the place of an ideograph for which a glyph can't be found.

GL area. In ISO 2022, the range running from 0x20 to 0x7F and set aside for the encoding of printing characters. In most ISO 2022-based encodings, the ASCII characters are placed into the GL range.

Glottal stop. The stoppage of sound caused by the closing of the glottis (the back of the throat). The hyphen in "uh-uh" is a glottal stop.

Glue character. Alternate term for non-breaking character.

Glyph. A concrete written or printed representation of a character or group of characters.

Glyph index. A number identifying a particular glyph description in a font file. The cmap table in a TrueType font maps from code points to glyph indexes.

Glyph metamorphosis table. In an AAT font, a table that performs complex mappings on glyph indexes. It is responsible for context-sensitive glyph selection, ligature formation, Indic vowel reordering, and so on.

Glyph selection. The process of choosing the proper glyph to display for a character in a particular place.

Glyph-substitution table. In an OpenType font, a table that performs complex mappings on glyph indexes. It is responsible for context-sensitive glyph selection, ligature formation, and so on.

Glyphic variant. A different glyph representing the same underlying character. The term is usually used in opposition to "different character." For example, $, $, and $ are all glyphic variants of the same character; $ and ¢ are different characters.

GR area. The part of the ISO 2022 encoding space running from 0xA0 to 0xFF and set aside for printing characters.

Grapheme. (1) A minimal unit of writing in some written language; a mark that is considered a single "character" by an average reader or writer of a particular written language. (2) In versions of Unicode prior to Unicode 3.2, the concept that is now called a grapheme cluster.

Grapheme cluster. A sequence of one or more Unicode code points that should be treated as an indivisible unit by most processes operating on Unicode text, such as searching and sorting, hit testing, arrow key movement, and so on. A grapheme cluster may or may not correspond to the user's idea of a "character" (i.e., a single grapheme). For instance, an Indic orthographic syllable is generally considered a grapheme cluster but an average reader or writer may see it as several letters. The Unicode standard puts forth a default definition of grapheme clusters, but permits language-sensitive tailoring. For example, a contracting character sequence in most sort orders is a language-specific grapheme cluster.

Grapheme joiner. See *combining grapheme joiner.*

Grapheme_Base. A property assigned to all characters that are grapheme clusters unto themselves unless they occur next to a Grapheme_Extend or Grapheme_Link character. This is a derived property—all characters that aren't Grapheme_Extend or Grapheme_Link characters are Grapheme_Base characters.

Grapheme_Extend. A property assignecd to all characters that belong to the same grapheme cluster as the characters that precede them. Combining marks are Grapheme_Extend characters.

Grapheme_Link. A property assigned to all characters that cause the characters that precede and follow them to be considered part of the same grapheme cluster. The combining grapheme joiner and the viramas are Grapheme_Link characters.

Graphic character. Alternate term for printing character.

Grave accent. A slanted line drawn over a vowel, usually to indicate secondary stress or change the sound in some way.

GSUB table. Abbreviation for glyph substitution table.

Guillemet. A v-shaped mark used in a number of languages, notably French, as a quotation mark.

H source. Collective name for the various sources of ideographic characters submitted to the IRG by the Hong Kong Special Administrative Region.

Hacek. Alternate term for caron.

Halant. Alternate term for virama.

Half mark. See *combining half mark*.

Half-form. The form that a consonant in Devanagari and some other Indic writing systems often takes when it's part of a conjunct consonant. The term comes from the fact that a half-form is usually an abbreviated version of the character's normal shape, often omitting the vertical stem. Half-forms are glyphic variants of normal consonants and do not have a separate encoding in Unicode.

Half-width. The term given to characters that occupy half of a normal display cell in East Asian typography. Latin letters, for example, are considered half-width. The Unicode standard draws a distinction between characters that are explicitly half-width—these have "HALFWIDTH" in their names—and those that are implicitly half-width. Half-width characters don't always take up exactly half the space along the baseline of full-width characters; often they're proportionally spaced, and the term merely indicates that they take up less space along the baseline than a normal ideograph.

Hamza. A mark used in Arabic to indicate a glottal stop.

Han character. Alternate term for Chinese character.

Han unification. The process of collecting Chinese characters from a variety of disparate sources and weeding out the characters that are really duplicates. The duplicate characters are encoded once in Unicode, not once for every source encoding in which they appear. The process of Han unification involves keeping careful track of just which characters from which sources are unified.

Handakuten. The small circle applied to certain Kana characters that turns the initial *h* sound into an initial *p* sound.

Hangul. The alphabetic writing system used for writing Korean.

Hangul syllable. (1) A cluster of Hangul jamo representing a single Korean syllable. (2) A single Unicode code point representing a Hangul syllable.

Hangul Syllables Area. The range of the Unicode encoding space running from U+AC00 to U+07FF and containing the Hangul syllables.

Hangzhou numerals. Alternate term for Suzhou numerals.

Hanja. Korean for Chinese character.

Hankaku. Japanese for half-width.

Hanzi. Mandarin for Chinese character.

Hard sign. A letter of the Cyrillic alphabet that indicates the absence of palatalization in a spot where it would normally occur.

Headstroke. The characteristic stroke at the top of all letters in most Indic writing systems. Depending on the script, the headstroke may be a different shape.

Hex_Digit. A property assigned to those characters that can be used as hexadecimal digits.

High surrogate. A code unit value that is used as the first code unit in a surrogate pair, or the code point value corresponding to it. The high surrogates run from U+D800 to U+DBFF.

Higher-level protocol. A protocol that is out of the scope of the Unicode standard but that uses the Unicode standard as its basis. XML is an example of a higher-level protocol.

Hindi numerals. The native digits used with the Arabic alphabet. *Not* the digits used with Devenagari.

Hint. Alternate term for instruction.

Hiragana. The more cursive form of Kana used for writing native Japanese words and grammatical endings.

Hit testing. The process of determining the position in the backing store that corresponds to a particular pixel position in a piece of rendered text.

HKSCS. Hong Kong Supplemental Character Set. A collection of characters used in the Hong Kong Special Administrative Region. Many of these characters are used specifically to write Cantonese.

Hollerith. Herman Hollerith, who developed a system of using punched cards for data processing.

Hollerith code. Any of a number of similar methods of representing alphanumeric data on punched cards.

HTML. Hypertext Markup Language. A method of representing styled text and hypertext links between documents. The standard method of representing Web page content.

HTTP. Hypertext Transfer Protocol. A protocol for requesting and transferring hypertext documents, and the standard communication protocol on the Web.

Hyphen (property in PropList.txt). A property assigned to Unicode dash-punctuation characters (and some connector-punctuation characters) that are hyphens.

Hyphenation. The process of dividing words between lines of text, usually at syllable boundaries and with a hyphen added at the end of the first line, in an effort to improve the appearance of justified text.

HZ. A code-switching scheme used with Chinese text.

IAB. Abbreviation for Internet Architecture Board.

IANA. Abbreviation for Internet Assigned Numbers Authority.

ICU. Abbreviation for International Components for Unicode.

IDC. Abbreviation for ideographic description character.

Identifier. A sequence of characters used to identify some entity. Variable and function names in programming languages are examples of identifiers.

Ideograph. (1) A character that represents an idea. (2) Alternate term for Chinese character.

Ideographic. A property assigned to ideographic characters in Unicode—specifically, the Han characters and radicals.

Ideographic description character. A special character that indicates how the two or three ideographic characters or ideographic description sequences following it are to be combined to form a single character. Officially, ideographic description characters are printing characters, but a smart rendering engine can use them to approximate the appearance of an otherwise-unrepresentable ideograph.

Ideographic description sequence. A sequence of Unicode characters that describe the appearance of otherwise-unrepresentable Chinese characters. An ideographic description sequence contains at least one ideographic description character.

Ideographic Rapporteur Group. A formal standing subcommittee of ISO/IEC JTC1/SC2/WG2 responsible for the maintenance and development of the unified Han repertoire in Unicode and ISO 10646. The IRG is made up of experts from Asian countries that use the Han characters, as well as a few representatives of the UTC.

Ideographic variation indicator. A special character used to indicate that the following character is only an approximation of the desired Chinese character, which can't be represented in Unicode.

IDS. Abbreviation for ideographic description sequence.

IDS_Binary_Operator. A property assigned to ideographic description characters that take two operands.

IDS_Trinary_Operator. A property assigned to ideographic description characters that take three operands.

IEC. Abbreviation for International Electrotechnical Commission.

IETF. Abbreviation for Internet Engineering Task Force.

Ignorable character. A character that is to be ignored by a language-sensitive string comparison routine, or that is to be considered significant only at certain levels of comparison. The Unicode Collation Algorithm defines a large collection of characters (mostly spaces and punctuation) as ignorable by default; tailorings may specify more ignorable characters or make certain characters significant that are ignorable by default.

Independent form. The glyph shape taken by a character in the absence of any surrounding characters to which it can connect cursively. Typically used with Arabic and Syriac letters.

Independent vowel. A full-fledged letter (as opposed to a mark that is applied to another letter) representing a vowel sound in an Indic script. Generally, independent vowels are used for word-initial vowel sounds and for vowel sounds that follow other vowel sounds. In some scripts, the "independent vowels" take the form of dependent vowels applied to a "null" consonant.

Index.txt. A file in the Unicode Character Database that lists all Unicode characters by name; a soft copy of the character names index in the Unicode book.

Indic script. One of a large collection of scripts used mostly in India, Southeast Asia, and certain islands in the Pacific and derived from the ancient Brahmi script.

Informative. A statement, property, or recommendation in a standard that need not be followed to conform to the standard. Informative elements are usually present to clarify or supplement the standard in some way.

Inherent directionality. The directionality that a character has by virtue of its definition in the Unicode standard, as opposed to its resolved directionality.

Inherent vowel sound. The vowel sound that a consonant in an Indic script has when no dependent vowels are attached to it. (Letters in Indic scripts actually represent syllables, not just consonants.)

Initial form. The glyph shape that a character takes when it appears at the beginning of a word, or when it's preceded by a character that doesn't connect to the following character.

Initial-quote punctuation. A property assigned to half of the quotation marks in Unicode. Whether the characters with this property are actually opening quotation marks or are instead closing quotation marks depends on the actual language of the text.

Input method. A piece of software that translates user actions on some input device into characters that are passed as input to a text-editing utility. The term is used specifically to refer to code that permits input of Chinese characters with a series of keystrokes (and often interactive menu choices).

Insertion point. In an interactive text-editing application, the position, usually marked by a blinking vertical line, where any text the user types will be inserted.

Instruction. An element of a font that indicates how to deform the ideal shape of a glyph to better fit the coordinate system of the output device when the output device has low resolution. Instructions are used, for example, to make the characters in an outline font designed for a printer look good (or at least legible) on the screen.

Interact typographically. To affect the shapes or positions of surrounding characters. Two characters are said to interact typographically if the glyph shapes when the characters are juxtaposed in memory differ from the glyph shapes the characters have in isolation. A character a and a character b that follows it in memory interact typographically if (1) b is drawn somewhere other than in the next position after a in the dominant writing direction (e.g., in a left-to-right script, if b is drawn above, below, to the left of, inside, or overlaying a), (2) the shape of a, b or both differs from the shape the character has in isolation, or (3) a and b combine into a ligature.

Interlinear annotation. Annotations appearing between lines of text that help to clarify the pronunciation or meaning of unfamiliar characters or words.

International Components for Unicode. An open-source library of routines for performing operations on Unicode text, including character encoding conversion, Unicode normalization, language-sensitive comparison and searching, boundary analysis, transliteration, and case mapping and folding.

International Electrotechnical Commission. An international body that issues international standards for various technical and engineering disciplines.

International Organization for Standardization. An international body that issues international standards in a variety of disciplines and serves as an umbrella organization for the various national standards bodies.

International Phonetic Alphabet. A special set of characters used for phonetic transcription.

International Telegraphy Alphabet #2. An international encoding standard used for several decades in telegraphy.

Internationalization. The process of designing software so that it can be localized for particular user communities without having to change or recompile the executable code.

Internet Architecture Board. The group responsible for the IETF's technical activities.

Internet Assigned Numbers Authority. A sister organization to the IETF that acts as a central registration authority for Internet-related identifiers and numbers, such as charsets, MIME types, and so forth. (The IANA was also once responsible for domain names, but no longer handles this duty.)

Internet Engineering Task Force. An informal organization consisting of engineers who do Internet-related work and that issues standards for the operation of different parts of the Internet. Most Internet-related standards, other than those relating to the World Wide Web, are IETF standards.

Internet-draft. A document issued by the IETF that either represents a standards-track proposal in its very earliest stages of discussion or that contains only informative information. Internet-drafts carry no normative force.

Inversion list. A data structure that represents a collection of values with an array containing only the initial values in each contiguous range of values.

Inversion map. An extension of the inversion list that represents a collection of mappings from one set of values into another with an array that contains only the initial values for each contiguous range of source values that map to the same result value.

Invisible formatting character. A Unicode code point value that has no visual presentation of its own, but affects the way some process operating on text treats the surrounding characters.

Invisible math operator. A Unicode code point value representing a mathematical operation whose application is implicit (i.e., indicated by the simple juxtaposition of symbols in a mathematical formula). Invisible math operators have no visual presentation (although sometimes they affect the spacing of the surrounding characters), but exist to help software parsing a mathematical expression.

IPA. Abbreviation for International Phonetic Alphabet.

IRG. Abbreviation for Ideographic Rapporteur Group.

IRV. International Reference Version. For international standards such as ISO 646 that allow for variations between countries, the IRV is the version to use in the absence of a country-specific version. The International Reference Version of ISO 646 is American ASCII.

ISCII. Indian Script Code for Information Interchange. An encoding standard issued by the Indian government for representing various Indic scripts used in India.

ISO. Abbreviation for International Organization for Standardization.

ISO 10646. Unicode's sister standard. ISO 10646 is an official international standard, rather than an ad hoc industry standard. Since the early 1990s, it has included exactly the same assignments of characters to code point values as Unicode and shares some other architectural characteristics with it as well. Unicode goes beyond ISO 10646 to specify more details of character semantics and implementation details, and other subtle differences distinguish the two standards. The current formal designations for ISO 10646 are ISO/IEC 10646-1:2000 and ISO/IEC 10646-2:2001 standards; "ISO 10646" is used informally to collectively refer to both (or to earlier versions).

ISO 10646 comment. Informative text about a character that occurs in the ISO 10646 code charts and is included as a formal Unicode character property for compatibility with ISO 10646.

ISO 2022. An ISO standard that specifies a general encoding-space layout for other encoding standards to follow, and that specifies an elaborate system of escape sequences for switching between coded character sets.

ISO 6429. A standard that specifies semantics for control characters in ISO 2022-derived encodings.

ISO 646. The international standard based on ASCII. The International Reference Version of ISO 646 is the same as ASCII, but the ISO 646 standard itself specifies a group of "national use" code points that can be assigned to characters other than the ones in the International Reference Version by national bodies. With a few exceptions, such as JIS-Roman, the national-use variants of ISO 646 have fallen into disuse.

ISO 8859. A family of ISO 2022-compatible encoding standards for European languages and languages used by large populations of people in Europe. The first 128 code point assignments in all of the ISO 8859 encodings are identical to the ISO 646 IRV, making all of them downward compatible with ASCII.

ISO 8859-1. An encoding standard for representing Western European languages using the Latin alphabet. The most common "extended ASCII" encoding standard, it was the default character encoding for HTML until recently. The first 256 code point assignments in Unicode are identical to ISO 8859-1. ISO 8859-1 is slowly being superseded by ISO 8859-15 (Latin-9), which is almost the same, but removes a few less frequently used character assignments and adds a few new characters, including the euro symbol.

ISO-2022-CN. A code-switching scheme for Chinese.

ISO-2022-CN-EXT. A code-switching scheme for Chinese similar to ISO-2022-CN, but including support for a larger number of characters.

ISO-2022-JP. A code-switching scheme for Japanese.

ISO-2022-KR. A code-switching scheme for Korean.

Isolated form. Alternate term for independent form.

Isshar. A mark used in Bengali to write the name of God.

ITA2. Abbreviation for International Telegraphy Alphabet #2.

J source. Collective name for sources of Han ideographs submitted to the IRG by the Japanese national body.

Jamo. The individual "letters" of the Hangul writing system. Two or more jamo, representing individual sounds, are arranged in a square display cell to form a Hangul syllable. Modern Hangul syllables can be represented in Unicode either with series of individual code points representing the jamo, or with a single code point representing the whole syllable.

Jamo short name. A property assigned to the Hangul jamo in Unicode that is used to derive names for the Hangul syllables.

Jamo.txt. A data file in the Unicode Character Database that specifies the Jamo short name property for the characters in Unicode that have this property.

Japanese Industrial Standards Commission. The main Japanese national standards-setting body, and the Japanese member of ISO.

Jinmei-yo Kanji. A list of characters officially sanctioned by the Japanese government for use in personal names.

JIS C 6226. Early term for JIS X 0208.

JIS X 0201. A Japanese encoding standard that includes code point values for the ASCII characters and the Katakana characters.

JIS X 0208. The main Japanese encoding standard that encodes kanji characters.

JIS X 0212. A supplemental Japanese standard that adds more kanji to those already encoded by JIS X 0208.

JIS X 0213. A supplemental Japanese standard that adds more kanji to those already encoded by JIS X 0208 and JIS X 0212.

JISC. Abbreviation for Japanese Industrial Standard Commission.

JIS-Roman. Alternate term for JIS X 0201.

Johab. An encoding scheme for Korean that makes it possible to encode all of the modern Hangul syllables as single code points.

Join_Control. A property assigned to invisible formatting characters that control cursive joining and ligature formation.

Joiner. See *zero-width joiner.*

Jongseong. A Hangul jamo representing a syllable-final consonant sound.

Joyo Kanji. A standardized list of Japanese characters used in government documents and newspapers.

JTC1. Joint Technical Committee #1 of the International Organization for Standardization and the International Electrotechnical Commission. This committee is responsible for developing and publishing information technology standards.

Jungseong. A Hangul jamo representing a vowel sound.

Justification. The process of distributing extra whitespace on a line of text, usually to cause the text to be flush with both margins.

K source. Collective name for sources of ideographs submitted to the IRG by the Korean national bodies.

Kana. Collective name for Hiragana and Katakana, the two syllabic writing systems used in Japanese.

Kangxi radical. One of the 214 radicals used to classify Chinese characters in the Kangxi dictionary.

Kangxi Zidian. A dictionary for Chinese completed in 1716 and widely considered definitive.

Kanji. Japanese for Chinese characters.

Kashida. A long connecting stroke used to elongate Arabic words to make them fit a specified space.

Kashida justification. The process of justifying a line of Arabic text by inserting kashidas.

Katakana. The more angular form of Kana used in Japanese to write foreign words and onomatopoeia.

Kerning. The process of adjusting the spacing between individual pairs of characters (usually by moving them closer together) to achieve a more pleasing appearance.

Key closure. The process of making sure that for every key in a trie-based data structure, all proper prefixes of that key are also included as keys.

Khan. A Khmer punctuation mark used at the ends of sentences.

Khomut. A Thai punctuation mark used at the end of a document.

Khutsuri. A style of Georgian writing that mixed asomtavruli and nuskhuri and was used primarily in ecclesiastical settings.

Killer. Alternate term for virama.

Koronis. A diacritical mark used in monotonic Greek to indicate elision of vowels.

KS C 5601. Old name for KS X 1001.

KS X 1001. One of the main Korean national character encoding standards.

Kunddaliya. A Sinhala punctuation mark that appears at the end of sentences.

L2. Committee L2 of the National Committee for Information Technology Standards, which is the American national body reporting to WG2.

Labialization. Beginning a vowel or ending a consonant with the lips puckered. English speakers tend to think of this action as inserting a *w* sound between a consonant and a vowel.

Lam-alef ligature. The glyph that is formed when the Arabic letter lam is followed by the Arabic letter alef. It is the one mandatory ligature in Arabic.

Last resort font. A font used (typically by a compound font) to provide glyphs for characters that couldn't be displayed by any other font. A typical last resort font includes glyphs for each of the scripts covered by Unicode, allowing the user to at least get an idea of which language (or script) included the missing characters and, therefore, what kind of font would need to be provided to see them.

Latin-1. Alternate term for ISO 8859-1.

Left-joining letter. An Arabic or Syriac letter that can connect to a letter only on its left.

Left-joining vowel. An Indic dependent vowel that attaches to the left-hand side of the consonant to which it is applied.

Left-to-right embedding. An explicit embedding character that starts a new embedding level and specifies its direction to be left-to-right.

Left-to-right mark. An invisible formatting character that has strong left-to-right directionality and that can be used to cause characters of neutral directionality to resolve to left-to-right directionality.

Left-to-right override. An explicit override character that causes all following characters to be treated as having strong left-to-right directionality.

Legacy encoding. Generally used to mean "any encoding other than Unicode." More specifically employed to refer to whatever encoding standard or standards were in use before Unicode.

Letter. (1) A single base character in an alphabetic or alphasyllabic writing system. Usually represents a single consonant or vowel sound (although in many alphabetic writing systems, vowel sounds are represented with diacritical marks). (2) In Unicode, a word used in many places (including the general categories) to refer to any character that makes up words and isn't a diacritical mark, whether that character is a "letter" in the traditional sense, a syllable, or an ideograph.

Letter number. A category containing characters that represent numeric values but have the form of one or more letters.

Letter–mark combination. A letter with one or more diacritical marks applied to it.

Level separator. A sentinel value used in collation keys to delimit the weight values for one level from the weight values for the next level. The value is usually lower than any of the weight values, so that shorter strings compare before longer strings. Level separators can be eliminated if the weight values for one level are disjoint from the weight values for the next level.

Lexical comparison. Alternate term for binary comparison.

LF. Line feed. A control function that signals the receiving equipment to advance the platen to the next line (on some systems, it also implies moving the carriage back to the home position). The LF character is used as the new-line function on some systems, particularly most UNIX-based systems and the Java programming language.

LI18NUX. Linux Internationalization Initiative. An offshoot of the Linux Standards Base movement which published a specification for the internationalization capabilities that should be included in a Linux implementation.

Ligature. (1) A single glyph that represents more than one character and is formed when a certain sequence of characters occurs in succession. A ligature often has a shape that is very different from the shapes of the component characters in isolation. (2) A glyph in a font file that is drawn when a certain sequence of two or more code point values occur together in the backing store. Note that these two definitions are not the same—a ligature in the normal sense may be drawn with two specially shaped glyph descriptions in certain fonts, and an accented letter may be drawn with a "ligature" in a font, even though an accented letter is not normally considered a "ligature."

Line break. The point in a piece of text where one line ends and another line begins.

Line-break property. A property applied to all Unicode characters that describes how they are to be treated as a line-breaking routine.

Line breaking. The process of dividing a piece of text into lines.

Line layout. The process of arranging a series of characters on a line of text.

Line separator. (1) A control function that signals the beginning of a new line, but not the beginning of a new paragraph. (2) The Unicode character, U+2028, intended to unambiguously represent this function.

Line starts array. An array that stores the offset in the backing store of the first character on each line of a piece of displayed text (or the number of code points in each line). Line breaking is the process of building the line starts array (or keeping it up to date as the text changes).

LineBreak.txt. The file in the Unicode Character Database that specifies each character's line-break property.

Linked list. A data structure that stores a sequence of values using a separate memory block for each value, with pointers from one memory block to the next.

Linux Standards Base. A specification that details a standard feature set for Linux implementations.

Little-endian. (1) A serialization format that sends and receives multiple-byte values with the least significant byte first. (2) A processor architecture that stores the least significant byte of a multibyte value lowest in memory.

Ll. The abbreviation used in the UnicodeData.txt file for the "lowercase letter" property.

Lm. The abbreviation used in the UnicodeData.txt file for the "modifier letter" property.

Lo. The abbreviation used in the UnicodeData.txt file for the "other letter" property.

Locale-dependent. Dependent on the language and dialect of the text, and often on the nationality of the person writing or reading the text. Collation behavior is locale-dependent.

Localization. The process of converting an application for use by a new user community. Localization involves not just translating any user-visible text, but also altering things such as pictures, color schemes, window layouts, and number, date, and time formats to match the cultural conventions of the new user community.

Logical character. Alternate term for grapheme cluster.

Logical order. The order in which the characters are pronounced and (usually) typed.

Logical selection. A selection that represents a contiguous range of code points in the backing store, but which may appear visually discontiguous.

Logical_Order_Exception. A property assigned to characters that in Unicode are stored in visual order rather than logical order. This property currently consists just of left-joining vowel signs in Thai and Lao.

Logograph. A character representing a single word. Sometimes used to describe Chinese characters.

Long s. An alternate glyph shape for the lowercase letter s that was used as a nonfinal form for the letter s in the eighteenth century. In handwritten text, it looks like an integral sign, and in printed text, it looks like the letter f.

Loop. A series of points in an outline describing a closed shape consisting of line and curve segments. A glyph description usually consists of one or more loops.

Low surrogate. A code unit value used to represent the second code unit in a surrogate pair, or the code point values corresponding to these code unit values. The low-surrogate range is from U+DC00 to U+DFFF.

Lowercase. In a bicameral script, the set of letters used to write most words.

Lowercase letter. The property given to lowercase letters in bicameral scripts.

LRE. Abbreviation for left-to-right embedding.

LRM. Abbreviation for left-to-right mark.

LRO. Abbreviation for left-to-right override.

LS. Abbreviation for line separator.

LSB. (1) Abbreviation for Linux Standards Base. (2) Abbreviation for "least significant bit" or "least significant byte."

Lt. Abbreviation used in the UnicodeData.txt file to represent the "titlecase letter" property.

LTRS. A control function in some old telegraphy codes that indicated to the receiving equipment that it should interpret succeeding code points as letters.

Lu. Abbreviation used in the UnicodeData.txt file to represent the "uppercase letter" property.

LZW. Lempel-Ziv-Welch. A general-purpose dictionary-based compression algorithm.

Macron. A line drawn above a vowel to indicate a long vowel sound.

Madda. A mark used with some Arabic letters to indicate a glottal stop.

Maiyamok. A mark used in Thai to indicate repetition of the syllable that precedes it.

Major version number. The part of the Unicode version number before the first decimal point. The major version number is incremented any time a new version of Unicode is published in book form.

Mark. A collection of Unicode general categories containing the various combining characters.

Markup. A higher-level protocol that uses certain sequences of characters to impose structure on the text or supplement it with additional information.

Maru. Alternate term for handakuten.

Mathematical symbol. A category containing symbols that are normally used in mathematical expressions.

MathML. Mathematical Markup Language. An XML-based file format for describing mathematical expressions.

Matra. Hindi name for dependent vowel

Medial form. The glyph shape used for a character when it occurs in the middle of a word, or for Arabic letters when it can connect to letters on both sides.

MICR. Magnetic Ink Character Recognition.

MIME. Multipurpose Internet Mail Extensions. A method of transmitting different data types in a standard RFC 822 mail message.

Minor version number. The second number in a Unicode version number. The minor version is updated whenever a new version of Unicode is issued that includes new characters or significant architectural changes, but isn't published in book form.

Mirrored. The property assigned to characters that have different glyph shapes when their resolved directionality is right-to-left than they have when their resolved directionality is left-to-right. The two glyph shapes are generally mirror images of each other, and often (but not always) mirrored characters come in pairs that can simply exchange glyphs in right-to-left text.

"Missing" glyph. A glyph that is drawn when the font doesn't have a glyph for a particular code point value.

Mkhedruli. The modern form of the Georgian alphabet.

Modifier letter. A spacing character that has no pronunciation of its own but changes the pronunciation of the preceding letter.

Modifier symbol. Similar to a modifier letter, but used for spacing clones of combining marks and other characters that aren't necessarily treated as letters.

Monospaced. Used to describe a font in which all characters are the same width.

Monosyllabic language. A language in which all of the words have only one syllable. Many Chinese and related languages are generally considered monosyllabic, although most of them do have some polysyllabic words.

Monotonic Greek. A simplified system of Greek spelling that went into effect in the 1970s and greatly simplified the use of diacritical marks with Greek letters.

Morse. Samuel Morse, who invented the telegraph in 1837.

Morse code. The code that was used to send text with Morse's telegraph (and is still used in certain applications today). It employed variable-length sequences of long and short signals to represent characters.

mort table. Abbreviation for glyph metamorphosis table.

Multilevel comparison. The process of comparing a pair of strings in multiple passes, where certain types of differences are significant only if no higher-level differences between the strings exist (for example, case differences count only if the strings are otherwise the same).

Murray. Donald Murray, who invented the first teletype machine around 1900.

Muusikatoan. A Khmer mark that converts a second-series consonant to the first-series consonant.

Name. A property given to each character that identifies it and attempts to convey something about its meaning or use.

NamesList.html. A file in the Unicode Character Database that describes the NamesList.txt file.

NamesList.txt. A file in the Unicode Character Database that is used to produce the code charts in the Unicode standard. It lists all of the characters by name, along with a variety of annotations.

Narrow. A property assigned to all characters that are implicitly half-width. Characters of neutral or ambiguous East Asian width resolve as narrow when used in Western typography.

Nasalization. Pronouncing a vowel sound with the nasal passage open. The first and last vowel sounds in the French phrase *en passant* are nasalized.

National Committee on Information Technology Standards. A U.S. standards body specializing in information technology standards. NCITS acts as an umbrella organization for various information-technology-related ANSI working groups, including L2, the group responsible for representing the American position to WG2.

National digit shapes. A deprecated invisible formatting character that causes the code point values in the ASCII range that represent digits to represent the native digits for the current language (usually Arabic) rather than the European digits they normally represent.

National-use character. (1) A code point value in ISO 646 (and some other encoding standards) that may represent a different character in different countries (i.e., different countries can have their own versions of ISO 646 that can be different from the International Reference Version and still conform to the standard). (2) A character represented by a national-use code point value.

NBSP. Abbreviation for non-breaking space.

NCITS. Abbreviation for National Committee on Information Technology Standards.

NCR. Abbreviation for numeric character reference.

Nd. The abbreviation used in the UnicodeData.txt file for the "decimal-digit number" general category.

NEL. New line. A character in the C1 space (and in EBCDIC) used on some systems to represent the new-line function.

Nestorian. One of the modern writing styles of the Syriac alphabet.

Neutral directionality. No inherent directionality. A character with neutral directionality takes on the directionality of the surrounding characters.

New-line function. A control function that indicates the end of a line of text and the beginning of a new line. Depending on the application, the new-line function may also indicate the beginning of a new paragraph.

NFC. Abbreviation for Normalized Form C.

NFC_MAYBE. A derived property assigned to characters that may occur in Normalized Form C, but only in certain contexts. If a string contains NFC_MAYBE characters and no MFC_NO characters, extra analysis must be done to determine whether it is, in fact, in Normalized Form C.

NFC_NO. A derived property assigned to characters that may not occur in Normalized Form C.

NFD. Abbreviation for Normalized Form D.

NFD_NO. A derived property assigned to characters that may not occur in Normalized Form D.

NFKC. Abbreviation for Normalized Form KC.

NFKC_MAYBE. A derived property assigned to characters that may occur in Normalized Form KC, but only in certain contexts. If a string contains NFKC_MAYBE characters and no NFKC_NO characters, extra analysis must be done to determine whether it is, in fact, in Normalized Form KC.

NFKC_NO. A derived property assigned to characters that may not occur in Normalized Form KC.

NFKD. Abbreviation for Normalized Form KD.

NFKD_NO. A derived property assigned to characters that may not occur in Normalized Form KD.

Nigori. Alternate term for dakuten.

Nikahit. A Khmer sign used to indicate nasalization.

Nl. Abbreviation used in the UnicodeData.txt file to represent the "letter number" general category.

NL. Alternate term for NEL.

NLF. Abbreviation for new-line function.

No. Abbreviation used in the UnicodeData.txt file for the "other number" general category.

Nominal digit shapes. A deprecated invisible formatting character used to cancel the effects of the national digit shapes character.

Non-breaking character. A character that prevents a line break from happening before or after it. It "glues" the characters before and after it together on one line.

Non-breaking hyphen. A hyphen with non-breaking semantics.

Non-breaking space. A space with non-breaking semantics.

Nonce form. A character coined for an ad hoc use in one particular paper or situation. This term is usually applied to rare Chinese characters or mathematical symbols.

Noncharacter. A code point value that is specifically defined never to represent a character (it is different from a private-use character). Noncharacter code point values are set aside for internal application use (as sentinel values, for example) and should never appear in interchanged Unicode text.

Noncharacter_Code_Point. The property assigned to all noncharacter code points.

Noncognate rule. Two similar-looking ideographs that would be unified based on glyph shape alone aren't unified if they have different meanings and etymological histories.

Noninflecting language. A language where the forms of words don't change depending on their grammatical context. Some Chinese languages are generally noninflecting.

Non-joiner. See *zero-width non-joiner*.

Non-joining letter. An Arabic or Syriac letter that does not connect cursively to the letters on either side.

Non-spacing mark. A combining character that takes up no space along the baseline. Non-spacing marks usually are drawn above or below the base character or overlay it.

Nonstarter decomposition. A decomposition that consists entirely of combining marks. Nonstarter decompositions are not allowed in Normalized Form C.

Normalization. The process of converting a piece of Unicode text to one of the Unicode Normalized Forms; the process of converting a sequence of Unicode code points that has other equivalent sequences to one particular equivalent sequence according to rules that dictate which sequences are preferred. Strings that are different but should be considered equivalent can be compared by normalizing them first (the normalized versions will be identical).

Normalization form. Alternate term for normalized form.

NormalizationTest.txt. A file in the Unicode Character Database that can be used to determine whether an implementation of Unicode normalization conforms to the standard.

Normalized form. One of four transformations on Unicode text, each of which converts all equivalent sequences of characters to a single preferred representation. The four Unicode normalized forms do so, however, according to different criteria.

Normalized Form C. A Unicode normalized form that prefers canonical composites over combining character sequences when possible. Combining character sequences are converted entirely to canonical composites or, if that isn't possible, to the shortest equivalent combining character sequence. Certain canonical composites, such as those with singleton decompositions, those with nonstarter decompositions, and those that aren't generally used in certain scripts, are prohibited from appearing in Normalized Form C.

Normalized Form D. A Unicode normalized form that disallows canonical composites. Canonical composites are replaced with their canonical decompositions, and combining character sequences are arranged into canonical order.

Normalized Form KC. A Unicode normalized form that disallows compatibility composites, but prefers canonical composites over combining character sequences when possible.

Normalized Form KD. A Unicode normalized form that disallows both canonical and compatibility composites. Canonical composites are replaced with their canonical decompositions, compatibility composites are replaced with their compatibility decompositions, and combining character sequences are arranged into canonical order.

Normative. Used to describe specifications and descriptions in a standard that must be followed to conform to the standard.

Nukta. A dot applied to letters in some Indic scripts, usually to create extra letters to write languages other than the language for which the script was originally created.

NULL. A control character that is intended to have no effect, represented with the all-bits-off code point value. Some programming languages and systems, such as C, treat NULL as a noncharacter code point signaling the end of a string.

Null consonant. A letter representing the absence of a consonant sound. Typically used as a base to which vowel marks are applied to represent word-initial vowel sounds or the second vowel sounds in diphthongs.

Null vowel. A vowel mark representing the absence of a vowel sound after a particular consonant. A virama can be considered a special kind of null vowel.

Number. (1) A property assigned to Unicode characters that are generally used to represent numeric values. (2) A numeric value.

Numeral. The written representation of a numeric value, which may consist of one or more characters.

Numeric character reference. A sequence of characters in XML or some other markup language that together represent a single Unicode code point by its code point value. In XML, a numeric character reference takes the form Ӓ.

Numeric value. A property assigned to digits and numerals that specifies the numeric value they represent.

Nuskhuri. An older style of Georgian writing used in ecclesiastical texts.

Nyis shad. A Tibetan punctuation mark analogous to the Indic double danda and used to mark a change in topic.

Object replacement character. A special Unicode character used to mark the position of an embedded object in a stream of Unicode text. This character should normally not occur in Unicode text for interchange—the function is best left to a markup language such as HTML—but is useful as an implementation detail, where it can provide an implementation with a character in the text to which to attach information about the embedded object.

OCR. Optical Character Recognition.

Off-curve point. A point in a loop in an outline font that defines the shape of a curve segment.

Ogonek. A hook-like mark that is attached to the bottom of some vowels in some languages to indicate a change in pronunciation.

On-curve point. A point in a loop in an outline font that defines the beginning of a curve or line segment and the end of another curve or line segment.

Onomatopoeia. A word whose pronunciation resembles the sound that the word describes. "Crash" is an example of onomatopoeia.

Opening punctuation. Alternate name for starting punctuation.

OpenType. An advanced font file format backed by Adobe and Microsoft.

Optical alignment. Adjusting the positions of characters along a margin so that they appear to line up. (If the leftmost pixels of a straight character like an H are aligned with the leftmost pixels of a round character like an O, they actually don't appear to line up. Instead, the O must be shifted slightly to the left.)

Orthographic syllable. A group of characters in an Indic script that corresponds roughly to a spoken syllable. The letters in an orthographic syllable don't necessarily match the sounds in a spoken syllable: A consonant sound that is spoken at the end of one syllable is actually written at the beginning of the next orthographic syllable. For example, the "n" in "Hindi" is at the end of the first spoken syllable but at the beginning of the second orthographic syllable. An Indic orthographic syllable is one kind of grapheme cluster.

Other letter. The category assigned to the majority of "letter" characters in Unicode, including syllables, ideographs, and uncased letters.

Other number. The category assigned to all Unicode characters that represent numeric values but can't be used as digits in positional notation.

Other punctuation. The category assigned to all Unicode punctuation that doesn't fit into one of the more specific punctuation categories (generally all punctuation, other than dashes and hyphens, that doesn't come in pairs).

Other symbol. The category assigned to all Unicode symbols (the majority) that don't fit into one of the more specific symbol categories (generally, all symbols that aren't math or currency symbols and aren't used to modify another character).

Other_Alphabetic. A property assigned to the characters with the Alphabetic property that can't be determined algorithmically (certain categories of character, such as cased letters, automatically have the Alphabetic property).

Other_Default_Ignorable_Code_Point. A property assigned to the characters with the Default Ignorable Code Point property that can't be determined algorithmically (certain categories of characters, such as formatting characters, automatically have the Default Ignorable Code Point property).

Other_Grapheme_Extend. A property assigned to the characters with the Grapheme_Extend property that can't be determined algorithmically (certain categories of characters, such as non-spacing marks, have this property automatically).

Other_Lowercase. A property assigned to the characters with the Lowercase property (generally symbols made up of lowercase letters) that aren't in the Lowercase Letter general category.

Other_Math. A property assigned to all characters with the Mathematical property that don't belong to the Mathematical Symbols general category.

Other_Uppercase. A property assigned to the characters with the Uppercase property (generally symbols made up of uppercase letters) that aren't in the Uppercase Letter general category.

Outline font. Any font technology whose glyph descriptions take the form of abstract descriptions of the ideal character shape rather than bitmapped images of the glyphs.

Out-of-band information. Information about a piece of text that is stored in a separate data structure (such as a style run array) from the characters themselves.

Oxia. Greek name for the acute accent.

Pair table. A two-dimensional table used in boundary analysis. Each axis is indexed by character or character category, and the cells of the table say whether (or under which conditions) a boundary separates those two characters (or characters belonging to those two categories).

Paired punctuation. Punctuation marks that come in matched pairs and mark the beginning and end of some range of text. Parentheses and quotation marks are examples of paired punctuation.

Paiyannoi. A Thai mark used to indicate elision of letters.

Palatalization. Modifying a consonant by ending it with the back of the tongue pressed toward the roof of the mouth, or beginning a vowel with the tongue in that position. English speakers tend to think of palatalization as inserting a *y* sound between a consonant and a vowel. The scraping sound at the beginning of "Houston" is a palatalized *h*.

Pamudpod. The Hanunóo virama.

Paragraph separator. The Unicode character, U+2029, that marks the boundary between two paragraphs. In many applications, the underlying system's new-line function is treated as a paragraph separator.

Pc. The abbreviation used in the UnicodeData.txt file to represent the "connector punctuation" general category.

Pd. The abbreviation used in the UnicodeData.txt file to represent the "dash punctuation" general category.

PDF. (1) Abbreviation for pop directional formatting. (2) Portable Document Format.

PDUTR. Abbreviation for Proposed Draft Unicode Technical Report.

PDUTR #25. A proposed Unicode technical report describing how Unicode should represent mathematical expressions.

PDUTR #28. The proposed Unicode technical report specifying Unicode 3.2.

Pe. The abbreviation used in the UnicodeData.txt file to represent the "ending punctuation" general category.

Perispomeni. The Greek circumflex accent (which actually may look like a circumflex or tilde depending on type style).

Pf. The abbreviation used in the UnicodeData.txt file to represent the "final-quote punctuation" general category.

Phonetic. A component of a Chinese character that supplies an approximate idea of the word's pronunciation.

Pi. The abbreviation used in the UnicodeData.txt file to represent the "initial-quote punctuation" general category.

Pictograph. A character that represents the word for an object by depicting the object pictorially.

Pinyin. A system for writing Mandarin Chinese words using Latin letters and digits, designed and promulgated by the Chinese government.

Place-value notation. Alternate term for positional notation.

Plain text. Pure text with no accompanying meta-data, such as formatting information, hyperlinks, or embedded nontext elements. Plain text is generally considered to be the minimal amount of information necessary to render a piece of text legibly (i.e., the written characters themselves, plus an extremely small amount of extra information necessary to render those characters legibly).

Plane. A particular range of code point values in a coded character set's encoding space. Usually if an encoding space is divided into several kinds of divisions (such as planes, rows, and columns), the plane is the largest such division. In Unicode, a plane is a range of 65,536 contiguous code point values whose first five bits (out of 21) are the same. These first five bits are considered to be the "plane number."

Plane 0. In Unicode, the range of code point values from U+0000 to U+FFFF. This Basic Multilingual Plane is the range of code points assigned to the characters of all modern writing systems (except for some relatively rare Chinese characters).

Plane 1. In Unicode, the range of code point values from U+10000 to U+1FFFF. This Supplementary Multilingual Plane is the range of code points assigned to various characters from historical (i.e., obsolete) writing systems and to various symbols that have fairly specialized uses.

Plane 2. In Unicode, the range of code point values from U+20000 to U+2FFFF. This Supplementary Ideograph Plane is the range of code point values assigned to a wide variety of less common Chinese characters.

Plane 14. In Unicode, the range of code point values from U+E0000 to U+EFFFF. This Supplementary Special-Purpose Plane is the range of code point values assigned to a number of special-purpose characters.

Platen. The rubber roller that paper is wrapped around in a typewriter or teletype machine.

Po. The abbreviation used in the UnicodeData.txt file for the "other punctuation" general category.

Point. Any vowel mark or diacritical mark used in Hebrew or Arabic.

Pointed Hebrew. Hebrew written with most or all of the points (which are generally optional and omitted most of the time).

Polytonic Greek. The older system of Greek spelling, which includes a complicated system of diacritical marks.

Pop directional formatting. A special Unicode character that terminates the effect of the most recent explicit override character or explicit embedding character in the text.

Positional notation. The practice of writing a numeric value using a small number of characters whose values are determined by their positions in the numeral. In a decimal integer, the rightmost digit is a multiple of 1, the next digit to the left is a multiple of 10, and the digits to the left represent multiples of progressively higher powers of 10.

Post-composition version characters. Canonical composites that are in the composition exclusion list because they were added to Unicode after Unicode 3.0, the version of Unicode on which Normalized Form C is based.

PostScript. A page description language and a collection of font formats developed by Adobe Corporation. The PostScript outline format is one of two outline formats supported by OpenType.

Precomposed character. Alternate term for composite character.

Precomposed Hangul syllable. One of the Unicode code points representing a whole Hangul syllable. The precomposed Hangul syllables are all canonical composites and have canonical decompositions to sequences of conjoining Hangul jamo.

Presentation form. (1) The glyph shape used for a character in a particular situation. (2) A code point representing a particular glyph shape for a character that can have more than one glyph shape. Presentation forms are compatibility characters, and are generally compatibility composites with compatibility decompositions to the code points representing the character irrespective of glyph shape.

Primary key. The main field by which records are sorted. If two records' primary keys are equal, the secondary key determines the order.

Primary source standard. One of the main sources of characters for Unicode, and one of the encoding standards for which it was deemed important to maintain round-trip compability.

Primary weight. The weight value that is compared first in a multilevel comparison. Only if two strings' primary weights are all the same are secondary weights compared. In a typical sort order (and in the UCA default sort order), different primary weights are assigned to code points that are considered to represent different characters. For example, "a" and "b" have different primary weights.

Primary-level difference. A difference in the primary weights of two collation keys (or the corresponding difference in the original strings).

Printing character. A character with a visible glyph. The term is usually used to distinguish code points that represent actual written characters from code points that represent control functions (control characters) or that alter the appearance or treatment of surrounding characters (formatting characters).

Private Use Area. A range of code points whose meaning is purposely unstandardized. The code points in the Private Use Area are available for ad hoc use by users and applications, which can assign any meaning desired to them. In Unicode, the Private Use Area runs from U+E000 to U+F8FF and is supplemented by two Private Use Planes.

Private-use character. Alternate term for private-use code point.

Private-use code point. A code point whose meaning is purposely unstandardized. In Unicode, the private-use code point values are collected together in the Private Use Area and Private Use Planes.

Private-use high surrogate. A surrogate code unit value that serves as the high-surrogate value for code points in the Private Use Planes. The private-use high surrogates run from U+DB80 to U+DBFF.

Private Use Planes. One of two planes of the Unicode encoding space set aside as extensions of the Private Use Area. The two Private Use Planes are plane 15, which runs from U+F0000 to U+FFFFF, and Plane 16, which runs from U+100000 to U+10FFFF.

PropertyAliases.txt. A file in the Unicode Character Database that gives short and long names for all of the Unicode character properties, for use in regular expression syntax, for example.

PropertyValueAliases.txt. A file in the Unicode Character Database that gives short and long names for all possible values for many of the Unicode character properties (numeric and Boolean values are left out, for obvious reasons), for use in regular expression syntax, for example.

PropList.html. A file in the Unicode Character Database that describes the various properties listed in PropList.txt.

PropList.txt. A file in the Unicode Character Database that lists a large number of character properties and the characters that have each of them.

Proportionally spaced. Used to describe a font in which the glyphs have different widths, generally corresponding to the relative widths of the characters in handwritten text.

Proposed Draft Unicode Technical Report. A Unicode Technical Report that has been published while still in draft form. Unlike a Draft Unicode Technical Report, where the general content has been agreed upon in principle, everything about a Proposed Draft Technical Report remains in flux. Unicode Technical Reports carry no normative force while still in draft form.

Prosgegrammeni. A small iota written after some capital vowels in ancient Greek to represent certain diphthongs.

Ps. The abbreviation used in the UnicodeData.txt file for the "starting punctuation" general category.

PS. Abbreviation for Paragraph Separator.

Psili. The Greek "smooth-breathing mark," which indicates the absence of an *h* sound at the beginning of a word.

PUA. Abbreviation for Private Use Area.

Punctuation. The property assigned to all Unicode characters that are used as punctuation marks.

Quotation_Mark. The property assigned to all Unicode characters that are used as quotation marks.

Quoted-printable. A transfer encoding syntax that encodes generic binary data as ASCII text. Byte values corresponding to most ASCII printing characters are represented with those characters; other byte values are represented with a sequence of ASCII characters that contains the spelled-out hexadecimal byte value. This transfer encoding syntax is generally used to represent text in an ASCII-based encoding, such as UTF-8 or ISO 8859-1, in an RFC 822 message.

Radical. (1) The component of a Chinese character by which it is classified in dictionaries. Usually the radical is thought to convey an idea of the meaning of the character. (2) The main consonant in a Tibetan syllable. (3) A component of a Yi syllable by which it is classified in dictionaries. (4) The property assigned to Unicode code points that represent Chinese radicals.

Rafe. A diacritical mark used in Hebrew.

ReadMe.txt. A file in the Unicode Character Database that provides important background and overview information on the database.

Reahmuk. A Khmer mark that indicates a glottal stop.

Rebus. A method of writing words that uses pictures of objects to represent the sounds of those object's names.

Regular expression. An expression in some structured syntax (many regular expression languages exist) that describes a pattern of characters. If a sequence of characters fits the pattern, it is said to "match" the regular expression. Regular expression matching enables complicated searches on text.

Rendering. The process of converting a sequence of code unit values in memory to a visible sequence of glyphs on some output device, such as the computer's screen or a printer.

Rendering process. The software responsible for converting a series of code units in memory to a series of visible glyphs on an output device. The rendering process encompasses breaking the text into pages and lines, choosing appropriate glyphs for each character, arranging those glyphs on a line, and drawing the glyph images on the output device. The software usually encompasses both system software and logic in the font files themselves.

Repertoire. See *Abstract character repertoire*.

Repetition mark. A mark that indicates that the preceding character, syllable, or word should be repeated.

Repha. In Devanagari and a few other Indic scripts, the form that the letter ra takes when it's the first letter in a conjunct consonant. This hook-shaped mark attaches to the top of the last consonant in the conjunct.

Replacement character. A Unicode character intended to stand in for an otherwise unrepresentable character. It's usually emitted by character code converters when they encounter an illegal sequence of code units or a character that can't be represented in Unicode.

Representative glyph. The glyph shape shown for a character in the Unicode standard's code charts. As the name suggests, the glyph is chosen to clarify to the reader which character a code point is supposed to represent; it's generally not the only glyph shape possible for the character, nor is it necessarily even the *preferred* glyph shape. Representative glyphs have no normative force.

Reserved. Set aside for future standardization. For example, all unassigned code point values (except for those in the Private Use Area) are reserved— the Unicode Technical Committee reserves for itself the right to make future character assignments to these code point values, and they are not free for other uses in the meantime.

Resolved directionality. The directionality that a character of neutral directionality takes on by virtue of its position in the text. For example, if a neutral character is preceded and followed by left-to-right characters, its resolved directionality is left-to-right.

RFC. Request for Comments. A document published by the IETF that is intended to become a standard at some point. Because documents tend to stay in RFC form for a long time, many become de facto standards well before they are approved as real standards, and those that do become actual IETF standards tend to continue to be referred to by their RFC number even after their official publication as standards.

RFC 822. An IETF standard that specifies a standard format for text messages, such as e-mail and Usenet messages. Mail messages on the Internet are almost always in RFC 822 format. Because RFC 822 is an ASCII-based format that requires explicit line breaks between the lines of a message, today most mail messages are sent in a format, such as MIME, that can encode much richer content within the framework of an RFC 822 text message.

Rhotacization. Pronouncing a vowel with the tongue curled upward. In American English, it is generally thought of as following the vowel with an *r* sound. The *a* in "car," as spoken by most Americans, is a rhotacized *a*.

Rich text. Text with accompanying meta-data, such as formatting information, language information, or embedded nontext objects.

Right-joining letter. An Arabic or Syriac letter that can connect to a character to its right, but not a character to its left.

Right-joining vowel. A dependent vowel in an Indic writing system that attaches to the right-hand side of the consonant it modifies.

Right-to-left embedding. An explicit embedding character that starts a new embedding level with left-to-right directionality.

Right-to-left mark. An invisible character with strong right-to-left directionality. This character can be used to alter the resolved directionality of neutral-directionality characters.

Right-to-left override. An explicit override character that causes all of the following characters to be treated as strong left-to-right characters.

RLE. Abbreviation for right-to-left embedding.

RLM. Abbreviation for right-to-left mark.

RLO. Abbreviation for right-to-left override.

Romaji. The Japanese term for Japanese written with Latin letters.

Romanization. Transliteration to Latin letters, particularly transliteration of languages that use Chinese characters to Latin letters. Pinyin is a system of romanization.

Rough-breathing mark. Alternate term for dasia.

Round-trip compatibility. The ability to perform some transformation, followed by its inverse, and end with the original data in its original form. Two encodings are said to have round-trip compatibility if you can convert from one to the other and back to the first without losing data. Unicode includes a number of characters specifically to make this guarantee with respect to some source encoding.

Ruby. Japanese term for interlinear annotation.

Run array. A data structure that associates information with contiguous sequences of records in some other data structure (such as a sequence of characters in a character array).

Run-length encoding. A data compression technique that compresses sequences of repeating values by storing the repeating value or pattern once, accompanied by a repeat count.

SAM. Abbreviation for Syriac abbreviation mark.

Sc. The abbreviation used in the UnicodeData.txt file for the "currency symbol" general category.

SC2. Subcommittee #2 of ISO/IEC Joint Technical Committee #1, which is responsible for international coded-character-set standards. WG2, which is responsible for ISO 10646, is a working group of SC2.

Script. Alternate term for writing system.

Scripts.txt. A file in the Unicode Character Database that identifies the script to which each character in Unicode belongs.

SCSU. Standard Compression Scheme for Unicode. A technique for compressing Unicode text that is backward compatible with ISO 8859-1 and allows text encoded with Unicode to be stored in roughly the same amount of space as it would occupy if encoded with an appropriate legacy encoding.

Second-series consonants. Khmer consonants that carry an inherent *o* sound.

Secondary key. A key that is used to determine the sorted order of two records only if their primary keys are the same.

Secondary weight. The weight value that is compared in the second pass of a multilevel comparison. Differences in secondary weights are significant in a comparison only if the primary weights are all the same. In most sort orders, differences in secondary weight correspond to variants of the same letter, such as the letter with different accents applied to it. For example, a and ä typically have the same primary weight but different secondary weights. Note that this feature is language-specific: In languages such as Swedish, where ä is a different letter, a and ä have different primary weights.

Secondary-level difference. A difference in the secondary weights of two collation keys, or the corresponding difference in the strings from which they were created.

Separator. A property given to characters that mark divisions between units of text. Three separator categories exist: the line and paragraph separators, which are each categories unto themselves, and a third category containing all of the spaces.

Serialization format. Alternate term for character encoding scheme.

Series-shifter. The Khmer muusikatoan and triisap characters, which change a consonant from one series to the other.

Serto. One of the modern writing styles of the Syriac alphabet.

Shad. A Tibetan punctuation mark analogous to the Devanagari danda that indicates the end of an expression.

Shadda. A mark written over an Arabic letter to indicate consonant gemination.

Sheva. A Hebrew point used to indicate the absence of a vowel sound after a letter.

Shifted. An alternate-weighting setting in the Unicode Collation Algorithm that causes strings with ignorable characters in analogous positions to sort together.

Shift-JIS. A character encoding scheme that represents characters from the JIS X 0201 and JIS X 0208 standards with various one- and two-byte combinations.

Shift-trimmed. An alternate-weighting setting in the Unicode Collation Algorithm that causes strings with ignorable characters in analogous positions to sort together.

Shin dot. A dot drawn over the leftmost tine of the Hebrew letter shin to indicate it has a *sh* sound.

SHY. Abbreviation for soft hyphen.

Simplified Chinese. A method of writing Chinese that uses simplified (sometimes greatly simplified) versions of many of the Chinese characters. This method is used today in most of the People's Republic of China and in Singapore.

Sin dot. A dot drawn over the rightmost tine of the Hebrew letter shin to indicate it has a *s* sound.

Singleton decomposition. A canonical decomposition consisting of a single character, or a canonical composite with a one-character decomposition. Singleton decompositions are generally variants of characters that are included elsewhere in Unicode and disunified for round-trip compatibility with some other standard. These variants are effectively discouraged from normal use by prohibiting their appearance in any of the Unicode normalized forms.

SIP. Abbreviation for Supplementary Ideographic Plane.

Sk. The abbreviation used in the UnicodeData.txt file for the "modifier symbol" general category.

Slur. A musical marking that indicates that two or more notes should be played with no separation between them.

Sm. The abbreviation used in the UnicodeData.txt file for the "mathematical symbol" general category.

Small. When used to talk about a letter in a bicameral script, a synonym for lowercase.

Smooth-breathing mark. Alternate term for psili.

SMP. Abbreviation for Supplementary Multilingual Plane.

So. The abbreviation used in the UnicodeData.txt file for the "other symbol" general category.

Soft hyphen. A code point that indicates to a text-rendering process a location where a word can be hyphenated. When a soft hyphen appears immediately before a line break, it is rendered as a regular hyphen; otherwise, the soft hyphen is invisible.

Soft sign. A Cyrillic letter used to indicate palatalization in a location where it isn't otherwise implied by the spelling.

Soft_Dotted. A property assigned to characters whose glyphs include a dot that usually disappears when a diacritical mark is applied. The lowercase i and j and their variants, whose dots go away when an accent is applied (for example, in "naïve"), have this property. (In a few languages, such as Lithuanian, the dot doesn't disappear—this character is represented with a specific combining-dot character following the i; case mappings then have to take care to add or remove the combining dot when appropriate.)

Sort key. Alternate term for collation key.

Source separation rule. Two characters that are disunified in one of Unicode's primary source standards will also be disunified in Unicode, even if they would otherwise be unified.

Space separator. The general category assigned to all of the space characters in Unicode, except for a few that explicitly have non-breaking semantics.

SpecialCasing.txt. A file in the Unicode Character Database that lists complex case mappings. For historical reasons, simple one-to-one case mappings reside in UnicodeData.txt; case mappings that are specific to certain languages, happen only in certain contexts, or result in a single character turning into two or more are listed in SpecialCasing.txt.

Split caret. In a text-editing application, an insertion point marking a position in the backing store that corresponds to two positions in the rendered text. Generally, an insertion point is drawn at both positions in the rendered text, often with a tick mark or arrow that indicates where different kinds of text will go if the user enters more text. Split carets appear at the boundaries of directional runs.

Split vowel. An Indic dependent vowel with components that appear on two different sides (such as both the left- and right-hand sides, or above and to the right) of the consonant modified. Often, but not always, the two components of a split vowel are vowels in their own right, used in combination to represent another vowel sound.

SSP. Abbreviation for Supplementary Special-Purpose Plane.

StandardizedVariants.html. A file in the Unicode Character Database that lists all combinations of a regular Unicode character and a variation selector that are legal and the exact glyph shape each combination should produce.

Starting punctuation. A category of characters that mark the beginning of some range of text, such as a parenthetical expression or a quotation.

State machine. A function that remembers things from invocation to invocation. A state machine can produce different outputs for the same input, as its behavior depends not only on the current input, but also on some number of previous inputs.

State table. A state machine implemented as an array. The function looks up a new state and perhaps an action based on the current state and the input value.

Stateful. When applied to an encoding scheme, a term indicating that the interpretation of particular code unit values can vary depending on which code unit values have been seen earlier in the text stream. The term typically doesn't refer to variable-length encoding schemes such as UTF-8, where several code units following a well-defined syntax are used to represent a single code point, but rather to schemes such as SCSU, ISO 2022, or the old Baudot code. In those schemes, one may have to scan backward an arbitrary distance (perhaps even to the beginning of the text stream) to know with certainty how a particular arbitrary byte in the middle of the stream should be interpreted.

Stem. The vertical stroke in the middle of most Devanagari consonants that represents the core of the syllable and usually disappears when the consonant is part of a conjunct.

STIX. Scientific and Technical Information Exchange. A consortium of experts on mathematical typesetting that has derived a standard set of mathematical symbols.

Storage format. Alternate term for character encoding form.

Strong directionality. Directionality sufficient to terminate an embedding level and to affect the resolved directionality of neutral-directionality characters. A sequence of strong-directionality characters placed into a sequence of characters of the opposite directionality will cause that sequence to be split into separate directional runs at the same embedding level. Compare *weak directionality*.

Style run. A contiguous sequence of characters with the same styling information.

Styled text. Alternate term for rich text.

SUB. Substitute. The ASCII control character (0x1A) that marks the position of an otherwise-unrepresentable character. The ASCII equivalent of Unicode's REPLACEMENT CHARACTER.

Subjoined consonant. In Tibetan, a consonant that occurs in a stack somewhere other than at the top. As Tibetan lacks a virama, consonant stacks are represented as a regular consonant followed by one or more subjoined consonants.

Sukun. The Thaana null-vowel character.

Supervisory code. Alternate term for control character used in FIELDATA and some other early encoding standards.

Supplementary Ideographic Plane. Alternate name for plane 2.

Supplementary Multilingual Plane. Alternate name for plane 1.

Supplementary planes. All of the planes in the Unicode encoding space except for the Basic Multilingual Plane.

Supplementary Special-Purpose Plane. Alternate name for plane 14.

Surrogate. (1) A code unit in UTF-16 that is half of the UTF-16 representation of a supplementary-plane character. In UTF-16, supplementary-plane characters are represented as a sequence of two code units, a high surrogate followed by a low surrogate. (2) A code point value in the range U+D800 to U+DFFF, corresponding to the surrogate code unit. (3) The general category assigned to code point values in the surrogate range.

Surrogate mechanism. The practice of representing supplementary-plane characters using pairs of code unit values from the surrogate range; now part of UTF-16.

Surrogate pair. A sequence of two UTF-16 code units from the surrogate range—a high surrogate followed by a low surrogate—used together to represent characters in the supplementary planes.

Surrogates Area. The range of the Unicode encoding space running from U+D800 to U+0FFF and set aside as unassigned and reserved.

Suzhou numerals. A collection of commercial numerals used in parts of China and Japan.

SVG. Scalable Vector Graphics. An XML-based format for describing object-based graphics.

Syllabary. A writing system whose characters represent whole syllables. In a true syllabary, the characters representing syllables cannot be further decomposed into components representing individual sounds.

Syllable cluster. Alternate term for orthographic syllable.

Symbol. A group of general categories containing symbols and other miscellaneous characters.

Symbols Area. The part of the Unicode encoding space running from U+2000 to U+2E7F and containing various punctuation marks and symbols.

Symmetric swapping. Alternate name for mirroring (i.e., the process of using mirror-image glyphs for characters with the "mirrored" property when they appear in right-to-left text). Two deprecated characters turn this behavior on and off.

Syriac abbreviation mark. A special character used with Syriac to indicate abbreviations. Syriac abbreviations are denoted with a bar drawn above the characters in the abbreviation. The Syriac abbreviation mark has no appearance of its own, but indicates to the rendering process that an abbreviation bar should be drawn over every character from the next character to the end of the word.

T source. Collective name for the various sources of ideographs submitted to the IRG by the Taiwanese national body.

Tag. Some sort of meta-information (such as a language tag) represented in Unicode plain text with tag characters.

Tag characters. A group of special characters that are invisible but can be used to place information about the text into the plain-text stream along with the text itself. Currently, Unicode supports only language tagging (using the tag characters to mark certain ranges of text as being in a particular language). Use of the tag characters is strongly discouraged in favor of higher-level protocols such as XML.

Tailoring. A set of modifications to the default behavior of a process, usually to adapt its behavior to the requirements of a particular language. The

Unicode Collation Algorithm provides a tailoring syntax to let you change the default sort order to a language-specific one, and the Unicode standard allows for tailoring of the rules for finding grapheme cluster boundaries, although no formalized syntax exists for this purpose yet.

Tate-chu-yoko. Japanese for "horizontal in vertical." The practice of setting two or more characters horizontally in a single display cell in vertical Asian text.

Tatweel. Alternate term for kashida.

TCVN 5712. The Vietnamese national character encoding standard.

Technical report. See Unicode Technical Report.

Teh marbuta. A special form of the Arabic letter teh used to write feminine endings.

Telegraph. An electrical device for sending and receiving written communication over long distances.

Telegraphy code. An encoding scheme used to represent text in the communication link between two telegraphs.

Teletype. A kind of telegraph where text being received is output as printed characters on a piece of paper and (usually) the text being sent is entered into the machine with a typewriter keyboard.

Terminal_Punctuation. A property assigned to punctuation marks used at the end of a sentence or clause.

Ternary tree. A linked data structure consisting of individual nodes that are arranged in a hierarchy and where each node points to no more than three other nodes.

Tertiary weight. The weight value that is compared in the third pass of a multilevel comparison. Differences in tertiary weights are significant in a comparison only if both the primary and secondary weights are the same. In most sort orders, differences in tertiary weight correspond to case differences or to differences between characters whose compatibility decompositions are the same.

Tertiary-level difference. A difference in the tertiary weights of two collation keys, or the corresponding difference in the original strings. For example, the strings "HELLO" and "Hello" have a tertiary-level difference at the second character position.

TEX. A computer language for describing typeset text, used especially for mathematical and technical typesetting.

Text rendering process. See *rendering process.*

Thanthakhat. A mark sometimes used in Thai to mark a silent letter.

Tie. A marking that connects two musical notes together and indicates that they should be played as a single note with the combined value of the two tied notes.

Tilde. A diacritical mark that looks like a sideways s drawn above a letter.

Tippi. The Gurmukhi candrabindu.

TIS 620. The Thai national encoding standard.

Titlecase letter. The property given to single Unicode code points representing digraphs where the first letter in the digraph is uppercase and the second is lowercase (for all other characters, "titlecase" is equivalent to "uppercase").

Tonal language. A spoken language where the pitch of the voice (or the change in pitch of the voice) is a significant component of pronunciation, such that a change in voice pitch or pitch contour by itself can turn a word into a different word. Many Asian and African languages are tonal languages.

Tone letter. A spacing character that indicates the tone of the preceding letter in the written form of a tonal language.

Tone mark. A diacritical mark that indicates the vocal pitch contour with which a letter or syllable should be spoken.

Tonos. The accent mark used in monotonic Greek.

Top-joining vowel. An Indic dependent vowel that joins to the top of the consonant it modifies.

Tracking. Widening a line of text by adding extra space between all characters.

Traditional Chinese. Chinese written using the more complicated traditional forms of the characters. The term is typically used to draw a distinction with Simplified Chinese. Traditional Chinese is used in Taiwan and Hong Kong, among other places.

Transfer encoding syntax. A transformation applied to a sequence of bytes being transmitted or stored, usually for compression or to fit the constraints of a communication protocol. Base64 and quoted-printable are examples.

Translation. Converting a particular series of thoughts expressed in one language to the same series of thoughts expressed in another language.

Transliteration. (1) Converting text in a particular language from one writing system to another. The words stay the same; the characters used to write them change. (2) Performing an algorithmic transformation on a sequence of text according to some set of rules. Software that carries out such a transformation can be used for actual transliteration as well as other types of transforms.

Trema. Alternate term for dialytika.

Trie. An *n*-way tree structure in which a node at any level of the tree represents the set of keys that start with a particular sequence of characters.

Triisap. A Khmer mark that converts a first-series consonant to a second-series consonant.

TrueType. A file format for describing an outline font. Both OpenType and AAT extend the TrueType file format with extra tables that allow for more complex typography than a traditional TrueType font, but in incompatible ways.

TrueType GX. Former name for AAT.

Tsheg. A dot used to mark word divisions in Tibetan.

Typeface. A collection of fonts with common design characteristics intended to be used together. For example, Times is a typeface; Times Roman and Times Italic are fonts.

Typographer's ellipsis. A single character representing the European ellipsis, a series of three periods in a row. Three normal periods in a row generally are spaced too close together; the typographer's ellipsis includes the optimal amount of spacing between the periods.

U source. Collective name given to sources of ideographs used by the IRG without their being submitted by a particular national body.

UAX. Abbreviation for Unicode Standard Annex.

UAX #9. The official specification of the Unicode bidirectional layout algorithm.

UAX #11. The official specification of the East Asian Width property.

UAX #13. A set of guidelines dictating how line and paragraph divisions should be represented in Unicode.

UAX #14. The official specification of the Unicode line-breaking properties.

UAX #15. The official specification of the Unicode normalization forms.

UAX #19. The official definition of UTF-32.

UAX #27. The official specification of Unicode 3.1.

UCA. Abbreviation for Unicode Collation Algorithm.

UCAS. Abbreviation for Unified Canadian Aborginal Syllabics.

UCD. Abbreviation for Unicode Character Database.

UCS. Abbreviation for Universal Character Set, an alternate name for ISO 10646.

UCS-2. One of the two character encoding forms specified by ISO 10646. UCS-2 represents characters in the Basic Multilingual Plane as 16-bit quantities. Characters in the supplemental planes can't be represented in UCS-2; the surrogate space is not used and is treated like a range of unassigned code point values. UCS-2 is now generally discouraged in favor of UTF-16. (Applications that can't handle surrogate pairs properly often bill themselves as "supporting UCS-2.")

UCS-4. One of the two character encoding forms specified by ISO 10646. It represents each abstract code point value as a 32-bit quantity, with the extra bits filled with zeros. With the most recent versions of ISO 10646 and Unicode, UCS-4 is equivalent to UTF-32. In earlier versions, code point values above 0x10FFFF were theoretically allowed in UCS-4 but not in UTF-32, although this factor was of little practical significance, as nothing was encoded there.

Umlaut. A brightening of a vowel sound in languages such as German, or the mark (a double dot) placed on a vowel to indicate umlaut. The diaeresis and the umlaut are essentially the same mark used to represent different things; Unicode unifies them and standardizes on the term "diaeresis" to refer to the mark itself.

Unassigned. A term for a code point value that hasn't been assigned to a character. Unassigned code point values in Unicode are reserved for possible future encoding and are not available for ad hoc uses.

Unicode 1.0 name. A property that gives the name a character had in Unicode 1.0, in the cases where it differs from the character's current name.

Unicode Character Database. A collection of data files that specify fully the character properties given to each of the Unicode code point values, along with other useful information about the characters.

Unicode Collation Algorithm. A specification for a standard method of performing language-sensitive comparison on Unicode text. The UCA comprises an algorithm for comparing strings, a default order for all Unicode code point values in the absence of tailoring, a syntax for specifying tailorings, and some useful implementation hints.

Unicode Consortium. The organization responsible for developing, maintaining, and promoting the Unicode standard. It is a membership organization generally made up of corporations, nonprofit institutions, and governments with an interest in character encoding.

Unicode mailing list. A mailing list for general discussion of Unicode. The address is unicode@unicode.org. Membership is open to anyone; to join, go to the Unicode Web site.

Unicode normalization form. One of four methods of standardizing the Unicode representation of text. Normalized Forms D and KD favor decomposed forms, while Normalized Forms C and KC favor composed forms. Normalized Forms C and D normalize only canonically equal strings to the same representation; Normalized Forms KC and KD extend this ability to characters whose compatibility decompositions are also the same.

Unicode scalar value. The term used in Unicode 2.0 for what is now called a code point.

Unicode standard. (1) *The Unicode Standard, Version 3.0* (Boston, MA: Addison-Wesley, 2000). (2) The full Unicode standard, comprising not only the book, but also the complete suite of current Unicode Technical Reports and the Unicode Character Database.

Unicode Standard Annex. A technical report that carries normative force and is considered an addition to the standard itself. Unicode 3.1 and 3.2 are published as Unicode Standard Annexes, as are certain sets of character properties added after Unicode 2.0, such as line-breaking and East Asian width properties.

Unicode Technical Committee. The group within the Unicode Consortium that makes decisions about changing and extending the standard. This group is made up of experts from the Unicode Consortium's member organizations.

Unicode Technical Report. (1) A document issued by the Unicode Consortium that amends or supplements the standard in some way. The term refers collectively to Unicode Standard Annexes, Unicode Technical Standards, and Unicode Technical Reports (in the more restrictive sense). This usage, and the fact that all three types of technical reports are numbered from the same series, stems from the fact that "Unicode Standard Annex" and "Unicode Technical Standard" are relatively new terms—everything was once called a Unicode Technical Report. (2) Those documents that are still called Unicode Technical Reports but are informative supplements to the Unicode standard, providing clarifying information, useful implementation information, or techniques for using Unicode in certain situations.

Unicode Technical Standard. A supplementary standard issued by the Unicode Consortium and based on Unicode. Unicode Technical Standards are not part of the Unicode standard itself, but are separate, independent standards with their own conformance rules. The Unicode Collation Algorithm is an example.

Unicode Web site. The Web site maintained by the Unicode Consortium. It serves as the definitive source for all things Unicode—in particular, the most recent versions of the Unicode Character Database and Unicode Technical Reports. The URL is `http://www.unicode.org`.

UnicodeCharacterDatabase.html. A file in the Unicode Character Database that gives an overview of all files in the database.

UnicodeData.html. A file in the Unicode Character Database that describes the contents and format of UnicodeData.txt.

UnicodeData.txt. A file in the Unicode Character Database that lists all characters in the current version of Unicode, plus their most important properties: name, general category, decomposition, numeric value, simple case mappings, and some other things.

Unicore mailing list. A mailing list for internal discussion by members of the Unicode Consortium. Membership is open only to designated representatives of Unicode Consortium members and certain invited experts.

Unification. (1) Declaring two "characters" from different sources (or with different appearances) to be the same character and assigning them a single code point. (2) Declaring two scripts to be variants of one another and unifying the characters they have in common.

Unified Han Repertoire. The complete set of Han characters in Unicode (excluding the characters in the Han Compatibility Ideographs blocks), which is the result of unifying a wide variety of collections of Han characters from different sources.

Unified_Ideograph. The property assigned to the Chinese characters in Unicode. The difference between this property and the Ideographic property is that this property excludes the Han radicals.

Unified Repertoire and Ordering. The name of the original set of Han characters in Unicode, developed by the CJK Joint Research Group.

Uniform early normalization. See *early normalization.*

Unify. See *unification.*

Unihan. Nickname for Unicode Han Repertoire.

Unihan.txt. A data file in the Unicode Character Database that lists all of the Han characters in Unicode, along with their counterparts in a wide variety of sources and other information about them.

Uniscribe. The advanced text-rendering engine in more recent versions of Microsoft Windows.

Update version number. The final component of a Unicode version number, after the second decimal point. The update version number is incremented whenever changes are made to the Unicode Character Database without changes being made to other parts of the standard.

Uppercase. In a bicameral script, the set of letters used at the beginnings of sentences and proper names and for emphasis.

Uppercase letter. The property assigned to uppercase letters in bicameral scripts.

URI. Uniform Resource Identifier. A string of characters that identifies a resource on the World Wide Web. URLs and URNs are types of URIs.

URL. Uniform Resource Locator. A URI that identifies a resource on the Web by specifying a location and a path to follow to reach the resource.

URN. Uniform Resource Name. A URI that identifies a resource on the Web using a location-independent name.

URO. Abbreviation for Unified Repertoire and Ordering.

User character. Alternate term for grapheme cluster.

UTC. Abbreviation for Unicode Technical Committee.

UTF-16. (1) A Unicode encoding form that represents Unicode code point values in the BMP with 16-bit code units and Unicode code point values in the supplementary planes with pairs of 16-bit code units. (2) A Unicode encoding scheme based on UTF-16 that uses the byte order mark to indicate the serialization order of bytes in each code unit.

UTF-16BE. A Unicode encoding scheme based on UTF-16 that serializes the bytes in each code unit in big-endian order.

UTF-16LE. A Unicode encoding scheme based on UTF-16 that serializes the bytes in each code unit in little-endian order.

UTF-32. (1) A Unicode encoding form that represents Unicode code points as 32-bit values. (2) A Unicode encoding scheme based on UTF-32 that uses the byte order mark to indicate the serialization order of bytes in each code unit.

UTF-32BE. A Unicode encoding scheme based on UTF-32 that serializes the bytes in each code unit in big-endian order.

UTF-32LE. A Unicode encoding scheme based on UTF-32 that serializes the bytes in each code unit in little-endian order.

UTF-7. A transfer encoding syntax that makes it possible to use Unicode text in environments, such as RFC 822 messages, that can handle only 7-bit values. It is rarely used today.

UTF-8. A Unicode encoding form that represents Unicode code points as sequences of 8-bit code units. Seven-bit ASCII characters are represented using single bytes, characters from the rest of the BMP are represented using sequences of two or three bytes, and characters from the supplementary planes are represented using sequences of four bytes.

UTF-8-EBCDIC. Alternate name for UTF-EBCDIC.

UTF-EBCDIC. A UTF-8-like encoding form that maintains backward compatibility with EBCDIC rather than with ASCII.

UTR. Abbreviation for Unicode Technical Report.

UTR #16. The description of UTF-EBCDIC.

UTR #17. A set of definitions of terms for discussing character encodings.

UTR #18. A set of guidelines for supporting Unicode in a regular-expression engine.

UTR #20. A set of guidelines for using Unicode in markup languages such as XML.

UTR #21. A more detailed discussion of case mapping in Unicode.

UTR #22. A specification for an XML-based file format for describing mappings between Unicode and other encoding standards.

UTR #24. Defines the script-name property.

UTS. Abbreviation for Unicode Technical Standard.

UTS #6. The official definition of the Standard Compression Scheme for Unicode.

UTS #10. The official definition of the Unicode Collation Algorithm.

V source. Collective term for sources of Han ideographs submitted to the IRG by the Vietnamese national body.

Varia. The Greek name for the grave accent character.

Variation selector. A special formatting character that has no appearance of its own, but tells the rendering engine to use a particular alternate glyph for the preceding character (if possible).

Vertical Extension A. Alternate name for the CJK Unified Ideographs Extension A block in Unicode. The "vertical" refers not to the fact that Han is often written vertically, but to the fact that the extension adds characters. A "horizontal" extension merely adds new mappings from Unicode to a source standard.

Vertical Extension B. Alternate name for the CJK Unicode Ideographs Extension B area in Unicode.

Virama. (1) A mark that cancels the inherent vowel sound of an Indic consonant, causing it to be counted as part of the same orthographic syllable as the consonant that follows it. (2) In Unicode, a code point representing a virama may not always result in a visible virama in the rendered output; the code point is also used to signal the formation of a conjunct consonant. (Conceptually, it is the same thing, the canceling of the inherent vowel on an Indic consonant; all that's different is how this concept is drawn.)

Virtual font. A font that doesn't include any glyph images of its own but merely refers to other fonts for the glyph images.

Visarga. A mark in various Indic scripts that indicates a *h* sound.

VISCII. Vietnamese Standard Code for Information Interchange. An informal character encoding standard for Vietnamese.

Visual order. The order in which the characters are displayed on the screen.

Visual selection. A selection that encompasses a group of characters that are continuous in the rendered text, but may be split into two or more separate ranges in the backing store.

Vowel bearer. One of three marks used in Gurmukhi with the dependent vowels to form independent vowels.

Vowel mark. A mark applied to a consonant to indicate the vowel sound that follows it.

Vowel point. Alternate term for vowel mark.

Vowel sign. Alternate term for dependent vowel.

VT. Vertical tab. An ASCII control character sometimes used as a line separator in applications that use the system new-line function as a paragraph separator.

Vulgar fraction. A single character representing an entire fraction: the numerator, fraction bar, and denominator.

W3C. Abbreviation for World Wide Web Consortium.

W3C character model. A W3C recommendation that specifies how text should be represented in all W3C data file formats. It mandates early uniform normalization, specifies UTF-16 or UTF-8 as the default character encoding, and requires that numeric character references also be in normalized form.

W3C normalization. The normalized form that Unicode should take on the World Wide Web. It is essentially Normalized Form C, but with the extra provision that numeric character references, when expanded, can't break normalization. Earlier versions of the W3C character model also included prohibitions on characters that made W3C normalization more restrictive than Normalized Form C, but these have since been moved to a separate document and are no longer a requirement.

wchar_t. A C and C++ data type representing a "wide character." Like char, which specifies an integral type large enough to hold a character and no larger than any of the other integral data types, wchar_t doesn't impose any semantics on the contents—it merely defines an integral type large enough to hold a "wide character." wchar_t must be at least as large as char, but isn't required to be any larger.

Weak directionality. Directionality that isn't strong enough to start a new embedding level. A sequence of characters with weak directionality is drawn with the correct directionality, but doesn't break up the enclosing directional run.

Weight. An arbitrary value assigned to a character that controls how that character sorts. For example, if B should sort after A, B is assigned a higher weight value.

WG2. Working Group #2 of Subcommittee #2 of ISO/IEC Joint Technical Committee #1; the group responsible for maintaining the ISO 10646 standard.

White_space. A property assigned to all characters that should be treated as "whitespace" by programming-language parsers and similar applications. It consists of all space characters, the tab character, the line and paragraph separators, and all of the control characters that are used as line and paragraph separators on various systems.

Wide. A property assigned to all characters that are implicitly full-width, and to which neutral and ambiguous characters resolve when used in vertical text.

WJ. Abbreviation for word joiner.

Word joiner. A special character that prevents word breaks from being placed between it and the preceding and following characters. It essentially "glues" those two characters together on one line.

Word-wrapping. Breaking text up into lines in such a way that words aren't divided across two lines (or are hyphenated). The term is functionally equivalent to "line breaking."

World Wide Web Consortium. An industry body that issues standards (called "recommendations") for various operations and data file formats on the World Wide Web.

Writing system.   A collection of characters and rules for writing them in one or more languages. The characters and rules may vary slightly between languages (for example, English and German have different letters in their alphabets, but both are considered to be written with the Latin alphabet), and the same language may be written with more than one writing system (Kanji and Hiragana for Japanese, or the Latin and Cyrillic alphabets for Serbo-Croatian).

WRU. "Who are you?" A control function used in early teletype machines as part of a handshaking protocol. In response to this signal, the receiving equipment would send back a short identifying string.

www.unicode.org. The URL of the Unicode Web site.

WYSIWYG. What you see is what you get. A term applied to applications where the document being operated on appears on the screen exactly the same way (or close enough) as it will look when printed.

X3. ANSI Committee X3, the committee responsible for information technology standards at the time ASCII was published. X3 has since morphed into NCITS.

X3.4. See *ANSI X3.4-1967.*

XCCS. Xerox Coded Character Set. One of the important predecessors of Unicode.

x-height. The height of the lowercase letter x in a Latin font and, by extension, the height of the other lowercase letters that don't have ascenders and descenders, and the height of the parts of the other lowercase letters other than the ascenders and descenders.

XHTML. Extensible Hypertext Markup Language. An XML-based page description language with functionality equivalent to HTML.

XML. Extensible Markup Language. A W3C standard for describing structured data in a text file. It forms the basis of many W3C data file standards.

XSL. Extensible Stylesheet Language. An XML-based language for describing the look of a page of text.

Xu Shen. The compiler of the first known Chinese dictionary in A.D. 100.

Yi Area. The area of the Unicode encoding space running from U+A000 to U+A4CF and containing the Yi syllables and radicals.

Ypogegrammeni. The iota subscript used with some vowels in ancient Greek to write some diphthongs.

Zenkaku. Japanese for full-width.

Zero-width joiner. A formatting character that has no appearance of its own, but indicates to a text-rendering process that the characters on either side should be joined together in some way, if possible. This combination may involve cursive joining or the forming of a ligature; if both are possible, it requests that both happen.

Zero-width non-breaking space. The character that, in versions of Unicode prior to Unicode 3.2, served the same purpose as the word joiner. The same code point also serves as the byte order mark.

Zero-width non-joiner. A formatting character that has no appearance of its own, but indicates to a text rendering process that the characters on either side should *not* be joined together. It is used to break a cursive connection that would otherwise happen or to prevent the formation of a ligature.

Zero-width space. An invisible character that indicates to a line-breaking algorithm where it is acceptable to put a line break. It is used in situations (such as Thai) where this location can't be determined from looking at the real characters.

Zl. The abbreviation used in the UnicodeData.txt file for the "line separator" general category, which consists solely of the line-separator character.

Zone row. A row of a punched card that is used to change the meanings of punches in other rows.

Zp. The abbreviation used in the UnicodeData.txt file for the "paragraph separator" general category, which consists solely of the paragraph-separator character.

Zs. The abbreviation used in the UnicodeData.txt file for the "space separator" general category.

ZWJ. Abbreviation for zero-width joiner.

ZWNBSP. Abbreviation for zero-width non-breaking space.

ZWNJ. Abbreviation for zero-width non-joiner.

ZWSP. Abbreviation for zero-width space.

ZWWJ. Zero-width word joiner. An old term for word joiner.

Bibliography

The Unicode Standard

The Unicode Consortium, *The Unicode Standard, Version 2.0,* Reading, MA:
  Addison-Wesley, 1996.

The Unicode Consortium, *The Unicode Standard, Version 3.0,* Boston, MA:
  Addison-Wesley, 2000.

Davis, Mark, "Unicode Standard Annex #9: The Bidirectional Algorithm,"
  version 3.1.0, March 23, 2001, `http://www.unicode.org/unicode/`
  `reports/tr9/`.

Freytag, Asmus, "Unicode Standard Annex #11: East Asian Width," version
  3.1.0, March 23, 2001, `http://www.unicode.org/unicode/reports/tr11/`.

Davis, Mark, "Unicode Standard Annex #13: Unicode Newline Guidelines,"
  version 3.1.0, March 23, 2001, `http://www.unicode.org/unicode/`
  `reports/tr13/`.

Freytag, Asmus, "Unicode Standard Annex #14: Line Breaking Properties,"
  version 3.1.0, March 23, 2001, `http://www.unicode.org/unicode/`
  `reports/tr14/`.

Davis, Mark, and Martin Dürst, "Unicode Standard Annex #15: Unicode Normalization Forms," version 3.1.0, March 23, 2001, http://www.unicode.org/unicode/reports/tr15/.

Davis, Mark, "Unicode Standard Annex #19: UTF-32," version 3.1.0, March 23, 2001, http://www.unicode.org/unicode/reports/tr19/.

Davis, Mark, Michael Everson, Asmus Freytag, John H. Jenkins, et. al., "Unicode Standard Annex #27: Unicode 3.1," version 3.1.0, May 16, 2001, http://www.unicode.org/unicode/reports/tr27/.

Wolf, Misha, Ken Whistler, Charles Wicksteed, Mark Davis, and Asmus Freytag, "Unicode Technical Standard #6: A Standard Compression Scheme for Unicode," version 3.2, August 31, 2000, http://www.unicode.org/unicode/reports/tr6/.

Davis, Mark, and Ken Whistler, "Unicode Technical Standard #10: Unicode Collation Algorithm," version 8.0, March 23, 2001, http://www.unicode.org/unicode/reports/tr10/.

Umamaheswaran, V. S., "Unicode Technical Report #16: UTF-EBCDIC," version 7.2, April 29, 2001, http://www.unicode.org/unicode/reports/tr16/.

Whistler, Ken, and Mark Davis, "Unicode Technical Report #17: Character Encoding Model," version 3.2, August 31, 2000, http://www.unicode.org/unicode/reports/tr17/.

Davis, Mark, "Unicode Technical Report #18: Unicode Regular Expression Guidelines," version 5.1, August 31, 2000, http://www.unicode.org/unicode/reports/tr18/.

Dürst, Martin, and Asmus Freytag, "Unicode Technical Report #20: Unicode in XML and Other Markup Languages," version 5, December 15, 2000, http://www.unicode.org/unicode/reports/tr20/.

Davis, Mark, "Unicode Technical Report #21: Case Mappings," version 4.3, February 23, 2001, http://www.unicode.org/unicode/reports/tr21/.

Davis, Mark, "Unicode Technical Report #22: Character Mapping Markup Language," version 2.2., December 1, 2000, http://www.unicode.org/unicode/reports/tr22/.

Davis, Mark, "Unicode Technical Report #24: Script Names," version 3, September 27, 2001, http://www.unicode.org/unicode/reports/tr24/.

Phipps, Toby, "Draft Unicode Technical Report #26: Compatibility Encoding Scheme for UTF-16: 8-Bit (CESU-8)," version 2.0, December 12, 2001, http://www.unicode.org/unicode/reports/tr26/.

Beeton, Barbara, Asmus Freytag, and Murray Sargent, III, "Proposed Draft Unicode Technical Report #25: Unicode Support for Mathematics," version 1.0, January 3, 2002, http://www.unicode.org/unicode/reports/tr25/.

The Unicode Consortium, "Proposed Draft Unicode Technical Report #28: Unicode 3.2," version 3.2.0, January 21, 2002, http://www.unicode.org/unicode/reports/tr28/.

The Unicode Character Database, http://www.unicode.org/Public/UNIDATA/.

Other Standards Documents

ECMA-35, "Character Code Structure and Extension Techniques," 6th ed., December 1994.

ECMA-94, "8-bit Single Byte Coded Graphic Character Sets—latin Alphabets No. 1 to No. 4," 2nd ed., June 1986.

IETF RFC 1034, "Domain Names: Concepts and Facilities."

IETF RFC 2825, "A Tangled Web: Issues of I18N, Domain Names, and the Other Internet Protocols."

Linux Internationalization Initiative, "LI18NUX 2000 Globalization Specification," version 1.0, amendment 2, http://www.li18nux.net/docs/html/LI18NUX-2000.htm.

W3C Working Draft, "Character Model for the World Wide Web," December 20, 2001, `http://www.w3.org/TR/charmod/`.

Books and Magazine Articles

Boyer, Robert S., and J. Strother Moore, "A Fast String Searching Algorithm," *Communications of the Association for Computing Machinery,* vol. 20, no. 10, pp. 762–772, 1977.

Daniels, Peter T., and William Bright, eds., *The World's Writing Systems,* Oxford: Oxford University Press, 1995.

Ifrah, Georges (trans. by David Bellos, E. F. Harding, Sophie Wood, and Ian Monk), *The Universal History of Numbers*, New York: Wiley, 2000.

Jenkins, John H., "Adding Historical Scripts to Unicode," *Multilingual Computing and Technology,* September 2000.

Kernighan, Brian W., and Dennis M. Ritchie, *The C Programming Language,* Englewood Cliffs, NJ: Prentice-Hall, 1978.

Ksar, Mike, "Untying Tongues: ISO/IEC 10646 Breaks Down Computer Barriers in Processing Worldwide Languages," *ISO Bulletin*, June 1993.

Lunde, Ken, *CJKV Information Processing,* Cambridge, MA: O'Reilly, 1999.

Nakanishi, Akira, *Writing Systems of the World,* Tokyo: Charles E. Tuttle Co., 1980.

Unicode Conference Papers

Davis, Mark, "Bits of Unicode," *Proceedings of the Eighteenth International Unicode Conference,* session B11, April 27, 2001.

Davis, Mark, "Collation in ICU 1.8," *Proceedings of the Eighteenth International Unicode Conference,* session B10, April 27, 2001.

Davis, Mark, and Alan Liu, "Transliteration in ICU," *Proceedings of the Eighteenth International Unicode Conference,* session B14, April 27, 2001.

Edberg, Peter K., "Survey of Character Encodings," *Proceedings of the Thirteenth International Unicode Conference,* session TA4, September 9, 1998

Gillam, Richard, "Text Boundary Analysis in Java," *Proceedings of the Fourteenth International Unicode Conference,* session B2, March 24, 1999.

Jenkins, John H., "New Ideographs in Unicode 3.0 and Beyond," *Proceedings of the Fifteenth International Unicode Conference,* session C15, September 1, 1999.

Ksar, Mike, "Unicode and ISO 10646: Continued Convergence," *Proceedings of the Twentieth International Unicode Conference,* session C2, January 30, 2002.

Milo, Thomas, "Creating Solutions for Arabic: A Case Study," *Proceedings of the Seventeenth International Unicode Conference,* session TB3, September 6, 2000.

Werner, Laura, "Unicode Text Searching in Java," *Proceedings of the Fifteenth International Unicode Conference,* session B1, September 1, 1999.

Other Papers

Emerson, Thomas, "On the 'Hangzhou-Style' Numerals in ISO/IEC 10646-1," white paper published by Basis Technology.

Halpern, Jack, "The Pitfalls and Complexities of Chinese to Chinese Conversion," undated white paper published by the CJK Dictionary Publishing Society.

Online Resources

Adobe Systems, "OpenType Specification v1.3," `http://partners.adobe.com/asn/developer/opentype/`.

Apple Computer, "Developer Documentation," `http://developer.apple.com/techpubs`.

Apple Computer, "TrueType Reference Manual," `http://developer.apple.com/ fonts/TTRefMan/index.html`.

Czyborra, Roman, "Good Old ASCII," `http://www.czyborra.com/charsets/ iso646.html`.

Czyborra, Roman, "ISO 8859 Alphabet Soup," `http://www.czyborra.com/ charsets/iso8859.html`.

Davis, Mark, and Markus Scherer, "Binary-Ordered Compression for Unicode," IBM DeveloperWorks, `http://www-106.ibm.com/developerworks/ unicode/library/u-binary.html`.

Dürst, Martin, "URIs and Other Identifiers," `http://www.w3.org/ International/O-URL-and-ident`.

Hietaniemi, Jarkko, "Unicode Support in Perl," `http://www.ilsi.fi/jhi/ perlunicode.pod`.

Jennings, Tom, "Annotated History of Character Codes," `http:// www.wps.com/texts/codes`.

Jones, Douglas W., "Punched Cards: An Illustrated Technical History" and "Doug Jones' Punched Card Codes," `http://www.cs.uiowa.edu/~jones/ cards`.

McGowan, Rick, "About Unicode Consortium Procedures, Policies, Stability, and Public Access," published as an IETF Internet-draft, `http:// search.ietf.org/internet-drafts/draft-rmcgowan-unicode- procs-01.txt`.

Microsoft, "Global Software Development," `http://www.microsoft.com/ globaldev`.

Opstad, Dave, "Comparing GX Line Layout and OpenType Layout," `http:// fonts.apple.com/WhitePapers/GXvsOTLayout.html`.

Searle, Steven J., "A Brief History of Character Codes," `http:// www.tronweb.super-nova.co.jp/characcodehist.html`.

SIL International, "Ethnologue," `http://www.ethnologue.com`.

Index

Also from Addison-Wesley

The Unicode Standard, Version 3.0

The Unicode Consortium

ISBN 0-201-61633-5
1,072 pages with CD-ROM
© 2000

Unicode

- Characters for all the languages of the world
- The standard for the new millennium
- Required for XML and the Internet
- The basis for modern software standards and products
- The official way to implement ISO/IEC 10646
- The key to global interoperability

The Unicode Standard, Version 3.0

The authoritative, technical guide to the creation of software for worldwide use.

• Detailed specifications for Unicode:
Structure, conformance, encoding forms, character properties, semantics, equivalence, combining characters, logical ordering, conversion, allocation, big/little endian usage, Korean syllable formation, control characters, case mappings, numeric values, mathematical properties, writing directions (Arabic, Japanese, English, and so on), character shaping (Arabic, Devanagari, Tamil, and so on)

• Expanded implementation guidelines by experts in global software design:
Normalization, sorting and searching, case mapping, compression, language tagging, boundaries (characters, word, lines, and sentences), rendering of non-spacing marks, transcoding to other character sets, handling unknown characters, surrogate pairs, numbers, editing and selection, keyboard input, and more

• Comprehensive charts, references, glossary, and indexes:
Codes, names, appearances, aliases, cross-references, equivalences, radical-stroke ideographic index, Shift-JIS index, and more

CD-ROM

• The comprehensive Unicode Character Database for:
Character codes, names, properties, decompositions, upper-, lower-, and title cases, normalizations, shaping

• International, national, and vendor character mappings for:
Western European, Japanese, Chinese, Korean, Greek, Russian, and others
Windows, Macintosh, Unix, and Linux

• Unicode Technical Reports that extend the standard for:
Sorting, displaying, normalizing, linebreaking, compression, serialization, regular expressions, CR/LF, XML, case mappings, and more

The Unicode Consortium is a nonprofit organization founded to develop, extend, and promote use of the Unicode Standard. Members include companies and organizations on the vanguard of globalization technology; together they comprise a source of unrivaled internationalization expertise. Visit the Consortium's Web site: http://www.unicode.org.

informIT

www.informit.com

YOUR GUIDE TO IT REFERENCE

Articles

Keep your edge with thousands of free articles, in-depth features, interviews, and IT reference recommendations – all written by experts you know and trust.

Online Books

Answers in an instant from **InformIT Online Book's** 600+ fully searchable on line books. For a limited time, you can get your first 14 days **free**.

POWERED BY

Safari
TECH BOOKS ONLINE®

Catalog

Review online sample chapters, author biographies and customer rankings and choose exactly the right book from a selection of over 5,000 titles.

Register
Your Book

at www.awprofessional.com/register

You may be eligible to receive:

- Advance notice of forthcoming editions of the book
- Related book recommendations
- Chapter excerpts and supplements of forthcoming titles
- Information about special contests and promotions throughout the year
- Notices and reminders about author appearances, tradeshows, and online chats with special guests

Contact us

If you are interested in writing a book or reviewing manuscripts prior to publication, please write to us at:

Editorial Department
Addison-Wesley Professional
75 Arlington Street, Suite 300
Boston, MA 02116 USA
Email: AWPro@aw.com

Addison-Wesley

Visit us on the Web: http://www.awprofessional.com